Professional Stage

Module E

Tax Planning
(Finance Act 1999)

ACCA Textbook

0254/J99

British Library Cataloguing-in-Publication Data

A catalogue record for this book is available from the British Library.

Published by AT Foulks Lynch Ltd
Number 4
The Griffin Centre
Staines Road
Feltham
Middlesex
TW14 0HS

ISBN 0 7483 4025 4

© AT Foulks Lynch Ltd, 1999

Acknowledgements

We are grateful to the Association of Chartered Certified Accountants, the Chartered Institute of Management Accountants and the Institute of Chartered Accountants in England and Wales for permission to reproduce past examination questions. The answers have been prepared by AT Foulks Lynch Ltd.

CONTENTS

PREFACE

This Textbook is the ACCA's official text for paper 11, Tax Planning, and is part of the ACCA's official series produced for students taking the ACCA examinations. It has been produced with direct guidance from the examiner specifically for paper 11, and covers the syllabus in great detail giving appropriate weighting to the various topics. It is fully up to date for the Finance Act 1999 which was enacted in July 1999. This textbook is suitable for the June and December 2000 examinations. Candidates for the December 1999 examination should use the separate Textbook updated for the Finance Act 1998.

This Textbook is, however, very different from a reference book or a more traditional style textbook. It is targeted very closely on the examinations and is written in a way that will help you assimilate the information easily and give you plenty of practice at the various techniques involved.

Particular attention has been paid to producing an interactive text that will maintain your interest with a series of carefully designed features.

- **Activities**. The text involves you in the learning process with a series of activities designed to arrest your attention and make you concentrate and respond.

- **Definitions**. The text clearly defines key words or concepts. The purpose of including these definitions is **not** that you should learn them - rote learning is not required and is positively harmful. The definitions are included to focus your attention on the point being covered.

- **Conclusions**. Where helpful, the text includes conclusions that summarise important points as you read through the chapter rather than leaving the conclusion to the chapter end. The purpose of this is to summarise concisely the key material that has just been covered so that you can constantly monitor your understanding of the material as you read it.

- **Self test questions**. At the end of each chapter there is a series of self test questions. The purpose of these is to help you revise some of the key elements of the chapter. The answer to each is a paragraph reference, encouraging you to go back and re-read and revise that point.

- **End of chapter questions**. At the end of each chapter we include examination style questions. These will give you a very good idea of the sort of thing the examiner will ask and will test your understanding of what has been covered.

Revision Series - The ACCA Revision Series contains all the relevant current syllabus exam questions from June 1994 to December 1998 with the examiner's own official answers, all updated as appropriate. The edition updated for the Finance Act 1999 will be available in late 1999/2000

What better way to revise for your exams than to read and study the examiner's own answers!

Lynchpins - The ACCA Lynchpins, pocket-sized revision aids which can be used throughout your course, contain revision notes of all main syllabus topics, all fully indexed, plus numerous examples and diagrams. They provide invaluable focus and assistance in keeping key topics in the front of your mind.

Audio Tapes - Our new 'Tracks' audio tapes are fully integrated with our other publications. They provide clear explanations of key aspects of the syllabus, invaluable throughout your studies and at the revision stage. The FA 99 edition of Tracks will be available in early 2000.

FORMAT OF THE EXAMINATION

The examination will have the following format:

Number of marks

Four (out of six) questions of 25 marks each   100

Time allowed: 3 hours

Tax rates and allowances will be given in the paper

Students are reminded that the questions for this and subsequent papers will normally focus on everyday situations and accordingly, it will be relatively unusual for a question to involve knowledge of only one tax. While there will generally be some computational elements in each question, long and involved calculations will not be called for. The emphasis will rather be on the appreciation of how the various taxes may impact on a given situation. Students will also be expected to appreciate the more common interactions between the taxes and be able to identify basic tax planning points where appropriate. Students will be expected to demonstrate their ability to communicate their findings and recommendations to clients, as well as to explain clearly the more important principles of tax law.

Students are advised that a knowledge of section numbers will not be needed to understand questions in this paper, nor will they be expected to use them in their answers. If students wish to refer to section numbers in their answers they may do so and will not be penalised if old, or even incorrect, section numbers are used.

SYLLABUS

Professional stage - Module E Paper 11: TAX PLANNING

Introduction

The syllabus includes everything examinable in Paper 7, the Tax Framework, but extends and deepens the coverage. It also includes some new areas. Topics will be examined so that emphasis is given to simple planning to minimise or defer tax; the application of the tax knowledge to problems encountered in practice; and the inter-relationship of taxes.

(1)   **OVERVIEW OF PERSONAL BUSINESS TAXATION**

      (a)   Interactions between different taxes in a range of situations or transactions.

      (b)   Tax planning; the application of tax planning measures appropriate to the particular situation.

(2)   **CAPITAL GAINS TAX**

Application of Capital Gains Tax to individuals and corporate taxpayers, with emphasis on business situations.

(3)   **INHERITANCE TAX**

      (a)   Principles and scope.

      (b)   Rules basis and application.

      (c)   Calculating the tax due by clients.

      (d)   Minimising/deferring tax liabilities by identifying/applying relevant exemptions, reliefs and allowances.

(4)   **TRUSTS**

Application to trusts of Income Tax, Capital Gains Tax and Inheritance Tax.

(5)   **VALUE ADDED TAX**

The application of Value Added Tax to transactions and other activities of corporate taxpayers.

(6)   **CORPORATE TAXATION**

      (a)   Groups and consortia.

      (b)   The provisions covering liquidations and areas such as disincorporations, purchases of own shares, sales and acquisitions of subsidiaries, and share for share amalgamations.

      (c)   Implications of a company being classed as an investment or close company.

(7)   **OVERSEAS ACTIVITIES GIVING RISE TO TAXATION LIABILITIES**

      (a)   Definition of residence, ordinary residence and domicile.

      (b)   The taxation of UK income and gains of non-domicile individuals.

(c)   Overseas income and gains: the UK tax treatment of overseas income and gains of UK resident individuals and companies, including relief for double taxation.

(d)   Overseas persons, the UK tax treatment of income and gains arising within the UK to non-resident individuals and companies.

(e)   The Inheritance Tax position regarding overseas assets of UK individuals and UK assets of non-resident individuals.

(f)   Business structures, including a UK branch/subsidiary of a foreign company/group and a foreign branch/subsidiary of a UK company/group.

(g)   Anti-avoidance legislation relating to overseas activities, income or persons.

(8)   GENERAL

(a)   Inter-relationship of taxes: the effect of any of the taxes in a given situation or on a particular transaction.

(b)   Anti-avoidance: appreciation of the main areas of anti-avoidance legislation and of the enquiry and investigation procedures of the Inland Revenue and Customs and Excise.

(9)   PERSONAL FINANCE

(a)   Assisting clients in the determination of personal financial objectives, taking into account such factors as individual circumstances, expectations and the economic environment.

(b)   Determining financial needs of clients (how much, when, for how long, and for what purpose?).

(c)   Regulations affecting investment advisers, and ethical considerations, including the definition of investment business.

(d)   Advising on sources and costs of different forms of finance and their applicability to different circumstances including

         (i)   bank borrowing
         (ii)   finance houses
         (iii)   mortgages
         (iv)   money and capital markets.

(e)   Advising on investment of clients' personal funds

         (i)   insurance policies
         (ii)   pension funds
         (iii)   unit trusts, investment trusts and open ended investment companies (OEICs)
         (iv)   Individual savings accounts (ISAs)
         (v)   equity shares
         (vi)   gilt edged securities and other bonds
         (vii)   real property
         (viii)   banks and building societies
         (ix)   National savings.
         (x)   Enterprise investment scheme
         (xi)   Venture capital trusts

THE OFFICIAL ACCA TEACHING GUIDE

Paper 11 - Tax Planning

	Syllabus Reference	*Chapter Reference*

The syllabus for this paper includes everything examinable in paper 7 Tax Framework and it is assumed that students have a basic knowledge of Income Tax, Capital Gains Tax, Corporation Tax and VAT. Revision of these areas are designated as self study.

Self-Study - Income Tax   1, 4, 5

- prepare a proforma income tax computation (revision)
- list those sources of income which are received net of lower or basic rate tax and those that are exempt (revision)
- explain the effect of each category of annual charge on the income tax computation (revision)
- list the personal allowances and the main rules relating to each (revision)
- list the principal payments that qualify as annual charges (revision)
- describe the conditions relating to each type of qualifying annual charge (revision)
- state the main provisions relating to the independent taxation of husband and wife (revision)
- compute the tax liabilities arising in the year of marriage, separation, divorce or death (revision)
- state the tax relief available for maintenance payments (revision)
- state the tax position of the recipient of maintenance payments (revision)
- state the tax position of children (revision)

Session 1   ***Taxation of Income from Employment in the UK***   6, 7

- state the factors taken into account by the Inland Revenue in determining whether an activity is treated as employment or self-employment (revision but more depth)   Paper 7
- quote case law in support of the above
- discuss whether other lump sum payments are assessable
- list the main features of a profit-sharing scheme
- list the main features of a share option scheme
- list the main features of an employee share ownership plan

Self-Study
- describe the income assessable under Schedule E (revision)
- describe the Schedule E basis of assessment for UK residents (revision)
- list the expenditure deductible under Schedule E to include the fixed profit car scheme (revision)
- quote case law in support of the above
- explain how to determine whether payments for loss of office are assessable (revision)
- calculate the amount of a payment on termination of office assessable under Schedule E (revision)
- state how benefits in kind are assessed (revision)
- describe the benefits in kind assessable on all employees (revision)
- identify P11D employees (revision)
- state the general principles by which benefits in kind are assessed on P11D employees (revision)
- describe the benefits in kind assessed on P11D employees that are calculated on a special basis (revision)

- calculate the benefits in kind assessed on an employee (revision)
- describe the basis by which employed persons are liable to pay national insurance contributions (revision)
- describe the basis by which employers are liable to pay national insurance contributions in respect of their employees, and state the relief that they receive for these contributions (revision)

Session 2   *Taxation of Income from Property and Investments*   2, 3

Paper 7

- state the main features of an occupational pension scheme
- explain the significance of an occupational pension scheme being approved by the Inland Revenue
- state the options available to an employee seeking to improve upon his or her pension entitlement
- describe the main features of a personal pension plan (revision)
- list the main features of a qualifying life assurance policy, and describe the tax relief available
- describe the tax relief given by an individual savings scheme, and the conditions that must be satisfied
- describe the features of the Enterprise Investment Scheme
- describe the main features of venture capital trusts

Self-Study
- compute the income assessable under Schedule A
- explain how relief for Schedule A losses is given
- compute the tax liabilities arising in respect of premiums on short leases (revision)
- state the taxation provisions relating to income from furnished holiday lettings (revision)
- list those investments that are tax-free (revision)
- list the main sources of income assessable under Schedule D Case III (revision)
- describe the basis of assessment under Schedule D Case III (revision)
- list the main sources of income assessable under Schedule D Case VI (revision)
- describe the basis of assessment under Schedule D Case VI (revision)

Self-Study - Capital Gains Tax
- define 'chargeable disposals', chargeable assets', and chargeable persons' (revision)
- state the circumstances when the market value of an asset should be used as the disposal value (revision)
- compute the appropriate rate of tax to be applied (revision)
- describe how capital losses can be relieved (revision)
- state the due date of payments (revision)
- prepare a basic capital gains tax computation (revision)
- compute tapering relief (revision)
- explain how the computation of capital gains for corporation tax purposes differs from that for income tax (revision)

- state the circumstances when an election for universal 31 March 1982 valuation may be made, and when such an election would be favourable (revision)
- state the circumstances when a disposal is treated as a no gain no loss (revision)
- prepare a capital gains tax computation on the part disposal of an asset (revision)
- state the circumstances when the alternative treatment for small disposals is available (revision)
- prepare capital gains tax computations on the disposal of assets acquired prior to 31 March 1982 (revision)
- list the identification rules applying to disposals of shares after 5 April 1998
- apply the pooling provisions for shares acquired prior to 6 April 1998
- explain the treatment of a bonus issue and a rights issue
- calculate the allowable cost where there have been capital reorganisations or takeovers
- list those securities that are exempt from capital gains tax (revision)

Session 3   *Hold-over Relief, Chattels, Wasting Assets, Land and Principal Private Residence*   16, 18, 20, 21

- describe the relief for held-over gains (revision)   2
- state the circumstances when hold-over relief is available in respect of gifts (revision)
- prepare capital gains tax computations where hold-over relief is available (revision)
- state the circumstances when relief for chattels is available, and compute the relief (revision)
- describe the basis on which a lease wastes away, and distinguish this from other wasting assets (revision)
- prepare a capital gains tax computation on the disposal of a lease (revision)
- state the circumstances when a principal private residence will be wholly or partly exempt (revision)
- prepare a capital gains tax computation on the disposal of a principal private residence (revision)

Session 4/5   *Inheritance Tax - General Principles*   29-33

- state the circumstances when a charge to IHT arises   3a, b, c
- define the terms 'chargeable transfer', 'transfer of value', 'chargeable property' and 'chargeable persons'
- list those assets which are excluded property
- calculate the liability when the donee pays the inheritance tax
- describe the concept of grossing up
- calculate the liability when the donor pays the inheritance tax
- list the property which comprises a person's estate at the date of death
- explain the interaction of PETs that become chargeable with chargeable lifetime transfers
- compute tapering relief
- calculate the IHT on an estate and state who pays it
- describe the transfers that are wholly exempt
- describe the exemptions that are available to the donor
- state the order in which the exemptions are applied
- calculate the liability to IHT after applying the exemptions

The official ACCA teaching guide

This section should concentrate on the regulations as they affect accountants/tax advisers. The coverage should generally be of a broad, rather than a full, nature.

Session 10   *Personal Finance - Determining the Appropriate*   38
                 Investments and Finance

- state which investments should be held by non tax-payers, starting rate   9b, d
  tax-payers, basic rate tax-payers, and higher rate tax-payers
- state when it is appropriate to invest for income, and when to invest for
  capital growth
- advise on the appropriate investments to be held taking into account an
  individual's age, wealth and risk profile
- advise on the appropriate investments taking into account the period over
  which an individual wishes to invest
- list the sources of finance available to an individual or a business
- state which sources of finance would be most appropriate in given
  circumstances
- distinguish between the tax implications of raising equity finance and of
  raising loan finance
- list the other accounting and legal factors which should be considered
  when raising finance

The syllabus includes sources of finance under personal finance, but there is scope for questions on business finance. One obvious area is start-up finance for a new business.

Session 11/12   *The Taxation of Trusts*   34

- describe the main features of trusts with an interest in possession,   4
  discretionary trusts, and accumulation and maintenance trusts
- describe how income tax applies to interest in possession trusts
- describe how income tax applies to discretionary trusts and accumulation
  and maintenance trusts
- describe the basic principles governing the application of CGT to trusts
- explain the CGT liability when a beneficiary becomes entitled to trust
  property
- describe how IHT applies to interest in possession trusts
- describe how IHT applies to discretionary trusts
- describe how trusts can be used in tax planning

Self-Study - Unincorporated Businesses
- list the factors which are taken into account when deciding if a
  transaction is considered to be in the nature of a trade (revision)
- list the expenditure which is allowable in calculating the adjusted
  Schedule D Case 1 profit (revision)
- quote case law in support of the above
- describe the adjustments peculiar to sole traders (this should include
  private use appropriation of profit, allowable expenditure not charged in
  the accounts, goods/services for personal benefit, and salary paid to a
  family member) (revision)
- compute the adjusted Schedule D Case 1 profit for a sole trader
  (comprehensive example) (revision)
- apply the normal rules in computing the assessable profit for a fiscal year
  (revision)
- compute the special relief that is available to farmers (revision)
- define plant and machinery for the purpose of capital allowances
  (revision)
- quote case law in support of the above principles
- define a motor car for the purposes of capital allowances (revision)

- apply the adjustments that result from the private use of assets (revision)
- compute capital allowances on plant and machinery for a period of account (revision)
- advise when an election in respect of short-life assets may be beneficial (revision)
- calculate capital allowances on the commencement and cessation of a business (revision)
- define industrial buildings and qualifying hotels for the purposes of industrial buildings allowance (revision)
- quote case law in support of the above principles
- calculate the industrial buildings allowances claimable for a period of account (revision)
- calculate the balancing adjustment arising on the disposal of an industrial building (revision)
- compute the qualifying expenditure for second and subsequent owners (revision)
- describe the effect of using an industrial building for non-industrial purposes (revision)
- define the expenditure that qualifies for agricultural buildings allowance (revision)
- calculate the agricultural buildings allowance claimable by first and subsequent owners (revision)
- compute the allowances claimable in respect of expenditure on patents, and the adjustment arising on disposal (revision)
- compute the allowances claimable in respect of expenditure on know-how, and the adjustment arising on disposal (revision)
- compute the allowances claimable in respect of expenditure on scientific research, and state how disposal proceeds are treated (revision)

Session 13   *The Taxation of Profits from Trades, Professions and Vocations*   9 - 12

- compute the assessable Schedule D Case 1 profit on the commencement of a business, and state the factors that will influence the choice of accounting date (part revision)   Paper 7 1a, b
- compute the assessable Schedule D Case 1 profit on the cessation of a business (revision)
- state the conditions that must be met for a change of accounting date to be valid (revision)
- compute the assessable Schedule D1 profit on the change of accounting date (revision)
- describe the scope for waiving capital allowances, and when it would be beneficial to do so
- describe the alternative ways in which relief for a loss can be obtained, and state the relevant time limits (revision - to include loss relief against chargeable gains)
- compute income tax computations for a number of years, optimising the loss relief claims
- list the commercial conditions that must be satisfied before a loss can be claimed against statutory total income (revision)
- explain how capital allowances can be used to vary the amount of the loss
- compute the assessments for a business that has incurred a loss in its first accounting period (revision)
- calculate the amount of loss relief available to be carried forward (revision)
- calculate the amount of loss relief available to be set off against statutory total income (revision)

- calculate the amount of terminal loss available on the cessation of a trade (revision)
- compute the last four years' assessments when a business has incurred a loss in its final accounting period (show the position under alternative loss relief claims)
- describe the provisions that apply to business start-up relief (revision)

Session 14   *Partnerships and National Insurance*   13

Paper 7
1a, b

- describe how a partnership is assessed to tax (revision)
- allocate the assessable profits between the partners following a change in their profit sharing ratio (revision)
- allocate the assessable profits between the partners following a change in the members of a partnership (revision)
- describe the alternative loss relief claims that are available to partners (revision)
- compute the allocation of trading losses between partners (revision)
- distinguish between the national insurance contributions paid by a self-employed person and those paid by an employed person
- compute the tax position for a self-employed person and for an employed person, both on similar gross incomes

Self-Study
- describe the basis on which self-employed persons are liable to pay national insurance contributions (revision)

Session 15   *The Disposal and Replacement of Business Assets*   20

2

- compute the capital gain arising on the disposal of a business asset (revision)
- describe the roll-over relief that is available on the replacement of a business asset (revision)
- compute the capital gain arising on the replacement of a business asset (revision)
- advise as to the most advantageous claims where there is more than one gain to be rolled over, or more than one asset to roll-over against
- describe the treatment of tangible moveable property which is both a business asset and a wasting asset (revision)
- state how the capital gains computation interacts with capital allowances on the disposal of business assets (should cover both plant and machinery and IBAs) (revision)
- state the implications of a disposal made by a partnership
- state the implications of a change in the profit-sharing ratio of a partnership
- state the implications of a change in the membership of a partnership

Session 16   *Disposal of All or Part of a Business; Retirement*   19

2

- compute the capital gains arising on the disposal of all or part of a business (revision)
- distinguish between the capital gains tax implications arising on the transfer of a business, and those on the transfer of shares in a company
- describe the relief available when a business is transferred to a limited company
- list the conditions which must be satisfied for relief to be available when a business is transferred to a limited company
- describe the relief available when gains are reinvested in Enterprise Investment Scheme shares or in Venture Capital Trusts

- list the conditions which must be satisfied for retirement relief to be available in respect of the disposal of an unincorporated business (revision)
- compute retirement relief on the disposal of an unincorporated business (revision)
- list the conditions which must be satisfied for retirement relief to be available in respect of the disposal of shares in a personal company (revision)
- compute retirement relief on the disposal of shares in a personal company (revision)
- state how retirement relief interacts with gift relief (revision)

Self-Study - Value Added Tax
- describe the scope of value added tax (to include the definition of a taxable person) (revision)
- list the circumstances in which a person must register/deregister for value added tax (revision)
- state when a person may voluntarily register/deregister for value added tax (revision)
- explain why it may be beneficial for a person to voluntarily register for value added tax (revision)
- describe the consequences of a person not registering for value added tax at the appropriate time (revision)
- list the documentation and accounting records that a registered person is required to keep (revision)
- list the principal zero rated and exempt supplies (revision)
- explain the meaning of 'a mixed supply', 'a composite supply', and 'a self supply' (revision)
- describe the principles which apply to the valuation of supplies (revision)
- describe the relief that is available for bad debts (revision)
- explain the rules relating to fuel bought by employees, and motor expenses where there is some private motoring (revision)
- state the circumstances in which input tax is non-deductible (revision)
- explain how VAT is applied to imports and exports, and to acquisitions within the European Union (revision)
- describe the cash accounting and annual accounting schemes (revision)
- state the consequences of a person being partially exempt (revision)
- explain the assessment and appeals procedures for value added tax (revision)
- state the circumstances in which a default surcharge, a serious misdeclaration penalty, and default interest will be applied (revision)
- list the other penalties that can be applied by the Customs and Excise (revision)

Session 17 *Value Added Tax*   35, 36

- list the advantages of group registration and divisional registration   5
- explain how a group should be structured in order to be efficient for the purposes of value added tax
- explain the application of the disaggregation rules
- state the effect on the Schedule D Case 1 tax liability of non-deductible value added tax
- explain how value added tax interacts with other taxes

Session 18   Tax Management

22

8b

- describe the features of self assessment (revision)
- calculate payments on account and the balancing payment/repayment (revision)
- calculate interest on overdue tax, and state the penalties that can be charged (revision).
- describe the powers of the Inland Revenue and the procedures followed when enquiring into self assessment returns
- state the interest and penalties that may result from an Inland Revenue enquiry
- explain the use of discovery assessments
- state who is liable to pay IHT, and who is required to report transfers to the Inland Revenue
- describe the procedure for appealing against an Inland Revenue notice of determination
- state the due date for the payment of IHT
- calculate the interest on overdue IHT and on repayments of IHT

Self-Study - Corporate Taxation
- summarise the scope of corporation tax (revision)
- define the terms 'period of account', 'accounting period', and 'financial year' (revision)
- compute a company's profits chargeable to corporation tax for an accounting period (comprehensive example) (revision)
- explain how the corporation tax treatment of the disposal of shares differs from the capital gains tax treatment
- compute a company's corporation tax liability for an accounting period (to include marginal relief) (revision)
- describe the features of self assessment as it applies to companies
- explain how large companies are required to account for corporation tax on a quarterly basis
- calculate the income tax payable by a company for an accounting period, and the due dates thereof (revision)
- compute the amount of loss relief available for set-off in the current, previous and subsequent accounting periods (revision)
- state the respective time limits for loss relief claims (revision)

Session 19   Computation of the Corporation Tax Liability

23, 24, 25

Paper 7
8b

- explain the treatment of a company's profits and losses from loan relationships
- list the factors that will influence the choice of loss relief claimed
- explain how the adjusted trading loss for an accounting period can be varied by the disclaiming of capital allowances
- explain the principles established by Ramsay v CIR and Furniss v Dawson (briefly)

Session 20   Investment Companies and Close Companies

27

6c

- describe how the profits chargeable to corporation tax are determined for an investment company
- list the consequences of being defined as a close company
- list the consequences of being defined as a close investment holding company

Session 21/22   *Groups and Consortia*   26

- define an associated company   6a
- explain the consequences of having associated companies
- define a 51% group, and explain the benefits of making a group election
- define a 75% group
- describe the relief that is available to members of a 75% group
- list the factors that will influence the choice of loss relief within a 75% group
- define a consortium company
- list the reliefs available within a consortium
- compute the corporation tax liabilities of a consortium company and the consortium members
- define a 75% group for capital gains purposes
- explain the treatment of assets transferred within a capital gains group
- describe the effect of a company leaving a capital gains group
- explain how roll-over relief is applied within a capital gains group
- compute the corporation tax liabilities of a capital gains group

Session 23   *Reorganisations*   28

- list the consequences of a company joining or leaving a group   6b
- compute the corporation tax liabilities of a group where a company has joined or left
- list the taxation consequences arising from a share for share amalgamation
- explain the taxation consequences arising from a company's purchase of its own shares
- list the conditions that must be met for a company's purchase of its own shares to receive the special treatment
- describe the taxation consequences of a company going into liquidation

Session 24   *Overseas Aspects of Personal Taxation*   37

- define 'residence', 'ordinary residence', and 'domicile'   7a, b, c, d
- explain how an individual's residence status is affected by the Inland Revenue's extra-statutory concession
- explain the residence status of persons leaving the UK
- explain the residence status of persons arriving in the UK
- state the basis of assessment of income from overseas employment
- state the basis of assessment of profits from trading abroad
- compare the expenses deductible for travel abroad by the employed with those deductible by the self-employed
- compute double taxation relief
- explain the application of capital gains tax to the disposal of assets situated overseas
- determine whether a trade is carried on within the UK, and list the relevant provisions of the OECD model double taxation agreement
- describe the regulations that apply to the remittance of UK income to non-UK residents
- state whether non-UK residents are entitled to personal allowances
- describe the liability of non-UK residents to capital gains tax

Session 25/26   *Company Residence and Its Implications*   37

- define residence for companies
- describe the implications of a company being UK resident   7c, d, f, g
- explain how relief for overseas taxation may be obtained
- calculate the amount of overseas taxation qualifying for double tax relief

- define a controlled foreign company, and explain the consequences of being so classified
- list the taxation factors which might determine whether to trade overseas through a branch or a subsidiary
- define the term 'trading at artificial prices', and explain the consequences of so doing
- list the factors which determine whether a trade is carried on with or within a country (to include the significance of the concept of permanent establishment)
- list the taxation factors which might determine whether to trade in the UK through a branch or a subsidiary

Session 27/28   Tax Planning   40

- compare the tax implications of employment vis-à-vis self employment   8a
- compare alternative remuneration packages from both the employee's and employer's point of view
- compare the tax position of a director/shareholder in a family company with that of a sole trader
- compute the most tax efficient way to extract profit from a company by way of either remuneration, dividend or liquidation
- list the tax implications arising from the disposal of shares in a business run as a company
- advise a group of companies on suitable strategies that will minimise their taxation liabilities
- explain the strategies that a company may adopt in order to minimise and/or defer its liability to corporation tax

List of Excluded Topics

NATIONAL INSURANCE
- The calculation of directors' NIC on a month by month basis.
- For the purposes of class 4 NIC: the offset of trading losses against non-trading income.
- Social Security: the areas of benefit.

INCOME TAX
- Pre 5 April 1988 maintenance payments and deeds of covenant.
- Relief for interest on home improvement loans.
- Detailed computations in respect of share options, share incentives, profit sharing and profit related pay. An employee share ownership plan (ESOP) will not be examined in its own right.
- A detailed knowledge of the conditions which must be met to obtain Inland Revenue approval for an occupational pension scheme.
- Profit related pay schemes.
- Commercial woodlands.
- Computations in respect of a non-qualifying life assurance policy or a qualifying policy which is surrendered within 10 years
- The PYB rules for Schedule D
- The transitional rules applicable to Schedule D
- Retirement annuity premiums
- Farmer's averaging where the lower profits are between 70% and 75% of the higher profits
- TESSAs and PEPs
- Relief for interest on a loan used to purchase a life annuity by a person aged 65 or over.

CAPITAL GAINS TAX
- The rules applicable to assets held on 6 April 1965
- The grant of a lease or sub-lease out of either a freehold, long lease or short lease
- A detailed knowledge of the statements of practice on partnership capital gains
- A question will not be set in respect of a principal private residence where the tax-payer was not in occupation on 31 March 1982.
- A detailed question will not be set on the pooling provisions for shares (for pre 6.4.98 acquisitions).
- Reinvestment relief.
- A detailed question will not be set on the relief available when gains are reinvested in Enterprise Investment Scheme shares or in Venture Capital Trusts.
- Small part disposals of land.
- Capital sums received in respect of damage to an asset.
- Capital sums received in respect of the loss or destruction of an asset.
- The 50% relief where holdover relief has been claimed in respect of a disposal made between 31 March 1982 and 6 April 1988.
- The 50% relief where rollover relief has been claimed in respect of an asset acquired before 31 March 1982 and disposed of before 6 April 1988.

INHERITANCE TAX
- A detailed knowledge of gifts with reservation
- Double grossing up on death
- Valuation of an interest in possession trust involving an annuity, and requiring the use of the higher and lower income yields
- DTR calculation involving $(A/A + B) \times C$ formula
- Conditional exemption of heritage property
- Woodlands relief
- A question will not be set involving the computation of the principal charge or an exit charge for a discretionary trust. (Note that a written question could be set on the principles involved.)
- An accumulation and maintenance trust ceasing to qualify
- The relief on BPR/APR given to exempt legacies

TRUSTS
- Tax liabilities arising during a period of administration
- The 'tax pool' where insufficient 34% income tax has been paid by a discretionary trust
- The IHT implications of adding property to a discretionary trust
- Retirement relief
- The residence of trusts
- The overseas aspects of trusts

VALUE ADDED TAX
- The special VAT schemes for retailers
- The capital goods scheme
- In respect of property and land; leases, do-it-yourself builders and demolition
- A detailed knowledge of penalties (apart from the default surcharge, serious misdeclarations and default interest)

CORPORATION TAX
- Advance corporation tax.

- A question will not be set involving the carry back of losses incurred in an accounting period commencing prior to 2 July 1997.
- S242 ICTA 1988 loss relief
- A question will not be set on the interaction of consortium relief and group relief, although this does not preclude the situation where (a loss making) company has both a (profit making) 75% subsidiary and is also a consortium member (re a profit making consortium company).
- The definition of a close company (although the consequences of a being a close company are examinable)
- Demergers and reconstructions (other than share for share amalgamations). On disincorporations, a question is unlikely to be set on the sale of a trade or business in return for shares. A question involving a double charge to CGT would not be set.
- On liquidations, a question would not be set on the more complex areas such as the different types of liquidation, the preference of debts, or income and expenses arising during the liquidation. A question involving a double charge to CGT would not be set.
- A computational question involving the carry back of a loss arising from a loan relationship for non-trading purposes

OVERSEAS ACTIVITIES

- A detailed knowledge of double tax agreements
- The 100% relief for a 365 day qualifying period
- The foreign income dividend scheme and international headquarters companies
- The migration of a company resident in the UK under the central management and control test.

GENERAL

- The names of cases or a detailed knowledge of the judgements, although a knowledge of the principles derived from the leading cases is required
- A question will not be set requiring a knowledge of anti-avoidance legislation (ie, artificial transactions in land). However, a question might be set requiring comment as to the Inland Revenue's possible attitude towards a particular transaction/situation taking into account the principles from decided cases.

RATES AND ALLOWANCES (up to and including Finance Act 1999)

(A) INCOME TAX

(1) Rates

Rate %	Band of income £	Cumulative tax £
10	1 - 1,500	150
23	1,501 - 28,000	6,095
		6,245
40	28,001 -	

(2) Personal allowances and reliefs

	£
Personal allowance	4,335
Married couple's allowance	1,970*
Age allowance (65 - 74)	
personal	5,720
married couple's	5,125*
income limit	16,800
Age allowance (75 or over)	
personal	5,980
married couple's	5,195*
income limit	16,800
Additional personal allowance	1,970*
Widow's bereavement allowance	1,970*
Blind person's allowance	1,380

* Relief restricted to 10%

(3) Pension contribution limits

Age at start of tax year	Personal pension schemes (%)
35 or less	17½
36 - 45	20
46 - 50	25
51 - 55	30
56 - 60	35
61 and over	40

(4) First year allowance rates

Date expenditure incurred on plant and machinery	FYA rate
2 July 1997 - 1 July 1998	50%
2 July 1998 - 1 July 2000	40%

(B)   CORPORATION TAX

	FY 1996	FY 1997	FY 1998	FY 1999
Rate	33%	31%	31%	30%
Small companies rate (up to £300,000)	24%	21%	21%	20%

Taper relief

$(M-P) \times \frac{1}{P} \times$ fraction

where M is £1,500,000

Fraction	$\frac{9}{400}$	$\frac{1}{40}$	$\frac{1}{40}$	$\frac{1}{40}$

The amounts of dividends received or paid represent the actual amounts without any adjustment for tax credits.

(C)   CAPITAL GAINS TAX

(1)   **Annual exemption**

1999/00   £7,100

(2)   **Retail price index** (RPI)

	1982	1983	1984	1985
January	-	82.61	86.84	91.20
February	-	82.97	87.20	91.94
March	79.44	83.12	87.48	92.80
April	81.04	84.28	88.64	94.78
May	81.62	84.64	88.97	95.21
June	81.85	84.84	89.20	95.41
July	81.88	85.30	89.10	95.23
August	81.90	85.68	89.94	95.49
September	81.85	86.06	90.11	95.44
October	82.26	86.36	90.67	95.59
November	82.66	86.67	90.95	95.92
December	82.51	86.89	90.87	96.05

	1986	1987	1988	1989	1990	1991	1992	1993
January	96.25	100.0	103.3	111.0	119.5	130.2	135.6	137.9
February	96.60	100.4	103.7	111.8	120.2	130.9	136.3	138.8
March	96.73	100.6	104.1	112.3	121.4	131.4	136.7	139.3
April	97.67	101.8	105.8	114.3	125.1	133.1	138.8	140.6
May	97.85	101.9	106.2	115.0	126.2	133.5	139.3	141.1
June	97.79	101.9	106.6	115.4	126.7	134.1	139.3	141.0
July	97.52	101.8	106.7	115.5	126.8	133.8	138.8	140.7
August	97.82	102.1	107.9	115.8	128.1	134.1	138.9	141.3
September	98.30	102.4	108.4	116.6	129.3	134.6	139.4	141.9
October	98.45	102.9	109.5	117.5	130.3	135.1	139.9	141.8
November	99.29	103.4	110.0	118.5	130.0	135.6	139.7	141.6
December	99.62	103.3	110.3	118.8	129.9	135.7	139.2	141.9

	1994	1995	1996	1997	1998	1999	2000
January	141.3	146.0	150.2	154.4	159.5	163.4	e165.9
February	142.1	146.9	150.9	155.0	160.3	e164.1	e166.1
March	142.5	147.5	151.5	155.4	160.8	e164.3	e166.1
April	144.2	149.0	152.6	156.3	162.6	e164.7	e166.3
May	144.7	149.6	152.9	156.9	163.5	e164.5	
June	144.7	149.8	153.0	157.5	163.4	e164.8	
July	144.0	149.1	152.4	157.5	163.0	e165.1	
August	144.7	149.9	153.1	158.5	163.7	e165.2	
September	145.0	150.6	153.8	159.3	164.4	e165.0	
October	145.2	149.8	153.8	159.5	164.5	e165.6	
November	145.3	149.8	153.9	159.6	164.4	e165.7	
December	146.0	150.7	154.4	160.0	164.4	e165.6	

e - estimated

(3) **Lease percentages**

Years	Percentage	Years	Percentage	Years	Percentage
50 or more	100.000	33	90.280	16	64.116
49	99.657	32	89.354	15	61.617
48	99.289	31	88.371	14	58.971
47	98.902	30	87.330	13	56.167
46	98.490	29	86.226	12	53.191
45	98.059	28	85.053	11	50.038
44	97.595	27	83.816	10	46.695
43	97.107	26	82.496	9	43.154
42	96.593	25	81.100	8	39.399
41	96.041	24	79.622	7	35.414
40	95.457	23	78.055	6	31.195
39	94.842	22	76.399	5	26.722
38	94.189	21	74.635	4	21.983
37	93.497	20	72.770	3	16.959
36	92.761	19	70.791	2	11.629
35	91.981	18	68.697	1	5.983
34	91.156	17	66.470	0	0.000

(4)   **Taper Relief**

Number of complete years after 5/4/98 for which asset held	Percentage of Gain chargeable	
	Business Assets	*Non-business Assets*
0	100	100
1	92.5	100
2	85	100
3	77.5	95
4	70	90
5	62.5	85
6	55	80
7	47.5	75
8	40	70
9	32.5	65
10 or more	25	60

(D)   CAR AND FUEL BENEFITS

(1)   **Car scale benefit**

35% of list price when new including accessories, delivery charges and VAT (subject to £80,000 maximum). Reductions in the charge are as follows:

Business mileage 2,500 to 17,999 pa	25% of list price
18,000 or more pa	15% of list price
Then, cars 4 years old and over at end of tax year	¼ reduction
Second car 18,000 or more pa	25% of list price

Cars over 15 years old at tax year end with an open market value of more than £15,000 (which is also higher than the original list price) taxed by reference to the open market value.

(2)   **Van scale benefit**

Vans (under 3.5 tonnes) including fuel	*Under 4 years*	*4 years and over*
	£500	£350

(3)   **Car fuel benefit**

	Petrol £	Diesel £
Cylinder capacity		
Up to 1400 cc	1,210	1,540
1401 - 2001 cc	1,540	1,540
over 2001 cc	2,270	2,270

(E)   INHERITANCE TAX

   (1)   **The nil rate band**   £231,000

   (2)   **Tax rates**

	Rate on gross transfer	Rate on net transfer
Transfers on death	40%	$\frac{2}{3}$
Chargeable lifetime transfers	20%	$\frac{1}{4}$

(F)   NATIONAL INSURANCE CONTRIBUTIONS

   (1)   **Class 1 employed**

      Employee
      £ per week earnings

	Contracted in
Up to £66.00	Nil
Earnings between £66.01 and £500.00	10%

      Employer

Up to £83.00	Nil
Earnings over £83.00	12.2%

   (2)   **Class 2 Self-employed**

      Weekly rate £6.55

      Small earnings exemption £3,770 pa

   (3)   **Class 3 Voluntary**

      Weekly rate £6.45

   (4)   **Class 4 Self-employed**

      6% on annual profits £7,530 – £26,000

1 AN OUTLINE OF INCOME TAX

INTRODUCTION

This chapter gives an outline of income tax, and looks at different types of income and how they are dealt with, within the tax system.

1 THE PRINCIPLES OF INCOME TAX

1.1 Introduction

Liability to income tax is computed by reference to income for a tax year (also known as the fiscal year). This is a year ended on 5 April and is labelled by the calendar years it straddles. Thus the year from 6 April 1999 to 5 April 2000 is referred to as the fiscal year 1999/00.

1.2 The income tax return

Every tax year each taxpayer is required to complete a tax return and submit it to the appropriate district inspector of taxes. Returns are not usually required from non-tax payers (eg, children) or those who are fully taxed at source (eg, employees). The taxpayer has a choice as regards the calculation of his tax liability.

(a) he can calculate his own tax liability, in which case the tax return must be submitted by 31 January following the end of the tax year, or

(b) he can get the Inland Revenue to calculate the tax liability for him, in which case the tax return must be submitted by 30 September following the end of the tax year.

The administration of income tax will be looked at in more detail in chapter 22.

1.3 The rates of income tax

The charge to income tax for 1999/00 comprises three tiers:

- A starting rate of 10%;
- A basic rate of 23%;
- A higher rate of 40%.

The starting rate of 10% applies to the first £1,500 of taxable income, and the basic rate of 23% applies to the next £26,500. The higher rate of 40% applies where taxable income exceeds. £28,000.

However, the tax calculation is complicated by the fact that different rates apply to savings income and dividends.

- Savings income is taxed at a lower rate of 20% if it falls below the higher rate threshold of £28,000. The 20% lower rate applies even if savings income falls within the first £1,500 of taxable income. Once the higher rate threshold is reached, savings income is taxed at the higher rate of 40%.

- Dividends are taxed at a special lower rate of 10% if they fall below the higher rate threshold, and at a special higher rate of 32.5% once the threshold is reached.

Savings income and dividends will be looked at in more detail later in this chapter and in chapter 3.

1.4   Independent taxation

Individual taxpayers, married or single, male or female, are taxed separately on their own income. Married men are not responsible for their wives' tax affairs.

Each individual is separately responsible for

- making a tax return, and
- declaring all their income to the Inspector of Taxes, and
- claiming their own allowances and reliefs, and
- paying any tax due on their own income (and capital gains) or receiving any repayments due.

1.5   Collection of income tax

Income tax may be collected either by deduction from the income at source, or by self-assessment.

(a)   **Deduction at source**

Where possible, the Inland Revenue collect income tax at source – that is immediately the income arises. This avoids the necessity of collecting the tax subsequently from each individual taxpayer receiving the income. The payer of the income acts, effectively, as an agent for the Revenue, deducting income tax usually either at the basic rate (23%) or lower rate (20%) and paying over that tax to the Revenue. The recipient will, therefore, receive only the net income.

It is vital to realise that deduction at source is a method of collection and not necessarily the final liability of the recipient. Thus the gross income must be brought into the taxpayer's computation, and once his total liability has been calculated the amount of income tax already deducted at source is offset against that total liability. Any overpayment can normally be reclaimed from the Revenue.

The most widely-known method of deduction at source is the Pay As You Earn (PAYE) system applied to income from employment. Under this system the employer is liable to account to the Revenue for the tax deducted at the starting, basic and higher rates.

In the following cases, where deduction at source applies, only lower rate tax at the rate of 20% is deducted.

- bank interest;
- building society interest;
- loan and debenture interest received from UK resident companies; and
- interest paid on local authority securities (interest on Government securities is normally paid gross).

Dividends received from UK resident companies are treated as if tax at the rate of 10% had been deducted at source.

(b)   **Self-assessment**

Under self-assessment the tax liability on income not taxed (or not taxed sufficiently) at source is payable through two payments on account, one due on 31 January in the tax year and one due on 31 July following the tax year, with a final (or balancing) payment due on 31 January following the tax year. The two payments on account will be estimated using the previous year's liability and the final payment (or repayment) adjusts the tax already paid to the correct liability for the year.

The 31 January following the tax year is a key date under self-assessment. By that date the tax return and tax calculation (income tax and capital gains tax) for the previous tax year must be submitted along with any further income tax due for that year and the first income tax payment on account for the current year as calculated from the tax return being submitted. The capital gains tax for that previous tax year is also payable on 31 January in one sum (ie, no requirement to make payments on account).

2   THE SCHEDULAR SYSTEM OF INCOME TAX

2.1   Schedular System

Income is classified for income tax purposes according to its nature and source. The classifications into which the income falls are known as Schedules. There are four Schedules and, in Schedules D and E, there are further subdivisions called Cases. The type of income to be included in each Schedule and Case is laid down by statute (Schedules B and C have been abolished).

According to the statutory rules of each Schedule and Case the income will be assessable on either an actual or a current year basis (ie the assessment will be on the actual income arising in the year of assessment or on the profits of an accounting period ending in the current year of assessment). The Schedules and Cases are summarised below

Schedule		Nature of income	Normal basis of assessment
A		Income from land and buildings in the UK	Actual
D	Case I	Profits of a trade	Current year
	Case II	Profits of a profession or vocation	Current year
	Case III	Interest received without deduction of tax at source	Actual
	Case IV	Interest on foreign securities (eg, debentures)	Actual
	Case V	Income from foreign possessions (eg, foreign dividends, rents, business profits and pensions)	Actual
	Case VI	Any taxable income not assessed under another Schedule or Case	Actual
E	(3 Cases)	Emoluments and benefits derived from an office or employment (including all UK pensions)	Actual
F		Dividends received (plus related tax credits) from UK resident companies	Actual

Under the old assessment based system applying for 1995/96 and earlier years the Revenue raised different assessments depending upon the Schedule under which the income was chargeable. Allowances and tax bands were allocated piecemeal and it could be difficult to reconcile the total liability with the tax appearing in the different assessments.

The schedular system is still important under self-assessment for computing assessable amounts but the tax liability is computed for the tax year in a single computation (by the taxpayer) instead of being fragmented over the different assessable sources.

2.2   Income taxed at source

Income received by a taxpayer under deduction of tax at source is not formally assessable under a Schedule or Case. Important exceptions are dividends received from UK resident companies (Schedule F), and emoluments of employment (Schedule E).

Income not formally assessable under a Schedule or Case is always assessable on an actual basis and the gross equivalent is included in the computation. The grossing up is usually at the lower rate (ie, 100/80) as most taxed at source income is taxed at the lower rate of 20%. Dividends must be grossed up at the rate of 10% (ie, 100/90).

The principal examples of taxed income not formally assessed under a Case or Schedule are

- loan stock and debenture interest received from a UK resident company
- bank interest
- building society interest.

3   EXEMPTIONS

3.1   Exempt income

The following income is exempt from income tax

(a)   interest on National Savings Certificates

(b)   interest on repayment of overpaid tax

(c)   redundancy payments under the *Employment Protection Act 1978*

(d)   scholarship income

(e)   state benefits paid in the event of accident, sickness, disability, infirmity or unemployment

(f)   income from Individual Savings Accounts (ISAs) (see chapter 3)

3.2   Exempt persons

The following persons are exempt from income tax

(a)   charities

(b)   approved pension funds and personal pension schemes

4   FORMAT OF THE INCOME TAX COMPUTATION

4.1   Basic computation

An individual's income tax liability for a year of assessment is determined by

(a)   computing statutory total income (STI) – income from all sources less allowable outgoings therefrom, and then deducting

(b)   the reliefs and allowances (eg the personal allowance) to which there is an entitlement in the current year of assessment.

The resultant figure is known as taxable income. Unless a taxpayer has savings income or dividends, the first £1,500 of taxable income is charged to income tax at the starting rate of 10%, the next £26,500 at the basic rate of 23%, and any excess over £28,000 at the higher rate of 40%.

4.2   Example: Income tax computation

Tony, who is single, has statutory total income of £9,335 in 1999/00. He does not have any savings income or dividends.

The personal allowance is £4,335. What is Tony's income tax liability for 1999/00?

4.3   Solution

		£
Statutory total income		9,335
Less: Personal allowance		4,335
Taxable income		5,000

Income tax liability	£	£
	1,500 at 10%	150
	3,500 at 23%	805
	5,000	955

4.4 Activity

Teresa, who is single has statutory total income of £38,335 in 1999/00. She does not have any savings income or dividends.

What is Teresa's income tax liability for 1999/00?

4.5 Activity solution

	£
Statutory total income	38,335
Less: Personal allowance	4,335
Taxable income	34,000

Income tax liability

	£	%	£
At starting rate	1,500	at 10	150
At basic rate	26,500	at 23	6,095
At higher rate	6,000	at 40	2,400
Income tax liability on	34,000	is	8,645

4.6 Statutory total income

This may be broken down into four constituent parts:

- Non-savings/dividend income plus
- Savings income *plus*
- Dividends *less*
- Allowable outgoings (called charges on income)

4.7 Non-savings/dividend income

It is important to separate non-savings/dividend income from savings income and dividends. The reason for this is that savings income is taxed at the lower rate of 20% when it falls below the higher rate threshold, whilst special rates of 10% and 32.5% apply to dividends. This is dealt with in more detail in chapter 3.

The following are the *main* types of *non-saving/dividend income:*

(a) **Schedule A** income from land and buildings

(b) **Schedule D Cases I and II** profits of a trade, profession or vocation

(c) **Schedule D Case VI** casual freelance earnings

(d) **Schedule E** emoluments from an individual's office or employment including

- wages and salaries
- assessed benefits in kind (eg the use of a company car)
- bonuses, commissions and expense allowances
- pensions arising from past employment.

It is necessary to deduct the following:

- allowable expenses of employment, professional subscriptions and occupational pension contributions – deducted from Schedule E income

- allowable personal pension plan contributions paid by the self-employed or people in employments where either no occupational pension is provided by the employer, or where personal provision for a pension has been opted for rather than entry into an employer's scheme.

4.8   Dividends and savings income

Dividends from UK companies are taxed at a special lower rate of 10% if they fall below the higher rate threshold. For this purpose, dividends are treated as the top slice of income. If dividends fall above the higher rate threshold, then they are taxed at a special higher rate of 32.5%.

Income from savings includes:

- Interest from bank and building societies
- Interest from government securities (gilts) and debentures

As already mentioned, savings income is taxed at the lower rate of 20% when it falls below the higher rate threshold. For this purpose, savings income is treated as the next top slice of income after dividends. If savings income falls above the higher rate threshold, then it is taxed at 40% as per normal.

4.9   Allowable outgoings: charges on income

Certain payments made by an individual are allowable deductions for income tax purposes. Some, like those mentioned above, are deductible from specific source(s) of income; others, referred to as charges on income, are deductible from **total** income (non-savings/dividend income, savings income and dividends). The most common example is a charitable deed of covenant. Relief is given in a tax year for payments made in that same year.

4.10   Layout of a personal tax computation

An example of a personal tax computation follows. Pay attention to the way it is set out. Much of the terminology is explained in later chapters.

Mr White: Income tax computation 1999/00

		£	£	£
Non-savings/dividend income				
Schedule D Case I				X
Schedule E Salary/bonus			X	
	Benefits in kind		X	
			X	
Less:	Expenses	X		
	Occupational pension scheme contributions	X		
			(X)	
				X
				X
Less:	Personal pension premiums			(X)
				X
Schedule A				X
				X
Savings income				
	Building society interest (including tax credit)		X	
	Bank interest (including tax credit)		X	
				X
				X

UK dividends (including tax credit)	X
	—
	X
Less: Charges on income (gross)	(X)
	—
Statutory total income	X
Less: Personal allowances	(X)
	—
Taxable income	X
	—
Tax liability	
	£
At starting rate (10%)	X
At basic rate (23%)	X
At lower rate - savings income (20%)	X
- dividends (10%)	X
At higher rate - all income except dividends (40%)	X
- dividends (32.5%)	X
	—
	X
Less: Relief for maintenance payments (@ 10%)	(X)
Tax credit for mortgage interest (@ 10%)	
(where not paid under MIRAS)	(X)
Tax credit on personal allowances (eg, MCA)	
(where tax relief is restricted to 10%)	(X)
	—
	X
Add: Basic rate tax retained on charges	X
	—
Income tax liability	X
Less: PAYE	(X)
Tax suffered on: dividends	(X)
bank interest	(X)
building society interest	(X)
other taxed income	(X)
Tax paid by two payments on account (31.1.2000 and 31.7.2000)	(X)
	—
Final income tax due on 31.1.2001	X
	—

This basic layout can be adapted to suit the particular requirements of each question.

4.11   Tax Liability and Tax Payable

The following standardised terms are used in the requirements of examination questions:

Tax Liability: The total income tax liability after deducting any allowances or reliefs, and adding any basic rate tax retained from charges on income (such as charitable deeds of covenant).

Tax Payable: The tax liability after deducting credits for any tax already suffered.

Payments on account under self-assessment should only be taken into account if a question specifies that this is to be done. Otherwise, they can be ignored.

5   SOCIAL SECURITY BENEFITS

5.1   Tax-free benefits

The following are the principal tax-free benefits:

(a)   family credit
(b)   incapacity benefit (initial period only)
(c)   child benefit
(d)   lump sum widow's payment.

Other benefits, such as the state pension and the jobseeker's allowance paid to the unemployed are taxable.

5.2   Statutory redundancy payments

An employee is entitled to a statutory redundancy payment if he loses his job through redundancy.

The amount of the payment depends on weekly pay, length of service, and the age of the employee.

Payments are exempt from income tax, although they may reduce the amount of any non-statutory redundancy payment that is otherwise exempt.

5.3   Enterprise Allowance Scheme

The scheme provides a flat rate weekly allowance for the first year of a new business venture set up by an unemployed person.

Payments under the scheme are taxable under Schedule D Case VI.

6   CONNECTED PERSONS

6.1   Introduction

There are several situations where it is necessary to establish with whom an individual is connected.

6.2   Connected persons

An individual is connected with family members and any company he controls. For this purpose family members are:

- ancestors, lineal descendants and their spouses;
- brothers, sisters and their spouses;
- his spouse; and
- the relatives (as in categories above) of his or her spouse.

These relationships are most easily seen in diagrammatic form as shown below.

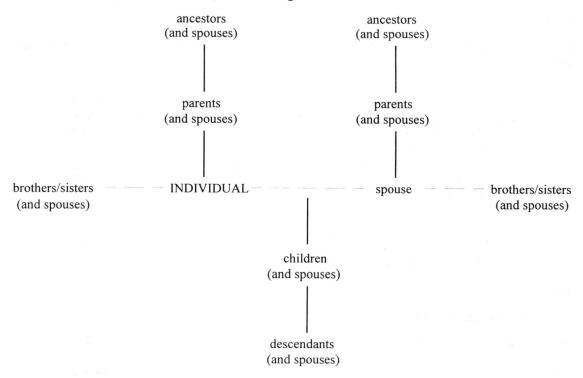

An individual is also connected with business partners and companies over which the individual has control.

These rules also apply to company and to partnerships. Companies are connected with one another when one controls the other or both are under common control. Two partnerships are deemed to be connected with one another where one person is common to both.

7   SELF TEST QUESTIONS

7.1   What is a tax year (also known as a fiscal year)? (1.1)

7.2   From what income is lower rate tax deducted? (1.5)

7.3   What Schedules and Cases is income classified into for the purposes of income tax? (2.1)

7.4   What type of income is included in each Schedule and Case? (2.1)

7.5   What is the normal basis of assessment for each Schedule and Case? (2.1)

7.6   What income is exempt from tax? (3.1)

7.7   How is an individual's income tax liability determined for a year of assessment? (4.1)

7.8   What are the main sources of savings income? (4.8)

7.9   Which social security benefits are tax-free? (5.1)

7.10   Which family members are connected persons? (6.2)

8   EXAMINATION TYPE QUESTION

8.1   Kate

Kate, a single person, has the following income, outgoings and allowances for the year ended 5 April 2000.

	£
Salary	34,400
Benefits in kind by reason of employment	875
Allowable expenses of employment	(95)
Taxed investment income - bank interest (gross)	520
- building society interest (gross)	890
Rents from UK unfurnished lettings	1,890
Personal allowance	4,335
Allowable charge on income paid (gross)	2,160

Calculate her income tax liability for 1999/00.

9   ANSWER TO EXAMINATION TYPE QUESTION

9.1   Kate

Income tax computation 1999/00

Non-savings/dividend income		£	£
Schedule E˙			
Salary			34,400
Benefit in kind			875
			35,275
Less: Allowable expenses			(95)
			35,180
Schedule A			1,890
			37,070
Savings income	- bank interest	520	
	- building society interest (actual)	890	
			1,410
			38,480
Less: Charge on income (gross)			(2,160)
Statutory total income			36,320
Less: Personal allowance			(4,335)
Taxable income			31,985

Income tax liability

	£	%	£
Starting rate	1,500	10	150
Basic rate	26,500	23	6,095
Higher rate	3,985	40	1,594
			7,839
Basic rate tax retained on charge 2,160 at 23%			497
Income tax liability			8,336

Notes:

(1)   The savings income is taxed at 40% since it is treated as the top part of taxable income and therefore falls entirely within the higher rate band.

(2)   The logic behind adding the basic rate tax retained on charges paid will be covered in chapter 4.

2 INCOME FROM LAND AND BUILDINGS

INTRODUCTION & LEARNING OBJECTIVES

All UK income from land and buildings is taxed under Schedule A for individuals, although special rules apply to furnished holiday lettings. As from 1 April 1998, the rules for companies are virtually identical to those for individuals. The few minor differences are dealt with in the corporation tax chapters.

When you have studied this chapter you should have learned the following:

- How Schedule A income is assessed, and the relief available for Schedule A losses.
- How premiums for the grant of leases are dealt with.
- The special treatment of furnished holiday accommodation.
- Rent a room relief.

1 SCHEDULE A

1.1 Income liable

The following income is liable to assessment under Schedule A

(a) rents under any lease or tenancy agreement
(b) premium received on grant of a short lease (this is covered in the next section).

1.2 Basis of assessment

The income from land and buildings is computed as if the letting of the property were a business, and the amount assessable under Schedule A will be the rental business profits of the year of assessment. If the landlord lets more than one property, the different lettings all form one single business, so that the assessable amount is the aggregate of the profits and losses from each separate property.

Thus the assessable income for 1999/00 is the rent due for the period 6 April 1999 to 5 April 2000, less the expenses payable for the same period. The due dates for payment of the rent, the date of actual receipt of the rent, and the date of payment of the expenses are irrelevant since business accounts should be drawn up on the accruals basis.

Note that although the computation is made as if the letting were a business, the net income is still generally assessable under Schedule A, and the letting is not treated as an actual business. The main exception to this is furnished holiday lettings (see beyond). Occasionally the letting may constitute an actual trade, for example where lodgers are taken in, in which case the net income will be assessable under Schedule D Case I.

1.3 Activity

Hembery owns a property which was let for the first time on 1 July 1999. The rent of £5,000 pa is paid alternatively (i) quarterly in advance; (ii) quarterly in arrears; (iii) annually in advance. Hembery paid allowable expenses of £200 in December 1999 (related to redecoration following a burst pipe), and £400 in May 2000 for repairs completed in March 2000.

Compute the Schedule A profit for 1999/00.

1.4   Activity solution

The rent assessable in each case is the rent due for the period 1 July 1999 to 5 April 2000. Expenses relating to the same period are deductible.

	£	£
Rent due 9/12 × £5,000		3,750
Expenses		
Redecoration	200	
Repairs	400	
	——	
		(600)
Schedule A profit for 1999/00		3,150
		——

1.5   Allowable deductions

The expenses allowable against the rental income are computed under the normal rules for businesses. These are discussed fully in the chapter on Schedule D Case I, but the main rules are given below.

(a)   To be allowable, the expenses must have been incurred wholly and exclusively in connection with the business.

This covers items such as:

- insurance;
- agents fees;
- other management expenses;
- repairs;
- interest on a loan to acquire or improve the property.

Where property is not let at a full rent (eg, to an aged relative) a portion of the expenses will be disallowed as not being wholly and exclusively incurred for the business. For example if rent charged is £250 pa but a commercial rent would be £1,000 pa, only 25% of expenses will be allowed. In practice the Revenue would allow the expenses but only up to the amount of the rent on that property.

(b)   Capital expenditure is not allowable.

The main distinction between capital and revenue expenditure is between improvements and repairs. Repairs are allowable expenses, whilst improvements are not. In some cases a repair will include an element of improvement, in which case it is necessary to apportion the expenditure between capital and revenue.

Depreciation may be charged in accounts as a means of writing off the cost of capital expenditure over the life of an asset. It is not an allowable deduction, but capital allowances may be claimed instead for expenditure on plant and machinery used for the purposes of the letting (see Capital Allowances chapter).

For furnished lettings, capital allowances are normally replaced by a 'wear and tear' allowance, which is calculated as 10% of the rent. If the landlord pays the council tax on the property, the wear and tear allowance is calculated as 10% of the rent net of the council tax.

(c)   Specific bad debts are allowable, whilst a general provision for bad debts is not allowable. If a tenant leaves without paying the outstanding rent, the amount owed can be deducted as an expense. However the landlord could not make a general deduction of (say) 5% of rent due in case a tenant should default.

(d)   Relief is available for any expenditure incurred before letting commenced, under the normal pretrading expenditure rules.

1.6   Activity

Giles owns a cottage which he lets out furnished at an annual rent of £3,600, payable monthly in advance. During 1999/00 he incurs the following expenditure:

May 1999	Replacement of windows with new UVPC double glazed units (it is estimated that the improvement element in the expenditure was £1,500)	£2,000
June 1999	Insurance for year from 5 July (previous year - £420)	£480
November 1999	Drain clearance	£380
May 2000	Redecoration (work completed in March 2000)	£750

The tenant had vacated the property during June 1999 without having paid the rent due for June. Giles was unable to trace the defaulting tenant, but managed to let the property to new tenants from 1 July 1999.

Calculate the Schedule A profit for 1999/00 assuming Giles claims the 10% wear and tear allowance.

1.7   Activity solution

	£	£
Rent due £300 × 12		3,600
Expenses		
Bad debt - June 1999 rent	300	
Window repairs £(2,000 − 1,500)	500	
Insurance 3/12 × £420 + 9/12 × £480	465	
Drain clearance	380	
Redecoration	750	
Wear and tear 10% × £(3,600 − 300)	330	
		(2,725)
Schedule A profit for 1999/00		875

1.8   Schedule A losses

If the landlord owns more than one property, the profits and losses on all the properties are aggregated to calculate the Schedule A assessment for the year. Effectively this allows the loss arising on one property to be set against the profits arising on other properties.

This set off applies irrespective of the nature of the underlying lease. Note, however that where a property is let at less than the market rental, the Revenue practice of restricting expenses to the amount of the rent means that such leases will not produce allowable losses.

If there is an overall Schedule A loss, the assessment for the year will be nil. The loss is carried forward, and set against the Schedule A assessment for the following year. If the income in the following year is insufficient to relieve the loss, the unrelieved balance is carried forward against future Schedule A income.

1.9   Activity

Sheila owns three properties which were rented out. Her assessable income and allowable expenses for the two years to 5 April 2000 were:

	Property		
	1	2	3
	£	£	£
Income			
1998/99	1,200	450	3,150
1999/00	800	1,750	2,550
Expenses			
1998/99	1,850	600	2,800
1999/00	900	950	2,700

What are Sheila's Schedule A profit/(loss) amounts for 1998/99 and 1999/00?

1.10   Activity solution

	Property		
	1	2	3
	£	£	£
1998/99			
Income	1,200	450	3,150
Less: Expenses	1,850	600	2,800
Profit/(loss)	(650)	(150)	350
Total			(450)
Schedule A profit (loss c/f £450)			Nil
1999/00			
Income	800	1,750	2,550
Less: Expenses	900	950	2,700
Profit/(loss)	(100)	800	(150)
Total			550
Less: Schedule A loss b/f			(450)
Schedule A profit			100

2   PREMIUMS RECEIVED ON THE GRANT OF A SHORT LEASE

2.1   Premiums

A premium is a lump sum payment made by the tenant to the landlord in consideration of the granting of a lease. Since the payment is in the nature of rent (a higher annual rent would be charged if no premium were paid) the landlord is assessed under Schedule A on the premium received, **unless the premium is for a long lease (exceeding 50 years).** (Premiums on long leases are treated as capital receipts and are dealt with only under the capital gains legislation.)

A premium received on the grant of a short lease (for 50 years or less) is treated as rent assessed under Schedule A in the fiscal year in which the lease is granted.

The amount assessable is

(a)   the amount of the premium *less*

(b)   2% of the premium for each complete year of the lease (other than the first).

This can be calculated either as:

$$\text{Premium} \times \frac{51 - \text{duration of lease}}{50}$$

or as

Premium	x
Less: Premium × 2% × (Duration of lease − 1)	(x)
	x

This rule does not apply if a lease is being assigned (ie, where the entire interest in a property is sold).

2.2   Activity

A 21 years 11 months lease is granted for a premium of £10,000 in 1999/00.

What is the amount assessable under Schedule A for 1999/00?

2.3   Activity solution

Assessable under Schedule A for 1999/00.

$$£10,000 \times \frac{51 - 21}{50} = £6,000$$

2.4   Leases determinable at intervals

In order to avoid income tax it would be a simple matter to grant a lease for over 50 years, but to give the landlord the right to determine (ie end) the lease before the expiration of 50 years.

Anti-avoidance legislation provides that where the lease can be terminated at some date during the lease, the period of the lease is taken to extend only to the earliest date on which the lease may be terminated, where the premium payable is obviously less than market value for a longer lease.

2.5   Example: Duration of a lease

Arnold grants a 99-year lease on property in Kensington for a premium of £4,000. The agreement states that the lessor may terminate the lease at the end of the fifth year. The current market value of a 99-year lease on a similar property in that area is £180,000.

What will be taken as the period of the lease, and what amount, if any is assessable under Schedule A?

2.6   Solution

In this case it is patently obvious that the landlord intends to terminate the lease after five years and that the premium charged relates only to that period and not 99 years. Thus the duration of the lease for Schedule A purposes will be five years and the computation will be:

Assessable under Schedule A

$$£4,000 \times \frac{51 - 5}{50} = £3,680$$

2.7   Premiums paid by traders

A proportion of a premium paid for the grant of a short lease (not exceeding 50 years) of business premises is deductible each year from business profits.

The amount allowable each year is computed by dividing the sum assessable on the landlord under Schedule A by the number of years of the lease.

2.8   Example: Premiums paid by traders

Rodney granted a 21-year lease of business premises to Charles on 1 July 1999 for a premium of £10,500. Charles uses the premises for his trade as a restaurateur.

What are the income tax consequences on Rodney and Charles?

2.9   Solution

The amount assessable under Schedule A on Rodney for 1999/00 is

$$£10,500 \times \frac{51 - 21}{50} = £6,300$$

The **annual** deduction given to Charles, the payer of the premium, in his Schedule D Case 1 computation is

$$\frac{\text{Amount assessable as income on recipient}}{\text{Duration of lease}} \text{ ie, } \frac{£6,300}{21} = £300 \text{ pa for 21 years.}.$$

If Charles prepares accounts to 30 September each year only a 3 months portion of the annual amount ie, £75 (3/12 × 300) will be allowed in the year ended 30 September 1999.

2.10   Premiums for granting subleases

If a tenant sublets his property and grants a lease to a subtenant, any premium he charges to the subtenant will be assessable under Schedule A under the normal rules for granting leases. However, if the tenant originally paid a premium on his own lease (known as the head lease) relief is given as follows:

$$\text{Taxable premium for head lease} \times \frac{\text{duration of sublease}}{\text{duration of headlease}}.$$

2.11   Example: Grant of a sublease

Victor granted a lease to Alec on 1 August 1993 for a period of 20 years. Alec paid a premium of £20,000.

On 1 August 1999 Alec granted a sublease to Max for a period of 5 years. Max paid a premium of £24,000.

Calculate the amount assessable under Schedule A on Alec for 1999/00 for the premium received from Max.

2.12   Solution

The taxable premium for the head lease

$$£20,000 \times \frac{51 - 20}{50} = £12,400.$$

Alec's Schedule A income for 1999/00.

	£
Premium received	
$£24,000 \times \dfrac{51 - 5}{50}$	22,080
Less: Relief for premium paid	
$£12,400 \times \dfrac{5}{20}$	3,100
	——
	18,980
	——

3   FURNISHED HOLIDAY ACCOMMODATION

3.1   Introduction

Profits arising from the commercial letting of furnished holiday accommodation are treated as **earned** income arising from the operation of a single and separate trade, even though still assessable under Schedule A.

3.2   Furnished holiday accommodation

The letting will only be treated as furnished holiday accommodation if it is furnished, let on a commercial basis with a view to the realisation of profits, and satisfies the following conditions.

(a)   It is **available** for commercial letting, to the public generally, as holiday accommodation for not less than 140 days a year;

(b)   the accommodation is **actually let** for at least 70 days in that 140 day period;

(c)   for at least seven months out of the twelve months qualifying period, the property must not normally be occupied by the same person continuously for more than 31 days.

3.3   Tax treatment of furnished holiday lettings

Any profits from commercially let furnished holiday accommodation remain assessable under Schedule A computed as if the letting were a business. Note, however, the following.

The profits deriving from all the qualifying holiday accommodation will be treated as earned income arising from a single trade carried on by the landlord. The following advantages and reliefs thereby become available.

(a)   The profits are relevant earnings for the purposes of relief for personal pension scheme contributions.

(b)   Relief may be claimed for any losses sustained as if they were trading losses (see chapter on trading losses).

(c)   Capital gains tax roll-over relief, retirement relief and the business rate of taper relief are available where appropriate.

(d)   Capital allowances will be available in respect of plant and machinery. This will normally be more beneficial than the wear and tear allowance.

| Conclusion | Profits from furnished holiday lettings, although assessable according to the Schedule A rules are treated as earned income. From an exam point of view the most important of the tax treatments listed are: |

- profits treated as relevant earnings for personal pension premium purposes; and

- any loss may be relieved as if it were a trading loss.

4   RENT A ROOM RELIEF

4.1   Introduction

If an individual lets furnished accommodation in his main residence, and the income is liable to tax under Schedule A or Schedule D Case I a special exemption applies.

If the gross annual receipts (before expenses or capital allowances) are £4,250 or below, they will be exempt from tax.

4.2   The rent a room scheme

The detailed rules for the rent a room scheme are as follows:

(a)   The individual's limit of £4,250 is reduced by half to £2,125 if, during a particular tax year any other person(s) also received income from letting accommodation in the property while the property was the first person's main residence.

  This rule allows a married couple taking in lodgers to either have all the rent paid to one spouse (who will then have the full limit of £4,250) or to have the rent divided between the spouses (and each spouse will then have a limit of £2,125).

(b)   An individual may elect to ignore the exemption for a particular year (for example if a loss is incurred when taking account of expenses).

(c)   If the gross annual receipts are more than £4,250, an individual may choose between:

  •   paying tax on the excess of his gross rent over £4,250; or
  •   being taxed in the ordinary way on their profit from letting (rent less expenses).

| Conclusion | Gross annual income from renting furnished accommodation in an individual's only main residence is exempt from tax if it amounts to £4,250 or less. |

5   CHAPTER SUMMARY

This chapter has dealt with income from land and buildings. The following areas were covered:

•   Income from land and property. Profits are assessable under Schedule A on an accruals basis. Note how losses are relieved;

•   Furnished holiday accommodation. This income is treated as earned income, although still assessable under Schedule A. Note the tax treatment of income from furnished holiday accommodation;

•   Rent a room relief. Where an individual receives gross annual receipts of £4,250 or less from renting furnished accommodation in his main residence, it will be exempt from tax.

6   SELF TEST QUESTIONS

6.1   What is the basis of assessment for income assessed under Schedule A? (1.2)

6.2   What deductions are allowable from income assessed under Schedule A? (1.5)

6.3   What deduction is available for depreciation from income from furnished lettings? (1.5)

6.4   What relief is available for Schedule A losses? (1.8)

6.5   How are premiums which are received in consideration of granting a lease taxed? (2.1)

6.6   What relief is given for premiums paid by traders? (2.7)

6.7   What are the conditions for lettings to be treated as furnished holiday accommodation? (3.2)

6.8   What is the tax treatment of furnished holiday lettings? (3.3)

6.9   What exemption applies if an individual lets furnished accommodation in his own residence? (4.1)

6.10   If gross rents from the letting of furnished accommodation in an individual's main residence exceed £4,250, how will the income be taxed? (4.2)

7   EXAMINATION TYPE QUESTIONS

7.1   Eastleigh

Eastleigh acquired two properties on 1 June 1999 which were first let on 1 July 1999.

Property A is let unfurnished for an annual rental of £4,000 payable quarterly in advance. He incurred the following expenditure in respect of this property.

		£
20.6.99	Repairs to roof following a violent storm on 15 June	1,600
29.6.99	Insurance for y/e 31.5.00	420
1.2.2000	Repainting exterior	810

Property B is let furnished for an annual rental of £5,000, payable quarterly in arrears. The tenants were late in paying the amount due on 31 March 2000 - this was not received until 15 April 2000.

Eastleigh incurred the following expenditure in respect of this property in 1999/00.

		£
4.6.99	Letting expenses paid to agent	40
29.6.99	Insurance for y/e 31.5.2000	585

You are required to calculate Eastleigh's Schedule A profit for 1999/00. (Make all calculations to the nearest month.)

7.2   Tom Jones

For many years Tom Jones has owned six houses in Upland Avenue which are available for letting unfurnished. He is responsible for the repairs to numbers 21, 23, 25 and 67. The tenants are responsible for the repairs to numbers 38 and 40.

Tom's mother lives at number 67. The rent she pays is about 25% of a commercial rate and the Revenue accept Tom's profits on the basis of allowing only 25% of expenses.

The following details have been provided by the client.

	Property number					
	21	*23*	*25*	*38*	*40*	*67*
	£	£	£	£	£	£
Rent due for y/e 5.4.2000	2,080	1,820	2,340	1,300	1,300	520
Insurance due for y/e 5.4.2000	280	220	340	150	150	140

(1)   Tom employs a gardener to look after all the properties and pays him £1,200 a year. There are also accountancy charges of £480 a year; both of these costs are allocated equally to each property.

(2)   Numbers 23 and 40 had new tenancies in the year. The cost of advertising for tenants was £50 in respect of number 23 and £100 for number 40. The new tenant at number 23 took over immediately the old tenant moved out. Unfortunately, the old tenant at No 40 defaulted on rent of £350 due before the new tenant moved in.

(3)   During the year Tom had to replace the boiler in number 40 at a cost of £800. During the year he also had to replace the water tank at number 21 at a cost of £100 and a new roof for number 25 cost him £5,000.

(4)   Tom has loans outstanding on each of the six properties and pays interest of £500 per year on each loan.

You are required:

(a)   to calculate Tom's Schedule A loss for 1999/00

(b)   to explain how relief can be obtained for the loss.

8   ANSWERS TO EXAMINATION TYPE QUESTIONS

8.1   Eastleigh

	£	£
Property A		
Rents 9/12 × £4,000		3,000
Less: Insurance (10/12 × £420)	350	
Repainting exterior	810	
Roof repairs (pretrading expenditure)	1,600	
		2,760
		240
Property B		
Rent 9/12 × £5,000		3,750
Less: Insurance (10/12 × £585)	487	
Letting expenses	40	
		527
		3,223
Wear and tear allowance 10% × 3,750		375
		2,848
Schedule A profit for 1999/00 (£240 + £2,848)		3,088

8.2   Tom Jones

Schedule A loss for 1999/00

Upland Avenue No	21 £	23 £	25 £	38 £	40 £	67 £
Rent due for y/e 5.4.2000	2,080	1,820	2,340	1,300	1,300	520
Expenses payable						
Insurance	280	220	340	150	150	35
Gardener	200	200	200	200	200	50
Accountancy	80	80	80	80	80	20
Advertising		50			100	
Repairs	100		5,000		800	
Bad debt					350	
Interest	500	500	500	500	500	125
	1,160	1,050	6,120	930	2,180	230
Profit/(loss)	920	770	(3,780)	370	(880)	290

Summary

	£
No 21	920
No 23	770
No 25	(3,780)
No 38	370
No 40	(880)
No 67	290
	(2,310)
Amount assessable under Schedule A for 1999/00	Nil
Loss carried forward for offset against future Schedule A profits	£2,310

As it is not necessary to consider profits and losses on each property individually the accounts could be drawn up to show the total rents etc for all the properties, instead of property by property. Care has to be taken to disallow a portion of expenses relating to the non-commercial letting.

3 FINANCIAL INVESTMENTS AND SUNDRY INCOME

INTRODUCTION & LEARNING OBJECTIVES

Funds may be invested in banks, building societies or stocks and shares; income received from such investments may be paid gross, paid under deduction of tax or be tax free. It is important to know how the various types of income are dealt with.

Individuals may pay premiums into a pension fund, which is a very tax effective way of investing. The provisions relating to pension premiums are quite complicated, but nevertheless, important for exam purposes.

When you have studied this chapter you should have learned the following:

- Investments that are tax-free
- What constitutes Schedule D Case III income and how it is taxed
- The scope of Schedule D Case VI income
- The types of income that are received under deduction of tax
- The special rules applying to 'savings' income
- How trust income is taxed
- The tax relief given by an individual savings account
- The tax relief given by the enterprise investment scheme
- The tax relief given by venture capital trusts
- Investment in pension funds.

1 TAX-FREE INVESTMENTS

1.1 Introduction

The following investment income is tax-free

- Proceeds of National Savings Certificates

- Premium Bond winnings

- First £70 of interest from an NSB ordinary account

- Income from an individual savings account

2 SCHEDULE D CASE III

2.1 Income assessable

Schedule D Case III is primarily concerned with interest not taxed at source.

The main examples are:

- National Savings Bank accounts; and
- most holdings of Government securities (gilts)

2.2 National Savings Bank interest

(a) The first £70 interest pa from an **ordinary** account with the NSB is exempt from tax.
(b) Interest from an **investment** account with the NSB is assessable in full.

2.3   Basis of assessment

The actual basis of assessment applies. The income assessable is the interest arising (ie, **received** or **credited** to the account) during the tax year.

No account is taken of accrued income under the income tax rules, ie income arises when it is received.

2.4   Other examples of income covered by Schedule D Case III

Interest on the following is also received gross:

- loans between individuals; and

- interest on National Savings Income Bonds.

> Conclusion   Interest received gross is taxed under Schedule D Case III on the actual basis.   The most important examples of interest assessable under Schedule D Case III are:
>
> - interest from National Savings Bank accounts; and
> - interest from gilts.

3   SCHEDULE D CASE VI

3.1   Introduction

Schedule D Case VI deals with income which is not taxed under any other Schedule or Case.

Examples of types of income which are assessed under Schedule D Case VI are:

- profits on the sale of patent rights;
- casual commission;
- sale of future earnings;
- post-cessation receipts; and
- the enterprise allowance

3.2   Basis of assessment

In all instances it is the income and profits received in the actual tax year which are assessable.

4   DIVIDENDS

4.1   Introduction

Dividends received from a company resident in the UK are charged to income tax. The actual basis applies.

4.2   Tax credit

(a)   A dividend received carries with it a tax credit which may be set against the recipient's total tax liability. It is not possible to reclaim the tax credit on dividends where it exceeds the total liability. It is the gross dividends (ie, dividend received plus the tax credit) received in the actual tax year which are assessable.

(b)   The tax credit is 10/90 of the dividend received (or 10% of the gross dividend). Thus if an individual received a dividend of £180 on 1 August 1999, the tax credit is £180 × 10/90 ie, £20, and the amount assessable in 1999/00 is £200 (£180 + £20).

4.3   Taxation of dividends

Special rules apply to the income taxation of dividends.

Dividends received by an individual from a UK resident company are taxed at a special lower rate of 10% if they fall below the higher rate threshold of £28,000. For this purpose, dividends are treated as the top slice of income. If dividends fall above the higher rate threshold, then they are taxed at a special higher rate of 32.5%.

Since dividends have a 10% tax credit, basic rate taxpayers have no further liability (the credit meets the 10% tax rate). Higher rate taxpayers have an additional liability of 22.5% (32.5% less the 10% tax credit).

As dividends (and savings income) receive a special tax treatment, it is useful to include extra columns in the standard taxable income layout to analyse between dividends, savings income and non-savings/dividend income.

4.4   Example: Taxation of dividends - starting rate taxpayer

Simone, a single person, received net dividends of £4,500 in 1999/00.

Calculate the income tax payable/repayable

4.5   Solution

	£
Dividends	4,500
Tax credit (4,500 x 10/90)	500
	5,000
Less: Personal allowance	4,335
Taxable income	665
Income tax liability £665 × 10%	66
Less: Tax credit on dividends	500
Income tax payable	Nil

The surplus tax credit of £434 (500 - 66) is not repayable.

4.6   Example: Taxation of dividends - basic rate taxpayer

Jeremy, a single person, received a salary of £14,000 (PAYE: £1,980) and net dividends of £6,750 in 1999/00.

Calculate the income tax payable.

4.7   Solution

The dividends are treated as the highest part of Jeremy's income. As he is only a basic rate taxpayer, all the dividends (grossed up) will be taxed at the special lower rate of 10%.

	£	£	Non-dividend £	Dividend £
Schedule E		14,000	14,000	-
Dividends	6,750			
Tax credit (6,750 × 10/90)	750			
		7,500	-	7,500
		21,500	14,000	7,500
Less: Personal allowance		4,335	4,335	-
Taxable income		17,165	9,665	7,500

		£
Income tax liability		
Taxable at starting rate (Sch E) £1,500 × 10%		150
Taxable at basic rate (Sch E) (9,665 − 1,500) = 8,165 × 23%		1,878
Taxable at special lower rate (dividend plus tax credit) £7,500 × 10%		750
		2,778
Less: Tax credit on dividends £7,500 × 20%		(750)
PAYE		(1,980)
Income tax payable		48

Note that the personal allowance is set first against the non-dividend income.

4.8   Example - Taxation of dividends - higher rate taxpayer

Jacob, a single person, received a salary of £22,000 (PAYE: £3,840) and net dividends of £15,750 in 1999/00.

Calculate the income tax payable.

4.7   Solution

	£	£	Non-savings £	Savings £
Schedule E		22,000	22,000	-
Dividends	15,750			
Tax credit (15,750 × 10/90)	1,750			
		17,500	–	17,500
		39,500	22,000	17,500
Less: Personal allowance		4,335	4,335	–
Taxable income		35,165	17,665	17,500

The dividends are treated as the highest part of Jacob's income. The first £10,335 (£28,000 − 17,665) of the gross dividend falls into the basic rate band, and will be taxed at the special lower rate of 10%, the remaining £7,165 (17,500 − 10,335) falls into the higher rate band and will be taxed at the special higher rate of 32.5%.

	£
Income tax liability	
Taxable at starting rate (Sch E) £1,500 × 10%	150
Taxable at basic rate (Sch E) (17,665 − 1,500) = £16,165 × 23%	3,718
Taxable at special lower rate (dividend) £10,335 × 10%	1,033
Taxable at special higher rate (balance of dividend) £7,165 × 32.5%	2,329
	7,230
Less: Tax credit on dividends £17,500 × 10%	(1,750)
PAYE	(3,840)
Income tax payable	1,640

Conclusion   Dividends received by an individual are taxable only at the special lower or higher rates of 10% and 32.5%. They are treated as the highest part of an individual's taxable income for the purpose of calculating the tax liability.

5   BANK AND BUILDING SOCIETY INTEREST

5.1   Introduction

Banks and building societies pay interest to individuals net of lower rate tax (10%).

5.2   Basis of assessment

(a)   An individual is taxed on the grossed up amount of the actual interest received in a tax year (ie, the amount credited to the account by the bank or building society during the tax year regardless of when the individual has his passbook written up). He will receive a lower rate tax credit for the lower rate tax suffered at source, or a repayment where tax is overpaid. Thus if an individual receives interest of £240, he will be taxed on £240 × 100/80 ie, £300 and has a tax credit of £60 (£300 × 20%).

(b)   Bank and building society interest is taxed at the lower rate of 20% to the extent that it falls below the higher rate threshold of £28,000. The 20% rate applies even if the interest falls in the first £1,500 of taxable income, since the starting rate of 10% does not apply to savings income. For this purpose, bank and building society interest, along with other savings income is treated as the next top slice of income after (ie, 'below') dividends.

(c)   Banks and building societies may pay interest gross to an individual who has supplied a certificate of non-liability to income tax. If it transpires that the individual is liable to income tax after all, then the gross interest is assessable under Schedule D Case III. Interest paid by the National Savings Bank is always paid gross and assessable under Schedule D Case III but it is still subject to the saving income tax regime.

5.3   Set off of annual charges, personal allowances and other deductions

Annual charges, personal allowances and other deductions are normally set firstly against non-savings income in preference to savings income (or dividends). This is because the basic rate of tax on non savings income (23%) is higher than the corresponding lower rate of tax on savings income (20%).

However, this will not be the case where the 10% starting rate of tax is concerned. Where possible, annual charges, personal allowances and other deductions should therefore be set off so as to leave £1,500 of non-savings income chargeable to tax.

5.4   Example: Utilising the starting rate tax band

Simon, a single person, received a salary of £5,000 and building society interest of £6,000 (net) in 1999/00.

Calculate the income tax repayable.

5.5   Solution

	Non-savings income	Savings
		£
Schedule E	5,000	
BSI 6,000 × 100/80		7,500
Less: Personal allowance	3,500	835
Taxable income	1,500	6,665
Income tax liability		
Taxable at starting rate (Sch E) £1,500 x 10%		150
Taxable at lower rate (BSI) £6,665 × 20%		1,333

	1,483
Less: Tax credit on BSI £7,500 x 20%	1,500
Income tax repayable	17

The personal allowance has been allocated between non-savings income and savings income so as to leave £1,500 of the Schedule E income chargeable to tax. If the whole personal allowance had been set off against the non-savings income, then Simon's income tax liability would have been £83 (835 x 10% (20% - 10%)) higher. Unlike the tax credit attached to a dividend, the tax credit on BSI (and other savings income) is repayable.

6   TAXED INCOME

6.1   Introduction

In addition to bank interest and building society interest certain other income is received net of lower rate tax. The gross amount of income is taxable, and the taxpayer will receive a lower rate tax credit for the lower rate tax suffered at source or a repayment where tax is overpaid.

Taxed income received net of lower rate tax includes the following:

- interest on company loans and debentures; and
- interest on local authority stocks.

Such income is taxed under the same special rules applying to savings income.

Interest is normally paid gross on UK government securities.

One type of taxed income, patent royalties, is received net of basic rate tax and is not treated as 'savings income'.

6.2   Income from unit trusts and open-ended investment companies

Dividends received by unit holders in unit trusts are treated in the same way as dividends received by shareholders in companies.

Open-ended investment companies (OEICs) are a relatively new type of investment, which are designed to eventually replace unit trusts. Unit trusts and OEICs are similar in nature, but OEICs are incorporated companies rather than trusts. They were introduced because they are easier to market overseas.

Dividends from OEICs are treated in exactly the same way as any other company dividends.

6.3   Example - Taxation of savings income and dividends - higher rate taxpayer

Andrew, a single man, receives the following income for 1999/00.

	£
Salary	18,000
Building society interest	2,400 (net)
UK government stock interest	2,000 (gross)
Patent royalties	770 (net)
UK dividends	9,000 (net)
Rental income	500

Calculate the income tax payable.

6.4   Solution

	Non-savings/ dividend income £	Savings £	Dividends £
	£		
Schedule E	18,000	18,000	–	–
BSI 2,400 × 100/80	3,000	–	3,000	–
UK government stock	2,000	–	2,000	–
Taxed income 770 × 100/77	1,000	1,000	–	–
Dividends 9,000 × 100/90	10,000	–	–	10,000
Schedule A	500	500	–	–
STI	34,500	19,500	5,000	10,000
Less: PA	4,335	4,335	–	–
Taxable income	30,165	15,165	5,000	10,000

Income tax liability

		£
Non-savings/dividend income:	1,500 @ 10%	150
	13,665 @ 23%	3,143
	15,165	
Savings:	5,000 @ 20%	1,000
	20,165	
	7,835 @ 10%	783
	28,000	
	2,165 @ 32.5%	704
	30,165	5,780

		£
Less: Tax credits:		
BSI		600
Patent royalties		230
Dividends		1,000
		1,830
Income tax payable		3,950

Note: This figure would be reduced by PAYE deducted and by any payments on account of tax Andrew had paid on 31 January 2000 and 31 July 2000. Any balance remaining would be payable on 31 January 2001. Dividends must be grossed up at the rate of 10% (ie, 100/90). The personal allowance is set off against non-savings/dividend income as there is clearly sufficient non-savings/dividend income for the 10% starting rate of tax to be used in full.

7   TRUST INCOME

7.1   Introduction

A trust is an obligation binding a person (the trustee) to hold or to deal with property (the trust property) settled by one person (the settlor) for the benefit of another person or persons (the beneficiaries).

There are three types of trust from which an individual (as a beneficiary) may receive income:

- an interest in possession trust;
- a discretionary trust; and
- an accumulation and maintenance trust.

Where an individual receives income from an interest in possession trust, it is net of basic rate tax (23%) or lower rate tax (20% or 10%) to the extent that it represents savings income or dividends. The savings income or dividend element is taxed on the individual just as for any other source of savings/dividend income.

Income from the other two types of trust is paid net of tax at 34%. For example, £132 net from a discretionary trust is grossed up to £200 (132 × 100/66) and carries a £68 tax credit. The trustees have to account for any deficit in their pool of tax credits when making the payment but that does not concern the beneficiary.

The gross amount of the income paid to the discretionary beneficiary is taxable as non-savings income (at 10%,23% or 40%) regardless of the type of income used by the trustees to make the payment. The beneficiary will receive a 34% tax credit for the tax suffered, and this may lead to a tax repayment where the tax is overpaid.

8   INDIVIDUAL SAVINGS ACCOUNTS

8.1   Introduction

From 6 April 1999 an individual savings account (ISA) can be opened by any individual aged 18 or over who is resident and ordinarily resident in the UK.

8.2   Exemption

An ISA offers the following tax reliefs:

- Income received is free of income tax.

- When income consists of dividends, the account manager can make a repayment claim to recover the tax credit from the Inland Revenue (however this is only possible until 5 April 2004).

- Disposals of investments within an ISA are exempt from capital gains tax.

- When investments are transferred out of the account their acquisition cost for capital gains tax purposes is the market value at the date of transfer.

There is no minimum holding period, so withdrawals can be made from the account at any time without affecting the tax relief.

8.3 Qualifying investments

An ISA can include three components:

(1)   Cash

This includes bank and building society accounts, as well as those National Savings products where the income is not exempt from tax.

(2)   Life assurance

(3)   Stocks and shares

Investment is allowed in shares and securities listed on a stock exchange anywhere in the world.

The following stocks and shares qualify:

- Ordinary shares

- Fixed interest preference shares and convertible preference shares

- Fixed interest corporate bonds and convertible bonds with at least five years to run until maturity.

- Gilts with at least five years to run until maturity.

In addition, investments in unit trusts, investment trusts and open-ended investment companies also qualify.

Unlisted shares and shares traded on the Alternative Investment Market do not qualify.

It is not possible to transfer newly issued shares (eg, privatisation issues) into an ISA.

8.4 Subscription limits

The subscription limit is £5,000 in each tax year. Of this, up to £1,000 may go into the cash component and £1,000 into life assurance. However, for 1999/00 only, the overall limit is increased to £7,000, with a maximum of £3,000 into the cash component (the life assurance component is still £1,000).

Husband and wives each have their own limits.

8.5 Account providers

Savers have a choice of account providers and account formats. They can either go to a provider offering all three components in a single account and where they can make their maximum subscription, or they can obtain separate accounts for each of the three components with the same or separate providers. Where a maximum subscription account is used the account is known as a MAXI ISA, whilst an account for investing for just one component is known as a MINI ISA. The main difference is that with a MINI ISA only £3,000 can be invested in the stocks and shares component each year, since the account provider will not necessarily know whether any investment has been made in the other two components (£5,000 - £1,000 - £1,000 = £3,000). There is more flexibility with a MAXI ISA since there is no reason why the subscription limit of £5,000 (£7,000 for 1999/00) should not be used entirely for the stocks and shares component. In this case the account provider will obviously be aware of any investment made in the other two components.

In each tax year an investor is only allowed one MAXI ISA **or** three MINI ISAs where each MINI covers a different component.

9   ENTERPRISE INVESTMENT SCHEME

9.1   Introduction

The Enterprise Investment Scheme (EIS) was introduced with the aim of encouraging investment in unquoted companies.

9.2   Income tax relief available to investors

(a)   Income tax relief of 20% of the amount, up to a tax year maximum of £150,000, subscribed for qualifying shares is available.

(b)   The relief operates by taking 20% of the amount invested in the scheme and deducting it from the individual's income tax liability. The relief can reduce an individual's tax liability to nil, but it can never result in a repayment of tax.

(c)   The deduction from the income tax liability is made before deducting tax credits for the following:

- personal reliefs (MCA, WBA, APA)
- qualifying maintenance payments
- mortgage interest paid (outside MIRAS).

These are explained in more detail in chapter 4.

9.3   Example: EIS relief

James, a married man, earns £42,605 in 1999/00. He invests £50,000 in shares qualifying for relief under the EIS.

Calculate James's income tax liability.

9.4   Solution

James's income tax liability is as follows:

	£
Schedule E	42,605
Less: PA	(4,335)
	38,270
Income tax liability	
£1,500 × 10%	150
£26,500 × 23%	6,095
£10,270 × 40%	4,108
	10,353
Less: EIS relief (50,000 × 20%)	(10,000)
MCA (1,970 × 10%)	(197)
Income tax liability	156

9.5   Capital gains tax relief available for investors

(a)   Gains accruing on a disposal of EIS shares more than five years after the issue of the shares are wholly exempt if relief was given on the amount subscribed for them. This applies even where relief was restricted as a result of the investor's tax liability for the year.

(b) If a loss arises on the disposal of shares which have received EIS relief, the loss is allowable but the acquisition cost of the shares is reduced by the amount of EIS relief attributable to the shares. This can be illustrated as follows:

Holly subscribed £20,000 for 10,000 shares qualifying for EIS relief on 1 January 1995, and receives EIS relief on the full amount of the subscription. On 1 February 2000 Holly sells the shares for £12,000. The allowable loss on the disposal of the shares is:

	£
Proceeds	12,000
Less: Cost less income tax relief of 20,000 × 20%	(16,000)
Allowable loss	(4,000)

The loss may either be relieved against capital gains or against income (see chapter 12). It does not matter whether the disposal is inside or outside the five-year period.

9.6   Further details of relief

(a) Amounts invested in ordinary shares in any unquoted company trading in the UK may qualify for relief. There is no requirement for the company to be resident in the UK.

(b) To qualify for relief, the investor must not be:

- an employee of the company (other than as a director not previously connected with the company before the share issue), or

- have an interest of 30% or more in the company.

An investor is allowed to become a paid director after the date of the share issue without affecting his or her entitlement to relief.

These conditions must be satisfied throughout the period commencing two years before the issue of the shares (or, if later, on the date of incorporation) and ending five years after the issue.

Relief is not available where certain arrangements exist before or at the time of the issue of shares. For example, where the shareholder's investment is guaranteed or where there is a pre-arranged exit.

(c) The company must meet the following conditions:

- It must be unquoted. Shares listed on the Alternative Investment Market count as unquoted for this purpose.

- It carries on a qualifying trade, or carries out research and development intended to lead to such a trade.

- These conditions must be met throughout the three years following the share issue.

(d) There are a number of activities which are excluded, and therefore do not constitute a qualifying trade. Excluded activities include:

- Financial activities

- Legal and accountancy services

- Dealing in commodities, futures, shares, securities and other financial instruments.

- Property backed activities such as farming and market gardening and property development.

Where a group is concerned, the group is looked at as a whole in order to decide whether qualifying activities are carried on. The existence of non-qualifying activities that do not form a substantial part of the activities of the group as a whole will not prevent qualification

(e)   Shares qualify for relief in the year that they are issued. An investor may elect to carry back to the previous year up to half of any amounts invested prior to 6 October in any year. He may carry back a total of £25,000.

(f)   EIS relief previously given is withdrawn if

- the shares on which relief has been given are disposed of within five years of issue;

- the individual receives value from the company;

- the investor ceases to be a qualifying investor within five years of the shares being issued;

- the company ceases to be a qualifying company within three years of the shares being issued.

Relief is not withdrawn if the investor dies or the company is wound up for bona fide commercial reasons.

The full relief is withdrawn in all cases except where the investor disposes of the shares in an arms length transaction. In this case the relief withdrawn is limited to the disposal proceeds multiplied by 20%.

Shares are treated as disposed of on a FIFO basis.

Withdrawal of relief can be illustrated as follows:

Jonathan subscribes £12,000 for eligible shares in Penn Ltd in July 1999. EIS relief on those shares is £12,000 × 20% = £2,400 in 1999/00. In August 2002, Jonathan sells the shares for £7,000.

Jonathan's relief is reduced by £7,000 × 20% = £1,400.

(g)   There is no limit as to the amount that a company can raise through the issue of EIS shares each year.

However, participation in the scheme is limited to those companies with gross assets or less than £15 million before the share issue, and no more than £16 million after the issue. This limits the EIS to smaller companies, and puts an overall maximum on the amount that can be raised (this will vary according to the amount of gross assets that a company has before the share issue).

(h)   It is also possible to obtain re-investment relief in respect of EIS shares, where the proceeds from the disposal of an asset are reinvested (see chapter 20).

Although the CGT on the disposal is only deferred, for a higher rate taxpayer the initial relief is effectively 60% - 20% income tax on the EIS investment, and 40% CGT deferred.

10   VENTURE CAPITAL TRUSTS (VCTs)

10.1   Introduction

Relief for investment in Venture Capital Trusts was introduced to encourage individuals to invest indirectly in unquoted trading companies.

By buying quoted shares in a venture capital trust, an individual will be able to invest in a spread of unquoted companies. It is therefore similar to an investment trust.

10.2 The reliefs available

The following tax reliefs are available for an individual who invests in a venture capital trust:

- Income tax relief at the rate of 20% is available on subscriptions for new ordinary shares in venture capital trusts of up to £100,000 per tax year. The shares must be held for at least five years, or the relief is withdrawn.

- Dividend income from a venture capital trust is exempt from income tax.

- Disposals of shares in a venture capital trust are exempt from CGT in respect of investments of up to £100,000 per year.

- Re-investment relief will be available where the proceeds from the disposal of assets is reinvested in the subscription of new ordinary shares in venture capital trusts (see chapter 20).

The tax reliefs are therefore similar to those available for investment under the enterprise investment scheme.

10.3 Comparison to the EIS

(a) The main differences between a VCT and investment under the EIS are as follows:

- The investment limit is £150,000 under the EIS, but only £100,000 for a VCT.

- Dividend income from a VCT is exempt from income tax. This is not the case with dividend income received from an investment under the EIS.

    Dividend income from a VCT is even exempt if the shares are not subscribed for, but are purchased on the Stock Exchange at a later date.

- There is no requirement for shares in a VCT to be held for five years in order for the disposal to be exempt from CGT. Instead, the exemption is based on the investment limit of £100,000 per year.

    The CGT exemption will also apply if the shares are not subscribed for, but are purchased on the Stock Exchange at a later date.

- If a loss arises on a disposal of shares in a VCT, no relief is available against either capital gains or income. This contrasts with the EIS where relief against either capital gains or income is available.

(b) Compared to the EIS, venture capital trusts should represent a less risky method of investing in unquoted companies, although such an investment is still relatively high-risk.

10.4 Qualifying conditions

(a) A VCT has to be quoted on the Stock Exchange.

(b) At least 70% of the investments of a VCT have to be in unquoted trading companies, with not more than 15% in any one company.

    At least 30% of this investment must be in the form of new ordinary shares.

    The unquoted trading company must not be carrying on an excluded activity (as defined for EIS - see 9.6 (d) above).

    Companies quoted on the Alternative Investment Market qualify as unquoted shares.

(c)   At least 10% of a VCTs total investment in any company must be held in the form of ordinary shares.

(d)   The unquoted trading companies that are invested in must have gross assets of less than £15 million before the share issue, and no more than £16 million after the issue.

(e)   A maximum of £1 million can be invested in any one company during the period:

- six months ending on the date of investment; or

- the period from the start of the tax year to the date of investment

whichever is the longer.

11   PENSIONS

11.1   Introduction

(a)   The point is often missed that payments into a pension scheme not only provide an individual with income during his retirement, but also represent a very tax efficient long term investment. Tax relief is available on contributions into a pension scheme (subject to certain restrictions), both capital gains and income from the pension fund's investments are tax free (although dividend tax credits are not recoverable) and on retirement a tax-free lump sum payment may be taken, though the pension itself is taxed as earned income.

(b)   The main ways of investing in a pension scheme are:

- an occupation pension scheme; or
- a personal pension scheme.

11.2   Occupational pension schemes

(a)   Occupational pension schemes are ones set up by employers for employees. Contributions must be made by the employer and, in addition, employees may contribute. If the scheme is Revenue approved, they enjoy considerable tax advantages.

(b)   For a Revenue approved occupational pension scheme the following apply:

- contributions made by an employee of up to a maximum of 15% of earnings are deductible from his Schedule E income. There is a restriction on the size of contribution that can be made, in that there is an earnings cap (£90,600 for 1999/00) which allows a maximum contribution of £13,590 (15% of £90,600) in 1999/00;

- employer's contributions are not treated as benefits in kind;

- employer's contributions are tax deductible;

- an employee may be paid a tax free lump sum on retirement (limited to 1½ of the lower of final salary or the earnings cap);

- the pension paid on retirement (limited to 2/3 of the lower of final salary or the earnings cap) is taxed as earned income.

- an employee benefiting from an occupational pension scheme may make further provision for his retirement by paying additional voluntary contributions (AVCs) either into his employer's scheme or into a separate scheme. They are tax deductible to the extent that they, plus any contributions made by him into his employer's scheme do not exceed 15% of earnings.

11.3 Personal pension schemes

Personal pension schemes are available to the self-employed and those in non-pensionable employment.

Non-pensionable employment includes employment where an occupational pension scheme is operating but where the employee has not joined the scheme.

Personal pension schemes are operated by individuals contracting with a pension provider and paying premiums into a fund. If an employer makes contributions into an employee's personal pension fund, the payments are not treated as benefits in kind providing that they are within the limit on contributions.

11.4 Tax relief available for personal pension schemes

The taxpayer may claim a deduction from net relevant earnings for premiums paid. There is a limit on the amount of premium that can be relieved which is a percentage (age-related) of net relevant earnings.

The pension fund is free from capital gains tax and income tax.

The pension received on retirement is taxed as earned income with facility for a tax-free lump sum (subject to limits) to be paid on retirement.

11.5 Allowable premiums

The maximum annual tax deductible premium is a percentage of net relevant earnings (limited by an earnings cap - £90,600 for 1999/00). The deductible percentages of net relevant earnings for 1999/00 are as follows:

Age at **start** of tax year	%
Up to 35	17½
36 to 45	20
46 to 50	25
51 to 55	30
56 to 60	35
61 and over	40

Where an employer makes contributions to the scheme these will operate to reduce the maximum relief otherwise allowable.

11.6 Method of giving relief

(a)   **Employees** – Relief is given at the basic rate by deduction at source when the contributions are paid.

Higher rate relief is given when calculating the tax liability for the year concerned.

(b)   **Self-employed** – Contributions are paid gross. Relief given as an allowable deduction (against net relevant earnings) in calculating the tax liability for the year concerned.

11.7 Net relevant earnings

(a)   Relevant earnings are

●   emoluments from an office or employment assessable under Schedule E (including benefits in kind)

Note: should an employee be a member of the employer's occupational pension scheme, then the income from that employment is *not* relevant earnings.

- profits of a trade, profession or vocation assessable under Schedule D (including profits from letting of furnished holiday accommodation).

(b)   Net relevant earnings – are relevant earnings less:

In the case of an employed person

- allowable expenses incurred wholly, exclusively and necessarily in the performance of the duties of the employment.

In the case of a self-employed person

- losses brought forward
- charges on income incurred wholly and exclusively for business purposes.

Note: In practice the Inland Revenue permit business charges to be deducted from non-relevant income in priority, leaving the excess only to reduce relevant earnings.

11.8   Carry forward of unused relief

Unused relief arises when the premiums paid in a tax year are less than the maximum calculated as a percentage of net relevant earnings. It may be carried forward and used to relieve contributions paid in any of the next six years of assessment. Relief is given for the year in which the contribution is paid **provided** the maximum relief for that year is fully absorbed first by the payments.

Unused relief brought forward from earlier years must be used before that from later years.

11.9   Carry-back of contributions

The individual may elect to have all or part of a contribution treated as if it were paid in the preceding year of assessment, or, if there were no NREs in that preceding year, in the year before that. The election must be made not later than 31 January following the end of the year of assessment in which the contribution was actually paid.

The election to carry back contributions allows the taxpayer to take advantage of the situation where he has income taxed at a higher rate in the preceding year against which he can relieve his contribution.

Under self-assessment (see chapter 22), the tax relief for the premium carried back is given either as a tax credit against the liability for the current year, or a claim can be made for a repayment. Although the tax relief is based on the individual's tax position for the preceding year, the self-assessment for the preceding year is not reopened.

11.10   Example: Personal pension premium

Bernice, who was born on 6 June 1954, has run her own hairdressing business for many years. Results for 1999/00 are as follows:

	£
Schedule D Case I	25,000

Bernice's other income and payments for 1999/00 are as follows:

	£
Schedule D Case III	600
Mortgage interest (gross) paid under MIRAS	3,500
Trade charges (gross)	1,800

There is no unused pension contribution relief brought forward. Calculate the maximum personal pension premium that Bernice can set off in 1999/00.

11.11   Solution

1999/00 Net relevant earnings

	£	£
Schedule D Case I		25,000
Schedule D Case III	600	
Trade charges	(1,800)	
Unrelieved trade charges		(1,200)
Net relevant earnings		23,800

Note that trade charges are set against non-trading income before trading income.

Bernice is 44 at the start of the tax year.

Maximum pension premium is £23,800 × 20% = £4,760.

11.12   Example: Unused relief

Benjamin, born in 1971 started making payments into a personal pension plan in August 1996 on taking up his first employment since leaving university.   He provides you with the following information:

	Net relevant earnings £	17½% of net relevant earnings £	Premiums paid £
1996/97	28,000	4,900	4,200
1997/98	30,000	5,250	5,125
1998/99	26,000	4,550	5,160
1999/00	32,000	5,600	5,760

How are the premiums paid relieved?

11.13   Solution

1996/97	£
17½% of net relevant earnings	4,900
Less premium paid	4,200
Unused relief	700

1997/98

17½% of net relevant earnings	5,250
Less premium paid	5,125
Unused relief	125

1998/99	£
17½% of net relevant earnings	4,550
Unused relief (1996/97) (amount needed to balance)	610
	5,160
Less: Premium paid	5,160
	-

1999/00

17½% of net relevant earnings	5,600
Unused relief (1996/97: balance remaining)	90
(1997/98) (amount needed to balance)	70
	5,760
Less: Premium paid	5,760

At 6.4.2000 there is (125 – 70 =) £55 of 1997/98 unused relief remaining to carry forward.

Conclusion   Pensions are a fairly tax effective way to make long term investments.

Individuals can either pay into:

- an occupational pension scheme; or
- a personal pension scheme.

Occupational pension schemes are set up by employers for their employees. Tax relief is limited to 15% of earnings.

Personal pension schemes are entered into by self-employed individuals and people in non-pensionable employment. Tax relief is limited to an age related percentage of net relevant earnings subject to an earnings cap.

12   THE ACCRUED INCOME SCHEME

12.1   Introduction

This scheme applies to marketable securities such as gilts and debentures. Interest is paid to the registered holder on a certain date. An individual who sells the security before that date will not receive the interest payment due on that date.

However, the price the vendor receives for selling the security will be increased to take account of the fact that the purchaser will receive the interest payment.

As the vendor has received no income this increase cannot be charged to income tax, and as gilts and debentures are exempt from CGT, any gain on the disposal will also escape tax.

12.2   The accrued income scheme

The scheme was introduced to prevent the practice of bondwashing. This is where securities are sold before the interest date so as to avoid any tax liability.

Under the scheme, interest is deemed to accrue on a daily basis. The purchase price (or disposal price) of the security is therefore apportioned between the income element and the capital element.

The scheme does not apply unless the total nominal value of securities held by an individual exceed £5,000 at some time during the year of assessment.

Any assessment is under Schedule D Case III and counts as 'savings income'.

12.3   Example

Joe purchased £6,000 of 8% loan stock on 15 May 1999 for £6,200.

Interest is payable on 30 April and 31 October.

The entire holding was sold for £6,300 on 15 August 1999.

12.4   Solution

The loan stock will pay interest of £240 (gross) at half yearly intervals (£6,000 at 8% × 6/12).

The interest element included in the purchase price is that accruing from 1 May 1999 to 15 May 1999. This is £19.57 (£240 × 15/184).

The interest element included in the selling price is that accruing from 1 May 1999 to 15 August 1999. This is £139.57 (£240 × 107/184).

Although Joe has received no interest payments, he will be assessed on £120.00 (139.57 – 19.57). This equates to the interest for the period he has held the loan stock (16 May 1999 to 15 August 1999 = 92 days).

13   CHAPTER SUMMARY

This chapter has dealt with financial investments and sundry income. The following areas were covered:

- Tax-free income

- Schedule D Case III income: note the main examples of income not taxed at source.

- Schedule D Case VI income: note that the basis of assessment is the income received in the tax year.

- Dividends: note that dividends are grossed up by 100/90 and taxed at either the special lower rate of 10% or the special higher rate of income tax of 32.5% depending on the individual's level of income.

- Bank and building society interest: note that 'savings income' received net is grossed up by 100/80 and taxed at either 20% or 40%, depending on the individual's level of income.

- Other taxed income: this is taxed in the same way as bank and building society interest. The exception is patent royalties which are received net of basic rate and **not** subject to the 'savings' income tax regime.

- Trust income.

- Individual savings accounts

- Enterprise investment scheme

- Venture capital trusts.

- Personal pensions.

14   SELF TEST QUESTIONS

14.1   What are the main examples of Schedule D Case III income? (2.1)

14.2   What exemption is available for National Savings Bank interest? (2.2)

14.3   What is the basis of assessment for bank and building society interest? (5.2)

14.4   Give examples of taxed income. (6.1)

14.5   What is the maximum amount that can be invested in an ISA? (8.4)

14.6   What is the difference between a Maxi ISA and a Mini ISA? (8.5)

14.7   What is the maximum tax deductible contribution that an individual may make into an occupational pension scheme? (11.2)

14.8   What tax relief is available for premiums paid into a personal pension scheme? (11.4)

14.9   What constitutes net relevant earnings for personal pension scheme purposes? (11.7)

14.10   How is unused personal pension scheme relief utilised? (11.8)

15   EXAMINATION TYPE QUESTION

15.1   Long Life

Long Life, a single man aged 35 on 6 April 1998, has been trading for many years as a barrel manufacturer. His adjusted trading results for 1998/99 and 1999/00 were £14,400 and £23,000 respectively.

During 1999/00 he received building society interest of £1,984. His only other income assessable in 1999/00 was £3,300 interest which arose on a holding of government stock. He also took out a £25,000 mortgage on 1 July 1999 for the purchase of his new residence. The net interest paid under MIRAS during 1999/00 was £1,725.

He also entered into two deeds of covenant in August 1999 as follows:

Save the Children (a charity)	£3,500 (gross)
His mother	£600 (gross)

He paid a personal pension contribution of £2,000 on 3 April 1999. He also paid personal pension contributions totalling £6,000 in 1999/00. There was no unused relief as at 6 April 1998.

Interim tax payments totalling £2,700 had been made on 31 January and 31 July 2000.

You are required to calculate the balance of tax payable by Long Life for 1999/00 (taking advantage of any unused pension relief brought forward).

16   ANSWER TO EXAMINATION TYPE QUESTION

16.1   Long Life

Income tax computation 1999/00

			£
Trading profits			23,000
Less: Personal pension plan contributions lower of:			
(i)	amount paid	£6,000	
(ii)	20% × £23,000 (aged 36)	4,600	
	Add: Relief b/f 1998/99 (W)	520	
		£5,120	(5,120)
			17,880
Building Society interest £1,984 × 100/80			2,480
Schedule D III - Government stock			3,300
			23,660
Charges - Charitable Deed of Covenant			(3,500)
			20,160
Less: PA			(4,335)
Taxable income			15,825

Income tax:

Non-savings:	1,500 × 10%	150
	8,545 × 23%	1,965
Savings:	5,780 × 20%	1,156
		3,271
Add:	Tax retained on charges £3,500 × 23%	805
Tax liability		4,076
Less:	Tax suffered at source on BSI received	(496)
	Interim payments	(2,700)
Balance of tax payable (on 31 January 2001)		880

Note: mortgage interest within MIRAS is ignored in the income tax computation.

WORKING

Net relevant earnings for 1998/99	14,400
Relief @ 17½% (age 35 on 6.4.98)	2,520
Relief taken in 1998/99	(2,000)
Unused relief c/f for up to 6 years	520

4 DEDUCTIONS FROM INCOME AND FROM INCOME TAX LIABILITY

INTRODUCTION

There are certain allowable outgoings and personal reliefs that individuals are allowed to deduct from their income in order to arrive at their amount of taxable income.

It is important to be aware not only of the payments that can be deducted from income, but also how they are dealt with in the income tax computation.

Relief is also available on certain allowances and interest payments, not as a deduction from taxable income but as a tax credit given against the individual's tax liability.

1 INTRODUCTION

1.1 Context

It will be remembered from an earlier chapter that charges are deducted from statutory total income. It is necessary to consider exactly what is meant by the term charges on income.

1.2 Classification of charges

The following outgoings of an individual fall within the category of charges on income:

(a) annual interest
(b) annual payments.

The charges may be further classified according to method of payment

(a) paid under deduction of either 23% or 10% tax at source (known as retainable charges), for example

- deeds of covenant to charities (paid net of 23% tax)
- mortgage interest paid under the MIRAS scheme (paid net of 10% tax)

(b) paid gross without deduction of tax at source (known as non-retainable charges), for example mortgage interest not coming under the MIRAS scheme

1.3 Treatment in tax computations

(a) Subject to points (b) and (c) below, charges paid under deduction of tax at source are grossed up for inclusion in the computation, and are deducted in arriving at a statutory total income.

Charges are **ALWAYS** dealt with on an actual year basis.

(b) Mortgage interest on a main residence attracts relief at 10% only. Where payments are made gross they are not allowed as a deduction from income; instead, a tax credit is given which reduces the individual's tax liability. (This is covered in more detail later in the chapter).

(c) Mortgage interest paid under MIRAS has already received relief at 10%, and therefore no further entry in the computation is required. (Again, this is covered in more detail later).

(d) Tax relief on mortgage interest is to be withdrawn from 6 April 2000.

2   ANNUAL INTEREST

2.1   Loans for qualifying purposes

Relief is given for interest **paid** on **loans** incurred to finance expenditure for a **qualifying purpose**. Relief may be claimed for **any** payment of interest other than interest paid in excess of a reasonable commercial rate.

However, if the purpose of the debt is to finance expenditure wholly and exclusively in the course of a trade, profession or vocation, interest is deductible as a trading expense in arriving at the profit assessable under Schedule D Case I or II and is **not** dealt with as a charge on income in the personal tax computation.

The **qualifying purposes** to which the loan must be applied are as follows.

(a)   **Only or main residence**

The purchase of land or buildings in the UK (including static caravans and houseboats) provided the property is **used** at the time the interest is paid is the **only** or **main** residence of the borrower.

There is a limit on the total amount of loans which can qualify for relief. This limit is £30,000 and it applies to the **residence**, not the borrower, and is for purchase only. This means that individuals sharing the cost of purchase of a residence will not get £30,000 relief each, but instead the limit of £30,000 is divided between the number of borrowers.

(b)   **Partnerships.** The purchase of a share in a partnership, the contribution of capital or loans by a partner for the purchase of plant or machinery for use in the partnership.

(c)   **Close companies.** The purchase of ordinary shares in, or loans to, a close (ie, controlled by a limited number of persons) trading company.

(d)   **Employee-controlled companies.** Relief is available to full-time employees for loans taken out to acquire ordinary shares in an employee controlled UK resident, unquoted trading company.

(e)   **Employees.** The purchase of plant or machinery by an employed person for use in his employment. Relief is not given beyond the three fiscal years following that in which the debt was incurred.

(f)   **Borrowers living in job-related accommodation**

(i)   Tax relief is also available where an individual is living in 'job related' accommodation and he is paying interest on a loan (up to £30,000) used to purchase a property which he intends will become his main residence.

(ii)   Accommodation is job related if it is provided for a person by reason of his employment where:

- it is necessary for the proper performance of the duties of his employment (eg, caretakers); or

- it is provided for the better performance of the employee's duties and it is customary for such employers to provide accommodation for their employees (eg policemen); or

- special security arrangements are in force and the employee resides in the accommodation as part of those arrangements because there is a threat to his security.

(iii)   Accommodation is also regarded as job related if a self-employed person is provided with accommodation by another person and required to trade on premises provided by that other person (eg, tenant of a brewery).

(g)   **Bridging loans**

Where, at a time when the borrower has a qualifying loan used to acquire his only or main residence, he raises a new qualifying loan to acquire a second property with the intention of using it as his new main residence and disposing of the only or main residence to which the first loan relates, relief is available temporarily for interest on both loans for 12 months (or such longer time as the Inspector may allow).

The Revenue apply the tax limit of £30,000 separately to both loans during this bridging period.

Relief is also available for mortgage interest for 12 months after moving out of the main residence, even when a loan has not been taken out to purchase a new home. This allows people moving into rented accommodation to continue benefiting from the relief while trying to sell their previous home.

2.2   Mortgage Interest Relief At Source (MIRAS)

Most mortgage interest is paid net of 10% income tax under the MIRAS (mortgage interest relief at source) scheme.

(a)   **Outline of the scheme**

The essence of the scheme is that

- the borrower is entitled to deduct and retain income tax at 10% on making the payment, and

- the lender will recover from the Inland Revenue the amount of income tax deducted by the borrower.

The MIRAS scheme confers relief at 10% on non-taxpayers as well as on taxpayers, and there is no provision to recover this relief because the borrower is not a taxpayer.

(b)   **Income tax relief**

Mortgage interest attracts relief at 10% only. Where mortgage interest is paid under MIRAS it must be ignored in calculating the individual's income tax liability; relief is given when the payment is made.

2.3   Methods of giving relief for interest paid

There are two methods of giving relief for interest paid. The method of relief depends on the purpose of the loan.

The first method applies to interest on a loan

- used to purchase the borrower's only or main residence;

- used to purchase a property which is intended to be used as the borrower's only or main residence where the borrower lives in job-related accommodation;

Where such interest is paid gross (ie, not under the MIRAS provisions) relief is given by deducting a tax credit of 10% of the gross amount from the individual's income tax liability.

Thus, if Gregory, who is single, and earns £34,335 a year pays mortgage interest of £2,500 (gross) in 1999/00 on a loan of £30,000 used to purchase his main residence, his tax position would be as follows:

(a)   If the loan is outside the MIRAS scheme

	£
Income	34,335
Less: Personal allowance	(4,335)
Taxable income	30,000

	£
Income tax liability	
£1,500 × 10%	150
£26,500 × 23%	6,095
£2,000 × 40%	800
	7,045
Mortgage interest £2,500 × 10%	(250)
	6,795

(b)   If the loan is within the MIRAS scheme

	£
Income tax liability (as above)	7,045

The interest payment is ignored in the income tax computation. Relief is given when the interest is paid, which in 1999/00 will be £2,500 × 90% ie, £2,250.

The second method applies to interest on a loan

- used to purchase machinery or plant for business purposes;
- used to purchase an interest in a close company;
- used to purchase a share in a partnership;
- used to purchase shares in an employee-controlled company.

Where such interest is paid, relief is given by deducting the interest from the borrowers' income for the year.

Thus, if Gregory, from the previous illustration paid interest of £2,500 on a loan taken out to purchase a share in a partnership, his tax position would be as follows:

	£
Income	34,335
Less: Interest	(2,500)
	31,825
Less: Personal allowance	(4,335)
Taxable income	27,500
Income tax liability	
£1,500 × 10%	150
£26,000 × 23%	5,980
	6,130

Note that where the interest is deducted from income, relief is automatically available at starting, lower, basic or higher rate as appropriate.

| Conclusion | The methods of giving relief depend on the purpose of the loan

- Interest on loans to purchase the borrower's main residence

    - loan within MIRAS: relief given at the time of payment; ignored in income tax computation.

    - loan outside MIRAS: relief given by deducting a tax credit of 10% of the gross amount of mortgage interest from the income tax liability.

- Interest on loans for other eligible purposes; relief is given by deducting the amount of interest paid from the borrower's income.

3   DEEDS OF COVENANT

3.1   Introduction

A deed of covenant is a legally binding agreement under which one person agrees to make a series of payments without receiving consideration in return.

All deeds of covenant, in order to obtain tax relief, must satisfy **FOUR** conditions, namely

- payments under the covenant must be for a period **capable** of exceeding three years.
- the covenant must be irrevocable.
- the covenant must not have been made for valuable consideration.
- the covenant must be payable to a recognised charity.

All charitable covenants are fully allowable as charges on income, thereby benefiting from tax relief at lower basic or higher rate as appropriate.

Because the covenantor deducts and retains basic rate relief at source at the time of payment, it is necessary to adjust for this in the individual's tax computation to prevent double relief being obtained. In order to calculate the final tax liability, the basic rate tax that has been retained by the taxpayer is added to the tax liability. This is because the taxpayer must account to the Inland Revenue for the tax retained.

Thus if Peter, who is single and earns £38,335 pays a charitable deed of covenant of £1,925 (net) each year, his tax position for 1999/00 would be as follows:

	£
Income	38,335
Less: Deed of covenant $(1,925 \times {}^{100}/77)$	(2,500)
Less: Personal allowance	(4,335)
	31,500
Income tax liability	
£1,500 × 10%	150
£26,500 × 23%	6,095
£3,500 × 40%	1,400
	7,645
Add: Tax retained on charges paid net (2,500 × 23%)	575
	8,220

The amount actually paid to the charity is £1,925 (ie, net of basic rate tax). In order to achieve relief at higher rate, for the taxpayer, the gross amount is included in the computation. As relief has already been given at basic rate at the time of payment, this must be added back at the bottom of the calculation.

Note that although the taxpayer only pays £1,925 to the charity, the charity can reclaim the tax from the Inland Revenue of £575 and thus receives £2,500 in total.

4   EXCESS CHARGES, S350 ADJUSTMENTS

4.1   S350, ICTA 1988 ADJUSTMENTS

If those charges on income which are paid under deduction of tax at source exceed an individual's total income from all sources, further special points arise.

(a)   Charges paid net (other than mortgage interest under MIRAS)

If a taxpayer has very little or no income (eg he is a trader and makes a loss), his charges on income may well exceed his income as follows:

1999/00	£
Schedule D Case I	Nil
Less: Charges on income:	
Deed of covenant to a charity	100
Statutory total income	Nil

Referring back to the example above it should be appreciated that the income tax computation becomes, in effect

	£
Income tax on nil taxable income	Nil
Add: Income tax relief deducted at source from	
deed of covenant £100 × 23%	23
Income tax liability	23

Under the self-assessment calculation a tax liability of £23 will arise (known as a s350 adjustment).

(b)   Mortgage interest paid net of income tax

Where mortgage interest is paid net under the MIRAS scheme, income tax is deducted upon payment and retained but the tax does not have to be recovered by means of a *Sec 350* adjustment in circumstances similar to those above.

This means that non-taxpayers and the lower paid will always benefit from tax relief on mortgage interest provided it is paid under the MIRAS arrangements.

5   PAYROLL GIVING

An employee, included in the PAYE system, may make donations to charity by having the employer deduct the donations from wages or salary prior to calculation of PAYE deductions.

The maximum permitted donations are £1,200 pa (although the government is planning to remove this limit). Donations made by deed of covenant do not qualify for this relief but are relieved separately as charges on income.

It is necessary for the employer to set up an Inland Revenue approved scheme to deal with such deductions and to channel funds via an approved agent to the charities.

6   GIFT AID

For those who wish to give one-off gifts of money to charity the Gift Aid scheme is available.

Single charitable lifetime cash gifts of at least £250 (net of basic rate tax) per year of assessment will attract tax relief at the donor's highest tax rate.

This minimum limit is reduced to £100 for donations made under the Millennium Gift Aid Scheme. This scheme is designed to support education and anti-poverty projects in the world's poorest countries, and runs until 31 December 2000.

The payments must be made with basic rate tax deducted at source (ie, out of taxed income); the gross amount is relieved as a charge on income.

Donations by deed of covenant or under the payroll giving scheme are not affected.

There is no upper limit on the amount gifted.

7   VOCATIONAL TRAINING EXPENSES

Relief is given to UK resident individuals who pay for their own vocational training. Detailed provisions are as follows:

- Training must be towards a National Vocational Qualification (NVQ), and may be up to degree level. Relief is not, however, conditional upon a qualification actually being obtained.

- Relief is restricted to the basic rate of 23%, and is given by deduction at source when course and examination fees are paid. The relief is to be withdrawn for payments made on or after 6 April 2000.

- Relief is given (by deduction at source) even if the trainee has no taxable income and/or where the training is unrelated to the trainee's present work.

Tax relief is not available for;

- Children under 16;
- Individuals aged 16 to 18 who are in full-time education at school;
- Training which is wholly or mainly for leisure purpose.

In addition, relief is given to individuals over the age of 30 who pay for their own retraining for new careers. Detailed provisions are as follows:

- Tax relief is given on fees paid for full-time vocational courses, lasting between four weeks and a year.

- Relief is available whether or not the training course leads to an NVQ.

Tax relief is not denied if a trainee is receiving a career development loan or access funding.

8   PERSONAL ALLOWANCES

8.1   Introduction

Various personal allowances (also known as personal reliefs) are available to taxpayers, depending on their status and circumstances. The method of giving relief depends on the type of allowance as follows:

- personal allowance and blind person's relief - deducted from statutory total income

- married couple's allowance, additional personal allowance and widow's bereavement allowance - a credit of 10% of the allowance is given against the income tax liability (for most taxpayers, these allowances will be withdrawn from 6 April 2000).

Note that the tax credit may reduce the tax liability to nil but it can never lead to a repayment of tax.

8.2   Personal allowances (PA)

Each taxpayer (including children) is entitled to a personal allowance. The amount for 1999/00 is £4,335. Relief is available at the starting, basic and higher rates of tax.

Surplus personal allowance cannot be transferred to any other taxpayer.

8.3   Married couple's allowance (MCA)

A man who is married and living with his wife for all, or any part of, a tax year is entitled to claim (on his tax return) the married couple's allowance in addition to his personal allowance.

The rate of married couple's allowance for 1999/00 is £1,970.

Relief is given by a deduction of 10% of the allowance from the income tax liability.

The allowance is restricted in the year of marriage.

If a husband's tax liability is too small to use the whole married couple's allowance tax credit he can give notice to his Inspector that he wishes the surplus to be transferred to his wife.

Furthermore the wife may elect that the allowance be split equally between the couple, or the spouses together may elect that the allowance should be allocated wholly to the wife.

Thus Julie, who is married and has jointly elected with her husband to claim all the MCA, and earns £29,335 will have a tax position as follows:

	£
Salary	29,335
Less: Personal allowance	(4,335)
Taxable income	25,000
Income tax liability	
£1,500 × 10%	150
£23,500 × 23%	5,405
	5,555
MCA (£1,970 × 10%)	(197)
	5,358

The tax credit calculation would be done in the same way, if instead of dealing with MCA, the widow's bereavement allowance or the additional personal allowance (see below) was available.

Tax credits should be deducted before adding back tax retained on charges on income.

8.4   Allowances depending upon age

Taxpayers aged 65 and over at any time in the year of assessment are entitled to higher rates of personal allowance and married couple's allowance.

Personal allowance:

Those aged 65 – 74 get a higher rate (£5,720)

Those aged 75 and over get the highest rate (£5,980)

The allowance is given for the year of assessment in which the 65th or 75th birthday falls even if the taxpayer dies before the birthday.

Married couple's allowance

The amount depends upon the age of the older of the husband and wife by the end of the year.

The allowance is given to the husband.

For those aged 65 to 74 the allowance is £5,125, for those aged 75 or over, the allowance is £5,195.

For both the age related personal allowance and married couple's allowance an income restriction operates to reduce the level of the allowances. If the taxpayer's statutory total income is above £16,800 the age related allowance is reduced by half the difference between the statutory total income and £16,800 – but not so as to reduce the allowance to less than the basic personal allowance or married couple's allowance.

8.5   Example: Age allowance

Mr and Mrs Grey are living together throughout 1999/00. Mr Grey, aged 70, has statutory total income of £20,000. Mrs Grey, aged 69, has statutory total income of £13,000. Assume all the income is in the form of pensions.

Calculate their income tax liability.

8.6   Solution

		£	£	£
Mr Grey:	Total income		20,000	
	Limit		16,800	
	Excess		3,200	
	PA (Aged 65 – 74)		5,720	
	Less: ½ excess (£1,600) limited to		1,385	
	Reduced PA cannot be less than		4,335	4,335
	MCA (Aged 65 – 74)		5,125	
	Less: ½ excess	1,600		
	Less: Reduction in PA	1,385	215	
	Reduced MCA		4,910	4,910

Notes:

(1)   The restriction of age related MCA depends only on the husband's total income.

(2)   The reduction in any MCA due to husband's total income is less any reduction already made to his PA.

Mrs Grey:	PA: Full PA allowance for 65 – 74.	5,720

Computations 1999/00

	Mr Grey £	Mrs Grey £
Statutory total income	20,000	13,000
Less: Allowances		
PA (65 – 74)	(4,335)	(5,720)
Taxable income	15,665	7,280
Income tax liability		
£1,500 × 10%	150	150
£14,165/£5,780 × 23%	3,258	1,329
	3,408	1,479
MCA £4,910 × 10%	(491)	
	2,917	1,479

8.7   Additional personal allowance (APA)

The following classes of taxpayer may claim the additional personal allowance (APA), also known as the additional child allowance (ACA), provided they have **resident** with them a **qualifying child** or children.

- A widow or widower
- A man not entitled to married couple's allowance (eg a divorced man)
- An unmarried, separated or divorced woman
- A married man or woman whose spouse is totally incapacitated.

A qualifying child is either

- the claimant's own child (including a stepchild or adopted child) who is born in or is under the age of 16 at the beginning of the year of assessment or who, being 16 or over, is either in full-time education or undergoing full-time training for a trade or profession, lasting for at least two years or

- any other child born in or under the age of 18 at the beginning of the year of assessment and maintained at the claimant's expense for at least part of the year.

The amount of the allowance is £1,970.

Relief is given by a deduction of 10% of the allowance from the income tax liability.

8.8   Widow's bereavement allowance (WBA)

This allowance is given to a widow for the year of assessment in which her husband died and for the next following year of assessment.

It is a condition that the husband was entitled for the year of his death to the married couple's allowance.

If the widow should remarry **in the year of bereavement** she will **not** be given the widow's bereavement allowance for the **next** following year.

There is no corresponding relief for widowers.

The amount of the allowance is £1,970. Relief is given by a deduction of 10% of the allowance from the income tax liability.

8.9   Blind person's relief (BPR)

Any person who is registered with the local authority as a blind person may claim this relief.

The full relief is given even though the claimant may have been registered for part only of the fiscal year. The amount of the allowance is £1,380

Relief is given by deducting the allowance from statutory total income.

Conclusion   Personal allowances are important reliefs available to all taxpayers; care must be taken in an income tax question to note whether the taxpayer is:

- married;
- aged 65 or over;
- is single and has a child resident with them; or
- is a recently widowed woman

as additional reliefs may be available.

9   CHAPTER SUMMARY

This chapter has dealt with deductions from income and deductions from income tax. The following areas were covered:

- the types of loan interest and their treatment: by far the most important type is mortgage interest;
- tax relief on charitable deeds of covenant;
- adjustments arising when charges paid net of basic rate tax exceed all other income;
- payroll giving;
- the gift aid scheme;
- relief for vocational training expenses;
- personal allowances.

10   SELF TEST QUESTIONS

10.1   What relief is available for interest paid where the purpose of the debt is to finance expenditure wholly and exclusively in the course of a trade? (2.1)

10.2   What are the qualifying purposes to which a loan must be applied if relief is to be given for interest paid on the loan? (2.1)

10.3   What constitutes job-related accommodation? (2.1)

10.4   What conditions must a deed of covenant satisfy in order to obtain tax relief? (3.1)

10.5   What is the payroll giving scheme? (5)

10.6   What is the gift aid scheme? (6)

10.7   What relief is available for vocational training expenses? (7)

10.8   Who is entitled to claim a married couple's allowance? (8.3)

10.9   Who is entitled to claim an additional personal allowance? (8.7)

10.10   For which years is the widow's bereavement allowance given? (8.8)

11   EXAMINATION TYPE QUESTION

11.1   Mr Brown

Mr Brown, who was born in 1936 is employed by the local bank.

For 1999/00 he received the following remuneration:

	£
Salary	30,000
Benefits in kind	3,720

PAYE of £6,600 was deducted.

He received the following amounts from his investments in 1999/00.

	£
Building society interest	1,568
Interest on holding of £10,000 13% Treasury Stock 2003	1,300 (gross)
National Savings Bank investment account	82

Mr Brown cashed in some National Savings Certificates, which he had purchased for £1,200 in 1994, from which he received £2,490.

In April 1999 Mr Brown invested £3,000 in an Individual Savings Account. The account was credited with £25 of interest by 5 April 2000.

Mr Brown took out an endowment mortgage on 1 March 1999 of £40,000 to buy the house he lives in at a fixed rate of 7%. He pays the loan under the MIRAS system and actually paid £2,590 in 1999/00 (gross interest of £2,800 with tax relief at source of £210).

Mr Brown also pays £55 each year to a charity under a deed of covenant. Mr Brown lives with his wife, Ivy, who was born in 1934: she has no income of her own.

No interim payments of income tax were required on 31 January or 31 July 2000.

You are required to calculate the income tax payable by Mr Brown for 1999/00.

12   ANSWER TO EXAMINATION TYPE QUESTION

12.1   Mr Brown

Income tax liability 1999/00	Savings £	Non-savings £	Total £
Schedule E - salary and benefits in kind		33,720	33,720
Building society interest (× 100/80)	1,960		1,960
Government stock interest	1,300		1,300
Schedule D Case III - NSB investment account	82		82
Less: Charge on income			
Deed of covenant to charity (£55 × 100/77)		(71)	(71)
STI	3,342	33,649	36,991
Less: Personal allowance	-	(4,335)	(4,335)
Taxable income	3,342	29,314	32,656

Income tax

£		£	£
1,500 × 10%			150
26,500 × 23%			6,095
4,656 × 40%			1,862
			————
32,656			8,107

Less: Tax credit re MCA (1,970 × 10%)   (197)
                                                                          ————
                                                                          7,910

Add: Basic rate tax retained
          Deed of covenant £71 × 23%   16
                                                                          ————
                                                                          7,926
Income tax liability
Less: PAYE   6,600
            BSI   392
                                                      ————
                                                                          6,992
                                                                          ————
Income tax payable   934
                                                                          ————

Notes:

(1)   Income from ISAs is exempt.

(2)   Encashments of National Savings Certificates are exempt.

(3)   The charge on income and the personal allowance are set off against non—savings income in preference to savings income. There is clearly sufficient non-savings income for the 10% starting rate band to be used in full.

(4)   Mr Brown is entitled to an age related married couple's allowance as his wife is 65; however, as his STI is £36,991 the allowance is restricted to the ordinary married couple's allowance of £1,970.

(5)   Mortgage interest paid under the MIRAS scheme is paid net of 10% tax. The payment is ignored in the tax computation.

(6)   As all the savings income does not include dividends and it clearly falls in the 40% band there is no need to show it separately in the computation of income tax due.

(7)   Where a taxpayer has no gross sources of income he is unlikely to have to make interim tax payments under self-assessment. Instead, all tax not collected at source or through PAYE, would be payable on 31 January following the tax year. Amounts under £1,000 are likely to be collected by restricting the PAYE tax code provided the Revenue receive the tax return by 30 September following the tax year.

5 HUSBANDS, WIVES AND CHILDREN

INTRODUCTION

All taxpayers are taxed separately on their own income, have their own personal allowance, and must make their own annual income tax return. However, there are still some very important tax implications that affect the married couple specifically and these are the subject of this chapter.

1 PERSONAL ALLOWANCES AND THEIR TRANSFER

1.1 Personal allowances

Unused personal allowances cannot be transferred between spouses.

1.2 Married couple's allowance

The following elections are available:

(a)   The wife may elect that the married couple's allowance should be split equally between the couple;

(b)   The couple may jointly elect that the married couple's allowance should be allocated wholly to the wife.

Elections under (a) and (b) should be made before the beginning of the first tax year to which it is to apply. Once made, the election remains in force for future years until revoked.

These elections do not apply to the age related element in married couple's allowances. For example even if £5,125 is available only £1,970 or £985 may be allocated to the wife.

(c)   Where the husband has insufficient income tax liability to deduct all of the £197 (£1,970 × 10%) tax credit, the amount of the credit not deducted may be transferred to his wife.

In the same way, if the wife has insufficient income tax liability to deduct all of her tax credit, she may elect that the excess is set against her husband's income tax liability.

This election applies not only to the basic married couple's allowance, but also to the age related married couple's allowances.

The election applies for one year only, and must be made within five years of 31 January following the relevant tax year.

1.3 Example: Transfer of excess married couple's allowance

The following information is relevant to Mr and Mrs Barefoot, both aged under 65, and living together throughout 1999/00. Mr Barefoot is a university undergraduate, his wife has a full-time job.

	Mr B £	Mrs B £
Salary		12,000
Vacation earnings	4,585	

Mr Barefoot gives notice that he wishes to transfer surplus MCA to his wife. Show the position for 1999/00.

1.4   **Solution**

	£	£
Transfer of married couple's allowance tax credit		
MCA tax credit (1,970 × 10%)		197
Mr Barefoot's total income:		
Vacation earnings	4,585	
Less: PA	4,335	
Taxable income	250	
Income tax liability £250 × 10%	25	
Less: MCA tax credit	(25)	(25)
Transferred to Mrs B		172

Tax position 1999/00	Mr B £	Mrs B £
Income	4,585	12,000
Less: PA	(4,335)	(4,335)
Taxable income	250	7,665
250/1,500 × 10%	25	150
6,165 × 23%		1,418
	25	1,568
Less: Tax credit re MCA	(25)	(172)
Income tax liability	Nil	1,396

2   **YEAR OF MARRIAGE**

2.1   **Personal allowance**

This is given for the year of marriage in the same way as for any other year.

2.2   **Married couple's allowance**

In the year of marriage the married couple's allowance is reduced by one-twelfth for each complete tax month (ending on the 5th) from 6 April to the date of marriage.

If the age-related married couple's allowance is due this is reduced first by any excess income restriction before applying the above rule.

2.3   **Activity**

Jack is considering marrying Jill on the following alternative dates:

(a)   4 May 1999

(b)   6 August 1999

To how much married couple's allowance will he be entitled in 1999/00 in each case?

2.4   Activity solution

(a)   **4 May 1999** – the allowance of £1,970 will not be restricted since the marriage takes place before a complete tax month (ending on the 5th) after 6 April has expired.

(b)   **6 August 1999** – the fourth complete month since 6 April 1999 expired on 5 August 1999 – the allowance will be £1,970 less $\frac{4}{12} \times £1,970 = £1,313$.

2.5   Additional personal allowance (APA)

In the year of marriage, a husband who is entitled to the additional personal allowance (for example, as a widower he had care of dependent children from a previous marriage) may choose to keep that allowance instead of (a reduced) married couple's allowance.

A woman can have the additional personal allowance for the year of marriage if she qualified by having a qualifying child living with her before the date of marriage. A wife cannot claim the additional personal allowance for any year throughout which she is living with her husband.

3   YEAR OF SEPARATION OR DEATH

3.1   Death of wife

If his wife dies a husband is still entitled to the full married couple's allowance for that year of assessment.

3.2   Death of husband

Any election for the wife to receive half or all of the MCA is automatically void. The husband receives the full MCA in the year of his death as well as the full personal allowance.

The wife is entitled to her full personal allowance for the year of assessment in which her husband dies. In addition she can get:

(a)   any of the credit re the married couple's allowance which cannot be used against her husband's income

(b)   the additional personal allowance, if she has a qualifying child living with her after her husband's death

(c)   the widow's bereavement allowance for the year of husband's death and also for the following year (if she has not re-married by the start of that year)

3.3   Separation

(a)   The wife gets her full personal allowance for the year of separation, and in addition:

•   any surplus married couple's allowance transferred to her by her husband; and

•   the additional personal allowance, if she has a qualifying child living with her after the separation.

If she elects to be allocated any of the married couple's allowance, the sum of this allowance and the additional personal allowance must not exceed £1,970.

(b)   The husband will get his full personal allowance in the year of separation and in addition, he may claim the additional personal allowance if there is a qualifying child resident with him at some time after the date of separation.

The sum of the married couple's allowance and the additional personal allowance claimed in the year must not exceed £1,970.

(c)   These provisions may be illustrated as follows:

Michael and Jane separate permanently during 1999/00.

John, their only son is to spend six months of the year with each parent. Jane has elected to have half of the married couple's allowance allocated to her.

In 1999/00, the allowances available are as follows:

	Michael £	Jane £
Married couple's allowance	985	985
Additional personal allowance	985	985
	1,970	1,970

Note: if Michael and Jane had elected for all the married couple's allowance to be transferred to Jane, then she could not claim any additional personal allowance, but John may claim the full £1,970.

3.4   Example: Year of death of husband

John died on 6 October 1999 aged 48. The assessable income and allowable charge of John and his wife Sarah, aged 47, for 1999/00 was as follows

Income	John £	Sarah £
Salaries from employment	17,000	18,395
Interest from National Savings Bank investment account	–	850
Bank deposit interest		400
Building Society interest	480	600

Outgoings

Building society interest paid under MIRAS before John's death on £18,000 mortgage (gross amount)	1,000	-

The mortgage on their house was paid off by Sarah using the proceeds of a mortgage protection insurance policy maturing on John's death.

COMPUTE the income tax liabilities of John and Sarah respectively for 1999/00.

3.5   Solution

(a)   **JOHN (deceased)**

	£
Income Tax Computation 1999/00	
Schedule E – actual – salary	17,000
Building society income	
$£480 \times \dfrac{100}{80}$	600
Statutory total income	17,600
Less: PA	4,335
Taxable income	13,265

	£
Starting rate £1,500 @ 10%	150
Basic rate £11,165 (17,000 − 4,335 − 1,500) @ 23%	2,568
Lower rate £600 @ 20%	120
	2,838
MCA £1,970 @ 10%	197
Income tax liability	2,641

(b)   **SARAH (widow)**

Income Tax Computation 1999/00	£	£
Schedule E − actual − salary		18,395
Bank deposit interest		
£400 × $\frac{100}{80}$	500	
Building society interest £600 × $\frac{100}{80}$	750	
Schedule D III interest	850	2,100
Statutory total income		20,495
Less: PA		4,335
Taxable income		16,160

	£
Starting rate £1,500 @ 10%	150
Basic rate £12,560 (18,395 − 4,335 − 1,500) @ 23%	2,889
Lower rate £2,100 @ 20%	420
	3,459
MCA £1,970 @ 10%	197
Income tax liability	3,262

4   MAINTENANCE PAYMENTS

4.1   Court Orders and Agreements

Payments under Court Orders and under maintenance agreements are dealt with as follows

- the recipient is not taxed on any payments received

- where payments are made to **a former or separated spouse** or to such a person for the maintenance of a **child (under 21) of the family** the payer gets tax relief, up to a maximum limit equal to the amount of the married couple's allowance

- tax relief is only given until the recipient spouse re-marries

- the relief is given by way of a tax credit of 10% of the payment (or of the amount of the married couple's allowance, ie, £1,970 if less)

- all payments are made GROSS.

In the year of separation or divorce a husband will get the married couple's allowance for the whole year (there is no apportionment); he will also get relief up to the limit for maintenance payments made in the part of the year during which he is separated or divorced, provided that these are made after the date of the court order or maintenance agreement. On re-marriage the husband will be able to claim the married couple's allowance, as well as relief (up to the maximum) for maintenance payments to his ex-wife, either for her benefit or for the benefit of a child of the family.

5   JOINT INCOME

5.1   Introduction

Although a husband's and wife's incomes are calculated separately, special rules exist for dealing with income arising from jointly held assets.

5.2   The 50:50 rule

Income from assets held in their joint names by a married couple who live together will normally be split equally between them for tax purposes.

It is the amount of income assessable, either on an actual or current year basis, that is split.

5.3   Declaration of beneficial interests

A married couple whose actual entitlement to a jointly held asset and the income from it is unequal may make a joint irrevocable declaration of their actual beneficial interests in the asset and their income from it.

If a declaration is made each spouse will be assessed on their actual entitlements from those assets covered by the declaration.

6   MORTGAGE INTEREST

6.1   Introduction

A husband and wife are entitled to claim relief on the interest they each pay on a loan used to purchase their only or main residence. They share a joint ceiling for relief of £30,000. If the loan is in their joint names the £30,000 limit is normally divided equally between them so that each gets relief for payments of interest on up to £15,000. If the loan is in the name of only one of them, then that person will normally get tax relief on the interest paid, up to the £30,000 limit.

6.2   Election available

A husband and wife can jointly elect to share both the limit and the tax relief between them in any way they choose. For example, a wife can have all the tax relief even though the loan is in her husband's name. This is called an allocation of interest election.

To make an election a married couple must complete and sign the appropriate form. An election must be made by 31 January following the end of the tax year to which it applies. Once made, an election will apply for subsequent years until it is changed or withdrawn.

If the interest is paid under MIRAS the election is of no practical relevance.

6.3   Year of marriage

Concessions apply in the year of marriage as follows:

- Where one spouse leaves their home to live with the other spouse, then relief continues to be given in respect of interest paid on a loan used to purchase the property vacated. The property must be sold within 12 months.

- Where both spouses leave their homes to live in a new home, then relief will continue to be given in respect of interest paid on loans used to purchase the two properties vacated (as well as on interest paid on a loan used to purchase the new property). Relief will continue for a maximum of 12 months.

7   CHARGES ON INCOME AND JOINT PAYMENTS

7.1   Introduction

Relief for charges on income is given to the spouse who qualifies for it. Where there is a limit to the amount of relief, each spouse separately is entitled to that limit (but see mortgage interest above).

7.2   Deeds of covenant

Each spouse gets relief on payments made under covenants separately entered into, and where spouses have jointly covenanted the amount actually paid by each person is the amount allowed. If this is not clear (eg, paid from joint bank account), the 50:50 rule will apply.

8   TAX PLANNING

8.1   Introduction

A married couple's overall tax liability can be reduced where one spouse is not fully utilising his or her personal allowances, starting rate tax band or basic rate tax band, and the other spouse is, for example, a higher rate tax payer.

8.2   Options available

The basic aim of tax planning with a married couple is to reduce the taxable income of the spouse with the higher income, and to correspondingly increase the taxable income of the spouse with lower income.

- Income producing assets can be transferred into joint names or entirely into the name of the lower income spouse.

  Putting assets into joint names has the advantage that control over an asset is not relinquished, and yet income will, subject to a declaration being made to the contrary, be split 50:50.

- If the higher income spouse is in business, it may be possible to employ the lower income spouse, or perhaps bring that spouse into partnership.

- Charges, such as a deed of covenant to charity, that attract tax relief at up to 40%, should be paid by the higher income spouse.

8.3   The lower tax rates on savings income and dividends

The 10% and 20% tax rates on savings income and dividends increases the scope for tax saving where a married couple are concerned.

The tax saving is 20% if savings income is transferred from a spouse paying tax at the rate of 40% to a spouse who is not fully utilising his or her basic rate tax band. Similarly a tax saving of 22½% can be made on dividend income.

9   CHILDREN'S INCOME

9.1   General rules

All income of a child is assessable on the child and is not aggregated with a parent's income. The child has full entitlement to a personal allowance.

Returns and claims may be made by a child, but normally these would be done by a parent or guardian.

Where the child has received taxed income in excess of the personal allowance, a repayment of tax will arise.

9.2 Aggregation with parent's income

Where a child under the age of 18 and unmarried has investment income and this is derived from capital provided by either parent, then the income is treated as that of the parent who provided the capital. The capital could be provided by means of a formal trust or settlement or could simply be a gift of money (eg opening a NSB account in the child's name) or shares.

If the income does not exceed £100 in a year of assessment, then it is ignored for aggregation purposes and remains taxed as the child's income.

10 CHAPTER SUMMARY

This chapter picks up the knowledge acquired in the earlier chapters and applies it to the family group.

The following areas were covered:

- transfer of the married couple's allowance between spouses;
- the allowances available in the year of marriage, of separation or of death of a spouse;
- tax relief for maintenance payments;
- tax treatment of joint income;
- the treatment of charges; and
- children's income.

11 SELF TEST QUESTIONS

11.1 What elections are available concerning the transfer of the married couple's allowance? (1.2)

11.2 How is the amount of tax credit for the married couple's allowance that can be transferred determined when a husband has insufficient income tax liability to use the full amount? (1.2)

11.3 How is the married couple's allowance in the year of marriage calculated? (2.2)

11.4 What allowances are available to a husband and wife in the year that they separate? (3.3)

11.5 What sort of maintenance payments qualify for tax relief? (4.1)

11.6 What is the tax position of the recipient of such payments? (4.1)

11.7 How is the income from assets held in the joint names of a married couple normally taxed? (5.2)

11.8 What declaration may a married couple make when the entitlement to the income of a jointly held asset is unequal? (5.3)

11.9 What election may a married couple make concerning tax relief on mortgage interest payments? (6.2)

11.10 How is the income of a child assessed? (9.1)

12 EXAMINATION TYPE QUESTIONS

12.1 Mr and Mrs Old

Mr Old died on 5 January 2000 at the age of 68. His income from 6 April 1999 to the date of death comprised:

	£
Pension	12,700
Rents from properties (net of expenses)	4,300

Mrs Old, who was five years younger than her husband, has the following income:

	£
Profits from hairdressing business	9,010
Loan stock interest of £800 pa (gross) received half yearly on 30 September and 31 March	
After her husband's death she received a pension of £75 per week (for 13 weeks in 1999/00)	

You are required to compute the income tax liability of Mr and Mrs Old for 1999/00.

12.2   Norman and Hilda

The tax returns of Norman, aged 45, show the following

	Year ended 5 April 2000 £
Income	
Salary and commission from Flyhigh Ltd	26,860
Benefits-in-kind, assessable under Schedule E	2,050
Rentals from unfurnished lettings, less expenses	4,100
Building society interest - amounts received	2,000
Payments	
Maintenance to former wife under Court Order dated 1.9.94 - amount paid	3,400

Mortgage interest of £4,760 (gross) is paid in respect of a mortgage of £32,000 on Norman's main residence, purchased in September 1994. The loan is included in the MIRAS scheme. The interest rate on the loan is fixed.

On 9 October 1999 Norman married his second wife, Hilda, whose income for the year ended 5 April 2000 was

	£
Salary at £1,250 per month up to 30 September 1999 (on that date she was made redundant)	
Building society interest	160

Hilda has a daughter, Ashleigh, aged 10. Ashleigh was given £5,000 of 3½% War Loan on 6 April 1999 as a birthday present by Hilda.

You are required to compute for 1999/00

(a)   the income tax liability of Hilda
(b)   the income tax liability of Norman.

13   ANSWERS TO EXAMINATION TYPE QUESTIONS

13.1   Mr and Mrs Old

Mr Old - Income tax computation 1999/00

	£
Schedule E pension	12,700
Schedule A - rents from properties	4,300
Statutory total income	17,000
Less: Allowances and reliefs:	
PA 5,720 - ½(17,000 – 16,800)	(5,620)
Taxable income	11,380

Income tax:

1,500 @ 10%	150
9,880 @ 23%	2,272
	2,422
MCA (5,125 × 10%)	(513)
Income tax liability	1,909

Mrs Old - Income tax computation 1999/00

	£
Schedule DI	9,010
Schedule E pension 75 × 13 weeks	975
Taxed interest	800
Statutory total income	10,785
Less: PA	(4,335)
Taxable income	6,450

Income tax

1,500 @ 10%	150
4,150 (6,450 – 800 – 1,500) @ 23%	954
800 @ 20%	160
	1,264
WBA (1,970 × 10%)	(197)
Income tax liability	1,067

13.2   Norman and Hilda

Hilda
Income tax computation 1999/00

	£	£
Schedule E - actual - salary (1,250 × 6)		7,500
Building society interest 160 × 100/80	200	
Schedule D III - War Loan interest *(note 1)*	175	375
Statutory total income		7,875
Less: PA		(4,335)
Taxable income		3,540

Income tax

1,500 @ 10%	150
1,665 (7,500 – 4,335 – 1,500) @ 23%	383
375 @ 20%	75
	608
WBA (1,970 × 10%) (Note 2)	(197)
Income tax liability	411

(Tutorial note:

(1)   The War Loan interest is assessed on Hilda because her daughter is under 18 and unmarried and the income is derived from capital provided by the parent.

The amount assessable under Schedule D III is the amount arising in the year ie, 3½% × £5,000 = £175.

(2)   A woman can have the additional personal allowance for a qualifying child for the year of marriage provided the child was living with her before the marriage.

Norman
Income tax computation 1999/00

	£
Schedule E	
Salary - actual	26,860
Benefits-in-kind	2,050
	28,910
Schedule A - net rents - actual	4,100
Building society interest received £2,000 × 100/80	2,500
	35,510
Statutory total income	
Less: PA	(4,335)
Taxable income	31,175
1,500 × 10%	150
26,500 × 23%	6,095
3,175 × 40%	1,270
	7,515
Maintenance payments (1,970 × 10%)	(197)
MCA (1,970 − 9/12 × 1,970) × 10%	(99)
Income tax liability	7,219

6 INCOME FROM EMPLOYMENT

INTRODUCTION

(a) This chapter, concerning income from employment has two themes. The first is setting limits to the Schedule E charge and so it reviews the nature of assessable emoluments, when payments are treated as emoluments, and the vital distinction between employment and self-employment. Establishing the link between tax years and emoluments is also considered.

(b) The second area covered by the chapter is the treatment of a variety of incentive schemes. What links them together is a lenient tax regime on certain payments (that would otherwise be charged more rigorously under Schedule E) when they are directly or indirectly tied to an employer's financial performance.

1 THE SCOPE OF SCHEDULE E

1.1 Assessable emoluments

(a) Directors and employees are assessed on the amount of emoluments **received** in the year of assessment. The term emoluments includes not only cash wages or salary, but bonuses and commission and benefits-in-kind made available by the employer.

(b) The following benefits are also taxed under Schedule E:

- statutory sick pay (SSP);
- statutory maternity pay (SMP);
- retirement pension and widow's pension; and
- the jobseeker's allowance which is paid to the unemployed.

1.2 When payments are emoluments

(a) There is a considerable body of case law on whether a payment is an 'emolument from an office or employment'. For example, payments may be received from persons other than an employer and still constitute emoluments from the office eg, tips of waiters and porters; on the other hand payments may be received which have some connection with the holding of the office but are not derived from holding it.

(b) Brief notes on the decisions reached in some leading cases are given below.

- Tips received by an employee taxi-driver where held to be assessable as remuneration for services rendered.

- The payment by a company for the defence of a director in a dangerous driving prosecution, a criminal offence, was held to be income of the director. (The expenditure would be allowable in the company's computation).

- Collections received by a professional county cricketer for meritorious performance as provided by the league rules, were held to be profits arising from his employment.

- An amount of £1,000, part of a bonus paid by the Football Association to the 'squad' from which the English side in the 1966 World Cup competition was chosen, and £750 paid by a manufacturer as prizes in a competition, were held not to be in the nature of rewards for services rendered and therefore, not assessable.

1.3   The time earnings are received

(a)   Because Schedule E assessments are on a receipts basis, the time that the emoluments are received is of critical importance. The statute stipulates that this time is when the **earliest** of the following events occurs:

- actual payment of, or on account of, emoluments; or
- becoming entitled to such a payment.

(b)   In the case of directors, who are in a position to manipulate the timing of payments, there are extra rules. They are deemed to receive emoluments on the earliest of the two general rules set out above and:

- when sums on account of emoluments are credited in the accounts;

- the end of a period of account, where emoluments are determined before the end of that period; and

- when the amount of emoluments for a period are determined, if that is after the end of that period.

(c)   These rules do not deal with the timing of when benefits-in-kind are assessable, which is dealt with under separate legislation (eg the provision of an asset as a benefit would normally be assessed initially when first made available). Similarly pensions are taxed on an accruals rather than receipts basis.

1.4   Employment or self-employment?

(a)   The distinction between employment and self-employment is fundamental - an employee is taxable under Schedule E whilst a self-employed person is assessed on the profits derived from his trade, profession or vocation under Schedule D Cases I or II.

(b)   In many instances, determining whether a person is either employed or self-employed is not difficult. However, in other cases the distinction is less clear. The following principles, laid down by case law decisions, are important matters taken into account in deciding whether a person is employed or self-employed.

(c)   The primary test of an employment as opposed to self-employment is the existence of a **contract of service** compared with a mere **contract for services**. However, even in the absence of a contract of service any of the following matters would corroborate the existence of a such a contract.

- obligations by the 'employer' to offer work and the 'employee' to undertake the work offered. An 'employee' would not normally be in a position to decline work when offered.

- the manner and method of the work being controlled by the 'employer'.

- the 'employee' being committed to work a specified number of hours at certain fixed times.

- the 'employee' is obliged to work personally and exclusively for the 'employer'.

- the work performed by the 'employee' is an integral part of the business of the 'employer' and not merely an accessory to it.

- the economic reality of self-employment is missing - namely the financial risk arising from not being paid an agreed, regular, remuneration.

(d)   A recent case concerned a vision mixer who was engaged under a series of short-term contracts in the film industry.

It was decided that the overall picture must be considered, and that in this case the number of separate engagements was the deciding factor. Persons engaged in a profession or vocation will often do without the trappings of a business, and will, for example, not supply all of their own equipment. It was therefore held that the vision mixer was self-employed.

2   LUMP SUM PAYMENTS ON TERMINATION OR VARIATION OF EMPLOYMENT

2.1   Principles

The tax treatment of a lump sum payment made to an employee on the cessation of employment depends on whether or not the payment is a genuine redundancy payment for ceasing to be an employee.

A genuine redundancy payment falls outside of the normal Schedule E rules (because it is not in return for services as an employee) but is subject to a special tax regime. If the payment is not a genuine redundancy payment then it will be taxed in the same way as any other employment income (since it is in return for services as an employee).

Payments made when an employee leaves are taxed in the year of receipt, rather than in the year of termination.

2.2   Ex-gratia payments

Genuine ex-gratia redundancy payments are subject to Schedule E tax, in principle, but the first £30,000 is exempt. Payments include not only cash but benefits in kind received (such as allowing the employee to keep his company car). Where an employee receives statutory redundancy pay the amount received counts as the first part of the £30,000 exempt band.

Where an ex-gratia payment is made to an employee approaching retirement age the Revenue can deem it to be made under an unapproved retirement benefit arrangement and thereby assessable in full under Schedule E (ie, without the £30,000 exemption). Retrospective approval can be given for the sum to be fully exempt provided there is no actual approved scheme and the amount is within the normal limits - eg, 3/80ths of final salary for each year of service.

2.3   Exempt payments

There are specific statutory provisions to exempt some payments made to former employees. These are:

- payments for injury, disability or death; and
- statutory redundancy payments.

Lump sum payments received from an approved pensions scheme are also exempt.

2.4   Example

Albert age 40 years received a lump-sum of £80,000 from his employers following his redundancy in December 1999. He has other remuneration of £34,000 and income from furnished accommodation of £4,335 for 1999/00.   There are no charges on income.   Albert also received £5,000 statutory redundancy pay.

Calculate Albert's taxable income for 1999/00 assuming all tax reliefs are claimed for the lump sum.

2.5 **Solution**

Income tax computation - 1999/00

	£	£	£
Remuneration			34,000
Lump sum		80,000	
Less: Exempt amount	30,000		
Less: Statutory redundancy pay	5,000		
		25,000	
			55,000
			89,000
Schedule A			4,335
STI			93,335
Less: Personal allowance			4,335
Taxable income			89,000

3 **INCENTIVE SCHEMES**

3.1 **Introduction**

(a) It has long been recognised by employers that there are commercial benefits in schemes to motivate employees that are linked to a company's profitability. These may take the form of profit-sharing, allocation of company shares or the grant of options to buy company shares in the future.

(b) Successive governments have encouraged this approach by giving tax privileges to such schemes, provided that they meet the relevant requirements. Schemes that do so are known as approved schemes and those that do not unapproved schemes.

(c) We look first at approved schemes and the conditions necessary for approval. At the end of this section there is an outline of the tax regime for unapproved schemes.

3.2 **Approved profit-sharing schemes**

(a) Each scheme is administered by a trust (set up by the relevant company) using funds provided by the company to buy shares in the company (or its parent) for appropriation to the company's participating employees. An approved profit-sharing scheme provides for an annual amount of a company's authorised shares to be allocated to eligible employee participants, with no income tax liability arising on the benefit so obtained.

(b) The employee must undertake not to dispose of, or assign, the shares allocated to him during the retention period, and must permit the trustees to hold the shares throughout that period. The retention period is from initial appropriation (to the employee) until the second anniversary of that date, the employee's death or reaching an age specified in the scheme (which must be between 60 and 75).

(c) The maximum initial market value of shares which may be appropriated to any one participant in a year of assessment is the greater of:

• £3,000, or

• 10% of the participant's remuneration for the relevant or preceding year of assessment;

subject to an overriding maximum of £8,000. Remuneration is that liable to PAYE ie, excluding benefits-in-kind and after deducting occupational pension contributions.

(d)   The shares must be quoted on a recognised stock exchange or be shares in a company not controlled by another.

(e)   An eligible employee is any person who is a full-time or part time employee or full-time director of the company concerned.

(f)   Any sums expended by a company participating in an approved scheme, by way of payment to the scheme trustees, are allowed as a deduction in computing assessable trading profits under Schedule D, as are the costs of establishing such a scheme.

(g)   When shares are appropriated to an individual by the trustees no charge under Schedule E arises, except where shares are appropriated to a participant in excess of the above mentioned limit.

(h)   A disposal of a participant's shares by the trustees before the third anniversary of the appropriation (the release date) gives rise to a Schedule E charge for the year of assessment in which the disposal takes place, on the locked-in value. The **locked-in value** is the initial market value of the shares or the disposal proceeds where they are lower.

3.3   Example

Goodenuff is a participant in his company's approved profit-sharing scheme. On 1 September 1996 the scheme trustees appropriated to him 5,000 25p ordinary shares (market value 40p). On 1 May 1999 the trustees sell 350 of the shares at 50p each on his behalf.

What Schedule E charge, if any, will Goodenuff be liable to tax on as a result of the sale of shares in May 1999?

3.4   Solution

The Schedule E charge will be:

	£
1999/00	
Market value on appropriation 350 x 40p	140

Locked-in value = £140 and so the Schedule E charge is £140, being lower than the proceeds (350 × 50p × 100% = £175).

3.5   Savings-related share option schemes

(a)   There is favourable tax treatment for share option schemes:

- that are linked to a SAYE (Save As You Earn) contract with a maximum monthly contribution by any employee of £250 per month for 3, 5 or 7 years; and

- where the purchase price of the shares is met by the employee, out of the SAYE accumulated savings, and the shares so acquired become additional share capital of the company,

provided the price at which options are offered is not less than 80% of market value when purchased.

(b)   If the options are exercised **more than three years** after the option was granted, no Schedule E assessments arise on

- grant of the option
- exercise of the option.

(c)   On subsequent disposal of the shares, the capital gains arising on the excess of net sale proceeds (or market value) at the date of disposal over the subscription price plus the cost of acquiring the options, will be taxable.

(d)   The costs of setting up such a scheme are allowable as trading expenses.

3.6   Company share option plan

(a)   This type of approved share option scheme differs from the SAYE schemes described above in that:

- the funds are provided by the employing company;
- the aggregate value of options granted is potentially much higher; and
- the company has much greater discretion in allocating options to employees.

(b)   An approved scheme is one where an option to purchase shares is granted to an individual:

- by reason of employment or directorship; and
- in accordance with a scheme approved under the legislation.

(c)   Participation in the scheme need not be extended to all employees nor be on equal terms to all participants. Eligible employees must be either full-time directors (ie, working at least 25 hours per week) or full-time or part time employees. Close company directors with a material interest (>10%) are ineligible. Subject to the above, the company has complete discretion as to participants.

(d)   The price payable for the shares on exercise of the option must not be materially less than their market value at the time the option was granted.

(e)   The tax implications for the employee are:

- on grant of an option: no charge under Schedule E

- on exercise of an option: no charge under Schedule E, provided the right is

   -     exercised not less than three nor more than ten years after grant, and

   -     is not exercised within three years of the date another option under the plan was last exercised.

- on final disposal of scheme shares, CGT will be charged on any gain then arising. The gain would be net disposal proceeds (or market value) less the price paid on exercise and the cost of the option.

(f)   There is a £30,000 limit to the value of shares for which a participant may hold unexercised options at the time of any grant of options.

(g)   The costs of administering the scheme are allowable trading expenses for the company.

3.7   Employee share ownership trusts (ESOTs)

(a)   The purpose of an ESOT is similar to that of an approved profit sharing scheme described above. However, there is no limit on the value of shares that may be distributed, which provides a significant incentive to establish them.

(b)   A company making a payment to a qualifying share ownership trust will be able to deduct the expenditure in its corporation tax computation. The receipts will not be taxed in the share ownership trust provided the funds are spent on qualifying purposes.

(c)   Individuals who sell shares in the founding company to a qualifying share ownership trust can roll over the gain against the cost of chargeable assets acquired with the sale proceeds. This encourages the sale of shares to the ESOT.

(d)   The plan should be established to receive or borrow funds from the founding company, which are used to buy shares in that company. Borrowing from other sources is permitted. The shares must be transferred to the beneficiaries within seven years, or sold to an approved profit sharing scheme at open market value.

3.8   Unapproved employee share schemes

The approved schemes described above enable limited benefits to be provided for directors and employees without attracting a tax charge. However, all the above schemes impose severe limitations on use. Consequently, many employers/employees prefer to use unapproved schemes for the benefit of senior executives and to accept the resultant tax charge.

3.9   Unapproved share option schemes

The main events giving rise to a tax charge on unapproved share option schemes are as follows.

(a)   Where a share option is exercisable more than 10 years after it was granted an immediate charge to income tax may arise under Schedule E. The tax charge will be collected under PAYE.

(b)   On exercise of a share option the gain is then taxed as income under Schedule E.

3.10   Unapproved share schemes

The main events giving rise to a tax charge on unapproved share schemes are as follows:

(a)   If the shares are acquired at less than their market value an income tax charge is levied on that undervalue. The tax charge is collected under PAYE.

(b)   If the shares are issued to the employee/director subject to restrictions, a Schedule E charge is raised whenever any of those restrictions are removed or varied such that the value of the shares increases.

(c)   Where an employee/director received any benefit arising from the shareholding which is not received by all holders of that class of shares - the benefit is charged as income under Schedule E.

4   SELF TEST QUESTIONS

4.1   What are the rules governing the time emoluments are deemed to be received by an employee? (1.3)

4.2   What factors do the Courts take into account in distinguishing between employment and self-employment? (1.4)

4.3   What impact does the receipt of statutory redundancy pay have on the taxation of an ex-gratia payment received on termination of employment? (2.2)

4.4   Which lump sum payments are completely exempt from tax? (2.3)

4.5   What conditions apply to shares of a company that has set up an approved profit sharing scheme? (3.2)

4.6   For what periods can a savings-related share option scheme be set up? (3.5)

4.7   What discretion does a company have in deciding on the participants in a company share option plan? (3.6)

4.8   Why might employers/employees prefer to use unapproved employee share schemes? (3.8)

4.9   What are the main events giving rise to a tax charge on unapproved share option schemes? (3.9)

4.10   What are the main events giving rise to a tax charge on unapproved share schemes? (3.10)

5   EXAMINATION TYPE QUESTION

5.1   ABC plc

ABC plc has 80 employees with an average remuneration of £45,000 pa.

ABC plc is proposing to:

(a)   Set up a profit sharing scheme whereby employees would receive free fully paid up ordinary shares in ABC plc.

(b)   Set up a share option scheme whereby employees would receive free options to purchase fully paid up ordinary shares in ABC plc at their present value. The options will be exercisable in five years time.

ABC plc's ordinary shares are presently quoted at £1.00 each, and are likely to be worth £6.00 each in five years time.

You are required to:

(a)   Explain the income tax implications for the employees if Inland Revenue approval is not obtained for either of the two schemes.

(b)   Calculate the tax saving if Inland Revenue approval is obtained for the two schemes.

6   ANSWER TO EXAMINATION TYPE QUESTION

6.1   ABC plc

The income tax implications for the employees if Inland Revenue approval is not obtained for either of the two schemes are as follows:

Profit sharing scheme

The employees will be charged under Schedule E on the difference between the market value of the shares issued to them, and the amount paid for them. The Schedule E charge will therefore be £1 for each share allocated.

Share option scheme

The options cannot be exercised more than ten years after their grant. There will therefore be no Schedule E charge at the time that they are granted.

When the options are exercised in five years time, there will be a charge based on the market value of the shares at that date, less the amount paid for them. The charge will be £5 (£6 − £1) for each share option exercised.

The tax saving if Inland Revenue approval is obtained for the two schemes is as follows:

Profit sharing scheme

Provided that the shares are held in trust for at least three years, there will be no liability to income tax.

The maximum market value of shares that can be allocated to an employee each tax year is the greater of £3,000 or 10% of remuneration, subject to an overall maximum of £8,000. The employees will be entitled to shares worth £4,500 (£45,000 × 10%) each year, which is a tax saving of £1,800 pa (£4,500 at 40%).

Note that there will still be a liability to CGT when the shares are sold. If the shares are sold after three years there will be a capital gain (before taper relief) of £22,500 (4,500 × (£6 − £1).

Share option scheme

There will be no liability to income tax as the share options are exercisable between three and ten years.

The maximum market value of share options that an employee may hold is £30,000. The tax saving when the share options are exercised in five years time will be £60,000 (£30,000 × £5 at 40%).

Note that there will still be a liability to CGT when the shares are sold. If the shares are sold immediately after the exercise of the options, there will be a capital gain (before taper relief) of £150,000 (£30,000 × (6 − 1)).

7 BENEFITS IN KIND

INTRODUCTION

This chapter looks at the principles of the taxation of benefits and expense deductions. A distinction is drawn between the way benefit charges are imposed on employees earning less than £8,500 pa on the one hand and those earning more, and directors, on the other.

1 PRINCIPLES OF TAXATION OF BENEFITS

1.1 Introduction

(a) The scope of the Schedule E charge, set out above, was defined in terms of the emoluments from an office or employment. In addition to salary, the term emoluments also covered perquisites and profits, which are better known as benefits-in-kind.

(b) The general rule for valuing benefits in kind provided to employees was established by case law (Tennant v Smith, 1892). Employees are taxed on the cash equivalent of the benefit, which is the cash value the employee would receive if he disposed of the benefit to a third party. Occasionally a benefit can be taxed without the need to consider the value to a third party. In Heaton v Bell (1969) an employee was assessed on an amount of income he would have received from his employer had he given up a benefit provided (the loan of a car).

1.2 Exceptions to the general principle

There are three types of exception to the general rule derived from case law outlined above:

(a) some benefits, that are assessable on all employees, are subject to specific statutory rules;

(b) benefits received by a group that broadly comprises employees earning £8,500 pa or more and directors are taxed, in general, under a different general principle imposed by statute; the cost of providing the benefit; and

(c) some specific benefits that are taxable only in the hands of employees earning £8,500 pa or more and directors are subject to specific statutory valuation rules.

2 BENEFITS ASSESSABLE ON ALL EMPLOYEES

2.1 Introduction

The general rule (the cash value of the benefit on disposal to a third party) is used as a fall back measure where the benefit provided does not fall into one of the categories below that have specific rules.

2.2 Vouchers and credit tokens

(a) Vouchers are broadly documents with which an individual can obtain goods and services. Cash vouchers are subject to PAYE when handed over to an employee and thus no further benefit arises on them since tax has already been paid. Non-cash vouchers are assessable on the employee at the cost of providing them. By concession luncheon vouchers are not taxed unless they are worth more than 15 pence per working day.

(b) Use of credit tokens (such as a company credit card) are assessable on the value of goods and services bought with them.

(c)   No assessable benefit arises where the employee can show that the use of either vouchers or credit tokens was wholly, exclusively and necessarily in the performance of the duties of his employment.

2.3   Living accommodation

(a)   Where an employee is provided with living accommodation as a result of his employment, he is assessed on the higher of:

- the accommodation's annual value; and
- the rent actually paid for it by the provider of the accommodation.

(b)   Normally annual value is assumed to be rateable value, in spite of the abolition of domestic rates.

(c)   To the extent that the accommodation is used wholly, exclusively and necessarily for business purposes the employee's benefit assessment is reduced. Similarly, it is reduced by any contribution the employee makes for the accommodation.

(d)   There is no assessable benefit at all if the accommodation is job-related. To qualify as such it must be provided:

- where it is necessary for the proper performance of the employee's duties (eg, a caretaker); or

- for the better performance of the employee's duties and, for that type of employment, it is customary for employers to provide living accommodation (eg hotel-worker); or

- where there is a special threat to the employee's security and he resides in the accommodation as part of special security arrangements.

(e)   A director can only claim one of the first two exemptions if:

- he has no material interest in the company; and

- he is a full-time working director or the company is a non-profit making organisation.

A material interest is broadly, more than 5% in the company's ordinary share capital.

(f)   There is an additional benefit assessed on expensive living accommodation. It applies where the cost of providing the accommodation exceeds £75,000 and there is a charge under the normal accommodation rules described above. So, however expensive the accommodation, it does not apply where it qualifies as job-related. It does, however, apply when there is no normal charge only because the employee pays rent equal to the rateable value of the property.

(g)   The benefit is calculated as the additional value of the accommodation to the employee which is:

(cost of provision - £75,000) × the appropriate percentage

Cost of provision is the purchase price of the property plus expenditure on improvements incurred before the start of the tax year. The appropriate percentage is the official rate of interest used for beneficial loans in force at the start of the tax year.

To prevent avoidance, where the accommodation has been owned by the provider throughout a period of six years preceding the employee's taking up residence in it, the calculation of the benefit uses the property's market value when first used by the employee rather than the original cost. This applies even if the value has declined.

Deductions from the assessable benefit are available both for bona fide business use of the accommodation and for rent paid by the employee that exceeds the benefit assessable under the normal charge.

(h)   It should be emphasised that the benefit for use of expensive accommodation is an extra assessable benefit, **not** a replacement for the 'normal' charge.

2.4   Activity

Barber, a sales manager, occupies a flat owned by his employer. Its annual value is £4,000 and Barber pays his employer £500 pa for use of the flat. The flat was purchased in 1994 for £120,000. It has been agreed that 25% of the use of the flat may be attributed to business use.

Calculate the total benefit assessable on Barber for 1999/00, assuming an official rate of interest of 10%.

2.5   Activity solution

	£	£
Normal accommodation benefit	4,000	
Less: 25% business use	1,000	
		3,000
Less: Contribution for personal use		500
		2,500
Additional accommodation benefit		
(120,000 - 75,000) × 10%)	4,500	
Less: 25% business use	1,125	
		3,375
Total assessable benefit		5,875

3   BENEFITS ASSESSABLE ON EMPLOYEES EARNING £8,500 OR MORE AND DIRECTORS

3.1   Principles of assessment

(a)   Instead of being taxed under the general principle for valuing benefits (effectively the second hand sale value of the benefit) these employees and directors are taxed under a separate set of statutory rules.

(b)   The measure of the benefit provided is the cost of providing it.

(c)   Where employers provide in-house benefits (such as free tickets for employees of a coach travel company) the measure of the benefit is the additional or marginal cost incurred by the employer as a result - not a proportion of the total cost (Pepper v Hart, 1993).

(d)   A benefit is deemed to have been provided to an employee not only when it is provided to him directly but also when it is provided to a member of his family or household. For the sake of brevity, throughout this section benefits are described as being made available to an employee but it should be borne in mind that on each occasion the charge to tax is also incurred when the benefit is provided to a member of the employee's family or household.

(e)   To be taxed under these principles a benefit must be provided to the employee by reason of his employment.

3.2   The threshold income level

In broad terms, the calculation to ascertain whether a person reaches the threshold income level of £8,500 assumes (in the calculation of benefits) that he does so. A calculation of the following kind is required in cases of doubt.

	£
Salary	x
Benefits assessable on all employees *	x
Benefits assessable only on £8,500 (or more) earners	x
	—
Total emoluments (for test purposes)	x
	—

* except the additional charge for living accommodation

If the total amounts to £8,500 or more the individual becomes subject to the benefits regime for the 'higher-paid'. Note that there is no deduction for business expenses in calculating this total.

3.3   Expenses connected with living accommodation

(a)   Under the general benefits in kind rule, expenses connected with living accommodation, such as lighting and heating, are taxable on an employee where the cost is met by his employer.

(b)   Such costs can total a considerable sum and so there is a limit on the amount taxable as a benefit where **the employee's accommodation is job-related**.

(c)   The limit applies to the following types of expense.

- heating, lighting and cleaning
- repairing, maintaining or decorating the premises
- furniture and other goods normal for domestic occupation.

(d)   The taxable limit is 10% of net emoluments (salary plus benefits other than the ancillary benefits in question less any expenditure deductible against employment income).

3.4   Use of assets

(a)   Many benefits in kind constitute payment of expenses on behalf of an employee. Sometimes, however, assets are provided for an employee's use while legal ownership remains with the employer. The most common example is the company car, which has special rules of its own considered later on in this chapter, but there is a general rule that applies to other assets.

(b)   Except for cars, car fuel, vans and accommodation, the general rule is that an employee is taxed on a benefit amounting to 20% of an asset's market value at the time it is first provided. So, if the employee is provided with a television costing £500, he is subject to a benefit in kind charge under Schedule E of £100 (£500 × 20%). The benefit is assessed for **each** tax year in which it is provided (not just the one in which it was first made available).

(c)   Where the employer rents the asset made available to the employee instead of buying it, the employee is taxed on the rental paid by the employer rather than 20% of market value if the rental is the higher figure. So if the annual rental for the television mentioned above is £120, that would be assessed on the employee.

(d)   Payments made by the employee for the use of the asset reduce (or eliminate) the taxable benefit.

3.5   Gifts of assets

(a)   If an employer purchases a new asset and gives it to an employee immediately, the employee is taxed on the cost.

(b) Where an asset is given to an employee that is second-hand, different rules may apply. In these circumstances the employee is taxed on the **higher** of the asset's market value when **given to him** and:

- the asset's market value at the time it was **first made available** to the employee

  less

- the benefit assessed on the employee during the time he had the use of it but did not own it.

(c) The purpose of the special rule for gifts of used assets is to prevent employee's gaining from gifts of assets that depreciate in value rapidly once they are used.

(d) Where the employee buys the asset, the payment is deducted in calculating the benefit.

3.6 Activity

Brian's employer, X Ltd, purchased a dishwasher for his use on 1 June 1998, costing £600. On 6 April 1999 X Ltd gave the dishwasher to Brian (its market value then being £150).

Calculate the benefit assessable on Brian on the basis of:

(a) the circumstances as set out above; and
(b) if Brian paid X Ltd £100 for the dishwasher.

3.7 Activity solution

(a) Gift of dishwasher

	£
Market value when first made available to Brian	600
Less: Benefit already assessed	
1998/99 £600 × 20% × 10/12	100
Taxable benefit - 1999/00	500

The benefit is £500 since this is greater than the dishwasher's market value when given to Brian (£150).

(b) Sale of dishwasher to Brian for £100

	£
Benefit as calculated in (a) above	500
Less: Price paid	100
Taxable benefit - 1999/00	400

Note: where the benefit of use is provided for only part of a tax year the benefit is reduced proportionately.

3.8 Cars

(a) The 'company car' has been one of the benefits most widely provided for employees. The amount of the benefit depends on the cost, age and amount of business use the car is put to.

(b) In line with the approach to taxing benefits, there is no assessment where a car is not intended to be available for private use and, as a matter of fact, there is none. Remember that travel between home and a permanent workplace counts as private use, **not** business use.

(c)   No individual using a 'pool car' is assessed on a car benefit. To qualify as a 'pool car' **all** of the following conditions must be met during the tax year in question.

- The car must be used by more than one employee (and not usually by one employee to the exclusion of the others).

- It must not normally be kept overnight at or near the residence of any of the employees making use of it.

- Any private use by an employee must be merely incidental to his business use of it.

(d)   Unless the employee is exempted (because he makes no private use of an employer's car, or it is a pool car), he is subject to a benefit in kind charge.

The car benefit charge is a percentage of the car's list price.

(e)   The list price of a car is defined as the inclusive price (ie, including taxes) appropriate for the car on the assumption that it is sold in the UK as an individual sale in the retail market. Consequently employees of large companies cannot benefit from bulk discounts their employer might negotiate. It is the list price **on the day before the car's first registration** that is used.

(f)   Where the car is fitted with accessories the list price of these is added to the list price of the car subject to a maximum price of £80,000.

(g)   An employee may reduce the price on which his car benefit charge is calculated by making a capital contribution. The price is reduced by the lower of:

- the capital contribution towards the cost of the basic car and its accessories; and
- £5,000.

(h)   The standard car benefit is 35% of the price of the car subject to a maximum price of £80,000.

(i)   The standard 35% charge applies where there is low business mileage (or none at all). Business mileage in excess of certain limits results in a reduced percentage charge as follows:

- The car benefit is 25% of the list price for business mileage of 2,500 to 17,999 miles in the tax year.

- The car benefit is 15% of the list price for business mileage of 18,000 miles or more in the tax year.

(j)   When more than one car is made available to an employee, the second car (the one with the least business use) is assessed at 35% of the list price. This is only reduced to a charge of 25% of the list price if business mileage is 18,000 miles or more.

(k)   The benefit may be reduced in the following circumstances:

- Where the car is four years old or more at the end of the tax year, the basic benefit is reduced by ¼.

- Where the car is unavailable for part of the tax year because it was first provided or ceased to be provided part way through a tax year the benefit (after taking account of business mileage and the car's age) is reduced proportionately.

  The car may also be unavailable for a period during the tax year but was available both before and after (for instance if it was under repair after a crash). The benefit charge that would otherwise apply is proportionately reduced provided that it was unavailable for a continuous period of 30 days.

- Lastly, a reduction is made where the employee makes a financial contribution as a condition of the car being available for his private use. (This should not be confused with a capital contribution made towards the purchase cost of the car, which is deducted from the price on which the percentage car benefit is based.)

(l) The charge for cars available for private use takes into account the running expenses of the vehicle, so there is no additional taxable benefit when the employer pays for insurance, road fund licence, maintenance etc. If a chauffeur is provided with the car however it constitutes an additional benefit. A separate benefit-in-kind charge is made for car fuel (see below).

(m) A special system applies to 'classic cars'. A classic car is one that is at least 15 years old at the end of the tax year, has a market value of £15,000 or more and has a higher market value than list price.

(n) The percentage benefit charge for classic cars is based on market value (on the last day of the tax year). As with ordinary cars, there is a reduction (up to a £5,000 maximum) for capital contributions towards the cost of the car made by the employee.

3.9 Car fuel

(a) Scale charges apply to car fuel provided for private motoring in a car provided by reason of a person's employment. They are based on engine size only, without reference either to the age of the car or its original market value or the amount of business mileage.

(b) The scale charges for **petrol** cars for 1999/00 are:

Engine size	£
1,400 cc or less	1,210
1,401cc - 2,000cc	1,540
2,001 cc or more	2,270

For **diesel** cars the equivalents are:

Engine size	£
2,000cc or less	1,540
2,001 cc or more	2,270

(c) Proportionate reductions in the fuel scale charge apply where the car is unavailable for part of the tax year. These are calculated on the same basis as reductions in the car charge.

(d) No reduction is made in the fuel scale charge for payments made by the employee unless he pays for **all** fuel used for private motoring. In which case the charge would be cancelled. Since the fuel scale charge applies only to vehicles for which there is a car benefit charge, it does not apply to 'pool cars'.

3.10 Activity

Charles took up employment with Weavers Ltd on 1 July 1999. His remuneration package included a 5 year old 2,500cc petrol-driven car, list price £24,000. He took delivery of the car on 1 August 1999 and during the remainder of the tax year drove 15,000 miles on business and 18,000 miles for private purposes. As a condition of the car being made available to him for private motoring, Charles paid £100 per month for the car and £50 per month for petrol.

Weaver's Ltd incurred the following expenses in connection with Charles' car

	£
Servicing	450
Insurance	780
Fuel (of which £1,150 was for business purposes)	2,500
Maintenance	240

Calculate Charles' assessable benefits for 1999/00 in connection with his private use of the car

3.11   Activity solution

	£	£
Benefit - £24,000 × 15% (W1)	3,600	
Less: Reduction for age of car £3,600 × ¼	900	
	2,700	
Less: Reduction for non-availability (W2)	900	
	1,800	
Less: Payment for use (W3)	800	
		1,000
Fuel - standard scale charge	2,270	
Less: Reduction for non-availability (W4)	757	
		1,513
Assessable benefit		2,513

WORKINGS

(W1)   Business mileage - car

The business mileage threshold is reduced due to non-availability to 18,000 × 8/12 = 12,000 miles. Thus Charles qualifies for the 15% basic charge.

(W2)   Reduction for non-availability - car

Car first made available on 1 August 1999. Thus not available for 4 months of 1999/00. Reduction is thus £900 (£2,700 × 4/12).

(W3)   Payment for use

Payment made for 8 months @ £100/month = £800.

(W4)   Reduction for non-availability - car fuel

Same proportionate reduction applies as for car benefit charge. Reduction is thus £2,270 × 4/12 = £757.

Notes:

(1)   The amount of Charles' private mileage has no impact on the calculations.

(2)   Charles does not qualify for the cancellation of the fuel scale charge because he does not pay for all fuel used for private motoring.

3.12   Cars and cash alternatives

Where employees are offered either a company car or a cash alternative, the employee will pay tax on the option that they have taken ie, either on the cash or the car benefit figure based on list price. Without this rule the Heaton v Bell principle would apply to reduce the value, of the car benefit to the (usually lower) amount of salary 'sacrificed'.

3.13   Activity

Sally and Ray are both employed by Buddle Ltd. As part of their remuneration package, they are offered the choice between a company car and a cash alternative of £400 per month.

Sally chooses a Volvo 850 with a list price of £19,500. She travels 2,000 business miles in 1999/00. Ray chooses the cash alternative.

Calculate the assessable benefit for Ray and Sally for 1999/00.

3.14   Activity solution

Sally's assessable benefit:

£19,500 × 35%   £6,825

Ray's assessable benefit

£400 × 12   £4,800

3.15   Vans and heavier commercial vehicles

(a)   Where employers' vans are made available to employees for their private use, a benefit in kind scale charge applies.

(b)   A distinction has to be drawn between cars, vans and heavier commercial vehicles. Vans are defined as vehicles primarily designed for carrying goods or burden (and cars are defined in opposite terms). Between vans and heavier commercial vehicles the distinction is one of weight. Vehicles up to 3.5 metric tonnes are vans. Any weight above this level counts as a heavier commercial vehicle.

(c)   Unless a heavier commercial vehicle is provided wholly or mainly for an employee's private use (which would be unusual) there is no taxable benefit. Vans, however, are subject to a taxable benefit, the size of which depends on the age of the van and whether it is made available for private use to just one employee or is shared. As with cars, there is an exemption from the charge for pooled vans and the same definition of pooled applies to both cars and vans.

(d)   Where a van is made available for private use to only one employee the scale charge is £500 if it is less than four years old at the end of the tax year. Older vans attract a £350 scale charge. Proportionate reductions in the scale charge are made where a van is unavailable (using the same definition as for cars). Again following the car benefit principle, a reduction is made for payments made by the employee for private use of the van.

(e)   Where employees share the private use of the van, or vans, a different calculation applies. The £500 scale charge is totalled for all the shared vans and the resulting figure is divided equally over all the employees who made any private use of any of the vans during the tax year regardless of the amount of private use.

(f)   A shared van is one that is available to more than one employee of the same employer.

(g)   No employee sharing the private use of vans can incur a scale charge higher than £500.

Official **ACCA** *Textbook, published by AT Foulks Lynch*

(h)   An employee can elect for his scale charge to be calculated on an alternative basis when he shares the private use of a van or vans. This basis looks to the number of days on which the employee has a shared van available for private use; the scale charge is £5 per day. The election will benefit employees who make relatively little private use of a shared van.

3.16   Beneficial loans

(a)   Beneficial loans are those made to an employee below the **official rate of interest** (broadly an approximation to the prevailing commercial mortgage rate).

(b)   Employees are liable to a benefit in kind charge on the difference between the interest that would be payable on the loan (had interest been charged at the official rate) and the interest actually paid in respect of the tax year, whether paid during it or afterwards.

An exemption for small loans applies where all the employee's cheap or interest free loans, excluding loans which qualify for tax relief, total no more than £5,000.

(c)   There are two methods of calculating the benefit, the averaging method and the accurate method. The former uses the average of the loan outstanding at the beginning and end of the tax year. If the loan was taken out or redeemed during the tax year that date is used instead of the beginning or end of the tax year. The latter method calculates the benefit day by day on the balance actually outstanding. Either the taxpayer or the Revenue can decide that the accurate method should be used.

(d)   If an interest-free or cheap loan is one that would ordinarily attract tax relief, tax relief is available on the appropriate amount of the loan at the official rate of interest.

(e)   If all or part of a loan to an employee (whether or not made on low-interest or interest-free terms) is written off, the amount written off is treated as a benefit in kind and charged to income tax.

3.17   Activity

Daniel was granted a loan of £35,000 by his employer on 31 March 1999 to help finance the purchase of a yacht. Interest is payable on the loan at 3% pa. On 1 June 1999 Daniel repaid £5,000 and on 1 December 1999 he repaid a further £15,000. The remaining £15,000 was still outstanding on 5 April 2000. Daniel earns £30,000 pa.

Calculate the assessable benefit for 1999/00 under

(a)   the averaging method; and
(b)   the accurate method

assuming that the official rate of interest was 10% pa.

3.18   Activity solution

(a)   Averaging method

		£	£
$\dfrac{35,000 + 15,000}{2} \times 10\%$			2,500

Less: interest paid

		£	£
6.4.99 - 31.5.99	£35,000 × 3% × $\frac{2}{12}$	175	
1.6.99 - 30.11.99	£30,000 × 3% × $\frac{6}{12}$	450	
1.12.99 - 5.4.2000	£15,000 × 3% × $\frac{4}{12}$	150	
			(775)
			1,725

(b) Accurate method

	£
6.4.99 - 31.5.99	
£35,000 × 10% × $\frac{2}{12}$	583
1.6.99 - 30.11.99	
£30,000 × 10% × $\frac{6}{12}$	1,500
1.12.99 - 5.4.2000	
£15,000 × 10% × $\frac{4}{12}$	500
	2,583
Less: Interest paid	(775)
	1,808

3.19 Loans with mortgage interest relief

The rules for taxing cheap and interest-free loans provided by employers where mortgage interest relief applies are as follows:

- First, the value of the loan for tax purposes is calculated; which is the difference between the interest (if any) paid by the employee and the interest which he would have paid at the official rate of interest.

  This amount is added to his other income and taxed at his marginal rate of tax.

- Second, the employee will be entitled to tax relief at 10% on the loan, up to £30,000, as if he had paid interest at the official rate.

3.20 Activity

Grace has a £50,000 home loan at 2% provided by her employer. She is a higher rate tax payer. Calculate the net tax payable on the loan assuming that the official rate of interest is 10%.

3.21 Activity solution

Tax liability

	£	£
Taxable benefit £50,000 @ (10% – 2%) 8%	4,000	
Tax due £4,000 @ higher rate 40%		1,600
Tax relief		
Interest actually paid £50,000 @ 2%	1,000	
Interest treated as paid	4,000	
Total	5,000	
Mortgage interest relief on £5,000 × $\frac{30}{50}$ @ 10%		300
Net tax payable		1,300

3.22   Exemption for commercial loans

There is an exemption for loans made to employees on commercial terms by employers who lend to the general public. The exemption will apply where

- the loans are made by an employer whose business includes the lending of money;

- loans are made to employees on the same terms and conditions as are available to members of the public; and

- a substantial number of loans on these terms are made to public customers.

3.23   Scholarships

(a)   In principle, if a scholarship is provided to a member of an individual's family or household, the cost of it is taxable as a benefit in kind.

(b)   There is an exemption, however, for the 'arm's length' grant of scholarships.   No taxable benefit arises where:

- the scholarship is awarded from a separate trust scheme;

- the person receiving it is in full-time education at a school, college or university; and

- not more than 25% of payments made in the tax year from the scheme are made by reason of a person's employment.

(c)   In the hands of the recipient scholarship income is exempt.

3.24   Payment of director's tax liability

(a)   Where tax should have been deducted from a director's emoluments under the PAYE system, but was not, and the tax is paid over to the Revenue by someone other than the director, the director is treated as receiving a benefit in kind.

(b)   The measure of the benefit is the amount of tax accounted for, less any reimbursement by the director (if any).

(c)   Note that this benefit in kind rule applies only to directors (not employees earning more than £8,500).

4   EXEMPT BENEFITS

The following are the more important exempt benefits-in-kind

(a)   the **employer's contribution** to an approved pension scheme. Although many schemes also require contributions by the employee (also tax deductible against his Schedule E salary), the ultimate benefit-in-kind will be a non-contributory scheme

(b)   the use of subsidised on-site **restaurant or canteen** facilities, provided such facilities are available for all employees

(c)   luncheon vouchers up to a value of 15p per working day

(d)   entertainment provided for an employee, by reason of his employment, by a **genuine third party** eg, a ticket or seat at a sporting or cultural event provided for a business contact or client to generate goodwill.

(e)   gifts received, by reason of his employment, from genuine third parties, provided the cost from any one source does not exceed £150 in a year of assessment

Long service awards in kind (eg gold watches) are exempt up to a cost of £20 for each year of service of 20 years or more

(f)   the provision of a benefit of a car parking space provided at or near the place of work, including the reimbursement of the cost of such a parking place

(g)   provision of travel, accommodation and subsistence during public transport disruption caused by industrial action

(h)   the provision of a mobile telephone by the employer to an employee.

(i)   the provision of a computer worth up to £2,500 by the employer to an employee.

(j)   there is no tax charge in respect of certain benefits aimed at encouraging employees to travel to work other than by private car. The exemption includes work buses, subsidies to public bus services, and the provision of bicycles and cycling safety equipment.

(k)   Employer funded training

Where the expenses of training are paid for by the employer, no taxable benefit arises on the employee. The exemption includes:

(i)   Training in practical or theoretical skills and competencies that a trainee is likely to need with that employer.

(ii)   Training in first aid and health and safety.

(iii)   Activities intended to develop leadership skills.

The exemption applies whether the training is full-time or part-time, and whether it is in-house or run externally. It also makes no difference whether the employer pays for the training directly, or reimburses the employee's expenses.

(l)   medical insurance for treatment and medical services where the need for treatment arises while abroad in performance of duties

(m)   Christmas parties, annual dinner dances etc for staff generally. Modest cost (up to £75 pa per head) will not be assessed

(n)   security assets and services

Where a security asset or security service is provided by reason of employment, or where reimbursement is made for the cost of such measures.

Relief is not, therefore, available where the director or employee himself bears the cost.

The asset or service must meet a special threat to the employee's personal physical safety (as opposed to his property). Security assets include such things as intruder alarms, bullet-resistant glass and floodlighting. Security services include such items as bodyguards and specially trained chauffeurs

(o)   work-place nurseries for child (under 18) care

Nurseries run by the employer (who must be responsible for finance and management) at the workplace or at other non-domestic premises will not be an assessable benefit-in-kind.

Included are facilities run jointly with other employers or local authorities and similar facilities for older children after school or during school holidays.

Note: the provision of cash allowances or vouchers to meet child care expenses are assessable.

(p)   Recreational or sporting facilities.

No benefit arises on the provision of such facilities by a person's employer (directly or indirectly).

(q)   Removal expenses and benefits.

No assessable benefit arises on payment or reimbursement of removal expenses and benefits provided that:

- the expenses are incurred in connection with a change in the employee's principal private residence resulting from:

    - taking up a new employment; or
    - an alteration in the duties of an employment; or
    - a change in the location at which the employee's duties are carried out;

- the costs met or reimbursed are qualifying expenses. These are widely drawn so as to include costs of disposing of the first house, travel and subsistence when looking for a new house, removal expenses and interest on a bridging loan whilst the employee owns both the old and new homes;

- the expenditure is incurred by the end of the tax year following the one in which the employment change occurred; and

- only the first £8,000 of the total expenditure met or reimbursed is exempt.

(r)   Counselling services for employees

No assessable benefit arises on counselling services provided to an employee made redundant provided that:

- the recipient has been a full-time employee throughout the previous two years;

- the services are provided in the UK;

- their purpose is to enable the employee to find another employment or become self-employed; and

- the services consist wholly or mainly of advice and guidance, developing skills or using office facilities.

(s)   Expenses incurred by employees whilst away overnight on company business

Where employers pay personal expenses, such as telephone calls home, laundry and so on, for employees who stay away from home on business, these expenses are not a taxable benefit for employees, provided that they fall below the de-minimis limit of £5 per night in the UK and £10 per night overseas.

This exemption applies regardless of how the employer meets the expenses. For instance, the employer may:

(i)   pay hotel bills directly; or
(ii)   provide a nightly allowance; or
(iii) reimburse the employee with the actual expenses incurred.

If an amount above the limit is paid, the whole amount is taxable.

(t)   Employee liability insurance (XE'Employee liability insurance')

Liability insurance is aimed at protecting an employee from a work-related liability.

The payment of liability insurance by an employer is exempt. Where liability insurance is paid by an employee then it qualifies as a deductible expense, with relief being given against income of the year in which the expenditure is incurred. Relief is available for up to six years after the year in which employment ceases.

Where payments are made by an employer or by an employee to meet uninsured liabilities (such as legal costs) of an employee, then the payments are treated in the same way as the payment of liability insurance.

5   DEDUCTIBILITY OF EXPENSES FROM EMPLOYMENT INCOME

5.1   Introduction

Relief for expenditure against employment income, taxed under Schedule E, is of two types. Firstly, certain types of expenditure are specifically permitted by statute. The most important of these are:

(a)   contributions to approved pension schemes or personal pensions plans (within certain limits);

(b)   fees and subscriptions to professional bodies and learned societies, provided that the recipient is approved for the purpose by the Revenue and its activities are relevant to the individual's employment; and

(c)   payments to charity made under a payroll deduction scheme operated by an employer (up to a maximum of £1,200 pa).

Secondly, unspecified expenditure on travel and other expenditure is deductible to the extent that it complies with very stringent rules. These are discussed below.

5.2   Travel expenditure

(a)   Travelling expenses may be deducted (s198 ICTA 1988) only where they:

- Are incurred necessarily in the performance of the duties of the employment. Typically this type of journey is where an employee travels to visit a client. Travel that is integral to the performance of the duties also falls under this heading, and will include commercial travellers and service engineers who move from place to place during the day.

- Are attributable to the necessary attendance at any place by the employee in the performance of their duties.

(b)   No relief is given for travelling between two separate employments. However, if an employee has more than one place where duties have to be performed for the same employer, then travelling expenses between them are allowable.

(c)   Relief is not given for the cost of journeys that are ordinary commuting or for the cost of private travel. Ordinary commuting is the journey made each day between home and a permanent workplace. Private travel is a journey between home and any other place that an employee does not have to be for the purposes of work.

(d)   Relief is given where an employee travels directly from home to a temporary place of work. A temporary workplace is defined as one where an employee goes to perform a task of limited duration, or for a temporary purpose.

However, a place of work will not be classed as a temporary workplace where an employee works there continuously for a period which lasts, or is expected to last, more than 24 months.

(e)   Where an employee passes their normal permanent workplace on the way to a temporary workplace, relief will still be available provided the employee does not stop at the normal workplace, or any stop is incidental eg, to pick up some papers.

(f)   An employee may travel to a temporary workplace without that journey being significantly different from his or her normal ordinary commuting. This may be the case where the temporary workplace is situated near the permanent workplace, and in these circumstances relief is denied.

(g)   Where an employee's business journey qualifies for relief, then the amount of relief is the full cost of that journey. There is no need to take account of any savings the employee makes by not having to make his or her normal commuting journey to work.

5.3   Other expenses

(a)   The rule covering deductibility of non-travelling expenses is even more strict. In addition to being incurred necessarily and in the performance of the duties of employment, such expenses must also be incurred wholly and exclusively in the performance of those duties. So severe are these tests that one judge thought that the words of the rule 'are found to come to nearly nothing at all'.

(b)   The test that expenditure must be incurred **'in the performance** of the duties' means that there is no deduction for expenditure incurred beforehand to gain the requisite knowledge or experience to do the work. So, for example, the cost of attending evening classes by a schoolteacher has been disallowed.

(c)   For expenditure to be 'necessarily' incurred it must be inherent in the job, not something imposed by the employee's circumstances. Thus an employee with poor eyesight was unable to deduct the cost of spectacles. In other words, to be necessary expenditure, each and every person undertaking the duties would have to incur it.

(d)   For expenditure to be incurred 'wholly and exclusively' it must be with the sole objective of performing the duties of the employment. It does not matter that some personal benefit is acquired from the expenditure as long as it is incidental. Two examples show this distinction. If an employee is required to wear clothes of a high standard, and so purchases them, the expenditure is **not** deductible. The employee's clothes satisfy both professional and personal needs. On the other hand expenditure on a home telephone can be partly deductible. Business calls are made 'wholly and exclusively' and so are deductible. But, on the same reasoning as applied to the clothes no part of the line rental for a home phone may be deducted.

6   THE FIXED PROFIT CAR SCHEME (FPCS)

6.1   Introduction

Employees who use their own motor cars for work will normally be paid a mileage allowance.

This will be assessed on the employee as a benefit in kind, against which can be made a claim for the business proportion of the cost of running the motor car.

Alternatively, the FPCS can be used. Provided the mileage allowance is within the rates set by the Inland Revenue, then no benefit in kind arises.

6.2   The mileage rates allowed

The rate per mile allowed under the scheme is as follows:

Size of engine	First 4,000 miles pa	Over 4,000 miles pa
up to 1,000cc	28p	17p
1001 – 1,500cc	35p	20p
1501 – 2,000cc	45p	25p
over 2,000cc	63p	36p

Details of the allowable mileage rates will be given if they are needed in an examination question.

6.3   Expense claim

The FPCS can also be used as a basis for expense claims where an employee is not reimbursed by his employer, or where the reimbursement is less than the tax-free mileage rates.

6.4   Example

An employee uses her own 1,800cc motor car for business travel. During 1999/00 she drove 6,000 miles on business. Her employer paid her 20p per mile.

6.5   Solution

The mileage allowance of £1,200 (6,000 at 20p) will be received tax free, but in addition the employee can make an expense claim of £1,100 as follows:

	£
4,000 miles at 45p	1,800
2,000 miles at 25p	500
	2,300
Mileage allowance	1,200
Expense claim	1,100

7   SELF TEST QUESTIONS

7.1   What general principle is applied (unless overridden by a specific statutory rule) to the valuation of benefits provided to employees earning £8,500 or more and directors? (1.2)

7.2   In what circumstances does the additional benefit on living accommodation apply? (2.3)

7.3   How is the additional benefit on living accommodation calculated? (2.3)

7.4   How is the £8,500 income threshold calculated? (3.2)

7.5   How is the value of the benefit calculated when an employee is given an asset? (3.5)

7.6   What deductions may be given when calculating the value of a car benefit? (3.8)

7.7   What deductions may be given when calculating the value of the car fuel benefit? (3.9)

7.8   What are the two alternative ways of calculating the value of the benefit from a beneficial loan? (3.16)

7.9   In what circumstances will removal expenses be an exempt benefit? (4)

7.10   What tests must travelling expenditure comply with to be deductible against Schedule E income? (5.2)

8   EXAMINATION TYPE QUESTIONS

8.1   Mr F Darcy

Mr F Darcy, managing director of the Pemberley Trading Co Ltd, is paid an annual salary of £36,000 and also bonuses based on the company's performance. Pemberley's accounting year ends on 31 December each year and the bonuses are normally determined and paid on 31 May thereafter. In recent years bonuses have been

Year to 31 December 1997	£4,000
Year to 31 December 1998	£8,000
Year to 31 December 1999	£4,000

Mr Darcy pays 7% of his basic salary to an approved occupational pension scheme. He uses a company car (3,500cc) purchased in 1997 for £20,000, for 25,000 miles during 1999/00, of which 25%

is for non-business use. Running expenses including car fuel paid by the company were £2,600 in the year.

On 2 April 1998 the company set up a scholarship fund for its employees and their relatives. Mr Darcy's son, who is 23 years old and has no income of his own, was awarded a scholarship of £2,940 per year for three years from 1 October 1999 to continue to study for a doctorate at the University of London while continuing to live with his father. It is paid each year on 1 December.

Under the terms of the company's approved profit-sharing scheme Mr Darcy was allotted 1,000 ordinary £1 shares of the company, the market value of which is £4.25 per share, on 21 January 2000.

Mr Darcy pays charitable deeds of covenant totalling £4,235 (net).

Mr Darcy's wife died in 1992.

You are required to compute Mr Darcy's income tax liability for 1999/00. Briefly give reasons for your treatment of items included or excluded in arriving at his taxable income.

8.2   Mr Drake

Mr Drake is employed as the sales director of Drakemain Ltd at a salary of £20,000 pa and his form P11D for the year ended 5 April 2000 shows the following entries

	£
Entertainment	683
Travelling and subsistence (including £385 rail fares home to office)	826
Benefit of motor car	4,800
Gross annual value of company house	650
BUPA subscription	409
Home telephone (rental and units)	160
Scale benefit for private fuel	2,270
	9,798

You are given the following further information

(i)   £10 per month is deducted from Drake's net salary to cover his private use of the motor car and £40 per month as rent for the house.

(ii)   Drake pays the council tax on the company house in the year 1999/00. This amounted to £325.

(iii)   The telephone installed in the company house is used only 40% for business.

(iv)   Unless otherwise indicated all expenses reimbursed to Drake were incurred for business purposes.

(v)   The company omitted one item from the form P11D. They had purchased a TV on 6 April 1998 and allowed Drake the use of it for the whole of the years ended 5 April 1999 and 2000. The set was then given to him on 5 April 2000. The set cost £500 and was worth £150 in April 2000.

You are required to calculate Mr. Drakes Schedule E assessment for 1999/00.

9   ANSWERS TO EXAMINATION TYPE QUESTIONS

9.1   Mr F Darcy

Computation of income tax payable for 1999/00

		£	£
Schedule E:			
Salary			36,000
Bonus *(note 1)*			8,000
			44,000
Benefits			
Car 20,000 × 15% (note 2)		3,000	
Car fuel		2,270	
Scholarship paid for son		2,940	
Excess shares under profit sharing scheme *(note 3)*		102	
			8,312
			52,312
Less: Pension contributions 7% × £36,000			2,520
			49,792
Less: Charitable deed £4,235 × 100/77			5,500
Statutory total income			44,292
Less: PA			4,335
Taxable income			39,957

£		£
1,500 @ 10%		150
26,500 @ 23%		6,095
11,957 @ 40%		4,783
Less: Tax credit re APA (1,970 × 10%)		
(son in full time education)		(197)
		10,831
Add: Tax withheld on £5,500 charitable covenant		1,265
Income tax liability		12,096

Explanation of treatment

(1)   Under the receipts basis for directors under Schedule E the bonus is treated as received, and therefore taxed, when it is determined. Thus the bonus determined in May 1999 is taxable in 1999/00.

(2)   The car benefit is 15% of the list price as Mr Darcy drove more than 18,000 business miles during the year.

(3)   The limit of value which may be apportioned under an approved profit sharing scheme is 10% of salary for PAYE purposes (ie, excluding benefits in kind, but after deduction of pension contributions).

ie: £36,000 + 8,000 − 2,520 = £41,480

	£
Value of shares allotted 1,000 × 425p	4,250
Limit 10% × £41,480 (less than the £8,000 overriding limit)	4,148
	102

9.2   Mr Drake

Mr Drake's Schedule E assessable amount will be

	£	£
Salary		20,000
Expenses and benefits per P11D		9,798
		29,798
Less: Entertaining (disallowed in the employer's computation)	683	
Travelling, etc (other than home to office)	441	
Telephone £160 less private 60%	64	
Payments for accommodation at £40 per month against the benefit of £650	480	
Payments for use of company car	120	1,788
		28,010
Benefit for use of TV (20% of 500)		100
Benefit for gift of TV (500 – 100 – 100)		300
Schedule E assessment		28,410

8 NATIONAL INSURANCE CONTRIBUTIONS

INTRODUCTION & LEARNING OBJECTIVES

Individuals who are either employed or self employed must pay national insurance contributions in addition to income tax. National insurance contributions are also payable by employers.

This tax is easily overlooked in an exam situation: remember that individuals (either employees, employers or the self-employed) and companies (as employers) pay national insurance contributions.

When you have studied this chapter you should have learned the following:

- The different classes of contribution.
- The operation of Class 1 primary contributions.
- The operation of Class 1 secondary contributions.
- The operation of Class 1A secondary contributions on company cars and private use fuel.
- The operation of Class 1B secondary contributions on PAYE Settlement Agreements.
- How Class 1 contributions are calculated.
- Voluntary Class 3 contributions.
- Class 2 contributions.
- The operation of Class 4 contributions.

1 INTRODUCTION

1.1 Classes of contribution

The amount a person pays and the statutory rules governing payment of contributions depend upon the class of contribution. These classes are

Class 1 **Primary**. A percentage-based contribution payable by employees earning over £66 a week (for 1999/00).

Secondary: A percentage-based contribution paid by employers in respect of employees earning over £83 a week (for 1999/00).

Class 2 Flat rate weekly contribution payable by a self-employed person whose annual accounting profits (for 1999/00) are over £3,770.

Class 3 Flat rate **voluntary** contribution which can be paid by anyone whose contribution record is otherwise insufficient for entitlement to the full range of benefits.

Class 4 A percentage-based contribution payable, in addition to Class 2 contributions, by a self-employed person on taxable profits between £7,530 and £26,000 (for 1999/00).

2 EMPLOYED PERSONS

2.1 Class 1 contributions: employed persons

A liability for Class 1 contributions arises where an individual

(a)   is employed and
(b)   is aged 16 or over and
(c)   has earnings at least as much as the lower earnings limit.

A person holding an office is classed as an employee for this purpose if the emoluments are assessed under Schedule E.

Exceptions. Primary and secondary contributions are not payable in respect of certain employed persons. The more important of these are persons:

(a)   aged under 16 or

(b)   employed outside the UK or

(c)   earning below the lower earnings limit (£66 per week for employees and £83 per week for employers).

2.2   Primary contributions

(a)   The rate of employee's Class 1 NIC is 10%.

The contributions are not allowable deductions for income tax purposes.

(b)   Contributions are calculated as a percentage of gross earnings.

There is no liability where gross earnings do not exceed the lower earnings limit of £66 per week. Where earnings exceed the lower limit then contributions are paid on earnings in excess of the limit, but only up to an upper earnings limit of £500 per week (for 1999/00). The maximum weekly employee Class 1 NIC for 1999/00 is therefore £43.40 (£500 – £66 = £434 at 10%).

Directors are dealt with somewhat differently (see below).

(c)   Where the employer provides an occupational pension scheme, or the employee provides his own personal pension scheme, then those employees who are members of such schemes can be 'contracted-out' of the State Earnings Related Pension Scheme (SERPS). Contracted out employees pay a lower rate of National Insurance contributions.

(d)   The earnings on which Class 1 contributions are calculated comprise ANY remuneration derived from employment and paid in MONEY. The calculation is on gross earnings, with no deduction allowed for any income tax payable. Specifically, gross earnings includes

- wages, salary, overtime pay, commission or bonus

- sick pay, including statutory sick pay

- tips and gratuities paid or allocated by the employer

- payment of the cost of travel between home and work, or on any profit element where business travel is reimbursed (for example, the payment of mileage allowances in excess of the fixed profit car scheme rates).

- remuneration, such as bonuses, made by using financial instruments such as shares, unit-trusts, options, gilts, gold, precious stones, fine wines and 'readily convertible' assets. An asset is 'readily convertible' if arrangements exist for its purchase.

- remuneration in the form of non-cash vouchers such as M & S vouchers but excluding vouchers for child care.

The following are DISREGARDED in calculating gross earnings for primary contributions.

- most benefits-in-kind (see above regarding use of financial instruments and vouchers)
- redundancy payments
- payments of any pension.

2.3   Employers' secondary contributions

(a)   The rate of employer's Class 1 NIC is 12.2%.

The contributions are a deductible expense for the employer when calculating taxable profits.

(b)   Contributions are calculated as a percentage of gross earnings.

There is no liability where gross earnings do not exceed the earnings threshold of £83 per week (this threshold is based on the personal allowance: £4,335/52 = £83). The monthly equivalent is defined as £361 (£4,335/12).

Where earnings exceed the earnings threshold then contributions are paid on earnings in excess of the threshold. There is no upper earnings limit, and so the amount of employers' Class 1 NIC payable is unlimited

As for primary contributions, reduced rates apply where the employee is contracted out of SERPS.

2.4   Example

Alex is paid £150 per week and Betty is paid £700 per week.

Calculate the employee's and the employer's Class 1 NIC liability due each week.

2.5   Solution

Alex

	£
Employee's Class 1 NIC	
(£150 − £66) = £84 at 10%	8.40
Employer's Class 1 NIC	
(£150 − £83) = £67 at 12.2%	8.17

Betty

Employee's Class 1 NIC	
(500 − £66) = £434 at 10% (maximum)	43.40
Employer's Class 1 NIC	
(£700 − £83) = £617 at 12.2%	75.27

2.6   Company cars and free fuel

Employers are required to pay Class 1A secondary contributions on the taxable benefit of cars and free fuel provided for the private use of their employees.

The main details concerning this charge are

(a)   The NICs are computed using the income tax car and fuel scale benefits.

(b)   No contributions are levied where employee's earnings are less than £8,500 a year.

(c)   Contributions are at the employer's rate (12.2% for 1999/00) and are collected annually in arrears.

For example, for an 1,800 cc car costing £16,000 new and under 4 years old on 5 April 2000 Class 1A contributions for 1999/00 will be:

	Business mileage		
	Less than 2,500	2,500- 17,999	18,000 or more
	£	£	£
Income tax scale charges:			
Car (£16,000 × 35%/25%/15%)	5,600	4,000	2,400
Fuel	1,540	1,540	1,540
	7,140	5,540	3,940
NIC at 12.2%	871	676	481

2.7 Deduction and payment by the employer

The employer calculates the primary and secondary contributions at each weekly or monthly pay date.

At the end of each PAYE month (5th) the total primary and secondary contributions become payable to the Collector of Taxes, along with income tax deducted under PAYE, not later than 14 days thereafter (ie, by 19th).

2.8 Persons with more than one job

(a) **Liability**

A person with more than one job is separately liable for primary contributions in respect of each job falling within the scope of Class 1 contributions (where earnings are over £66 per week). Each employer is also separately liable for secondary contributions where he pays earnings in excess of the £83 per week earnings threshold.

(b) **Annual maximum**

The total Class 1 contributions from all employments is subject to an overall annual maximum. Employees with more than one job can prevent overpayment of contributions by

- applying for deferment of contributions; or
- claiming a refund after the end of the tax year.

2.9 Company directors

Where a person is a company director he is deemed to have an **annual** earnings' period and the **annual** upper and lower earnings' limits apply. For 1999/00 these are

	£	
Lower - Employee	3,432	(52 × £66)
- Employer	4,335	
Upper - Employee only	26,000	(52 × £500)

The rules prevent directors avoiding NIC by paying themselves a low weekly or monthly salary, and then taking a large bonus.

2.10 Example

June is paid a monthly salary of £1,000. During March 2000 she was also paid a bonus of £10,000.

Calculate the employee's Class 1 NIC for 1999/00 if June is (1) an employee, and (2) a director.

2.11 Solution

If June is an employee she would pay NIC of £973.50. Her NIC for March 2000 is limited to the monthly upper limit of £2,167 (£26,000/12).

Therefore, £8,833 (£11,000 – £2,167) of the bonus is not subject to employees Class 1 NIC.

	£
£9,735 (£22,000 – £3,432 – £8,833) at 10% =	973.50

If June is a director, she would pay NIC of £1,856.80

	£
£18,568 (£22,000 – £3,432) at 10% =	1,856.80

2.12 Employees reaching pensionable age

An employee who continues to work after attaining pensionable age (65 for a man, 60 for a woman) has no liability for primary Class 1 contributions.

The employer is still liable for full secondary contributions.

2.13 Dividends

Dividends are not subject to NIC, even if they are drawn by director/shareholders in place of a monthly salary.

Therefore, for director controlled companies, drawing at least some profits out of a company by way of dividend rather than salary can be a useful tax planning device.

However, if no NIC is paid, entitlement to some state benefits (such as the state pension) will be lost or reduced. Also, the level of salary will impact upon entitlement to contribute towards a personal pension.

The normal practice is therefore to draw a regular salary, and then to take a year end bonus by the most tax efficient means - be it additional salary or a dividend.

2.14 Class 1B contributions

Employers who provide small and irregular benefits to their employees can be allowed by the Revenue to exclude them from PIID reporting if they make a PAYE Settlement Agreement (PSA) with the Revenue. The benefits covered by a PSA are totalled and taxed at the average marginal tax rate of the employees concerned. The income tax is due on 19 October following the tax year.

Employer's contributions at 12.2% are collected at the same time (under Class 1B) on the tax itself and that part of the global benefits figure which would be 'earnings'. No primary contributions are payable.

2.15 Voluntary Class 3 contributions

The only purpose of voluntary contributions is to enable a person to maintain a contribution record sufficient for entitlement to various state benefits, such as the basic retirement pension.

Such contributions are of particular importance, therefore, for individuals who are excluded from paying as employed or self-employed persons, and for those who do not make sufficient contributions under another Class.

3 SELF EMPLOYED PERSONS

3.1 Liability

All self-employed persons over the age of 16 must pay both Class 2 and Class 4 contributions, unless a certificate of exemption is held.

3.2   Class 2 contributions

Class 2 contributions are payable at a weekly flat rate (£6.55 for 1999/00).

Contributions may be paid by means of direct debit from a bank account or by quarterly billing in arrears.

The following persons are not liable to pay Class 2 contributions

(a)   Children under 16 and men aged 65 or over and women aged 60 or over.

(b)   Those with low earnings who obtain certificates of exemption.

The annual low earnings limit for 1999/00 is £3,770.

Only **one** Class 2 contribution is payable weekly regardless of the number of self-employed occupations; however, the earnings from all such occupations are aggregated to decide whether or not the low earnings limit is exceeded.

Earnings for the small earnings exception are the accounts profits (ie, not tax adjusted) actually falling in the fiscal year. Apportionment may be necessary where the year end is not 5 April.

3.3   Class 4 contributions

These contributions are, in effect, a form of additional taxation, since they bring no entitlement to any benefits. The contributions are calculated as a percentage of profits assessed to income tax under Schedule D Case I and II within upper and lower limits specified. The calculation is made without any allowance for income tax payable.

The contribution rate for 1999/00 is 6% on earnings between £7,530 and £26,000.

Earnings for this purpose are Schedule D Case I or II profits after losses. Trading charges on income are also deductible.

Class 4 NIC is payable at the same time as the income tax due under self assessment. There is no income tax allowance for Class 4 NIC paid.

3.4   Persons not liable to pay Class 4 contributions

(a)   Children under 16, men aged 65 or over and women aged 60 or over at the start of the tax year.

(b)   Those whose earnings do not exceed the lower Class 4 profits threshold.

(c)   Those whose earnings are not immediately derived from carrying on a trade, profession or vocation (eg, a sleeping partner in a partnership).

3.5   More than one business

Class 4 contributions are payable on the aggregate of all profits from self-employment up to the upper profits limit, irrespective of the number of self-employed occupations.

4   CHAPTER SUMMARY

This chapter has dealt with national insurance contributions. The following areas were covered:

- Classes of contribution;
- Primary Class 1 contributions payable by employees;
- Secondary Class 1 contributions payable by employers;
- Class 1A secondary contributions payable by employers on company cars and free fuel;
- The national insurance position for company directors;
- Voluntary Class 3 contributions;
- Class 1B on PAYE Settlement Agreements;

- Class 2 contributions payable by the self-employed; and
- Class 4 contributions payable by the self-employed.

5   SELF TEST QUESTIONS

5.1   What are the four classes of contribution? (1.1)

5.2   When does liability for Class 1 contributions arise for an individual? (2.1)

5.3   What earnings are Class 1 primary contributions calculated on? (2.2)

5.4   How are Class 1 secondary contributions calculated? (2.3)

5.5   How are Class 1A contributions calculated? (2.6)

5.6   How are national insurance contributions for company directors calculated? (2.9)

5.7   What Class 1 contributions are payable once employees reach pensionable age? (2.10)

5.8   Which people are not liable to pay Class 2 contributions? (3.2)

5.9   What tax relief is available for Class 4 contributions? (3.3)

5.10   What earnings are Class 4 contributions calculated on? (3.3)

6   EXAMINATION TYPE QUESTION

6.1   Mr Mouland

Mr Mouland is in business as a forest fencer, and prepares accounts to 31 March each year.

Mr Mouland has given you the following information:

(a)   His Schedule D Case I profit for the year ended 31 March 2000 was £18,329.

(b)   Mr Mouland employed Jack and Jill during 1999/00. Their gross wages were £5,200 and £12,480 respectively. Jack was also paid a bonus of £1,000 in the week commencing 1 May 1999 after the early completion of a job.

Jack's and Jill's wages and employer's national insurance were included in the profit figure which Mr Mouland has given you.

You are required to calculate the following:

(a)   The total Class 1 contributions payable for 1999/00;
(b)   The Class 2 and Class 4 contributions payable by Mr Mouland for 1999/00.

7   ANSWER TO EXAMINATION TYPE QUESTION

7.1   Mr Mouland

(a)   **Class 1 contributions**

Employees'

		£	£
Jack	£34 × 51 × 10%	173.40	
	£434 × 1 × 10%	43.40	
			216.80
Jill	£174 × 52 × 10%		904.80
			1,121.60

Employer's

Jack	£17 × 51 × 12.2%	105.77	
	£1,017 × 1 × 12.2%	124.07	
		229.84	
Jill	£157 × 52 × 12.2%	996.01	
			1,225.85

Total Class 1 contributions   2,347.45

(b)   **Class 2 contributions**

52 × £6.55   £340.60

Class 4 contributions

	£
Schedule D Case I (y/e 31.3.2000)	18,329
Less: Lower limit	7,530
	10,799

Class 4 contributions £10,799 × 6%   £647.94

9 SCOPE OF BUSINESS INCOME TAX

INTRODUCTION & LEARNING OBJECTIVES

(a)   The following chapters are concerned with the detail of the income tax regime as it applies to unincorporated businesses (ie, sole traders). Before that can be considered, however, the limits of the system must be defined.

(b)   Definition: Schedule D Case I: the annual profits arising or accruing in respect of any trade carried on in the UK or elsewhere;

Schedule D Case II: the annual profits arising or accruing in respect of any profession or vocation not contained in any other Schedule.

When you have studied this chapter you should be able to do the following:

- Identify whether an activity will be regarded as trading or non-trading by using the 'badges of trade'
- Adjust an accounting profit for the deductions and additions required to calculate Schedule D Case I profit
- Calculate the basis periods and overlap relief in the opening and subsequent years of a business
- Calculate the assessment upon the cessation of a business
- Understand the conditions for changing the accounting date of a business and calculating the assessments in such circumstances.

1   BADGES OF TRADE

1.1   Introduction

(a)   It is Schedule D Case I that most concerns us and it can be seen from the definition above that the key element is the concept of a trade.

> **Definition**   'Trade includes every trade, manufacture, adventure or concern in the nature of trade'.

(b)   Although the above is the statutory definition of a trade, in practice it is not a very helpful one. What constitutes a trade has been reviewed by the Courts in many decided cases. The criteria that emerge from these were set out by a Royal Commission and are known as the 'badges of trade'. They are:

- the subject matter of the realisation;
- the length of the period of ownership;
- the frequency or number of similar transactions by the same person;
- supplementary work on or in connection with the property realised;
- the circumstances that were responsible for the realisation; and
- motive.

(c)   Each of these principles is dealt with individually below. It is vital to appreciate that no one 'badge' is decisive. In any set of circumstances one 'badge' may indicate trading and another the opposite. It is the overall impression, using all relevant factors, that is important.

(d)   It is important to decide whether an activity amounts to a trade. Depending on the circumstances, the profit or gain on a transaction may, if not caught under Schedule DI, be assessable under another income tax Schedule or Case, or be assessable as a capital gain, or be quite simply exempt tax altogether.

1.2   Subject matter

The type of goods involved in a transaction is relevant in deciding whether the transaction concerns an investment (in which case it is capital in nature and not subject to Schedule D Case I) or goods for the private use of the individual (or his family) or stock in trade. Normally, to be considered as an investment, the goods must either be income producing (such as land or shares) or liable to be held for aesthetic reasons (such as works of art). So, for example, when an individual acquired 1,000,000 rolls of toilet paper and resold them at a profit he was held not to have acquired and resold an investment and consequently was judged to have made a trading profit (Rutledge v CIR, 1929).

1.3   Length of period of ownership

As a general rule the longer the period between acquisition and disposal of assets the greater the likelihood that the resale will not be treated as a trading transaction. Care must be taken in applying this principle and in particular the nature of the assets has to be taken into account. For instance, it would be necessary to hold land for far longer than quoted shares to obtain the benefit of this rule, since normally the market in land operates much more slowly than that in shares.

1.4   Frequency of similar transactions

A single transaction may be enough for a person to be regarded as trading, as was seen in the toilet rolls case above, but the more often similar transactions are entered into the more likely they will be regarded as trading activities. Again the nature of the assets involved is important. In Salt v Chamberlain (1979) the taxpayer was held to be trading on the evidence of over 200 Stock Exchange sales and purchases over a period of three years. But in Pickford v Quirke (1927) the director of a spinning company was engaged in buying the shares of a mill-owning company and then causing it to sell its assets (asset stripping). One transaction of this kind might have been regarded as capital in nature but when he had done the same thing four times over he was held to be trading.

1.5   Supplementary work on assets before resale

If work is done on an asset before it is sold this may indicate a trade. In Cape Brandy Syndicate v CIR (1921) the purchase of brandy in bulk and subsequent blending and re-casking before resale was held to be a trade.

1.6   Circumstances in which the assets were acquired

An individual who deliberately purchases goods is more likely to be regarded as trading than one who acquires them accidentally, for example by inheritance or by gift.

1.7   Motive

The more obvious an individual's intention to profit from a transaction the more likely it is that it will be viewed as trading. When the comedian, Norman Wisdom, purchased a large quantity of silver bullion as a hedge against devaluation of sterling, the profit resulting from its resale was regarded as a trading profit. The Court of Appeal held that the motive for the transaction was to make a profit in sterling terms and that, since it could not be characterised as an investment, it was a trading profit.

It is important to appreciate, however, that the absence of a profit motive does not **of itself** preclude the transaction from being treated as trade.

1.8   Employment or self-employment

The whole issue of whether an individual can claim that he is trading under Schedule D or is assessable under Schedule E on his earnings raises significant issues concerning the information that the individual presents to the Revenue. In marginal cases the Revenue will consider closely the evidence to see whether it supports a Schedule D or Schedule E assessment. (This was discussed in chapter 6.)

2   COMPUTING TAXABLE TRADING INCOME

2.1   Introduction

(a)   Schedule D Case I profit is rarely the same figure as the profit shown in a trader's profit and loss account, although accounting profit before tax is the starting point for the series of adjustments that are normally necessary. The adjustments that need to be made to move from accounting profit to taxable profit are of four types, as follows:

- expenditure that has been charged in the profit and loss account but which tax law prevents from being an allowable deduction;

- income taxable under Schedule D Case I that has not been included in the accounts;

- expenditure that is deductible for tax purposes but not charged in the profit and loss account; and

- profits taken into the profit and loss account that are not subject to Schedule D Case I.

The first two types of adjustment increase the Schedule D Case I profit and the second two reduce it.

(b)   Before considering the adjustments in detail two important points need to be emphasised. Firstly, it is only an individual's Schedule D Case I profit that is being calculated. The fact that an item of income (such as interest received) is excluded does not mean that it is not taxable; only that it is not taxable under Schedule D Case I. Secondly, the starting point for all adjustments is the principles of normal commercial accountancy. These apply unless overridden by tax law (derived either from statute or decided cases).

2.2   Deductible and non-deductible expenditure

Non-deductible expenditure (also known as disallowable expenditure) is by far the most common form of adjustment to accounts. The necessary adjustments reflect a series of principles which are examined below.

(a)   **Expenditure not incurred 'wholly and exclusively' for trading purposes**

Such expenditure may be disallowed because it is too remote from the purposes of the trade (the remoteness test) or because it has more than one purpose and one of them is not trading (the duality principle).

Expenditure is regarded as being too remote from the trade when it is incurred in some other capacity than that of a trader.

The duality principle is also best illustrated by decided cases. A self-employed person was unable to eat lunch at home and claimed the extra cost as a tax deduction. It was held that the expenditure was not allowable. The duality of purpose lay in the fact that the taxpayer needed to eat to live, not just to work! Similarly, a female barrister was refused a tax deduction for her expenditure on the black clothing necessary for court appearances. It was held that the expenditure had been for her personal needs as well as professional ones.

Although there is this general principle that prohibits the deduction for tax purposes of expenditure that has a dual purpose, in practice some types of expenditure, notably on cars, is apportioned between the amounts that relate to business and private use, with the business element treated as being allowable.

(b)   **Subscriptions and donations**

Subscriptions and donations to political parties are generally not deductible.

Trade or professional association subscriptions are normally deductible since they will be made wholly and exclusively for the purposes of the trade.

A charitable donation must meet three tests to be allowable. Firstly, it must be 'wholly and exclusively' for trading purposes (for example promoting the business' name). Secondly, it must be local and reasonable in size in relation to the donor's business. Thirdly, it must be made to an educational, religious, cultural, recreational or benevolent organisation.

Non-charitable gifts are not allowable except as set out below.

(c) **Capital expenditure**

Expenditure on capital assets is not allowed in computing Schedule D Case I profits, so any amount charged in the form of depreciation, loss on sale of fixed assets or lease amortisation must be added back to profit for tax purposes. Similarly the profit on sale of a fixed asset should be deducted from the accounting profits.

Adjustments are also necessary, when expenditure is on the borderline between what might be regarded as revenue and capital expenditure. Most commonly this occurs in distinguishing between repairs expenditure (treated as revenue expenditure and so allowable) and renewals expenditure (treated as capital expenditure and so disallowed).

The cost of initial repairs to an asset are not deductible where they are necessary to make it serviceable for the trade (Law Shipping Co Ltd v CIR, 1923). But the cost of initial repairs is deductible if the assets can be put into use before the repairs are carried out, if they are to make good normal wear and tear and the purchase price was not reduced to take account of the necessary repair work (Odeon Associated Theatres v Jones, 1971).

Other than initial repairs the principal source of dispute is the treatment of restoration costs. Here the principle to be applied is whether the restoration renews a subsidiary part of an asset (in which case it is an allowable repair to the larger asset) or whether it is the renewal of a separate asset (in which case it is treated as non-allowable capital expenditure. So, for example, the replacement of a factory chimney was held to be a repair to the factory but the replacement of an old stand with a new one at a football club was held to be expenditure on a new asset and thus disallowable capital expenditure.

Expenditure on certain categories of capital assets such as plant and machinery or industrial buildings attract tax allowances known as capital allowances (see following chapter). Capital allowances are deductible as if they were a trading expense.

(d) **Entertaining and gifts**

Expenditure on gifts and entertainment needs to be looked at in terms of the recipient.

Small gifts, normally but not exclusively, to customers (with a cost of not more than £10 per recipient) are allowable provided that firstly, the gift is not of food, drink, tobacco or vouchers exchangeable for goods and secondly, the gift carries a conspicuous advertisement for the donor. The cost of gifts which do not meet these restrictive conditions are disallowed unless they are to charities (examined above) or to employees. Gifts to employees will normally be allowable in the hands of an employer but will usually result in an income tax charge to an employee under the benefits in kind rules (looked at in an earlier chapter).

Entertainment expenditure is disallowed. The only exception is for expenditure relating to an employer's staff, provided it is not merely incidental to the entertainment of others.

(e)   **Legal and professional charges**

Legal and professional charges are allowable provided that they are incurred in connection with the trade and are not related to capital items. So, for example, the following commonly met types of professional charge are allowed:

- legal fees to collect trade debts
- charges incurred in defending title to fixed assets

Using the same principle, the following are not deductible:

- Fees incurred when acquiring new fixed assets
- (For companies) fees arising as a result of issuing new share capital

The principle of allowing or disallowing professional fees by relating them to the type of expenditure with which they are connected is broken in the case of fees incurred in obtaining loan finance. Fees and other incidental costs of obtaining loan finance are specifically allowable.

(f)   **Appropriations**

Appropriations are the withdrawal of funds from a business's profits rather than expenses incurred in earning them. The obvious examples are charges described as a proprietor's salary, or interest on capital invested in the business. Similarly any private element of expenditure relating to a proprietor's car, telephone and so on is also disallowed under this heading.

Other items commonly found in a profit and loss account also count as appropriations rather than expenses. These are notional expenses (in the sense that they do not represent money spent by the business) such as general provisions against doubtful trade debts. In contrast, writing off a trade debt and specific provisions are allowable (on the grounds that they represent a best estimate of an actual cost to the business). Consequently, when making adjustments to the figure of accounting profits in respect of write offs of, or provisions against, trade debts all that needs to be done is to add back any increase or deduct any decrease in the **general** provision that has occurred during the course of the year. Bad debts that are not trade debts are not allowable (which includes debts to employees).

(g)   **Charges on income**

Charges on income are deducted for tax purposes from all income. Consequently, in computing Schedule D Case I income, they must be added back to the figure of accounting profit. Common examples are patent royalties and charitable deeds of covenants. Remember that the amount deductible for charges against total income is the amount paid in the period (rather than the amount accrued in the accounts which is added back in the Schedule D Case I computation).

(h)   **Interest payable**

Interest on borrowings such as business account overdrafts, credit cards or hire purchase contracts is allowable on an accruals basis and thus no adjustment is needed to the accounts.

For unincorporated businesses interest on overdue tax is never allowable and likewise interest received on overpaid tax is not taxable. (This is not the case for companies with accounting periods ending on or after 1 July 1999 - see chapter 24).

(i)   **Pre-trading expenditure**

Pre-trading expenditure is specifically deductible by statute. Provided that the expense is of a kind that would have been deductible had the trade been carried on at the time, pre-trading expenditure incurred in the seven years before the trade begins is allowable. The expenditure is treated as a trading expense incurred on the first day of business.

(j)   **Car leasing**

The rental charges payable for leasing a car are allowed on the basis of the normal adjustment principles - ie, disallow the private use portion.

However, if the car cost more than £12,000 when new the business use portion is reduced to the amount given in the following formula:

$$\text{Business portion of rental charge} \times \frac{£12,000 + \frac{1}{2}(\text{Cost of car} - £12,000)}{\text{Cost of car (when new)}}$$

Example

Roy enters into a leasing contract for a Turbo Saab car with an original cost of £30,000, paying £8,000 pa in rental charges. His business use amounts to 80%.

The annual allowable amount would be:

$$8,000 \times 80\% \times \frac{12,000 + \frac{1}{2}(30,000 - 12,000)}{30,000} = £4,480$$
$$(\text{ie, disallow } 8,000 - 4,080 = £3,520)$$

Note that if, instead, the vehicle was being acquired under a hire purchase agreement all of the business portion of the hire-purchase interest would be allowed. The car is treated instead as if the trader owned it from the start of the HP contract and capital allowances would be given (restricted for a car over £12,000) - see Chapter 10.

(k)   **Other items**

The items dealt with above are the more important ones that you are likely to meet in the course of adjusting expenditure charged in a trader's accounts. Set out below is a list of some other items you may meet and a brief description of how to treat them.

Type of expenditure	Treatment in computation	Notes
Compensation for loss of office	Allow	Only if for benefit of trade
Cost of registering patents and trademarks	Allow	
Cost of seconding employees to charities	Allow	
Counselling services provided in the UK for redundant employees	Allow	
Damages paid	Allow	Only if paid in connection with trade matter
Defalcations	Allow	Only if by employee, not a director or proprietor
Educational courses	Allow	Only if for trade purposes
Fines	Disallow	Unless parking fines incurred on business by employee (not director or proprietor)
Payment that constitutes a criminal offence	Disallow	

Pension contributions to an approved pension scheme	Allow	Provided paid (not accrued) by the year end
Premiums for insurance against an employee's death or illness	Allow	Receipts will be taxable
Redundancy pay in excess of the statutory amount	Allow	On the cessation of trading the limit is 3 × the statutory amount
Removal expenses	Allow	Provided not an expansionary move or expenses relating to personal move of proprietor
Salaries accrued at year end	Allow	Provided paid not more than nine months after year end
Travelling expenses to trader's place of business	Disallow	Unless trader has no fixed place of business

2.3 Income taxable under Schedule D Case I but not included in accounts

Other than errors arising due to faulty accounting, this adjustment is normally needed only when a trader removes goods from the business for his own use. So, for example, if a car dealer removes a vehicle from stock to become his own vehicle he will not have recorded it as a sale. Nevertheless in computing Schedule D Case I profits he must include the market value of the vehicle as income (and likewise is entitled to a deduction for its purchase cost).

2.4 Deductible expenditure not charged in the profit and loss account

(a) There are two common types of expenditure that fall into this category. The first concerns a premium paid for a short lease. A trader is entitled to deduct a proportion of the amount assessable on his landlord in his trading accounts. This will not be reflected in his accounts, however, since the cost of the lease will be reflected in an annual amortisation charge. The adjustments for the lease are thus to add back the amortisation charged in the accounts (disallowable as capital) and deduct the proportion of the Schedule A charge (which does not feature in the accounts at all).

The Schedule A charge assessable on the landlord is calculated either as $P \times \dfrac{51 - D}{50}$ or as $P - (P \times 2\% \times (D - 1))$

where P = total premium
D = duration of lease in years

The allowable deduction is the Schedule A charge spread evenly over the period of the lease.

(b) The second example is rentals on finance leases that have been capitalised in the trader's accounts in accordance with SSAP 21. The trader's accounts will show a depreciation charge for the capitalised asset and an interest charge that is the part of the lease rental that represents a finance charge. In principle, both of these need to be added back and the lease payments, which did not appear in the profit and loss account, are deducted. However, the Inland Revenue will allow the use of the deductions calculated in accordance with SSAP 21, provided that they do not materially differ from the actual lease payments.

2.5   Profits recognised in the accounts but not charged under Schedule D Case I

These tend to fall into three categories as follows:

(a)   capital receipts (which may be subject to capital gains tax for individuals or corporation tax for companies);

(b)   income taxed other than under Schedule D Case I (such as rents charged under Schedule A, interest received under Schedule D Case III or income taxed at source); and

(c)   income that is exempt from tax (notably interest received on overpaid tax where this is received by an uncorporated business).

Such receipts must be deducted from the figure for accounting profit. Amounts that are subject to income tax must then be included elsewhere in an individual's personal income tax computation.

2.6   Activity

You are presented with the accounts of Mr Cornelius for the year to 31 December 1999, as set out below. Mr Cornelius runs a small printing business and wishes to know the amount of his Schedule D Case I profit.

	£	£
Gross profit on trading account		25,620
Profit on sale of premises		1,073
Building society interest received		677
		27,370
Advertising	642	
Staff wages	12,124	
Rates	1,057	
Repairs and renewals	2,598	
Motor car expenses	555	
Bad debts	75	
Telephone	351	
Heating and lighting	372	
Miscellaneous expenses	347	
Depreciation - printing presses	1,428	
- office equipment	218	
- Mr Cornelius' motor car	735	
		20,502
Net profit before tax		6,868

Notes:

(1)   Staff wages includes an amount of £182 for a staff Christmas lunch.

(2)   Mr Cornelius uses his motor car 75% for business purposes and 25% for private purposes.

(3)   Repairs and renewals comprises the following expenditure:

	£
Refurbishing second hand press before use in the business	522
Redecorating administration offices	429
Building extension to enlarge paper store	1,647
	2,598

(4)   Miscellaneous expenses included:

	£
Subscription to Printers' Association	45
Contribution to local Enterprise Agency	50
Gifts to customers - calendars costing £7.50 each	75
- 2 food hampers	95

(5)   The profit on the sale of premises relates to the sale of a small freehold industrial unit in which Mr Cornelius used to store paper before building his extension.

(6)   The charge for bad debts was made up as follows:

	£
Write off of specific trade debts	42
Increase in general provision for bad debts	50
	92
Less: recovery of bad debt previously written off	17
Charge to profit and loss account	75

Calculate Mr Cornelius' Schedule D Case I income

2.7   Activity solution

Mr Cornelius - Schedule D Case I income - Year ended 31 December 1999

		£
Net profit before tax		6,868
Add: Disallowable expenditure		
repairs and renewals (522 + 1,647)	2,169	
motor car expenses (555 × 25%)	139	
bad debts	50	
gifts to customers (food hampers)	95	
depreciation (1,428 + 218 + 735)	2,381	
		4,834
		11,702
Less: Income not chargeable under Schedule D Case I		
profit on sale of premises	1,073	
interest received	677	
		1,750
Schedule D Case I income		9,952

Notes:

(1)   The expenditure on the Christmas lunch is allowable in the hands of the employer. Provided it is not excessive it will not produce a benefit in kind in the hands of employees.

(2)   Refurbishment of the second hand press is disallowed on the grounds that the expenditure was necessary before it was brought into use in the business. The extension of the stockroom created a new asset and was not the repair of part of an existing one.

(3)   Gifts to customers are disallowed unless they amount to £10 or less per customer during the year and display a conspicuous advert for the business. Gifts of food (or drink or tobacco) are disallowed irrespective of their cost.

3   BASIS PERIODS AND TAX YEARS

3.1   Introduction

(a)   Income tax is charged for tax years (also known as fiscal years or years of assessment) that run from 6 April to the following 5 April. Since traders normally do not make up their profit and loss accounts to coincide with the tax year there needs to be a system for attributing profits earned in a period of account to a particular tax year. Both Schedule D Case I and Schedule D Case II use the same method and so for simplicity they are both referred to here as Schedule D Case I.

(b)   The profit-earning (or loss-making) period that is attributed to a particular tax year is known as the 'basis period' for that tax year.

3.2   Apportionment on a daily basis

For Paper 7, apportionment of Schedule D Case I profits, losses and capital allowances for income tax businesses, where required, was performed on a daily rather than monthly basis.

As regards Paper 11, the examiner has stated that it is unlikely that a question will require calculations on the daily basis.

The justification for this is that because of the nature of the paper, questions usually include forecast or estimated figures. Although the daily basis of apportionment is applicable to Paper 11, it would be unrealistic to expect calculations involving forecast or estimated figures to be calculated on a daily basis.   Therefore, where questions involve forecast or estimated figures, the monthly basis will continue to be acceptable.

We use the monthly basis in the following examples to avoid confusion. In fact the Paper 7 examiner has now dropped the requirement for daily apportionment.

4   CURRENT YEAR BASIS - ONGOING YEAR RULES

4.1   The basic principles

The basic rule is that the profits for a year of assessments are the adjusted profits shown by the accounts ending in that year.

4.2   Example

Jerry prepares accounts to 30 September annually. His profits for the 2 years to 30 September 1999 were:

	£
Year to 30 September 1998	20,000
Year to 30 September 1999	22,000

These form the basis for the assessable amounts for 1998/99 and 1999/00:

	£
1998/99	
(Year to 30.9.98)	20,000
1999/00	
(Year to 30.9.99)	22,000

5   CURRENT YEAR BASIS - OPENING YEAR RULES

5.1   Introduction

There are special provisions to deal with the opening and closing years.

The basis of assessment in the opening years is normally as follows:

Year 1   Actual profits from commencement to 5 April

Year 2   Either:

        (a)   Where there is an accounting date in the year, the 12 months ending on that accounting date; or

        (b)   Where there is an accounting date in the year that is not preceded by 12 months of profits, the first 12 months from the commencement date; or

        (c)   Where there is no accounting date in the year, the fiscal basis applies.

Year 3   12 months ending with the accounting date in the year.

The following examples illustrate the three possible situations that can arise in Year 2. Remember that strictly any apportionments should be made on a daily basis. However, we use the monthly basis as the daily basis is unlikely to be required in the Paper 11 exam. Indeed, in practice the Revenue do not insist on the daily basis of apportionment.

5.2   Example 1

Arthur commenced trading on 1 July 1997. He prepares accounts to 30 June each year. His adjusted trading profits for the first two years were as follows:

	£
Year ended 30.6.98	24,000
Year ended 30.6.99	28,000

The Schedule DI assessable amounts are as follows

	£
1997/98	
(1.7.97 - 5.4.98)	
24,000 × 9/12	18,000
1998/99 (see note)	
(year to 30.6.98)	24,000
1999/00	
(year to 30.6.99)	28,000

Note. Because there is an accounting date which is preceded by 12 months of profits in the year, the assessment is the 12 months ending on that accounting date (rule (a)). If the strict daily basis had been used the assessment for 1997/98 would be £18,345 (£24,000 × 279/365).

On a monthly basis there is a significant reduction in the 1997/98 assessment but there is a corresponding reduction in the overlap relief (see example 5 below) so the basis of apportionment makes no difference to the total profits assessed over the life of the business.

5.3   Example 2

Edwina commenced trading on 1 July 1997. She prepared accounts to 31 March 1999 and annually thereafter. Her adjusted trading profits for the first two periods were as follows:

	£
21 months ended 31.3.99	42,000
Year ended 31.3.2000	27,000

The Schedule DI assessable amounts are as follows:

		£
1997/98		
(1.7.97 - 5.4.98)		
42,000 × 9/21		18,000
1998/99 (see note)		
(year to 31.3.99)		
42,000 × 12/21		24,000
1999/00		
(year to 31.3.00)		27,000

Note. There is an accounting date in the second year of assessment which is preceded by at least 12 months of profits, so the assessment is the 12 months ending on that accounting date (rule (a) again). Note that it doesn't matter whether the 12 months preceding the accounting date form the whole or part of an accounting period.

5.4   Example 3

Pattie commenced trading on 1 September 1997. She prepared accounts to 30 June 1998 and annually thereafter. Her adjusted trading profits for the first two periods were as follows:

	£
10 months ended 30 June 1998	30,000
Year ended 30 June 1999	48,000

The Schedule DI assessable amounts are as follows:

	£
1997/98	
(1.9.97 - 5.4.98)	
30,000 × 7/10	21,000
1998/99 (see note)	
(1.9.97 - 31.8.98)	
30,000 + (2/12 × 48,000)	38,000
1999/00	
(year to 30.6.99)	48,000

Note. Because the accounting date ending in the second year of assessments is not preceded by 12 months of profits, the assessment is the first 12 months of profits from the date of commencement (rule (b)).

5.5   Example 4

Cordelia commenced trading on 1 July 1997. She prepared accounts to 30 April 1999 and annually thereafter. Her adjusted trading profits for the first two periods were as follows:

	£
22 months ended 30.4.99	55,000
Year ended 30.4.2000	32,000

The Schedule DI assessable amounts are as follows:

	£
1997/98	
(1.7.97 - 5.4.98)	
55,000 × 9/22	22,500

1998/99 (see note)
(6.4.98 - 5.4.99)
55,000 × 12/22   30,000

1999/00
(year to 30.4.99)
55,000 × 12/22   30,000

Note. Because there is no accounting date in the second year of assessment, the assessment is the profits for the period 6.4.98 to 5.4.99 - the fiscal basis (rule (c)).

5.6   Overlap profits

In each of the above four opening year examples it can be seen that some of the profits have been included in the assessments for more than one year. The portion of profits which were assessed in more than one year are known as the 'overlap profits'.

The overlap profits are carried forward and are normally deducted from the assessment for the period in which the business ceases (see below) to equalise the profit earned with the profits taxed over the life of the business. Relief may not therefore be obtained for many years if the business continues for a long while. Overlap profits may also be relieved when a business changes its accounting date (see later).

Example 5

The assessable amounts for the first two years in example 1 were:

	£
1997/98	
(1.7.97 - 5.4.98)	
24,000 × 9/12	18,000
1998/99	
(year to 30.6.98)	24,000

The overlap profits which were assessed twice are those of the period 1.7.97 - 5.4.98 ie, 24,000 × 9/12 = £18,000.

Example 6

The assessable amounts for the first two years of trading in example 2 were:

	£
1997/98	
(1.7.97 - 5.4.98)	
42,000 × 9/21	18,000
1998/99	
(year to 31.3.99)	
42,000 × 12/21	24,000

In this case there are no overlap profits. (Check: £18,000 + £24,000 − £42,000 = Nil.)

Strictly there are 5 days of overlap profits (1.4.98 - 5.4.98) but the Revenue will not allow the daily basis to be used to calculate overlap profits if assessments have been calculated on a monthly basis.

Example 7

The assessable amounts for the first three years in example 4 were:

	£
1997/98 (1.7.97 - 5.4.98) 55,000 × 9/12	22,500
1998/99 (6.4.98 - 5.4.99) 55,000 × 12/22	30,000
1999/00 (year to 30.4.99) 55,000 × 12/22	30,000

The overlap profits are those of the period 1.5.98 - 5.4.99 ie, 55,000 × 11/22 = £27,500. (Check: £22,500 + £30,000 + £30,000 − £55,000 = £27,500.)

5.7   Choice of accounting date

An accounting date of just after, rather than just before, 5 April will ensure the maximum interval between earning profits and having to pay the related tax liability.

However, an accounting date just after 5 April will result in increased overlap profits upon the commencement of trading.

Although there is relief for overlap profits, there may be a long delay before relief is obtained.

The choice of accounting date is therefore not clear-cut.

5.8   Tax planning re the commencement of trading

It is usually beneficial to ensure that profits for the first period of trading are kept to a minimum where they are assessed more than once under the commencement rules.

Profits can be minimised by, for example, renting equipment for the first period of trading rather than purchasing it, or by the payment of bonuses to employees.

6   CURRENT YEAR BASIS - CLOSING YEAR RULES

6.1   Introduction

The basis of assessment in the closing years is as follows:

Closing year   Actual profit from the end of the basis period of the previous year of assessment until cessation.

Deduct any unrelieved overlap profits

6.2   Example 8

Michael ceased trading on 31 March 2000. His adjusted trading profits for the final three periods are as follows:

	£
Year ended 30.4.98	40,000
Year ended 30.4.99	42,000
Period ended 31.3.2000	38,000

Assume his overlap profits are £27,000

The Schedule DI assessable amounts are as follows:

	£
1998/99	
(year to 30.4.98)	40,000
1999/00	
(23 months from 1.5.98 to 31.3.2000)	
(42,000 + 38,000)	80,000
Less overlap profits	27,000
Final assessable amount	53,000

7 CURRENT YEAR BASIS - TREATMENT OF CAPITAL ALLOWANCES

Capital allowances are treated as a trading expense of the accounting period.

This can be illustrated as follows:

	£
Adjusted profits for year ended 31.3.2000	X
Less: capital allowances (basis period y/e/ 31.3.2000)	(X)
DI profit for year ended 31.3.2000	X

This amount will be assessable in 1999/00.

8 CHANGE OF ACCOUNTING DATE

8.1 Introduction

Provided certain conditions are met, a self-employed person is allowed to change his or her accounting date. There may be tax advantages in doing so, or the change may be made for commercial reasons. For example, it may be easier to take stock at certain times of the year.

8.2 Conditions to be met

A change in accounting date will only be valid if the following conditions are met:

(a)   The change of accounting date must be notified to the Inland Revenue on or before 31 January following the tax year in which the change is to be made.

(b)   The first accounts to the new accounting date must not exceed 18 months in length.

        If the period between the old accounting date and the proposed new accounting date is longer than 18 months, then two sets of accounts will have to be prepared.

(c)   There must not have been another change of accounting date during the previous five tax years.

        This condition may be ignored if the Inland Revenue accept that the present change is made for genuine commercial reasons. Not surprisingly, obtaining a tax advantage is not accepted as a genuine commercial reason.

8.3 Failure to meet the conditions

If the conditions are not met, the old accounting date will continue to apply. If accounts are made up to the new accounting date, then the figures will have to be apportioned accordingly.

8.4   Calculation of assessable profits

If the conditions are met, then the basis period for the tax year in which the change of accounting date is made will either be less than or more than 12 months in length.

8.5   Basis period of less than 12 months

Where the period between the end of the previous basis period and the new accounting date is less than 12 months, the basis period will be the 12 month period ending with the new accounting date.

Because this will result in some profits being assessed more than once, overlap profits will arise. These will be carried forward and offset in exactly the same way as overlap profits arising upon the commencement of trading.

8.6   Example: Basis period of less than 12 months

Andrea, a sole trader, has always made up her accounts to 31 March. She decides to change her accounting date to 30 June by making up accounts for the three month period to 30 June 1999. Andrea's tax adjusted profits are as follows:

	£
Year ended 31 March 1999	60,000
Three months to 30 June 1999	20,000
Year ended 30 June 2000	85,000

The Schedule D1 assessable amounts will be as follows:

		£
1998/99	Year to 31.3.99	60,000
1999/00	12 month period to new accounting date of 30.6.99	
	Year to 31.3.99 $60,000 \times 9/12$	45,000
	Period to 30.6.99	20,000
		65,000
2000/01	Year to 30.6.2000	85,000

The profits of £45,000 taxed in 1999/00 are overlap profits, since they were also taxed in 1998/99. They will be carried forward and would normally be offset when Andrea ceases trading.

If Andrea had instead made up accounts for the 15 month period to 30 June 2000, then the result would have been virtually the same. Suppose the tax adjusted profit for the 15 month period ended 30 June 2000 is £105,000:

		£
1998/99	Year to 31.3.99	60,000
1999/00	12 month period to new accounting date of 30.6.99	
	Year to 31.3.99 $60,000 \times 9/12$	45,000
	Period to 30.6.2000 $105,000 \times 3/15$	21,000
		66,000
2000/01	Year to 30.6.2000 $105,000 \times 12/15$	84,000

The basis period for 1999/00 is to the new accounting date of 30 June, since there are no accounts made up to a date in 1999/00. Overlap profits are still £45,000.

8.7   Basis period of more than 12 months

Where the period between the end of the previous basis period and the new accounting date is more than 12 months, then that period becomes the basis period.

Because the basis period is more than 12 months, it will be possible to offset a corresponding proportion of any overlap profits that arose upon the commencement of trading.

8.8   Example: Basis period of more than 12 months

Peter, a sole trader, commenced trading on 1 July 1996, and has always made up his accounts to 30 June. He has now decided to change his accounting date to 30 September by making up accounts for the 15 month period to 30 September 1999. Peter's tax adjusted profits are as follows:

	£
Year ended 30 June 1997	18,000
Year ended 30 June 1998	24,000
Period ended 30 September 1999	30,000
Year ended 30 September 2000	36,000

The Schedule D1 assessable amounts will be as follows:

		£
1996/97	1.7.96 to 5.4.97	
	£18,000 × 9/12	13,500

The profits of £13,500 are overlap profits

1997/98	Year to 30.6.97	18,000
1998/99	Year to 30.6.98	24,000
1999/00	15 month period to 30.9.99	30,000
	Less: Overlap profits 13,500 × 3/9	4,500
		25,500
2000/01	Year to 30.9.2000	36,000

In 1999/00 profits for 15 months are assessed. Because the normal basis of assessment is that only 12 months profits are assessed, Peter is allowed to offset 3 months worth of his overlap profits that arose when he commenced trading. These overlap profits are for a period of 9 months, so the offset is based on a fraction of 3/9.

9   AVERAGING RELIEF FOR FARMERS

9.1   Introduction

(a)   Compare two businesses that each earn profits over two years of £40,000. One earns £20,000 each year and the other £40,000 in the first year and £nil in the second. The second business pays more tax than the first because there is a liability to higher rate tax in year one whereas the first business doesn't pay tax above the basic rate in either year.

(b)   Farmers are particularly vulnerable to volatile changes in the profitability of their businesses from year to year due to good or bad weather. Consequently, they are entitled to a special relief that protects them from the effects of higher rate tax in the sort of circumstances described above.

9.2 Principles of averaging relief

(a) The relief is available to farmers and market gardeners, either trading alone or in partnership. It comes into play when one of two consecutive year's profits is 70% or less of the other's. The profits figure on which the comparison is made is the tax-adjusted figure but before taking into account loss relief of any kind. It is not available in the first or last tax year of trade.

(b) Once a profit figure has been subject to averaging it is used for all tax purposes.

(c) Where averaging has occurred the later year's result (after averaging) can be compared with the next year's result and, if it meets the criteria, re-averaged. However, the earlier year cannot be reaveraged with the year that preceded it, so the practical consequence is that when dealing with several years the earliest year of the series is taken first (subject to the time limit mentioned below).

(d) The farmer or market gardener must specifically claim the relief by the 31 January which is nearly two years from the end of the later tax year affected.

(e) there is also a more restrictive form of relief that applies where the lower profits are between 70% and 75% of the higher profits, but this is not examinable.

9.3 Mechanics of the relief

Where one of two consecutive years profits is 70% or less of the other the profits of both are adjusted to the average of the two. If one of the years is loss making it is treated as zero and so both years are treated as making half the profits of the other year.

9.4 Activity

Smith is a market gardener his tax-adjusted profits are as follows:

Year to 31 October 1998	£15,000
Year to 31 October 1999	£40,000

Calculate the final assessments for 1998/99 and 1999/00, assuming that any possible averaging claim is made within the appropriate time limit.

9.5 Activity solution

The profit for 1998/99 (£15,000) is less than 70% of that for 1999/00 (£40,000) and so the averaging procedure applies, as follows.

	£
1998/99	15,000
1999/00	40,000
	55,000
£55,000/2 =	27,500

Thus £27,500 is the final assessment for 1998/99. The averaged assessment for 1999/00 is also £27,500 but it may be possible to average this averaged profit with 2000/01.

10   CHAPTER SUMMARY

(a)   Schedule D Case I tax is chargeable only on the profits of trade, but since 'trade' is defined by statute in a circular fashion it has been left to the Courts to define the limits of what is considered to be trading activity. The Courts look at the overall outcome from the following tests:

	Test	*Comment*
(i)	What type of goods are the subject matter of the transaction?	If of a type normally traded rather than held as an investment, it implies trading.
(ii)	How long were the goods owned?	The shorter the period of ownership the more likely that trading is taking place.
(iii)	How many transactions of a similar kind have there been?	The more transactions there have been, the more likely it will be treated as trading.
(iv)	Has there been any supplementary work done to the goods?	Supplementary work increases the likelihood that the activity will be treated as trading.
(v)	In what circumstances were the goods sold?	A person who has deliberately acquired goods is more likely to be treated as trading than one who acquires them by gift or inheritance.
(vi)	What was the motive behind the transaction?	The more obvious an individual's intention to profit from a transaction the more likely that it will be treated as trading.

Remember that it is the **overall** impression from these tests that determines whether or not an activity is treated as trading, not the result of one test in isolation.

(b)   A series of adjustments are normally needed to a trader's accounting profit to calculate his profit taxable under Schedule D Case I. The adjustments are of four types:

(i)   expenditure charged in the profit and loss account that is disallowed in computing Schedule D Case I tax. Such adjustments may arise because the expenditure is not allowed for tax purposes at all (such as on entertaining) or relief is given in some other way (such as patent royalties allowable as a charge on income).

(ii)   income taxable under Schedule D Case I that is not recognised in the accounts. This normally concerns stock removed by a proprietor for his own use (treated as a sale at market value for tax);

(iii)   deductible expenditure under Schedule D Case I that is not charged in the profit and loss account. Such adjustments are relatively rare and occur most often when a trader deducts a proportion of the amount assessable on his landlord for the lease of his business premises; and

(iv)   profits recorded in the profit and loss account that are not subject to Schedule D Case I, such as capital receipts, income taxed in another way and exempt income.

(c)   Because businesses do not normally make up accounts for years coinciding with the tax year, a system is needed to link a period of account with a tax year.

Businesses are taxed on the current year basis with special rules in opening years, closing years and on a change of accounting date.

(d)   Averaging relief for farmers allows farmers (and market gardeners) to average the tax profits (before loss relief) of two adjacent years if one of them is 70% or less of the other.

11   SELF-TEST QUESTIONS

11.1   How is a trade defined for tax purposes? (1.1)

11.2   What are the six badges of trade? (1.1)

11.3   What are the four types of adjustment needed to calculate Schedule D Case I from accounting profit? (2.1)

11.4   What are the two tests used to decide whether or not expenditure is incurred wholly and exclusively for trading purposes? (2.2)

11.5   What types of item tend to be recognised as profit in accounts but are not charged to tax under Schedule D Case I? (2.5)

11.6   How is pre-trading expenditure treated? (2.2)

11.7   What is the basis of assessment for the second year of a new business? (5.1)

11.8   Which profits are assessed in the year that a business ceases to trade? (6.1)

11.9   How are capital allowances treated under the current year basis? (7)

11.10   When is it possible for farmers to average their profits? (9.2)

12   EXAMINATION TYPE QUESTION

12.1   Capone

Capone is in business as a wine merchant preparing accounts to 30 June annually. His profit and loss account for the year ended 30 June 1999 is as follows:

	£		£
Rent and business rates	2,740	Gross profit b/d	51,929
Light and heat	120	Bank deposit interest	160
Office salaries	19,660	Dividends (net)	140
Repairs to premises (a)	2,620		
Motor expenses	740		
Depreciation - motor vans	2,800		
- equipment	750		
Amortisation of lease	120		
Loss on sale of equipment	40		
Bad and doubtful debts (b)	680		
Professional charges (c)	375		
Interest on bank overdraft (d)	240		
Sundry expenses (e)	770		
Salary - Capone	14,000		
- wife, as secretary	1,450		
Net profit	5,124		
	52,229		52,229

The following information is given

(a)   **Repairs to premises**

	£
Alterations to flooring in order to install new bottling machine	1,460
Decorations	475
Replastering walls damaged by damp	685
	2,620

(b)   **Bad and doubtful debts account**

	£			£
Trade debts written off	1,300	Provision b/d - general		3,600
Loan to employee		- specific		1,520
written off	400	Trade debts recovered		60
Provision c/d - general	3,350	Loan to employee recovered		170
- specific	980	Profit and loss account		680
	6,030			6,030

(c)   **Professional charges**

	£
Accountancy	200
Cost of Court action for failing to observe Custom's regulations	110
Legal costs of obtaining new lease [see note (f)]	20
Debt collection	45
	375

(d)   **Interest on bank overdraft**

The overdraft was obtained in order to finance the purchase of stock.

(e)   **Sundry expenses**

	£
Fine re breach of Custom's bonding regulations	250
Subscription to Wine Retail Trade Association	50
Donation to police welfare fund	20
Entertaining customers	300
Calendars bearing firm's name sent to 300 customers	120
Miscellaneous allowable expenses	30
	770

(f)   On 25 March 1999 Capone was granted a 21 year lease on new larger premises. He paid a premium of £12,600 which was charged to the leasehold property account.

(g)   During the year Capone withdrew goods from stock for his own consumption. The cost of this stock was £455. The business makes a uniform gross profit of 35% on selling price. No entry had been made in the books in respect of the goods taken, other than the resulting reduction in closing stock.

You are required to compute Capone's Schedule D Case I adjusted profit before capital allowances for the year ended 30 June 1999.

13   ANSWER TO EXAMINATION TYPE QUESTION

13.1   Capone

Computations

(a)   **Expenditure charged but not allowable.**

REMEMBER THE MAIN RULE of admissibility - the expenditure must be 'incurred WHOLLY AND EXCLUSIVELY for the purposes of THE trade'; in this case the trade of wine merchant.

The adjustments under (a) in this question are

	£ (+)	£ (−)	Reason
Repairs to premises: Floor alterations	1,460		Capital
Depreciation - vans & equipment	3,550		Capital
Amortisation of lease	120		Capital
Loss on sale of equipment	40		Capital
Bad and doubtful debts:			
Decrease in general provision		250	Reverse of an appropriation
Loan to employee written-off	400		Not W and E
Loan to employee recovered		170	Reverse original disallowance
Professional charges:			
Cost of court action	110		Not W and E
Costs of new lease	20		Capital
Sundry expenses:			
Fine	250		Not W and E
Donation	20		Not W and E
Entertaining	300		Statutory
Salary - Capone	14,000		Appropriation

(b)   **Income credited but not assessable under DI.** It is fairly certain that all credit items will either be assessed under a different Schedule or Case, or will be capital items or will not be taxable.

	£ (+)	£ (−)	Reason
Bank deposit interest		160	Taxed investment income. Assessable under Schedule D III
Dividends (net)		140	Assessable under Schedule F

(c)   **Expenditure not charged but allowable.**

The most usual item here is the one illustrated in this question. Premiums on SHORT leases are treated partly as rent, and if for business purposes are allowable ie,

(i)   Show as WORKINGS

Lease premium paid assessed on landlord under Sch A

$£12,600 \times \dfrac{51-21}{50}$ £7,560
                                                    ‾‾‾‾‾

Treated as rent paid by Capone
Allowed over period of lease

$£7,560 \times \dfrac{1}{21}$ each year   £360

Allowed in first year for 3 months
$(25.3.99 - 30.6.99)$ $\frac{3}{12} \times £360 =$ £90

(ii)   Show £90 as adjustment on (−) side of computation.

(d)   **Income not credited but assessable.** An adjustment under this head will normally arise because goods have been taken for the proprietor's own use. Case law precedent has established that this 'sale' is to be brought to account for tax purposes at full market price ie,

$£455 \times \dfrac{100}{65} = £700.$

The £700 will be an adjustment on the (+) side of the computation.

The final computation appears as follows.

Adjustment of profits for year ended 30 June 1999	£ +	£ −
Net profit per accounts	5,124	
Repairs - alterations to flooring	1,460	
Depreciation of vans and equipment	3,550	
Amortisation of lease	120	
Loss on sale of equipment	40	
Bad and doubtful debts		
Decrease in general provision		250
Loan to employee written off	400	
Loan to employee recovered		170
Professional charges - Cost of Court action	110	
- Costs of obtaining new lease	20	
Sundry expenses		
Fine	250	
Donation	20	
Entertaining customers	300	
Salary - Capone	14,000	
Bank deposit interest		160
Dividends		140
Proportion of lease premium		90
Goods withdrawn by Capone at selling price	700	
	26,094	810
	810	
Schedule D Case I profit	25,284	

10 CAPITAL ALLOWANCES ON PLANT AND MACHINERY

INTRODUCTION & LEARNING OBJECTIVES

(a)   This chapter is concerned with capital allowances available to traders and others on the purchase of plant and machinery. There are, however, a number of preliminary points that need to be considered. Is the person who has incurred the expenditure eligible for capital allowance? Does the asset acquired count as plant or machinery? If it does qualify, what allowances are available and for which tax year(s) are they given?

(b)   Once the rules for deciding these questions are appreciated the arithmetical calculations are fairly straight forward. Provided that the computations are laid out clearly and with an appropriate structure, the resulting figures should readily fall into place.

When you have studied this chapter you should be able to do the following:

- Identify whether capital expenditure falls within the definition of plant and machinery evolved by the Courts
- Determine whether an item is included in any of the types of expenditure deemed to be plant by specific pieces of legislation
- Allocate expenditure to the general pool, the car pool or specific items as appropriate
- Calculate writing down allowances on the basis of the unrelieved expenditure available and restrict the allowances where particular rules make this relevant
- Deal with disposals of plant and machinery and calculate the balancing charge or balancing allowance that may arise
- Apply the rules for determining the circumstances in which balancing allowances occur
- Calculate first year allowances
- Calculate capital allowances applying to assets acquired by hire purchase
- Restrict the allowances given where the asset in question is an expensive car or an asset used partly for private purposes by the trader
- Apply the rules for long-life assets and fixtures forming part of a building

1 ELIGIBILITY

1.1 Qualifying assets

Capital allowances are given at statutory rates on qualifying expenditure on certain fixed assets. The allowances are not only given on original cost, but also on all subsequent qualifying expenditure of a capital nature which has been disallowed in the adjusted profits computation (eg, improvements). Contributions towards cost received from public, government, or local authority sources must be deducted from the cost to obtain the expenditure eligible for capital allowances.

The allowances are available for expenditure on:

(a)   plant and machinery;
(b)   industrial buildings and structures;
(c)   qualifying hotels;
(d)   agricultural buildings and works; and
(e)   patents and know-how.

Plant and machinery is considered in this chapter and the other categories in the following chapter.

1.2 Who may claim capital allowances

Capital allowances are available to persons who:

(a)   buy and use capital assets (as indicated above) in a trade or profession assessable under Schedule D Case I or II, or in an employment the income from which is assessable under Schedule E;

(b)   have profits assessed under Schedule A and incur expenditure on plant used for property maintenance, or

(c)   receive royalty income from patents.

1.3   Mechanism for giving relief

(a)   Capital allowances are given as a trading expense in calculating the Schedule D Case I profit.

(b)   Capital allowances are given for each period of account instead of for a tax year. Where there is a short or long period of account, the writing down allowance is contracted or expanded on a pro rata basis. However, if the period of account exceeds eighteen months it must be divided, for capital allowance purposes into a 12 month period of account and a second period of account to deal with the remaining months.

1.4   Activity

Grace commenced trading on 1 August 1998. Results, adjusted for income tax purposes but before capital allowances, have been as follows:

	£
Year ended 31 July 1999	25,500
Year ended 31 July 2000	30,000

On 9 November 1998 she bought a motor car for £6,000.

Calculate the amounts assessable under Schedule D Case I for 1998/99 and 1999/00.

1.5   Activity solution

Capital allowances for 12 months ended 31 July 1999 are £1,500 (£6,000 × 25%)

Schedule D Case I amounts assessable.

	£
1998/99	
1.8.98- 5.4.99 8/12 × (25,500 – 1,500)	16,000
1999/00	
y/e 31.7.99 (25,500 – 1,500)	24,000

Note: If the first period of account was instead, say, for the 14 month period to 30 September 1999, the capital allowances would be £1,750 (£6,000 × 25% × 14/12).

2   MEANING OF PLANT AND MACHINERY

2.1   Introduction

There is no statutory definition of plant except that it includes vehicles and ships. The most informative definition was given in the case of Yarmouth v France (1887). Plant was said to include

> Whatever apparatus is used by a businessman for carrying on his business - not his stock-in-trade which he buys or makes for sale - but all goods and chattels, fixed or moveable, live or dead, which he keeps for permanent employment in his business.

This is obviously a very far-reaching definition. It includes not only the obvious items of plant and machinery, but also such items as moveable partitions, office furniture and carpets, heating installations, motor vehicles, computers, lifts and any expenditure incurred to enable the proper functioning of the item such as reinforced floors or air conditioning systems for computers.

2.2   The Courts' interpretation of 'plant'

(a)   The original definition of plant in **Yarmouth v France** provides a good starting point but has been refined by the Courts. In particular, the test that has been applied is a **functional** one. It asks, is the item simply part of the setting or premises **in which** the trade is carried on or is it something **with which** the trade is carried on? If it is part of the setting or premises it is not plant, and thus no capital allowances are available, but if it fulfils a function it is plant.

(b)   The dividing line between an asset that is functional and one that is merely part of the setting in which the trade is carried on is not always clear. Examples below show how the Courts have reacted to claims for capital allowances in these circumstances.

  (i)   A canopy covering petrol filling pumps was held to be part of the setting and not plant and machinery. (It did not assist in serving petrol to customers.)

  (ii)   False ceilings in a restaurant were held not to be plant. (All it did was to hide unsightly pipes.)

  (iii)   Swimming pools at a caravan park were held to be plant and machinery - the caravan park as a whole was the setting.

  (iv)   Moveable partitioning in an office was held to be plant and machinery.

2.3   Assets deemed to be plant

There are various types of expenditure that would not be thought of as plant using the approach set out above but are treated as plant by specific legislation. These are:

(a)   thermal insulation in an industrial building;

(b)   cost of complying with fire regulations;

(c)   expenditure to comply with regulations on safety at sports grounds;

(d)   expenditure on a security asset which is one used to counter a threat to an individual's security that arises due to the trade involved. Some items are excluded from being treated as security assets notably cars and dwellings;

(e)   cost of alterations to buildings needed for the installation of plant;

(f)   expenditure on acquiring computer software outright or under licence (to the extent that it is capital rather than revenue expenditure).

On disposal the first four categories above are treated as being sold for nothing which means that no balancing charge can arise. Balancing charges are considered later in the chapter.

2.4   Clarification on the meaning of plant

There is no general statutory definition of plant for tax purposes. However, provisions have been introduced with the intention of making the issue clearer by providing that land, buildings and structure cannot be plant. In particular the provisions (see below) give detailed lists of items associated with buildings which are part of the building and not plant. However, it is not intended that expenditure on buildings and structures which specific decisions of the courts have shown to be plant should cease to qualify.

The term 'buildings' includes:

- Walls, floors, ceilings, doors, windows and stairs.
- Mains services, and systems, of water, electricity and gas.

The following may fall within the definition of a building but will nevertheless normally qualify as plant:

- Electrical, cold water and gas systems provided mainly to meet the particular requirements of the trade, or to serve particular machinery used for the purposes of the trade.

- Space or water heating systems, systems of ventilation and air cooling, and any ceiling or floor comprised in such systems.

- Manufacturing or processing equipment, storage equipment, display equipment, counters, check-outs and similar equipment.

- Cookers, washing machines, diswashers, refrigerators and similar equipment.

- Wash-basins, sinks, baths, showers, sanitary ware and similar equipment.

- Furniture and furnishings.

- Lifts and escalators.

- Sprinkler equipment and fire alarm systems.

- Movable partition walls.

- Decorative assets provided for the enjoyment of the public in a hotel, restaurant or similar trade.

- Advertising hoardings, signs and similar displays.

3   CALCULATING THE ALLOWANCES

3.1   Pooling expenditure

(a)   Generally, the cost of all plant and machinery purchased by a trader becomes part of a *pool of expenditure* on which capital allowances may be claimed. When an addition is made, the pool increases; on disposal the pool is reduced by the sale proceeds.

(b)   Exceptionally, certain items are not included in the pool. They are:

- motor cars;
- assets with private usage by the proprietor; and
- expenditure incurred on **short-life** plant where an election to de-pool is made.

These exceptional treatments are dealt with below.

3.2   Writing down allowances (WDA)

(a)   An annual WDA of 25% is given on a reducing balance basis by reference to the unrelieved expenditure in the pool brought forward at the beginning of the year (ie, cost of all pool assets less allowances already given against the pool) adjusted for additions and disposals during the year. The WDA is first given on the allowable cost in the year of purchase.

(b)   Looking at a proforma helps to understand how the WDA is calculated. Suppose that Brian prepares accounts to 31 December each year, and has a balance of unrelieved expenditure brought forward at 1 January 1999.

Year ended 31 December 1999	*Pool* £
Unrelieved expenditure b/f, say	50,000
Less: Disposal proceeds	14,000
	36,000
WDA @ 25%	9,000
Unrelieved expenditure c/f to 1 January 2000	27,000

(c)   The important point to note is when in the sequence the WDA is available on assets disposed of during the year. Their disposal proceeds are deducted first from the pool balance. Note that if the disposal proceeds for any asset are greater than its original cost, the amount deducted from the pool is limited to **original cost**.

(d)   Next the WDA is calculated on the balance remaining after excluding disposals.

(e)   No WDA may be claimed in the final period of trade.

(f)   If the profits basis period for a tax year is less than 12 months long the WDA is scaled down proportionately. This rule affects the first tax year of a new business (where it is based on less than 12 months of profits) and companies' accounting periods that are shorter than 12 months.

(g)   Where a new trade is being established capital expenditure incurred before it starts is treated as being made on the first day of trade.

3.3   Waiver of capital allowances

An individual may claim (in his income tax return) the whole or only part of the allowance to which he is entitled. If a partial claim is made in one year, WDAs in subsequent years will be calculated on a higher figure than if the allowances had previously been claimed in full, but as a consequence relief for the expenditure incurred will be delayed.

3.4   Example

John's Schedule DI profits for the year ended 31 December 1999 are £6,000 before taking account of capital allowances. The WDV of plant and machinery at 1 January 1999 is £10,000.

John is single and has no other income or outgoings.

John could claim capital allowances of £2,500 (10,000 at 25%). However, he should restrict the claim to £1,665 so that his personal allowance is not wasted. His taxable income for 1999/00 will be:

	£
Schedule DI (6,000 – 1,665)	4,335
Personal allowance	4,335
Taxable income	Nil

The WDV carried forward is increased from £7,500 (10,000 – 2,500) to £8,335 (10,000 – 1,665).

3.5   Expenditure on plant and machinery: notification

No claim for a WDA in respect of expenditure on plant or machinery may be made unless the expenditure is notified to the Inspector by the 31 January which is nearly two years after the tax year in which the period of account ends.

3.6   Length of ownership in the basis period

The WDA is never restricted by reference to the length of ownership of an asset in the basis period.

3.7   Activity

Bertram commenced trading on 1 January 1997, preparing accounts to 31 December annually.   He purchased the following items of machinery:

1 November 1997	cost £1,333
1 April 1998	cost £6,000
1 March 1999	cost £4,000

Compute the capital allowances for the years ended 31 December 1997 to 31 December 1999.   You should ignore first year allowances (see (4)).

3.8   Activity solution

	Pool £	Allowances £
Year ended 31 December 1997		
Additions - Cost 1 November 1997	1,333	
WDA - 25%	333	333
Written down value (WDV) c/f	1,000	
Year ended 31 December 1998		
Additions - Cost 1 April 1998	6,000	
	7,000	
WDA - 25%	1,750	1,750
WDV c/f	5,250	
Year ended 31 December 1999		
Addition - Cost 1 March 1999	4,000	
	9,250	
WDA - 25%	2,313	2,313
WDV c/f	6,937	

3.9   Sale of plant

(a)   Where plant is sold during the basis period the disposal value is deducted from the balance of unrelieved expenditure in the pool.   The WDA for the year is then calculated on the resultant figure (ie, pool brought forward less sale proceeds of current year disposals).   The normal rule is that the sale proceeds must be deducted from the pool after bringing in acquisitions in the same basis period but **before** calculating the WDA.

(b)   The disposal value deducted from the pool must never exceed the original cost of purchasing the asset.   An excess of proceeds over original cost may be charged to capital gains tax, but not income tax.   Thus on a disposal always deduct from the pool the lower of the disposal value and the original cost.

3.10   Activity

Sandy prepares accounts to 30 April annually. In the year to 30 April 1999 the following transactions took place.

15 May 1998	Plant sold (originally purchased for £4,000) for £800
10 June 1998	Plant purchased for £2,000

Compute the capital allowances for the year ended 30 April 1999 assuming that the WDV on 1 May 1998 was £4,900. You should ignore first year allowances.

3.11   Activity solution

	Pool £	Allowances £
Year ended 30 April 1999		
WDV b/f at 1.5.98	4,900	
Additions - 10 June 1998	2,000	
	6,900	
Less: Sale proceeds - 15 May 1998	800	
	6,100	
Less: WDA - 25%	1,525	1,525
Pool WDV c/f at 30.4.99	4,575	

3.12   Balancing charges

(a)   If, on disposal of an asset in the pool, disposal proceeds exceed the pool balance brought forward, the excess allowances previously given will be recovered and charged to tax by means of a balancing charge.

(b)   A balancing charge is assessed separately as an addition to the Schedule D Case I assessment and the capital allowances are deducted from the total.

3.13   Activity

Nelson prepares accounts to 30 April annually. In the year ended 30 April 1999 he had the following transactions

1 May 1998	Sold plant (originally purchased for £6,000) for £6,200
1 June 1998	Purchased new plant for £2,500

The WDV of plant at 1 May 1998 was £3,000.

Compute the capital allowances available for the year ended 30 April 1999, if any. You should ignore first year allowances.

3.14   Activity solution

	Pool £
Year ended 30 April 1999	
WDV b/f at 1.5.98	3,000
Additions: 1 June 1998	2,500
	5,500

Less: Sale proceeds 1 May 1998: limited to cost	6,000
Balancing charge	500

3.15   Balancing allowances

(a)   The basic idea underlying capital allowances is that over the life of a business a trader will obtain relief for the total cost less subsequent sale proceeds of his plant. Where the trade is permanently discontinued and there is still a balance of unrelieved expenditure in the pool (ie, a balance after deducting final sale proceeds), the trader is entitled to claim relief for that unrelieved balance by means of a balancing allowance (it is effectively a last year allowance).

(b)   To summarise

- The only time a balancing allowance will arise in the general pool is in the period of account at the end of which the trade is permanently discontinued.

- A balancing allowance is computed by reference to the excess of the pool balance at the end of the final period of account over the sale proceeds received on ultimate disposal of the plant.

- No WDA is available for the period of account, the cost of any additions being merely added in. This is logical, since relief for unrelieved expenditure will be given by means of a balancing allowance instead.

3.16   Example

Joad prepares accounts to 30 April annually. He ceased to trade on 30 April 1999, on which date he sold the whole of his plant for £10,000. The WDV at the beginning of the final period of account (ie, on 1 May 1998) was £14,000 and he had purchased plant in May 1998 for £5,000.

Compute the balancing allowance for the year ended 30 April 1999.

3.17   Solution

	£
WDV b/f	14,000
Addition during year	5,000
	19,000
Less: Sale proceeds	10,000
Balancing allowance for the year ended 30 April 1999	9,000

3.18   Assets acquired by hire purchase and leased assets

(a)   The essence of a **hire purchase** contract is that on making the final payment the payer becomes the asset's legal owner. Although the payer only hires the asset beforehand this is effectively ignored for capital allowances purposes and he is treated as though he had bought the asset in the first place. Consequently:

- the hire purchase interest is treated as a trading expense of the period of account in which it accrues (and is deductible in computing Schedule D Case I profits);

- the full cash price of the asset is brought into the pool in the period of first use; and

- capital allowances are made on the full cash price irrespective of the actual instalments paid in the period of account.

(b)   Legal title to **leased assets** remains with the lessor. The lessee (the user of the asset) is hiring it and this is reflected in the tax treatment. Lease payments are treated as deductible, on an accruals basis, in computing Schedule D Case I profits and no capital allowances are available to the lessee.

4   FIRST YEAR ALLOWANCES

4.1   Introduction

First-year allowances (FYA) were abolished in 1986, but have been temporarily reinstated for certain businesses in respect of expenditure on plant and machinery incurred during the period 2 July 1997 to 1 July 2000.

4.2   The relief

(a)   In the year of acquisition, a FYA is given instead of the WDA. The rate of FYA is 50% for additions during the period 2 July 1997 to 1 July 1998, and 40% for additions during the period 2 July 1998 to 1 July 2000. These rates and periods will be given to you in the rates and allowances section of the examination paper.

(b)   The balance of expenditure remaining after claiming the FYA is then added into the general pool, and will qualify for WDA in subsequent periods.

(c)   FYAs cannot be claimed in respect of motor cars or assets which are leased out.

(d)   The full FYA does not have to be claimed if it is not beneficial to do so.

(e)   Unlike the WDA, the full FYA is still available if the period of account is less than twelve months.

4.3   Small and medium-sized businesses

(a)   FYAs are only available to small and medium-sized sole traderships, partnerships and companies.

(b)   The definition of small and medium-sized businesses is similar to that used for Companies Act purposes, in that two out of the following conditions must be met in the current or previous year:

(i)   Turnover must not exceed £11.2 million.
(ii)   Assets must not exceed £5.6 million.
(iii)   Employees must not exceed 250.

If a company is a member of a group, then the group must meet the above conditions.

4.4   Activity

Alex prepares accounts to 31 May annually.

His general pool of unrelieved expenditure on plant and machinery brought forward on 1 June 1998 was £11,000.

During the year ended 31 May 1999 the following transactions took place:

15 June 1998   Purchased plant costing £6,500.
31 August 1998   Purchased plant costing £12,000.
30 November 1998   Sold plant for £2,800 (originally purchased for £4,600).

Compute the capital allowances for the year ended 31 May 1999.

| **4.5** | **Activity solution** |

	£	General pool £	Total allowances £
Year ended 31 May 1999			
WDV b/f at 1.6.98		11,000	
Sale proceeds - plant		(2,800)	
		8,200	
WDA 25%		(2,050)	2,050
Additions qualifying for FYA			
15.6.98 Plant	6,500		
FYA 50%	3,250		3,250
		3,250	
31.8.98 Plant	12,000		
FYA 40%	4,800		4,800
		7,200	
WDV c/f at 31.5.99		16,600	
Total allowances			10,100

5 CARS AND ASSETS WITH PRIVATE USE BY TRADER

5.1 Cars costing £12,000 or less

(a) The cost of acquisition of a car is put into a separate **car pool,** unless the cost of the car exceeds £12,000, or the car is used for private as well as business purposes by the owner.

(b) If there is a balance brought forward on the car pool the cost of acquisition is added before dealing with disposals or computing the WDA. This rule ensures that balancing charges are avoided or minimised where acquisitions and disposals occur in the same period of account.

(c) The 'car pool' is deemed to be a separate trade for the purposes of capital allowances so that if all the cars in the pool are disposed of the 'trade' ceases and a balancing allowance or balancing charge must be computed.

5.2 Cars costing more than £12,000

(a) The cost of a car, where it exceeds £12,000, must not be brought into either the general pool or the car pool. The capital allowances on each such car must be separately computed.

(b) The WDA is restricted to a maximum, in a one year period of account, of £3,000. Once the car has been written down to below £12,000 the WDA will be computed in the normal way (ie, 25% of written down value) but the car remains in its separate column of the computation. It must not be brought into the general or car pool.

(c) Each car costing over £12,000 is deemed to be used in a separate trade so that when the car is sold a balancing allowances or charge must be computed on the difference between the written down value and the sale proceeds.

5.3 Private use of an asset by the owner

Where an asset is used by the proprietor/owner partly for business and partly for private purposes (eg, a motor car), only a proportion of the available capital allowances is given. This proportion is computed by reference to the percentage of business use to total use. Where an asset is used partly privately, the following rules must be followed in computing the allowances available and the allowances given

(a)   The cost must not be brought into the general or car pool, but must be the subject of a separate computation (in the same way as a car costing over £12,000).

(b)   The written down value of the asset is based on its full cost but only the business proportion of any allowance is actually given.

(c)   On disposal of the asset, a balancing adjustment is computed by comparing sale proceeds with the written down value (if a profit, there is a balancing charge and vice versa). Having computed the balancing adjustments, the amount assessed or allowed is then reduced to the business proportion.

(d)   Where the asset concerned is an 'expensive' car WDAs are first restricted to the £3,000 limit (for written down values still over £12,000) and then the business proportion of £3,000 is actually given as an allowance.

(e)   Private use by an employee of an asset owned by the business has no effect on the business's entitlement to capital allowances (although there will normally be a benefit-in-kind charge on the employee).

5.4   Activity

Mr Fish prepared annual accounts to 30 September. As at 1 October 1997 the following written down values were brought forward for capital allowance purposes

	£
General pool (of plant)	20,000
Car (costing £7,000 in May 1997) with 30% private use by Fish	5,250

Subsequently the following additions and disposals of plant and machinery were made

Additions   12.10.97 Die-casting machine, cost £7,500
3.6.98 Car, cost £14,000 (no private use)
12.6.98 Car, cost £7,500 (no private use)

Disposals   1.1.98 Milling machine sold for £4,300 (original cost £11,000)
1.1.99 Car purchased May 1997 sold for £2,750

Mr Fish claims maximum allowances. He is not a large business for capital allowance purposes.

Compute the capital allowances available for the years ended 30 September 1998 and 30 September 1999.

5.5   Activity solution

	General pool	Car pool	Expensive Car	Car with 30% private use	Allowances
	£	£	£	£	£
Year ended 30 September 1998					
WDV b/f at 1.10.97	20,000			5,250	
Acquisitions (6.98)		7,500	14,000		
Disposal of plant (1.98)	4,300				
	———				
	15,700				

WDA - 25%		(3,925)	(1,875)	(3,000)		8,800
				(max)		
- 25%					(1,313) (70%)	919
Addition qualifying for FYA						
(10.97)	7,500					
FYA 50%	(3,750)	3,750				3,750
WDV c/f at 30.9.98		15,525	5,625	11,000	3,937	13,469
Year ended 30 September 1999						
Disposal of car (1.99)					(2,750)	
Balancing allowance					1,187 (70%)	831
WDA - 25%		(3,881)	(1,406)	(2,750)		8,037
WDV c/f at 30.9.99		11,644	4,219	8,250		8,868

6   SUMMARY OF COMPUTATIONAL TECHNIQUE

(a)   Bring forward unrelieved expenditure from the previous year for

    (i)   the general pool
    (ii)   the car pool
    (iii)   cars costing over £12,000 (separate column for each)
    (iv)   assets used partly privately (separate column for each).

(b)   Add, in the appropriate column, costs of items acquired (unless FYA is available).

(c)   Deduct, in the appropriate column, the sale proceeds (or cost if lower) of any assets disposed of during the period, calculating the balancing charge where one arises (or balancing allowance in the case of (iii) and (iv) only.

(d)   Compute the WDAs available (restricting to £3,000 pa each in the case of expensive cars), and then reduce for any private use by the owner.

(e)   Compute FYAs on plant and machinery acquired during the period 2 July 1997 to 1 July 2000. The balance of expenditure is added to unrelieved expenditure of the general pool to be carried forward to next year.

7   LONG-LIFE ASSETS

(a)   The WDA for plant and machinery with a working life of 25 years or more is 6% rather than 25%, although the allowance is still given on a reducing balance basis.

(b)   A FYA at the rate of 12% is given for expenditure incurred during the period 2 July 1997 to 1 July 1998. Note that there is no FYA for long-life assets acquired during the period 2 July 1998 to 1 July 2000.

(c)   The 25 year working life is from the time that the asset is first brought into use to the time that it ceases to be capable of being used. It is not sufficient to just look at the expected life in the hands of the current owner.

(d)   The reduced rate does not apply to businesses that spend less than £100,000 pa on long life assets. This limit is reduced for accounting periods of less than twelve months, and for companies with associated companies.

(e)   The following can never be classed as long-life assets:

(i)   Motor cars

(ii)   Plant and machinery situated in a building that is used as a retail shop, showroom, hotel or office.

(f)   Long-life assets are kept in a separate pool, which operates in exactly the same way as the general pool.

(g)   Examples of long-life assets might include aircraft used by an airline, and agricultural equipment used by a farm and pipes or power transmission cables used by a privatised utility company.

8   FIXTURES FORMING PART OF A BUILDING

8.1   Restriction to original cost

Where fixtures which form part of a building are concerned, capital allowances are restricted to the original cost of the fixtures.

8.2   Joint election

The purchaser and the vendor of a building can make a joint election so as to determine how much of the sale price relates to fixtures. This figure cannot exceed the sale price of the property or the original cost of the fixtures. The election must be made within two years of the disposal.

8.3   Anti-avoidance provisions

Anti-avoidance provisions may apply if the vendor attempts to accelerate capital allowances on fixtures by selling them at an artificially low price.

8.4   Activity

White Ltd sells a building to Black Ltd for £300,000. The building includes fixtures (qualifying as plant and machinery) which originally cost White Ltd £60,000. At the date of the sale the fixtures had a WDV of £12,000, and a market value of £8,000.

On what value can Black Ltd claim capital allowances?

8.5   Activity solution

White Ltd and Black Ltd can make a joint election as to how much of the sale price of £300,000 is to be allocated to fixtures.

The figure can be anything between the market value of £8,000 and the original cost of £60,000. A figure less than £8,000 may fall foul of the anti-avoidance provisions.

9   ELECTION FOR DE-POOLING OF SHORT-LIFE ASSETS

9.1   The election

(a)   The election is designed to enable traders to accelerate capital allowances on certain short-life machinery or plant, where it is the intention to sell or scrap the item within five years of acquisition.

(b)   An election must be made by the 31 January which is nearly two years after the tax year containing the end of the period of account in which the expenditure was incurred, and is irrevocable.

(c)   Any plant and machinery can constitute a short-life asset, except, principally:

- motor cars;
- assets with private use; and
- ships.

9.2   Computations

(a)   The treatment of short-life assets corresponds in most respects to that applied to motor cars costing over £12,000 and assets with private use. Thus:

- each short life asset is the subject of a separate computation; and
- on disposal within five years a separate balancing allowance is given or balancing charge arises.

(b)   However, unlike the treatment of expensive cars and assets with private use, if no disposal has taken place by the fourth anniversary of the end of the period of account in which the acquisition took place, the unrelieved balance is transferred back to the general pool in the first period of account following that anniversary. This ensures that no tax advantage arises from making the election where it ought not, in retrospect, to have been made.

(c)   The making of a short-life asset election has no bearing on whether or not FYA can be claimed.

9.3   Activity

Tango prepares annual accounts to 30 June. At 1 July 1996 he had a general pool of qualifying expenditure of £8,000. On 1 August 1996 he purchased two microcomputers with peripheral hardware for £4,000 each. Tango's policy is to replace computers every two to three years. One computer was sold for £200 on 20 September 1999 but the other was still in use at 30 June 2001. Short life asset elections were made in respect of both computers.

Calculate the capital allowances available to Tango for all the years ended 30 June 1997 to 30 June 2002.

9.4   Activity solution

	General pool £	Short life assets No 1 £	No 2 £	Allowances £
Year ended 30 June 1997				
WDV b/f at 1.7.96	8,000			
Additions - microcomputers:		4,000	4,000	
WDA - 25%	2,000	1,000	1,000	4,000
	6,000	3,000	3,000	
Year ended 30 June 1998				
WDA - 25%	1,500	750	750	3,000
	4,500	2,250	2,250	
Year ended 30 June 1999				
WDA - 25%	1,125	563	563	2,251
	3,375	1,687	1,687	

Year ended 30 June 2000
Disposal proceeds (20.9.99)   200

Balancing allowance		1,487	1,487
WDA - 25%	844	422	1,266
	2,531	1,265	2,753
Year ended 30 June 2001			
WDA - 25%	633	316	949
	1,898	949	
Year ended 30 June 2002			
Transfer of short life asset to qualifying pool	949	949	
	2,847		
WDA - 25%	712		712
WDV c/f at 30.6.2002	2,135		

Notes:

(a) The disposal of one microcomputer within the short life period has resulted in full allowances being given during the period of use in the business (1 August 1996 - 20 September 1999).

(b) Since the other microcomputer is used beyond its anticipated short life, the unrelieved balance is transferred over to the general pool immediately after the fourth anniversary of the end of the period of account in which it was acquired.

(c) The short-life asset claim must be made by 31 January 2000.

(d) If the purchases had been made a year later on 1 August 1998 they would have qualified for FYA whether or not a short life asset claim was made.

10   SUCCESSIONS TO TRADE

10.1   Introduction

(a) Where a business ceases to trade without someone else taking it over, balancing adjustments arise. Depending on the amount of unrelieved expenditure and the proceeds obtained on the sale of the assets, these may be either balancing charges or balancing allowances.

(b) If the trade is taken over but none of the special rules considered below apply there is nothing abnormal from a capital allowances viewpoint; the sales proceeds (or market value if higher) of assets are entered in the computation of the person ceasing to trade and (the same) purchase price starts off the new trader's computation.

10.2   Special situations

Special rules apply where there is a succession to trade and the predecessor and successor are connected with one another.

10.3   Successions to trade between connected persons

(a) If the predecessor and successor to a trade are connected, the approach for capital allowances purposes is broadly to ignore the change of ownership. The actual sale price (if any) is ignored and the plant and machinery is deemed to have been sold for the predecessor's written down value. Consequently no balancing charge or allowance arises on the predecessor, and the successor uses the same written down values to begin his computation. As the successor is treated as standing in the shoes of the predecessor, the maximum amount that can be used as a disposal value in the future is the **predecessor's** original cost.

(b)   This is a privileged treatment and so there are conditions attached. These are:

- an election must be made jointly by the predecessor and successor within two years of the time the succession took place;

- both parties must be within the charge to UK tax on the profits of the trade; and

- the assets must be in use in the trade immediately before and after the succession.

If no election is made assets are deemed to have been sold at market value as normal.

11   CHAPTER SUMMARY

(a)   Capital allowances are available only for capital expenditure on certain types of fixed asset. The most important of these is plant and machinery. Allowances are given as a trading expense in computing the Schedule D Case I profits for traders and from Schedule E income of employees (where applicable).

For Schedule D Case I businesses they are given for periods of account by reference to transactions in that period of account.

(b)   There is no statutory definition of 'plant' and so the Courts have devised tests to establish what falls within the scope of the term. The principal test applied is whether the item concerned performs a **function** in the trade (plant) or merely forms part of the setting in which the trade is carried on (not plant). Certain items are specifically treated as plant by the legislation whatever function, or lack of it, they might be thought to have.

(c)   Most plant and machinery expenditure is pooled. The principal exceptions are cars costing over £12,000, assets partly used privately by the proprietor and assets for which a 'short-life' election has been made. Cars costing £12,000 or less are pooled but in a separate pool of their own.

(d)   Writing down allowances are calculated on the pool balance brought forward plus purchases less disposal proceeds (or original cost if lower). The rate of WDA is 25% pa although a 6% rate applies to the separate pool of 'long life' assets.

(e)   For a non-12 month period of account WDA is reduced or increased proportionately. The time during a period of account after an asset is purchased is never relevant in calculating the amount of allowance due.

(f)   Balancing charges arise whenever disposal proceeds (or original cost, if lower) exceed the balance on the pool. In contrast balancing allowances occur only when there is an unrelieved pool balance when trade ceases (or is deemed to have ceased on the disposal of any asset whose capital allowances are calculated individually).

(g)   FYAs are available to small and medium-sized businesses in respect of expenditure on plant and machinery incurred during the period 2 July 1997 to 1 July 1998 at the rate of 50%) and during the period 2 July 1998 to 1 July 2000 (at the rate of 40%).

(h)   An election can be made to de-pool plant and machinery (other than, principally, cars and assets with private use). It ensures that full relief can be gained whilst an asset is in use in the trade. An asset not disposed of by the fourth anniversary of the end of the period of account in which it was acquired is then transferred to the general pool at its written down value (and thus the benefit of the election is lost).

12   SELF-TEST QUESTIONS

12.1   Who may claim capital allowances? (1.2)

12.2   How is relief for capital allowances given to unincorporated traders? (1.3)

12.3   What distinction does the functional test make in determining whether an asset qualifies as plant or not? (2.2)

12.4   What assets are specifically deemed to be plant by legislation? (2.3)

12.5   On what amount are writing down allowances calculated? Is the taxpayer required to use his entitlement? (3.2)

12.6   When plant is sold what are the alternative amounts that may be deducted from unrelieved expenditure? (3.98)

12.7   In what circumstances do balancing allowances arise? (3.15)

12.8   How are allowances calculated on assets used partly for private purposes by the trader? (5.3)

12.98   What is the definition of a long-life asset? (7)

12.10   How does the calculation of capital allowances on short-life assets differ from that of 'normal' assets? (9.2)

13   EXAMINATION TYPE QUESTION

13.1   Bill

Bill prepares accounts to 30 April annually.

His general pool of unrelieved expenditure on plant and machinery brought forward on 1 May 1997 was £23,500.

In the two years ended 30 April 1999 the following transactions took place.

Year ended 30 April 1998

1 Nov 1997	Purchased plant costing £6,000
10 Nov 1997	Sold two lorries (purchased for £8,450 each) for £2,500 each. Purchased two replacement lorries for £5,250 each.
1 Dec 1997	Purchased two cars costing £6,600 each. One of the cars is used 30% for private purposes by Bill.

Year ended 30 April 1999

1 Nov 1998	Purchased plant costing £1,000
18 Nov 1998	Purchased two cars costing £5,200 each (used wholly for business purposes)
1 Dec 1998	Sold both cars purchased in December 1997 for £2,000 each.

Bill is not a large business for capital allowance purposes.

You are required to compute the capital allowances available to Bill for the years ended 30 April 1998 and 30 April 1999.

13   ANSWER TO EXAMINATION TYPE QUESTION

13.1   Bill

Bill - capital allowances on plant and machinery

	General pool £	Car pool £	Car (30%) private use £	Total allowances £
Year ended 30 April 1998				
WDV b/f at 1.5.97	23,500			
Additions				
1.12.97 Motor cars		6,600	6,600	
Sale proceeds - lorries	(5,000)			
	18,500			
WDA (25%)	(4,625)	(1,650)	(1,650) (× 70%)	7,430
Additions qualifying for FYA				
1.11.97 Plant 6,000				
10.11.97 10,500				
16,500				
FYA 50% (8,250)	8,250			8,250
WDV c/f at 30.4.98	22,125	4,950	4,950	15,680
Year ended 30 April 1999				
Addition 18.11.98		10,400		
		15,350		
Sale proceeds 1.12.98		(2,000)	(2,000)	
		13,350	2,950	
Balancing allowance			(× 70%)	2,065
WDA (25%)		(5,531)	(3,338)	8,869
Addition qualifying for FYA				
1.11.98 Plant 1,000				
FYA 40% (400)				400
	600			
WDV c/f at 30.4.99	17,194	10,012		11,334

11 CAPITAL ALLOWANCES ON INDUSTRIAL BUILDINGS AND MISCELLANEOUS ASSETS

INTRODUCTION & LEARNING OBJECTIVES

Allowances on plant and machinery were dealt with in the previous chapter. This chapter considers the other principal categories of asset for which capital allowances are available.

When you have studied this chapter you should be able to do the following:

- Decide whether a building will qualify under the statutory definition of an industrial building or qualifying hotel
- Calculate the proportion of expenditure incurred that is eligible for industrial buildings allowances
- Decide whether the initial allowance is available on a particular item of expenditure and if so decide the rate of allowance
- Decide whether a writing down allowance may be made in respect of a particular period of account and calculate it when appropriate
- Determine whether a sale of an industrial building gives rise to a balancing adjustment
- Calculate the balancing charge or allowance arising on sale and deal with the different calculations required when the building has been used throughout its period of use for industrial purposes, and when non-industrial use has occurred.
- Judge whether allowances are available to a purchaser of a used industrial building and, where appropriate, calculate them
- Determine whether particular expenditure qualifies for capital allowances as expenditure on agricultural buildings and works
- Be able to compute the capital allowances due to both the seller and purchaser of an agricultural building when it is sold
- Calculate allowances due to and charges arising on owners of patent rights and know-how

1 INDUSTRIAL BUILDINGS

1.1 Definition of an industrial building

The Capital Allowances Act 1990 states that buildings used for a variety of specific purposes qualify as industrial buildings. The more important of these are:

(a)   a trade carried on in a mill, factory or similar premises,

(b)   a trade which consists in the manufacture of goods or materials or the subjection of goods or materials to any process,

(c)   a trade which consists in the storage of

- goods or materials used for manufacturing purposes, or which are to be subjected to any process, or

- finished goods or materials which have been manufactured or subjected to any process.

In addition, the following structures are also industrial buildings:

(a)   any building or structure provided by the person carrying on one of the above trades for the welfare of the employees and in use for that purpose, eg, a canteen or workplace nursery

(b)   a drawing office used for the preparation of plans for manufacturing or processing operations

(c)   a sports pavilion used in any trade

(d)   a building or structure in use for the purpose of a (private) toll road undertaking

(e)   a warehouse used to store imported goods at their point of arrival in the UK.

The Courts have amplified the definitions set out in the statute and the following illustrate the views of the Court in setting limits to them.

- Where claims are made for a building on the grounds that it is used to subject goods to a process the nature of the 'goods' is important.

    -     The screening and packing coal into paper bags is subjecting goods to a process.

    -     On the other hand a building used for the cremation of human bodies does not qualify - human bodies are not goods. Neither does a building used for packing wages into envelopes - notes and coins are not goods.

- A building for maintaining and repairing hired out plant did not qualify because the plant was not being subjected to a process.

- Buildings used for storage of manufactured goods before delivery to a customer qualify. Where a retailer or wholesaler stores goods the building **doesn't** qualify as the storer is the customer to whom the manufacturer has delivered the goods.

1.2   Excluded buildings

Specifically excluded from classification as industrial buildings are

(a)   dwelling houses
(b)   retail or wholesale premises
(c)   showrooms
(d)   hotels (except qualifying hotels)
(e)   offices (except offices directly involved in production).

1.3   Qualifying hotels

Provided that an hotel meets the conditions for qualification, it is treated as an industrial building qualifying for allowances.

A qualifying hotel is one that satisfies **all** the following four conditions.

(a)   The building must be a hotel.

(b)   The hotel must be open for at least 4 months (120 days) in the season (1 April to 31 October each year).

(c)   When open in the season the hotel must have at least 10 bedrooms which are available for short-term letting to the public (ie, not more than 30 days per letting).

(d)   When open in the season, the services provided for guests must normally include breakfast, evening meal, room cleaning and the making of beds.

1.4   Enterprise zones

(a)   Enterprise zones have been designated for the purpose of encouraging and accelerating economic redevelopment within certain mainly urban areas.

(b)   Advantageous capital allowances on the cost of construction of industrial and commercial buildings in these zones form part of the package of incentives.

(c)   The buildings that qualify for IBAs (industrial building allowances) are:

- industrial buildings

- qualifying hotels

- any other commercial buildings used for trading or professional purposes. (This covers hotels that do not count as 'qualifying hotels', retail premises, and offices generally.)

- offices - whether or not they are used for trading or professional purposes.

Dwelling houses are **not** covered

(d)   The expenditure must be incurred within 10 years of the date on which the area is designated an enterprise zone if it is to rank for the enhanced allowances.

2   QUALIFYING COST OF CONSTRUCTION

2.1   Principles

(a)   Expenditure must be incurred in construction; thus the cost of the land and the incidental expenses associated with its acquisition do not rank for IBAs. However, costs of work on the land that is preliminary to construction do qualify, as follows:

- the preparation of the site in order to lay foundations; and
- cutting, tunnelling and levelling the land in connection with the construction.

(b)   Professional fees, notably those of architects, incurred as part of a construction project for an industrial building.

(c)   Where part of a single building is not used for a qualifying purpose and the expenditure on that non-industrial part does not exceed 25% of the total qualifying cost of the whole building, then the IBAs will be given on the cost of the whole building. Conversely, if the non-industrial part costs more than 25%, IBAs will be given on the industrial part, only.

(d)   Capital expenditure on alterations to an existing industrial building also qualifies for IBAs.

(e)   The total cost of constructing a qualifying building is eligible for IBAs (subject to the rule on non-qualifying parts of a building) if built by or for the trader. If it was acquired after construction (but before use) the eligible expenditure depends on the type of vendor. When purchased from a builder it is the purchase price (including the builder's profit margin), otherwise it is the **lower** of the purchase price and the construction expenditure incurred.

2.2   Example

Jumbo erected a factory block for use in his manufacturing business. The total price of £370,000 was apportioned as follows

	£
Freehold land (including cost of conveyancing)	60,000
Cutting and tunnelling of site	2,000
Construction of building comprising	
Factory	267,000
Employee's canteen	12,000
General offices	29,000
	370,000

2.3   **Solution**

The expenditure qualifying for IBAs would be as follows

		£
Total cost		370,000
Less: Land and associated legal costs		60,000
Cost of construction of whole structure		310,000

The cost of the non-qualifying part of the structure (ie, the offices) of £29,000 does not exceed 25% of the cost of the whole structure of £310,000. Therefore IBAs are available on the cost of the whole structure.

3   **CALCULATING INDUSTRIAL BUILDINGS ALLOWANCES FOR A NEW BUILDING**

3.1   **Initial allowance**

The initial allowance for general industrial buildings and hotels (but not enterprise zone buildings) was phased out in the mid 1980s. However, it was temporarily reintroduced for expenditure incurred under a contract entered into between 1 November 1992 and 31 October 1993. The rate was 20% of the eligible expenditure on the building.

3.2   **Writing down allowance**

(a)   Unlike WDAs on plant and machinery, those for industrial buildings are given on a **straight line basis** on the cost of the qualifying capital expenditure. The WDA is proportionately reduced where the period of account is of less than 12 months duration and proportionately increased where the period of account exceeds 12 months.

(b)   A WDA is given provided the building is in use as an industrial building at the end of the period of account. **Temporary** disuse of an industrial building does **not** affect the allowances given but use for non-industrial purposes does. Non-industrial use is dealt with below. Unlike plant, it is possible to get both IA (where available) and WDA given for the same period of account.

(c)   The rate of WDAs is 4% for industrial buildings and hotels.

(d)   The WDA is given to the person who possesses the relevant interest at the end of the period of account.

(e)   The relevant interest in the building (eg, freehold, leasehold) is that which the person who incurred the capital expenditure was entitled to at the time the expenditure was incurred (ie, the WDA will normally go to the person who incurred the cost of construction).

3.3   **Writing down period**

Industrial buildings are deemed to have a tax life of 25 years from the date the building was first used. The tax life is important insofar as no balancing adjustment will arise on the sale of the building after the 25-year period has elapsed. Similarly, no allowances will be available to a purchaser of a building where its tax life has already expired.

3.4   **Sales of buildings without non-industrial use**

(a)   On disposal of an industrial building a balancing adjustment is computed by comparing disposal proceeds with its WDV (known as the 'residue before sale').

(b)   Where the disposal proceeds are **less** than the residue before sale a balancing allowance is given.

(c)   A balancing charge arises when the disposal proceeds are **more** than the residue before sale. The balancing charge can never exceed the allowances previously given on the building (this restriction applies where the building is sold for more than original cost). The surplus over original cost may be charged to capital gains tax.

3.5   Example

Expenditure as in the earlier example (see 2.2). The factory block was completed and paid for on 1 June 1996 and taken into use on 1 August 1996. Jumbo prepares accounts to 30 April annually.

On 1 August 1999 the factory was sold for £500,000 (including £100,000 for the land) to Mumbo.

Compute the IBAs available to Jumbo for each of the years concerned.

3.6   Solution

	£	£
Year ended 30 April 1997		
Qualifying expenditure incurred 1.6.96		310,000
WDA (4%) on cost (in use 30.4.97)	12,400	
Years ended 30 April 1998 and 1999		
WDA - £12,400 pa for two years	24,800	
		37,200
WDV before sale		272,800
Year ended 30 April 2000		
Qualifying sale proceeds - 1.8.99 - £400,000. Restricted to allowable cost (no WDA: building not in use by Jumbo on 30.4.2000)		310,000
Balancing charge (recovers all IBAs given)		37,200

3.7   Building sold after non-industrial use - for more than cost

(a)   Where an industrial building is being used for non-industrial purposes at the end of a period of account **no WDA is given**. However, the cost of the building is written down by a **notional WDA** (calculated in the normal way - but not given to the taxpayer).

(b)   If, after non-industrial use, the building is sold for more than it originally cost, any balancing charge that arises is limited to the total allowances **actually given**.

3.8   Example

Facts as in the example above, except that Jumbo used the building as retail premises between 1 March 1999 and 31 July 1999. Calculate the balancing charge arising on disposal.

3.9   Solution

	£	*Allowances given* £
Year ended 30 April 1997		
Qualifying expenditure (1.6.96)	310,000	
WDA (4%)	12,400	12,400
	297,600	
Year ended 30 April 1998	12,400	12,400
	285,200	

Year ended 30 April 1999 notional WDA	12,400	-
	272,800	
Year ended 30 April 2000		
Sale proceeds - limited to cost	310,000	
Balancing charge	37,200	
Balancing charge limited to allowances given		24,800

3.10 Building sold after non-industrial use - for less than cost

Where an industrial building is sold for less than original cost, having been, for part of its tax life, not used for a qualifying industrial purpose, the balancing charge is calculated as the excess of allowances actually given over the adjusted net cost.

Adjusted net cost is 'cost minus sales proceeds' multiplied by the fraction

$$\frac{\text{Period(s) of qualifying industrial use since date of first use}}{\text{Total period of use since date of first use}}$$

Note that questions are rarely set on this aspect of industrial buildings.

4 ALLOWANCES FOR USED INDUSTRIAL BUILDINGS

4.1 Principles

Provided the building is to be used in a qualifying trade, a subsequent purchaser of the building (the tax life of which has not expired) is entitled to an annual WDA (having acquired the relevant interest). This annual allowance is computed as follows

$$\frac{\text{Residue of expenditure after sale}}{\text{Remaining tax life of building from date of first use}} = \text{Annual WDA}$$

The residue of expenditure after sale is the written down value of the building prior to a sale, plus any balancing charge assessed on the vendor (or minus any balancing allowance) but if this results in a figure greater than the price the purchaser paid for the building it is restricted to purchase price.

Remaining life of the building means the unexpired part of the 25 year tax life.

4.2 Example

Jones sells an industrial building for £750,000 on 1 December 1999. The building was constructed for his use at a cost of £300,000 and brought into use on 1 June 1993. The residue before sale is £228,000.

Calculate the annual WDA for the purchaser.

4.3 Solution

	£
Residue before sale	228,000
Add: Balancing charge (300,000 - 228,000)	72,000
Residue after sale	300,000

$$\text{Annual WDA} = \frac{300,000}{25 - 6\frac{1}{2} \text{ years}} = £16,216$$

Note: the purchaser obtains IBAs only on the original construction price of the building (£300,000) rather than the £750,000 he paid for it.

5   IBAs ON BUILDINGS IN ENTERPRISE ZONES

5.1   Initial allowance

The rate of initial allowance is 100% . It is available on the eligible cost of qualifying buildings incurred within 10 years of the site being included in the enterprise zone or under a contract entered into during that period.

5.2   Writing down allowance

Writing down allowance becomes relevant only when the initial allowance is wholly or partly unclaimed. It is then calculated at 25% pa on cost, any residual amount being taken as a final allowance.

5.3   Purchase of buildings in enterprise zones within two years of use

Provided that the building is purchased within two years of first being used, enterprise zone allowances are also extended to the purchaser of a used building. Any balancing charge on the seller is computed in the normal way but the purchaser obtains allowances on the same basis as the purchaser of an unused building.

6   AGRICULTURAL BUILDINGS AND WORKS

6.1   Introduction

This is a capital allowance on expenditure on the construction (including alterations and improvements) of qualifying works and buildings. The allowance is available to owners or tenants of agricultural land and is given to the person who incurred the expenditure.

6.2   Qualifying expenditure

(a)   The Capital Allowances Act 1990 refers to buildings and other works in the UK. These include:

> farmhouse (see below)
> farm buildings
> fences
> drainage works
> water and electrical installations
> farm cottages used by employees (need not be on the land being farmed)
> shelter belts of trees

The cost of the land is not included.

(b)   Not more than one third of the capital expenditure on a farmhouse qualifies for relief. The proportion may be further reduced where the accommodation and amenities are not in keeping with the size and nature of the agricultural undertaking.

6.3   Allowances

(a)   Allowances for agricultural buildings (ABAs) closely follow the system for industrial buildings allowances. However, there is sometimes a departure from the industrial buildings system when agricultural buildings are sold and this is dealt with below.

(b)   An initial allowance of 20% was available on capital expenditure incurred by the owner of agricultural land on the construction of the types of work set out above. As for industrial buildings, the expenditure must have been incurred under a contract made between 1 November 1992 and 31 October 1993.

(c)   Annual writing down allowances of 4% are made where the building is in use for agricultural purposes at the end of the period of account. Following the industrial buildings system, the

WDA is made for the period of account in which the expenditure was incurred if the building has been brought into agricultural use by the end of the period of account.

6.4 Method of giving relief

Allowances are given as a trading expense of the period of account (ie, deducted in arriving at the Schedule D Case I profits).

6.5 Disposal of agricultural buildings

(a) The WDA for the period of account in which the disposal takes place is apportioned between the vendor and purchaser - the new owner is then entitled to the WDA for the balance of the 25 year writing down period. The apportionment is made as follows

Vendor: from start of (vendor's) period of account to date of sale
Purchaser: from date of sale to end of (purchaser's) period of account

Where the buyer and seller make up accounts to different dates this apportionment results in a total WDA being claimed in the year of sale that is more (or less) than normal. A compensating adjustment is made on the buyer in the last year for which WDA is available. The purchase price of the building is **irrelevant**.

(b) Alternatively, the two parties concerned may elect to regard the transaction as a balancing event. In this case there is no WDA in the period of account of transfer, and the former owner is subject to a balancing adjustment. The balancing adjustment is computed as for industrial buildings. The new owner will be entitled to a WDA based upon the residue of expenditure, which must be written-off over the rest of the 25 year writing down period.

(c) The transaction is treated as a balancing event only if a joint election is made by vendor and purchaser by 31 January following the year of assessment in which the period of account of sale ended.

6.6 Example

Sugden, who prepares accounts to 31 December annually, erected a new dairy building, for use in his farming business, at a cost of £10,000 on 1 January 1998. Sugden sold the building for £9,500 on 1 January 2000 to NY Estates a partnership which prepares accounts to 30 June. A joint election is made to treat the disposal as a balancing event.

Calculate the agricultural buildings allowances for both parties.

6.7 Solution

	Allowances £	WDV £
Year to 31 December 1998		
Cost of dairy		10,000
WDA 4%	400	
Year to 31 December 1999		
WDA 4%	400	
		800
	800	
WDV before sale		9,200
Year to 31 December 2000		
Sale proceeds		9,500
Balancing charge	(300)	(300)
ABAs are equal to net cost of	500	

NY Estates

Annual WDA : $\dfrac{\text{WDV before sale } + \text{ balancing charge}}{\text{remainder of writing - down period}}$

ie, $\dfrac{£(9,200+300)}{1.1.2000-31.12.2022} = \dfrac{£9,500}{23\,years}$

ie,   £413 pa for 23 years starting in the year to 30 June 2000.

7   PATENT RIGHTS

7.1   Introduction

Patent rights means the right to do, or authorise the doing of, anything which would, but for that right, be an infringement of a patent. Allowances are available on the capital expenditure incurred on the purchase of existing patent rights.

7.2   Allowances available and balancing adjustments

(a)   For any period of account a writing down allowance of 25% is given in respect of

- the tax written down value of patent rights brought forward in the pool of patent right expenditure, plus

- the cost of patent rights incurred in the relevant period of account, less

- the sale proceeds (or, if lower, the original qualifying cost) of patent rights sold in the period of account.

(b)   On disposal of patent rights in whole or in part, if disposal proceeds exceed the balance of cost in the pool (including current basis period expenditure) a balancing charge arises. A balancing allowance is made for the period of account in which the trade ceases or the last patent is sold, where the sale proceeds are less than the patents' written down value.

(c)   If disposal proceeds exceed the original qualifying cost of the patent rights, the capital profit is assessed as income under Schedule D Case VI in six equal annual instalments, commencing with the actual tax year (not period of account) in which the disposal took place. However, the taxpayer may elect, by 12 months after 31 January following the end of that fiscal year, for the whole excess to be assessed in the tax year of disposal.

7.3   Activity

Brainstawm, who prepares accounts to 30 September annually, has the following transactions in patent rights

1 May 1997   Acquired the rights to a new machine design for £12,500

1 October 1998   Acquired the rights to a new manufacturing process for £25,000

1 December 1999   Sold the patent rights to the manufacturing process for net sale proceeds of £32,500

Calculate the allowances attributable to Brainstawm's patent rights.

7.4 **Activity solution**

	Pool of patent rights £	Allowances (charges) £
Year ended 30 September 1997		
1.5.97 Cost of rights	12,500	
Less: WDA - 25%	3,125	3,125
	9,375	
Year ended 30 September 1998		
WDA - 25%	2,344	2,344
	7,031	
Year ended 30 September 1999		
1.10.98 Cost of rights	25,000	
	32,031	
Less: WDA - 25%	8,008	8,008
	24,023	
Year ended 30 September 2000		
1.12.99 Net sale proceeds, restricted to original cost	25,000	
Balancing charge	977	(977)

8 KNOW-HOW

8.1 Introduction

(a) An alternative to the normal course of undertaking a programme of research is to buy the results of someone else's research in the form of know-how. This is more widely defined as industrial information or techniques likely to assist in

- the manufacture or processing of goods or materials
- the working of (or searching for) mineral deposits
- agricultural, forestry or fishing operations.

(b) Know-how purchased as a separate entity qualifies for relief under this heading. However, if it was an asset acquired as part of a purchase of a business, it is part of a transaction dealt with under capital gains rules unless both parties elect, within two years of the transfer, for it to be dealt with under income tax rules.

8.2 Allowances available and balancing adjustments

(a) Qualifying expenditure on acquiring know-how attracts tax relief in the same way as expenditure on patents described above.

(b) However, the full amount of disposal proceeds is deducted from the know-how pool even if it exceeds the relevant original amount of qualifying expenditure. Thus, any capital gain may be assessed as a balancing charge.

9 SCIENTIFIC RESEARCH

9.1 Introduction

Expenditure on scientific research can take two forms: revenue and capital. Revenue expenditure (eg, salaries of research personnel, rent of premises for research purposes, etc) is allowed in the normal way in computing profits. Capital expenditure that does not rank for other reliefs (as plant and/or industrial buildings) qualifies for a capital allowance under this heading.

9.2   Allowances available and recovery of allowances

(a)   Capital expenditure on scientific research related to the trade qualifies for a 100% allowance in the period of account in which the expenditure is incurred.

(b)   No allowance is given for expenditure on the acquisition of land.

(c)   When an asset which qualified for a scientific research allowance ceases to belong to the claimant, the disposal proceeds are treated as a trading receipt.

10   CHAPTER SUMMARY

(a)   Industrial buildings include:

- mills, factories or similar premises used for a trade;
- buildings in which a trade of manufacturing or processing goods is carried on;
- canteens used in the trades mentioned above; and
- sports pavilions used in any trade.

(b)   Some buildings are specifically disqualified from industrial buildings' status. These are:

- dwelling houses;
- retail or wholesale premises;
- hotels (except qualifying hotels); and
- offices.

(c)   Qualifying hotels are treated as industrial buildings for IBA purposes. Broadly, to qualify it must have at least 10 bedrooms, be open for at least 4 months in the period April to October and provide usual services (breakfast, evening meal, room cleaning, making of beds).

(d)   Enterprise zones have a privileged IBA regime. Any commercial building (but **not** dwelling houses) qualifies as an industrial building. Accelerated allowances (100% in year of expenditure) are available during their 10-year designation period. Any 100% allowance not taken can be written off in future years (at 25% of qualifying cost per annum).

(e)   Qualifying cost is normally the cost of construction. The cost of land on which the building stands does **not** qualify but professional fees incurred in connection with the construction do qualify. Where part of the cost is incurred on non-qualifying construction (such as administrative offices) it will nevertheless qualify if it does not exceed 25% of the total cost of construction (ie, including the doubtful costs). A similar rule applies to hotels; expenditure of more than 25% of the total on parts of the building occupied by the proprietor or his family is disallowed.

(f)   Where an industrial building is purchased unused from the person that built it the qualifying cost to the purchaser is the lower of the purchase cost and the cost of construction. If it is bought unused from a builder the price paid is the qualifying amount and the cost of construction by the builder is irrelevant.

(g)   Initial allowances are available on qualifying costs of construction between 1 November 1992 and 31 October 1993 at a rate of 20%.

(h)   Writing down allowances at 4% of cost (on a straight line basis) may be claimed provided that the building is in use as an industrial building at the end of the period of account. It is not available if the building is being used for non-industrial purposes at the end of a period of account, but temporary disuse is ignored.

(i)   Buildings have a tax life of 25 years from the date of first use. Its significance lies in the fact that a balancing adjustment arises on sale within this period but not after it has expired.

(j)   When industrial buildings are sold, without ever having been used for non-industrial purposes, any balancing adjustment is computed by comparing disposal proceeds with the tax written down value (known as the residue before sale) at the time of sale. A balancing allowance or charge arises depending on whether the building is sold for more or less than its written down value. A balancing charge must not exceed the allowances previously given on the building.

(k)   If the building is sold for more than cost after non-industrial use any balancing charge is limited to the total allowances actually given. If the sale is for less than cost the balancing charge is the excess of allowances actually given over the adjusted net cost.

(l)   Writing down allowances to a second or subsequent user of an industrial building are given over its remaining tax life in equal annual amounts.

(m)   Capital allowances on agricultural buildings closely follow the industrial buildings allowances system. Initial and writing down allowances are given in the same way. On a sale of an agricultural building a balancing charge or allowance may be calculated if the buyer and seller elect for this treatment. Otherwise the writing down allowance of the year of sale is apportioned between them.

(n)   Patent rights and know-how are pooled in a similar way to plant and machinery with WDAs of 25% pa.

11   SELF TEST QUESTIONS

11.1   What buildings are specifically disqualified from being industrial buildings? (1.2)

11.2   What conditions must an hotel meet to be treated as a qualifying hotel? (1.3)

11.3   What costs are eligible for industrial buildings allowances? (2.1)

11.4   What is the limit on the expenditure incurred on a non-industrial part of a building if the whole of it is to qualify for IBAs? (2.1)

11.5   What is the relevant interest for the purposes of the writing down allowance? (3.2)

11.6   How long is the tax life of an industrial building and what is its significance? (3.3)

11.7   In what way is a balancing charge restricted where a building is sold for more than original cost after non-industrial use? (3.7)

11.8   How are writing down allowances calculated for the second or subsequent user of an industrial building? (4.1)

11.9   What buildings and works qualify for agricultural buildings allowances? (6.2)

11.10   What are the two alternative methods of calculating allowances due to the seller and purchaser of an agricultural building for the period of account in which it is sold? (6.5)

12   EXAMINATION TYPE QUESTION

12.1   The Straight-Furrows

Simon Straight-Furrow and his wife Cynthia separated permanently on 3 August 1999 and on 12 August 1999 he executed an agreement to pay his wife a separation allowance of £300 per month commencing on that date with subsequent payments being due on the twelfth of each month.

Cynthia was granted custody of their only child (a girl born in 1989), who has lived with her permanently since the separation.

Simon owns and operates a farm. Recent profits, as adjusted for income tax but before deducting capital allowances, have been as follows

	£
Year ended 31 March 1999	11,035
Year ended 31 March 2000	18,860

Simon wishes to make a claim to average the profits assessable for 1998/99 and 1999/00.

For the year ended 31 March 1999 agricultural buildings allowances of £1,030 resulting from a barn constructed for £25,750 in September 1998 have been agreed. Expenditure qualifying for agricultural buildings allowance was incurred during the year ended 31 March 2000 is as follows:

	£
Fencing and draining	1,850
Extension of farmworker's cottage	17,450

Cynthia does part-time work for a charity and was paid £500 per month throughout 1999/00, tax under PAYE of £15 being deducted each month.

During 1999/00 Simon received building society interest of £16,800. Cynthia received the following amounts of building society interest

	£
In June 1999	3,105
In February 2000	3,975

Simon and his wife had always lived away from the farm, and the ownership of their residence was transferred into Cynthia's name on 30 September 1999; on the same date the mortgage of £20,000 was transferred from Simon to Cynthia. Interest on this mortgage during 1999/00 was £2,543 (gross), of which Simon paid £1,180 up to 30 September 1999 and Cynthia paid £1,363 after that date. The MIRAS scheme applies.

In October 1999 Simon borrowed £15,000 towards the purchase of a flat which became his only residence, paying interest of £1,110 (gross) up to 5 April 2000. The loan is outside the MIRAS scheme.

During 1999/00 Simon paid £250 (gross amount) under four-year covenants in favour of charities.

You are required:

(a)   to calculate the income tax payable by Simon for 1999/00
(b)   to calculate the repayment of income tax due to Cynthia for 1999/00.

13   ANSWER TO EXAMINATION TYPE QUESTION

13.1   The Straight-Furrows

(a)   **Simon - income tax computation 1999/00**

		£
Schedule DI (W1)		13,531
Building society interest $(16,800 \times {}^{100}/_{80})$		21,000
		34,531
Less:	Charges paid	
	Deeds of covenant to charities	250
Statutory total income		34,281

Less: PA	4,335
Taxable income	29,946

£1,500 × 10%	150
£7,446 × 23%	1,713
£19,054 × 20%	3,811
£1,946 × 40%	778
	6,452
Less: Tax credit on mortgage interest (W3) £1,110 × 10%	(111)
Relief for maintenance payments £1,970 × 10%	(197)
Tax credit on MCA £1,970 × 10%	(197)
	5,947
Add: Tax retained on charge paid £250 × 23%	57
Income tax liability	6,004
Less: Tax deducted at source £21,000 × 20%	(4,200)
Income tax payable	1,804

(*Tutorial notes:*

(1) Only £1,970 of the maintenance is given as a tax credit (at 10%). The amounts are not taxable in the hands of the recipient.

(2) The married couples' allowance (MCA) is allowed in full for the year of separation.)

(b) **Calculation of income tax repayment due to Cynthia**

	£	£
Schedule E 12 × £500		6,000
Building society interest (3,105 + 3,975) × $^{100}/_{80}$		8,850
Statutory total income		14,850
Less: PA		4,335
Taxable income		10,515
£1,500 × 10%		150
£165 × 23%		38
£8,850 × 20%		1,770
		1,958
Less: Tax credit on APA (dependent daughter) 1,970 × 10%		(197)
Income tax liability		1,761
Less: Tax credits		
BSI £8,850 × 20%	1,770	
PAYE £15 × 12	180	
		1,950
Income tax repayment due		189

(*Tutorial note:* Cynthia is entitled to APA because the daughter was resident with her after the date of separation.)

WORKINGS

(W1)   **Averaging of farming profits for 1998/99 and 1999/00**

		£
Before averaging		
1998/99 (year to 31 March 1999) 11,035 − 1,030		10,005
1999/00 (year to 31 March 2000) 18,860 − 1,802		17,058

The lower profits are about 59% of the higher profits, so the profits can be averaged.

	£
	10,005
	17,058
	27,063 / 2 = 13,531

(W2)   **Agricultural buildings allowances for the year ended 31 March 2000**

	£	£
Barns	25,750	
Fencing and drainage	1,850	
Extension	17,450	
	45,050	
WDA @ 4%		1,802

(W3)   **Relief for loan interest**

	Simon £	Cynthia £
Loan interest on original house (MIRAS)	1,180	1,363
Loan interest on Simon's flat (not MIRAS)	1,110	-
	2,290	1,363

(Tutorial notes:

(1)   The £30,000 test applies separately to each spouse after the separation.

(2)   Interest paid under MIRAS is ignored in the income tax computation.

(3)   Relief for interest paid outside MIRAS is given as a tax credit against the income tax liability.*)*

12 TRADING LOSSES

INTRODUCTION & LEARNING OBJECTIVES

(a)   When dealing with the income tax regime for traders in this text it has so far been assumed that their trades are profitable and we have therefore been concerned with the calculation of the tax due on those profits. However, there are also provisions for dealing with losses incurred by traders and this is the subject of this chapter.

(b)   A tax loss arises in a trade when an accounting result is adjusted for tax purposes in the usual way but the adjusted figure is negative. One of the most important points to appreciate in dealing with trading losses is that where the result for a period of account is a loss the assessable profit for that period is nil.

(c)   Although you are not required to learn the sections of legislation for your examination, it is usual for loss reliefs to be referred to by their section number and, since there are relatively few of them, it takes no great feat of memory.

When you have studied this chapter you should be able to do the following:

- Calculate the amount of loss that may be carried forward under S385 ICTA 1988 against future trading profits and deal with its set off
- Ascertain the charges on income that may be carried forward with a S385 loss
- Calculate the amount of loss for the purposes of relief against total income under S380 ICTA 1988
- Set the S380 relief off correctly against the taxpayer's statutory total income
- Judge when a claim may be made to set off trading losses against net chargeable gains for the year
- Calculate the relief due under S381 ICTA 1988 and set it off correctly against the total income of the three preceding tax years.
- Calculate the relief for losses in closing years under S388 ICTA 1988.

1 THE RELIEFS AVAILABLE

1.1 Introduction

The reliefs available for a trading loss, as explained in the following sections, are as follows:

(a)   S385 ICTA 1988 carry forward against future trading profits;
(b)   S380 ICTA 1988 relief against STI;
(c)   S381 ICTA 1988 opening year loss relief against STI;
(d)   S388 ICTA 1988 terminal loss relief against previous trading profits.

Remember that capital allowances will be deducted as an expense in calculating the tax adjusted loss. Separate loss claims are therefore not possible for capital allowances, although capital allowances may turn a profit into a loss.

2 LOSS RELIEF BY CARRY FORWARD: S385 ICTA 1988

2.1 Principles of the relief

(a)   This is the most straightforward of the loss reliefs. A trading loss may be carried forward and set against the **first** taxable profits arising in the **same** trade. If the subsequent profits are not high enough to use all the loss then so much of the loss is used so as to reduce the profits to nil, with the remainder being carried forward again until further profits arise, and so on.

(b)   The loss itself may be carried forward indefinitely (until such time as there are profits against which to set it off) but a claim must be made to establish the amount of the loss to be carried forward within five years of 31 January following the end of the tax year in which the loss arose. Once the claim has been established the loss will be used automatically against the future trading profits without the need for a further claim.

(c)   When dealing with set off of losses it is useful to adopt a columnar layout, presenting each year in a separate column. Keep a separate working to show when, and how much, of the loss has been used up.

2.2   Activity

Edward, has had the following recent tax adjusted results:

Year to 31 December 1997	Loss	£5,000
Year to 31 December 1998	Profit	£3,000
Year to 31 December 1999	Profit	£10,000

Assuming that Edward wishes to claim loss relief only under S385 ICTA 1988, calculate his assessable amounts for 1997/98 to 1999/00 inclusive.

2.3   Activity solution

	1997/98 £	*1998/99* £	*1999/00* £
Schedule D Case I	nil	3,000	10,000
Less: S385 relief	nil	3,000	2,000
Net Schedule D Case I amounts	nil	nil	8,000

Working - loss memorandum

	£
Trading loss	5,000
Less: S385 relief in 1998/99	3,000
	2,000
Less: S385 relief in 1999/00	2,000
Loss carried forward to 2000/01	nil

Note: The loss is set off against the first profits to arise, to the maximum extent possible. Thus £3,000 of the loss is set off in 1998/99 and the remainder carried forward to 1999/00, where it is set off against more substantial profits.

3   TRADE CHARGES: S387 ICTA 1988

3.1   Introduction

(a)   Charges on income, whether trade charges (such as patent royalties) or non-trade charges (such as charitable covenants) are both deducted from the aggregate of a taxpayer's income rather than from any particular type of income.

(b)   Where aggregate income is low, the charges to be deducted may exceed the available income. For non-trade charges this is simply bad luck for the taxpayer; no relief is obtained for them. But excess **trade** charges are treated as though they were a trading loss and may be carried forward to be relieved against future trading profits in exactly the same way as a trading loss carried forward under S385.

(c)   If the taxpayer had both trade and non-trade charges, the non-trade charges are deducted in priority against any aggregate income to avoid wasting them.

3.2   Activity

Arnold has the following income and expenditure

	1998/99 £	1999/00 £
Schedule D Case I	1,000	21,000
Investment income	3,000	3,000
Charitable covenant	5,000	5,000
Patent royalty	6,000	6,000

What is Arnold's statutory total income for each year?

3.3   Activity solution

	1998/99 £	1999/00 £
Schedule D Case I	1,000	21,000
Less: 'Loss' (trade charge brought forward)		6,000
	1,000	15,000
Investment income	3,000	3,000
	4,000	18,000
Less: Non-trade charges	4,000 *	5,000
	-	13,000
Trade charges		6,000
Statutory total income	nil	7,000

* there is sufficient income to deduct only £4,000 of non-trade charges.   Relief for the remaining £1,000 is lost. The trade charges not deducted in 1998/99 are carried forward in the same way as a s 385 loss (and so are deducted in 1999/00).

4   RELIEF AGAINST TOTAL INCOME: S380 ICTA 1988

4.1   Introduction

In a prolonged difficult period for a business relief under S385 may take a long time to materialise. Consequently there is another potential option made available to taxpayers; they may relieve trading losses against the statutory total income of the tax year of the loss and/or the previous one. This claim is made under S380 ICTA 1988.

4.2   Calculating the loss

The loss is calculated on an accounting period basis (ie, in the same way as profits). A loss for the year ended 31 December 1999 is relieved against STI of 1999/00 and/or 1998/99.

4.3   Example

Graham makes up his accounts to 31 December annually. His recent tax adjusted results are as follows:

Year to 31 December 1998	Profit	£10,000
Year to 31 December 1999	Loss	£6,000
Year to 31 December 2000	Profit	£12,000

What loss relief is available under s.380?

4.4   Solution

The loss is £6,000 for the tax year 1999/00 (in which Graham's loss-making period of account ended). This is available under s.380 against STI of 1999/00 and/or 1998/99.

4.5   Obtaining relief for the loss

(a)   As shown above, the loss may be set off against the taxpayer's statutory total income of the year of the loss. If that relief is chosen the taxpayer cannot decide to set only part of his loss against total income; it must be set off to the maximum possible extent. Remember that statutory total income comprises income from all sources less charges on income. However, personal allowances are deducted after any loss relief and so a claim under S380 may involve wasting them.

(b)   The loss could instead be carried back against the STI of the previous year whether or not the trade was being carried on in that previous year. A claim under S380 may be made for either the tax year of the loss or the previous year or both. The two years are treated separately and thus a claim is required for each year. A written claim must be made within one year of 31 January following the end of the tax year of loss.

(c)   A taxpayer may have losses for two consecutive tax years and wish to relieve both under S380. In these circumstances statutory total income of a year is relieved by the loss of that year in priority to the loss carried back from the following year.

4.6   Activity

Adrian makes up accounts annually to 31 December. His recent results have been:

Year ended 31 December 1998	Profit	£34,000
Year ended 31 December 1999	Loss	£48,000
Year ended 31 December 2000	Profit	£60,000

For 1998/99 Adrian has other income of £5,000 and charges on income of £2,800. In 1999/00 the figures are £6,000 and £2,500 respectively.

Show how relief for the loss would be given under S380 ICTA 1988, assuming that Adrian makes all claims to the extent that they are beneficial. What loss, if any, is available for carry forward against trading profits after all S380 claims have been made?

4.7   Activity solution

The loss is incurred in 1999/00. Thus S380 claims may apply for 1999/00 and 1998/99.

	1999/00 £
Schedule D Case I (y/e 31 December 1999)	nil
Non-trading income	6,000
	6,000
Less: Charges on income	2,500
STI	3,500
Less: S380 relief - ignore as STI covered by PA	-
	3,500
Less: PA	3,500 (max)
Taxable income	nil

	1998/99
	£
Schedule D Case I (y/e 31 December 1998)	34,000
Non-trading income	5,000
	39,000
Less: Charges on income	2,800
STI	36,200
Less: S380 relief (W)	36,200
Taxable income	nil

Losses of £11,800 (W) remain unrelieved after a claim for 1998/99 has been made under S380 and they are thus available for carry forward under S385.

Working - loss memorandum

	£
1999/00 - loss of y/e 31.12.99	48,000
Less: Used in 1998/99	36,200
Available for carry forward against future trading profits	11,800

Note: by making a claim for only 1998/99 under S380 Adrian obtained relief for his loss as rapidly as possible, without needlessly wasting his personal allowances for those years. In this way he has maximised the amount of loss to carry forward to use against future trading profit. The best course of action would depend on the personal circumstances of each case but as a general principle there is clearly no point in claiming S380 where personal allowances already cover all or most of the STI (as here in 1999/00).

4.8   S380 relief in opening years

(a)   In the first year of trade, the assessable profit (or loss) period starts on the day trade commences and finishes on 5 April following. Unless the trader prepares his accounts to 5 April, this will require the profit (or losses) of a period straddling 5 April to be apportioned.

(b)   A loss may only be relieved once. If, in the opening years, a loss has been relieved, it is treated as nil when calculating the next assessment.

4.9   Activity

Geraldine starts trading on 1 August 1998. Her results, as adjusted for tax purposes, are:

		£
10 months to 31 May 1999	Loss	(20,000)
Year ended 31 May 2000	Profit	48,000

Calculate Geraldine's Schedule D Case I assessable amounts for 1998/99 and 1999/00 on the assumption that she claims relief under S380 against STI of £30,000 of 1998/99.

4.10 Activity solution

Schedule D Case I assessable amounts

	£
1998/99 (actual basis)	
1.8.98 - 5.4.99 8/10 × (20,000) = (£16,000)	Nil
1999/00 (accounts in second fiscal year less than 12 months	
after commencement; therefore first 12 months)	
1.8.98 - 31.7.99	
Loss	(20,000)
Less: Relieved under s.380	16,000
	————
	(4,000)
Profits 2/12 × 48,000	8,000
	————
	4,000
	————

(***Tutorial note:*** When calculating the amount assessable under Schedule D Case I for 1999/00, the loss already relieved under S380 must be deducted.)

4.11 Relief of trading losses against capital gains

(a)   A limited relief is available to permit traders to set off trading losses against chargeable gains, the purpose of which is to put unincorporated businesses on a closer footing to companies.

(b)   The relief works by acting as an extension to S380 relief described above (under rules given in S72 FA 1991). It only becomes available, however, if the statutory total income of the year in question has been reduced to zero by the trading loss under a normal S380 claim and yet the loss is not fully relieved. There is no need to make a S380 claim for the previous year (or any other claim for loss relief) but relief against capital gains is only granted to the extent that the loss remains after being used to relieve income.

(c)   The remaining unrelieved trading loss may be set off as a deemed capital loss against the taxpayer's net chargeable gains for the year; that is after setting off current year capital losses against current year capital gains. It takes precedence over both the CGT annual exemption and any capital losses brought forward. The loss relief is therefore given before the calculation of taper relief.

4.12 Example

Charles, who makes up accounts annually to 31 December, made a trading profit of £3,000 and loss of £14,000 in his periods of account ended 31 December 1999 and 2000 respectively. He has income taxed at source of £4,500 (gross) in 1999/00 and also realised capital gains of £16,000 and capital losses of £5,000 in that tax year.

Calculate the amounts that remain in charge to tax for 1999/00, assuming that Charles claims relief against both income and gains under S380 for that year and no other year.

4.13 Solution

	1999/00
	£
Schedule D Case I (y/e 31.12.99)	3,000
Income taxed at source	4,500
	————
	7,500

Less: s 380 relief against income	7,500
Taxable income	nil
Capital gains	16,000
Less: Capital losses	5,000
Net gains	11,000
Less: S380 relief against chargeable gains (14,000 - 7,500)	6,500
Gains remaining in charge before annual exemption	4,500

5 RELIEF OF TRADING LOSSES IN THE EARLY YEARS OF TRADE

5.1 Introduction

(a) Particular consideration is given to taxpayers who have recently established businesses since they are more likely to incur losses. There are special loss relief rules that apply to the first four tax years of a trade.

(b) The special relief, under S381 ICTA 1988, is available only in these early years of trade. It is important to appreciate, however, that this is only one alternative; the reliefs under S385 and S380 described earlier in this chapter can be used if the taxpayer prefers. Which claim or combination of claims is most appropriate depends on the taxpayer's personal circumstances.

5.2 Relief under S381 ICTA 1988

(a) A trading loss suffered may be set off under S381 against the taxpayer's statutory total income of the three tax years preceding the tax year of the loss. So if a loss is suffered in, say, 1999/00 it may be set off against the total income of 1996/97, 1997/98 and 1998/99. There is no need for the trade to have been carried on in earlier years. Potentially, for example, the relief can be set against income under Schedule E if a taxpayer gave up employment to start a business.

(b) Unlike S380 relief, where separate claims are required for relief in the current year and the previous year, relief under S381 operates automatically for all three years, beginning with the earliest and ending with the latest.

(c) The loss available for S381 relief must be computed in the same way as described for S380 relief ie, in the same way as profits.

(d) Remember that capital allowances are automatically deducted in arriving at the Schedule D Case I profit or loss figure.

(e) The additional relief against chargeable gains is **not** available under S381.

5.3 Example

Caroline started in business as a sheep shearer on 1 July 1998. Her results, as adjusted for tax purposes, for the first two years are as follows:

		£
Year ended 30 June 1999	Loss	(12,000)
Year ended 30 June 2000	Profit	2,500

Before becoming a sheep shearer, Caroline had been employed as a dress maker. Her remuneration from this employment, which ceased on 30 September 1997, for recent years was:

	£
1997/98	5,868
1996/97	11,050
1995/96	9,520

Caroline is single and has other income of £4,500 (gross) pa.

Calculate taxable income for all years:

(a)   after claiming relief under S381 ICTA 1988; and

(b)   after claiming relief under S380 ICTA 1988, instead of claiming under S381 ICTA 1988.

Assume and allowances for 1999/00 apply throughout.

5.4   Solution

(a)   **Taxable income computations**

	1995/96	1996/97	1997/98	1998/99
Schedule E	9,520	11,050	5,868	-
Other income	4,500	4,500	4,500	4,500
	14,020	15,550	10,368	4,500
Less: S381 (W2)	(9,000)	(3,000)	-	-
	5,020	12,550	10,368	4,500
Less: PA	(4,335)	(4,335)	(4,335)	(4,335)
Taxable income	685	8,215	6,033	165

	1999/00	2000/01
Schedule D Case II	-	2,500
Other income	4,500	4,500
	4,500	7,000
Less: PA	(4,335)	(4,335)
Taxable income	165	2,665

*(**Tutorial note:** The loss of 1998/99 is set against STI of 1995/96, then if any loss remained, it would be set against STI of 1996/97 then 1997/98.)*

WORKINGS

(1)   **New business: assessments**

	£
1998/99 1.7.98 - 5.4.99	Nil
1999/00 (y/e 30.6.99)	Nil
2000/01 (CYB: y/e 30.6.2000)	2,500

(2) **Loss**

1998/99 (1.7.98 - 5.4.99)
  (9/12 × 12,000)   9,000

1999/00 (y/e 30.6.99)
  (12,000 – 9,000)   3,000

(b)

	1995/96	1996/97	1997/98	1998/99
Schedule E	9,520	11,050	5,868	-
Other income	4,500	4,500	4,500	4,500
	14,020	15,550	10,368	4,500
S380			(9,000)	(3,000)
Less: PA	(4,335)	(4,335)	(1,368)	(1,500)
Taxable income	9,685	11,215	Nil	Nil

	1999/00	2000/01
Schedule D Case II	-	2,500
Other income	4,500	4,500
	4,500	7,000
Less: PA	(4,335)	(4,335)
Taxable income	165	2,665

Tutorial notes:

(1) The personal allowance is assumed throughout to be £4,335.

(2) Under S380:

(a) the loss for 1998/99 (£9,000) is set against STI of 1998/99 and/or 1997/98;

(b) the loss for 1999/00 (£3,000) is set against STI of 1999/00 and/or 1998/99.

In the example, relief is taken in the earliest year possible.

There is no requirement that the trade be carried on in the earlier year that a S380 claim is made.

6 LOSSES IN CLOSING YEARS : S388 ICTA 1988

6.1 Introduction

(a) Without special provision, the only effective relief for trading losses incurred in the final year of trade would be a current year (or previous year) claim under S380. No claim is possible under S385 (because there will be no trade to generate future profits).

(b) To alleviate this lack of opportunity to relieve final year trading losses there is a special relief provided under S388 ICTA 1988. Broadly, it permits the trading loss and trade charges of the final 12 months of trade that remain unrelieved to be set against the available profits (as defined) for the year of cessation and then carried back and set against the available profit for the three tax years preceding.

(c)   There are two elements in dealing with S388 relief:

- calculating the amount of the 'terminal loss'; and
- calculating the amount of 'available profit' against which the terminal loss may be set off.

6.2   Calculating the terminal loss

(a)   The terminal loss is made up by totalling the following elements:

(i)   trading loss incurred in the final tax year (ie from 6 April to date of cessation);

(ii)   unrelieved business charges of the final tax year;

(iii)   trading loss incurred from 12 months before cessation to the start of the final tax year;

(iv)   a proportion of the business charges of the penultimate tax year.

(b)   In calculating these amounts bear the following in mind.

(i)   Any overlap relief created when the trade commenced is deductible in the final year of assessment thereby increasing any trading loss (or, perhaps, turning a trading profit into a loss) appearing in (i) above.

(ii)   If the calculation of trading losses in either (i) or (iii) above in fact shows a profit, treat it as £nil.

(iii)   The proportion of business charges of the penultimate tax year is calculated at the **lower** of:

- any amount unrelieved; and

- $\dfrac{\text{number of months in (iii) above}}{12} \times \text{total charges for the year}$

(iv)   If any of the losses that might appear in the terminal loss calculation have been relieved by some other means (eg, s 380), they must be excluded.

6.3   Available profit

Definition   The available profit for each year of assessment is the adjusted Schedule D Case I profit less the excess of trading charges over non-trading income (ie, those amounts which would have been carried forward for relief had cessation not intervened). The assessments are also reduced by any loss relief given in those years under S380.

6.4   Activity

Yves ceased trading on 30 June 2000. His final period of trade was the 9 months to 30 June 2000 and beforehand he made up accounts annually to 30 September. His tax-adjusted trading results and charges on income are as follows

Period of account	Trading result	£
9 months to 30.6.2000	Loss	7,200
Year to 30.9.99	Profit	100
Year to 30.9.98	Profit	7,300
Year to 30.9.97	Profit	7,500

Tax Year	Trade charges
	£
2000/01	420
1999/00	560
1998/99	560
1997/98	560

There was overlap relief of £1,800 brought forward.

Calculate the terminal loss claim available to Yves and show how relief may be obtained for it. Yves had no other sources of income.

6.5   Activity solution

		1997/98		1998/99	1999/00	2000/01
		£		£	£	£
Income available (W1)		6,940		6,740	nil	nil
Less: terminal loss relief (W2)	(ii)	3,075	(i)	6,740	nil	nil
		3,865		nil	nil	nil

WORKINGS

(W1)   Income available for terminal loss relief

	1997/98	1998/99	1999/00	2000/01
	£	£	£	£
Schedule D Case I	7,500	7,300	100	-
Less: charges not set against non-trading income	560	560	560	-
Available income	6,940	6,740	nil	nil

(W2)   Calculation of terminal loss

	£	£
Loss in 2000/01 (3/9 × £7,200)		2,400
Overlap relief		1,800
Unrelieved trading charges of 2000/01		420
Loss in 1999/00: 1.7.99 - 5.4.2000		
(6/9 × £7,200) - (3/12 × £100)		4,775
Trade charges of 1999/00.		
Lower of:		
Unrelieved charges (£560 – £100 (W1))	460	
9/12 × total charges (£560)	420	
		420
Terminal loss		9,815

The remaining loss of £25 (£7,200 – 2,400 – 4,775) could be relieved under s.380 had Yves any other sources of income.

7   BUSINESSES TRANSFERRED TO COMPANIES: S386 ICTA 1988

7.1   Overview of the relief

(a)   When a business ceases to trade any accumulated losses are normally lost. If, however, the business is sold to a company controlled by the former proprietor(s) the losses may be carried forward and set against the first available income of the former proprietor(s) from the company. Note that the losses are not set against the company's own profits.

(b)   The relief applies to trading losses at the date of cessation.

(c)   For the relief to apply the consideration for the business given by the company must be wholly or mainly shares in the company. The Revenue normally treat this condition as being fulfilled if at least 80% of the consideration is in the form of shares.

(d)   The losses may be carried forward indefinitely (awaiting sufficient income from the company) provided that:

- the former proprietor retains his shares in the company; and
- the company continues to carry on the former business' trade

(e)   Losses brought forward are set off against earned income (salaries, directors' fees) and then unearned income (interest, dividends).

8   LOSSES ON SHARES IN QUALIFYING TRADING COMPANIES: S574 ICTA 1988

8.1   Introduction

Relief is available where an individual incurs a loss in respect of shares that have been subscribed for in a qualifying trading company.

8.2   The relief available

The loss is calculated using the normal CGT rules (see chapter 15).

A claim may be made to treat the loss as a trading loss which is then set off against the individual's total income for the year of the loss and/or the preceding year.

The claim for a loss incurred in 1999/00 must be made by 31 January 2002.

As for relief under S380, partial claims are not allowed.

A claim under S574 takes priority over claims under S380 or S381.

8.3   Qualifying shares

The shares must be subscribed for, and not purchased.

The company must be unquoted or on the Alternative Investment Market, and must carry on its business wholly or mainly in the UK.

The company must be an eligible trading company. Basically, this means that the company must be a qualifying company for the purposes of relief under the enterprise investment scheme (see Chapter 3). The company must:

- Be an eligible trading company for the six years prior to the disposal, or

- An eligible trading company for a shorter period provided it has never been a non-qualifying company.

9   PLANNING POINTS

(a)   Planning relief for trading losses concerns, broadly, four points:

- ensuring that the taxpayer does not fall foul of the restrictions on certain reliefs;
- obtaining relief as rapidly as possible;
- attempting to ensure that the taxpayer's personal allowances are not wasted; and
- obtaining relief at the highest marginal rate of tax.

(b)   Although the reliefs against statutory total income, S380 and S381, obtain relief more quickly than relief by carry forward under S385, they frequently involve loss of personal allowances. Care must be taken, however, to review the trend of likely future profits. There is no point in choosing the S385 route for a large loss that will eliminate several years modest trading profits if there is no non-trading income in those future years to obtain relief for personal allowances. All that will have happened is that future personal allowances rather than current ones will have been wasted.

(c)   The taxpayer can choose whether to claim relief first under S380 against total income of the tax year of the loss or alternatively of the preceding one; the legislation does not dictate that either takes priority. Depending on both the size of previous profits and non-trading income, a previous year claim often results in a larger claim. So, if the loss is small enough to be wholly absorbed by the Schedule D Case I assessment a previous year claim is probably the right choice.

(d)   If neither a current nor a previous year claim under S380 appears appropriate (on the grounds of wasting personal allowances), look further afield. Where the taxpayer has made a large chargeable gain a claim under s 72 FA 1991 may be suitable. Since the claim can only be made once total income for the year is reduced to zero, it will undoubtedly involve wasting personal allowances of at least one year. However, consider the following illustration.

C has profits of £15,000 for the year to 31 December 1998 and a loss of £20,000 for the year to 31 December 1999. In 1999/00 he makes net chargeable gains of £38,000. He has no non-trading income.

Option 1 is to obtain relief as quickly as possible; a S380 claim for the previous year:

	1998/99
	£
Schedule D Case I (y/e 31.12.98)	15,000
Less: S380 relief	15,000
	———
Taxable income	nil
	———

C has £5,000 losses left to carry forward and his 1998/99 personal allowances have been wasted.

Option 2 is to claim relief under s 72 FA 1991 (as an extension to S380) for 1999/00. C has no income in 1999/00 and so, irrespective of the choice he makes, the 1999/00 personal allowances will be wasted. He can make a S72 claim:

	£
Net chargeable gains	38,000
Less: S72 relief	20,000
	———
Chargeable gains before annual exemption	18,000
	———

C has not wasted personal allowances by his choice (they were wasted anyway). He has saved himself some tax at 40% (less any reduction as a result of losing taper relief on £20,000 of gain) on the chargeable gains at the expense of having to pay basic and lower rate tax on the 1998/99 Schedule D Case I profits (as reduced by his personal allowances). As an added bonus, the gains relieved do not even have to arise on the disposal of business assets; he might have had a Stock Exchange windfall!

10 SELF TEST QUESTIONS

10.1 Is it possible to deal with capital allowances separately from a trading loss? (1.1)

10.2 By what time must a claim be made to establish the amount of loss that may be carried forward under S385 ICTA 1988? (2.1)

10.3 How are trade charges given relief under S387 ICTA 1988? (3.1)

10.4 If a taxpayer has claimed loss relief against total income of the same tax year is there any restriction on his claiming relief against total income of the previous year? (4.1)

10.5 What is the time limit for a claim under S380 ICTA 1988? (4.5)

10.6 How are losses calculated in the first year of trade for the purposes of S380 ICTA 1988? (4.8)

10.7 In what circumstances may a trading loss be relieved against chargeable gains? (4.11)

10.8 For which tax years may a S381 ICTA 1988 claim be made? (5.1)

10.9 Does the taxpayer need to make separate claims for each of the three tax years that may be relieved under a S381 ICTA 1988 claim? (5.2)

10.10 Which years can be relieved by a s.388 ICTA 1988 claim. (6.1)

11 EXAMINATION TYPE QUESTION

11.1 Sigmund

Sigmund, a single man, began trading on 1 January 1999. He prepares accounts to 31 December annually, with results as follows.

	Schedule D Case I £
Year ended 31 December 1999 Loss	(12,000)
Year ended 31 December 2000 Loss (estimated)	(4,000)
Year ended 31 December 2001 Profit (estimated)	8,000
Year ended 31 December 2002 Profit (estimated)	11,500

Details of the amounts of other income and payments for the years 1995/96 to 1998/99 were as follows

	Salary from employment £	Dividends received (incl tax credit) £	Gross loan interest paid £
1995/96	9,000	3,000	2,800
1996/97	13,000	3,400	2,600
1997/98	8,800	3,800	2,500
1998/99	3,300	700	2,600

From 1 January 1999 the business is Sigmund's only source of income. The gross loan interest paid is eligible loan interest which qualifies to be treated as a charge on income. Gross interest paid after 1998/99 can be taken at £2,300 a year.

Sigmund wishes to obtain relief for his initial trading losses as soon as possible.

You are required:

(a)   to calculate the Schedule D Case I assessments for 1998/99 to 2002/03 before giving relief for any losses under S380 or S381 ICTA 1988.

(b)   to show how the losses incurred in the first two years of trading are to be relieved so as to provide earliest relief.

12   ANSWER TO EXAMINATION TYPE QUESTION

12.1   Sigmund

(a)   **Schedule D Case I assessments**

	Case I assessments £	Trading loss £
1998/99 (1.1.99 - 5.4.99)	Nil	3,000
3/12 × £(12,000) (loss)		
1999/00 (1.1.99 - 31.12.99)	Nil	9,000
(12,000 – 3,000)		
2000/01	Nil	
y/e 31.12.2000 (loss)		4,000
		16,000
2001/02		
y/e 31.12.2001	8,000	
Less: S385 relief	(8,000)	(8,000)
	Nil	
2002/03		
ye 31.12.2002	11,500	
Less: S385 relief	(8,000)	(8,000)
	3,500	
Loss to c/d under S385		Nil

(b)   **Utilisation of losses**

1998/99 loss of £3,000.

This can be claimed under S380 for 1998/99 and/or 1997/98, or under S381 for 1995/96, 1996/97, 1997/98 in that order.

A claim under S381 which would be fully utilised in 1995/96 appears to be the most beneficial.

1999/00 loss of £9,000.

This can be claimed under S380 for 1999/00 and/or 1998/99, or under S381 for 1996/97, 1997/98, 1998/99 in that order.

A claim under S381 which would be fully utilised in 1996/97 appears to be the most beneficial.

2000/01 loss of £4,000.

This can be claimed under S380 for 2000/01 and/or 1999/00, or under S381 for 1997/98, 1998/99, 1999/00 in that order.

A claim under S381 which would be fully utilised in 1997/98 appears to be the most beneficial.

The revised statutory total income for 1995/96 to 1997/98 will be as follows:

	£	*Losses* £
1995/96		
Loss sustained in 1998/99		3,000
Salary	9,000	
Dividends (gross)	3,000	
	12,000	
Less: Loan interest	2,800	
	9,200	
Less: S381 relief	(3,000)	(3,000)
Revised STI, (PA preserved)	6,200	Nil
Loss sustained in 1999/00		9,000
1996/97		
Salary	13,000	
Dividends (gross)	3,400	
	16,400	
Less: Loan interest	2,600	
	13,800	
Less: S381 relief	(9,000)	(9,000)
Revised STI (PA preserved)	4,800	Nil
Loss sustained in 2000/01		4,000
1997/98		
Salary	8,800	
Add: Dividends (gross)	3,800	
	12,600	
Less: Loan interest	2,500	
	10,100	
Less: S381 relief	(4,000)	(4,000)
Revised STI (PA preserved)	6,100	Nil

13 PARTNERSHIPS

INTRODUCTION

A partnership is a body of persons carrying on business together with a view to profit (Partnership Act 1890).

Although a partnership is a single trading entity, for tax purposes each individual partner is effectively treated as trading in their own right.

1 THE ALLOCATION OF PROFITS AND LOSSES

1.1 The computation of partnership profits and losses

(a) The principles of computation of a partnership's tax adjusted profit or loss are the same as those for a sole trader.

(b) Partners' salaries and interest on capital are not deductible, since these are an allocation of profit.

1.2 The allocation of the profit or loss

(a) The tax adjusted profit or loss is allocated between the partners according to their profit sharing arrangements for that period of account.

(b) Partners may be entitled to salaries (a fixed allocation of profit) and interest on capital. The balance will be allocated in the profit sharing ratio.

(c) A partnership may have non-trading income such as a Schedule A profit or bank interest.

Such income will be allocated between the partners according to the profit sharing ratio.

(d) A partnership may pay annual charges, such as an annuity to a retired partner.

These are also allocated between the partners according to the profit sharing ratio.

1.3 A change in the profit sharing ratio

If a partnership changes its basis of profit sharing during a period of account, then the profit or loss will need to be time apportioned accordingly prior to allocation.

1.4 Example

David and Peter are in partnership Their tax adjusted profit for the year ended 30 September 1999 was £16,500.

Up to 30 June 1999 profits were shared between David and Peter 3:2, after paying salaries of £3,000 and £2,000.

From 1 July 1999 profits were shared 2:1 after paying salaries of £6,000 and £4,000.

Show the allocation of profits for 1999/00.

1.5   Solution

The 1999/00 partnership profits will be allocated as follows:

	Total £	David £	Peter £
1.10.98 to 30.6.99			
(profits £16,500 × 9/12 = £12,375)			
Salaries (9/12)	3,750	2,250	1,500
Balance (3:2)	8,625	5,175	3,450
	12,375	7,425	4,950
1.7.99 to 30.9.99			
(profits £16,500 × 3/12 = £4,125)			
Salaries (3/12)	2,500	1,500	1,000
Balance (2:1)	1,625	1,083	542
	4,125	2,583	1,542
Total allocation	16,500	10,008	6,492

1.6   Partnership capital allowances

(a)   Capital allowances are deducted as an expense in calculating the tax adjusted profit or loss.

The profit allocated between the partners is therefore after capital allowances.

(b)   Individual partners cannot claim capital allowances on their own behalf.

If assets are owned privately (such as motor cars), then the business proportion of such assets must be included in the partnerships capital allowances computation. The total capital allowances are then deducted as an expense.

2   COMMENCEMENT AND CESSATION

2.1   Introduction

(a)   The normal commencement and cessation rules apply upon the commencement and the cessation of a partnership.

(b)   The rules are applied after the allocation of the profit or loss between the partners.

(c)   Each partner is therefore effectively taxed as a sole trader in respect of their share of profit or loss.

A partner will be treated as commencing when he or she joins the partnership (which will be upon the commencement of the partnership for the original partners), and will be treated as ceasing when he or she leaves the partnership (or the partnership ceases).

(d)   Each partner may therefore have his or her own overlap relief.

2.2   A change in the membership

(a)   The membership of a partnership may change as the result of the admission, death or retirement of a partner.

(b)   Provided that there is at least one partner common to the business before and after the change, the partnership will automatically continue.

(c) However, the commencement and cessation rules will apply to the individual partner who is joining or leaving the partnership.

2.3 Example

Able and Bertie have been in partnership since 1 July 1997 making up their accounts to 30 June each year. On 1 July 1999 Carol joins the partnership.

The partnership's tax adjusted profits are as follows:

	£
Year ended 30 June 1998	10,000
Year ended 30 June 1999	13,500
Year ended 30 June 2000	18,000

Profits are shared equally.

Show the amounts assessed on the individual partners for 1997/98 to 2000/01.

2.4 Solution

Profits will be allocated between the partners as follows:

	Total £	Able £	Bertie £	Carol £
y/e 30.6.98	10,000	5,000	5,000	–
y/e 30.6.99	13,500	6,750	6,750	–
y/e 30.6.2000	18,000	6,000	6,000	6,000

Able and Bertie will both be assessed as follows, based upon a commencement on 1 July 1997:

		£
1997/98	1 July 1997 to 5 April 1998 £5,000 × 9/12	3,750
1998/99	Year ended 30 June 1998	5,000
1999/00	Year ended 30 June 1999	6,750
2000/01	Year ended 30 June 2000	6,000

They will both be entitled to overlap relief of £3,750.

Carol will be treated as commencing on 1 July 1999, and will be assessed on her share of the partnership profits as follows:

		£
1999/00	1 July 1999 to 5 April 2000 £6,000 × 9/12	4,500
2000/01	Year ended 30 June 2000	6,000

She will be entitled to overlap relief of £4,500.

2.5 Sole traders

If a sole trader takes someone into partnership, the commencement rules will apply to the new partner, whereas the sole trader will be treated as continuing.

Similarly, when a business goes from partnership to sole trader, the sole trader will be treated as continuing, while the other partner(s) will have a cessation.

3   PARTNERSHIP LOSSES

3.1   Notional losses

(a)   Loss relief is only available if the partnership as a whole makes a loss.

(b)   The basis of allocating profits between partners may result in one partner showing a loss, and yet the partnership as a whole has made a profit.

(c)   The loss is only notional, and is reallocated to the other partners according to the amount of profits each partner was originally allocated.

3.2   Example

Maud, Nigel and Olive are in partnership. Their adjusted profit for the year ended 30 April 1999 is £1,200. They share profits equally after salaries of Maud £4,200, Nigel £3,000 and Olive £1,800.

Show the allocation of profits between the partners for 1999/00

3.3   Solution

	Total £	Maud £	Nigel £	Olive £
Salaries	9,000	4,200	3,000	1,800
Share of balance (1/3 Each)	(7,800)	(2,600)	(2,600)	(2,600)
	1,200	1,600	400	(800)
Olive's loss is reallocated to Maud and Nigel 1,600:400		(640)	(160)	800
	1,200	960	240	–

3.4   The allocation of trading losses

Losses are allocated between partners in exactly the same way as profits.

3.5   Loss relief claims available

(a)   The loss relief claims available to partners are the same as those for sole traders.

(b)   A partner joining a partnership may be entitled to claim under S381 ICTA 1988 where a loss is incurred in the first four years of his membership of the partnership.

This relief would not be available to the existing partners.

(c)   A partner leaving the partnership may be entitled to claim for a terminal loss under S388 ICTA 1988.

Again, this relief will not be available to the partners remaining in the partnership.

3.6   Example

Peter, Paul and Mary are in partnership making up their accounts to 5 April. During 1999/00 Paul left the partnership and Maggie joined in his place.

For the year ended 5 April 2000 the partnership made an adjusted loss of £20,000.

State the loss relief claims that will be available to the partners.

3.7   Solution

Paul will be entitled to terminal loss relief under S388 ICTA 1988 since he has actually ceased trading.

Maggie will be entitled to claim opening years relief under S381 ICTA 1988 since she has actually commenced trading.

Peter and Mary will not be entitled to either of the above reliefs.

All the partners will be entitled to relief under S380 ICTA 1988.

All the partners except Paul will be entitled to relief under S385 ICTA 1988.

4   PARTNERSHIP CAPITAL GAINS

4.1   Each partner is assessed separately on his or her share of the partnership's capital gains.

You may prefer to come back to this section after studying the chapters on capital gains.

4.2   A disposal by the partnership

(a)   Capital gains are normally allocated according to the profit sharing ratio unless a different basis has been agreed.

(b)   Strictly, the proceeds and cost of the asset should be allocated between the partners so that each partner has his or her own separate capital gains computation.

It is usually acceptable, however, to calculate the gain and then allocate this one figure between the partners.

4.3   Example

Jim, James and June are in partnership. During 1999 they disposed of a freehold building and made a chargeable gain of £60,000.

The partners share profits 40:35:25.

Allocate the gain between the partners.

4.4   Solution

The gain will be allocated:

	£
Jim (40%)	24,000
James (35%)	21,000
June (25%)	15,000

4.5   Reliefs

(a)   Each partner will be entitled to their own annual exemption of £7,100 to use against their gains on partnership and other assets.

(b)   Each partner will qualify for retirement relief individually. A partner under 50 will not qualify as a result of all the other partners being over 50.

(c)   Rollover relief will be available to each partner as they choose. Thus some partners may claim to rollover their share of a gain against their share of a replacement asset whilst others may not.

(d)   The same principle will apply to any other reliefs that are available, such as holdover relief in respect of the gift of business assets and taper relief.

4.6 A change in the profit sharing ratio

(a) Partners in relation to the acquisition and disposal of partnership assets pursuant to bona fide commercial arrangements, are generally not classed as connected persons.

(b) This means that where there is a disposal between partners, the market value of the asset will not be used as the disposal price. The disposal price will instead be the value of that asset as shown in the partnership balance sheet.

(c) A change in the partners profit sharing ratio does not by itself give rise to a charge to CGT, even though this will result in some partners having a reduced share (a disposal) of the partnership assets.

(d) However, a revaluation of assets on the partnership balance sheet followed by a change in the partners profit sharing ratio will result in a charge to CGT.

The disposal price for partners who reduce their share of partnership assets will be the value in the balance sheet.

4.7 Example

Adam and Barry are in partnership. In December 1998 they decided to include the value of the partnership goodwill in their balance sheet at a value of £100,000.

The partners have always allocated profits and losses equally, but decided to change this in December 1999 to Adam 70% and Barry 30%.

Calculate the chargeable gains that will be assessed on the partners.

4.8 Solution

The inclusion of goodwill in the balance sheet in December 1998 does not give rise to a chargeable gain.

The subsequent change in profit sharing in December 1999 will result in a chargeable gain based on the value of goodwill reflected in the balance sheet of £100,000.

Barry' share of goodwill is reduced from 50% to 30% and so he will be treated as making a disposal of 20%, as follows:

		£
Share of goodwill before change in profit sharing	$100,000 \times 50\% =$	50,000
Share of goodwill after change in profit sharing	$100,000 \times 30\% =$	30,000
Deemed proceeds		20,000

Since the goodwill has no cost, he will be treated as making a chargeable gain of £20,000 for 1999/00.

Goodwill is a business asset, and so Barry will be entitled to taper relief based on two years of ownership. This will reduce the chargeable gain to £17,000 ($20,000 \times 85\%$).

Adam's share of the goodwill is increased from 50% to 70% and he therefore does not have a capital gain He will now have a base cost for goodwill equivalent to Barry's deemed proceeds of £20,000. For taper relief purposes on a subsequent disposal Adam will be treated as owning his current share of goodwill from the date he first acquired **any** interest in the goodwill.

4.9 A change in the membership

(a) The CGT rules relating to a change in the members of a partnership are exactly the same as for a change in the partners profit sharing ratio.

(b) The admission or retirement of a partner will only result in a charge to CGT if the partnership has previously revalued assets on the balance sheet.

(c) Where partnership assets have not been revalued, an incoming partner will simply take over a share of the cost of the partnership assets.

4.10 Example

Cathy and Des are in partnership, and allocate profits equally.

In June 1997 they admitted Eve as a partner. Profits were still allocated equally.

At the date that Eve was admitted to the partnership, goodwill was valued at £120,000, but this was not revalued in the partnership balance sheet neither did it have a CGT base cost.

The partners decided to cease trading in May 1999 and sold the goodwill for £150,000.

Show the chargeable gains that will be assessed on the partners.

4.11 Solution

On Eve's admission to the partnership there was no charge to CGT since goodwill was not revalued in the partnership balance sheet.

The cessation in May 1999 is a straightforward disposal of a partnership asset resulting in a chargeable gain of £150,000 This will be shared equally between the partners (£50,000 each), and will be assessed in 1999/00. Taper relief based on two years of ownership will be given.

5 SELF TEST QUESTIONS

5.1 How are profits allocated between partners? (1.2)

5.2 How are annual charges allocated between partners? (1.2)

5.3 How are capital allowances given for assets owned privately by partners? (1.6)

5.4 When will the commencement rules apply to a partner? (2.1)

5.5 When will a partnership automatically continue when there is a change in the membership? (2.2)

5.6 How is a notional loss reallocated? (3.1)

5.7 What loss relief claims are available to partners? (3.5)

5.8 How are a partnership's capital gains assessed? (4.1)

5.9 When will a partner qualify for retirement relief? (4.5)

5.10 When will the change in the profit sharing ratio result in a charge to CGT? (4.6)

6 EXAMINATION TYPE QUESTION

6.1 Alf and Bob

Alf aged 56 and Bob aged 57 have been in partnership together since 1 December 1994.

The partners sold their business on 30 November 1999 for its market value of £520,000.
The partnership assets at 30 November 1999, and the chargeable gains (after indexation) arising on the disposal), were as follows:

	Market Value £	Chargeable Gain £
Freehold property	322,000	133,000
Goodwill	100,000	100,000
Plant and machinery	58,000	–
Net current assets	40,000	–
	520,000	233,000

The Schedule D Case I amounts for the final four years before dividing between the partners are as follows:

	Profit/(Loss) £
1996/97	15,000
1997/98	14,000
1998/99	11,200
1999/00	(33,500)

Profits and losses have always been shared 40% to Alf and 60% to Bob.

Alf is single and had no other income or outgoings.

Bob is single and also has no other income or outgoings apart from bank interest of £1,250 (gross) received on 1 December 1999.

Assume the 1999/00 rates and allowances apply to all years. Ignore overlap relief.

You are required to:

(a)   Calculate the chargeable gains that will be assessed on Alf and Bob for 1999/00.

(b)   (i)   Advise the partners of the possible ways of relieving the partnership loss for 1999/00.

(ii)   Advise the partners as to which loss relief claims would be the most beneficial.

(iii)   After taking into account the advice in (ii), calculate the partners' taxable income for 1996/97 to 1999/00, and their net chargeable gains for 1999/00.

7   ANSWER TO EXAMINATION TYPE QUESTION

7.1   Alf and Bob

(a)   The capital gains of £233,000 arising on the disposal of the business will be split between the partners in their profit sharing ratios as follows:

	£
Alf – 40%	93,200
Bob – 60%	139,800

Both partners are over 50 and will therefore qualify for retirement relief, with the relevant qualifying period being 5 years.

Alf's chargeable gains of £93,200 are fully covered by retirement relief (£200,000 × 50% = £100,000).

Bob's chargeable gains for 1999/00 are as follows:

	£	£
Share of capital gains		139,800
Retirement relief		
200,000 × 50%	100,000	
(139,800 − 100,000) × 50%	19,900	
		119,900
Chargeable gains		19,900

(b)   There are two possible ways that the partnership loss can be relieved.

(i)   A claim can be made under S380 ICTA 1988 against total income for 1999/00 and/or 1998/99.

Subject to this claim being made, it would then be possible to extend the claim under S72 FA 1991 against chargeable gains of the same year.

(ii)   Terminal loss relief can be claimed under S388 ICTA 1988.

The final Schedule D Case I assessments will be split between the partners as follows:

	Alf *40%* £	*Bob* *60%* £
1996/97	6,000	9,000
1997/98	5,600	8,400
1998/99	4,480	6,720
1999/00	(13,400)	(20,100)

The most beneficial loss relief claim available to Alf would appear to be a terminal loss claim under S388 ICTA 1988.

Bob could also make a terminal loss claim, but this would waste his personal allowances for several years. He would be advised to make a claim under S380 ICTA 1988 against his statutory total income of £1,250 for 1999/00, and then claim under S72 FA 1991 against his chargeable gains of £19,900 for 1999/00.

Alf - taxable income:

	1996/97 £	*1997/98* £	*1998/99* £	*1999/00* £
Schedule D Case I	6,000	5,600	4,480	–
Terminal loss	(3,320)	(5,600)	(4,480)	–
	2,680	–	–	–
PA	(2,680)	–	–	–
Taxable income	–	–	–	–

Bob - taxable income:

	1996/97 £	1997/98 £	1998/99 £	1999/00 £
Schedule D Case I	9,000	8,400	6,720	–
Bank interest	–	–	–	1,250
	9,000	8,400	6,720	1,250
Loss claim S380 ICTA 1988				(1,250)
PA	(4,335)	(4,335)	(4,335)	–
Taxable income	4,665	4,065	2,385	–
Chargeable gains				19,900
Loss claim S72 FA 1991 (20,100-1,250)				18,850
				1,050
Taper relief × 85%				892
Annual exemption				892
				-

14 OVERVIEW OF CAPITAL GAINS TAX

INTRODUCTION & LEARNING OBJECTIVES

When capital assets are sold at a profit, the profit is taxed; if the disposer is an individual, the profit will be charged to capital gains tax, if a company, to corporation tax. These chapters are concerned with explaining how the profit (the gain) is calculated, and the reliefs that are available.

When you have studied this chapter you should have learned the following:

- The scope of capital gains tax.
- In what circumstances a person is a chargeable person.
- The principal categories of exempt persons.
- Which assets are chargeable, and which exempt.
- The scope of the term 'disposal'.
- The position of companies with respect to capital gains.
- How loss relief is given and its interaction with the annual exemption.
- How assets are valued.
- The scope and significance of the term 'connected persons'.
- Rates of capital gains tax and when tax may be paid in instalments.

1 SCOPE OF CAPITAL GAINS TAX

1.1 Introduction

(a) Although it needs some elaboration, the scope of capital gains tax can be stated briefly. Capital gains tax is charged on gains arising on chargeable disposals of chargeable assets by chargeable persons. Such gains are not taxed individually, however. They are aggregated for each tax year.

(b) The taxpayer's capital transactions for the tax year are entered in a computation, as follows.

Proforma CGT computation - Mr Brown - 1999/00

	£
Total 1999/00 chargeable gains	20,000
Less: Total 1999/00 allowable losses	4,000
	16,000
Less: Allowable losses brought forward at 6 April 1999	5,000
	11,000
Less: Annual exempt amount for 1999/00	7,100
Taxable gains for 1999/00	3,900

(c) Loss relief for capital gains tax and the annual exempt amount are considered later in this chapter.

1.2 Chargeable and exempt persons

Only a chargeable person can be subject to capital gains tax, and liability will extend to the disposal of assets situated anywhere in the world.

The following may be chargeable persons:

- individuals
- companies
- trustees.

1.3   Chargeable and exempt assets

(a)   All forms of property are chargeable assets unless exempted. The list of exempt assets is therefore long, but the main ones are set out below.

- foreign currency for personal expenditure.

- motor vehicles including veteran and vintage cars (except those unsuitable for private use)

- decorations for valour (unless acquired by purchase)

- some chattels (dealt with later in the text)

- gilt edged securities and qualifying corporate bonds

- debts (other than debts on a security)

- principal private residences (see chapter 16)

- investments held in an individual savings account

- pension and annuity rights

- National Savings certificates.

- Prizes and betting winnings.

(b)   Exempt assets are outside the scope of capital gains tax. Consequently, whilst gains are not taxable, losses are not allowable either.

1.4   Chargeable disposal

(a)   An asset may be regarded as disposed of when its ownership changes. Consequently the following are 'disposals';

- sales of assets
- gifts of assets

(b)   However, legislation and case law takes the meaning of 'disposal' further than might be thought from its everyday use. In particular, the following are also regarded as 'disposals' for capital gains tax purposes:

- sale of part of an asset (such as a half share in a painting)
- receipt of a capital sum derived from an asset
- loss or total destruction of assets.

Remember that capital gains tax can only be charged if there is a chargeable disposal of a chargeable asset by a chargeable person. All three elements must be present and even then there may be a relief from tax.

1.5   Exempt disposals

Transfers of assets on death are exempt disposals, so no capital gain or allowable loss can arise. The beneficiaries inherit the assets with a base cost equivalent to the market value at the date of death.

Gifts to charities and national heritage bodies are also exempt disposals.

1.6   Annual exempt amount

Every individual is entitled to an exempt amount for each tax year. For 1999/00 it is £7,100. If his gains for the year do not exceed that amount, he is not chargeable to tax. Otherwise, he is chargeable on gains over and above the exempt amount.

1.7   Taper relief

Where an individual disposes of a chargeable asset after 5 April 1998, the amount of gain chargeable may be reduced by a taper relief. The amount of taper relief depends on how long the asset has been owned after 5 April 1998, and in many cases will not be available for disposals made before 6 April 2000.

Taper relief will be looked at in detail in the next chapter.

1.8   Companies

The gains and losses of a company are broadly computed in the same way as for individuals. However, they are not subject to capital gains tax as such, but rather suffer corporation tax on their chargeable gains. The tax year is not the basis period for companies; their gains form part of their profits chargeable to corporation tax for the accounting period in which they arise.

From 6 April 1998 there are some important differences between the way in which capital gains tax is charged on individuals and on companies. In particular, companies cannot benefit from taper relief. These differences will be looked at in the corporation tax chapters.

Companies receive no annual exempt amount, and are thus taxable on chargeable gains in full.

2   LOSSES

2.1   Introduction

(a)   Losses and gains are calculated in the same way, as set out in the next chapter.

(b)   Where allowable losses arise they are set off against chargeable gains arising in the same tax year (or accounting period for companies).

(c)   Set off against gains is made to the maximum possible extent. There is no possibility of restricting the set off to avoid wasting all or part of the annual exemption. For example, if in 1999/00, Bill has chargeable gains of £14,000 and allowable losses of £9,000, his net chargeable gains are £5,000. This is covered entirely by his annual exemption of £7,100. Bill does **not** have the option of deducting only £6,900 of losses so that his net gains are £7,100 (which would be covered exactly by the annual exemption).

(d)   Where a taxpayer cannot set off allowable losses against gains in the tax year they arise (because the gains are insufficient), he is entitled to carry the loss forward.

(e)   Losses brought forward are deducted only if the taxpayer has net chargeable gains for the tax year (or accounting period for companies). Current year losses are deducted in priority. For individuals, losses brought forward reduce net chargeable gains only to the level of the annual exemption for the year. Any additional losses brought forward are carried forward again to the next year. Since companies have no annual exemption this point does not apply to them.

2.2 Activity

Tom and Jerry made chargeable gains and allowable losses for the years 1998/99 and 1999/00 as set out below.

		Tom	Jerry
1998/99			
	Chargeable gains	12,000	4,000
	Allowable losses	8,000	7,000
1999/00			
	Chargeable gains	10,000	9,300
	Allowable losses	2,000	1,000

Calculate the taxable gains for Tom and Jerry for both 1998/99 and 1999/00 and the amount of any losses carried forward at the end of 1999/00. Ignore taper relief.

2.3 Activity solution

Tom

1998/99	£
Chargeable gains	12,000
Allowable losses	8,000
	———
Net chargeable gains	4,000

Net chargeable gains are covered by the annual exemption. No losses to carry forward to 1999/00.

1999/00	£
Chargeable gains	10,000
Allowable losses	2,000
	———
Net chargeable gains	8,000
Less: Annual exemption	7,100
	———
Taxable gains	900

Tom is taxed on gains of £900 in 1999/00.

Jerry

1998/99	£
Chargeable gains	4,000
Allowable losses	4,000
	———
Net chargeable gains	Nil

Jerry is unable to use his 1998/99 annual exemption since his gains are all covered by current year losses. He has losses of £3,000 (7,000 – 4,000) to carry forward to 1999/00.

1999/00

	£
Chargeable gains	9,300
Allowable losses	1,000
Net chargeable gains	8,300
Less: Losses brought forward (1998/99)	1,200
	7,100
Less: Annual exemption	7,100
Taxable gains	Nil

Jerry used £1,200 of his losses brought forward, to reduce his net chargeable gains to the level of the annual exemption. He still has losses of £1,800 (3,000 – 1,200) to carry forward to 2000/01.

2.4   Losses in the year of death

In general the rule for capital gains tax is that allowable losses may not be carried back to earlier periods for relief. This applies to companies and, with one exception, to individuals. The exception is for losses incurred in the tax year in which an individual dies. Note that this does **not** apply to losses brought forward to that year.

Losses an individual suffers in the year of death may be carried back to the three tax years preceding the tax year of death. However, the carry back is possible only after the losses have been relieved to the maximum extent against gains of the same tax year (even if this entails wasting part or all of the annual exemption).

When losses are carried back they are relieved against the net gains of the earlier year (that is, the earlier years' own losses are relieved first). Losses carried back are relieved against the most recent year first and only to the extent that net gains are reduced to the level of the annual exemption for that year. Any remaining losses are then carried back to the next earliest year, and so on.

2.5   Activity

Jenny has made chargeable gains and suffered allowable losses as follows. She died on 31 March 2000.

	1996/97 £	1997/98 £	1998/99 £	1999/00 £
Chargeable gains	20,300	4,200	9,100	7,000
Allowable losses	4,000	-	2,000	19,000

(a)   What are Jenny's taxable gains for 1996/97 to 1999/00 inclusive?
(b)   What difference would it make, if any, had Jenny died on 8 April 2000?

Ignore taper relief.

Note: the annual exemption was £6,300 for 1996/97, £6,500 for 1997/98 and £6,800 for 1998/99.

2.6   Activity solution

(a)   The year of death is dealt with first.

1999/00

	£
Chargeable gains	7,000
Less: Allowable losses of the year	7,000
Taxable gains	Nil

Losses carried back to 1998/99 £12,000 (19,000 – 7,000).

1998/99	£
Chargeable gains	9,100
Less: Allowable losses for the year	2,000
	7,100
Less: Annual exemption	6,800
	300
Less: Losses carried back from 1999/00	300
Taxable gains	Nil

Losses carried back to 1997/98 £11,700 (12,000 – 300).

1997/98	£
Chargeable gains	4,200
Less: Annual exemption	6,500
Taxable gains	Nil

No carried back losses used as chargeable gains covered by the annual exemption. Losses carried back to 1996/97.

1996/97	£
Chargeable gains	20,300
Less: Allowable losses	4,000
	16,300
Less: Annual exemption	6,300
	10,000
Less: Losses carried back	10,000
Taxable gains	Nil

Losses of £1,700 (11,700 – 10,000) remain unrelieved as they cannot be carried back further. As capital gains tax will already have been paid for 1996/97 and 1998/99, it will now be repaid.

(b)   If Jenny had died on 8 April 2000 rather than 31 March 2000 the losses incurred in 1999/00 could not have been carried back as they would not be losses of the tax year in which the death occurred.

2.7   Connected persons and loss relief

Except for disposals between spouses, which are subject to separate rules set out later in the text, where a transaction between connected persons results in a loss it is not available for general relief of chargeable gains as set out above. Its use is restricted to relief of gains on disposals to the **same** connected person.

3   VALUATION OF ASSETS

3.1   Introduction

In most circumstances the value of an asset is what a purchaser is prepared to pay for it. However, if transferor and transferee strike a bargain that is not 'at arm's length' the asset's market value is substituted. This happens by default where they are connected persons. A bargain made 'at arm's length' is effectively one made at market value. An asset's market value is that which it might reasonably be expected to fetch on a sale in the open market.

3.2   Negligible value

If the value of an asset becomes negligible for whatever reason, the owner may claim to the Inspector that this has occurred. Provided that the Inspector agrees the owner is then treated as having disposed of, and immediately reacquired, the asset at its negligible value. This treatment crystallises a loss.

The deemed disposal is treated as occurring at the date of the claim although the taxpayer can treat it as having occurred up to two years before the start of the tax year in which the claim was made (accounting period for companies). The back dating of the loss applies only if the asset was actually of negligible value at both the date of the claim and the earlier date.

4   PAYMENT OF TAX

4.1   Introduction

Capital Gains Tax is administered as part of the self assessment system. Self assessment is covered in detail in chapter 22.

4.2   Payment of CGT

Under self-assessment CGT is automatically due on 31 January following the tax year - eg, by 31 January 2001 for 1999/00. Payments on account are not necessary for CGT.

CGT is therefore paid at the same time as any balancing payment of income tax. If a refund of income tax is due, then this is set off against the CGT liability.

4.3   Rates of tax

In broad terms, an individual's capital gains are taxed as if they were savings income. The rate of capital gains tax is therefore either 20% or 40% depending on whether the taxpayer is a basic rate taxpayer or a higher rate taxpayer. The starting rate of income tax of 10% is not applicable to savings income, and is therefore not applicable to capital gains.

Capital gains are taxed at 20% where the gains when added to taxable income are below the basic rate limit and at 40% where they exceed the limit. Although capital gains are taxed as if they were savings income, this does not mean that unused personal allowances can be used to reduce capital gains.

4.4   Example

Lucy has chargeable gains of £8,000 for 1999/00 (after allowing for taper relief and deducting the annual exemption). What capital gains tax does she pay if her 1999/00 taxable income (from employment) is:

(a)   £Nil (unused PA is £600)
(b)   £12,000
(c)   £23,000

4.5   Solution

(a)   Income of £Nil.

Lucy has no income chargeable to income tax but cannot use her surplus PA against the gains. Her capital gains tax payable is thus:

	£
£8,000 @ 20%	1,600

(b)   Income of £12,000

If treated as income, the whole of Lucy's gains would fall in the basic rate band. Her CGT payable is thus:

£8,000 @ 20%	£1,600

(c)   Income of £23,000

Part of her gains, if treated as the top part of her income, will cause her to pay at the 40% higher rate. Her capital gains tax payable is thus:

	£
First £5,000 (remainder of basic rate band) @ 20%	1,000
Remaining £3,000 @ 40%	1,200
	2,200

4.6   Payment of tax by instalments

It was noted earlier in the chapter that capital gains tax is due on 31 January following the tax year.

In two sets of circumstances, however, the tax may be paid in instalments.

(a)   If the seller is paid the consideration for the sale in instalments over a period of more than 18 months, the seller has the option to pay the associated CGT in instalments too. The instalments may then be spread over the shorter of:

- eight years; and
- the period over which payment of the disposal proceeds is spread.

(b)   In some circumstances, capital gains tax due on gifts may be paid by instalments. The donor must not be entitled to hold over relief for business assets (explained in chapter 21) and the gift must fall into one of the following categories.

- land, or an interest in land; or

- shares or securities in a company that gave the donor control of it immediately before the sale; or

- shares or securities in a company that did **not** give control, but which are not quoted on a recognised stock exchange or the Unlisted Securities Market.

Where tax is paid in instalments because the consideration is paid by instalments, no interest on overdue tax is paid. But for disposals by gift all instalments other than the first carry interest.

5   CHAPTER SUMMARY

(a)   Capital gains tax is charged when a chargeable disposal of a chargeable asset is made by a chargeable person. Broadly, a disposal occurs where ownership of an asset changes hands but

CGT legislation deems disposals to occur in other, specific circumstances. A chargeable person is one who is UK resident for the chargeable period in which the gain arises (unless specifically exempted). All forms of property are chargeable assets unless exempted.

(b) Companies pay corporation tax on their chargeable gains. Whereas an individual is chargeable for a tax year, companies' gains are chargeable for accounting periods. Their gains form part of profits chargeable to corporation tax. Individuals receive an annual exemption (£7,100 for 1999/00) but companies do not.

(c) Allowable losses are set off first against chargeable gains of the same tax year (accounting period for companies). In the case of individuals this can involve wasting all or part of the annual exemption. Where losses cannot be set off entirely in the year in which they arise they may be carried forward indefinitely. In future years they are set off only to the extent required to reduce net chargeable gains to the level of the annual exemption. Losses incurred by an individual in the tax year in which he or she dies may be carried back to the three previous tax years, taking later years before earlier ones. The annual exemption is not displaced when losses are carried back.

(d) The value of an asset is normally the price at which it is sold. Where it is gifted, sold at an undervalue or exchanged, its value is deemed to be market value. Quoted shares and securities have their own method of valuation.

(e) Connected persons are deemed not to have made a bargain 'at arm's length' and market value is used to calculate gains and losses for their transactions. Broadly, relatives, business partners and companies that an individual controls are 'connected' with him. Losses that arise on a disposal to a connected person may be relieved only against gains made to the **same** connected person.

(f) Under self assessment CGT is payable on 31 January following the tax year.

(g) Capital gains are taxed as if they were savings income, with the rate of tax being either 20% or 40%.

(h) CGT is not normally payable in instalments but this facility may be available where consideration is received in instalments or on certain assets where holdover relief for gifts of business assets does not apply.

6 SELF TEST QUESTIONS

6.1 On what gains is CGT charged? (1.1)

6.2 Other than individuals, who may be a chargeable person for CGT purposes? (1.2)

6.3 What forms of property are chargeable assets? (1.3)

6.4 Other than sales and gifts, in which circumstances may there be a disposal for CGT purposes? (1.4)

6.5 What is the annual exempt amount? (1.6)

6.6 How are companies' chargeable gains taxed? (1.8)

6.7 In what circumstances may losses be carried forward to a later period? (2.1)

6.8 In what circumstances can losses be carried back, and for what period? (2.4)

6.9 Against what gains may losses incurred in a disposal to a connected person be relieved? 2.7)

6.10 At what rate does an individual pay capital gains tax? (4.3)

15 THE CALCULATION OF GAINS AND LOSSES

INTRODUCTION & LEARNING OBJECTIVES

This chapter deals with the capital gains tax calculation. It covers disposal proceeds, acquisition costs and the indexation allowance and taper relief. It is essential to fully master this chapter, which covers the basic calculation, before moving on to the various reliefs available.

When you have studied this chapter you should have learned the following:

- The form of a capital gains tax calculation.
- The rule for determining when a disposal occurs.
- How disposal proceeds are measured.
- Which types of expenditure are deductible in a capital gains tax calculation and which disallowed.
- How to identify and treat incidental costs of disposal and acquisition.
- The tests that improvement expenditure must meet to be allowable.
- How the indexation allowance is calculated and used in a capital gains tax calculation.
- How taper relief reduces the amount of gain chargeable.
- The special rules for assets held since 31 March 1982.
- How to calculate allowable expenditure when the disposal is a part disposal of the asset.
- The treatment of improvement expenditure on a part disposal.
- The circumstances in which a disposal is deemed to take place on a 'no gain/no loss' basis.

1 INTRODUCTION

1.1 Overview of the calculation

In principle, although not in detail, capital gains tax is straightforward. The essence of a capital gain is the increase in value of an asset during the time it has been owned by the taxpayer and is therefore a comparison between the price he paid for it and the price he is now selling it for.

An illustrative computation, showing the main elements of the calculation, is set out below. The chargeable gain or allowable loss arising from the calculation then forms part of the individual's personal capital gains tax computation which was outlined in the previous chapter. In the case of the company it forms part of the company's profit chargeable to corporation tax for the accounting period in question.

1.2 Illustrative capital gains tax calculation

	£
Disposal proceeds	80,000
Less: Incidental disposal costs (see note below)	500
	79,500
Less: Allowable expenditure	30,000
Unindexed gain	49,500
Less: Indexation allowance	26,000
Chargeable gain	23,500
Taper relief × 85%	19,975
Annual exemption	7,100
	12,875

Note: incidental disposal costs form part of the allowable expenditure but they are shown separately in the calculation for reasons connected with the calculation of the indexation allowance.

The remainder of this chapter is devoted to outlining the basic rules for calculating each of the elements of the computation.

1.3   Date of disposal

Unlike income tax and corporation tax, there is no question of apportioning a gain between different tax periods; the whole gain falls into the tax year (for individuals) or accounting period (for companies) in which the disposal takes place. Thus it is vital to be able to determine the date on which the disposal occurs.

The normal rule for capital gains tax is that the date of disposal is the date the contract is made (rather than the date of transfer of the asset which may be different).

2   DISPOSAL PROCEEDS

2.1   The general rule

The general rule, in the sense that it applies to the vast majority of disposals, is that the disposal proceeds taken into account in the computation is the amount of consideration received for the asset. This rule is applied provided that the disposal occurs through a bargain made at arm's length. So, if Mr Jones sells some shares to Mr Smith for £20,000, it is £20,000 that Mr Jones takes into his capital gains computation.

It should be noted that it is the gross disposal proceeds that are taken into the computation, before taking into account any costs associated with the disposal. Allowance may be made for these (see later in this chapter) but not by way of adjustment to the disposal proceeds themselves.

2.2   Other situations

Where actual consideration is not used the market value of the asset is usually substituted. The market value is the price which the asset might reasonably be expected to fetch on a sale on the open market, without any reduction being made for the effect of placing the whole of the asset on the market at one time.

Market value is substituted for actual proceeds either because, in fact, the bargain was not made at arm's length or because the law assumes that it was not made at arm's length. In particular, it is assumed that transactions between connected persons and gifts are bargains not made at arm's length and so market value is used for disposal proceeds in the capital gains tax computation.

3   ALLOWABLE EXPENDITURE

3.1   Introduction

As can be seen from the proforma capital gains tax computation earlier in this chapter allowable expenditure is deducted from the disposal consideration to calculate the unindexed gain.

The four types of expenditure which rank as allowable deductions are:

(a)   the purchase cost of the asset;
(b)   expenditure on enhancing the value of the asset (improvement expenditure);
(c)   expenditure incurred to establish, preserve or defend the taxpayer's title to the asset; and
(d)   incidental costs arising both on the acquisition of the asset and its disposal.

In all cases the expenditure has to be incurred 'wholly and exclusively' for the required purpose.

No deduction is permitted (even if the expenditure would fall within one of the categories set out above) if it is any of the following:

(a)   payments under insurance policies against damage, injury, loss or depreciation of the asset;

(b)   payments of interest; or

(c)   payments which are deductible in computing income tax.

The taxpayer is also prevented from deducting any amount representing the notional amount of his own labour.

3.2   Incidental costs

Broadly the same types of expenditure are deductible as incidental costs of acquisition or disposal. For the most part these are fairly obvious and consist of the following:

(a)   fees and commissions for professional services (surveyors, valuers, auctioneers, accountants, legal advisors, stockbrokers, or other agents);

(b)   advertising costs to find a buyer or seller;

(c)   the costs of a legal conveyance or transfer (including stamp duty); and

(d)   reasonable costs incurred in making valuations necessary for computing the gain particularly where market value is required.

Although incidental in nature, one must make a distinction between the incidental costs of acquisition and those of disposal because they are treated differently for the purposes of the indexation allowance (see later in this chapter).

3.3   Acquisition cost

In the great majority of cases acquisition cost is simply the price paid when the asset was originally purchased. Where, however, the owner acquired the asset by a transaction which required the previous owner to use the asset's market value in calculating his own gain, that same market value is used by the current owner as his cost of acquisition.

3.4   Improvement expenditure

To be deductible improvement expenditure must meet two tests:

(a)   it must be spent with the purpose of enhancing the value of the asset; and

(b)   it must be reflected in the state or nature of the asset at the time of disposal.

3.5   Preservation of title

This category of allowable expenditure, is fairly rare. Such expenditure is deductible if it is incurred in either establishing, or preserving, or defending the owner's title to or right over the asset in question. So, for example, legal costs in successfully resisting a claim to ownership of a piece of land is allowed under this heading.

The main reason for its comparative rarity is that such payments would often be deductible in computing income tax and are therefore disallowed in computing capital gains tax (see earlier in this chapter).

4   INDEXATION ALLOWANCE

4.1   Introduction

The indexation allowance is a rough and ready measure that attempts to ensure that capital gains are subject to tax only to the extent that they represent an increase in real terms of an asset's value. Notional or inflationary gains are excluded.

For capital gains tax inflation is measured via the Retail Prices Index (RPI).

A fraction is used to calculate the indexation factor, as follows:

$$\frac{\text{RPI in month of disposal - RPI in month of expenditure*}}{\text{RPI in month of expenditure*}}$$

* as the relief was introduced by the FA1982 the month of expenditure is taken as March 1982 or the month in which the expenditure was actually incurred, whichever is the later.

The fraction is rounded to three decimal places before use in a capital gains tax computation.

You will find the retail price indices in the rates and allowances tables at the front of this text.

4.2   Withdrawal of the indexation allowance

The Finance Act 1998 made some important changes to the capital gains tax system for individuals.

For disposals made after 5 April 1998, the indexation allowance is replaced by taper relief. This means that indexation is given up to April 1998, but not thereafter. The RPI for the month of disposal is therefore the RPI for the earlier of:

- The actual month of disposal, and
- April 1998.

Taper relief is explained later in this chapter.

The changes only affect individuals and trusts. Companies continue to receive the indexation allowance up to the actual month of disposal, and are not entitled to taper relief. To avoid confusion, the chapters on capital gains tax cover the rules as they apply to individuals and trusts. The rules for companies are covered in the chapters on corporation tax.

The examiner has stated that indexation is still examinable, but not in detail. In many cases the indexation figure will be given as part of a question.

4.3   Example

Jones sold a chargeable asset in June 1999 which he had bought in February 1987.

What is the indexation factor used in the calculation of his chargeable gain?

4.4   Solution

RPI in month of expenditure (February 1987) = 100.4
RPI in month of disposal (April 1998) = 162.6

Indexation factor is thus

$$\frac{162.6-100.4}{100.4} = 0.620 \text{ (rounded to three decimal places)}.$$

The RPI for the month of disposal is taken as that for April 1998, since April 1998 is earlier than June 1999.

4.5   Calculation of the indexation allowance

The indexation factor, as calculated above, is applied to each element of allowable expenditure other than the incidental costs of disposal.

In the interests of accuracy the indexation allowance is calculated separately for each element of allowable expenditure that was incurred at a different time.

Since indexation is not given for periods after April 1998, no allowance will be available for allowable expenditure incurred after 31 March 1998.

4.6   Example

Pye bought an investment property for £25,000 on 1 April 1983. On 15 July 1986 he spent £7,000 on a loft extension. He sold the property on 30 September 1999.

What indexation allowance is Pye entitled to on disposal of the property?

4.7   Solution

Indexation factor for acquisition expenditure:

$$\frac{162.6 \text{ (RPI for April 1998)} - 84.28 \text{ (RPI for April 1983)}}{84.28 \text{ (RPI for April 1983)}}$$

= 0.929 (rounded to three decimal places)

The indexation allowance for the acquisition expenditure is:

£25,000 × 0.929 = £23,225

Indexation factor for improvement expenditure:

$$\frac{162.6 \text{ (RPI for April 1998)} - 97.52 \text{ (RPI for July 1986)}}{97.52 \text{ (RPI for July 1986)}}$$

= 0.667 (rounded to three decimal places)

The indexation allowance for the improvement expenditure is:

£7,000 × 0.667 = £4,669

Pye's total indexation allowance is thus £27,894 (£23,225 + £4,669).

4.8   Indexation allowance and capital losses

Indexation is only available to extinguish a capital gain, it is not available to create or increase a capital loss.

4.9   Activity

Cedric purchased an asset for £10,000 and later sold it for £12,000, the indexation allowance is £4,000

What is the capital gains tax position?

4.10   Activity solution

	£
Proceeds	12,000
Less: cost	(10,000)
	———
Unindexed gain	2,000
Indexation allowance (restricted)	(2,000)
	———
	Nil
	———

4.11   Indexation allowance on no gain/no loss disposals

In such cases it is assumed that the disposal proceeds of the vendor (and thus the base cost to the purchaser) are such that the vendor makes neither a gain nor a loss.

The most common instance of no gain/no loss disposals are those between spouses (see later in this section of the text).

The indexation allowance is calculated in the normal way and added to the vendor's allowable expenditure to calculate the deemed disposal proceeds.

5   ASSETS HELD AT 31 MARCH 1982

5.1   Introduction

When capital gains tax was first introduced in 1965 the level of inflation was relatively low. Since that time, however, it has periodically reached high levels and consequently the value of most assets has increased greatly in nominal, if not real, terms. The capital gains tax system therefore operates to exclude gains made prior to 31 March 1982.

5.2   Rebasing

The rules, which involve a system known as 'rebasing', apply to assets held on 31 March 1982. The system works by assuming that the person sold the asset on 31 March 1982 and immediately re-acquired it for its market value on that date. For assets held on 31 March 1982 the deemed acquisition cost (market value on that date) normally replaces original cost in the CGT computation. This ensures that the 'base date' for capital gains tax is effectively 31 March 1982.

5.3   Use of original cost

Before rebasing was introduced capital gains tax calculations were normally based on the purchase price of an asset. Occasionally, where the value of an asset went down between the date of purchase and March 1982, substituting its 31 March 1982 value for the original cost will cause the taxpayer to be taxable on a higher gain. So, to ensure fairness, there is a requirement to calculate the gain using original cost too.

The results of the two calculations are compared and the one used depends on the outcome, as follows:

(a)   if both calculations result in gains - the smaller gain;
(b)   if both calculations result in losses - the smaller loss.
(c)   if either result produces a result of £nil or one of them a gain and the other a loss - neither result is used, the transaction is assumed to be for no gain/no loss;

Suppose an asset were sold such that a loss of £1,500 was the result of the 'cost calculation' and a loss of £1,200 the result of the 'March 1982 value' calculation, the loss of £1,200 (the smaller of the two) would be used.

5.4   Indexation allowance under 'rebasing'

Although the results of the two calculations have to be compared, the same indexation allowance is used in each of them. The indexation allowance is always based on the higher of original cost or 31 March 1982 value.

5.5   Election for March 1982 value for all disposals

If the taxpayer wishes, the complexities of making these comparisons each time an asset owned on 31 March 1982 is sold can be avoided. He can make an election to have all gains and losses computed on the basis of their March 1982 values.

The election is relevant to all assets held on 31 March 1982. Once made, it is irrevocable. The time limit for making the election is two years after the end of the tax year (or accounting period for companies) in which the first disposal was made to which it could apply (that is an asset held on 31 March 1982).

Where such an election is made the indexation allowance is automatically based on the asset's value at 31 March 1982.

5.6   Example

In 1974 White purchased a second home for £14,000 which he planned to use in his retirement. In 1978 the Department of Transport announced plans for a bypass which would pass near to the property and, in consequence, the house was worth only £10,000 on 31 March 1982. In 1984 a different route was chosen for the by-pass and when, on 2 June 1999, White sold the property he obtained a price of £50,000.

(a)   Calculate the chargeable gain arising.

(b)   What would the chargeable gain have been had a different route for the by-pass been chosen in 1981, and the 31 March 1982 value been £20,000?

You should ignore taper relief.

5.7   Solution

(a)

	Cost £	31.3.82 value £
Disposal proceeds	50,000	50,000
Less: Purchase price/ March 1982 value	14,000	10,000
Unindexed gain	36,000	40,000
Less: Indexation allowance to April 1998		
$\dfrac{162.6 - 79.44}{79.44} (= 1.047) \times £14,000$	14,658	14,658
Chargeable gain	21,342	25,342

The result used is thus a gain of £21,342.

(b)

	Cost £	31.3.82 value £
Disposal proceeds	50,000	50,000
Less: Purchase price/March 1982 value	14,000	20,000
Unindexed gain	36,000	30,000
Less: Indexation allowance to April 1998		
$\dfrac{162.6 - 79.44}{79.44} (= 1.047) \times £20,000$	20,940	20,940
Chargeable gain	15,060	9,060

In this case the result used is a gain of £9,060. Again the smaller gain is taken, but this time it is based on the March 1982 value. The indexation allowance is higher because it is always based on the higher of the two alternatives (in this case £20,000).

5.8   Example

Meo bought a painting for £9,000 in January 1976 and sold it for £65,000 on 30 June 1999. In March 1982 it was professionally valued at £50,000.

Calculate the chargeable gain arising.

You should ignore taper relief.

5.9   Solution

	Cost £	31.3.82 value £
Disposal proceeds	65,000	65,000
Less: Purchase price/March 1982 value	9,000	50,000
Unindexed gain	56,000	15,000
Less: Indexation allowance to April 1998 $\frac{162.6-79.44}{79.44}$ (= 1.047) × £50,000	52,350	52,350
Chargeable gain	3,650	Nil

The indexation allowance in the 31 March 1982 calculation can only extinguish a gain, it cannot create a loss.

In this case the result from the cost calculation is a gain, and that from the 31 March 1982 calculation is nil. Thus the result used is nil; neither a gain nor a loss.

6   TAPER RELIEF

6.1   Introduction

For disposals after 5 April 1998, net chargeable gains are reduced by taper relief.

The relief progressively reduces the amount of the chargeable gain according to how long the asset has been held since 5 April 1998.

Taper relief is computed before the annual exemption is deducted.

6.2   The amount of relief

Taper relief is more generous for business assets than for non-business assets. The percentage of the gain chargeable is as follows:

Complete years after 5 April 1998 for which asset held	Gains on business assets	Gains on non-business assets
0	100.0%	100.0%
1	92.5%	100.0%
2	85.0%	100.0%
3	77.5%	95.0%
4	70.0%	90.0%
5	62.5%	85.0%
6	55.0%	80.0%
7	47.5%	75.0%

8	40.0%	70.0%
9	32.5%	65.0%
10 or more	25.0%	60.0%

The amount of taper relief is based on the number of complete years that an asset is held. For example, an asset bought on 8 May 1998 and sold on 4 May 2000 will have only been held for one complete year. If the sale was delayed until after 7 May 2000, then the holding period would be two years.

Assets acquired before 17 March 1998 qualify for an addition of one year to the period for which they are held after 5 April 1998. For example, an asset purchased on 1 January 1994 and sold on 1 July 1999 will be treated as having been held for two years post 5 April 1998.

For disposals during 1999/00, taper relief will therefore be based on two complete years of ownership where a business asset owned prior to 17 March 1998 is disposed of.

Non-business assets cannot attract taper relief for disposals during 1999/00.

The date of 17 March 1998 need not be learnt, since the examiner has stated that a question will not be set where an asset is acquired during the period 17 March to 5 April 1998.

6.3   Business assets

Business assets for taper relief purposes are broadly defined as:

- Those used for the purposes of a trade carried on by a sole trader or partner.

- Those used for the purposes of a trade carried on by a qualifying company of the individual concerned.

- Shares in a qualifying company.

- Those held for the purposes of an office or employment in which the individual was required to devote substantially the whole of his or her time.

This definition is similar to the retirement relief definition of business assets (see Chapter 19).

A qualifying company is one that is a trading company in which an individual must either have a 25% shareholding or have a 5% holding and also be a full-time working director or employee.

The company need not be wholly trading but any non-trading activities must have a 'non-substantial' effect on the company. The Revenue set a 20% limit for non-trading activities before the company ceases to be a qualifying company. How the 20% test is applied - value of investments over total assets or portion of company's income - is not explained.

6.4   Example

Andy disposes of a business asset in January 2000 for £95,000. The asset had cost £35,000 in March 1985. Andy is a 40% taxpayer and has made no other disposals during 1999/00.

Calculate Andy's capital gains tax liability for 1999/00.

6.5   Solution

Andy's capital gains tax liability for 1999/00 is as follows:

	£
Disposal proceeds	95,000
Less: Purchase price	35,000
Unindexed gain	60,000

Less: Indexation allowance to April 1998

$$\frac{162.6 - 92.80}{92.80} (=0.752) \times 35,000 \qquad 26,320$$

Chargeable gain	33,680
Taper relief × 85%	28,628
Annual exemption	7,100
	21,528
Capital gains tax at 40%	8,611

The asset was acquired before 17 March 1998, and so it is deemed to have been held for two years after 5 April 1998. As it is a business asset, only 85% of the gain is chargeable.

6.6   Taper relief and current year losses

Taper relief is computed on the net gains that are chargeable after the deduction of any losses of the same year.

For this purpose, capital losses are allocated against chargeable gains in the most favourable manner. It will normally be beneficial to allocate losses against those assets that qualify for the least amount of taper relief.

6.7   Example

For 1999/00 Claude has made the following chargeable gains and capital losses:

- A chargeable gain of £11,000 on a business asset.
- A chargeable gain of £12,500 on a non-business asset.
- A capital loss of £7,000.

All three assets were purchased prior to 17 March 1998, and were sold during September 1999.

Calculate the gains chargeable to capital gains tax after applying taper relief.

6.8   Solution

	£
Business asset	11,000
Taper relief × 85%	9,350
Non-business asset (12,500 - 7,000)	5,500
	14,850
Annual exemption	7,100
	7,750

The capital loss has been allocated against the non-business asset since this does not attract any taper relief. The business asset was acquired before 17 March 1998, and so it is deemed to have been held for two years after 5 April 1998.

6.9   Taper relief and brought forward losses

Losses brought forward are also deducted prior to the calculation of taper relief.

This complicates the calculation, since such losses are only deducted to the extent that the annual exemption is not wasted (see the previous chapter).

6.10   Example

During June 1999 Maud sold a business asset that resulted in a chargeable gain of £12,800. The asset was acquired in 1985.

She has capital losses of £8,500 brought forward from 1998/99.

Calculate the gains chargeable to capital gains tax after applying taper relief.

6.11   Solution

		£
Chargeable gain		12,800
Loss brought forward		5,700
		7,100
Annual exemption		7,100
		Nil

Taper relief of 85% is available against the £7,100 of gain which remains chargeable but there is no point in calculating the figure as the annual exemption covers the full gain. The balance of loss of £2,800 (8,500 - 5,700) is carried forward.

6.12   Interaction with other reliefs

The claiming of various other capital gains tax reliefs will also complicate the calculation of taper relief. The interaction of taper relief with these other reliefs is dealt with in the subsequent chapters on capital gains tax.

6.13   Companies

Companies are not entitled to taper relief when they make chargeable disposals. They instead receive the indexation allowance calculated up to the date of disposal. This is covered in the chapters on corporation tax.

7   PART DISPOSALS

7.1   Introduction

It is not simply the complete disposal of assets that triggers a charge to capital gains tax; part disposals do too.

The problem with part disposals is identifying the part of the allowable expenditure to deduct from the sale proceeds. This is done by calculating the fraction set out below and multiplying it by the whole cost. The fraction is:

$\dfrac{A}{A + B}$, which equals

$$\frac{\text{Disposal consideration for the part disposed of}(A)}{\text{Disposal consideration for the part disposed of}(A) \; + \; \text{Market value of the remainder* (B)}}$$

* at the time of disposal.

7.2   Example

Carruthers purchased a commercial building for £250,000. He later sold part of it for £100,000 and at that time the part he retained was worth £200,000.

Calculate the allowable expenditure available to Carruthers on the part disposal.

7.3   Solution

The part disposal fraction is:

$$\frac{\text{Disposal consideration } (£100,000)}{\text{Disposal consideration } (£100,000) \ + \ \text{Market value of remainder } (£200,000)}$$

$$= \frac{100,000}{300,000} = \frac{1}{3}$$

Thus the allowable expenditure is:

$$\text{Original cost } (£250,000) \times \frac{1}{3} = £83,333.$$

7.4   Improvement expenditure

Care is needed when dealing with improvement expenditure on a part disposal. There are three possibilities:

(a)   the improvement expenditure applies equally to the whole asset (in which case it too is apportioned using the part disposal fraction); or

(b)   the improvement expenditure applies wholly to the part disposed of (in which case all of it is deducted in the part disposal computation); or

(c)   the improvement expenditure applies wholly to the part retained (in which case none of it is deducted in the part disposal computation).

7.5   Example

Higgins purchased a commercial building and annexe for £175,000 on 1 September 1988. On 31 December 1989 he incurred costs of £30,000 on installing air conditioning in the main building (but not the annexe). He sold the main building (without the annexe) for £300,000 on 10 October 1999. At that time the annexe was worth £50,000.

Calculate the chargeable gain arising.

7.6   Solution

	£	£
Disposal proceeds		300,000
Less: Allowable expenditure (W)		180,000
Unindexed gain		120,000
Less: Indexation allowance to April 1998		
(a) on original cost		
$\frac{162.6 - 108.4}{108.4}$ $(= 0.500) \times £150,000$ (W)	75,000	
(b) on improvement expenditure		
$\frac{162.6 - 118.8}{118.8}$ $(= 0.369) \times £30,000$	11,070	
		86,070
Chargeable gain		33,930

No taper relief is available, since the building (which is a non-business asset) has not been owned for a sufficient period after 5 April 1998.

Working - allowable expenditure

Higgin's expenditure comprises a part of his original purchase plus the whole of the improvement expenditure

	£
Part of the original cost: $£175,000 \times \dfrac{300,000}{300,000 + 50,000}$	150,000
Improvement expenditure	30,000
	180,000

8   HUSBANDS AND WIVES

8.1   Introduction

Certain transactions, notably between spouses (provided they are not separated) are effectively ignored for capital gains tax purposes. The rationale is that married couples are essentially single economic entities and thus capital gains tax is imposed only when there is a disposal to a third party.

The way capital gains tax is side-stepped in these circumstances is to treat disposals between spouses as occurring at a price that provides the disposer with neither a gain nor a loss. When the transfer is made the transferor is deemed to dispose of the asset at its purchase cost plus indexation allowance from the date of acquisition to the date of transfer (or April 1998 if earlier). The transferee is deemed to have paid the same amount to acquire the asset (and so this amount is used in any later disposal to a third party).

For the purposes of taper relief, where there has been a transfer between spouses the relief is based on their combined period of ownership.

8.2   Activity

Jack acquired a holiday cottage for £25,000 on 1 September 1987 and transferred it to his wife, Jill, on 31 January 1990. Jill sold the cottage to a third party on 1 August 1999 for £42,000.

Compute the chargeable gain on Jill's disposal in August 1999.

8.3   Activity solution

	£
Disposal proceeds	42,000
Less: Deemed acquisition cost (W)	29,175
Unindexed gain	12,825
Less: Indexation allowance (April 1998 - Jan 1990) $\dfrac{162.6 - 119.5}{119.5} \ (= 0.361) \times £29,175$	10,532
Chargeable gain	2,293

Working - deemed acquisition cost

	£
Purchase price in September 1987	25,000
Add: Indexation allowance (Jan 1990 - Sept 1987)	

$$\frac{119.5 - 102.4}{102.4} \ (= 0.167) \times £25,000$$

	£
	4,175
	29,175

No taper relief is available, since the cottage (which is a non-business asset) has not been owned for a sufficient period after 5 April 1998.

In examinations it is normally acceptable to take a short cut as follows:

	£
Disposal proceeds	42,000
Less: Original acquisition cost	25,000
Unindexed gain	17,000
Less: Indexation (April 1998 - Sept 1987)	

$$\frac{162.6 - 102.4}{102.4} \ (= 0.588) \times 25,000$$

	£
	14,700
Chargeable gain	2,300

The difference of £7 (2,300 – 2,293) is due to the rounding of the indexation allowance.

8.4 Assets transferred after 31 March 1982

It was noted above that the rationale for no gain/no loss transfers is to treat the transferor and transferee as one economic entity and so effectively ignore transfers between them. The transferee 'stands in the shoes' of the transferor.

A particular problem arises where the transferor acquired an asset on or before 31 March 1982 and it is acquired by the transferee after that date. Since the rebasing rule requires the disposer to have owned the asset on 31 March 1982 the transferee would not obtain any benefit from them were it not for a special set of rules. These simply deem the transferee to have owned the asset on 31 March 1982. If the March 1982 value is the one used (rather than the transferor's original cost) indexation allowance for the transferee applies from that date too.

8.5 Activity

Stuart purchased a chargeable business asset on 1 November 1980 for £18,000 and transferred it to his wife, Hannah, on 1 June 1999 for use in her business. On 31 March 2000 Hannah sold the asset for £50,000. Its value on 31 March 1982 was £21,000.

Calculate the chargeable gain arising on Hannah's disposal in March 2000.

8.6   Activity solution

	Cost	31.3.82 value
	£	£
Disposal proceeds	50,000	50,000
Less: Cost/March 1982 value	18,000	21,000
Unindexed gain	32,000	29,000
Less: Indexation allowance to April 1998		
$\dfrac{162.6 - 79.44}{79.44}$ (= 1.047) × £21,000	21,987	21,987
Chargeable gain	10,013	7,013

The lower gain of £7,013 is taken. Taper relief is based on the combined period of ownership, so the gain chargeable in 1999/00 will be reduced to £5,961 (7,013 × 85%). The asset was acquired prior to 17 March 1998, and so two years' taper relief is available.

9   CHAPTER SUMMARY

The general form of a capital gains tax calculation is essentially straightforward. It involves deducting a person's allowable expenditure from his disposal consideration to obtain an unindexed gain and from this the indexation allowance is deducted to find the chargeable gain. This figure may then be reduced by taper relief.

It is helpful to view the calculation as a series of separate elements, taken in the following order.

(a)   Decide the date of disposal (the date the contract for sale is made). The tax year or accounting period is then known.

(b)   Ascertain the disposal consideration to be taken into account (normally it is the sale price but the asset's market value is used when the disposal is a gift, a sale at an undervalue or a transaction between connected persons).

(c)   Calculate the allowable expenditure, remembering in particular that to qualify, improvement expenditure must be reflected in the state or nature of the asset at the time of disposal.

(d)   Calculate the indexation allowance separately for allowable expenditure incurred at different times. Remember that incidental costs of disposal do not attract indexation allowance, and that (for individuals and trusts) indexation is only given up to April 1998.

For assets owned on 31 March 1982 the rebasing rules apply. A comparison is made to decide which result is used (or, if appropriate no gain/no loss) unless the taxpayer has elected for all disposals to be calculated using March 1982 values.

For disposals after 5 April 1998, the net chargeable gains are reduced by a taper relief. This progressively reduces the amount of the chargeable gain according to how long an asset has been held since 5 April 1998. Taper relief is more generous for business assets than for non-business assets.

Capital gains tax applies to part disposals as well as disposals of entire assets. The form of the calculation is the normal one but care must be taken to ascertain the proportion of allowable expenditure to deduct.

10   SELF-TEST QUESTIONS

10.1   On what date does a disposal occur for capital gains tax? (1.3)

10.2   What are the two alternatives that may be used as disposal consideration? (2.2)

10.3   What are the four categories of allowable expenditure? (3.1)

10.4   Why must incidental costs of acquisition and disposal be treated separately? (3.2)

10.5   What tests must improvement expenditure meet to be deductible? (3.4)

10.6   What is the definition of a business asset for the purposes of taper relief? (6.3)

10.7   When is indexation allowance restricted or denied on a disposal? (4.8)

10.8   What is the 'base date' for capital gains tax? (5.2)

10.9   An election may be made to have all disposals of assets held on 31 March 1982 computed on the basis of their value on that date. What is the time limit for the election? (5.5)

10.10   What fraction is used to apportion part of the cost of an asset when a part disposal is made? (7.1)

16 PRINCIPAL PRIVATE RESIDENCES

INTRODUCTION

Relief is available on the disposal of certain assets, and on certain types of disposal, so that the full gain is not taxed at the time of the disposal.

The types of relief fall into two broad categories:

- Exemption; and
- Deferral.

If a gain is exempt it means that it is not chargeable now, nor in any time in the future; the gain is eliminated. This type of relief is available on the disposal of a principal private residence (see below) and also on the disposal of a business, or shares in a business, when the vendor is at least 50 years old and certain conditions are met (retirement relief).

If a gain (or part of a gain) is deferred, it will not be taxed at the time of disposal, but may be taxed on some future event. One instance where this relief is available is where there is a disposal followed by reinvestment in a new asset; the gain is rolled over to reduce the base cost of the new asset. When the new asset is eventually sold the gain is generally crystallised. A good example is where the proceeds from the disposal of business assets are reinvested in further business assets.

When studying the various capital gains tax reliefs in the ensuing chapters, it is important to establish whether the particular relief exempts the gain, or simply defers it.

This chapter deals with the relief for principal private residences. With this relief the gain (or part of the gain) on the disposal of a principal private residence is exempt.

1 INTRODUCTION

1.1 Overview

Any gain on the disposal of a private residence, which has been an individual's principal residence throughout his period of ownership, is exempt from capital gains tax. The sale of most private homes benefit from this exemption and thus relatively little capital gains tax is paid on the transfer of private residential property. Equally, any losses sustained by the taxpayer on the disposal of such property are not allowable for CGT. This chapter is concerned with the scope of the CGT exemption and the conditions and restrictions which deny it or reduce it in particular cases.

1.2 Scope of the exemption

Normally the taxpayer's principal private residence and up to half a hectare of adjoining ground may benefit from the exemption. If, however, the size and character of the house warrant it, a larger area may be permitted. The test is whether a larger area is needed 'for the reasonable enjoyment of it.'

2 DWELLING HOUSE

2.1 Introduction

In order to obtain the relief, the property disposed of must be a dwelling house.

2.2   Meaning of 'dwelling house'

The meaning of 'dwelling house' is not defined in the legislation and so it has been left to the courts to determine the limits of the expression. A number of principles have emerged from decided cases.

(a)   Caravans connected to mains services such as electricity and water qualify as dwellings.

(b)   A taxpayer sold a bungalow and a small amount of land that was within the grounds of his house and which had been occupied by a part-time caretaker. It was held that the bungalow provided services for the benefit of the main house, was occupied by the taxpayer through his employee, and so qualified as part of the taxpayer's residence. A test resulting from this case is that buildings must together form an entity which can be regarded as a dwelling house, albeit divided into different buildings performing different functions.

(c)   Where a taxpayer owns a large property which is divided into several self contained units, only those parts which the taxpayer actually occupies qualify for exemption.

(d)   A taxpayer first sold his house and part of his garden and then, about a year later, sold the remainder of the garden at a substantial profit. It was held that the principal private residence exemption applied only to the first disposal, because when the remainder of the land was sold, it no longer formed part of the individual's principal private residence. It is likely that if the order of sales were reversed, the land sold independently of the buildings would still not qualify for relief.

3   RESTRICTIONS ON EXEMPTION

3.1   Periods of non occupation

In general, if the owner does not occupy his property for a period, any gain arising ceases to be exempt from capital gains tax. The exempt gain is then calculated by a fraction as follows:

$$\frac{\text{Total gain} \times \text{period of occupation}}{\text{Total period of ownership}}$$

The period before 31 March 1982 is ignored in calculating both periods of occupation and periods of ownership.

There are a number of sets of circumstances, in which despite being absent, an individual is nevertheless treated as being in occupation. These are:

(a)   the 36 months directly preceding the disposal of his property;

(b)   any period or periods which together do not last more than 3 years;

(c)   an unlimited period throughout which the individual was employed abroad;

(d)   any period or periods that together do not last more than 4 years, throughout which the individual was prevented from residing in his property because:

* his place of work was too far from his property; or
* his employer required him to reside elsewhere

Relief for the final 36 months is extremely useful, especially for relatively short term ownership of property. Unlike the rules for most of the other periods of deemed occupation, there is no need for the owner to occupy or reoccupy the property at the end of it. He may even let his property or elect for another property to be treated as his principal residence without losing the benefit of the exemption. It should be noted, however, that the exemption is lost for any part of the property used for business purposes during this period.

For any of the permitted periods of absence in (b), (c) and (d) above to apply, it is vital that at some time both before and after the absence the property must have been the individual's only or main residence. This is a question of fact and so a period of deemed occupation under one heading does not count as a period of residence, either before or after, for another heading. There is one exception to this, provided by extra statutory concession, which removes the need for actual residence after a period of absence so long as an individual is unable to resume residence in his previous home because the terms of his employment require him to work elsewhere. Where an individual is absent for longer than the periods permitted by (b) or (d) the Revenue regard only any gain accruing in the additional absence as taxable (not the whole of it).

Note that actual occupation before 31 March 1982, although ignored for exemption purposes, will qualify as actual owner occupation preceding a period of absence.

It is important to appreciate that the periods of deemed occupation are cumulative and so, in exceptional circumstances, a taxpayer could find himself benefiting from all of them at different times.

Permitted absence whilst staying in job related accommodation can apply to both the employed and the self employed.

3.2   Example

In September 1978 Mr Flint purchased a house in Southampton for £15,000, which he lived in until he moved to a rented flat on 1 July 1982. He remained in the flat until 1 October 1984 when he accepted a year's secondment to his firm's New York office. On coming back on 1 October 1985 he moved into a relative's house, where he stayed until he returned to his own home on 31 January 1986. On 1 July 1986 he changed jobs and rented a flat near his new employer's offices in Newcastle. Here he remained until he sold his Southampton house on 1 February 2000 for £95,000. In March 1982 it was estimated to be worth £25,000.

Calculate the gain arising on the disposal, if any.

3.3   Solution

Calculation of chargeable gain

	£
Disposal proceeds	95,000
Less: 31 March 1982 value *	25,000
Unindexed gain	70,000
Less: Indexation allowance to April 1998 $\dfrac{162.6 - 79.44}{79.44}$ (=1.047) × £25,000	26,175
Indexed gain	43,825
Less: Principal private residence (PPR) exemption (W)	17,817
Chargeable gain	26,008

* March 1982 value clearly produces lower gain than cost.

No taper relief is available, since the house (which is a non-business asset) has not been owned for a sufficient period after 5 April 1998.

Working - chargeable and exempt periods of ownership

		Chargeable months	Exempt months
Sept 1978 - March 1982	(irrelevant)	-	-
April 1982 - June 1982	(resident)	-	3
July 1982 - Sept 1984	(absent - any reason)	-	27
Oct 1984 - Sept 1985	(absent - employed abroad)	-	12
Oct 1985 - Jan 1986	(absent - any reason)	-	4
Feb 1986 - June 1986	(resident)	-	5
July 1986 - Jan 1997	(absent - see note)	127	-
Feb 1997 - Jan 2000	(final 36 months)	-	36
		127	87

Total period of ownership (127 + 87) = 214 months.

Exempt element of gain is thus $87/214 \times £43,825 = £17,817$.

Note: after Mr Flint left his residence to work in Newcastle he never returned. Consequently he broke the condition for exemption that work away from home is granted only when there is actual residence both before and after the absence. In contrast the exemption for the final 36 months of ownership has no such restriction and was thus still available.

4   BUSINESS USE AND LETTING

4.1   Business use

Where a house, or part of it, is used wholly and exclusively for business purposes, it clearly cannot be used as residential accommodation at the same time.

Consequently, to the extent it is used for business purposes and for the period of use, it loses its CGT exemption and becomes taxable. It should be noted particularly that the taxpayer cannot benefit from any of the rules of deemed occupation (including that of the final 36 months of ownership) for any part of his property used for business purposes.

Common methods of calculating the business proportion are to use the percentage of the floor area occupied for business purposes or to use the same percentage used in the taxpayer's income tax computation to apportion running costs to the area used for business purposes.

4.2   Example

On 30 June 1999 Alex sold his house for £125,000, resulting in a capital gain (after indexation) of £70,000. The house had been purchased on 1 July 1991, and one of the five rooms had been used for business purposes from 1 January 1995 to the date of sale.

Calculate the chargeable gain arising on the disposal.

4.3   Solution

Alex owned the house for 96 months, and used the room for business purposes for 54 months. The chargeable gain is:

$£70,000 \times 1/5 \times 54/96 = £7,875$.

4.4   Letting

Where an individual lets out his house for residential use (but not commercial use) the principal private residence exemption is extended to cover gains accruing while the property is let. Before considering the details of this relief, two points need to be made. Firstly, where the individual takes in a lodger who shares the family's accommodation and takes meals with them the letting exemption is unnecessary. In these circumstances the whole of the property is treated as remaining the individual's principal private residence throughout the period of letting. Secondly, the exemption for letting relieves gains which would otherwise be chargeable to tax and therefore does not apply during periods of deemed occupation, which are already exempted.

The gain which is exempt as a result of letting relief is subject to an overriding monetary limit, currently £40,000, and cannot in any case exceed the amount of the main residence exemption. Note that the relaxation comes in the form of exempting a gain which would otherwise be chargeable to tax; it cannot convert a gain into an allowable loss.

The letting exemption applies whether the owner is absent from his property and lets the whole of it or lets part of it and still occupies the remainder. To benefit from the relief, however, the letting must form a part of the individual's own residence.

The letting exemption is restricted to the lowest of:

(a)   £40,000;
(b)   the amount of the gain exempted by the normal principal private residence rules;
(c)   the part of the gain attributable to the letting period.

4.5   Example

Referring back to the example of Mr Flint, calculate the chargeable gain if the house in Southampton had been let during all of Mr Flint's periods of absence.

4.6   Solution

The letting relief would have been the lowest of:

(a)   £40,000
(b)   £17,817
(c)   £26,008

So the chargeable gain would be:

	£
Indexed gain (as before)	43,825
Principal private residence exemption	17,817
	26,008
Letting exemption	17,817
Chargeable gain	8,191

5   OWNERSHIP OF MORE THAN ONE RESIDENCE

5.1   Nomination of main residence

Where an individual has more than one residence he is entitled to nominate which of them is to be treated as his principal residence for capital gains purposes by notifying the Inspector of Taxes in writing. The election must be made within two years of acquiring an additional residence otherwise it is open to the Inspector as a question of fact to decide which residence is the main residence.

5.2   Married couples

Provided that they are not treated as being separated or divorced, a married couple is entitled to only one residence between them for the purposes of the private residence exemption.

6   **PLANNING POINTS**

6.1   **Introduction**

Capital gains tax planning concerning an individual's private residence concerns two main areas. On the one hand, if the taxpayer's circumstances are such that any gain realised will be exempt he should ensure that this is maximised. On the other hand, where he is absent from the property he should attempt to structure his absences in such a way that he benefits as much as possible from the deemed occupation rules and the letting exemption.

6.2   **Specific points**

(a)   Where the taxpayer has more than one residence he should ensure that he nominates the property with the greatest potential for gain as his main residence. It should be noted, however, that any property subject to an election must be used by the taxpayer at some time as his residence. It is not acceptable to purchase a property as a financial investment, nominate it as the main residence of the taxpayer, and never set foot in it.

(b)   If an individual's finances permit, he should purchase a new residence before disposing of the old one. He can elect for the new residence to be treated as his main residence for the CGT exemption but this does not prevent him gaining exemption on the old residence for the final 36 months of his ownership. In this way he can effectively gain exemption on two residences at once for a maximum of three years.

(c)   Subject to tax and other financial considerations, business use of the property should be avoided. Where business use is necessary thought should be given to the proportion of household expenses claimed under the income tax rules because these will be a material factor in determining the extent to which the principal private residence exemption is lost.

(d)   When the taxpayer is absent in circumstances that make him ineligible for exemption under the deemed occupation rules, he should give serious thought to letting his property. Whether this constitutes good tax planning will depend, on the one hand, at the rate his property is rising in value, and on the other hand, on the income and expenditure connected with the letting.

7   **SELF TEST QUESTIONS**

7.1   What is the normal maximum permitted area of ground that may be sold with a main residence and qualify for PPR exemption? (1.2)

7.2   Will a garden qualify for PPR if sold separately from the main residence? (2.2)

7.3   Is the owner required to occupy his property during the final 36 months of ownership to qualify for the PPR exemption? (3.1)

7.4   What is the earliest date that can be relevant in calculating the 'period of ownership'? (3.1)

7.5   If the property is used for business purposes during the final 36 months of ownership is PPR exemption affected? (4.1)

7.6   What is the maximum letting exemption? (4.4)

7.7   What happens if the taxpayer does not elect within two years of acquiring a second residence as to which is his main residence? (5.1)

7.8   What principal private residence relief is a married couple entitled to? (5.2)

8   **EXAMINATION TYPE QUESTION**

8.1   **Jane**

On 30 September 1999 Jane Smith made a gift of a house to her grandson Norman. The house had been bought by Jane on 1 September 1981 for £32,800, and was extended at a cost of £10,600 during

June 1987. Market values of £45,000 at 31 March 1982 and £140,000 at 30 September 1999 have been agreed by the Inland Revenue.

Jane occupied the house as her main residence until 30 September 1989 when she went to live with her sister. The house remained empty for four years, but has been rented out continuously since then.

Calculate the chargeable gain.

9   ANSWER TO EXAMINATION TYPE QUESTION

9.1   Jane

	£	£
Deemed proceeds		140,000
Market value 31.3.82	45,000	
Enhancement expenditure	10,600	
		55,600
		84,400
Indexation to April 1998 $45,000 \times \dfrac{162.6-79.44}{79.44}(1.047)$		(47,115)
$10,600 \times \dfrac{162.6-101.9}{101.9}(0.596)$		(6,318)
		30,967

Only the period from 31 March 1982 is relevant, so there is a total period of ownership of 17 years 6 months (31.3.82 to 30.9.99). Of this the period from 1.10.89 to 30.9.96 (7 years) is chargeable, the last three years being exempt. There are no other deemed periods of occupation since Jane never returned to live in the house.

Letting relief is available for the period from 1.10.93 to 30.9.96 (3 years). The chargeable gain is:

	£
$30,967 \times 7/17.5 =$	12,387

Letting relief being the lowest of:

(a)   £40,000

(b) $30,967 - 12,387 = £18,580$ (the part of the gain exempt as a principal private residence)

(c) $30,967 \times 3/17.5 = £5,309$ (the gain attributable to the period of letting)   5,309

Chargeable gain	7,078

No taper relief is available.

17 SHARES AND SECURITIES

INTRODUCTION & LEARNING OBJECTIVES

Shares and securities are chargeable assets and any gain made on their disposal is taxable, and any loss, allowable. It is important to understand the matching rules and rules for bonus and rights issues.

When you have studied this chapter you should have learned the following:

- The reason for needing matching rules to deal with the sale of shares and securities.
- The order in which matching takes place.
- How to construct the 1985 share pool and deal with purchases and sales affecting it.
- What 'operative events' are and how they affect the calculation of the indexation allowance.
- What shares constitute the 1982 holding.
- The rules for dealing with bonus and rights issues.
- The rules for dealing with changes in share capital (reorganisations and takeovers)
- The terms of the exemption given to gilts and qualifying corporate bonds.

1 INTRODUCTION

1.1 Overview

Shares and securities present a particular problem for capital gains tax computations because any two shares in a company (of a particular class) are indistinguishable. Where shares have been acquired on more than one occasion this creates difficulties in identifying just which have been disposed of on a sale. For instance Jones buys ordinary shares in Smith plc as follows.

	Shares	Cost £
16 December 1985	1,000	2,500
17 June 1988	1,500	4,500

If, in January 2000 Jones sells 600 shares, which has he sold; some from the earlier purchase, some from the later purchase or a mixture of the two?

The answer matters because, in order to calculate Jones' chargeable gain or allowable loss his allowable expenditure, indexation allowance and taper relief must be known.

This chapter is devoted to setting out the capital gains tax rules as they apply to shares and securities. The essential principles of capital gains tax remain but they are overlain by a system needed to keep track of just which shares or securities are being sold.

1.2 Valuation rules

Where it is necessary to establish the value of quoted shares and securities, their value is taken from prices quoted in the Stock Exchange Daily Official List and is the lower of:

(a) the lower quoted price plus a quarter of the difference between the lower and higher quoted prices; and

(b) the average of the highest and lowest recorded bargains.

1.3   Activity

Shares in XYZ plc are quoted in the Stock Exchange Daily Official List at 230p – 270p. On the same day the highest and lowest recorded bargains were 224p and 276p.

If a disposal of XYZ plc shares were made on that day other than on an arm's length bargain, what would be their value for capital gains tax?

1.4   Activity solution

Value of XYZ plc shares is the lower of:

(a)	Lower price	230p
	Add: $(270p - 230p) \times 1/4$	10p
		240p
(b)	Average of lowest and highest recorded bargains	
	$(224p + 276p) \times 1/2$	250p

Their value is thus 240p.

2   THE MATCHING RULES

2.1   Introduction

The matching rules are needed to solve the problem of being unable to identify acquisitions with disposals, as illustrated above. They apply when a person has made more than one purchase of shares or securities of the same class in the same company. But no matching rules are needed where, for example, someone buys both preference shares and ordinary shares in a company as they are distinguishable.

Shares and securities are subject to the same rules and so, for the rest of the chapter, the term 'shares' covers both.

2.2   The matching order

Where shares are sold after 5 April 1998 they are matched against acquisitions in the following order:

(a)   shares acquired on the same day (as the sale);
(b)   shares acquired within the following 30 days
(c)   shares acquired after 5 April 1998 (taking the most recent acquisition first on a LIFO basis);
(d)   shares in the 1985 pool;
(e)   shares in the 1982 pool.

2.3   Shares acquired within the following 30 days

It may appear strange that a disposal is matched with acquisitions following the date of sale. The reason for this is that it prevents a practice known as bed and breakfasting.

Typically, shares would be sold at the close of business one day and then bought back at the opening of business the next day. A gain or loss was thus established without making a genuine disposal of the shares. It might be useful for an individual to establish a capital loss, for example, in the same tax year that he or she has chargeable gains.

The 30 day matching rule makes the practice of bed and breakfasting much more difficult, since the subsequent acquisition cannot take place within 30 days.

2.4   Companies

The matching rules for companies are different from those for individuals. These are looked at separately in chapter 23 on corporation tax.

3   ACQUISITIONS AFTER 5 APRIL 1998

3.1   Introduction

As explained in chapter 15, taper relief may be given in respect of disposals made after 5 April 1998. Acquisitions made after that date therefore need to be separately identifiable, and so the system of share pooling that applied before that date (see later in this chapter) is no longer applied.

3.2   Calculation of the chargeable gain

A disposal is matched with acquisitions made after 5 April 1998 on a LIFO basis.

3.3   Example

Zoe sold 1,000 shares in XYZ plc on 31 January 2000 for £20,000.

She had acquired 1,500 shares in XYZ plc on 30 April 1999 for £18,000, and 500 shares on 31 May 1999 for £7,000.

On 10 February 2000 Zoe bought a further 200 shares in XYZ plc for £3,600.

The shares in XYZ plc are not a business asset for the purposes of taper relief.

Calculate Zoe's chargeable gain.

3.4   Solution

(a)   Match with acquisitions within following 30 days.

	£
Disposal proceeds (£20,000 × 200/1,000)	4,000
Less: Purchase price	3,600
Chargeable gain	400

(b)   Match with acquisition 31 May 1999

	£
Disposal proceeds (£20,000 × 500/1,000)	10,000
Less: Purchase price	7,000
Chargeable gain	3,000

(c)   Match with acquisition 30 April 1999

	£
Disposal proceeds (£20,000 × 300/1,000)	6,000
Less: Purchase price (£18,000 × 300/1,500)	3,600
Chargeable gain	2,400

No taper relief is available since the shares have not been held by Zoe for three complete years post 5 April 1998. It is necessary to calculate each element of the gain separately so taper relief could be correctly applied were it to be available.

Zoe's chargeable gain for 1999/00 is therefore £5,800 (400 + 3,000 + 2,400). The balance of cost remaining from her 30 April 1999 acquisition is £14,400 (18,000 - 3,600).

4   THE 1985 POOL

4.1   Introduction

Prior to 6 April 1998, shares were pooled together. This made the indexation calculations much more straightforward. As explained in chapter 15, indexation for individuals is only given up to April 1998.

4.2   Examiner's comments

The examiner has stated that a question will not be set that requires detailed calculations of either the 1985 pool or the 1982 pool (see later in this chapter).

4.3   Composition of the 1985 pool

The 1985 pool (the rules were introduced in the Finance Act 1985) contains shares that were acquired between 6 April 1982 and 5 April 1998.

The pool only ever contains shares of the same class of the same company, so any person may have several 'pools', each one concerned with a different class of share or shares in different companies.

4.4   Setting up the pool

The pool records, at any time, the number of shares held, their unindexed cost, and their indexed cost (that is original cost plus indexation to date).

Shares are added to the pool when a purchase is made and removed from it on a sale. The allowable cost is added to the totals in the unindexed pool and indexed pool and an indexation allowance (known as an 'indexed rise') is added to the pool of indexed cost immediately before each 'operative event' and so covers inflation on the total investment from one operative event to the next. For the most part operative events are purchases or sales but, strictly, they can be any event that changes the total indexed.

Note that the indexed rise is calculated in just the same way as any other indexation allowance, except for three features:

(a)   the fraction is not rounded to three decimal places; and

(b)   it is multiplied by the indexed cost total immediately after the previous operative event (even if this was a sale); and

(c)   there is no wait until the asset is sold to calculate the allowance (its added bit by bit as the indexed cost total alters).

As already explained, however, indexation is given up to April 1998, but not thereafter.

4.5   Example

Daisy bought the following shares in Handley plc:

- 3,200 shares on 30 April 1985 for £8,750
- 500 shares on 6 July 1985 for £1,300
- 1,300 shares on 10 October 1988 for £3,300

What is the value of the indexed cost pool on 10 October 1988?

4.6   Solution

	Shares	Unindexed cost £	Indexed cost £
30 April 1985 - purchase	3,200	8,750	8,750
6 July 1985 - purchase			
indexed rise £8,750 × $\frac{95.23 - 94.78}{94.78}$			42
			8,792
additional shares	500	1,300	1,300
	3,700	10,050	10,092
10 October 1988 - purchase			
indexed rise £10,092 × $\frac{109.5 - 95.23}{95.23}$			1,512
			11,604
additional shares	1,300	3,300	3,300
Total holding at 10 October 1988, and unindexed cost	5,000	13,350	
Indexed cost at 10 October 1988			14,904

4.7   **Making disposals from the pool**

When shares are sold that are matched against the pool, the number of shares sold is deducted from the share column, a proportionate part of the unindexed cost is deducted from the unindexed cost column, and a proportionate part of the indexed cost is deducted from the indexed cost column. As this is a part disposal the proportionate cost should be calculated using the A/(A + B) formula (as seen in a previous chapter). However, we are not usually given the value of the remaining shares (B in the formula), in which case average cost is used.

The gain or loss on disposal is calculated as follows:

	£
Proceeds	X
Less: Unindexed cost	(X)
Less: Indexation allowance	
(Indexed cost - unindexed cost)	(X)
	X

4.8   Example

Following on from the previous example, let us suppose that Daisy sold 3,000 shares in Handley plc for £14,000 on 1 February 2000.

Calculate the chargeable gain arising on the disposal.

	Shares	Unindexed cost £	Indexed cost £
b/f at 10 October 1988	5,000	13,350	14,904
1 February 2000 - sale			
indexed rise to April 1998			
$£14,904 \times \dfrac{162.6 - 109.5}{109.5}$			7,227
			22,131
sale of shares	3,000		
reduction of unindexed and indexed cost			
$\dfrac{3,000}{5,000} \times £13,350/22,131$		8,010	13,279
Bal c/f	2,000	5,340	8,852

	£
Sale proceeds	14,000
Less: Unindexed cost (above)	8,010
Unindexed gain	5,990
Less: Indexation allowance (13,279 – 8,010)	5,269
Chargeable gain	721

No taper relief is available, since the shares (which are a non-business asset) have not been owned for a sufficient period after 5 April 1998.

5   THE 1982 POOL

5.1   Introduction

As indicated earlier in the chapter shares acquired (in the same company and of the same class) before 6 April 1982 are not put into the 1985 pool. The reason for the rule is straightforward. The indexation on such shares is based on the higher of cost or market value at 31 March 1982, and so it is simpler to maintain a separate pool for these shares.

No new shares are ever added to the 1982 pool; its shares have been 'frozen' and it remains in existence only until those shares are disposed of.

The 1982 pool normally contains shares purchased between 6 April 1965 (when capital gains tax was introduced) and 1982 (as set out above). When a partial disposal of the holding occurs the proportion of the cost that is deductible is calculated by using the A/(A + B) formula if the values are given, but otherwise by taking an average of the cost of the shares in the pool. Then, as for other assets held at 31 March 1982, a comparison is made between the gain arising using purchase cost and that arising from using the March 1982 market value.

5.2   Example

Parrott bought 650 shares in Zenith plc on 1 March 1978 for £2,000 and a further 1,000 shares on 1 February 1982 for £3,200. On 1 December 1999 he sold 1,200 shares for £8,800. The price of Zenith plc shares on 31 March 1982 was £3.50.

Calculate the chargeable gain arising on the disposal.

5.3   **Solution**

Chargeable gain

	Cost	31.3.82 value
	£	£
Disposal proceeds	8,800	8,800
Less: Cost (W)	3,782	
March 1982 value (£3.50 × 1,200)		4,200
Unindexed gain	5,018	4,600
Less: Indexation allowance to April 1998		
$\dfrac{162.6 - 79.44}{79.44}$ (= 1.047) × £4,200	4,397	4,397
Chargeable gain	621	203

Both results produce chargeable gains and so the smaller one, £203, is taken.

No taper relief is available, since the shares (which are a non-business asset) have not been owned for a sufficient period after 5 April 1998.

Working - 1982 pool

	Shares	Cost
		£
1 March 1978 - purchase	650	2,000
1 February 1982 - purchase	1,000	3,200
	1,650	5,200
1 December 1999 - sale	1,200	*3,782
Remaining shares c/f	450	1,418

* Cost of shares sold: $\dfrac{1,200}{1,650}$ × £5,200 = £3,782

6   CHANGES IN SHARE CAPITAL

6.1   Introduction

So far we have looked at how capital gains are calculated when a person acquires shares, sometimes in several transactions spread over a lengthy period, and then sells some or all of them. Although matching rules are needed to keep track of which shares have been sold (and from that the attributable cost, indexation allowance and taper relief) the shares sold were at least the ones originally purchased.

On occasion, however, entirely new shares enter the picture, such as on bonus or rights issues. It helps to understand the rules for dealing with these issues if one remembers that the shareholder acquires them as a direct result of the holding he already owns.

6.2   Bonus issues

Bonus issues (sometimes known also as scrip or capitalisation issues) are fairly straightforward to deal with. Additional shares are issued, but at no extra cost to the shareholder.

The only complication produced by bonus issues is how to treat the extra shares for the purpose of the matching rules when a disposal is made. Quite simply, every purchase of shares made before the bonus issue takes place has the appropriate number of bonus shares added to it.

6.3   Example

Blackburn had the following transactions in the shares of Gray plc.

November 1980	purchased 2,200 shares for £3,400
January 1989	purchased 1,300 shares for £2,450
May 1998	purchased 500 shares for £1,750
June 1998	bonus issue of one for five
September 1999	sold 2,600 shares for £10,400

The price of Gray plc shares on 31 March 1982 (as adjusted for the bonus issue) was £1.50.

Calculate the chargeable gain or allowable loss arising on the sale in September 1999.

6.4   Solution

Calculation of chargeable gain

(a)   Shares matched against the post 5 April 1998 acquisition

		£
Proceeds $\dfrac{600}{2,600} \times £10,400$		2,400
Less: Cost		1,750
Chargeable gain		650

500 shares were acquired in May 1998, and this is increased to 600 as a result of the one for five bonus issue.

(b)   Shares matched against the 1985 pool

	£
Proceeds (1,560 shares (W1)) $\dfrac{1,560}{2,600} \times £10,400$	6,240
Less: Cost (W1)	2,450
Unindexed gain	3,790
Less: Indexation allowance (3,589 – 2,450)	1,139
Chargeable gain	2,651

(c)   Shares matched against the 1982 pool

	Cost	31.3.82 value
		£
Proceeds (2,600 – 600 – 1,560 = 440)		
$\dfrac{440}{2,600} \times £10,400$	1,760	1,760
Less: Cost/March 1982 value $£567$ (W2)/£1.50 × 440	567	660
Unindexed gain	1,193	1,100
Less: Indexation allowance to April 1998 $\dfrac{162.6 - 79.44}{79.44}$ (= 1.047) × £660	691	691
Chargeable gain	502	409

The smaller gain is taken, £409.

Total gain on disposal is thus £3,710 (650 + 2,651 + 409).

No taper relief is available, since the shares (which are a non-business asset) have not been owned for a sufficient period.

Workings - construction of pool costs

The disposal must be worked through in the order prescribed by the matching rules.

		Shares	Unindexed cost £	Indexed cost £
(W1)	**Shares held in the 1985 pool**			
	January 1989			
	purchase	1,300	2,450	2,450
	attributable bonus shares (1 for 5)	260		-
		1,560	2,450	2,450
	September 1999			
	indexed rise (January 1989 to April 1998)			
	$\dfrac{162.6 - 111.0}{111.0} \times £2,450$			1,139
				3,589
	sale	1,560	2,450	3,589

		Shares	Cost £
(W2)	**Shares in 1982 pool**		
	November 1980		
	purchase	2,200	3,400
	attributable bonus shares (1 for 5)	440	-
		2,640	3,400
	September 1999		
	sale (2,600 − 600 − 1,560 (W1))	440	*567
		2,200	2,833

* Cost of shares sold is $\dfrac{440}{2,640} \times £3,400 = £567$.

6.5   Rights issues

Rights issues have an essential feature in common with bonus issues; new shares are acquired as a result of an existing holding (and the number of new shares acquired is proportionate to the existing holding). Accordingly the same rule applies for rights issues as bonus issues; the new shares are deemed to have been acquired at the same time as the original shares.

But in contrast with bonus issues, the shareholder has to subscribe new money to acquire them. Subscribing new money has two important consequences for capital gains tax:

(a)   the cost of the total shareholding is increased by the amount subscribed for the rights issues shares; and

(b)   the shareholder may obtain additional indexation allowances, based on the amount of new expenditure.

Care is needed in dealing with (b) above. Although for matching purposes the rights issue shares are deemed to have been acquired at the same time as the original shares, the indexation allowance is computed from the time they were actually issued. To do otherwise would be illogical as the shareholder would be receiving indexation allowance for a period before he made his investment in the rights issue shares.

Conversely, taper relief is calculated from the date that the original holding was acquired.

6.6   Example

Carmichael had the following transactions in the shares of Rudderham plc.

October 1979	purchased 600 shares for £1,200
January 1987	purchased 2,100 shares for £3,200
May 1998	purchased 600 shares for £1,500
June 1998	took up 1 for 3 rights issue at £2.30 per share
August 1999	sold 4,000 shares for £14,000

As 31 March 1982 the value of Rudderham plc shares (as adjusted for the rights issue) was £1.55.

Calculate the chargeable gains or allowable loss on the disposal in August 1999.

6.7   Solution

Calculation of chargeable gain

(a)   Shares matched against the post 5 April 1998 acquisition

	£
Proceeds £14,000 $\times \dfrac{800}{4,000}$ (W1)	2,800
Less: Cost (W1)	1,960
Chargeable gain	840

(b)   Shares matched against the 1985 pool

	£
Proceeds £14,000 $\times \dfrac{2,800}{4,000}$ (W2)	9,800
Less: Unindexed cost (W2)	4,810
Unindexed gain	4,990
Less: Indexation allowance (6,813 – 4,810)	2,003
Chargeable gain	2,987

(c)   Shares matched against 1982 pool

	Cost £	31.3.82 value £
Proceeds (14,000 – 2,800 – 9,800)	1,400	1,400
Less: Cost (W3)/31.3.82 value	830	
£1.55 × 400		620
	570	780

Less: Indexation allowance to April 1998

    (i)   On original cost

$$\frac{162.6-79.44}{79.44} \ (=1.047) \times 1{,}200 \times \frac{400}{800} \qquad 628 \qquad 628$$

    (ii)   On cost of rights shares

        Nil, as acquired after 31 March 1998

                                  Nil   152

There is nil and a gain and thus no gain/no loss is taken. The total gain is thus £3,827 (840 + 2,987 + nil).

No taper relief is available since the shares have not been owned for a sufficient period. However, if taper relief were available the date of the rights issue is irrelevant to the calculation. For example, taper relief on the post 5 April 1998 gain would be calculated from May 1998.

WORKINGS

(W1) Post 5 April 1998 acquisition

	Shares	Cost £
May 1998 purchase	600	1,500
June 1998 rights issue	200	460
	800	1,960

(W2) Shares held in the 1985 pool

	Shares	Unindexed cost £	Indexed cost £
January 1987 purchase	2,100	3,200	3,200
June 1998 rights issue Indexed rise to April 1998 $\frac{162.6-100.0}{100.0} \times £3{,}200$			2,003
			5,203
Issue of shares (1 for 3)	700	1,610	1,610
	2,800	4,810	6,813
August 1999 disposal	2,800	4,810	6,813

(W3) Shares in 1982 pool

		Shares	Cost £
October 1979	purchase	600	1,200
June 1998	rights issue (1 for 3)	200	460
		800	1,660

August 1999	disposal (4,000 – 800 (W1) – 2,800 W2)	400	830
		400	830

7   REORGANISATIONS AND TAKEOVERS

7.1   Reorganisations

A reorganisation involves the exchange of existing shares and securities for others of another class. No CGT is charged until the replacement shares or securities are disposed of, unless the reorganisation involves a cash payout to shareholders.

Taper relief will be based on the date that the original shares were acquired.

The key aspect of reorganisations is attributing the cost of the original holding to the different component parts of the new holding. The rules differ according to whether the shares are quoted or unquoted. For quoted shares the apportionment of cost is made according to the relative values of the replacement shares and securities on the first day of quotation. For unquoted shares the apportionment is based on the relative values of the replacement shares and securities at the time the first disposal is made from them.

7.2   Example

Major purchased 2,000 ordinary shares in Blue plc (a quoted company) for £5,000 in June 1990. In July 1998 Blue plc underwent a reorganisation and Major received 2 'A' ordinary shares and 1 preference share for each ordinary share. Immediately after the reorganisation 'A' ordinary shares were quoted at £2 and preference shares at £1. In December 1999 Major sold all his holding of 'A' ordinary shares for £8,000.

Calculate the chargeable gain or allowable loss arising on the disposal in December 1999.

7.3   Solution

	£
Disposal proceeds	8,000
Less: Cost (W)	4,444
Unindexed gain	3,556
Less: Indexation allowance to April 1998	
$\dfrac{162.6 - 126.7}{126.7} \times £4{,}444$	1,259
Chargeable gain	2,297

Working - cost of 'A' ordinary shares

Major received:

4,000 'A' ordinary shares, valued at 4,000 × £2 =	£8,000
1,000 preference shares, valued at 1,000 × £1 =	£1,000

Cost attributable to the 'A' ordinary shares is thus:

$$£5{,}000 \times \frac{8{,}000}{9{,}000} = £4{,}444$$

No taper relief is available since the shares have not been owned for a sufficient period.

7.4   Takeovers

Where a takeover is a 'paper for paper' transaction shareholders of the company taken over acquire shares in the acquiring company. This does not constitute a disposal for capital gains tax purposes provided that:

(a)   the acquiring company obtains more than 25% of the target company's ordinary share capital as a result of the offer; or

(b)   there is a general offer to members of the target company which would give control to the acquirer if accepted; or

(c)   the acquirer can exercise more than 50% of the voting power in the target company.

The new shares are deemed to have been acquired at the same time and at the same cost as the original shares, provided that there is no substantial cash element in the consideration given by the acquiring company. If there is a cash element there are two possibilities:

(a)   the cash represents 5% or less of the value of the holding (ie, it is 'small'), in which case the cash is deducted from the allowable cost of the holding for future disposals; or

(b)   in other cases, there is a part disposal and the gain relating to the cash element must be calculated. In these circumstances the part of the cost of the original holding apportioned to the cash is calculated as:

$$\frac{\text{Cash received}}{\text{Cash received} + \text{market value of new shares}} \times \text{original cost}$$

In February 1997 the Revenue introduced a practice of treating cash proceeds of less than £3,000 as 'small' whether or not the 5% test was satisfied.

7.5   Example

Patrick bought 10,000 shares in Target plc in May 1998 for £20,000. On 3 November 1999 the entire share capital of Target plc was acquired by Bidder plc. Target plc shareholders received 2 Bidder plc shares and £0.50 cash for each share held. Bidder plc shares were quoted at £1.25.

Calculate the chargeable gain accruing to Patrick as a result of the takeover in November 1999.

7.6   Solution

The total consideration provided by Bidder plc is:

	£
Shares (20,000 @ 1.25)	25,000
Cash (10,000 × £0.50)	5,000
	30,000

As the cash Patrick has received exceeds 5% of the total (£30,000) (and exceeds £3,000) he has made a part disposal.

	£
Disposal proceeds (cash)	5,000
Less: Original cost:	
$\frac{5,000}{30,000} \times £20,000$	3,333
Chargeable gain	1,667

Patrick's allowable cost on the future disposal of his shares in Bidder plc will be £16,667 (20,000- 3,333).

No taper relief is available since the shares have not been owned for a sufficient period. Taper relief on the shares held in Bidder plc will be based on an acquisition date of May 1998, and not November 1999.

8   QUALIFYING CORPORATE BONDS AND LISTED GOVERNMENT SECURITIES

8.1   Introduction

It was mentioned earlier in the chapter that securities are subject to the same capital gains tax rules as shares. Listed government securities (gilt edged securities or gilts) and qualifying corporate bonds are the exception to this rule. As far as individuals are concerned, they are not subject to capital gains tax and thus no chargeable gains or allowable losses arise on their disposal.

8.2   Scope of qualifying corporate bonds

A qualifying corporate bond is one which:

(a)   represents a normal commercial loan;

(b)   is expressed in sterling and has no provision for either conversion into, or redemption in, any other currency; and

(c)   was issued after 13 March 1984 or was acquired by the disposer after that date (whenever it was issued).

The term 'corporate bond' is also extended to permanent interest-bearing shares in building societies, provided they meet the condition set out in (b) above.

The situation might arise where a non-qualifying corporate bond is changed into a qualifying bond. Any capital gain in respect of the non-qualifying corporate bond will become chargeable when the security is disposed of.

9   CHAPTER SUMMARY

9.1   Introduction

Shares and securities present a special problem in the context of capital gains tax because one is indistinguishable from another (if they are of the same class in the same company). The capital gains tax system gets around this problem by inventing a procedure, known as the matching rules, for identifying the shares involved in any particular sale.

9.2   Matching rules

Disposals are first matched against shares acquired within the following 30 days, and then against shares acquired after 5 April 1998 (taking the most recent acquisition first on a LIFO basis). Disposals are next matched against shares in the 1985 pool, then the 1982 pool.

The 1985 pool contains all shares acquired between 6 April 1982 and 5 April 1998. Unlike other assets, for which an indexation allowance is calculated on sale, shares in the share pool have the indexation allowance added to cost each time there is an operative event. Operative events are mostly purchases and sales but include any transaction that affects the total cost of the shareholder's investment.

The 1982 pool contains shares acquired between 6 April 1965, the date capital gains tax was introduced, and the start of the 1985 pool in 1982. No new shares are added to it; it continues in existence until such time as the shares held in 1982 are deemed to have been disposed of under the matching rules.

9.3   Alterations to share capital

Rights and bonus issues present different problems for capital gains tax but there is a common theme. In each case the shares resulting from the new issue are deemed to have been acquired at the time the shareholding giving rise to them was acquired. In the case of rights issues the indexation allowance complicates the picture because it is calculated from the time the new investment was made (not the time of the original acquisition).

Conversely, taper relief is calculated from the date that the original holding was acquired.

Where there is a reorganisation or takeover the problem is to apportion the cost of the original shares among whatever shares and securities replace them. For quoted shares this is done on the basis of the market values of the new shares and securities immediately afterwards. For unquoted shares no apportionment of cost is done until a disposal is made from the replacement holding and it is then based on the relative market values at that time.

9.4   Gilts and qualifying corporate bonds

Dealing with gilts and qualifying corporate bonds is easy for capital gains tax. Both are exempt and so no chargeable gains or allowable losses arise.

10   SELF-TEST QUESTIONS

10.1   Why are the matching rules necessary? (2.1)

10.2   What is the matching order? (2.2)

10.3   Why is a disposal matched firstly with acquisitions within the following 30 days? (2.3)

10.4   Shares acquired during which period are aggregated in the share pool? (4.3)

10.5   How is the calculation of the indexed rise for a share pool different from the normal indexation allowance calculation? (4.4)

10.6   What calculation is required to ascertain the indexed cost of a parcel of shares sold from the share pool? (4.7)

10.7   The 1982 holding contains shares acquired between certain dates. What are the dates? (5.1)

10.8   How do the matching rules apply to bonus issues? (6.2)

10.9   In what two ways does the treatment of a rights issue differ from that of a bonus issue? (6.5)

10.10   What is a qualifying corporate bond? (8.2)

11   EXAMINATION TYPE QUESTION

11.1   Jasper

Jasper had the following transactions in securities during the year 1999/00

(1)   Sold all of his 2,145 25p ordinary shares in Carrot plc on 19 November 1999 for net sale proceeds of £8,580.

His previous dealings in these shares were as follows

October 1981	purchased 1,250 shares for £1,650
July 1986	purchased 500 shares for £700
May 1998	purchased 200 shares for £640
June 1998	took up 1 for 10 rights issue at £3.40 per share

The shares were quoted at 149 – 153 on 31 March 1982.

(2)   Sold 400 £1 ordinary shares in Grasp plc for £3,600 on 31 March 2000. Jasper had acquired these Grasp plc shares as a result of a successful takeover bid by Grasp plc of Cawte plc on 5

December 1999. Prior to the takeover Jasper had owned 12,000 £1 ordinary shares in Cawte plc, which he had acquired for £15,700 on 3 May 1998. The terms of the take-over bid were

- one £1 ordinary share in Grasp plc, plus
- two 10% preference shares in Grasp plc, plus
- 40p in cash

for every £1 ordinary share in Cawte plc.

The following are the quoted prices for the shares of Grasp plc at 5 December 1999

£1 ordinary shares	350p
10% preference shares	110p

Jasper has elected for the market value basis of computation to be used for disposals of all assets held on 31 March 1982.

You are required to calculate the chargeable gains and allowable losses arising in respect of the disposals in 1999/00.

12   ANSWER TO EXAMINATION TYPE QUESTION

12.1   Jasper

Capital gains computation 1999/00

(1)   **Shares in Carrot plc**

Shares matched against the post 5 April 1998 acquisition

	£	£	Gain/(loss) £
Proceeds £8,580 × $\dfrac{220}{2,145}$		880	
Less: May 1998 purchase	640		
June 1998 rights issue (20 at 340p)	68		
		708	
			172

1985 pool	Shares No	Unindexed cost £	Indexed cost £
July 1986 Purchase	500	700	700
Indexed rise (July'86 − Apr'98)			
$\dfrac{162.6-97.52}{97.52} \times £700$			467
			1,167
June 1998 Rights issue			
1-for-10 at 340p per share	50	170	170
	550	870	1,337
November 1999 Disposal	550	870	1,337
Proceeds 8,580 × $\dfrac{550}{2,145}$			2,200
Less: Unindexed cost			870
Unindexed gain			1,330

Less: Indexation allowance
1,337 − 870 467

.... 863

1982 pool (MV 31.3.82 election in force)

October 1981 purchase	1,250	1,875
June 1998 Rights issue		
1−for−10 at 340p per share	125	425
	1,375	2,300

November 1999 Sold

$8,580 \times \dfrac{1,375}{2,145}$ 5,500

MV 31.3.82 2,300

Unindexed gain 3,200

Less: Indexation to April 1998

(i) MV 31.3.82
(March'82 − Apr'98)
$\dfrac{162.6 - 79.44}{79.44} (= 1.047) \times £1,875$ ..... (1,963)

(ii) Rights issue cost .... Nil

.... 1,237

Net result on disposal of 2,145 shares 2,272

(2) **Grasp plc**

Apportionment of cost of Cawte plc securities
to new securities and cash

	5.12.99 Purchase consideration £	Cost £
For 12,000 Cawte plc ordinary shares:		
12,000 Grasp £1 ordinary shares at 350p	42,000	9,008
24,000 Grasp 10% preference shares at 110p	26,400	5,662
Cash − 12,000 × 40p	4,800	1,030
	73,200	15,700

5% of (12,000 × 610p) = £3,660

As cash exceeds this figure (and exceeds £3,000), roll-over relief does not apply

Disposal for cash on 5 December 1999

	£	
Cash received	4,800	
Deemed cost	1,030	
Chargeable gain		3,770

Disposal on 31 March 2000

	£	
Proceeds	3,600	
Deemed cost £9,008 × 400/12,000	300	
		3,300
Chargeable gain		7,070

18 CHATTELS AND WASTING ASSETS

INTRODUCTION

This chapter covers chattels and wasting assets. Special attention should be paid to the more straightforward aspects of chattels, especially marginal relief, as these are the areas that tend to be examined.

When you have studied this chapter you should have learned the following:

- The definition of chattels and wasting assets.
- The scope of the exemption for chattels.
- How to calculate marginal relief and losses for chattels.
- To distinguish between wasting assets with different CGT treatments.
- The calculation for reducing the allowable cost of a wasting asset when it is sold.
- To distinguish between disposals of different kinds of leases and their CGT treatments.

1 CHATTELS

1.1 Chattel exemption

Chattels are defined as tangible, movable property. Paintings, furniture and jewellery are examples of chattels. Note the requirement that a chattel is tangible; therefore shares and leases are not chattels.

Chattels (which are defined as tangible movable property), do **not** have a general exemption from capital gains tax. There is, however, an exemption where a chattel is sold at a gain for a consideration (proceeds or market value, as appropriate) of £6,000 or less. The limit of £6,000 applies to the gross consideration (ie, before deducting disposal expenses).

Remember that cars have a separate specific exemption and are thus not chargeable assets, whatever their value.

2 MARGINAL RELIEF AND LOSS RELIEF

2.1 Marginal relief

Where a chattel is sold for more than £6,000 a marginal relief is available. In these circumstances the gain is **limited** to

$$5/3 \times (\text{gross disposal consideration} - £6,000)$$

Thus two calculations are needed, one using the marginal relief formula and the other computed in the normal way. Provided that both results produce a gain, the lower one is taken. Where the ordinary CGT computation produces a loss different rules apply.

The relief helps the taxpayer on the disposal of low value chattels. Just where it ceases to be advantageous depends on the levels of disposal consideration and allowable expenditure.

2.2 Activity

Andrew sells a picture on 1 February 2000 for £6,600 that he acquired on 1 March 1990 for £3,200.

Calculate the chargeable gain arising, if any.

2.3   Activity solution

		£
Disposal proceeds		6,600
Less: Cost		3,200
Unindexed gain		3,400
Less: Indexation allowance to April 1998		
$\dfrac{162.6 - 121.4}{121.4}$ $(= 0.339) \times £3,200$		1,085
Indexed gain		2,315

Marginal relief imposes a limit on the gain of:
$5/3 \times (6,600 - 6,000) = £1,000$

2.4   Loss relief

Where a chattel is sold for £6,000 or more at a loss, the loss is computed in the normal way. However, if it is sold for less than £6,000 the allowable loss is restricted. This is achieved by substituting notional proceeds of £6,000 for the actual, lower, proceeds.

The substitution of £6,000 for actual proceeds is not allowed to turn a loss into a gain. If the calculation produces an apparent gain the result is no gain/no loss.

2.5   Activity

Brian bought an antique table for £6,500 in September 1990 and sold it for £5,600 in December 1999. He incurred £250 to advertise it for sale.

Calculate the allowable loss arising, if any.

2.6   Activity solution

	£	£
Notional sale proceeds		6,000
Less: Cost	6,500	
Expenses of sale	250	6,750
Unindexed loss		750

The unindexed loss is the allowable loss, as an indexation allowance is not available to increase a loss.

3   WASTING ASSETS

3.1   Introduction

Definition   A wasting asset is an asset with a predictable life not exceeding 50 years. 'Life' means the asset's useful life, having regard to the purpose for which the disposer acquired it.

In addition to the general definition, the legislation deals with two specific cases, as follows.

(a)   Freehold land is **never** a wasting asset (irrespective of its nature or that of any buildings on it).

(b)   Plant and machinery is **always** a wasting asset.

The importance of the definition of a wasting asset lies in two points. Firstly certain wasting assets are exempt from capital gains tax. Secondly non-exempt wasting assets have a modified calculation of the gain or loss on disposal which reflects the fact that their relatively short life causes them generally to decline in value.

What distinguishes the treatment of wasting assets for capital gains tax is firstly whether the wasting asset is also a chattel (a 'wasting chattel') and secondly whether capital allowances may be claimed on it.   From this three categories of wasting asset may be identified, with differing CGT treatments. These are:

(a)   wasting chattels on which capital allowances could **not** be claimed by the disposer;

(b)   wasting assets and chattels on which capital allowances could be claimed by the disposer; and

(c)   wasting assets that are not chattels and have no entitlement to capital allowances.

The first category is easily dealt with as wasting chattels on which capital allowances could not be claimed are exempt.

3.2   Wasting assets and chattels with capital allowances

This category includes both wasting assets and chattels on which capital allowances have been claimed and those on which capital allowances could have been claimed (but, in fact, they have not been).

Where the disposal is of a chattel and gives rise to a gain it is computed in the normal way for chattels, with the benefit of the £6,000 exemption described earlier in the chapter.

Capital allowances may be ignored when the asset is disposed of at a gain as they are clawed back. However, if a loss is suffered, some or all of the loss may be disallowed because relief has been given under the capital allowances system.

Where net capital allowances are made (ie, net of balancing charges on disposal) they are deducted from the asset's allowable expenditure.

3.3   Example - reduction in value relieved by capital allowances

Fred bought some machinery for use in his trade for £35,000 in April 1992. In October 1999 he decides to replace it and sells the old machinery for £26,500.

Calculate the chargeable gain or allowable loss arising on the disposal in October 1999.

3.4   Solution

Fred obtains net capital allowances of £8,500 (35,000 - 26,500) during his ownership of the machinery.

	£	£
Disposal proceeds		26,500
Less: Cost	35,000	
Less: Net capital allowances	8,500	
		26,500
Allowable loss		Nil

3.5   Wasting assets (not qualifying for capital allowances)

The special point about wasting assets which are not chattels and which do not qualify for capital allowances is that the allowable expenditure is deemed to waste away over the life of the asset. Consequently, when a disposal is made, the allowable expenditure is restricted to take account of the asset's natural fall in value. Otherwise allowable losses could be accumulated merely by holding wasting assets (irrespective of financial and commercial conditions).

The depreciation of most wasting assets is deemed to occur on a straight line basis over its predictable life (the exception being leases of land, which are considered later in the chapter). Total depreciation over a wasting asset's entire life is cost minus scrap value (if any). The part of this depreciation that is attributable to the disposer's period of ownership is then:

$$\frac{P}{L} \times (C - S)$$

where: P is the disposer's period of ownership;
        L is the asset's predictable life;
        C is the cost of the asset; and
        S is any residual or scrap value at the end of the asset's predictable life.

3.6   Example

On 1 February 1992 Ian bought a wasting asset at a cost of £25,000. It had an estimated useful life of 30 years and an estimated scrap value of £1,000. He sold the asset for £38,000 on 1 February 2000.

Calculate the chargeable gain or allowable loss arising from the disposal in February 2000.

3.7   Solution

	£	£
Disposal proceeds		38,000
Less: Purchase cost	25,000	
Less: Wasting asset depreciation		
$\frac{8}{30} \times (25{,}000 - 1{,}000)$	6,400	
Allowable element of acquisition cost		18,600
Unindexed gain		19,400
Less: Indexation allowance to April 1998:		
$\frac{162.6 - 136.3}{136.3}\ (= 0.193) \times £18{,}600$		3,590
Indexed gain		15,810

4   LEASES OF LAND

4.1   Introduction

Leases of land are considered separately here because in some cases, even where they have less than 50 years to expiry (and so count as wasting assets) the capital gains tax computation is different to other wasting assets.

There are essentially two different situations to consider:

(a)   assignment of a lease with more than 50 years to expiry (a 'long' lease); and
(b)   assignment of a lease with less than or exactly 50 years to expiry (a 'short' lease);

The duration of a lease is normally obvious. If, however, the landlord has an option to terminate the lease early, the lease is deemed, for CGT purposes, to expire at the first time the landlord can exercise his option.

An assignment occurs when the seller disposes of his lease; it is the disposal of his whole interest.

Where a taxpayer occupies his principal private residence under the terms of a lease, any gain on its disposal qualifies for the principal private residence exemption (see earlier chapter on principal private residence).

4.2   **Assignment of a lease with more than 50 years to expiry**

This is the most straightforward case. The disposal is of the seller's whole interest and, since the lease has more than 50 years to run, it is not a wasting asset. The calculation of the gain or loss follows the normal capital gains tax rules.

4.3   **Assignment of a lease with 50 years or less to expiry**

A lease with 50 years or less to expiry is a wasting asset and the capital gains tax calculation reflects this. For most wasting assets, considered earlier in the chapter, depreciation is assumed to occur on a straight line basis. Leases are treated differently; the value assumed to be left in a lease of less than 50 years is given by a table set out in the legislation. It assumes that the lease loses value gradually at first and much more quickly close to the time of expiry.

The deductible part of the original cost (that is the actual cost less the assumed depreciation) is given by the formula

$$\frac{A}{B} \times \text{original cost (or 31 March 1982 value if appropriate)}$$

where: A is the table percentage for the number of years left to expiry at the time of disposal; and

B is the table percentage for the number of years left to expiry at the time of acquisition (or 31 March 1982 if appropriate)

If the dates of disposal or acquisition do not fall conveniently to make whole years, the calculation is done to the nearest month. One twelfth of the difference between the percentages for the years either side of the actual duration is added for each extra month. Fourteen or more days count as a month.

4.4   **Example**

Geoffrey purchased a lease with 48 years to run on 1 September 1995 for £62,000. On 28 January 2000 he sold the lease for £75,000.

Calculate the chargeable gain or allowable loss arising on the sale.

4.5   **Solution**

	£
Disposal proceeds	75,000
Less: Cost (W)	60,815
Unindexed gain	14,185
Less: Indexation allowance to April 1998	
$\dfrac{162.6 - 150.6}{150.6}\ (= 0.080) \times £60,815$	4,865
Indexed gain	9,320

Working - deductible lease cost

Years to run at acquisition	48 years
Years to run at disposal	43 years 7 months

Thus percentage for 43 years 7 months is:

$$97.107 + (97.595 - 97.107) \times 7/12 = 97.392$$

Deductible cost is thus $\dfrac{97.392}{99.289} \times £62,000 = £60,815$

Note that as for other wasting assets, the indexation allowance is based on the cost after depreciation, not the whole original cost.

5   CHAPTER SUMMARY

(a)   Chattels (tangible movable property) are exempt when they are sold at a gain for £6,000 or less. The limit of £6,000 applies to the gross consideration (before taking into account any disposal expenses).

(b)   Gains on chattels sold for more than £6,000 are restricted to 5/3 x (disposal consideration - £6,000) if this is less than the gain calculated using normal CGT principles.

(c)   Losses on chattels sold for less than £6,000 are restricted (by substituting £6,000 for the actual sale proceeds).

(d)   Wasting assets (assets with predictable lives of not more than 50 years) have a deduction made from allowable cost to reflect their depreciation during the disposer's period of ownership. Indexation allowance is based on cost less the depreciation deduction.

(e)   Wasting assets that are also chattels are exempt (unless they have, or could have, capital allowances claimed on them).

(f)   Disposal of leases of more than 50 years to expiry are treated like any other asset. Other leases (commonly known as short leases) are wasting assets. These have a separate treatment. The depreciation deduction is based on a table set out in the legislation (rather than assuming the straight line depreciation used for other wasting assets).

6   SELF TEST QUESTIONS

6.1   What are chattels? (1.1)

6.2   How are gains on chattels sold for more than £6,000 restricted? (2.1)

6.3   How are losses restricted for disposals of chattels for less than £6,000? (2.4)

6.4   What is a wasting asset? (3.1)

6.5   When are wasting assets exempt from CGT? (3.2)

6.6   In what way is allowable expenditure on a wasting asset (other than a lease) restricted when it is sold? (3.3)

6.7   How is the gain calculated when a lease with more than 50 years to expiry is assigned? (4.2)

6.8   How is the gain calculated when a lease with 50 years or less to expiry is assigned? (4.3)

7   EXAMINATION TYPE QUESTION

7.1   Mr and Mrs Steel

Mr and Mrs Steel had the following transactions in assets in the year ended 5 April 2000

Mr Steel

(a)   A house, which had been bought for £4,000 on 3 April 1983 and let to tenants thereafter, was sold on 1 July 1999. On 2 April 1984 an extension costing £2,000 was built, and on 12 June 1986 the loft was converted into a bedroom at a cost of £3,000. The net proceeds of sale were £62,750.

(b)   Sold a piece of sculpture for £6,500 on 30 August 1999 which he had bought for £3,900. The indexation factor is 0.424.

(c)   Sold a one-tenth share in a racehorse on 31 August 1999 for £6,200. The interest had cost £1,340 in November 1996.

(d)   Sold a vintage Alfa Romeo motor car for £76,500 on 19 December 1999. The car had cost £17,400 on 31 March 1983. During his period of ownership Steel had never actually used the car on the road.

Mrs Steel

(e)   Sold a rare Russian icon on 24 May 1999 for £5,600 which had cost £6,300. The indexation factor is 0.618.

(f)   Sold three acres out of a twelve acre plot of land on 14 December 1999 for £10,000. The whole plot had been purchased for £2,000. On 14 December 1999 the unsold acres had an agreed market value of £20,000. The indexation factor is 0.682.

(g)   Sold a piece of Chinese jade for £11,000 on 1 September 1999. This was purchased at auction in May 1970 for £4,100. The market value on 31 March 1982 was £6,500.

Mr Steel had capital losses brought forward at 6 April 1999 of £2,610. His taxable income for 1999/00 is £23,300. Mrs Steel has no income.

None of the above assets are business assets for the purposes of taper relief.

You are required:

(a)   to calculate Mr Steel's CGT liability for 1999/00.
(b)   to calculate Mrs Steel's CGT liability for 1999/00.

8   ANSWER TO EXAMINATION TYPE QUESTION

8.1   Mr and Mrs Steel

Mr Steel

(a)   **House**

	£	£	Gain/(loss) £
Net sale proceeds (1.7.99)		62,750	
Cost (3.4.83)	4,000		
Extension (2.4.84)	2,000		
Loft (12.6.86)	3,000		
		(9,000)	
Unindexed gain		53,750	

Less: Indexation allowance to April 1998

Cost $4,000 \times \dfrac{162.6 - 84.28}{84.28}$ (0.929)   3,716

Extension $2,000 \times \dfrac{162.6 - 88.64}{88.64}$ (0.834)   1,668

Loft $3,000 \times \dfrac{162.6 - 97.79}{97.79}$ (0.663)   1,989   (7,373)

| Chargeable gain | | 46,377 | 46,377 |

(b)   **Sculpture**

Sale proceeds	6,500	
Less: Cost	3,900	
	‾‾‾‾	
Unindexed gain	2,600	
Less: Indexation allowance 3,900 × 0.424	1,654	
	‾‾‾‾	
	946	
	‾‾‾‾	
Gain cannot exceed (6,500 − 6,000) × ⅚		833

(c)   **One-tenth interest in racehorse**

Exempt as a chattel which is also a wasting asset   -

(d)   **Alfa-Romeo vintage car**

Exempt asset   -

Net gains   47,210

Mrs Steel

(e)   **Icon**

	£	£	£
Deemed sale proceeds		6,000	
Cost		6,300	
		‾‾‾‾	
Allowable loss		(300)	(300)

(f)   **Plot of land**

		£	£
Sale proceeds of 3 acres		10,000	
Less: Cost of 3 acres			
$2,000 \times \dfrac{10,000}{10,000+20,000}$		667	
		‾‾‾	
Unindexed gain		9,333	
Less: Indexation allowance 667 × 0.682		455	
		‾‾‾	
Chargeable gain		8,878	8,878

(g)   **Jade**

	Cost basis £	31.3.82 basis £
Sale proceeds	11,000	11,000
Less: Cost/MV 31.3.82	4,100	6,500
	‾‾‾‾	‾‾‾‾
Unindexed gain	6,900	4,500
Less: IA (Mar 1982 – Apr 1998) Use higher MV 31.3.82 $6,500 \times \dfrac{162.6-79.44}{79.44}$ (1.047)	(6,806)	(6,806)
	‾‾‾‾	‾‾‾‾
Neither gain/nor loss	94	Nil

Net gains   8,578

		Mr Steel £		Mrs Steel £
Net gains for 1999/00		47,210		8,578
Less: Losses b/f		(2,610)		-
		44,600		8,578
Less: Annual exemption		(7,100)		(7,100)
Taxable amount		37,500		1,478

	£	£	£	£
Tax	4,700 × 20%	940	1,478 × 20%	296
	32,800 × 40%	13,120		—
	37,500	14,060		

19 RETIREMENT RELIEF

INTRODUCTION & LEARNING OBJECTIVES

This relief applies to the gains realised on the transfer of a business, or shares in a personal company. Earlier in the text it was explained that capital gains tax reliefs either exempt the gain or defer it; retirement relief exempts gains made on the transfer of a business or shares in a personal company. It is frequently examined and should be studied carefully.

When you have studied this chapter you should have learned the following:

- The purpose and scope of retirement relief.
- The monetary limits and the circumstances in which these are scaled down.
- The conditions applying to sole traders.
- The additional conditions applying to certain shareholders of personal companies.
- The conditions that must be met by assets to qualify for relief.
- The definition of a personal company.
- The restriction for non-business assets owned by a personal company.
- When two periods of business ownership may be aggregated to calculate the qualifying period.
- The circumstances in which retirement relief is extended to associated disposals.

1 INTRODUCTION

1.1 Purpose of retirement relief

Retirement relief provides generous relief from capital gains tax for people retiring from business towards the end of their careers. Broadly it applies only to chargeable gains realised by people actively involved in the business; generally gains realised by passive investors do not qualify for relief.

It is particularly valuable in assisting families to pass businesses on from one generation to the next. Such transfers are often made by gift. Although there is a separate relief for gifts of business assets, it is not so comprehensive as retirement relief. Since market value is substituted for disposal proceeds when a gift is made, if it were not for retirement relief the disposer would often find himself paying a large tax bill without having received any cash.

1.2 Scope of retirement relief

The most important groups of people covered by the retirement relief rules are:

(a) sole traders; and
(b) certain shareholders of personal companies.

Each group has its own set of conditions which must be met before retirement relief is available.

For both groups, however, the size of the eligible gain that can be relieved is the same. The first £200,000 is entirely exempt and, if the gain is large enough, an additional £600,000 attracts relief at 50%. Thus a total of £800,000 chargeable gains may be wholly or partly sheltered. The relief is deducted from the indexed gain.

1.3   Activity

Griffiths made indexed gains of £1,200,000 on the disposal of his business on 1 February 2000. He met all the conditions for retirement relief in full.

Calculate the chargeable gain after retirement relief.

1.4   Activity solution

		£	£
Gain before retirement relief			1,200,000
Less: Retirement relief			
(i)	first £200,000	200,000	
(ii)	(£800,000 – £200,000) × 50%	300,000	
			500,000
Chargeable gain after retirement relief			700,000

1.5   Taper relief

Retirement relief is given before any taper relief that is due. In the above example, taper relief would be calculated on the chargeable gain after retirement relief of £700,000.

Retirement relief is applied so as to provide the maximum possible benefit from taper relief.

2   PHASING OUT OF RETIREMENT RELIEF

2.1   Introduction

Retirement relief is currently being phased out by a gradual reduction of the relief thresholds. Relief will cease to be available altogether from 6 April 2003.

Prior to 6 April 1999 the first £250,000 of gains were fully exempt, with the next £750,000 attracting relief at the rate of 50%.

2.2   Examiner's comments

The examiner has stated that retirement relief will be fully examinable for the June and December 2000 examinations.

You only need to know the current year thresholds (1999/00) of £200,000 and £800,000, and these will be given to you in the rates and allowances section of the examination paper.

3   SOLE TRADERS AND PARTNERS

3.1   Conditions applying to the individual

The normal rule is that an individual must have reached 50 years of age (at the time of the disposal) for retirement relief to be available. Oddly, however, there is no need for the individual actually to retire. Afterwards he may engage in another business or take up employment if he wishes to do so.

To avoid unfairness, the age limit does not apply to those who retire due to ill-health. In these circumstances the age of the disposer is irrelevant.

For those aged 50 or more, retirement relief is automatic (ie, it does not need to be claimed). When the ill-health provisions are used, however, a claim does have to be made, backed up with the appropriate medical evidence.

The condition that the disposer must be at least 50 years old or be retiring due to ill-health is absolute. If it is not met there is no relief.

In contrast, there is a condition that the disposer must have owned the business for at least ten years to obtain full retirement relief. If he has owned it for a shorter period his entitlement to relief is scaled down proportionately (provided that he has owned it for an absolute minimum period of one year). For instance, an individual who had owned a business for four years at the time of retirement would qualify for complete exemption on the first £80,000 of gains (4/10 × £200,000) and 50% exemption on the next £240,000 (4/10 × £600,000). Note that it is the retirement relief limits that are scaled down, not the gain.

3.2   Conditions applying to the assets producing a chargeable gain

To qualify for relief the disposal must be a 'material disposal of business assets'. In the context of a disposal by a sole trader or a partner, business assets are:

(a)   a disposal of the whole or part of a business; and

(b)   a disposal of one or more assets which, at the time the business ceased to be carried on, were in use for the purposes of that business.

Assets can thus be disposed of by way of a going concern or piecemeal after it has ceased. Importantly, however, if the disposal is made while the individual remains in business, it must be of a business unit ('the whole or part of a business'). Disposing of single assets or a group of assets which could not be run as a business does not qualify for relief.

3.3   Chargeable business assets

Gains eligible for retirement relief are restricted to those on chargeable business assets. Chargeable business assets are those used for the purposes of the taxpayer's trade or profession (including goodwill but excluding shares, securities and other assets held as investments).

An asset cannot be a chargeable business asset where a gain that might arise on its disposal would not be a chargeable gain. This provision rules out exempt assets but not those that could produce a gain on disposal but currently stand at a loss.

3.4   Activity

Which of the following constitute chargeable business assets for retirement relief purposes?

(a)   an item of plant, purchased originally for £10,000 and now valued at £4,000
(b)   bank balance of £3,000
(c)   stock, valued at £25,000
(d)   current creditors of £15,000
(e)   goodwill, valued at £60,000
(f)   trade debtors of £18,000
(g)   shares in a supplier with a market value of £9,000
(h)   freehold premises, valued at £45,000

3.5   Activity solution

(a), (e) and (h) count as chargeable business assets. As for the others:

(b) -   cash is not normally an asset subject to capital gains tax

(c) -   any profit on disposal of stock is subject to income tax (and thus not to CGT)

(d) -   creditors are not an asset at all

(f) - trade debts are not subject to CGT

(g) - although a gain might arise on the disposal of these shares, shares are specifically excluded from the definition of chargeable business assets.

3.6 Example

Joe Smith purchased a steel stockholding business on 1 February 1994. As part of the purchase he acquired freehold premises, valued at £200,000, stock of £150,000 and goodwill of £80,000. On 31 January 2000, when he was 59 years old, he sold the business. The assets sold were valued as follows:

(i)	freehold premises	£480,000	
(ii)	stock	£175,000	
(iii)	shares in a supplier	£40,000	(acquired for £20,000 in January 1995)
(iv)	goodwill	£555,000	

Calculate:

(a) the retirement relief due to Joe Smith; and

(b) the chargeable gain arising on the disposal of his business.

3.7 Solution

	£	£
Premises		
Proceeds	480,000	
Less: Purchase price	200,000	
	———	
Unindexed gain	280,000	
Less: Indexation allowance to April 1998		
$\dfrac{162.6 - 142.1}{142.1}\ (= 0.144) \times £200,000$	28,800	
	———	
		251,200
Goodwill		
Proceeds	555,000	
Less: Purchase price	80,000	
	———	
Unindexed gain	475,000	
Less: Indexation allowance to April 1998		
$0.144 \times £80,000$	11,520	
	———	
		463,480
		———
Gains qualifying for retirement relief		714,680
Less: Retirement relief		
(i) first £200,000 × 6/10	120,000	
(ii) next ((800,000 × 6/10) – 120,000) × 50%	180,000	
	———	
		300,000
		———
Chargeable gains after retirement relief		414,680
Shares		
Proceeds	40,000	
Less: Purchase price	20,000	
	———	
Unindexed gain	20,000	

Less: Indexation allowance to April 1998

$$\frac{162.6 - 146.0}{146.0} \times £20,000$$ 2,274

17,726

Total chargeable gains   432,406

Notes:

(1)   Where there are several assets to be dealt with, only some of which qualify for retirement relief, it is simpler to deal first with all the qualifying assets. This approach makes it easier to deal with the limits for retirement relief.

(2)   In this case Joe Smith has owned the business for only six years and so he is entitled only to reduced retirement relief. Remember this is calculated by scaling down the retirement relief limits (by the fraction 6/10) **not** the gains. Thus his upper limit is £480,000.

(3)   The shares, purchased in January 1995, are held in a share pool. Thus the indexation factor is **not** rounded to three decimal places.

(4)   The premises and goodwill are business assets, and so Joe will be entitled to two years' taper relief. This will reduce the chargeable gains by £62,202 (414,680 × (100 - 85%)).

4   RELIEF FOR DISPOSALS OF SHARES IN A PERSONAL COMPANY

4.1   Introduction

Retirement relief applies to the owners of both unincorporated and incorporated businesses. Broadly, the conditions examined earlier in the chapter relating to disposals by sole traders are mirrored for shareholders in personal companies. The rules ensure, however, that retirement relief for shareholders is given only where the individual has both an ownership stake in the company and is intimately concerned with its management. How this is achieved is looked at below.

4.2   Conditions applying to the individual

The same basic conditions apply to a shareholder as to the owner of an unincorporated business. At the time of disposal the individual must be at least 50 years old (or be retiring due to ill-health). Unless this condition is met no retirement relief is available. Again mirroring the position for unincorporated business, maximum relief is available for ownership of ten years or more and is scaled down proportionately for shorter periods (with an absolute minimum ownership period of one year).

There are other conditions, however, that apply only to shareholders. These are:-

(a)   the shares disposed of must be in the individual's personal company. A company qualifies as an individual's personal company if not less than 5% of the voting rights are exercised by the individual.

(b)   The individual must be a full-time officer or employee of the company, working in a technical or managerial capacity.

The qualifying period (from a minimum of one year to a maximum of ten) applies not only to the individual's shares qualifying his holding as a personal company but also to his acting as a full-time working officer or employee. Consequently, if either (or both) periods are less than ten years, the shorter period is the qualifying period for retirement.

4.3   Activity

In each of the following cases would the disposal of the shares mentioned below qualify for retirement relief? If so, what is the qualifying period? Assume that all shares carry the same voting rights and the conditions stated are satisfied up to the date of any disposal.

(a)   Mr A has owned 10% of A Ltd for 8 years and been a full-time working director for 11 years.

(b)   Mr B has owned 6% of B Ltd for 10 years and has been a full-time working manager for the same period.

(c)   Mr C has owned 30% of C Ltd for 7 years and has been a full-time working director for 5 years.

(d)   Mr D owns 7% of D Ltd. He purchased the shareholding 9 months ago and has been a full-time working director for 11 years.

4.4   Activity solution

(a)   Restricted retirement relief available. Mr A has owned more than the 5% threshold for a qualifying period of 8 years.

(b)   Full retirement relief available (ie, qualifying period of 10 years). Mr B has owned a stake of at least 5% and has been a full-time working employee in a managerial capacity for more than 10 years.

(c)   Restricted retirement relief available. He owns more than 5% of the company. Relief is restricted to 50% (qualifying period of 5 years) because he has been a full-time working officer for only 5 years.

(d)   No retirement relief available. The shares have been owned for less than the absolute minimum period of one year.

4.5   Restrictions of relief for non-business assets

Where the qualifying disposal is of specific assets (in the case of sole traders) dealing with non-business assets is straightforward. It was seen earlier in the chapter that they are simply not taken into account when quantifying the amount of retirement relief available.

In the case of a disposal of shares in a personal company the position is different. The gain on the shares automatically reflects gains attributable to business and non-business assets alike. Consequently a restriction is needed to ensure that non-business assets do not attract retirement relief by being sheltered in a personal company. The gain on which retirement relief is given is:

$$\text{Total indexed gain on share disposal} \times \frac{\text{Chargeable business assets}}{\text{Chargeable assets}}$$

If either all chargeable assets are chargeable business assets or alternatively the company has no chargeable assets at all (perhaps a service company in rented accommodation) there is no restriction on retirement relief.

4.6   Example

Fred owned 35% of his family company, Fred Ltd, of which he had been managing director since 1977. On 20 February 2000, his sixtieth birthday, he sold his shares, which he had owned for the past 19 years. At the time of disposal Fred Ltd owned the following assets.

	Value at disposal £
Freehold trading premises	400,000
Goodwill	150,000
Plant and equipment (see note)	64,000
Investments	88,000
Stock and work in progress	75,000
Debtors	105,000
Cash	28,000
	910,000

Note: Plant and equipment contained one item valued at £8,000 (original cost £18,000 in 1991). All other items were worth less than £6,000.

Fred purchased his shares in 1981 for £41,000. On 31 March 1982 they were worth £43,500 and he sold them on 20 February 2000 for £258,000.

Calculate the chargeable gain arising on the disposal, if any.

4.7   Solution

	£
Sale proceeds	258,000
Less: March 1982 value (see note)	43,500
Unindexed gain	214,500
Less: Indexed allowance to April 1998 $\dfrac{162.6 - 79.44}{79.44}\ (= 1.047) \times £43,500$	45,545
Indexed gain	168,955
Less: Retirement relief (W)	145,939
Chargeable gain	23,016

Notes:

(1)   In this case both cost and March 1982 value clearly produce gains and the lower is that found by using the March 1982 value.

(2)   Taper relief (at 15%) is available on the gain of £23,016. The shares are in a qualifying company and therefore attract taper relief as a business asset. The taper relief legislation does not require the gain to be split notionally between 'business' and 'non-business' as applies for retirement relief purposes. This assumes, of course, that the investments do not have a 'substantial' effect on the company's trading status.

Working - retirement relief

It is first necessary to categorise Fred Ltd's assets into assets not subject to CGT, chargeable assets and chargeable business assets.

	Non-chargeable assets £	Chargeable assets £	Chargeable business assets £
Freehold trading premises		400,000	400,000
Goodwill		150,000	150,000
Plant and equipment	56,000	8,000	8,000
Investments		88,000	
Stock and WIP	75,000		
Debtors	105,000		
Cash	28,000		
	264,000	646,000	558,000

Fred has fulfilled the conditions for retirement relief for more than ten years and is thus entitled to full relief. His modest gain falls wholly within the wholly relieved first £200,000 but is restricted due to the investment portfolio of Fred Ltd.

Relief is thus $£168,955 \times \dfrac{558}{646} = £145,939$

5   AGGREGATION OF QUALIFYING PERIODS

5.1   Introduction

Suppose a businessman, aged 49, sold the business he had owned for 15 years and immediately purchased another business. Two years later he decided finally to retire and sold the second business, realising a substantial capital gain. On the basis of the rules set out above, it would appear that the retirement relief limits would be scaled down to 20% of the full values.

5.2   Recognition of ownership of a previous business

This position is recognised as unfair by the retirement relief legislation, since, had the businessman simply retained his earlier business he would have been entitled to full retirement relief.

Ownership of a previous business within ten years of the disposal of the current one counts towards an individual's qualifying period, provided that the 'gap' between the disposal of the earlier business and the acquisition of the later one is not more than two years. Note, however, that the gap period itself does not count as part of the qualifying period.

Retirement relief can be given on more than one disposal. However, if it is given on an earlier disposal it must be taken into account on a later qualifying disposal. The qualifying gains on the earlier disposal are aggregated as part of the qualifying gains on the later disposal to compute the amount of relief based on the qualifying period for the later disposal. The relief given on the earlier disposal is then deducted.

5.3   Activity

Charles set up a business on 1 May 1990. On 30 April 1994 he sold the business but purchased another on 1 November 1995. He sold the second business and retired, aged 57, on 30 April 1999.

How long is Charles's retirement relief qualifying period for the disposal on 30 April 1999?

5.4   Activity solution

Charles's qualifying period for his second business runs from 1 November 1995 to 30 April 1999 (ie, 3.5 years). The qualifying period for his earlier business (falling in the 10 years up to 30 April 1999) began on 1 May 1990 and ended on 30 April 1994 (ie, 4.0 years).

His total qualifying period is thus 7.5 years

5.5   Transfer of a business between spouses

Where an individual makes a disposal of business assets (including shares in a personal company) that were acquired from his or her spouse less than ten years before the disposal, the spouse's period can be the aggregate of:

(a)   his or her own qualifying period; and

(b)   the period of ownership of the transferor spouse that falls within the ten-year period before the disposal.

For this extension of the qualifying period to apply, the transfer between the spouses must occur either as a lifetime gift (not sale) or on the transferor spouse's death. Whichever of these circumstances applies, the couple must have been living together during the tax year in which the transfer took place.

5.6   Activity

Suzie owns 35% of S Ltd, which she sells on 1 February 2000, her sixtieth birthday. She acquired the shares from her husband on his death on 31 January 1997. He had acquired them on 1 August 1992. Both had been managing director of S Ltd while they owned the shares in the company.

What is Suzie's qualifying period for retirement relief on the disposal of the shares?

5.7   Activity solution

Suzie's qualifying period is the aggregate of:

(i)   her own period of ownership (3.0 years); and
(ii)   her husband's period of ownership within the last ten years (4.5 years).

Her total qualifying period is thus 7.5 years.

6   ASSOCIATED DISPOSALS

6.1   Introduction

Where an individual carries on a business through the vehicle of a personal company it is sometimes useful to own assets personally and allow their use by the company. Disposal of such assets also qualifies for retirement relief, subject to meeting the conditions set out below. Such disposals are known as 'associated disposals'.

6.2   Conditions for associated disposals

For retirement relief to be a available, the following conditions must be fulfilled.

(a)   The normal age or ill-health criteria must be met.

(b)   The asset in question must have been in use in the personal company's trade immediately before the disposal (or when trade ceased, if appropriate). If the business paid the individual any consideration for the asset's use (such as rent for premises) the relief may be restricted.

(c)   The asset must be a chargeable business asset in the normal way.

(d)   The disposal must be part of the individual's withdrawal from his business.

(e)   The individual making the disposal must qualify for retirement relief on disposing of his interest in the personal company.

(f)   Normally full relief or restricted relief is given on the same basis as for the principal disposal that attracts retirement relief (which is dependent on the length of time the individual has met the necessary conditions).

(g)   The same relief applies where a partner disposes of a personally owned asset that has been used for business purposes by the partnership. The disposal must be part of the partner's withdrawal from the business carried on by the partnership.

7   PLANNING POINTS

(a)   No relief is available at all until an individual reaches 50 years of age, so, unless the ill-health provisions apply, delay disposals until the age threshold is reached.

(b)   Since full relief becomes available only after a qualifying period of ten years, early planning is essential. This involves ensuring that the various conditions are met as soon as possible.

(c)   Ensure that both spouses have interests in the business that qualify for relief, providing that the likely gains make this necessary.

(d)   The associated disposal rules can be used to keep fast-appreciating assets outside a company (so that they escape an effective double charge to CGT).

(e)   Where practicable, ensure that a personal company disposes of chargeable assets that are not chargeable business assets before the 'retirement relief disposal' is made. This avoids the gain eligible for retirement relief being restricted but it is likely to cost the company money due to an increased corporation tax charge.

(f)   Directors of personal companies need to be careful not to 'wind down' their activity in a personal company too quickly. Retirement relief remains available only to individuals who, after ceasing to be full-time working officers or employees remain as officers or employees and devote an average ten hours per week to the company until the share disposal is made.

(g)   Partners should be careful in incorporating their business shortly before retirement. There is no lower limit to the interest a partner needs to have to qualify for retirement relief but a shareholder needs to have a 'personal company' (and thus normally a 5% stake) to qualify.

8   CHAPTER SUMMARY

Retirement relief is available to:

(a)   sole traders and partners; and
(b)   certain shareholders of personal companies.

Where an officer or employee of a personal company is withdrawing from his business, assets which he or she owned personally and were used in the business's trade may also qualify for relief. These are known as associated disposals.

Sole traders and partners obtain relief on the gains that arise on the sale of their chargeable business assets. Non-business assets are not covered by the relief. Shareholders obtain relief on the gain realised on the shares in their personal company. Where the company owns chargeable assets that are not business assets the gain eligible for retirement relief is scaled down by the fraction:

$$\frac{\text{Chargeable business assets}}{\text{Chargeable assets}}$$

Relief may be obtained only where the disposal is a 'material disposal of business assets'. In relation to a sole trader or partner this is normally the whole or part of the business. For a shareholder of a personal company it is the whole or part of his shareholding.

Owners of both incorporated and unincorporated businesses must be at least 50 years old to benefit from retirement relief (or their retirement must be caused by ill-health if they are younger). To be eligible for full retirement relief the business (for sole traders and partners) or the shares (for owners of personal companies) must have been owned throughout a qualifying period of ten years ending at the time of disposal. Ownership between one year and ten years entitles the disposer to partial relief; the normal retirement relief limits are scaled down arithmetically. There is no relief for ownership of less than one year.

In addition to the age and period of ownership requirements, shareholders are subjected to two further hurdles before they qualify for retirement relief. The company must count as their personal company (the individual must own not less than 5% of the voting power) and he must be a full-time working officer or employee.

Where an individual previously owned a business (or personal company shares) during the ten years before the disposal of the one he is selling, the period of ownership of that first business can count towards the qualifying period of retirement relief on the disposal of the second one. Similarly, where one spouse makes a gift of his or her interest in a business (or personal company) to the other, the transferor spouse's period of ownership can count towards the qualifying period of the transferee spouse on a disposal that is eligible for retirement relief.

Retirement relief is given before taper relief.

9   SELF TEST QUESTIONS

9.1   What groups of people may be eligible for retirement relief? (1.2)

9.2   What are the normal 1999/00 monetary limits for retirement relief? (1.2)

9.3   When is a claim for retirement relief necessary? (3.1)

9.4   How is retirement relief restricted when an individual's qualifying period is less than ten years long? (3.1)

9.5   What are chargeable business assets in the context of retirement relief? (3.3)

9.6   What additional conditions apply to owners of incorporated businesses? (4.2)

9.7   How are gains on the disposal of personal company shares restricted for non-business assets? (4.5)

9.8   What conditions apply to the extension of the qualifying period when a business has been given by one spouse to the other? (5.5)

9.9   What are associated disposals? (6.1)

9.10   What conditions must be met for retirement relief to be available on an associated disposal? (6.2)

10   EXAMINATION TYPE QUESTION

10.1   MacLathe

MacLathe owned 85% of the issued share capital of Bodgitt Ltd, a small manufacturing company. MacLathe had owned the shares and had been production director of the company from its formation in 1972 until December 1999 when he reached the age of 65, the retirement age for the company's directors. At that date he gave his shares equally to his two children. The shares had cost MacLathe their subscription price of £48,000 and the agreed market value in December 1999 was £540,000. The company's assets have the following market values as at 31.12.99 and 31.3.82:

	31.12.99 £	31.3.82 £
Freehold factory	350,000	77,000
Manufacturing plant (fixed)	140,000	12,000
Fixtures and fittings *(note 1)*	34,000	3,000
Motor cars	15,000	8,000
Goodwill	125,000	18,000
Investment in electrical wholesale company	14,000	-
Stock	16,000	6,000
Debtors	1,500	1,750
Cash	500	750
	696,000	126,500

Notes:

(1) The fixtures and fittings include various items of office equipment with a total value of £10,000 at 31.12.99. None of the items included in the £10,000 have either cost or have current value in excess of £6,000.

(2) MacLathe's shares were valued at £100,000 as at 31.3.82.

You are required to compute the chargeable gain on the gift of the shares after taking account of retirement relief. Holdover relief (see later) should be ignored.

10   ANSWER TO EXAMINATION TYPE QUESTION

10.1   MacLathe

	Cost £	31.3.82 MV £
MV of shares on disposal (December 1999)	540,000	540,000
Less: Cost/MV at 31.3.82	48,000	100,000
	492,000	440,000
Less: Indexation allowance (April 1998 – March 1982) $\frac{162.6-79.44}{79.44}=1.047\times£100,000$	(104,700)	(104,700)
Chargeable gain before retirement relief (lower gain)	387,300	335,300

Less: Retirement relief

(a) **Gain on shares attributable to chargeable business assets:**

$£335,300 \times \frac{639,000}{653,000}$ (W1) → 328,111

(b) **Basic relief - 10 years qualifying period**

(1) £200,000 × 100%	200,000	
(2) (£328,111 − 200,000) × 50%	64,056	(264,056)

Chargeable gain	71,244
Taper relief (85%)	60,557

Note: As the gain is on the disposal of shares in a qualifying company (for taper relief purposes) the 'business' taper relief rate of 85% applies. This assumes that the investments do not have a 'substantial' effect on the company's trading status.

WORKING

Chargeable business assets and chargeable assets are

	£
Freehold factory	350,000
Plant	140,000
Fixtures £(34,000 – 10,000)	24,000
Goodwill	125,000
Chargeable business assets	639,000
Investment	14,000
Chargeable assets	653,000

20 ROLLOVER RELIEFS

INTRODUCTION & LEARNING OBJECTIVES

This chapter covers two roll-over reliefs; one allows the gain realised on the disposal of business assets to be rolled over when the proceeds are reinvested in business assets; and the second is a rollover relief which is available for any chargeable disposal where the proceeds are reinvested in EIS or VCT shares. Notice that these reliefs do not exempt the gain, but only defer it.

When you have studied this chapter you should have learned the following:

- The purpose and basic form of rollover relief.
- The time limit for claiming the relief.
- The categories of asset that qualify.
- The time period during which reinvestment must occur.
- The restriction on rollover relief when not all of the proceeds of sale are reinvested.
- The way relief is restricted when only part of the asset is used for trade, or the asset is used for trade for only part of the period of ownership.
- How the modified relief, hold over relief, is applied when reinvestment is made in depreciating assets.
- The definition of depreciating assets.
- The rollover relief available in respect of EIS and VCT investments.

1 PURPOSE AND FORM OF THE RELIEF FOR REPLACEMENT OF BUSINESS ASSETS

1.1 Introduction

The first relief we study is the relief allowing the gain on the disposal of business assets to be rolled over when the proceeds are reinvested in business assets. This relief is covered in paragraphs 1 - 5. The relief, commonly known as rollover relief, exists to allow taxpayers to update and improve assets used in their trade without incurring a liability to capital gains tax.

There are a number of conditions and restrictions, which are considered in this chapter but the essentials of rollover relief are straightforward. Where a taxpayer disposes of a qualifying chargeable asset used in his trade at a gain, and reinvests the proceeds in another asset, the gain is not taxed immediately but is deferred until he eventually makes a disposal of the replacement asset without reinvesting.

The deferral is achieved by deducting the gain made on the old asset from the cost of the new one.

This treatment is not automatic, but must be claimed.

1.2 Taper relief

A claim for rollover relief will mean that the individual loses any entitlement to taper relief in respect of the original asset.

When the individual subsequently sells the replacement asset that has been subject to a rollover relief claim, only the period of ownership of the replacement asset will count in deciding how much taper relief is due.

1.3 Example

Smith purchased an asset qualifying for rollover relief in January 1987 for £100,000. In May 1999 he sold the asset for £180,000 and spent £200,000 in August 1999 on a new qualifying asset.

Official ACCA Textbook, published by AT Foulks Lynch

Calculate the amount of expenditure that will be deductible when the new asset is sold.

1.4   Solution

	£
Cost of new asset	200,000
Less: Gain on old asset (W)	17,400
Deductible cost of new asset	182,600

Working - gain on old asset

	£
Disposal proceeds	180,000
Less: Cost	100,000
Unindexed gain	80,000
Less: Indexation allowance to April 1998	
$\dfrac{162.6 - 100.0}{100.0}$ $(= 0.626) \times £100,000$	62,600
Indexed gain rolled over	17,400

2   REINVESTMENT: QUALIFYING ASSETS AND TIME PERIOD

2.1   Qualifying assets

Not all assets qualify for rollover relief, even if they are chargeable assets used for trading purposes.

The following are qualifying assets:

(a)   land and buildings that are both occupied and used for trading purposes;

(b)   fixed plant and machinery;

(In this context 'fixed' means immovable)

(c)   goodwill;

(d)   satellites, space stations, spacecraft, ships, aircraft and hovercraft.

The first three categories are the most important for exam purposes. To benefit from rollover relief the taxpayer's old and new assets must fall within one of the categories set out above (but not necessarily the same one). Thus a taxpayer could sell a factory and reinvest in an aircraft. It's not even necessary that the assets should be used in the **same** trade, because rollover relief treats all trades carried on by a taxpayer as one.

Where a group of companies is concerned, members of a 75% group (see chapter 26) are treated as carrying on a single trade for the purposes of rollover relief.

2.2   Time period for reinvestment

The acquisition of the replacement asset must occur during a period that begins one year **before** the sale of the old asset and ends three years after the sale.

3   PARTIAL REINVESTMENT OF PROCEEDS

3.1   Introduction

The purpose of rollover relief is to allow reinvestment in capital assets without the trader or company facing a tax bill. In part this is because if the proceeds are reinvested the transaction will not have generated cash with which to pay any tax. This is not true, however, where only part of the sale proceeds are used to purchase a new asset and thus, when this occurs, some immediate tax liability may arise.

3.2   Restriction where partial reinvestment

Where the disposal proceeds of the old asset are not fully reinvested, the surplus retained reduces the gain allowed to be rolled over. Thus if the surplus proceeds are greater than the gain there is no rollover relief at all.

3.3   Example

Jarvis bought a factory in September 1987 for £400,000. In December 1999, wishing to move to a more convenient location, he sold the factory for £750,000. He moved into a rented factory until March 2000 when he purchased and moved into a new factory.

What is the base cost of the new factory if it was purchased for

(a)   £700,000; or

(b)   £550,000.

3.4   Solution

	£
Disposal proceeds (old factory)	750,000
Less: Cost	400,000
Unindexed gain	350,000
Less: Indexation allowance to April 1998	
$\dfrac{162.6 - 102.4}{102.4} \ (= 0.588) \times £400,000$	235,200
Indexed gain	114,800

(a)   New factory purchased for £700,000.

Not all proceeds reinvested, thus restricted rollover relief.

	£	£
Purchase cost of new factory		700,000
Less: Gain on old factory	114,800	
Less: Restriction on rollover		
(750,000 − 700,000)	50,000	
Gain rolled over		64,800
Base cost of new factory		635,200

Two years' taper relief (85%) will be available in respect of the chargeable gain of £50,000 that is immediately chargeable for 1999/00.

(b)   New factory purchased for £550,000

In this case the amount of proceeds not reinvested of £200,000 (750,000 - 550,000) exceeds the gain made on the old factory. Thus none of the gain is eligible to be rolled over and so there is no adjustment to the base cost of the new factory. It remains at the purchase price of £550,000.

4   NON-BUSINESS USE

4.1   Introduction

Full rollover relief is only available where the asset being replaced (the old asset) was used entirely for business purposes throughout the trader's period of ownership. Where this condition is not met rollover relief is still available but is scaled down in proportion to the non-business use. Periods before 1 April 1982 are ignored.

The rollover relief rules achieve this effect by assuming that the asset is in fact two assets, one that qualifies for relief (the part wholly used in the trade) and another that does not. Normally proceeds and costs of the old asset for the qualifying and non-qualifying parts are in the same proportion and thus the same scaling down factor may be used.

4.2   Example

Hadley purchased a factory in November 1988 for £350,000. Not needing all the space, he let out 15% of it. In August 1999 he sold the factory for £560,000 and bought another in October 1999 for £600,000.

Calculate:

(a)   the chargeable gain arising on the disposal in August 1999; and

(b)   the allowable expenditure (base cost) of the new factory.

4.3   Solution

(a)   First, split the old factory into qualifying and non-qualifying parts and compute the gains on them separately.

	Qualifying £	Non-qualifying £
Disposal proceeds (85%/15%)	476,000	84,000
Less: Cost	297,500	52,500
Unindexed gain	178,500	31,500
Less: Indexation allowance to April 1998		
$\dfrac{162.6 - 110.0}{110.0}$ $(= 0.478) \times £297,500/£52,500$	142,205	25,095
Indexed gain	36,295	6,405

The gain of £6,405 is taxable immediately, as it does not qualify for rollover relief. There is no taper relief as it arises on a 'non-business' asset and there has been only two years of ownership since 5 April 1998.

(b)   The base cost of the new factory is reduced by the amount of the gain rolled over. It is thus:

	£
Purchase cost	600,000
Less:Gain rolled over	36,295
	563,705

4.4   Disposal of more than one business asset

Rollovoer relief is very flexible. Where several assets are sold and several more acquired using the full aggregate proceeds the gains can be rolled over against new assets in whatever order (or proportion) the taxpayer chooses.

Where two or more assets are disposed of, but only, say, one new asset is acquired for less than the aggregate proceeds, it may then be necessary to choose which gain should be rolled over. The following points should be considered:

- the amount of the gain on each asset disposed of; and
- if the amount of gain rolled over is to be restricted because all proceeds are not reinvested.

5   REINVESTMENT IN DEPRECIATING ASSETS

5.1   Introduction

Rollover relief is modified where the new asset purchased is a 'depreciating asset'.

Definition   a depreciating asset is one which is either:

(a)   a wasting asset (ie, having a predictable life of not more than 50 years); or
(b)   will become a wasting asset within 10 years.

Thus any asset with a predictable life of not more than 60 years is a depreciating asset.

The purpose of the modification to rollover relief where the new asset is a depreciating asset is to ensure that any gain accrued on the old asset does not escape tax because the new one loses value over a short life. In practice, it mostly occurs when the new asset is either fixed plant and machinery or a short lease.

5.2   Treatment of gain on reinvestment in a depreciating asset

The gain on the old asset is normally rolled over against the cost of the new asset. This does not happen when the new asset is a depreciating one. In these circumstances it is simply deferred (held over) until the **earliest** of three events. These are:

(a)   the disposal of the depreciating asset;
(b)   the depreciating asset ceases to be used for trading purposes; or
(c)   10 years has elapsed since the depreciating asset was acquired.

At this time the gain on the old asset simply becomes taxable. It is not deducted from the cost of the depreciating asset, even where the event that triggers the charge is its sale.

As with rollover relief proper, if only part of the proceeds are reinvested, or the asset was not wholly used for the trade, an element of the gain becomes taxable immediately.

5.3   Taper relief

Because the gain on the original asset is only deferred (and not deducted against the cost of the replacement asset), taper relief remains available when the gain subsequently becomes chargeable.

Taper relief on the original gain is calculated according to the period of ownership of the original asset.

5.4   Example

Cooper purchased a freehold factory in June 1985 for £150,000. In May 1998 he sold it for £420,000 and in June 1998 bought fixed plant and machinery for £450,000. In August 1999 he sold the fixed plant and machinery for £475,000.

Calculate the chargeable gains or allowable losses arising in 1999/00:

5.5   Solution

		£
Disposal proceeds		475,000
Less: Cost		450,000
Chargeable gain		25,000

One year's taper relief will be available based on the period that Cooper has owned the plant and machinery (one complete year). This will reduce the chargeable gain to £23,125 (25,000 × 92.5%).

The held over gain on the sale of the factory in May 1998 also becomes chargeable in 1999/00, because the depreciating asset has been sold. This is £164,400 (see working below).

Working - gain on sale of factory in May 1998

	£
Disposal proceeds	420,000
Less: Cost	150,000
Unindexed gain	270,000
Less: Indexation allowance to April 1998	
$\dfrac{162.6 - 95.41}{95.41}$ (= 0.704) × £150,000	105,600
Chargeable gain held over	164,400

One year's taper relief will be given.

5.6   Acquisition of a new non-depreciating asset

The held over gain normally becomes chargeable after 10 years, when the depreciating asset is sold or when it ceases to be used in the trade, whichever is the earliest. If, before this happens, a new non-depreciating asset is acquired rollover relief can be reinstated. The gain on the original asset is then rolled over into the new non-depreciating asset and the depreciating asset is, effectively, ignored. One can think of the impact of the depreciating asset as simply giving the taxpayer an extended period for reinvestment.

If the whole of the proceeds of the original asset are not reinvested in the new, non-depreciating asset, the excess is still treated as being held over. This is still an improvement on the 'basic' rollover relief position, since the existence of the depreciating asset prevents the excess proceeds from being taxable immediately.

5.7   Example

Smith purchased a factory in February 1988 for £195,000. In May 1998 he sold it for £380,000 and acquired a lease of commercial property (with 55 years to expiry) in June 1998 for £385,000. In April 1999 he purchased a new factory for £390,000 and he sold the lease for £430,000 in December 1999. In May 2002 he sold the second factory for £425,000.

Calculate the chargeable gain on:

(a)   the disposal of the first factory:
(b)   the disposal of the lease; and
(c)   the disposal of the second factory.

5.8   Solution

(a)   Gain on first factory - disposal in May 1998

	£
Disposal proceeds	380,000
Less: Cost	195,000
Unindexed gain	185,000
Less: Indexation allowance to April 1998	
$\dfrac{162.6 - 103.7}{103.7}$ (= 0.568) × £195,000	110,760
Gain available for hold over relief	74,240

(b)   Disposal of the lease - December 1999

	£
Disposal proceeds	430,000
Less: Allowable expenditure (see note)	385,000
Chargeable gain	45,000

One year's taper relief will be available based on the period that Smith has owned the lease (one complete year). This will reduce the chargeable gain to £41,625 (45,000 × 92.5%).

(c)   Disposal of second factory - May 2002

	£	£
Disposal proceeds		425,000
Less: Cost	390,000	
Less: Rolled over gain	74,240	
		315,760
Chargeable gain		109,240

Three year's taper relief will be available based on the period that Smith has owned the second factory (three complete years). This will reduce the chargeable gain to £84,661 (109,240 × 77.5%).

No taper is available in respect of the first factory as the gain was rolled over rather than deferred.

Notes:

(1)   The lease, although a depreciating asset for rollover relief purposes, is not a wasting asset because it had more than 50 years to expiry when it was sold. Its cost is therefore not scaled down when computing the gain or loss on disposal.

(2)   Because Smith reinvested the proceeds of the first factory in a depreciating asset (the lease) the gain on the first factory is held over. Smith then purchased another non-depreciating asset (the second factory) before the depreciating asset was sold. He could therefore rollover the gain on the first factory into the second.

6   EIS SHARES

6.1   Introduction

Where eligible shares are subscribed for, reinvestment relief will be available. Eligible shares are those of companies that qualify under the enterprise investment scheme (see chapter 3).

Reinvestment relief is broadly similar to rollover relief, but there are two important differences:

- The gain on the original asset is deferred rather than rolled over. This means that taper relief is given in the same way as where reinvestment is made in a depreciating asset.

  Taper relief therefore remains available when the gain subsequently becomes chargeable, and it is calculated according to the period of ownership of the original asset.

- It is only necessary to reinvest the amount of the gain, rather than the sale proceeds, in order to obtain full relief.

6.2   Details of the rollover

The amount of the relief is the lower of:

- the chargeable gain;
- the amount of the EIS investment; or
- the amount specified in the claim for the relief.

The amount of the relief is effectively unlimited, since there is no requirement that the EIS investment qualifies for income tax relief.

6.3   Time limits

The investment must be made within the period beginning one year before and ending three years after the date of the original disposal.

6.4   Example: deferral relief on reinvestment

Guy bought 4,000 ordinary £1 shares in Workhorse plc for £80,000 in June 1986.

He sold his entire holding in December 1999 for £250,000, and subscribed for eligible shares under the EIS scheme on 1 March 2000 costing £125,000.

You are required to calculate

(a)   How much deferral relief Guy will claim
(b)   The base cost of the new qualifying reinvestment.

Guy made no other capital disposals in 1999/00.

6.5   Solution

			£
(a)	Disposal proceeds		250,000
	Less: Cost		(80,000)
	Less: Indexation allowance to April 1998		
	$80,000 \times \dfrac{162.6 - 97.79}{97.79}$		(53,020)
	Gain		116,980

The amount that can be deferred is the lower of

(a)   the chargeable gain (£116,980) and
(b)   the acquisition cost of the qualifying investment (£125,000)

The gain deferred can be restricted so that the CGT annual exemption is not wasted. Guy would therefore defer £109,880 (£116,980 – £7,100) leaving £7,100 to be taxed in 1999/00, which is covered by the annual exemption.

In this example, no taper relief is available since the shares in Workhorse plc (which are a non-business asset) have not been owned for a sufficient period after 5 April 1998. If taper relief were available, it would be given (in 1999/00) to any gain remaining chargeable. For example, if taper relief of 95% were available the annual exemption of £7,100 would have to be grossed up when calculating the amount of the reinvestment relief claim. The relevant figure would be £7,474 (7,100 × 100/95).

Note: The same principle of restricting the amount of the deferred gain would apply if retirement relief or capital losses were available. The taxpayer should leave sufficient chargeable gains to utilise the relief or losses available.

(b)   The base cost of the qualifying investment is £125,000.

Note: The gain is merely deferred. It is not rolled over, ie, it is not deducted from the base cost of the EIS shares.

6.6   Withdrawal of the relief

The gain deferred will become chargeable in the following circumstances:

*   The EIS shares are disposed of.

     Although a disposal of EIS shares is normally exempt from CGT, the disposal will still result in the deferred gain becoming chargeable.

*   The investor ceases to be resident in the UK within five years of the share issue.

*   The shares cease to be eligible shares.

6.7   Double relief

An investment in EIS shares may therefore attract tax relief of up to 60%. This is because 20% income tax relief is given, and chargeable gains may be deferred, saving CGT at a top rate of 40%.

However, the 20% income tax relief is an actual tax reduction (provided the relief is not withdrawn), but the deferral relief only delays the chargeability of the gain until a later date.

6.8   Serial entrepreneurs

When a gain is deferred as a result of reinvestment in EIS shares, the taper relief calculation when the gain subsequently becomes chargeable is based on the period of ownership of the original asset (see (6.1))

However, the EIS shares themselves are exempt CGT provided they are held for at least five years. Should they be sold within 5 years the gain can be deferred by acquiring new EIS shares. If sufficient cash is subscribed for the new EIS shares both the gain on the old EIS shares and the original gain they deferred can be deferred against the new EIS shares. Under the original taper relief rules both such deferred gains would only attract taper relief based on the ownership of the respective original asset. Thus when the old EIS shares gain eventually crystallised, taper relief would be based on the period of ownership of the old EIS shares.

This was thought to discourage 'serial entrepreneurs' who wanted to switch between EIS investments more frequently than every five or more years.

The FA 1999 changed the EIS rules to allow taper relief to be calculated on a cumulative basis where an investor defers a chargeable gain arising on the disposal of an *EIS investment* itself by reinvesting in new EIS shares in another company. For taper relief purposes on the EIS share gain, the period of ownership runs from when the shares in the first company were acquired to when the shares in the second company are sold.

Example

Igor realises a gain of £65,000 on disposal of a painting in May 1999 and deters the full gain by subscribing in August 1999 for £73,000 of shares in Rostor Ltd, an EIS company.

In February 2003 Igor sells the Rostor Ltd shares realising a gain of £93,000 as well as crystallising the original £65,000 of gain. In November 2003 he subscribes £200,000 in Pantaloons Ltd, another EIS company and defers all the gains arising from the Rostor shares disposal. In July 2009 he sells his entire holding of Panraloons Ltd and makes no further reinvestment.

What gains arise in 2009/10?

Solution

(a)   On the Pantaloon shares - exempt as EIS shares held for more than 5 years.

(b)   Original gain on painting - £65,000 gain chargeable but taper relief (if any) based on ownership up to May 1999.

(c)   Gain on Rostor shares - £93,000 gain crystallises with taper relief based on ownership of nine years (Aguust 1999 - July 2009).

6.9   VCT shares

A similar type of reinvestment relief is available where shares are acquired in a venture capital trust (see chapter 3). The main differences are:

- Gains can only be deferred up to a maximum of the amount of the investment qualifying for income tax relief. This means that the deferred gain will become chargeable if the VCT relief is withdrawn.

- The qualifying period for reinvestment runs from one year before and ends one year after the date of the disposal.

7   APPROPRIATIONS TO AND FROM TRADING STOCK

7.1   Appropriations to trading stock

When a person appropriates a chargeable asset to trading stock, the normal rule is that he is treated as having sold the asset for its market value at the time of appropriation. In the trading account, for income or corporation tax purposes, market value is also used as the 'purchase' cost.

An election can be made by the taxpayer that overrides the normal rule. Where this is made no chargeable gain nor allowable loss arises at the time of appropriation. Instead the gain or loss is taken into account in computing profits subject to income tax or corporation tax. The mechanism for doing so is to reduce the market value of the asset (by the gain) in the taxpayer's trading account.

7.2   Activity

Alexander, a jeweller, bought a gem for £18,000 as a personal investment in May 1990. In October 1999, when it was worth £25,000 he appropriated it to his trading stock.

Calculate the acquisition cost for the gem in his trading accounts, assuming that he elects to override the normal rule.

7.3   Activity solution

	£
Market value at appropriation	25,000
Less: Chargeable gain (W)	1,816
Acquisition cost in trading account	23,184

Working - gain on appropriation

	£
Market value	25,000
Less: Cost	18,000
Unindexed gain	7,000
Less: Indexation allowance to April 1998 $\frac{162.6-126.2}{126.2}$ (= 0.288) × £18,000	5,184
Gain	1,816

7.4   Assets appropriated from trading stock

The rule in these circumstances is that where an appropriation is made from trading stock it is:

(a)   treated as a sale at market value in the trading account (following the rule in Sharkey v Wernher, 1955); and

(b)   market value is used as the acquisition cost for any subsequent sale of the asset that is subject to capital gains tax.

8   TAX PLANNING POINTS

Much of tax planning for replacement of business assets involves taking care to ensure that the various conditions are met.

(a)   Disposals and acquisitions need to be planned well in advance to ensure that the time limit for reinvestment is adhered to. It may be necessary to advance or delay capital expenditure to do so (where commercially possible).

(b)   It is not possible to choose to roll over only part of a gain leaving sufficient to cover the annual exemption. It might be possible to reinvest all but £7,100 of proceeds in replacement assets, however.

(c)   It is usually better to roll over gains into assets with a long life, particularly where the owner is approaching retirement. This increases the possibility that when the asset is sold the accrued gains will be permanently relieved via retirement relief.

9   CHAPTER SUMMARY

Relief for replacement of business assets

(a)   Rollover relief is designed to help taxpayers renew and update assets without incurring an immediate chargeable gain. It achieves this, provided the various conditions for the relief are met, by assuming that the disposal of an old asset occurred at no gain/no loss and deducting the indexed gain actually made from the allowable expenditure incurred on the replacement asset. Rollover relief must be claimed.

(b)   Only assets that fall within certain classes qualify for rollover relief. The most common ones are land and buildings, fixed plant and machinery and goodwill. Both the original and the replacement asset must be qualifying assets, but not necessarily of the same class.

(c)   Reinvestment in a qualifying asset must normally take place within a period that begins one year before and ends three years after the disposal of the original asset.

(d)   Rollover relief is restricted where the taxpayer fails to reinvest all of the proceeds of sale of the original asset in a replacement one. In these circumstances the proceeds not reinvested are taxable immediately (ie, at the time of the original asset's disposal) unless they are larger than the gain itself (in which case the whole of the gain is taxable immediately and there is no rollover relief). If the proceeds not reinvested are smaller than the gain, the balance of the gain may be rolled over.

(e)   Rollover relief is similarly restricted when either:

•   only part of the asset was used for the trade (such as a factory partly let out); or

•   the asset was used for the purposes of the trade for only part of the taxpayer's period of ownership.

The restriction is applied in either of these circumstances by treating the asset as two separate parts, one which qualifies for rollover relief and one which does not. The gains on each are calculated separately. The 'non-qualifying' asset's gain is taxable immediately but the gain on the qualifying part may be rolled over (subject to the other conditions for relief being met).

(f)   If the reinvestment is in a depreciating asset (one with a predictable life of not more than 60 years) rollover relief does not apply. The gain on the original asset is 'held over' (ie, put to one side) until the earliest of the dates when:

•   the depreciating asset is sold; or
•   the depreciating asset is no longer used in the trade; or
•   10 years have elapsed since the depreciating asset was acquired.

When the first of these three events occurs, the gain held over on the original asset becomes taxable.

(g)   If, before a held over gain crystallises, the taxpayer makes a further investment in a non-depreciating asset, the gain on the original asset that was held over can be rolled over into the new, non-depreciating asset.

(h)   A claim for rollover relief will mean that the individual loses any entitlement to taper relief in respect of the original asset. When the individual subsequently sells the replacement asset that has been subject to a rollover relief claim, only the period of ownership of the replacement asset will count in deciding how much taper relief is due.

When reinvestment is made in a depreciating asset, taper relief remains available when the gain subsequently becomes chargeable. Relief is calculated according to the period of ownership of the original asset.

Deferral relief on reinvestment in EIS shares

(a)   A form of deferral relief is also available where individuals dispose of any assets and reinvest in EIS shares.

(b)   The reinvestment must be within the period beginning 12 months before and ending 3 years after the disposal.

(c)   Full deferral relief is available by reinvesting the amount of the gain.

(d)   A similar relief is also available in respect of VCT investments.

10   SELF TEST QUESTIONS

10.1   How is the deferral of a rolled over gain achieved? (1.1)

10.2   How does a claim for rollover relief affect taper relief? (1.2)

10.3   What are the classes of assets qualifying for rollover relief? (2.1)

10.4   What is the period during which acquisition of the replacement asset must occur? (2.2)

10.5   How is rollover relief restricted when only part of the disposal proceeds of the original asset are reinvested? (3.2)

10.6   What is a depreciating asset ? (5.1)

10.7   How is relief given when reinvestment is in a depreciating asset ? (5.2)

10.8   What is a qualifying investment for reinvestment relief? (6.1)

10.9   What is the maximum amount that may be rolled over? (6.2)

10.10   What election can be made when a chargeable asset is appropriated to trading stock? (7.1)

11   EXAMINATION TYPE QUESTION

11.1   Medway

Your client, Medway, has been offered £160,000 for a freehold factory he owns and is considering disposing of it in early October 1999. He acquired the factory in early October 1966 for £10,000, and it was valued at £60,000 in March 1982. The factory has always been used for business purposes.

You are required

(a)   to compute the chargeable gain which will arise if Medway disposes of the factory.

(b)   to indicate to Medway the capital gains consequences of each of the following alternative courses of action he is considering taking, following the sale, and give any advice you consider to be relevant.

(i)   acquiring a larger freehold factory in 2000 for £172,000.

(ii)   acquiring a smaller freehold factory in 2000 for £155,500 and using the remainder of the proceeds as working capital.

(iii)   using the proceeds to pay a premium of £180,000 for a 40-year lease of a new factory (it is possible that a freehold warehouse will be bought in the next two or three years for an estimated cost of £200,000).

12   ANSWER TO EXAMINATION TYPE QUESTION

12.1   Medway

(a)   **Chargeable gain on disposal of factory**

	Cost £	MV 31 March 1982 £
Proceeds (October 1999)	160,000	160,000
Less: Cost	10,000	
MV 31 March 1982		60,000
Unindexed gain	150,000	100,000
Less: Indexation allowance to April 1998		
$\dfrac{162.6 - 79.44}{79.44} = 1.047$		
£60,000 × 1.047	(62,820)	(62,820)
Gain	87,180	37,180
The smaller gain is chargeable		37,180

(b)   (i)   All of the gain will be rolled over against the base cost of the new factory as all the proceeds are reinvested

	£
Cost of factory	172,000
Gain rolled over	37,180
Base cost of new factory	134,820

The claim for rollover relief will mean that Medway loses any entitlement to taper relief in respect of the original freehold factory.   When he subsequently sells the replacement factory, taper relief will be based on the period of ownership of the replacement factory.

(ii)   As only part of the proceeds are reinvested, the gain element which cannot be rolled over will be £4,500, £(160,000 – 155,500).   The balance of the gain will be rolled over as above

	£
Cost of factory	155,500
Gain rolled over £(37,180 – 4,500)	32,680
Base cost of new factory	122,820

Taper relief will reduce the gain chargeable in 1999/00 to £3,825 (4,500 × 85%).

(iii)   If all the proceeds are used to acquire a depreciating asset (ie, one with an expected life of less than 60 years), the gain is not rolled over but is instead held in suspense to become chargeable on the earlier of

(1)   when the asset is sold

(2)   when the asset ceases to be used in Medway's trade

(3)   the expiry of ten years from acquiring the asset.

Thus the base cost of the lease remains at £180,000. If, before the held over gain becomes chargeable, a non-depreciating asset is acquired, the gain can be rolled over in the usual way.

Taper relief will remain available when the gain on the original factory subsequently becomes chargeable.

21 OTHER RELIEFS

INTRODUCTION & LEARNING OBJECTIVES

This chapter deals with the relief for gifts of business assets, and the relief available on the transfer of a business to a limited company. Although these capital gains tax reliefs are not examined as frequently as reliefs covered earlier in the text, they are still of relevance to the exam.

When you have studied this chapter you should have learned the following:

- The purpose and nature of the relief for gifts of business assets.
- Who may claim relief for gifts of business assets and the time limit for claims.
- What assets are qualifying assets for the relief.
- How the relief is computed, for both gifts and sales at undervalue.
- The restriction on relief that applies when assets are not wholly used for trading purposes.
- How retirement relief interacts with relief for gifts of business assets.
- How gift relief is available when there is an immediate charge to inheritance tax.
- The purpose of, and conditions that apply to, the relief on transfer of a business to a company.
- How the relief for transfer of a business to a company operates.
- How the relief interacts with retirement relief.
- The purpose and scope of the relief for irrecoverable loans to traders.
- The conditions for the relief.
- How it operates and how relief is withdrawn where the loan is later repaid.

1 RELIEF FOR GIFTS OF BUSINESS ASSETS

1.1 Introduction

There is a general problem with gifts for capital gains tax. A gift is an occasion of charge (except when it occurs on death) and so tax may be payable. The donor, however, has received no funds with which to meet his tax bill. For many gifts the problem is unresolved but for gifts of certain business assets there is a deferral of tax until a future disposal.

1.2 Nature of the relief

The relief works by treating the disposal by way of gift as though it occurred at a value giving no gain and no loss to the donor. At the same time, the donee is treated as having paid the donor the market value of the asset but has the actual gain accruing to the donor deducted from his allowable expenditure.

1.3 Activity

Jones bought an asset for £25,000 in September 1988. In June 1999 he gifted it to Smith, when its market value was £40,000. The asset qualified for relief for gifts of business assets.

Show Jones's capital gains tax position on the gift to Smith and calculate Smith's allowable expenditure.

1.4 Activity solution

Jones has made a disposal in June 1999 as follows:

	£
Market value of asset	40,000
Less: Cost	25,000
Unindexed gain	15,000

Less: Indexation allowance to April 1998

$$\frac{162.6 - 108.4}{108.4} \ (= 0.500) \times £25,000 \qquad 12,500$$

	£
Indexed gain	2,500
Less: Hold over relief for business assets	2,500
Chargeable gain	Nil

Smith has allowable expenditure to set against a future disposal, calculated as follows.

	£
Market value of asset acquired	40,000
Less: Rolled over gain	2,500
	37,500

1.5 Taper relief

A claim for holdover relief will mean that the donor loses any entitlement to taper relief.

When the donee subsequently sells the asset that has been subject to a holdover relief claim, only his or her period of ownership will count in deciding how much taper relief is due. In the above example, when Smith disposes of the asset only the period of ownership from June 1999 will be counted.

1.6 Who may claim the relief?

The relief is available to individuals, not companies. Both the donor and donee must claim and this must be done within five years of 31 January following the end of the year in which the gift was made. Although, for the sake of simplicity, the relief is described as a relief for gifts, it also applies to sales made below market value (ie, where there is an element of gift).

1.7 Qualifying assets

An individual may only claim the relief where the gift is of a qualifying asset. The following are the principal categories of qualifying asset.

(a) Assets used in the trade of:

- the donor (ie, where he is a sole trader); or

- the donor's personal company; or

- a company in a trading group, of which the holding company is the donor's personal company.

The second and third of these cases extend the relief to assets owned by the individual but not used by him **directly** for trading purposes.

(b) Shares and securities of trading companies (or the holding companies of trading groups) provided that one of the following conditions apply.

- The shares or securities gifted are those of the individual's personal company.

- The shares or securities are not quoted on either a recognised stock exchange or the unlisted securities market.

An individual's personal company is defined in the same way as for retirement relief.

1.8   Computation of the relief

The basic form of the relief works in the way shown earlier in the chapter. If, however, the disposal is by way of a sale at undervalue, rather than a straight gift, the computation is adjusted to reflect this. In these circumstances any proceeds received over and above original cost are chargeable to tax immediately. The held over gain is reduced by this amount (and thus so is the deduction from allowable expenditure for the donee).

1.9   Example

Webster purchased shares in an unquoted trading company in November 1989 for £50,000. In January 2000 he sold them to his grandson for £70,000 when their value was £165,000. Webster and his grandson claimed relief for a gift of business assets.

Calculate:

(a)   the chargeable gain, if any, incurred by Webster; and

(b)   the allowable expenditure incurred by Webster's grandson.

1.10   Solution

(a)   Webster - gain on shares sold in January 2000

	£	£
Market value of shares in January 2000		165,000
Less: Cost		50,000
Unindexed gain		115,000
Less: Indexation allowance to April 1998		
$\dfrac{162.6-118.5}{118.5} \times £50,000$		18,608
Indexed gain		96,392
Less: Gain rolled over		
Indexed gain	96,392	
Less: Proceeds received - cost		
(70,000 – 50,000)	20,000	
Gain rolled over		76,392
Chargeable gain		20,000

Two years' taper relief will be available in respect of the chargeable gain of £20,000 if the shares qualify as a business asset.

(b)   Webster's grandson - allowable cost

	£
Market value of shares, January 2000	165,000
Less: Gain rolled over	76,392
Allowable expenditure	88,608

1.11   Assets not wholly used for trading purposes

Where only part of an asset (such as a building) is used for trading purposes the relief is restricted. There is a similar restriction where an asset (such as plant and machinery) has been used for trading purposes for only part of the donor's period of ownership.

The gain eligible for relief is scaled down arithmetically. So where an asset owned for ten years has been used in the trade for only six years, 60% of the chargeable gain is eligible for relief. The other 40% is chargeable to tax immediately.

As with retirement relief, the way of reducing the eligible gain described above applies only to individual trading assets. When the subject of the gift is shares in a company, the position is different. Unless the donor has a significant stake in the company, there is no restriction. But if, in a 12-month period before the disposal takes place the company has qualified as the donor's personal company then the gain on the shares eligible for relief is scaled down by the following fraction.

$$\frac{\text{Market value of company's chargeable business assets}}{\text{Market value of company's chargeable assets}}$$

1.12   Interaction of retirement relief and gift relief

The interaction works to the taxpayer's advantage. First the indexed gain on the disposal is calculated. From that retirement relief is deducted and any balance that qualifies for gift relief is then held over.

1.13   Example

Willis gave his business valued at £1,000,000 to his son in December 1999 when he was 58 years old. Chargeable gains of £250,000 and £150,000 arose on the disposal in respect of premises and goodwill respectively. Willis had owned the business since 1980.

Calculate:

(a)   the gain or loss accruing to Willis on the disposal, if any, and

(b)   the allowable expenditure available to Willis's son.

Assume that any available claims are made.

1.14   Solution

(a)   Disposal by Willis - December 1999

		£	£
Gain on premises			250,000
Gain on goodwill			150,000
			400,000
Less:	Retirement relief		
	Limit for full relief	200,000	
	50% on gains over £200,000		
	(400,000 – 200,000)	100,000	
			300,000
Gain eligible for holdover relief			100,000
Less:	Holdover relief			100,000
Chargeable gain			Nil

(b)   Allowable expenditure - Willis's son

	£
Total expenditure	1,000,000
Less: Rollover relief	100,000
Allowable expenditure	900,000

2   GIFT RELIEF AND INHERITANCE TAX

Inheritance tax is covered later in the text and students may wish to re-read this section when they have studied IHT.

2.1   IHT transfers of value which qualify for deferral relief

In addition to the relief available for gifts of business property outlined above, gift relief can also be claimed where a transfer would be subject to an immediate charge to inheritance tax.

The relief applies even if the transfer falls within the nil rate band of £231,000.

2.2   Example: gift relief

On 1 January 2000 Daisy Diamond transferred ordinary shares in Van Meers plc to the trustees of the Diadem Discretionary Trust. The shares had cost Daisy £52,350 in May 1987 and have a market value on 1 January 2000 of £125,000. Daisy has made no other gifts in her lifetime. A claim is made for gift relief. Use an indexation factor of 0.580.

2.3   Solution

Daisy's tax position is

For IHT	£
MV of shares	125,000
Less: Annual exemptions 1999/00 and 1998/99 b/f	6,000
No tax as below £231,000 threshold	-
Cumulative transfers c/f	119,000

For capital gains:	£
MV of shares	125,000
Less: Cost	52,350
Unindexed gain	72,650
Less: Indexation to April 1998: £52,350 × 0.580	30,363
	42,287
Gain held over (Claim made by Daisy only, trustees' consent not required)	42,287
Chargeable gain	Nil

The cost of the shares in the trust for the purposes of any future disposals by the trustees is

	£
MV of shares acquired	125,000
Less: Gain deferred	42,287
	82,713

3   TRANSFER OF A BUSINESS TO A COMPANY

3.1   Introduction

If an individual wishes to incorporate his business a capital gains tax liability can arise because the transfer is deemed to take place at market value irrespective of the consideration actually paid.

As a consequence, to avoid creating disincentives to incorporation, there is a rollover relief when a business is transferred to a company. The relief is automatic so no claim for it is required.

3.2   Conditions for the relief

There are three types of condition. These concern the transferor, the assets transferred, and the consideration given by the company for the transfer.

Any transferor other than a company is eligible to benefit from the relief. Principally the relief is for sole traders.

The assets transferred have to meet two conditions. Firstly, all the assets of the business (other than cash) must be transferred. Secondly, the transfer must be of a business as a going concern.

The form of the consideration given by the acquiring company is also important. To qualify for the relief it must be wholly or partly in shares issued to the transferor (not someone else). Whereas the conditions relating to the transferor and the assets transferred are absolute (ie, if not met in full there is no relief) the condition concerning the consideration received may be relaxed. To the extent that consideration for the transfer is not in the form of shares, the potential relief is scaled down.

3.3   Operation of the relief

The relief operates by rolling over the gain accruing to the transferor and deducting it from the allowable cost of the shares he acquires in exchange.

Initially, one calculates the gains accruing on the assets to be transferred (as reduced by losses where appropriate). If the exchange is wholly for shares the whole gain may be rolled over, provided that the value of the shares received in exchange is high enough. Where a company takes over significant liabilities as well as assets, the value of the shares will be reduced and this may prevent the whole of the gain being held over.

Where some of the consideration given by the company for the assets is not shares (for example debentures or cash) the gain eligible for rollover relief is calculated by the formula:

$$\text{Gain} \times \frac{\text{Value of shares issued}}{\text{Total consideration}}$$

3.4   Example

Smithers started a retail business in 1985. On 1 January 1991 he transferred his business to a company, Smithers Ltd. The assets transferred are set out below. In exchange he received 4,000 £1 ordinary shares (fully paid), valued at £80,000 and £20,000 cash. On 1 February 2000 Smithers sold his entire holding in Smithers Ltd for £150,000.

Calculate:

(a)   Smithers' gains realised in January 1991 after rollover relief; and

(b)   the chargeable gain arising on the disposal of the shares in Smithers Ltd in February 2000.

Assets transferred	Market value at 1.1.91 £	Chargeable gain £
Freehold premises	35,000	25,000
Furniture and fittings	8,000	-
Plant and machinery	14,000	-
Stock	25,000	-
Goodwill	18,000	18,000

3.5   Solution

(a)   Gain - January 1991

	£
Total chargeable gain (25,000 + 18,000)	43,000
Less: Gain rolled over $\dfrac{80,000}{80,000+20,000} \times 43,000$	34,400
Chargeable gain on Smithers (1990/91)	8,600

(b)   Disposal of shares - February 2000

	£	£
Disposal proceeds		150,000
Less: Cost	80,000	
Less: Rolled over gain	34,400	
		45,600
Unindexed gain		104,400
Less: Indexation allowance to April 1998 $\dfrac{162.6-130.2}{130.2} \times £45,600$		11,347
Chargeable gain		93,053

Two years' taper relief will be available in respect of the chargeable gain of £93,053 as the shares are a business asset.

3.6   Taper relief

A claim for rollover relief on incorporation will mean that the individual loses any entitlement to taper relief in respect of the unincorporated business.

When the individual subsequently sells the shares that have been subject to a rollover relief claim, only the period of ownership of the shares will count in deciding how much taper relief is due.

3.7   Interaction with retirement relief

The interaction of incorporation relief with retirement relief operates to the taxpayer's advantage. Retirement relief is deducted first, making any restrictions necessary. The gain that is left is then available for rollover relief. If rollover relief is also restricted (because part of the consideration given by the transferee company is not in the form of shares) the restricting fraction is applied to the gain left in charge after retirement relief (not the full gains accrued on the transferred assets).

3.8 Example

Embleton started a manufacturing business in November 1993. On 30 November 1999, when he was aged 62, he transferred all the assets of his business to Embleton Ltd, making (indexed) gains on the disposal of £350,000. Embleton Ltd issued shares in full consideration for the transfer. All the assets transferred qualified for retirement relief.

Calculate the chargeable gain on Embleton arising from the disposal on 30 November 1999.

3.9 Solution

		£	£
Total chargeable gains			350,000
Less: Retirement relief			
(i)	6/10 × £200,000	120,000	
(ii)	(£350,000 − £120,000) × 50%	115,000	
			235,000
			115,000
Less: Incorporation relief			115,000
Chargeable gain			Nil

Note: retirement relief limits are restricted as Embleton owned the business for only six years. The upper retirement relief limit of £480,000 (£800,000 × 6/10) is higher than the gains actually realised of £350,000.

3.10 Tax planning

Where the person incorporating a company has not used the annual exemption for the year of incorporation, or has unused capital losses, then it is beneficial to ensure that a sufficient chargeable gain arises. This can be arranged by taking some of the consideration as a loan.

3.11 Example

Sue is to transfer her business to a company during March 2000. The business is valued at £500,000, and the capital gains arising on the transfer will total £120,000. She has not used her annual exemption for 1999/00.

Assume that two years' taper relief (85%) is available.

What proportion of the consideration from the company should be taken as a loan?

3.12 Solution

The availability of taper relief complicates the calculation. It is necessary to gross up the annual exemption of £7,100 by the amount of taper relief, so the relevant figure is £8,353 (7,100 × 100/85).

The amount taken as a loan should be £34,804, calculated as follows:

£500,000 × £8,353/£120,000 = £34,804.

Applying the normal formula, the gain rolled over will then be:

$$£120,000 \times \frac{£500,000 - £34,804}{£500,000} = £111,647$$

This leaves a chargeable gain of £8,353 (120,000 - 111,647), which will be reduced to £7,100 after applying taper relief (£8,353 × 85%).

3.13   Drawbacks of rollover relief on incorporation

The main drawbacks of incorporation relief are that:

- All assets must be transferred.
- The sole trader may wish to retain some assets in private ownership and rent them to the company.

Holdover relief for gifts provides an alternative way of deferring gains on the incorporation of a business, especially where it is desirable that not all the assets are transferred.

4   RELIEF FOR IRRECOVERABLE LOANS TO TRADERS

4.1   Introduction

Debts, other than debts on a security and foreign currency bank accounts, are exempt from capital gains tax. Nevertheless, there are specific provisions that allow both lenders to traders and guarantors of traders' debts to claim CGT loss relief if their debt becomes irrecoverable (or the guarantee has to be fulfilled).

4.2   Conditions for the relief

These are the following.

(a)   The loan that has proved irrecoverable must have been used for the purposes of the borrower's trade.

(b)   The borrower must be UK resident.

(c)   For the relief to lenders (but not for guarantors) the debt must not be a debt on a security. (Otherwise it would be a chargeable asset anyway and these special rules would be unnecessary.)

If these conditions are fulfilled the loan is a 'qualifying loan'.

In addition the creditor or guarantor must be able to meet certain conditions. In the case of a creditor these are:

(a)   that all or part of the loan is irrecoverable;

(b)   that the creditor has not assigned his right to receive repayment; and

(c)   that the creditor and borrower were (at no time since the loan was made) neither spouses living together nor companies in the same group.

Essentially the same conditions apply to guarantors.

4.3   Operation of the relief and its withdrawal

Provided the conditions set out above are met the lender or guarantor is treated as incurring an allowable loss for capital gains tax purposes. It is treated as a loss of the tax year specified in the claim, provided that, in the case of a loan, the claim is made within two years of the end of the tax year (and that the loan was irrecoverable at that time). In the case of a guarantee, the claim must be made within 5 years of 31 January following the tax year in which the payment was made.

5   CHAPTER SUMMARY

(a)   Because a gift or sale at undervalue is not made at arm's length, market value is substituted for proceeds in the CGT computation. The disposer may thus incur a CGT liability without receiving funds to pay it. To overcome this problem, in some cases, there is a relief for gifts of business assets. It is available to individuals, not companies, and must be claimed jointly by the donor and donee within five years of 31 January following the end of the tax year in which the gift was made.

(b)   Relief for gifts of business assets works by treating the donor as though he made neither gain nor loss on the gift. The actual indexed gain is deducted from the allowable expenditure of the donee. The donee is treated as having paid market value for the asset. When the donee eventually sells the asset the gain that had accrued to the donor automatically becomes taxable as a result of the reduction in the donee's allowable expenditure.

(c)   Only certain assets qualify for the relief. Broadly speaking, these are assets used for trading purposes by a business run by the donor. Shares and securities of a company also qualify, provided they are shares or securities of an unquoted trading company or of the donor's personal company.

(d)   Relief is restricted (and so part of the gain is immediately chargeable on the donor) where the qualifying assets have not been wholly used for business purposes or have not been so used throughout the donor's period of ownership.

(e)   Where relief for gifts of business assets and retirement both apply to a disposal, retirement relief is deducted first and only the balance is eligible for rollover relief.

(f)   Holdover relief is available on any type of asset where there is an immediate charge to inheritance tax, even if the transfer falls within the nil rate band.

(g)   When the donee subsequently sells the asset that has been subject to a holdover relief claim, only his or her period of ownership will count in deciding how much taper relief is due.

(h)   Relief is also given when an unincorporated business is taken over by a company. In these circumstances too a CGT bill could be payable by the transferor, without his having funds to meet it, were it not for a specific relief.

(i)   Individuals, but not companies, may obtain relief for the transfer of a business to a company. No formal claim is necessary and thus the relief is automatic where the conditions are met.

(j)   All assets other than cash must be transferred to the company. Full relief is obtained where the consideration given by the company to the owner of the unincorporated business is in the form of shares. Relief is scaled down proportionately where consideration is provided in other forms (for example cash or debentures). The gains not eligible for relief are taxable immediately on the transferor.

(k)   The relief is provided by deducting the accrued gains on the assets transferred from the allowable expenditure incurred on the shares (which is normally their market value at the time of issue).

(l)   Where retirement relief also applies to the disposal it is deducted first.

(m)   When the individual subsequently sells the shares that have been subject to a rollover relief claim, only the period of ownership of the shares will count in deciding how much taper relief is due.

(n)   Relief is given to lenders or guarantors where a loan has become irrecoverable or a guarantee payment has had to be made. The relief applies to qualifying loans. Broadly, a qualifying loan is one which was made to a UK resident trader and used for trading purposes. The irrecoverable loan or guarantee payment is treated as a capital loss.

6   SELF TEST QUESTIONS

6.1   How does relief for gifts of business assets work? (1.2)

6.2   Who may claim relief for gifts of business assets? (1.6)

6.3   What is the time limit for making a claim for relief for gifts of business assets? (1.6)

6.4   What assets qualify for gift relief of business assets? (1.7)

6.5   How is relief restricted when a disposal is a sale at undervalue rather than an outright gift? (1.8)

6.6   Where a disposal qualifies for both gifts of business assets relief and retirement relief, which takes priority? (1.12)

6.7   What are the conditions that must be met for relief on transfer of a business to a company? (3.2)

6.8   How is relief restricted when some of the consideration received from the acquiring company is not in the form of shares? (3.3)

6.9   What is a qualifying loan for the purposes of the relief given for irrecoverable loans to traders? (4.2)

6.10   What form does the relief take? (4.3)

7   EXAMINATION TYPE QUESTION

7.1   Tristan

Tristan, who was born in 1953, bought a travel agency in Cornwall in 1975 paying £11,000 for goodwill.

On 15 July 1999 he sold the business as a going concern to Kareol Travel Ltd, an existing company, which took over all of the assets, except for cash, at the following agreed values

	MV 15.7.99 £	MV 31.3.82 £
Freehold premises	142,000	-
Goodwill	22,000	11,500
Estate car	3,000	2,000
Stock and debtors	3,000	3,000
	170,000	

The freehold premises cost £66,000 in May 1983.

The consideration for the sale was settled by Kareol Ltd allotting to Tristan 70,000 ordinary shares of 20p each, valued at 175p per share, and paying him cash of £47,500. The shares are not quoted.

On 25 March 2000 Tristan sold 10,000 ordinary shares in Kareol Ltd for £20,664 to an unconnected person. On the same day Tristan gave a further 10,000 shares in Kareol Ltd to his daughter.

Tristan's other capital transactions in the year ended 5 April 2000 were

(1)   On 16 January 2000 he sold, for net proceeds of £475,000, a 1966 Ferrari motor car which he had bought for £4,000 in January 1966. The market value on 31 March 1982 was £120,000.

(2)   On 1 July 1999 he assigned the lease of a shop for £58,250; the lease expires on 30 June 2015. Tristan had acquired the lease for £24,000 on 1 July 1986. The shop had not been used in any trade conducted by Tristan.

Tristan has made no election with regard to the assets he held on 31 March 1982 and no such election is to be considered.

Tristan's taxable income for 1999/00 is in excess of £50,000.

You are required to prepare a computation showing the tax payable by Tristan as a result of the above disposals, assuming that, all available reliefs are claimed.

8   ANSWER TO EXAMINATION TYPE QUESTION

8.1   Tristan

Capital gains tax computation 1999/00

		Cost £	MV 31.3.82 £	£
(a)	Sale of business to Kareol Travel Ltd			
	Freehold premises			
	Deemed proceeds (market value)	142,000		
	Less: Cost (May 1983)	66,000		
	Unindexed gain	76,000		
	Less: IA (Apr '98 – May '83)			
	$\dfrac{162.6-84.64}{84.64}$ (=0.921) × £66,000	(60,786)		
	Chargeable gain	15,214		15,214
	Goodwill			
	Deemed proceeds	22,000	22,000	
	Less: Cost/MV 31.3.82	11,000	11,500	
	Unindexed gains	11,000	10,500	
	Less: IA (Apr '98 – March '82)			
	Use higher MV 31.3.82			
	$\dfrac{162.6-79.44}{79.44}$ (=1.047) × £11,500	(11,000)	(10,500)	
	Indexation allowance restricted	Nil	Nil	Nil
	Estate car: Exempt asset			–
	Aggregate gains			15,214
	Less: Gains rolled over on the transfer of a business to a limited company			
	$15,214 \times \dfrac{122,500}{170,000} \left(\dfrac{\text{Value of shares}}{\text{Total consideration}}\right)$			(10,963)
				4,251
	Taper relief (two years) × 85%			3,613
(b)	Sale of Kareol Ltd shares			
	Shares acquired 15.7.99	122,500		
	Less: Rolled-over gain	(10,963)		
		111,537		
	Cost of sales: 10,000/70,000	(15,934)	15,934	
	Cost c/f	95,603		
	Sale proceeds		20,664	
	Chargeable gain (held for less than one year so no taper relief)		4,730	4,730
(c)	Gift of Kareol Ltd shares			
	Gain computed as in (b) above		4,730	
	Less: Relief for gift of business assets		4,730	
	Chargeable gain		Nil	

(d)   Ferrari motor car: Exempt asset

(e)   Assignment of shop lease

	Cost £	
Consideration (16 yrs to run)	58,250	
Less: Unwasted cost		
$£24,000 \times \dfrac{64.116\,(\%\ 16\ yrs)}{86.226\,(\%\ 29\ yrs)}$	17,846	
Unindexed gain	40,404	
Less: IA (Apr '98 – July '86)		
$\dfrac{162.6 - 97.52}{97.52}\,(=0.667) \times 17,846$	(11,903)	
Chargeable gain	28,501	28,501
Aggregate gains		36,844
Less: Annual exemption		(7,100)
Taxable amount		29,744
Tax liability at 40%		11,898

Note: no taper relief is available in respect of the lease, since (being a non-business asset) it has not been owned for a sufficient period after 5 April 1998.

22 ADMINISTRATION OF TAX

INTRODUCTION

This chapter brings together the main rules regarding the administration of the tax system and the methods and dates of payment. It will give you an understanding of the mechanism by which the UK tax system operates.

1 THE PRINCIPLES OF REVENUE LAW

1.1 Scope

Taxation is the raising of money by the State from businessess and from the general public. The principal taxes in the UK which are examinable in Paper 11 are:

Tax	Nature	Suffered by	Impact	Administered by
Income tax	Annual	Individuals Trusts	Direct	Board of Inland Revenue
Corporation tax	Annual	UK Companies	Direct	Board of Inland Revenue
Capital gains tax	Annual	Individuals Trusts Companies (which pay corporation tax on their capital gains)	Direct	Board of Inland Revenue
Inheritance tax	Permanent	Individuals Discretionary trusts	Direct	Board of Inland Revenue
Value added tax	Permanent	Anyone who is liable to register	Indirect	Commissioners of Customs & Excise

1.2 Statute law

(a)   The main statutes relating to tax are:

Income and Corporation Taxes Act 1988 (ICTA 88)
The Taxation of Chargeable Gains Act 1992 (TCGA 92)
Inheritance Tax Act 1984 (IHTA 84)
Capital Allowances Act 1990 (CAA 90)
Taxes Management Act 1970 (TMA 70)
Value Added Tax Act 1994 (VATA 94).
Annual Finance Acts

(b)   The *ICTA 88* is a consolidation of the tax legislation relating to income tax and corporation tax up to April 1988. Since then amendments have been added by the *Finance Acts 1988 to 1999.*

(c)   A similar consolidation has been enacted by means of the *TCGA 92* and this Act contains the body of the law on Capital Gains Tax together with the amendments implemented by subsequent Finance Acts.

(d)   The *CAA 90* sets out the main reliefs for capital expenditure given by means of the capital allowance system.

(e)   The *TMA 70* contains the law relating to the administration of income tax, corporation tax and capital gains tax.

(f)   Amendments and additions to the law are given effect by means of the annual Finance Act. Each Finance Act is the vehicle by which the annual taxes are reimposed and each provides that it shall be construed as one with all previous legislation so that the total body of tax law is brought into force each year.

1.3   Statutory instruments

The statutory legislation often empowers the Treasury or The Board to make orders or regulations to give effect to the legislation; these are usually made by means of Statutory Instruments.

1.4   The European Union

The Council of Ministers, representing the member states of the European Union, is the main decision-making body. The legally binding acts of the Council comprise

(a)   **regulations** – these are community laws binding on member states which take effect without the need for any action by member states

(b)   **directives** – these are as binding as regulations but it is left to the governments of member states to take the necessary action on implementation. For example the Treaty of Rome makes harmonisation of VAT throughout member states mandatory. The main method of implementation is via the 'Sixth Directive' with the *VATA 94* being the UK's method of taking action.

1.5   Case law

Judges interpret the law which applies to the circumstances of the particular case.

A considerable body of case law has been built up around taxation and many of the decisions are embodied in the text of this manual. The syllabus does not require identification of specific cases or a detailed knowledge of the judgements, although a knowledge of the principles derived from the leading cases is expected.

1.6   Extra statutory concessions

In cases where there is doubt as to the meaning of the law and no case law precedent is available, or where a strict application of the law produces an unacceptable result, the Inland Revenue do not always seek to apply the law strictly but instead make an **extra-statutory concession**.

1.7   Inland Revenue Statements of Practice

These are public announcements of the Revenue's interpretation of the legislation; they have no legal force and do not remove the taxpayer's right of appeal.

2   ORGANISATION OF THE INLAND REVENUE

2.1   Overview

The **Treasury** is the ministry responsible, under the Chancellor of the Exchequer, for the imposition and collection of taxation. The Treasury appoint permanent civil servants, as the **Board of Inland Revenue**, to administer the UK's direct taxation system; they are responsible for income tax, corporation tax, capital gains tax and inheritance tax.

For the purposes of administrative control the UK is divided into regions, with each region sub-divided into **districts**. Each district is under the control of a **district inspector**, assisted by other inspectors, tax officers and clerical grade civil servants. An inspector is more formally described as Her Majesty's Inspector of Taxes, or HMIT.

2.2   The Inspector of Taxes

The Board of Inland Revenue appoint the Inspectors of Taxes. The Inspectors' main duties are to:

- issue tax returns; and
- examine returns and accounts of individuals, businesses and companies.

2.3   The Collector of Taxes

The Board of Inland Revenue also appoint the Collectors of Taxes. Their responsibility is to collect tax which is:

- due under self assessment;
- due under the PAYE system; and
- due from companies.

Following recent changes in Revenue administration there is less separation between the Inspector and Collector roles.

3   PAYMENT OF INCOME TAX

3.1   Introduction

Wherever possible tax is deducted at source (eg, interest on building society deposit accounts is paid net of 20% income tax). However, deduction at source does not satisfy a taxpayer's higher rate liability. There are also situations where deduction at source is impractical (eg, on business profits or rents.)

Up to and including 1995/96 the Revenue raised assessments to collect income tax on income received gross or on income which had suffered insufficient tax deduction at source.

For 1996/97 onwards a new system called 'self-assessment' applies under which the responsibility for calculating and accounting for income tax has been shifted from the Revenue to the individual taxpayer. This has not altered the system of deducting tax at source. In fact the average taxpayer with a salary taxed under PAYE (see below) and small amounts of investment income taxed at source is unlikely to have been affected by the change to self-assessment as his tax liability will still be settled in full at source.

4   PAYE

4.1   Introduction

(a)   PAYE is a system of collection of income tax at source from the emoluments of employed individuals.

(b)   **All payments of emoluments** assessable under Schedule E are subject to deduction of tax under the PAYE system.

(c)   **All employers making payments of such emoluments** are required to deduct the appropriate amount of tax from each payment (or repay over-deductions) by reference to PAYE Tax Tables, which are so constructed that, as near as may be, tax deducted from payments to date corresponds with the correct time proportion to date of the net total tax liability (after allowances and reliefs) of the recipient on those emoluments for the year.

4.2   Coding notice

From the information supplied in his tax return, each employee is sent a coding notice which sets out the total reliefs and allowances available to him for the year. The last digit is removed to arrive at the code

number shown. Thus, allowances of £3,099 become 309. Using this code number and a set of tax tables the employer will be able to calculate the correct amount of tax each week or month.

Most code numbers issued to the employer will carry a suffix of which the most usual are H or L. The letter H denotes that the married couples allowance has been given, and L that just the ordinary personal allowance has been given. These letters are added to simplify the revision of codes, eg when the personal allowance was increased.

Some code numbers carry a K prefix. This indicates that the deductions to be made from allowances actually exceed the allowances. The code number is effectively 'negative'.

4.3 Example: Tax code

Albert is a married man employed as a purchasing manager of Fellows Ltd. He is paid a monthly salary of £1,150 (gross). He is provided with a 1600 cc company car costing £14,500 in 1997 and pays for all private fuel. His business mileage in 1999/00 is expected to be 12,000. He pays 3% of his gross salary to a pension scheme run by his company and approved by the Inland Revenue, and a professional subscription of £50.

Show how Albert's tax code is calculated for 1999/00.

4.4 Solution

NOTICE OF CODING – YEAR TO 5 APRIL 2000

ALLOWANCES	£	£
Expenses (professional subscriptions)		50
Personal		4,335
Married couple's		1,970
TOTAL ALLOWANCES		6,355
Less:		
Restriction of relief for married couple's allowance (note (c))	1,113	
Car benefit £14,500 × 25% (see note (a))	3,625	4,738
NET ALLOWANCES		1,617
Code		161H

Notes:

(a) The taxable value of most **recurring benefits-in-kind** are usually subject to tax under PAYE. Car benefits are an important example and their taxable value reduces the total of allowances set against total pay for Schedule E purposes.

(b) No relief in the coding is given for the allowable pension contributions made by the employee to occupational pension funds. Employers deal with pension contributions by deducting them from total pay, the net pay forming total pay for PAYE purposes.

(c) The married couple's allowance is not deducted in arriving at taxable income. Instead, relief is given via a tax credit against income tax liability. However, relief will be given through the PAYE code with a restriction depending on the employee's likely marginal tax rate to give an effective rate of 10%. For example, as above, (1,970 − 1,113) × 23% = £197; just as relief is restricted to £1,970 × 10% = £197.

4.5 Payments to Collector of Taxes

The amounts of tax and national insurance that the employer was *liable* to deduct during each tax month ending on the 5th of a calendar month are due for payment to the Collector of Taxes not later than 14 days after the tax month ends, ie by the 19th of each calendar month.

Employers whose average monthly payments of PAYE and NICs are less than £1,000 in total are allowed to make quarterly, rather than monthly, payments. Payments are due by the 19th of the month following the quarters ending 5 July, 5 October, 5 January and 5 April.

4.6   Interest on PAYE unpaid by employer

Interest will be charged on PAYE which remains unpaid more than 14 days after the end of the year of assessment for which the amount was due.

4.7   Procedure to be adopted when employee leaves

When an employee leaves an employment the PAYE system is interrupted. A form P45 must be completed for each employee in order that either

- a new employer can carry on making deductions using the appropriate code and cumulative totals from the last employment or

- the employee can claim a tax repayment and/or the jobseeker's allowance that is paid to the unemployed.

4.8   End of year procedure

The following returns will need to be completed at the end of each tax year.

P35 – Employer's Annual Statement, Declaration and Certificate (to be submitted by 19 May). The P35 includes the following:

- an overall summary of tax and NIC deducted by the employer for the year

- a questionnaire to ensure compliance with PAYE arrangements

- a declaration and certificate signed by the employer confirming that all year-end returns have been completed and submitted and that other post- year returns will be despatched.

P11D – a form P11D must be submitted for each employee by 6 July (and a copy given to the employee) if the employee is in receipt of expense allowances or reimbursed expenses, or is provided with benefits-in-kind and

- either he or she is an employee, whether or not a director receiving gross emoluments at the rate of £8,500 or more per annum or

- is a director who is not earning as above, unless such director has no material interest (5% of ordinary share capital) *and* is a full-time working director of the company.

P9D – a form P9D must be completed by 6 July (also copied to the employee) for any employee who is not a P11D employee where that employee received in a fiscal year expenses and benefits which are assessable because they represent a reward for services. That is benefits in

- money or capable of being converted into money (ie money's worth) or
- the satisfaction by the employer of a liability incurred by the employee or
- any other benefit which is assessable on employees regardless of their status.

P14–P60 – Certificate of Pay and Tax Deducted

P14 Not later than 19 May the employer must send the first two copies (P14) of this three-part form to the Collector of Taxes, showing for each employee

- personal details
- total emoluments for the year
- final PAYE code

- total tax deducted for the year
- total national insurance contributions.

P60 – this third part of the form, which must show in addition to the above the employer's name and address and the employee's national insurance number, is given to each employee.

4.9   PAYE audit

The Revenue has power to conduct a PAYE audit and inspect wages books, workings sheets and other records to ensure that the PAYE regulations are being complied with.

5   SELF ASSESSMENT

5.1   Introduction

Self assessment puts the onus on the taxpayer to calculate his or her own tax liability. Each year the taxpayer will be sent a self assessment tax return. This must be completed and submitted by 31 January following the tax year. This is also the due date for the payment of the year's income tax, Class 4 NIC and CGT liability, although interim payments on account may be required on 31 January in the tax year and 31 July following the tax year.

5.2   The self assessment tax return

(a)   The return for 1999/00 must be submitted by 31 January 2001. If the return is issued late, then the due date will be three months after the issue of the return should this be later.

(b)   The return should contain all information required to calculate the taxpayer's taxable income (from all sources) and any chargeable gains for the tax year concerned. Reliefs and allowances will also be claimed in the return.

(c)   For self-employed people, the return includes a section for standardised accounts information. Therefore, the information contained in a taxpayer's financial accounts has to be submitted in a standardised format. However, separate accounts may have to be submitted if the business is large or complex.

(d)   For employees who pay their tax liability under PAYE, a self assessment tax return will often not be required because they will have no further tax liability.

(e)   Although partners are dealt with individually, a partnership return will have to be completed to aid self assessment on the individual partners. This will give details of the partners, and a partnership statement detailing the partnership's tax adjusted income and how this is allocated between the partners.

5.3   Calculating the tax liability

(a)   The return includes a section for the taxpayer to calculate his or her own tax liability (hence the term 'self assessment'). This self assessment is required even if the tax due is nil or if a repayment is due.

(b)   The Inland Revenue will calculate the tax liability on behalf of the taxpayer if the return is submitted by 30 September following the tax year (rather than 31 January). The calculation by the Inland Revenue is treated as a self assessment on behalf of the taxpayer. The Inland Revenue will not make any judgement of the accuracy of the figures included in the return, but will merely calculate the tax liability based on the information submitted.

(c)   The Inland Revenue may correct any obvious errors or mistakes within nine months of the date that the return is filed with them. For example, they will correct arithmetical errors or errors of principle. This process of repair does not mean that the Inland Revenue has necessarily accepted the return as accurate.

(d)   The taxpayer can amend the return within twelve months of the filing date. For 1999/00, amendments must therefore be made by 31 January 2002.

        If an error is discovered at a later date then the taxpayer can make an error or mistake claim (see later) to recover any tax overpaid.

(e)   The Revenue normally communicate with the taxpayer by issuing a statement of account. This will show the self-assessed tax charges and any charges of interest or surcharges (see later) and will show any payments made by the taxpayer - much in the style of a credit card statement. The statement is not a notice to pay but merely a reminder of the taxpayer's indebtedness. Statements are issued as appropriate.

5.4   Notification of chargeability

(a)   Taxpayers who do not receive a return are required to notify the Inland Revenue if they have income or chargeable gains on which tax is due.

(b)   The time limit for notifying the Inland Revenue of chargeability is six months from the end of the tax year in which the liability arises.

(c)   Notification is not necessary if there is no actual tax liability. For example, if the income or chargeable gain is covered by allowances or exemptions .

5.5   Penalties for failure to submit a return

(a)   The initial penalty for not filing a return by the due date is £100.

(b)   A daily penalty of up to £60 per day can be imposed provided leave is given by the General or Special Commissioners (see later).

(c)   If a daily penalty has not been imposed within six months of the filing date, and the return is not submitted by this date, then there is a further penalty of £100.

(d)   The fixed penalties of £100 cannot exceed the amount of tax due.

(e)   If the failure to file a return continues for more than twelve months after the filing date, then a tax geared penalty may be imposed. The tax geared penalty is in addition to the fixed and daily penalties, although it cannot exceed the tax liability for the tax year in question.

5.6   Example: Penalties

A taxpayer does not submit his return for 1999/00 (which was issued during April 2000) until 10 October 2001. The tax due is £175.

Solution

Two fixed penalties of £100 will be due as the return is submitted more than six months after the filing date of 31 January 2001. The penalties will be reduced to the tax due of £175.

If a daily penalty was imposed, then this would run from the date when the Commissioners make a direction to 10 October 2001. The second fixed penalty of £100 will not be due if the daily penalties commenced before 31 July 2001 (six months after the filing date).

5.7   Determination of tax due if no return is filed

(a)   Where a self assessment tax return is not filed by the filing date, the Inland Revenue may determine the amount of tax due. This determination is treated as a self assessment by the taxpayer, and will be replaced by the actual self assessment when it is submitted by the taxpayer.

(b)   There is no appeal against a determination. Instead, the taxpayer should displace it with the actual self-assessment.

(c)   A determination can be made at any time within five years of the filing date.

5.8   Records

(a)   Taxpayers are required to keep and preserve records necessary to make a correct and complete return. For a business (including the letting of property), the records that must be kept include records of:

- All receipts and expenses.

- All goods purchased and sold

- All supporting documents relating to the transactions of the business, such as accounts, books, contracts, vouchers and receipts.

Other taxpayers should keep evidence of income received such as dividend vouchers, P60s, copies of PIIDs and bank statements.

(b)   For taxpayers with a business (ie the self employed), all their records (not just those relating to the business) must be retained until five years after the filing date. For 1999/00 records must therefore be retained until 31 January 2006.

(c)   For other taxpayers, records must be retained until the later of:

- Twelve months after the filing date (31 January 2002 for 1999/00).

- The date on which an enquiry into the return is completed (see later).

- The date on which it becomes impossible for an enquiry to be started.

(d)   A penalty of up to £3,000 may be charged for failure to keep or retain adequate records. The maximum penalty is only likely to be imposed in the most serious cases such as where a taxpayer deliberately destroys his records in order to obstruct an Inland Revenue enquiry.

6   PAYMENT OF TAX

6.1   Payments on account

(a)   Payments on account are required if the taxpayer had an income tax liability in the previous year in excess of any tax deducted at source.

(b)   The due dates for payments on account for 1999/00 are:

- First payment on account - 31 January 2000
- Second payment on account - 31 July 2000

(c)   No payments on account are ever required for CGT.

(d)   For self-employed taxpayers each payment on account will include a payment on account of the Class 4 NIC liability due for the year.

(e)   Payments on account are based on the previous year's tax liability, so the payments on account for 1999/00 are based on the tax liability for 1998/99.

The tax liability used for calculating payments on account excludes tax that was deducted at source - eg, PAYE, tax deducted from bank and building society interest, and tax credits on dividends.

The tax liability for the previous year, net of tax deducted at source, is known as the relevant amount

(f)   Each payment on account is 50% of the relevant amount of income tax and Class 4 NIC, if appropriate.

6.2   Payments on account not required

(a)   Payments on account are not required if:

  •   The relevant amount for the previous year is less than £500.

  •   More than 80% of the income tax liability for the previous year was met by deduction of tax at source. This will mean that most employed people will not have to make payments on account, since at least 80% of their tax liability is paid through PAYE.

(b)   Payments on account are also not required if there is no relevant amount in the previous year. A taxpayer who commences self-employment on 1 May 1999 will not have to make payments on account for 1999/00, since he or she will not have a relevant amount for 1998/99.

6.3   Example: Payments on account

A taxpayer's tax liability for 1998/99 was as follows:

	£
Income tax	9,400
Less: Tax deducted at source	2,100
	7,300
Class 4 NIC	700
CGT	3,500
	11,500

Solution

The relevant amount for income tax is £7,300.

The relevant amount for Class 4 NIC is £700.

Payments on account will be due for 1999/00 as follows:

31 January 2000 (£7,300 + £700 = £8,000/2)	£4,000
31 July 2000	£4,000

6.4   Claims to reduce payments on account

(a)   At any time before 31 January following the tax year, a taxpayer can claim to reduce the payments on account.

In the above example, the taxpayer would claim to reduce the payments on account if he expected his actual income tax and Class 4 NIC liability (net of tax deducted at source) for 1999/00 to be less than £8,000.

(b)   The claim must state the grounds for making the claim.

(c)   Following a claim, the payments on account will be reduced. Each payment on account will be for half the reduced amount, unless the taxpayer claims that there is no tax liability at all.

If payments on account are paid before a claim is made, then the Inland Revenue will refund the overpayment.

(d)   In certain circumstances, the relevant amount may alter as a result of an amendment to the self assessment for the previous year. Such an amendment will automatically result in a corresponding increase or decrease in the payments on account due for the current year.

6.5   Incorrect claims

(a)   A taxpayer should only claim to reduce payments on account if the tax liability (net of tax deducted at source) for the current year is expected to be less than the payments on account.

(b)   Where a claim is made and the actual tax liability for the current year turns out to be higher than the original payments on account, then interest will be charged on the tax underpaid (see later).

(c)   In addition, a penalty will be charged if a taxpayer fraudulently or negligently claims to reduce payments on account. The maximum penalty is the difference between the amounts actually paid on account, and the amounts that should have been paid.

(d)   A penalty will not be sought in cases of innocent error. The aim is to penalise taxpayers who claim large reductions in payments on account without any foundation to the claim.

6.6   Balancing payments

(a)   The balancing payment is due on 31 January following the tax year. For 1999/00 this will be 31 January 2001.

(b)   The balancing payment will be the total tax liability for the year (income tax, Class 4 NIC and CGT), less amounts deducted at source and less payments made on account.

It is possible that a balancing repayment will be due, in which case the Inland Revenue will repay the amount of tax overpaid.

(c)   Where the amount of tax due changes as a result of an amendment to the self assessment (by either the taxpayer or the Inland Revenue), any additional tax due must be paid within 30 days of the notice of amendment if this is later than the normal due date.

6.7   Example: Balancing payment

Continuing with example 6.3, suppose that the taxpayer's tax liability for 1999/00 is as follows:

	£
Income tax	10,800
Less: Tax deducted at source	2,500
	8,300
Class 4 NIC	800
CGT	4,600
	13,700

Solution

The balancing payment for 1999/00 due on 31 January 2001 will be as follows:

	£
Total tax liability as above	13,700
Less: Payments on account	8,000
Balancing payment due 31 January 2001	5,700

7   INTEREST AND SURCHARGES

7.1   Interest on tax paid late

(a)   Interest will automatically be charged if tax is paid late (whether it is income tax, Class 4 NIC or CGT).

Interest can arise in respect of payments on account, balancing payments, any tax payable following an amendment to a self assessment, and any tax payable following a discovery assessment (see later).

(b)   For payments on account, interest runs from the due date of 31 January in the tax year or 31 July following the tax year.

(c)   In other instances, interest runs from 31 January following the tax year to the date of payment. This is the case even if the tax was not actually due until a later date (ie following the amendment of the self assessment).

The only exception to this is where the return was issued late, in which case the due date will be three months after the issue of the return should this be later.

(d)   Interest is charged on penalties from the date they become due to the date that they are paid.

7.2   Example: Interest on tax paid late

A taxpayer pays his 1999/00 payments on account on 15 March 2000 and 10 August 2000. The balancing payment is paid on 15 April 2001.

Solution

Interest will be charged as follows:

- First payment on account from 1 February 2000 to 14 March 2000.
- Second payment on account from 1 August 2000 to 9 August 2000
- Balancing payment from 1 February 2001 to 14 April 2001

7.3   Interest on incorrect claims to reduce payments on account

(a)   Interest is charged where an excessive claim is made to reduce payments on account.

(b)   The charge is based on the difference between the amounts actually paid and the amounts that should have been paid. The amount that should have been paid is the lower of:

- The original payments on account based on the relevant amount for the previous year, and

- 50% of the final tax liability (excluding CGT, and net of tax deducted at source) for the current year

(c)   Interest runs from the due dates of 31 January in the tax year and 31 July following the tax year to the date of payment. The date of payment will be 31 January following the tax year when the balancing payment is due, unless the balancing payment is made late.

7.4   Example: Interest on incorrect claim to reduce payments on account

A taxpayer's relevant amount for 1998/99 is £5,000 (payments on account are therefore £2,500), but a claim is made to reduce the payments on account to £1,000 each. These payments are made on time.

The actually tax liability (net of tax deducted at source) for 1999/00 is £4,500. This is paid on 31 January 2001.

Solution

Payments on account should have been reduced to £2,250 (£4,500/2) rather than £1,000. Interest will therefore be charged as follows:

- On £1,250 from 1 February 2000 to 30 January 2001.
- On £1,250 from 1 August 2000 to 30 January 2001.

7.5   Interest paid on overpayments of tax

(a)   Interest is paid by the Inland Revenue on any overpayment of tax.

(b)   Interest runs from the date of actual payment to the date of repayment.

(c)   Interest is only paid on the amount of tax that should have been paid (ie, deliberate overpayments will not attract interest).

(d)   Tax deducted at source (eg, PAYE) are deemed to have been paid on 31 January following the tax year for the purpose of calculating interest on over payments.

7.6   Surcharge on unpaid tax

(a)   Interest on tax paid late is not a penalty, since it merely compensates for the advantage of paying late. Therefore, to further encourage compliance, surcharges can also be imposed where income tax, Class 4 NIC or CGT is paid late.

(b)   The surcharge does not apply to payments on account.

(c)   Where a balancing payment is not paid until more than 28 days after the due date (31 January following the tax year), a surcharge equal to 5% of the tax unpaid is imposed.

(d)   A further 5% surcharge arises if the tax is still unpaid after six months.

(e)   Where additional tax becomes due as a result of an amendment to a self assessment, a surcharge is only imposed if the additional tax is not paid within 28 days of the due date, which is 30 days after the amendment. This differs from interest which runs from the 31 January following the tax year.

(f)   Interest is charged if a surcharge is not paid within 30 days of the date that it is imposed.

(g)   A surcharge may be mitigated by the Inland Revenue, for example if there is a reasonable excuse for the non-payment of the tax. Insufficiency of funds is not a reasonable excuse.

7.7   Example: Surcharge on unpaid tax

A taxpayer's balancing payment due for 1999/00 is £5,000. Only £1,200 of this was paid on 31 January 2001.

Solution

Interest will be charged on £3,800 from 1 February 2001 to the date of payment.

A surcharge of £190 (£3,800 at 5%) will be due if the tax of £3,800 is not paid by 28 February 2001.

A further surcharge of £190 will be due if the tax is not paid by 31 July 2001.

8   CLAIMS

8.1   Making claims

(a)   Wherever possible claims must be included in the self assessment tax return.

(b)   A claim for a relief, allowance or repayment must be quantified at the time that the claim is made. For example, if loss relief is claimed, then the amount of the loss must be stated.

8.2   Claims for earlier years

(a)   Certain claims will relate to earlier years. The two most obvious examples of this are the carry back of personal pension contributions to the previous year and the claiming of loss relief for earlier years.

(b)   The basic rule is that such a claim is established in the later year, but is given effect by reference to the tax liability of an earlier year.

(c)   The taxpayer can make a claim in the return for the later year or can make a separate claim.

(d)   Although the claim is quantified by reference to the earlier year, it is given effect by reference to the later year. This means that the tax liability for the earlier year is not adjusted. Instead, the tax reduction resulting from the claim will be set off against the tax liability for the later year. Alternatively, if a separate claim is made, the Inland Revenue will refund the tax due.

The logic behind this is that it avoids re-opening self assessments for earlier years.

(e)   Because the claim is only quantified by reference to the earlier year, payments on accounts based on the relevant amount for the earlier year will not change.

8.3   Example: Claim for earlier years

A taxpayer's relevant amount for 1998/99 is £4,400. During 1999/00 the taxpayer pays a personal pension premium of £1,000, and makes a claim to carry this back to 1998/99.

Solution

The taxpayer's payments on account for 1999/00 are £2,200 (£4,400/2), and these will not alter as a result of the carry back of the personal pension premium.

The tax refund due will be calculated at the taxpayer's marginal income tax rate(s) for 1998/99. The tax refund due will either be set off against the 1999/00 tax liability, or will be repaid .

8.4   Error or mistake claims

(a)   Where an assessment is excessive due to an error or mistake in a return, the taxpayer can claim relief.

(b)   The claim must be made within five years of the filing date for the tax year concerned. For 1999/00 an error or mistake claim must be made by 31 January 2006.

(c)   A claim can be made in respect of errors made, and mistakes arising from not understanding the law.

9   ENQUIRIES INTO RETURNS

9.1   The Inland Revenue's right of enquiry

(a)   The Inland Revenue have the right to enquire into the completeness and accuracy of any self assessment tax return.

(b)   The enquiry may be made as a result of a suspicion that income is undeclared or deduction incorrectly claimed, because of information in the Inland Revenue's possession, or the choice of return may be completely random.

The Inland Revenue do not have to state a reason for the enquiry and are unlikely to do so.

An enquiry can be made even if the Inland Revenue calculated a taxpayer's tax liability.

(c)   The Inland Revenue must give written notice before commencing an enquiry.

(d)   The written notice must be issued within twelve months of the filing date. This deadline is extended if a return is filed late or is amended. Once this deadline is passed, the taxpayer can normally consider the self assessment for that year as final.

9.2   Enquiry procedures

(a)   The Inland Revenue can demand that the taxpayer produce documents, accounts or other written particulars. This includes being entitled to receive full answers to specific questions.

(b)   The information requested should be limited to that connected with the return.

(c)   The taxpayer has 30 days to comply with the request. An appeal can be made against the request.

(d)   The enquiry ends when the Inland Revenue give written notice that it has been completed. The notice will state the outcome of the enquiry. If the taxpayer believes that the Inland Revenue have no grounds for continuing an enquiry, he is entitled to ask the General or Special Commissioners that a date be set for its completion.

(e)   The taxpayer has 30 days from the completion of the enquiry to amend his or her self assessment. If the tax payer declines to do so or makes an amendment which is not to the satisfaction of the Revenue, the Revenue have a further 30 days to impose their amendement. The tax payer then has a further 30 days to appeal against the Revenue's amendment. The appeal must be in writing.

9.3   Discovery assessments

(a)   Despite the fact that the Inland Revenue must normally begin enquiries into a self assessment return within twelve months of the filing date, a discovery assessment can be raised at a later date to prevent the loss of tax. The use of a discovery assessment is restricted where a self assessment has already been made.

(b)   Unless the loss of tax is due to fraud or negligence, a discovery assessment cannot be raised where full disclosure was made in the return, even if this is found to be incorrect.

The Revenue will only accept that full disclosure has been made if any contentious items have been clearly brought to their attention - perhaps in a covering letter or in the 'white space' on the tax return. Information lying in the attached accounts will not constitute full disclosure if its significance is not emphasised.

Only a taxpayer who makes full disclosure in the self assessment tax return therefore has absolute finality twelve months after the filing date.

(c)   The time limit for making a discovery assessment is five years from the filing date. This is extended to 20 years from the filing date in the case of fraud or negligence.

(d)   A discovery assessment may be appealed against.

9.4   Penalties

In addition to interest on the late payment of tax, the Inland Revenue can impose a tax geared penalty for omitting information from a return, or where the return includes false information.

The maximum penalty is the difference between the tax actually due, and the tax that was shown as due. The maximum penalty may be reduced by the Inland Revenue, depending on the taxpayer's co-operation, the extent that information is disclosed voluntarily and the extent of fraud.

If a penalty is imposed, then no surcharge will be charged.

When anyone (eg a professional adviser) assists someone in making a false declaration or return, there is a £3,000 penalty.

10   APPEALS

10.1   Introduction

The taxpayer can appeal against an amendment to the self assessment following an Inland Revenue enquiry, and against discovery assessments.

Disputes that cannot be settled between the Inspector and taxpayer, are usually adjudicated by either the General or Special Commissioners, which are bodies set up for this purpose.

The Commissioners will hear the appeal at which the Inspector and the taxpayer (or his representative, eg, his accountant) present their cases. The Commissioners then adjudicate on the dispute.

Their findings are conclusive on a point of **fact**, but disputes on points of **law** (ie, interpretation of the Taxes Acts) may be continued through the High Court - Chancery Division, the Court of Appeal and finally to the House of Lords.

10.2   The Commissioners

(a)   **The General Commissioners**

These are **lay** persons appointed by the Lord Chancellor who have no special legal or taxation qualifications. The appointments are honorary and part-time. They function as follows.

All appeals are heard by them automatically, unless an election is made for the appeal to be determined by the Special Commissioners. This election, however, is not available unless the General Commissioners direct that they are satisfied that the case should be heard by the Special Commissioners. Also, the General Commissioners are able to transfer appeals to the Special Commissioners subject only to obtaining their agreement. They are likely to do this because of the complexity of the appeal or the length of time likely to be required for hearing it.

(b)   **The Special Commissioners**

These are full-time paid officials who are appointed by the Lord Chancellor. They are quite independent of the Inland Revenue. Special Commissioners must be barristers, advocates or solicitors of not less than ten years standing.

They hear all appeals where an election has been made for them to do so.

Certain appeals on special points **must** be heard by the Special Commissioners - normally those involved with complex interpretations of the Taxes Acts.

10.3   General points on appeals

Assuming that a decision is made to go beyond the District Inspector, the taxpayer will in many cases have a choice as to whether the General or Special Commissioners hear the appeal.

As a general rule, if one's case is considered to be good in equity, the General Commissioners should be chosen. Being experienced laymen they will be able to give a fair decision in equity.

Conversely, if one's case turns on a point of law - especially a strict or controversial interpretation - the case should be put before the more expert Special Commissioners.

At the Commissioners' stage of appeal, both sides will normally meet their own costs although the Special Commissioners can award costs against a party that has acted unreasonably in bringing or persisting with the case. Special Commissioner cases are published where the decision is likely to be of interest to other taxpayers.

Before requesting the Commissioners to state a case for the High Court, the taxpayer should carefully consider the costs involved against the potential tax savings and the effect of publicity. The costs of appeal incurred by the taxpayer are not allowable expenses for tax purposes.

11   SELF TEST QUESTIONS

11.1   How is the Inland Revenue organised? (2.1)

11.2   What is the significance of an employee's code number and how does it operate? (4.2)

11.3   When an employee leaves employment, what PAYE procedure must be adopted? (4.7)

11.4   What are the penalties for failing to submit a return? (5.5)

11.5   What records must a taxpayer keep? (5.8)

11.6   When are payments on account not required? (6.2)

11.7   When is the balancing payment for 1999/00 due? (6.6)

11.8   When is a surcharge imposed? (7.6)

11.9   When are discovery assessments made? (9.3)

11.10   What are the two bodies of appeal commissioners and what is their function? (10.2)

12   EXAMINATION TYPE QUESTION

12.1   Fred Foyle

Fred was employed until 31 March 1999. He purchased an existing business on 1 June 1999. Accounts have been prepared for the ten month period to 5 April 2000, and the results show a marked decline compared to the results of the previous owner for the year ended 31 May 1999:

	Previous owner Year ended 31 May 1999 £	Fred Period ended 5 April 2000 £
Sales - Cash	600,000	400,000
- Credit	120,000	100,000
Gross profit	300,000	150,000
Net profit	216,000	80,000

Fred included the figures in his self assessment tax return for 1999/00 which was submitted on 31 January 2001.

The Inland Revenue proceeded to carry out an enquiry into Fred's 1999/00 return, and have stated that they consider the sales shown in the accounts to be understated by £100,000.

The Inland Revenue gave written notice that the enquiry was complete on 31 July 2001. Fred did not raise an appeal, and paid the additional tax due 31 August 2001.

Fred is single, and has no other income or outgoings.

Required:

(a)   State the likely reasons why the Inland Revenue have investigated Fred's 1999/00 tax return.

State possible criteria that he could put forward in order to justify the fall in profits from those of the previous owner.

(b)   Calculate the interest on overdue tax (assuming a rate of 10%).

State the maximum amount of penalty that the Inland Revenue can charge Fred, and state the factors that will be taken into account in deciding if this maximum amount should be mitigated.

13   ANSWER TO EXAMINATION TYPE QUESTION

13.1   Fred Foyle

The Inland Revenue will probably have enquired into Fred's 1999/00 return because of the fall in the GP% compared to the accounts of the previous owner.

Fred's GP% is 30% (£150,000/(£400,000 + £100,000) × 100), compared to 41.7% (£300,000/(£600,000 + £120,000) × 100) for the previous owner.

The fall in the GP% has arisen because Fred's cash sales are £400,000 compared to an expected £500,000 (£600,000 × 10/12), which is a shortfall of £100,000.

The Inland Revenue will therefore assume that cash sales of £100,000 have not been recorded. The adjustment will increase Fred's GP% to the required 41.7%.

Fred could put forward the following points to justify the fall in GP%:

(1)   He may be selling goods at a lower margin than the previous owner.
(2)   He may be selling a different mix of goods.
(3)   He may have suffered an increase in theft or wastage.

Interest will run from 1 February 2001 to 30 August 2001, and will be as follows:

£100,000 at 40% = £40,000 × 10% × 7/12 = £2,333

Fred has negligently or fraudulently submitted an incorrect return. The maximum penalty is £40,000.

The Inland Revenue will mitigate this maximum penalty depending on Fred's co-operation in the enquiry, whether information was disclosed voluntarily, and to what degree his actions are considered to be fraudulent.

23 OUTLINE OF CORPORATION TAX

INTRODUCTION & LEARNING OBJECTIVES

Companies receive different types of income and incur different sorts of expenditure. This chapter explains how these items are dealt with in arriving at the profits chargeable to corporation tax and how the corporation tax liability is calculated.

A thorough understanding of this chapter is essential as it is a building block towards an understanding of more advanced aspects of corporation tax.

When you have studied this chapter you should have learned the following:

- The scope of corporation tax;
- How to determine the residence of a company;
- The basis of assessment to corporation tax;
- How profits chargeable to corporation tax are computed;
- How to deal with a period of account longer than 12 months;
- The rates of corporation tax; and
- When the small companies' rate of tax applies.

1 THE CHARGE TO TAX

Corporation tax is charged on the **profits** of **companies resident** in the UK by reference to the **total profits** arising in each **accounting period**.

> **Definition** A company is any body corporate, limited or unlimited, or unincorporated association. This does not include a partnership, a local authority or a local authority association.

2 COMPANY RESIDENCE

2.1 Determination of company residence

There are two criteria important in determining the residence of a company:

- the country in which the company is incorporated; and
- the country in which the company is centrally managed and controlled.

A company incorporated in the UK is resident here for corporation tax purposes irrespective of where it is centrally managed and controlled.

If a company is incorporated elsewhere, it is regarded as resident in the UK if it is centrally managed and controlled here. This will be looked at in more depth in chapter 37.

3 THE BASIS OF ASSESSMENT

3.1 Introduction

Having discussed the meaning of the word 'company' and 'residence' it is now necessary to look at how the profits are assessed. Earlier in the text it was stated that corporation tax is charged by reference to the total profits arising in each accounting period. It is essential to differentiate between an 'accounting period' and a 'period of account'.

Definition   A period of account is any period for which a company prepares accounts. It is usually 12 months in length, but may be shorter or longer than this.

Definition   An accounting period is the period for which a charge to corporation tax is made. It may never be longer than 12 months.

3.2   Accounting period

(a)   An accounting period begins when:

- a company starts to trade, or when the profits of a company first become liable to corporation tax; or

- the previous accounting period ends, providing that the company is still liable to corporation tax.

(b)   An accounting period ends on the earliest of:

- 12 months after the beginning of the accounting period;
- the end of the company's period of account;
- the company ceasing to trade
- the company ceasing to be resident in the UK;
- the company ceasing to be liable to corporation tax; or
- the commencement of the winding up of the company.

(c)   As an accounting period must not exceed 12 months, if a company has a period of account longer than 12 months, this must be split into two accounting periods, the first of 12 months and the second of the remainder of the accounting period. Note that the period of account **must** be split in this way.

3.3   Activity

A Ltd prepares accounts for the 15 month period from 1 October 1998 to 31 December 1999. What are the accounting periods of A Ltd?

3.4   Activity solution

(a)   12 months from 1 October 1998 to 30 September 1999
(b)   3 months from 1 October 1999 to 31 December 1999.

4   RATES OF CORPORATION TAX

The rate of corporation tax is fixed by reference to financial years.

Definition   A financial year runs from 1 April to the following 31 March and is identified by the calendar year in which it begins.

The year commencing 1 April 1999 is the financial year 1999 (FY 1999). Financial years should not be confused with fiscal years, the tax years for income tax which run from 6 April to the following 5 April.

The full rate of corporation tax ('Rate of corporation tax') for the current financial (FY 1999) is 30%. A reduced rate of 20% known as the small companies rate applies to companies with lower profits.

5   PAYMENT OF DIVIDENDS

5.1   Introduction

Until 5 April 1999, when a company paid a dividend to its shareholders it also had to make an advance payment of corporation tax (ACT) to the Inland Revenue.

The requirement to pay ACT was abolished for dividends paid after 5 April 1999. This means that the majority of companies simply pay their corporation tax liability in one lump sum (see the next chapter).

The payment of a dividend no longer gives rise to any tax implications for the paying company.

5.2   Examiner's comments

The examiner has stated that ACT is not longer examinable.

ACT is therefore not dealt with in this textbook.

6   PROFITS CHARGEABLE TO CORPORATION TAX

6.1   Introduction

A corporation tax computation is necessary to calculate the amount of profits that are charged to corporation tax for an accounting period. Included in the computation are the world-wide income of a company plus any chargeable gains. Note that dividends received from a company resident in the UK are not included.

6.2   Layout of a corporation tax computation

X Ltd corporation tax computation for the 12 months ended 31 March 2000

	£
Schedule D Case I	X
Schedule D Case III	X
Schedule D Case V	X
Schedule D Case VI	X
Schedule A	X
Taxed income (gross)	X
Chargeable gains	X
	X
Less: Charges on income (gross)	(X)
Profits chargeable to corporation tax (PCTCT)	X

(a)   The use of this layout is essential in any corporation tax exam question. The company and the chargeable accounting period should be identified. Each separate source of income should be identified by Schedule or otherwise.

(b)   Any amounts received or paid net such as taxed income and charges on income, should be grossed-up for inclusion in the computation. Taxed interest must be grossed up by 100/80 and charges on income must be grossed up by 100/77.

Remember the 20% **lower** rate of tax applies to savings income (eg, most interest other than bank or building society interest) whereas charges (eg, patent royalties and gift aid) are paid net of **basic** rate tax.

(c)   The different types of profits are dealt with separately according to the different Schedules or other category. Income assessed under a particular Schedule must be included according to the rules of that Schedule. Other income and charges must be included according to the rules given later in this chapter. They are then totalled to give the total profits chargeable to corporation tax.

(d)   The Schedules used in the corporation tax computation are broadly the same as those you are familiar with from income tax although there are some computational differences.

All interest received by a company - whether received net or gross or whether from a UK or foreign source - is normally assessable under Schedule D Case III. Note that while grossed up taxed interest might be shown in the layout as 'taxed income', it is technically Schedule D Case III income.

(e)   Care is also needed to include certain payments or receipts in the correct accounting period. The following is a useful summary of items that give particular problems:

-   Interest paid on borrowings (paid net or gross) for a trading purpose (eg, to provide working capital or buy plant) should be charged as a trading expense in the company accounts on an 'accruals' basis. No tax adjustment is therefore needed.

-   Interest received (net or gross) is usually credited in the company accounts on an 'accruals' basis. In which case no adjustment is needed for tax purposes.

-   Charges on income (eg, patent royalties or gift aid payments) have to be included in PCTCT on a paid basis regardless of whether the company accounts show them debited on a paid or accruals basis. Note that interest (whether paid net or gross) is never a charge on income. Instead, if it is for a trading purpose it is a trading expense. However, if it is for a non-trading purpose (eg, on a loan to buy commercially let property) it is deducted from interest received (if any) with any excess relieved under special loss relief rules.

6.3   Schedule D Case I: adjustment of accounting profit

(a)   The net profit disclosed by a company's profit and loss account will need adjustment to arrive at the net trading profit for Schedule D I purposes. The adjustments necessary can be classified, **as for income tax,** under the following headings:

		£	£
Net profits per accounts			X
Add:	Expenditure not allowable for taxation purposes	X	
	Income not credited in the accounts but taxable under Schedule D Case I	X	
			X
			X
Less:	Income credited in the accounts but not taxable under Schedule D Case I	X	
	Expenditure not charged in the accounts but allowable for the purposes of taxation	X	
	Capital allowances	X	
			X
Schedule D Case I			X

(b)   The rules regarding expenditure in the accounts not allowed for corporation tax purposes are basically the same as those for income tax, covered earlier in the study text. However, the following points should be noted:

•   When adjusting profits for corporation tax purposes, no adjustment is necessary for private expenses. Thus where a car is provided for an employee and the company pays all the expenses, for both business and private use, the full amount is deductible. The employee is **then** taxed under Schedule E on any benefit he has received.

- Appropriations of profit are not allowable expenditure. The sort of appropriations a company may make are payment of dividends, transfers to reserves and general provisions.

- Any costs incurred directly by a company in obtaining long term finance are allowable, even if the loan finance is not eventually obtained. The sort of costs allowed are fees, commission, legal expenses and advertising, but any indirect costs such as stamp duty are excluded. The costs are allowed as a trading expense if the loan interest is a trading expense.

- Any revenue expenditure incurred in the seven years before a company commences to trade is treated as an expense on the day that the company starts trading. For example if a company which started to trade on 1 April 1999 had spent £6,000 in the previous six months advertising the fact that it was about to trade, this expenditure would be treated as if it had been incurred on 1 April 1999.

- Payments to Employee Share Ownership Trusts and other approved arrangements for providing benefits to employees in the form of shares in the company are allowable trading expenses.

(c)   Certain items of income may be included in the accounts, but are not taxable under Schedule D Case I. The main items are as follows:

- Income taxed under another Schedule or Case such as interest, taxed under Schedule D Case III, and rent, taxed under Schedule A.

- Capital receipts, which are taxed as chargeable gains.

- Items which are exempt, such as profits on the sale of capital items which are exempt (motor cars) and dividends from UK companies.

6.4   Capital allowances

Capital allowances are computed as follows for companies:

- Allowances are given for accounting periods by reference to acquisitions and disposals in that accounting period.

- If the accounting period is less than 12 months the writing down allowance is proportionately reduced.

- Where there is private use of an asset, there is no reduction in the writing down allowance.

6.5   Example: Capital allowances for companies

Conifer Ltd prepared accounts for the nine month period ended 31 March 2000. On 1 November 1999 a car costing £10,000 was bought for the managing director, who used the car 80% for business purposes.

You are required to calculate the capital allowance available.

6.6   Solution

Conifer Ltd

Capital allowances for the nine month period to 31.3.2000
$£10,000 \times 25\% \times \frac{9}{12} =$ £1,875

6.7   Schedule D Case V

Where a company trades abroad they may do so either through an overseas branch or an overseas subsidiary.

Profits of an overseas branch are included in the Schedule D Case I figure. Where a company has an overseas subsidiary any dividends received are not exempt, (only dividends from a UK company are exempt) the gross amount is taxable under Schedule D Case V.

6.8   Schedule A

The Schedule A rules for companies are virtually identical to those for individuals (see chapter 2).

The only difference is in respect of interest payable on a loan to acquire or improve property. This is not allowed as a Schedule A deduction, but is instead set against interest received (see earlier in this chapter and chapter 25 on corporation tax losses).

There are also some special rules where a company incurs a Schedule A loss (see chapter 25).

7   OTHER INCOME AND PAYMENTS

7.1   Taxed income

(a)   Examples of taxed income which a company may receive and which must be included in the computation of profits calculation are:

- interest received from another UK company, for example debenture or loan stock interest (received net of lower rate tax);

- patent royalties (received net of basic rate tax).

Interest on gilt edged securities is paid gross where the company acquires the securities after 5 April 1998 or where it elects for gross payment on securities acquired before 6 April 1998.

(b)   The interest received is grossed-up by 100/80, so that if a company receives £8,000 (net) the gross equivalent to include in chargeable profits is £10,000. The £2,000 of income tax suffered at source is recoverable by the company (see the following chapter). Remember, the grossed-up interest is included in chargeable profits for an accounting period on an *accruals* basis. Interest received is normally assessable under Schedule D Case III whether it is received gross or net.

(c)   Patent royalties received are grossed up at 100/77 and are chargeable on a received basis. Thus, if a company receives £10,780 (net) of patent royalties on 10 April 1999 in respect of the usage of a patent during its accounting period to 31 March 1999, it has income of £14,000 (£10,780 × 100/77) for its year to 31 March 2000 (year of receipt). The accruals basis does not apply to taxed income other than interest.

(d)   Remember:

- dividends received from UK companies are **not** included in the profits calculation (see below).

- bank interest and building society is received gross by companies, and, being interest, are taxed under Schedule D Case III.

- as gilt edged security interest may be received net or gross after 5 April 1998 (as explained above) care must be taken to see whether or not gilt interest appearing in a question needs to be grossed up.

7.2   Franked investment income

Definition   Dividends received from UK companies plus the associated 10% tax credit is known as franked investment income.

(a)   It has already been mentioned that dividends received from UK companies are not included in the profits calculation. Such dividends are paid out of post-tax profits of the company paying them, and are not subject to further tax. The dividends received by a company plus the tax credit are known as franked investment income. Note that although a company is not liable to tax on UK dividends received, an individual is.

(b)   It is only dividends paid out of profits which have suffered UK corporation tax that are treated in this way. If dividends are received from foreign companies, they are taxed under Schedule D Case V.

(c)   Franked investment income does not include dividends received from 51% group companies (see chapter 26). Such dividends are completely outside the scope of corporation tax, and can therefore be ignored.

7.3   Charges on income

(a)   Companies may make payments which are charges on income: these are deducted from the total of profits from all sources to arrive at the profits chargeable to corporation tax figure.

The payments are made net of basic rate income tax, and the company accounts to the Revenue for the amount deducted. This is dealt with in more detail in the following chapter.

Note that it is the gross amount, before deduction of tax, that is included in the profits chargeable to corporation tax computation.

Examples of payments which are treated as charges on income are:

- patent royalties;
- charitable deeds of covenants; and
- one off donations to charities under the Gift Aid Scheme.

The accounts of the company will have been prepared on the accruals basis, and will include amounts due but not yet paid. For corporation tax purposes, the gross amount of charges actually paid in the chargeable accounting period must be included in the profits computation.

For example, a company may show patent royalties of £23,300 in the accounts for the year ended 31 March 2000 made up as follows:

	£
Amount paid December 1999	23,000
Accrual 31 March 2000	2,100
Less: accrual 1 April 1999	(1,800)
	23,300

The amount to be included as a charge in the profits computation is £23,000.

Note that although a company usually pays loan or debenture interest net of (lower rate) tax it is not a charge on income. The gross amount of interest is generally allowed as a trading expense charged on an accruals basis. Thus if the amounts in the above example had instead been loan interest the trading deduction of £23,300 would not be adjusted.

(b)   The Gift Aid Scheme allows companies to make one off payments to charities which are treated as charges on income and thus qualify for tax relief. The company must deduct basic rate income tax from the payments and account for the deduction via the quarterly accounting system (see next chapter).

There is no upper limit for relief under the Gift Aid Scheme. There is a minimum limit for certain companies (close companies) of a net payment of £250.

7.4 Activity

The following information relates to Holly Ltd for the year ended 31 March 2000.

	£
Trading profit (adjusted for taxation purposes)	1,500,000
Capital allowances	60,000
Bank interest receivable	25,000
Dividend received from overseas subsidiary (gross amount)	15,000
Dividend received from UK subsidiary (gross amount)	20,000
Interest on gilts (net amount receivable)	44,800
Debenture interest payable (gross amount)	35,000
Patent royalties payable (gross amount)	32,000

The amount of net patent royalties actually paid in the year ended 31 March 2000 amounted to £29,260.

You are required to calculate the profits chargeable to corporation tax.

7.5 Activity solution

Holly Ltd: Profits chargeable to corporation tax for the year ended 31 March 2000.

	£
Adjusted trading profit	1,500,000
Less: Capital allowances	(60,000)
Debenture interest payable	(35,000)
	———
Schedule D Case I	1,405,000
Schedule D Case III - bank interest	25,000
- taxed interest (£44,800 × 100/80)	56,000
Schedule D Case V	15,000
	———
	1,501,000
Less: Patent royalties paid (£29,260 × 100/77)	(38,000)
	———
Profits chargeable to corporation tax	1,463,000
	———

7.6 Detailed profit adjustment

It is unlikely that you will get a question requiring a detailed adjustment of trading profits at Paper 11, but some aspects could be examined.

7.7 Example: calculation of PCTCT with capital allowances computation

Superscoff plc is a trading company operating a fast food retailing business. The profit and loss account for the 12 months to 31 March 2000 shows the following.

	£		£
Salaries and wages	146,323	Gross profit	1,490,515
Rates, light and heat	11,650	Bank deposit interest	1,200
Travelling expenses	13,200	Dividends from UK	
Entertaining	6,000	companies	
Advertising	18,600	(received June 1999)	6,000
Depreciation	27,800	Gain on investments	798
Director's remuneration	40,000		
General expenses	3,150		
Debenture interest paid	8,800		
Net profit	1,222,990		
	———		
	1,498,513		1,498,513
	———		———

The following information is also relevant.

(a)   The entertaining expenses comprise £4,750 cost of entertaining customers, and £1,250 for the staff Christmas party.

(b)   Advertising includes the cost of 500 calendars, bearing the company's name, at a cost of £2 each.

(c)   General expenses comprise

	£
Subscriptions to BHRCA, the trade association	40
Donation to Oxfam (net) 1 January 2000	500
Fine for breach of hygiene regulations	250
Allowable expenses	2,360
	3,150

(d)   The debenture interest is on £88,000 10% Debentures issued in 1987. The interest is payable half-yearly on 30 September and 31 March.

(e)   The gain on the investments arises on the sale of 5,000 shares in Finefish Ltd, purchased and sold, in May 1999.

(f)   The written down value of the plant and machinery, for capital allowances purposes, on 1 April 1999 was as follows.

	£
General pool	200
General car pool	11,200
Car costing £18,750 used 60% privately by managing director	6,750

During the year ended 31 March 2000 the following transactions took place

1 August 1999   Sold the MD's car for £6,350 and purchased a replacement for £18,000. Private use remains at 60%.

1 March 2000   Sold a cold food display cabinet for £1,200 (cost £2,500).

You are required to compute the total profits liable to corporation tax for the 12 months ended 31 March 2000.

7.8   Solution

Superscoff plc

Corporation tax computation: 12 months ended 31 March 2000.

	£
Schedule D Case I trading profit (W1)	1,243,092
Schedule D Case III - bank deposit interest	1,200
Chargeable gain	798
	1,245,090
Less: Charges on income (gross):	
Gift aid payment (gross) £500 $\times \dfrac{100}{77}$	(649)
Profits chargeable to corporation tax	1,244,441

WORKINGS

(W1)   Schedule D Case I profit

	£
	£
Net profit per accounts	1,222,990
Add: Entertaining customers	4,750
General expenses:	
Gift aid payment	500
Fine	250
Depreciation	27,800
	1,256,290

Less: Bank deposit interest	1,200	
Dividend received	6,000	
Profit on investments	798	
		(7,998)
		1,248,292

Less: Capital allowances (W2)	(6,200)
Add: Balancing charge (W2)	1,000
Schedule D Case I profit	1,243,092

(W2)   Capital allowances: Plant and machinery

	General pool £	Car pool £	Car over £12,000 £	Allowances £
WDV b/f 1 April 1999	200	11,200	6,750	
Sale proceeds (1.8.99 + 1.3.2000)	(1,200)		(6,350)	
Balancing charge	(1,000)			(1,000)
Balancing allowance			400	400

			Car over £12,000 £	
Cost of new car (1.8.99)			18,000	
WDA 25%		(2,800)	(3,000) (max)	5,800
				6,200
WDV c/f at 31 March 2000	Nil	8,400	15,000	

8   CHARGEABLE GAINS

8.1   Introduction

(a)   Companies are not entitled to taper relief when they make chargeable disposals. They instead receive the indexation allowance calculated up to the date of disposal.

(b)   Subject to this difference, when a company disposes of a capital asset the chargeable gain is calculated on a similar basis as for individuals (ie, disposal proceeds less allowable deductions).

(c)   However, companies do not pay capital gains tax. Instead, their chargeable gains form part of their profits chargeable to corporation tax for an accounting period, and are therefore subject to corporation tax.

(d)   Companies do not receive an annual exemption as individuals do.

8.2   Example

Lex Ltd disposes of a factory in January 2000 for £245,000. The factory had cost £85,000 in March 1985. The company makes up its accounts to 31 March.

Calculate the chargeable gain that will be included in Lex Ltd's profits chargeable to corporation tax for the year ended 31 March 2000.

8.3   Solution

	£
Disposal proceeds	245,000
Less: Purchase price	85,000
Unindexed gain	160,000
Less: Indexation allowance	
(January 2000 - March 1985)	
$\dfrac{165.9 - 92.80}{92.80}$ (=0.788) × 85,000	66,980
Chargeable gain	93,020

8.4   Rollover relief

Of the various capital gains tax reliefs covered in chapters 19 to 21, the only important one relevant to companies is rollover relief for the replacement of business assets.

The relief is calculated on a similar basis as for individuals. The old asset qualifies for indexation up to the date of sale and the new asset from the date of purchase. For the new asset, indexation is calculated on the cost as reduced by the rolled over gain.

8.5   Example

Lex Ltd in the previous example purchases a replacement factory for £225,000 in March 2000.

What claim can be made for rollover relief?

8.6   Solution

The proceeds not reinvested of £20,000 (245,000 - 225,000) will remain chargeable in the year ended 31 March 2000.

The balance of the gain of £73,020 (93,020 - 20,000) can be rolled over. The base cost of the replacement factory will be £151,980 (225,000 - 73,020), and indexation will be based on this figure from March 2000.

8.7   Shares and securities

Unlike individuals, any shares and securities that a company acquires after 5 April 1998 will continue to be added to the relevant 1985 pool. The matching rules when a company disposes of shares are therefore relatively straightforward. Sales are matched against acquisitions in the following order:

(a)   Shares acquired on the same day (as the sale).
(b)   Shares acquired during the nine days before the sale.
(c)   Shares in the 1985 pool.
(d)   Shares in the 1982 holding.

The 1985 pool is operated in the same way as for individuals (see chapter 17), except that indexation continues to be given up to the date of the operative event, rather than ceasing at April 1998.

The examiner has stated that a question will not require detailed calculations of either the 1982 pool or the 1985 pool.

8.8   Example

Kola Ltd has the following investment in ABC plc:

Number of shares	1,000
Unindexed cost	£11,000
Indexed cost (up to May 1997)	£13,500

The shares were originally acquired in 1990, and the last operative event took place during May 1997.

During January 2000 Kola Ltd sold 500 of the shares in ABC plc for £19,000. The company makes up its accounts to 31 March.

Calculate the chargeable gain that will be included in Kola Ltd's profits chargeable to corporation tax for the year ended 31 March 2000.

8.9   Solution

1985 Pool	Shares	Unindexed cost £	Indexed cost £
B/f at May 1997	1,000	11,000	13,500
January 2000 - Sale			
Indexed rise (to January 2000)			
$13,500 \times \dfrac{165.9-156.9}{156.9}$			774
			14,274
Sales of shares	500	5,500	7,137
Balance c/f	500	5,500	7,137

	£
Disposal proceeds	19,000
Less: Unindexed cost	5,500
Unindexed gain	13,500
Less: Indexation allowance (7,137 - 5,500)	1,637
Chargeable gain	11,863

9 LONG PERIODS OF ACCOUNT

9.1 Introduction

Where a company prepares accounts for a period of more than 12 months, this must be split into two chargeable accounting periods of the first 12 months and the remainder of the period of account, as was explained earlier in this chapter.

A problem arises over how to allocate profits and charges between the two chargeable accounting periods.

The following rules apply:

<table>
<tr><td></td><td></td><td>**Method of allocation**</td></tr>
<tr><td>•</td><td>Trading profits before capital allowances.</td><td>Adjust profit for period of account for tax purposes and then apportion on a time basis.</td></tr>
<tr><td>•</td><td>Capital allowances and balancing charges.</td><td>Separate calculation for each chargeable accounting period. (WDAs will be restricted if accounting period less than 12 months).</td></tr>
<tr><td>•</td><td>Schedule A profit.</td><td>Apportion on a time basis.</td></tr>
<tr><td>•</td><td>Interest receivable.</td><td>Allocated to the period in which receivable.</td></tr>
<tr><td>•</td><td>Schedule D Case VI income.</td><td>Apportioned on a time basis.</td></tr>
<tr><td>•</td><td>Chargeable gains.</td><td>Dealt with in accounting period in which disposal takes place.</td></tr>
<tr><td>•</td><td>Charges on income.</td><td>Deducted from profits of the accounting period in which they are paid.</td></tr>
</table>

Conclusion Where a period of account is longer than 12 months, it must be split into two chargeable accounting periods. Profits and charges must be allocated between the two accounting periods. There are then two separate calculations for profits chargeable to corporation tax.

9.2 Activity

Oak Ltd prepared accounts for the 15 month period to 30 June 2000, with results as follows:

	£
Trading profit (adjusted for tax purposes but before capital allowances)	383,880
Bank interest (received 31 December 1999)	22,000
Schedule A (profit)	10,000
Schedule D Case VI income (received 1 June 1999)	30,000
Chargeable gain (asset disposed of 1 June 2000)	16,000
Patent royalties (net amount paid 1 February 2000)	18,480

Bank interest accrued was as follows:

At 1 April 1999	£5,200
At 1 April 2000	£4,100
At 30 June 2000	£9,780

The company bought plant costing £120,000 for use in its trade on 31 August 1999. It had made no previous acquisitions qualifying for capital allowances. Oak Ltd is not a large company for capital allowance purposes.

You are required to calculate the profits chargeable to corporation tax.

9.3   **Activity solution**

Oak Ltd: profits chargeable to corporation tax for the

	Year ended 31.3.2000 £	3 months ended 30.6.2000 £
Trading profit (12:3)	307,104	76,776
Less: Capital allowances		
FYA £120,000 × 40%	(48,000)	
WDA £72,000 × 25% × 3/12		(4,500)
Schedule D Case I	259,104	72,276
Schedule D Case III - (22,000 − 5,200 + 4,100)	20,900	–
- (9,780 − 4,100)	-	5,680
Schedule A (12:3)	8,000	2,000
Schedule D Case VI (12 : 3)	24,000	6,000
Chargeable gain		16,000
	312,004	101,956
Less: Patent royalties paid (£18,480 × 100/77)	(24,000)	–
Profits chargeable to corporation tax	288,004	101,956

10   **CHAPTER SUMMARY**

This chapter has dealt with the basics of corporation tax. The following areas were covered:

- The charge to tax. Corporation tax is charged on the total profits of UK companies arising in each accounting period.

- Company residence. A company is resident in the UK if incorporated here or centrally managed and controlled here.

- The basis of assessment. Remember that a chargeable accounting period can never exceed 12 months.

- The computation of profits chargeable to corporation tax. Remember that figures in the company accounts may need adjusting and that all figures in the computation are gross.

- Long period of account. If a period of account is longer than 12 months, it must be split into two accounting periods of the first 12 months and the remainder. Profits and charges must be allocated between the two accounting periods in accordance with the rules given in the chapter.

- The rates of corporation tax. Remember that the rates are fixed by reference to financial years.

11   **SELF-TEST QUESTIONS**

11.1   How is a company's residence determined? (2.1)

11.2   What is the definition of an accounting period? (3.2)

11.3   What is a financial year? (4)

11.4   What adjustments are needed for the net profit per the company's accounts to arrive at the Schedule D Case I figure (6.3)

11.5   How are capital allowances computed for companies? (6.4)

11.6   What is franked investment income? (7.2)

11.7   How are charges on income treated when calculating profits chargeable to corporation tax? (7.3)

11.8   How does the calculation of a company's chargeable gains differ from the calculation for individuals? (8.1)

11.9   When a company prepares accounts for a period that exceeds 12 months, what will be the company's chargeable accounting periods? (9.1)

11.10   How will trading profits be allocated when the period of account exceeds 12 months? (9.1)

12   EXAMINATION TYPE QUESTION

12.1   Springvale Ltd

Springvale Ltd has been carrying on a manufacturing business since 1970 and the following is a summary of the profit and loss account for the year to 31 March 2000.

	£		£
Director's remuneration	37,840	Trading profit	362,372
Depreciation	44,400	Debenture interest (gross)	
Loan stock interest payable (gross)	480	(31 March 2000)	1,200
Entertaining expenses (all customers)	420	Bank deposit interest receivable	359
Gift aid paid to charity (net)	3,850	Dividend from UK trade	
Patent royalty paid (gross)	300	investment (excluding tax credit)	400
Salaries and wages	16,460		
Rent and business rates	1,650		
Audit fee	350		
Trade expenses	15,418		
Net profit before taxation	243,163		
	364,331		364,331

Of the loan stock interest payable of £480, £80 was accrued at 31 March 2000. There was no opening accrual. Debenture interest is receivable annually on 31 March.

The trade expenses include the following items

	£
Christmas gifts	
Wines and spirits for UK customers	280
5,000 ball-point pens with company's name	250
Legal costs	
Re long-term loan finance secured by a floating charge	500
Re loan to employee	40
Re staff service agreements	90

The written down value on 1 April 1999 of plant and machinery was £24,220.

On 10 July 1999 the company purchased a new lathe for £1,200 and plant for £2,000. On 1 December 1999 plant that had cost £11,000 was sold for £1,500. On 1 February 2000 plant costing £5,200 and a motor car costing £13,000 were purchased (the private use of this car by the sales director was agreed at one-third). Springvale Ltd is not a large company for capital allowance purposes.

During the year the company made a chargeable gain after indexation of £51,160.

You are required to compute the profits chargeable to corporation tax for the year ended 31 March 2000.

13   ANSWER TO EXAMINATION TYPE QUESTION

13.1   Springvale Ltd

WORKINGS

(W1)   Capital allowances

		General pool £	Car costing £12,000 £	Total £
Plant and machinery				
WDV b/f at 1.4.99		24,220		
1.2.2000 Purchase			13,000	
1.12.99 Sale		(1,500)		
		22,720		
WDA 25%/restricted		(5,680)	(3,000)	8,680
Additions qualifying for FYA				
10.7.99 (1,200 + 2,000)	3,200			
1.2.2000	5,200			
	8,400			
FYA 40%	(3,360)	5,040		3,360
WDV c/f at 31.3.2000		22,080	10,000	
TOTAL ALLOWANCES				12,040

(W2)   Schedule DI profit

	£ −	£ +
Net profit per accounts		243,163
Depreciation		44,400
Entertaining		420
Gift aid to charity paid (net)		3,850
Patent royalty (gross)		300
Trade expenses		
Gifts of alcohol		280
Employee loan expenses		40
Debenture interest received	1,200	
Bank deposit interest received	359	
Dividend (FII) received	400	
Capital allowances (W1)	12,040	
	13,999	292,453
		13,999
Schedule D Case I profits		278,454

Springvale Ltd
Profits chargeable to corporation tax for year ended 31 March 2000

	£	£
Schedule D Case I (W2)		278,454
Schedule D Case III (bank deposit interest receivable)		359
(debenture interest receivable)		1,200
Chargeable gain		51,160
		———
		331,173
Less: Charges on income		
Gift aid (gross) 3,850 × 100/77	5,000	
Patent royalty paid	300	
	——	
		5,300
		———
PCTCT		325,873
		———

24 THE CORPORATION TAX LIABILITY

INTRODUCTION & LEARNING OBJECTIVES

This chapter covers the way in which the corporation tax liability is calculated. It explains the calculation of the corporation tax liability for small and marginal rate companies, and the way in which the corporation tax system is administered. Also covered is how a company has to retain income tax on certain payments and how it suffers income tax on certain income. The method of accounting for this income tax is dealt with, and the manner in which it is either paid over to the Inland Revenue or, alternatively, how it is set-off against the corporation tax liability.

When you have studied this chapter you should have learned the following:

- How to calculate the corporation tax liability for small and marginal rate companies.
- When corporation tax is due.
- How self-assessment impacts upon companies.
- How large companies make quarterly instalment payments of corporation tax.
- How to account for income tax.

1 THE SMALL COMPANIES' RATE

1.1 Introduction

The full rate of corporation tax for the current financial (FY 1999) is 30%. A reduced rate of 20% known as the small companies rate applies to companies with profits below £300,000. The rates for previous years are as follows:

Financial year	Full rate	Small companies rate
1998	31%	21%
1997	31%	21%
1996	33%	24%

> **Definition** 'Profits' are defined as profits chargeable to corporation tax plus franked investment income excluding any dividends from companies in the same 51% group.

> **Definition** Franked investment income is the grossed up amount of dividends received from UK companies. The tax credit is 10%, so dividends must be grossed up by 100/90 in order to calculate franked investment income.

1.2 Example: calculation of corporation tax

Beach Ltd had the following results for the year ended 31 March 2000:

	£
Schedule D Case I	169,000
Dividend from UK company (amount received)	5,400

Compute the corporation tax payable.

1.3   Solution

	£
PCTCT	169,000
FII (£5,400 × 100/90)	6,000
'Profits'	175,000

The 'profits' are below £300,000, so the small companies' rate applies.

Corporation tax payable

£169,000 × 20%   £33,800

Note: the FII is included to arrive at the 'profits' figure. The 'profits' determine what corporation tax rate applies. Corporation tax is, of course, payable on the PCTCT figure (and **not** the 'profits' figure).

1.4   Marginal relief

If the 'profits' of an accounting period are more than £300,000 but less than £1,500,000 a year, then marginal relief applies (sometimes called taper relief). The profits chargeable to corporation tax are first charged at the full rate of tax. From that amount, the following is deducted:

$$\text{Marginal relief fraction} \times (\text{Upper limit} - \text{Profits}) \times \frac{\text{PCTCT}}{\text{Profits}}$$

Where Profits = PCTCT plus franked investment income (see above).

For FY 1999

Marginal relief fraction = 1/40

Upper limit = £1,500,000

Conclusion   Where 'profits' are at least £1,500,000 a year, the full rate of corporation tax applies (FY 1999: 30%). Where 'profits' are £300,000 or less a year, the small companies rate applies (FY 1999: 20%).

Where 'profits' are between the two limits, PCTCT are first charged at the full rate of corporation tax which is then reduced by the marginal relief calculated:

$$\text{Marginal relief fraction} \times (\text{Upper limit} - \text{'Profits'}) \times \frac{\text{PCTCT}}{\text{'Profits'}}$$

The effective marginal rate of corporation tax on profits that fall between the lower and upper band limits is 32.5% (33.5% for the financial years 1997 and 1998).

1.5   Activity

Sycamore Ltd has the following results for the year ended 31 March 2000.

	£
Schedule D Case I	320,000
Chargeable gain	10,000
Dividends from UK companies (amount received)	18,000

You are required to calculate the corporation tax liability.

1.6   Activity solution

	£
Schedule D Case I	320,000
Chargeable gain	10,000
PCTCT	330,000
FII (£18,000 × 100/90)	20,000
'Profits'	350,000

Marginal relief applies as 'profits' are above £300,000 but below £1,500,000.

	£
Corporation tax on PCTCT £330,000 × 30%	99,000
Less: Marginal relief $1/40 \times (1,500,000 - 350,000) \times \dfrac{330,000}{350,000}$	(27,107)
Corporation tax payable	71,893

1.7   Accounting period straddling 31 March

When a company's chargeable accounting period falls into two financial years, then the corporation tax liability must be calculated in two parts if either the corporation tax rate changes or the limits for small companies relief changes between the two financial years.

Note: it is only the corporation tax liability that is affected: the calculation of profits chargeable to corporation tax remains unchanged.

1.8   Example: corporation tax liability with change in rates

Oak Ltd has the following results for the year ended 31 December 1999:

	£
Schedule D Case I	170,000
Schedule D Case III	70,000
Patent royalties paid (gross)	10,000
Franked investment income	80,000

The rates, limits and fraction for FY 1998 and FY 1999 are as follows:

	FY 1998	*FY 1999*
Full rate of corporation tax	31%	30%
Small companies rate	21%	20%
Lower limit	£300,000	£300,000
Upper limit	£1,500,000	£1,500,000
Marginal relief fraction	1/40	1/40

You are required to calculate the corporation tax liability for the year.

1.9   Solution

	£
Schedule D Case I	170,000
Schedule D Case III	70,000
	240,000

Less: Charges paid	(10,000)
PCTCT	230,000
FII	80,000
'Profits'	310,000

	£
FY 1998 (3 months)	
Corporation tax at 31% on £230,000 × 3/12	17,825
Less: Marginal relief 1/40 × (£1,500,000 − 310,000)	
$\times \dfrac{230,000}{310,000} \times 3/12$	(5,518)
FY 1999 (9 months)	
Corporation tax at 30% on £230,000 × 9/12	51,750
Less: Marginal relief 1/40 × (1,500,000 − 310,000)	
$\times \dfrac{230,000}{310,000} \times 9/12$	(16,554)
Corporation tax payable	47,503

1.10   Short accounting periods

The upper and lower limits of £1,500,000 and £300,000 apply for an accounting period of 12 months. If the accounting period is for less than 12 months, the limits must be reduced proportionately.

1.11   Associated companies

If a company has any associated companies, then the upper and lower limits are divided by the number of companies associated with each other.

Definition   Companies are associated with each other for small companies rate purposes if either

- one company controls the other; or
- they are both under common control.

In the second situation the companies may be controlled by an individual, a partnership or another company.

When determining if companies are associated, the following applies.

- control is established by holding:

    - over 50% of the share capital; or
    - over 50% of the voting rights; or
    - being entitled to over 50% of the distributable income, or net assets on a winding up.

- both UK resident and companies resident overseas are included.

- dormant companies are excluded.

- companies which have only been associated for part of an accounting period are deemed to have been associated for all of the accounting period for those purposes.

1.12 Activity

Chestnut Ltd prepared accounts for the nine months to 31 December 1999. The company acquired a subsidiary in 1998 which is resident in France, and a further subsidiary, on 1 July 1999 which is resident in the UK. You are required to calculate the upper limit for small companies rate purposes for the period to 31 December 1999.

1.13 Activity solution

The upper limit must be divided by the number of companies associated with each other

£1,500,000 × 1/3 = £500,000

The upper limit must be further reduced because the accounting period is only nine months long.

£500,000 × 9/12 = £375,000.

1.14 Example: corporation tax liability, upper and lower limits restricted

Chestnut Ltd, in the activity above, had PCTCT of £140,000 for the period to 31 December 1999 and received franked investment income of £10,000. None of the dividends were received from the subsidiary companies. You are required to calculate the corporation tax payable.

1.15 Solution

	£
PCTCT	140,000
FII	10,000
'Profits'	150,000

Lower limit: £300,000 × 1/3 × 9/12 = £75,000.

Upper limit: £375,000 (as above).

£150,000 lies between £75,000 and £375,000, therefore marginal relief applies.

	£
£140,000 × 30%	42,000
Less: Marginal relief 1/40 (£375,000 − 150,000) × $\frac{140,000}{150,000}$	(5,250)
	36,750

2 PAYMENT OF CORPORATION TAX

2.1 Due date

Corporation tax is due for payment nine months after the end of the chargeable accounting period to which it relates.

2.2 Long periods of account

When a company prepares accounts for a period exceeding 12 months this period of account (ie, period for which accounts are prepared) is divided into two successive accounting periods, ie,,

- first of 12 months
- then a balance of (say) 6 months.

Separate corporation tax liabilities must be computed for each accounting period and each liability will fall due for payment nine months from the end of that accounting period.

3   SELF ASSESSMENT FOR COMPANIES

3.1   Introduction

Self assessment for companies applies to accounting periods ending on or after 1 July 1999. Previously, companies had to work out their own corporation tax liabilities under a system of pay and file, so the move to self assessment was a relatively small step (compared to when individuals moved to the self assessment system).

3.2   Due date

As already mentioned, a company is required to pay its corporation tax liability on a fixed date (9 months after the end of the accounting period).

3.3   Interest

Interest runs from the due date on any tax paid late. Similarly any repayment of tax made by the Inland Revenue will attract interest from the original date of payment.

For periods covered by self assessment, interest on tax paid late is a deductible expense in calculating profits chargeable to corporation tax. Correspondingly, interest received on overpaid corporation tax is taxable.

3.4   Company tax returns

The Inspector will issue a formal notice requiring a company to make a self assessment tax return.

A company is required to submit its tax return and accounts to the Inland Revenue within 12 months after the end of the accounting period (there are special rules for long periods of account) or, if later, three months after the date of issue of the notice.

The return must include a self assessment of the amount of tax payable for that period.

If any sections on the return are not completed or amounts are estimated or marked 'information to follow' the return is not complete, and penalties may ensue. Generally, any amendment to a tax return must be made within 12 months of the filing date.

It is, therefore, not just a matter of filing the return within one year after the accounting period end but also filing the accounts and tax computations!

If the company fails to file within the specified time, then, unless it can show reasonable excuse, an automatic fixed penalty arises.

3.5   Table of penalties for late filing

Return overdue by	*Penalty*	
	First and second consecutive offences	*Third (or more) consecutive offence*
Up to 3 months	£100	£500
3 to 6 months	£200	£1,000
Over 6 months	£200 plus 10% unpaid tax	£1,000 plus 10% unpaid tax
Over 12 months	£200 plus 20% unpaid tax	£1,000 plus 20% unpaid tax

Unpaid tax is the tax due but not paid as at 18 months after the end of the return period (6 months after the date when the return was due).

3.6 Records

A company must keep and preserve similar records to those for a taxpayer in business (see chapter 22). The records must normally be retained for six years after the end of the accounting period.

3.7 Enquiries into returns

The system of Inland Revenue enquiry into company tax returns is the same as that for individuals (see chapter 22).

Written notice of the Inland Revenue's intention to make an enquiry must normally be given within 12 months of the filing date. This deadline is extended if a return is filed late or amended.

4 QUARTERLY INSTALMENT PAYMENTS

4.1 Introduction

Coinciding with the introduction of self assessment (for accounting periods ending on or after 1 July 1999), large companies are required to make quarterly instalment payments of their corporation tax liability.

4.2 Large companies

A large company is one paying the full rate of corporation tax. Small and medium sized companies (those paying the small and marginal rates of corporation tax respectively) are not required to pay corporation tax by instalments.

A company without any associated companies will therefore pay tax by instalments if profits are at least £1.5 million. This limit will be reduced where a company has associates, but instalments will not be due if a company's corporation tax liability is below £5,000.

4.3 Phasing in

Quarterly instalments are being phased in over a four-year period.

During the first year of the new scheme (the first accounting period ending on or after 1 July 1999), large companies only pay 60% of their corporation tax liability by instalments. The remaining 40% is due nine months after the end of the accounting period as per normal.

The amount paid by instalments will rise to 100% by year four of the transitional period.

4.4 Instalment dates

The four quarterly instalments are made in months 7, 10, 13 and 16 following the start of the accounting period.

Special rules apply where the accounting period is less than 12 months.

The instalments are due on the 14th of the relevant month.

4.5 Basis of payment

Instalments are based on the expected corporation tax liability for the current accounting period. It is therefore necessary for companies to produce an accurate forecast of their tax liability.

Companies that become large during an accounting period do not have to make instalment payments provided:

- Their profits for the accounting period do not exceed £10 million (reduced accordingly if there are associated companies), and

- They were not a large company for the previous year.

Companies will normally be able to obtain a refund if they subsequently find that instalments have been overpaid.

4.6   Example

ABC plc estimates that its corporation tax liability for the year ended 31 December 1999 will be £800,000.

ABC plc is a large company for the purposes of quarterly instalment payments.

You are required to show when ABC plc's corporation tax liability will be due.

4.7   Solution

60% of ABC plc's corporation tax liability is due by instalments. This amounts to £480,000 (800,000 × 60%), and will be paid as follows:

£120,000 on 14 July 1999
£120,000 on 14 October 1999
£120,000 on 14 January 2000
£120,000 on 14 April 2000

The remaining 40% (£320,000) is due on 1 October 2000 (ie, nine months after the end of the accounting period).

5   INCOME TAX

5.1   Introduction

(a)   A company may receive income which has suffered basic rate or lower rate income tax. This is known as taxed income or unfranked investment income. Examples of such income were given in the previous chapter. This income is part of a company's chargeable profits and the gross amount must be included in the PCTCT computation. As the company only receives the net amount of income, the income tax suffered is deducted from the corporation tax liability, to avoid the company being charged to tax twice.

(b)   When a company pays charges on income, the gross amount is deducted in the PCTCT computation. Charges are generally paid net of basic rate tax, for example gift aid payments and patent royalties (both net of basic rate). The company deducts basic rate income tax and must account for it to the Revenue.

(c)   When a company pays interest it is generally required to deduct lower rate income tax and account for it to the Revenue. The main exception to tax deduction at source is where the company pays interest to a UK bank.

(d)   When a company both pays charges on income or interest where basic rate or lower rate income tax has been retained and receives income which has suffered basic rate or lower rate income tax, the two amounts of tax can be netted off and the company only has to account to the Revenue where the income tax on charges or interest paid exceeds the income tax on income received.

       The company accounts for the income tax on form CT61 through a quarterly accounting system. Returns are made for each of the quarters ended 31 March, 30 June, 30 September and 31 December. If the company's accounting date does not coincide with one of these dates, the company must make an additional return for the period that ends on its accounting date. The tax is due within 14 days of the end of the return period.

(e)   If a company's income tax suffered on income exceeds the income tax retained on charges on income and interest, then the net amount of income tax will be repaid. The repayment can be made through the quarterly accounting system, (this is restricted to the amount of income tax already paid in the same accounting period) or by deduction from the corporation tax liability. If the income tax is greater than the corporation tax liability, then the balance is repaid.

(f)   Payments or receipts subject to deduction are always dealt with through the quarterly accounting system on a paid basis. Thus, the amounts of charges on income and taxed income (other than interest) used in calculating PCTCT for an accounting period are the same amounts dealt with under quarterly accounting for that accounting period. This is because the paid basis is used for both purposes. However, as shown in the following examples, interest paid or received net of income tax is dealt with on a paid basis for quarterly accounting but on an accruals basis for constructing PCTCT.

5.2   Example: quarterly returns for income tax

Wood Limited has the following taxed income, charges and interest paid for the year ended 31 March 2000.

		£	£
1.5.99	Patent royalties paid (net)	15,400	
1.7.99	Interest on local authority stock received (net)		28,000
1.11.99	Debenture interest paid (net)	20,000	
2.2.2000	Interest on local authority stock (net)		52,000

The company had PCTCT of £360,000 for the year ended 31 March 2000. The company has no associated companies. You are required to calculate the company's corporation tax liability and the amounts of tax payable to the Collector under the quarterly accounting system.

5.3   Solution

Return period ended	Tax deducted on charges and interest paid £	Tax suffered on income received £	Cumulative net £	IT paid/ (repaid) £	Due date
30.6.99	4,600		4,600	4,600	14.7.99
30.9.99		(7,000)	(7,000)	(4,600)	14.10.99
			(2,400)		
31.12.99	5,000		5,000		
			2,600	2,600	14.1.2000
31.3.2000		(13,000)	(13,000)	(2,600)	14.4.2000
Net income tax suffered			(10,400)		

Notes:

(1)   Interest on local authority stock and debenture interest are multiplied by 20/80 to calculate the income tax. Patent royalties are multiplied by 23/77.

(2)   The repayment for the quarter ended 30 September 1999 is restricted to the income tax already paid in the same accounting period.

(3)   The repayment for the quarter ended 31 March 2000 is restricted in the same way.

(4)   The net income tax suffered of £10,400 can be set against the company's corporation tax liability. If there is insufficient liability to set the £10,400 against, the balance will be repaid.

Wood Limited: calculation of mainstream corporation tax liability for the year ended 31 March 2000

	£
Corporation tax at 30% on £360,000	108,000
Less: marginal relief 1/40 (1,500,000 – 360,000)	(28,500)
	79,500
Less: Income tax suffered (net)	(10,400)
Corporation tax payable	69,100

Conclusion   Where a company receives taxed income and pays charges the income tax suffered and deducted is accounted for via the quarterly accounting system on form CT61. If the income tax suffered exceeds income tax deducted there will be a net amount of income tax suffered which is set against the company's corporation tax liability. In the absence of any corporation tax liability, the income tax suffered is repaid.

5.4   Interest paid and received

It was mentioned earlier that for the purpose of quarterly accounting, interest paid or received is dealt with on a paid basis. When calculating PCTCT it is dealt with on an accruals basis.

5.5   Activity

In the example of Wood Ltd above the company had an accrual for gross local authority stock interest of £13,600 at 1 April 1999 and of £7,200 at 31 March 2000. The same amount of debenture interest (£25,000 gross) is paid every year on 1 November. You are required to reconstruct Wood Ltd's PCTCT for the year to 31 March 2000 assuming that the only other income is trading profits.

5.6   Activity solution

	£	£
Schedule D Case I (balancing figure)		286,400
Schedule D Case III		
Received (28,000 + 52,000) × 100/90	100,000	
Deduct opening accrual	(13,600)	
Add: Closing accrual	7,200	
		93,600
		380,000
Less: Charges paid 15,400 × 100/77		(20,000)
PCTCT		360,000

Notes:

(1)   Although relief is given for tax suffered on £100,000 of taxed interest (partly through the quarterly accounting system and partly against corporation tax), the gross amount of taxed interest included in PCTCT is only £93,600.

(2)   The £25,000 (gross) of debenture interest paid has been deducted as a trading expense in arriving at the Schedule D Case I figure. As the same amount of interest is paid each year the paid basis (for quarterly accounting) and the accruals basis (as a trading expense) produce the same figure.

(3)   Charges are included on a paid basis for both PCTCT and quarterly accounting purposes.

6   CHAPTER SUMMARY

This chapter has dealt with the way in which the corporation tax liability is calculated, and the way in which the corporation tax system is administered.

- Marginal relief applies where profits of an accounting period are more than £300,000 but less than £1,500,000 a year. These limits are reduced according to the number of associated companies that a company has.

- A company is required to pay its corporation tax liability 9 months after the end of the accounting period. Interest runs from the due date on any tax paid late, or on any repayment made by the Inland Revenue.

- A company is normally required to submit its tax return and accounts to the Inland Revenue within 12 months after the end of the accounting period.

- Large companies must make quarterly payments on account for accounting periods ending on or after 1 July 1999.

  During the first year of the new scheme, large companies only pay 60% of their corporation tax liability by instalments. The remaining 40% is due nine months after the end of the accounting period.

  The four quarterly instalments are made in months 7, 10, 13 and 16 following the start of the accounting period.

- **Income tax**. Where a company receives taxed income and pays charges net of basic rate income tax or interest net of lower rate tax it must account to the Revenue for the income tax through the quarterly accounting system on form CT61. When income tax suffered exceeds income tax retained in an accounting period, the net income tax suffered may be used to reduce the corporation tax liability. In the absence of sufficient corporation tax, the balance will be repaid.

7   SELF TEST QUESTIONS

7.1   How is marginal relief calculated? (1.4)

7.2   How is corporation tax calculated when an accounting period straddles 31 March? (1.7)

7.3   What is the definition of an associated company? (1.11)

7.4   When is corporation tax normally due? (2.1)

7.5   When must a company submit its tax return? (3.4)

7.6   Which companies must make quarterly instalment payments? (4.2)

7.7   When are instalments due? (4.4)

7.8   How does a company account for income tax suffered on income and income tax deducted from charges? (5.1)

7.9   When a company suffers income tax on taxed income in excess of income tax retained on charges paid earlier in the accounting period, how much of the income tax repayment may be made through the quarterly accounting system? (5.1)

7.10   When a company suffers tax on taxed income that cannot be repaid through the quarterly accounting system, what relief is available for the company? (5.1)

8   **EXAMINATION TYPE QUESTION**

8.1   **Excel Holidays Ltd**

Excel Holidays Ltd operates a holiday camp. In order to reflect more effectively the seasonal nature of the trade, it changed its accounting date from 31 March to 30 September. Accordingly, accounts were drawn up for the twelve months ended 31 March 1998 and for the eighteen months ended 30 September 1999.

	12 months ended 31 March 1998		18 months ended 30 September 1999	
	£	£	£	£
Trading profit		50,000		63,000
Less: Repairs and renewals	15,000		12,000	
Travelling	2,000		3,000	
Sundry expenses	4,000		5,000	
Depreciation	8,000		10,000	
		29,000		30,000
		21,000		33,000
Deposit account interest (gross)		1,000		3,000
		22,000		36,000

The following transactions had taken place

(a)   Sundry expenses included in the accounting period ended 31 March 1998

		£
(i)	defalcation by staff	1,000
(ii)	travelling expenses of two directors to the French Riviera to attend a conference on holiday camp management	3,000

and included in the accounting period ended 30 September 1999

		£
(i)	loan to employee (camp comedian) written off	500
(ii)	fines for serving contaminated food	1,500

(b)   Interest on the bank deposit account was credited as follows.

		£
30 September	1997	400
31 March	1998	600
30 September	1998	500
31 March	1999	600
30 September	1999	1,900

(c)   Included in the accounting period ended 30 September 1999 under repairs and renewals is an accrual of £4,000 for painting and decorating. This work was completed during September 1999 but not invoiced until October 1999.

(d)   The general pool written down value of plant and machinery at 1.4.97 was nil, and additions were as follows:

				£
On 30 April	1997	- second hand minibus		20,000
31 May	1998	- swimming pool extension		41,000
30 September	1999	- two gas-fired barbecues		3,125

Excel holidays Ltd is not a large company for capital allowance purposes.

You are required to compute the corporation tax liabilities for all accounting periods covered by the periods of account ended 31 March 1998 and 30 September 1999.

9   ANSWER TO EXAMINATION TYPE QUESTION

9.1   Excel Holidays Ltd

Accounting periods	y/e 31.3.98	y/e 31.3.99	6 months 30.9.99
	£	£	£
Adjusted profit (W1)	29,000	30,000	15,000
Less: Plant and machinery (W2)	(5,000)	(24,250)	(5,219)
Schedule DI profit/(loss)	24,000	5,750	9,781
Bank deposit interest receivable	1,000	1,100	1,900
PCTCT	25,000	6,850	11,681
Corporation tax at 21%/21%/20%	5,250	1,438	2,336
Due date	1.1.99	1.1.2000	1.7.2000

WORKINGS

(W1)   Adjusted profit computation before capital allowances

	12 m/e 31.3.98	18 m/e 30.9.99
	£	£
Profits per accounts	22,000	36,000
Add: Depreciation	8,000	10,000
Fine/loan to employee	-	2,000
	30,000	48,000
Less: Interest received	1,000	3,000
Adjusted profit	29,000	45,000

No adjustment is necessary for the repairs accrual, since the accruals basis is the correct method of calculating the Schedule D Case I profit.

The adjusted profit for the 18 month period ended 30.9.99 needs to be time apportioned between the two accounting periods.

(i)   y/e 31.3.99 $12/18 \times £45,000$ =   £30,000
(ii)   6 m/e 30.9.99 $6/18 \times £45,000$ =   £15,000

(W2)   Capital allowances

Plant and machinery

	£	General pool £	Allowances £
y/e 31.3.98			
WDV B/F		Nil	
30.4.97 Addition		20,000	
WDA 25%		(5,000)	5,000
		————	————
WDV c/f		15,000	
y/e 31.3.99			
WDA 25%		(3,750)	3,750
Addition qualifying for FYA			
31.5.98	41,000		
FYA 50%	(20,500)	20,500	20,500
	————		
		————	————
WDV c/f		31,750	24,250
		————	————
6 months 30.9.99			
WDA - 25% ($^{6}/_{12}$)		(3,969)	3,969
Addition qualifying for FYA			
30.9.99	3,125		
FYA 40%	(1,250)	1,875	1,250
	————	————	————
WDV c/f		29,656	5,219
		————	————

25 CORPORATION TAX LOSSES

INTRODUCTION & LEARNING OBJECTIVES

This chapter deals with the different ways that companies which incur trading losses can obtain relief. Earlier chapters have dealt with the basic computation of profits chargeable to corporation tax and the calculation of corporation tax liability. Exam questions will require a thorough understanding of these topics. The examiner will also expect detailed knowledge of the various loss reliefs that are available.

In this chapter you should learn:

- Carry forward of trading losses (S393(1) ICTA 1988) where the loss is carried forward and set against future trading income.
- Loss relief against total profits (S393A ICTA 1988) where the loss is set off against current profits and may be carried back and set against profits of the previous twelve months.
- Unrelieved charges on income paid (S393(9) ICTA 1988) where unrelieved trade charges are carried forward and set against future trading income.
- Unrelieved interest on non-trading loans set first against current profits.

1 INTRODUCTION

1.1 Loss reliefs available

This chapter deals primarily with trading losses incurred by a company. However, trading losses are not the only losses that a company can incur, and it would be useful at this point to discuss how relief for other types of losses is obtained.

1.2 Capital losses

Where a company disposes of a capital asset and incurs a loss, this capital loss can only be set off against current chargeable gains, or where none are available, future chargeable gains.

Note: that

- a capital loss may never be carried back and relieved against chargeable gains for earlier periods; and

- capital losses may not be set against income.

An exam question may give a company's results in columnar form, and include a capital loss. When transferring these figures across into a computation of PCTCT, never include the capital loss, unless there are current chargeable gains to set it against.

1.3 Schedule A losses

Schedule A losses may be first set against other income or gains for the same period as the loss. Any excess loss may be carried forward to set against any future income or gains.

1.4 Schedule D Case V losses

Trading losses incurred may be carried forward and set against future trading profits from the same trade.

1.5   Schedule D Case VI losses

Where a Schedule D Case VI loss is incurred it may be set-off against other Schedule D Case VI income in the same accounting period. In the absence of such income in the current accounting period, the loss may be carried forward and set against future Schedule D Case VI income.

Note: that in this instance the set-off is not limited to profits of the same source; the loss can be relieved against any source of Schedule D Case VI income.

1.6   Schedule D Case III losses

Interest and other costs payable on loans taken out for a non-trading purpose are automatically set off against interest receivable which is assessable under Schedule D Case III. There are special rules (explained below in section 5) for obtaining relief where interest payable exceeds interest receivable.

2   CARRY FORWARD OF TRADING LOSSES; S393(1) ICTA 1988

2.1   Details of the relief

- Where a company incurs a trading loss, it may carry the loss forward and set it off against profits from the same trade in future accounting periods.

- The loss can be carried forward indefinitely, there is no time limit for obtaining relief, but it must be set-off against the first available trading profits.

- A claim to establish the amount of the loss available to carry forward should be made within six years of the end of the loss making accounting period.

2.2   Computation of the loss

A company's trading loss is computed in the same way as a company's trading profit ie, after deducting capital allowances and interest payable on loans etc taken out for the purposes of the trade.

2.3   Example: carry forward of trading losses

Rose Ltd has the following results for the two years to 31 March 2000.

	Year ended	
	31.3.99	31.3.2000
	£	£
Trading profit/(loss)	(20,000)	18,000
Schedule D Case III income	6,000	9,000
Capital loss	(2,000)	
Chargeable gains		7,000
Patent royalties paid (gross)	(1,000)	(1,000)

You are required to calculate the profits chargeable to corporation tax for the two periods, assuming that the loss is relieved under S393(1) ICTA 1988 showing any losses carried forward at 1 April 2000.

2.4   Solution

Under S393(1) trading losses are relieved against the first available trading profits.

Capital losses can only be set against current or future chargeable gains.

Rose Ltd: profits chargeable to corporation tax for the two years ended 31 March 2000.

	Year ended	
	31.3.99	*31.3.2000*
	£	£
Schedule D Case I	-	18,000
Less: S393(1) loss relief		(18,000)
		Nil
Schedule D Case III	6,000	9,000
Chargeable gains (£7,000 – £2,000)		5,000
	6,000	14,000
Less charges paid	(1,000)	(1,000)
PCTCT	5,000	13,000
Loss carried forward under S393(1) (£20,000 – £18,000)		£2,000

Conclusion Where a company incurs a trading loss, in the absence of any other relief being claimed, the loss is carried forward and set against the first available trading profits of the same trade.

3   LOSS RELIEF AGAINST TOTAL PROFITS: S393A ICTA 1988

3.1   Introduction

Where a company incurs a trading loss it may claim to set the loss against total profits (before all charges) of the accounting period producing the loss.

Any trading loss remaining unrelieved may then be carried back and set against total profits (this time before non-trading charges) of the twelve months preceding the loss making accounting period. This means that when a loss is carried back, the set-off is restricted so that trade charges do not become unrelieved.

Definition Trade charges are payments made wholly and exclusively for the purposes of the trade (for example patent royalties).

Definition Non-trading charges are payments not made wholly and exclusively for the purposes of the trade (for example deed of covenant to charity).

3.2   Relief available

(a)   When a trading loss is incurred, the company may claim to set the loss against total profits (before all charges) of the accounting period producing the loss.

When relief is claimed for a trading loss against total profits of the current accounting period, trade charges may become unrelieved. They may be relieved under S393(9) (see later in this chapter) and carried forward and set against the first available trading profits of the same trade.

(b)   A trading loss may also be carried back and set against total profits (this time before non-trade charges) of the twelve months preceding the loss making accounting period.

This means that when a loss is carried back, the set off is restricted so that trade charges do not become unrelieved.

(c)   If a company has prepared accounts for a period other than twelve months during the twelve months preceding the loss making accounting period, then the results of the accounting period which falls partly outside the twelve month period are apportioned, and loss relief is limited to the proportion of profits which falls within the twelve month period. There is some dispute as to whether profits are taken as before or after trade charges (see example below).

(d)   A claim must be made to relieve the loss against profits arising in the loss making period before a claim can be made to carry the loss back to the preceding period.

(e)   Losses must be dealt with in the order that they arise. Thus a loss in 1998 must be relieved, either against total profits, or carried forward and relieved against future trading income, before a loss arising in, say 1999, can be carried back for the previous twelve months.

(f)   Any loss remaining unrelieved after a S393A claim is carried forward under S393(1) and relieved against future trading profits of the same trade.

(g)   A claim for loss relief under S393A (either against current year profits, or carried back to the previous twelve months) must be made within two years of the end of the loss making accounting period.

(h)   A claim under S393A must be for the whole loss, including capital allowances. The amount of the loss may be reduced by not claiming the full amount of capital allowances available. A company may claim any amount of capital allowances, up to the full amount; a reduced claim would leave a higher tax written down value on which to claim allowances next year.

3.3   Example: Loss relieved against total profits

Lily Ltd has the following results for the periods to 31 March 2000

	Year to 30.9.98 £	6 months to 31.3.99 £	Year to 31.3.2000 £
Trading profit/(loss)	20,000	16,000	(50,000)
Non-trade charges	500	1,000	1,000
Trade charges	1,000	2,000	-

You are required to calculate the profits chargeable to corporation tax for all three periods, assuming that relief under S393A is claimed for the loss in the year ended 31 March 2000. Show any losses available to carry forward at 1 April 2000.

3.4   Solution

As the loss may be carried back against profits of the twelve months before the year to 31 March 2000, the profits of the year to 30 September 1998 must be apportioned. The loss may be set against 6/12 × profits (after trade charges) for this period.

Lily Ltd: PCTCT computation for the three periods ending 31 March 2000.

	Year to 30.9.98 £	6 months to 31.3.99 £	Year to 31.3.2000 £
Schedule D Case I	20,000	16,000	-
Non-trade charges	(500)	-	-
Trade charges	(1,000)	(2,000)	-
	18,500	14,000	-
Less: S393A relief	(9,500)	(14,000)	-
PCTCT	9,000	Nil	Nil
Unrelieved non-trade charges		1,000	1,000

Loss memorandum		£

Loss for y/e 31.3.2000 — 50,000

Less: S393A relief: 6 months to 31.3.99 — (14,000)

y/e 30.9.98 (£20,000 − £1,000) = £19,000 × 6/12 — (9,500)*

Loss available to carry forward under S393(1) — 26,500

This loss memorandum is essential in an exam question, as it shows the reasoning behind the reliefs claimed.

* An alternative view is that this should be £20,000 × $^6/_{12}$ = £10,000.

Either approach is acceptable in the examination.

3.5 Losses carried back and carried forward

(a) Care needs to be taken over the order of set off when there are losses for more than one year.

(b) Losses carried forward under S393(1) are set off before loss claims against current year profits or losses carried back under S393A.

(c) If the correct layout is used, then the order of set off is dealt with automatically.

3.6 Example: Loss relieved against total profits

Dahlia Ltd has the following results for the four accounting periods ended 31 March 2000.

	Year to 30.9.97 £	6 months to 31.3.98 £	Year to 31.3.99 £	Year to 31.3.2000 £
Trading profit/(loss)	14,000	(10,000)	23,500	(25,000)
Taxed income (gross)	2,200	1,800	2,000	2,400
Schedule A	800	400	800	800
Chargeable gains	-	700	-	1,900
Charges on income:				
Patent royalties (gross)	2,000	-	2,000	2,000
Charitable covenant (gross)	200	200	200	200

There was a loss brought forward under S393(1) at 1 October 1996 of £7,000.

You are required to calculate the profits chargeable to corporation tax, assuming that loss relief is claimed as early as possible.

3.7 Solution

There are three losses to consider;

£7,000 brought forward at 1 October 1996;

£10,000 in the 6 months ended 31 March 1998; and

£25,000 in the year ended 31 March 2000.

Relief must be given for earlier losses before relief is obtained for later losses.

The PCTCT layout should be drawn up for the four accounting periods and the various sources of income filled in. The losses should then be dealt with in the order that they arose, and as each loss is relieved the loss memorandum should be completed.

Official ACCA *Textbook, published by AT Foulks Lynch*

	Year to 30.9.97 £	6 months to 31.3.98 £	Year to 31.3.99 £	Year to 31.3.2000 £
Schedule D Case I	14,000	-	23,500	-
Less: S393(1) relief	(7,000)	-	-	-
	7,000			
Taxed income	2,200	1,800	2,000	2,400
Schedule A	800	400	800	800
Chargeable gains	-	700	-	1,900
	10,000	2,900	26,300	5,100
Less: S393A relief	(7,100)	(2,900)	(19,900)	(5,100)
	2,900	-	6,400	-
Less: Patent royalites	(2,000)	-	(2,000)	-
Charitable covenant	(200)	-	(200)	-
PCTCT	700	Nil	4,200	Nil

Loss memorandum	£
Loss carried forward at 1.10.96	7,000
Less: S393(1) y/e 30.9.97	(7,000)
	-

	£
Loss for six months ended 31.3.98	**10,000**
Less: S393A six months ended 31.3.98	(2,900)
S393A y/e 30.9.97	(7,100)
	-

	£
Loss for y/e 31.3.2000	25,000
Less: S393A y/e 31.3.2000	(5,100)
S393A y/e 31.3.99	(19,900)
	-

Notes:

(1)   The loss brought forward is dealt with first. Relief under S393(1) is against future trading income. The loss of £7,000 is fully relieved in the year ending 30.9.97.

(2)   The loss brought forward must be set-off in this way before relief under S393A is claimed for the loss in the six months ended 31.3.98.

Conclusion Where a company incurs a trading loss it may claim under S393A to set the loss against the total profits (before all charges) of the loss making accounting period. Having relieved the loss against current profits, the company may claim to set the loss against the total profits of the twelve months preceding the accounting period producing the loss. When the loss is carried back, trading charges in the earlier year must not become unrelieved. Any loss not relieved under S393A is carried forward under S393(1) and set against future profits of the same trade.

4 UNRELIEVED CHARGES ON INCOME PAID: S393(9) ICTA 1988

4.1 Introduction

Charges on income paid are usually relieved against total profits in computing the profits chargeable to corporation tax. Both trade charges and non trade charges are relieved in this way. For a definition of trade and non-trade charges see earlier in this chapter.

4.2 Details of the relief

- Where there are insufficient profits in an accounting period to relieve all charges paid, non-trade charges are set against profits before trade charges.

- Where trade charges are unrelieved in an accounting period, relief is available under S393(9). The unrelieved trade charges are carried forward and set against the first available trading profits of the same trade in the same way as a S393(1) loss.

 This relief is not available for non-trade charges.

- When relief for a trading loss is claimed under S393A against total profits of the accounting period producing the loss, trade charges may become unrelieved. Relief is available for these unrelieved trade charges under S393(9) and they may be carried forward and set against the first available trading profits of the same trade.

4.3 Activity

A company paid the following charges on income.

Charitable deed of covenant.

Patent royalties.

Gift aid.

Which of these payments are trade charges?

4.4 Activity solution

Patent royalties.

4.5 Example: unrelieved trade charges

Aster Ltd has the following results for the three years ended 31 March 2000.

	Year ended		
	31.3.98	*31.3.99*	*31.3.2000*
	£	£	£
Trading profit/(loss)	(10,000)	12,000	1,200
Charitable covenant (gross)	500	500	500
Patent royalties paid (gross)	1,000	1,000	1,000

Calculate the profits chargeable to corporation tax for all three years, assuming that loss relief is claimed as early as possible.

4.6   Solution

The trading loss is relieved against future trading profits of the same trade.

Non-trade charges are set-off in priority to trade charges. Unrelieved trade charges can be carried forward and relieved against future trading profits of the same trade.

There is no relief available for unrelieved non-trade charges.

	31.3.98 £	*Year ended* *31.3.99* £	*31.3.2000* £
Schedule D Case I	-	12,000	1,200
Less: S393(1) & (9) loss relief	-	(11,000)	(500)
	-	1,000	700
Less: Charitable covenant	-	(500)	(500)
Patent royalties	-	(500)	(200)
PCTCT	Nil	Nil	Nil
Unrelieved non-trade charges	500		

Loss memorandum	£
Loss for y/e 31.3.98	10,000
Unrelieved trade charges y/e 31.3.98	1,000
	11,000
Less: S393(1) & (9) relief y/e 31.3.99	(11,000)
	-
Unrelieved trade charges y/e 31.3.99	500
Less: S393 (9) relief y/e 31.3.2000	500
	-
Unrelieved trade charges y/e 31.3.2000	800
Loss carried forward under S393 (9)	800

4.7   Examination approach

Corporation tax questions involving losses may seem daunting at first. The key to answering them successfully is to use a systematic approach as follows.

(1)   Prepare a PCTCT proforma for the relevant accounting periods. In the proforma, enter relief under S393(1) and S393A in the appropriate place as follows:

PCTCT proforma	£
Schedule D Case I	X
Less: S393(1) relief	(X)
	X
Schedule A; Schedule D Case III etc	X
Net chargeable gains	X
	X
Less: S393A relief	(X)
	X

Less: Trade charges	(X)
Non-trade charges	(X)
PCTCT	X

(2)   The various amounts of income are then entered into the proforma.

(3)   Identify the losses.

Where there is more than one loss, deal with the earliest loss first, claiming relief in the appropriate place in the proforma.

(4)   As the losses are relieved, complete a loss memorandum, detailing how the loss has been relieved.

5   UNRELIEVED INTEREST ON NON-TRADING LOANS

5.1   Introduction

If interest is paid on a trading loan (ie, one taken out for a trading purpose) it is deductible (on an accruals basis) as a trading expense. If this creates or increases a trading loss, trading loss reliefs, as described earlier in this chapter, are available.

However, interest paid on a non-trading loan (eg, a loan taken out to buy commercial letting property) is relieved against interest assessable under Schedule D Case III. If there is insufficient income assessed under Schedule D Case III relief for the surplus is given as follows.

5.2   Relief for surplus non-trading interest

Interest is relieved as follows:

(a)   against any profits of whatever description of the same accounting period;

(b)   against Schedule D Case III income of the previous twelve months;

(c)   against any future profits of the company (other than trading profits) as soon as they arise.

Relief is given under (a) above after relieving any trading loss brought forward but before relieving any trading loss arising in the same period or carried back from a future period.

Relief under (a) for the excess interest of the current period takes priority over a claim under (b) where future excess interest is being carried back.

Claims under (a) or (b) must be made within two years of the end of the accounting period in which the excess interest arose.

The examiner has stated that a computational question will not be set involving the carry back of a loss arising from a non-trading loan.

6   RESTRICTIONS ON LOSS RELIEF

6.1   Introduction

There are restrictions on the carry forward of trading losses when there is a change in the ownership of a company in order to prevent avoidance of tax.

6.2   Change in ownership

(a)   Trading losses arising before a change in ownership cannot be carried forward under S393(1) to periods after the change, nor can losses arising after a change in ownership be carried back under S393A to periods before the change.

The relief under S393(1) and S393A for trading losses is denied in either of the following situations:

- where there is both a change in ownership and a major change in the nature or conduct of the trade within a period of three years; or

- when at any time after the scale of activities of the trade has become small or negligible, and before any considerable revival of the trade, there is a change in the ownership of the company.

The three year period can be either before or after the change of ownership.

(b)   In this context, a change in ownership means that more than one half of the ordinary share capital of the company is acquired by a person or persons, ignoring any person acquiring 5% or less.

(c)   A major change in the nature or conduct of the trade includes:

- a major change in the type of property dealt in or services provided; and
- a major change in customers, outlets or markets.

6.3   Change in trade

Relief under S393(1) is only available against future trading income of the same trade. If the nature of the trade changes to such an extent that the original trade ceases and a new trade commences, relief under S393(1) is denied for losses of the original trade.

7   TERMINAL LOSS RELIEF

7.1   Introduction

When a company incurs a trading loss during the final twelve months of trading, then it is possible to make a claim under S393A. However, such a loss can be carried back and set against total profits of the three years preceding the loss making period, rather than the preceding twelve months.

7.2   Relief available

(a)   Terminal loss relief applies to trading losses incurred during the final twelve months of trading.

(b)   The company must first claim to set the trading loss against total profits (before all charges) of the accounting period of the loss.

(c)   Unrelieved trade charges of the final twelve months may be added to the terminal loss claim. Non-trade charges are wasted.

(d)   The terminal loss can be carried back and set against total profits (before non-trade charges) of the three years preceding the loss making period.

(e)   The set-off is against later periods before earlier periods.

(f)   Apportionment will be necessary in two circumstances:

(i)   Where the loss making accounting period falls partly outside the final twelve months of trading. Only that proportion of the loss falling within the final twelve months can be carried back for three years. The proportion falling outside the twelve months can only be carried back under S393A for twelve months.

(ii)   Where the company has prepared accounts for a period other than twelve months during the three years preceding the loss making period. Apportionment will be necessary in the same way as for a normal S393A loss claim, so that losses are only carried back against the proportion of profits falling within the three year period.

7.3   Activity

Daisy Ltd made up accounts to 30 September each year but ceased to trade on 31 March 2000.

Results have been as follows:

	Year ended 30.9.97 £	30.9.98 £	Period ended 30.9.99 £	31.3.2000 £
Trading profits/(loss)	6,200	5,700	4,200	(30,000)
Schedule A	2,000	1,800	1,900	500
Schedule D Case III	750	900	840	400
Chargeable gains	3,000	-	2,000	
Charges on income:				
Patent royalties (gross)	1,000	1,000	1,000	500
Charitable covenant (gross)	300	300	300	300

Show the profits chargeable to corporation tax for all years, assuming that the loss is relieved under S393A.

7.4   Activity solution

Unrelieved trade charges in the accounting period in which a trade ceases can be added to the loss. When the loss is carried back, trade charges in earlier periods must remain relieved.

	Year ended 30.9.97 £	30.9.98 £	Period ended 30.9.99 £	31.3.2000 £
Schedule D Case I	6,200	5,700	4,200	-
Schedule A	2,000	1,800	1,900	500
Schedule D Case III	750	900	840	400
Chargeable gains	3,000	-	2,000	-
Less: S393A relief	(10,950)	(7,400)	(7,940)	(900)
	1,000	1,000	1,000	-
Less: Patent royalties	(1,000)	(1,000)	(1,000)	-
Charitable covenant	-	-	-	-
PCTCT	Nil	Nil	Nil	Nil
Unrelieved non-trade charges	£300	£300	£300	£300

Loss memorandum	£
Loss incurred in 6 months to 31.3.2000	30,000
Unrelieved trade charges 6 months to 31.3.2000	500
	30,500
Less: S393A 6 months to 31.3.2000	(900)
y/e 30.9.99	(7,940)
y/e 30.9.98	(7,400)
y/e 30.9.97	(10,950)
Loss remaining unrelieved	3,310

No relief is available for the £300 charitable covenants paid in the last four accounting periods, nor is relief available for the remaining loss of £3,310.

8 FACTORS INFLUENCING CHOICE OF LOSS RELIEF

8.1 Introduction

There may be several alternative loss reliefs available for a loss. Various factors will influence the loss relief chosen, as follows:

- **Cash flow**

    Relief under S393A will probably result in a repayment of tax, whereas relief under S393(1) will result in a reduction of a future liability

- **Rate of relief**

    The rate of relief will depend on the level of profits before the claim is made, and the year in which the claim is made.

- **Non-trade charges**

    Only unrelieved **trade** charges can be carried forward and relieved against future trading profits. Claims for loss relief may lead to relief for non-trade charges being lost.

9 TAX AVOIDANCE

9.1 Introduction

It is necessary to differentiate between tax avoidance and tax evasion.

Tax avoidance: the reduction of tax liabilities within the framework of the law.

Tax evasion: the reduction of tax liabilities by not informing the Revenue of all relevant facts.

Tax avoidance may not always succeed, but is legal; tax evasion is never legal.

9.2 Ramsay v CIR

This tax avoidance case concerned a scheme that involved a circular series of self-cancelling transactions. A capital loss was established, but the steps achieved nothing else. The courts held that the loss should not be allowed, as the transactions were entered into solely to achieve the loss.

9.3 Furniss v Dawson

The Ramsay principle was considered again in this case. Again, the intention of the scheme was to avoid tax but here, the transactions were not self-cancelling, but had legal effect.

The courts held that the loss should not be allowed.

This case extended the Ramsay principle to the situation where there are a series of transactions which have enduring legal consequences. The courts specified when this approach would be applied:

- There must be a pre-ordained series of transactions which can be regarded as a single composite transaction.

- There must be steps inserted in this series that have no commercial purpose other than the avoidance of tax.

10   CHAPTER SUMMARY

This chapter has dealt with corporation tax losses. The following areas were covered:

- Carry forward of trading losses: S393(1) ICTA 1988. A trading loss may be carried forward and relieved against future trading losses of the same trade.

- Loss relief against total profits: S393A ICTA 1988. A trading loss may be relieved against total profits (before all charges) of the loss making accounting period. Any unrelieved loss may be carried back and relieved against total profits of the preceding twelve months (trade charges may not become unrelieved). Any remaining loss is carried forward under S393(1).

- Unrelieved charges on income paid S393(9) ICTA 1988. Unrelieved trade charges may be carried forward and set against the first available trading profits of the same trade.

- Unrelieved non-trading interest can be set against any profits of the same period or against Schedule D Case III income of the previous twelve months with any remaining amount set against future profits other than trading profits.

- The carry forward or the carry back of trading losses may be prevented where there is both a change of ownership of a company and a major change in the nature or conduct of the trade within a period of three years.

- Terminal loss relief. When a company incurs a trading loss during the final twelve months of trading, then it is possible to make a claim under S393A against total profits of the three years preceding the loss making period, rather than the preceding twelve months.

- Tax avoidance is the reduction of tax liabilities within the framework of the law, whilst tax evasion is the reduction of tax liabilities by not informing the Inland Revenue of all relevant facts.

11   SELF-TEST QUESTIONS

11.1   If a company cannot relieve a trading loss against current profits, or profits from an earlier period, how is relief for the loss obtained? (2.1)

11.2   When a company relieves a trading loss under S393A in the loss making accounting period, what is the loss relieved against? (3.1)

11.3   When a company relieves a trading loss under S393A against the accounting period preceding the loss making accounting period, what is the loss relieved against? (3.1)

11.4   What is the definition of a trade charge? (3.1)

11.5   What is the definition of a non-trade charge? (3.1)

11.6   May a company claim to carry back a trading loss to the preceding period if it has not claimed to relieve the loss in the period in which the loss was incurred? (3.2)

11.7   If a company claims to relieve a trading loss against the current year's profits, must any remaining loss be carried back and relieved against profits of the preceding period? (3.2)

11.8   If there are insufficient profits in an accounting period to relieve trade charges, how may they be relieved? (4.2)

11.9   How is relief given for surplus non-trading interest? (5.2)

11.10   When a company carries back a terminal trading loss to the three preceding accounting periods, what is the order of set-off? (7.2)

12   EXAMINATION TYPE QUESTIONS

12.1   Segovia Ltd

The recent results of Segovia Ltd are as follows:

	31.3.97	*Years ending* *31.3.98*	*31.3.99*	*9 months ended* *31.12.99*
	£	£	£	£
Schedule D Case I	40,800	61,200	342,720	
Trading loss				(325,500)
Schedule A	7,750	6,800	7,100	5,440
Bank interest receivable	2,440	1,350	2,170	2,050
Schedule D Case V	680	880	800	275
Capital (loss)/gain	-	(3,200)	7,280	7,860
Patent royalties (gross)	(2,750)	(2,750)	(2,750)	(2,750)

Segovia Ltd had trading losses to carry forward of £7,000 at 1 April 1996.

You are required to calculate the corporation tax liability for all four periods, assuming that all beneficial claims are made.

12.2   Loser Ltd

Loser Ltd made up its accounts to 31 March 1998 but has since changed to a 30 September accounting date. The company has suffered declining results in recent years, and is therefore planning to restructure its business operations during September 1999 by closing three branches of its business, and disposing of the related assets. (You should assume that today's date is 1 August 1999.)

Loser Ltd forecasts a substantial tax adjusted Schedule DI trading loss for the current year to 30 September 1999. A small trading profit is forecast for the following year to 30 September 2000, with steadily increasing profits thereafter.

The company's tax adjusted Schedule DI trading profits for recent years have been as follows:

	£
Year ended 31 March 1998	550,000
Period ended 30 September 1998	70,000

You are required to:

(i)   Advise Loser Ltd as to which loss relief claims would be the most beneficial.

(ii)   Advise Loser Ltd as to when it would be beneficial for tax purposes to delay certain aspects of its restructuring until after 30 September 1999.

(iii)   Advise Loser Ltd as to whether the delaying of certain aspects of its restructuring until after 30 September 1999 would be considered to be tax avoidance or tax evasion.

13   ANSWERS TO EXAMINATION TYPE QUESTIONS

13.1   Segovia Ltd

Corporation tax payable

	31.3.97	*Years ended* *31.3.98*	*31.3.99*	*Period ended* *31.12.99*
	£	£	£	£
Schedule D Case I	40,800	61,200	342,720	—
Less S393(1)	(7,000)			
	33,800			

Schedule A	7,750	6,800	7,100	5,440
Bank interest receivable	2,440	1,350	2,170	2,050
Schedule D Case V	680	880	800	275
Capital gain			4,080	7,860
	44,670	70,230	356,870	15,625
Less: S393A	–		(309,875)	(15,625)
	44,670	70,230	46,995	–
Less: Trade charges	(2,750)	(2,750)	(2,750)	–
PCTCT	41,920	67,480	44,245	Nil
Corporation tax at 24%/21%/21%	10,061	14,171	9,291	–

Loss memorandum

		£
Schedule D Case I loss	9 m/e 31.12.99	325,500
Less: S393A	9 m/e 31.12.99	(15,625)
	y/e 31.3.99	(309,875)
Add: Trade charge	9 m/e 31.12.99 now unrelieved	2,750
Loss carried forward		2,750

13.2   Loser Ltd

(i)   Relieving the loss against total profits of the period ended 30 September 1998 and six months of the total profits of the year ended 31 March 1998 under S393A ICTA 1988 obtains relief partly at 21% and partly at the marginal rate of 33.5%.

This is compared to relief at 21%/20% if the loss relief claim is restricted to total profits (if any) of the current year, or relief at 20% if the loss is carried forward against future trading profits.

The most beneficial loss relief claim is therefore to claim under S393A against total profits of the year ended 30 September 1999, and then against the total profits of the preceding twelve months.

(ii)   It would be beneficial for Loser Ltd to delay until after 30 September 1999 any aspect of its restructuring that would decrease the amount of its Schedule DI trading loss available for the year ended 30 September 1999.

This will result in increased loss relief at up to 33.5%, with a corresponding increase in profits for the year ended 30 September 2000 assessable at 20%.

(iii)   Loser Ltd's strategy in maximising its trading loss available for carry back under S393A ICTA 1988 would appear to be within the ambit of tax avoidance, since it involves the careful timing of transactions in order to optimise the company's tax position.

However, if the reality of the situation was misrepresented, for example assets were sold in September 1999 but the sales invoice was dated October 1999, then this comes within the scope of tax evasion.

26 GROUPS AND CONSORTIA

INTRODUCTION

This chapter deals with three claims or elections that companies which are members of a group can make. They result in either a reduction or deferment of the corporation tax liability. The legislation is complex and it can be difficult to remember the rules for the different claims and elections. A suggested approach is to ensure that for each situation the following is noted:

- how the group is defined; and
- which members of the group can make the claim or election.

This is a difficult chapter, but it is essential that its contents are mastered.

1 GROUP RELIEF FOR LOSSES: S402 ICTA 1988

1.1 Introduction

Under group relief, loss relief is available for both members of a group and members of a consortium.

1.2 Members of a group: definition of a group.

(a) Two companies are members of a group where

- one is a 75% subsidiary of the other; or
- both are 75% subsidiaries of a third company.

One company is a 75% subsidiary of another if at least 75% of its ordinary share capital is owned directly or indirectly by the other company.

Ordinary share capital is any share capital other than fixed rate preference shares.

The following constitute a group for group relief purposes:

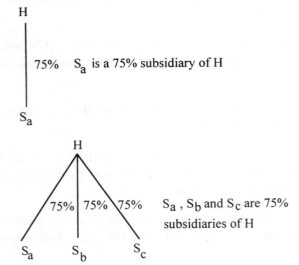

(b)   The following constitutes two groups for group relief purposes:

H

$\qquad$ 75% S_a is a 75% subsidiary of H

S_a S_b is a 75% subsidiary of S_a

$\qquad$ 75% S_b is not a 75% subsidiary of H as H owns only 56.25% (75% x 75%) of S_b

S_b

In addition, the following conditions must be satisfied:

- the holding company must have the right to receive at least 75% of the profits distributable to ordinary shareholders; and

- the holding company must have the right to receive at least 75% of the net assets on a winding up.

1.3   The relief

(a)   Trading losses may be surrendered to other companies in the group, which may then relieve the losses against their own taxable profits.

(b)   Any member company may surrender its loss to any other member of the group.

- A holding company may surrender a loss to its subsidiary company;
- A subsidiary company may surrender a loss to its holding company;
- A subsidiary company may surrender a loss to its fellow subsidiary company.

Definition   The surrendering company is the company which surrenders its loss.

The claimant company is the company to which the loss is surrendered.

1.4   ICI v Colmer

Until a recent case, the Inland Revenue's view was that all companies in a group must be resident in the UK in order for group relief to be available between them. However, the decision of the case of ICI v Colmer (heard in the European Court of Justice) was that as far as the European Union was concerned, this view was contrary to Community law. A final decision is still awaited from the House of Lords, but it would appear that the following group structure would now qualify for group relief:

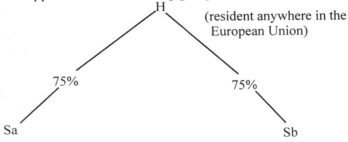

Despite the holding company not being resident in the UK, the two UK subsidiaries can claim and surrender group relief between each other.

1.5   The surrendering company

(a)   The surrendering company may surrender as much of the loss as it wants to. There is no requirement to relieve the loss against its own profits first. This is an important point to appreciate from a tax planning point of view, as it allows a company whose profits are taxed at the small companies rate to surrender its loss to other group members whose profits are taxed at the marginal rate or full rate of corporation tax.

(b)   The losses which may be surrendered are:

- trading losses;
- unrelieved charges on income (both trade **and** non-trade charges);
- unrelieved Schedule A losses;
- unrelieved interest paid on non-trading loans; and
- excess management expenses of an investment company.

Note that there is no group relief for capital losses.

(c)   Only current period losses are available for group relief.

1.6   The claimant company

(a)   Relief for the surrendered loss is against the total profits of the claimant company, ie, against profits chargeable to corporation tax after deducting charges on income.

(b)   The surrendered loss is relieved against the available profits (ie, profits **after** charges) of the claimant company. The available profits are calculated on the assumption that any current year losses and losses brought forward of the claimant company are relieved first.

Note that the claimant company's own losses are taken into account, but need not actually be claimed before the surrendered loss is relieved.

1.7   Activity

Red Ltd, a member of a group, has the following results for the year ended 31 March 2000.

	£
Trading loss	(12,000)
Schedule A	40,000
Schedule D III	15,000
Chargeable gains	7,000
Patent royalties paid (gross)	(2,000)

Calculate the profits available to absorb group losses for the year ended 31 March 2000.

1.8   Activity solution

	£
Schedule A	40,000
Schedule D III	15,000
Chargeable gains	7,000
	62,000
Less: S393A relief	(12,000)
	50,000
Less: Patent royalties paid	(2,000)
Profits available to absorb group losses	48,000

Note: The amount of profit available to absorb group losses is £48,000. Although relief under S393A of £12,000 is used in the calculation, it is not necessary to actually claim the relief before the surrendered loss is relieved.

1.9   Factors that will influence the choice of loss relief within a 75% group

The following points should be taken into account when a trading loss occurs within a 75% group

- losses should be surrendered to group members as follows:

    - first to companies paying tax in the marginal relief band (effective rate 32.5% FY 1999) to bring their profits down to the small companies rate lower limit

    - second to companies paying tax at 30% again to bring their profits down to the lower band limit

    - and then to companies paying tax at 20%

- where a group member suffering a loss has the choice to make a S393A claim against its own profits, or to surrender the loss to another group member consideration should be given to:

    - the rate of tax saved; and
    - the cash flow position (a claim under S393A could lead to a repayment of tax)

- a company claiming group relief must have sufficient profits to absorb the loss surrendered. The claimant company may find it advantageous not to claim all or to only claim part of the capital allowances available for a particular period in order to leave sufficient profits to absorb a surrendered loss. If this is done, the written down value carried forward and therefore the capital allowances in future years will be correspondingly higher.

- losses should not be surrendered to a group company where this results in that company being unable to utilise double taxation relief (see later in text).

- The rate of relief for losses carried back to FY 1998 under S393A is slightly higher (ie, 21%, 33.5% and 31%) than the equivalent rates for FY 1999.

1.10   Example: Group relief

A group, consisting of five companies had the following results for the year ended 31 March 2000.

	Profit/(loss)
	£
A Ltd	(100,000)
B Ltd	20,000
C Ltd	83,000
D Ltd	96,000
E Ltd	375,000

Calculate the corporation tax payable.

(a)   If no election for group relief is made; and

(b)   If an election for group relief is made, on the assumption that the loss is allocated in such a manner as to save the maximum amount of tax.

1.11   Solution

Step 1   Calculate the upper and lower limits for small companies rate and calculate the tax payable.

Upper limit $\dfrac{£1,500,000}{5} = £300,000$.

Lower limit $\dfrac{£300,000}{5} = £60,000$.

Corporation tax liability without group relief:

	A Ltd £	B Ltd £	C Ltd £	D Ltd £	E Ltd £
PCTCT	Nil	20,000	83,000	96,000	375,000
Corporation tax					
at 20%		4,000			
at 30%			24,900	28,800	112,500
Less:					
1/40 × (300,000 – 83,000)			(5,425)		
1/40 × (300,000 – 96,000)				(5,100)	
Corporation tax liability	Nil	4,000	19,475	23,700	112,500

Step 2   The loss should be surrendered first to companies paying tax in the marginal relief band so as to bring their profits down to the lower limit, as they are paying an effective rate of 32.5% in the marginal band. The loss should then be surrendered to companies paying tax at 30%. Any remaining loss should be surrendered to companies paying tax at 20%.

	A Ltd £	B Ltd £	C Ltd £	D Ltd £	E Ltd £
Profits	Nil	20,000	83,000	96,000	375,000
Less: Group relief			23,000	36,000	41,000
PCTCT	Nil	20,000	60,000	60,000	334,000
Corporation tax					
at 20%		4,000	12,000	12,000	
at 30%					100,200
	Nil	4,000	12,000	12,000	100,200

The loss is first surrendered to C Ltd and D Ltd to bring their profits down to £60,000, the balance of the loss is surrendered to E Ltd.

1.12   Corresponding accounting period

Losses available for group relief must be set against profits of a corresponding accounting period.

Definition   A corresponding accounting period is any accounting period falling wholly or partly within the surrendering company's accounting period.

If the accounting periods of the claimant company and the surrendering company do not coincide, both profits and losses must be apportioned. The apportionment is generally on a time basis.

1.13   Example: corresponding accounting periods

	£
White Ltd incurs a trading loss for the year to 30 June 1999	(24,000)
Black Ltd makes taxable profits:	
For the year ended 30 September 1998	36,000
For the year ended 30 September 1999	20,000

What group relief can Black Ltd claim from White Ltd?

1.14   Solution

Examine the corresponding accounting periods.

(1)   Year ended 30 September 1998 and year ended 30 June 1999. The common period is 1 July 1998 to 30 September 1998, ie, 3 months.

(2)   Year ended 30 September 1999 and year ended 30 June 1999. The common period is 1 October 1998 to 30 June 1999, ie, 9 months.

Black Ltd can claim the following group relief:

y/e 30.9.98

	£
Profits of the corresponding accounting period £36,000 × 3/12	9,000
Losses of the corresponding accounting period £24,000 × 3/12	(6,000)

Black Ltd can claim group relief of £6,000 against its profits for the year ended 30 September 1998.

y/e 30.9.99

	£
Profits of the corresponding accounting period £20,000 × 9/12	15,000
Losses of the corresponding accounting period £24,000 × 9/12	(18,000)

Black Ltd can claim group relief of £15,000 against its profits for the year ended 30 September 1999. Thus a total of (£6,000 + £15,000 = £21,000) can be relieved by group relief. The remaining £3,000 of the loss must be relieved against White Ltd's current, or earlier or later profits.

1.15   Claim for group relief

(a)   The claim for group relief is made by the claimant company; the consent of the surrendering company is required.

Under self assessment, the relevant details are included in the tax returns of the companies concerned.

(b)   Under self assessment, a claim must normally be made, withdrawn or amended within one year of the filing date for the claimant company's tax return (ie, two years after the end of the accounting period).

(c)   The claimant company may make a payment to the surrendering company for group relief. Any payment, up to the amount of the loss surrendered, is ignored for corporation tax purposes.

1.16   Anti-avoidance provisions

Provisions exist to ensure that only genuine group members can take advantage of group relief. Companies which are only temporary group members are generally denied group relief.

Group relief is denied if 'arrangements' exist between two companies whereby:

- either company might leave the group and enter into a group relationship with another unrelated company; or

- any person controls, or could obtain control of, one of the two companies, or

- a third company takes over the trade of one of the two companies.

There is no statutory definition of the term 'arrangement'. Indeed, the Revenue are not prepared to give a comprehensive statement of what constitutes 'arrangements'. It is a very wide term and includes both formal and informal agreements between two companies.

2   CONSORTIUM RELIEF

2.1   Introduction

(a)   **Definition**

A consortium-owned company is a company with:

- at least 75% of its ordinary share capital owned by UK resident companies (the decision in ICI v Colmer is likely to extend this to companies resident anywhere in the European Union), none of which has a holding of less than 5%; and

- where each member of the consortium is entitled to 5% or more of any profits available for distribution to ordinary shareholders, and 5% or more of the net assets on a winding up.

A consortium can be illustrated as follows:

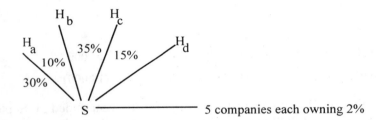

H_a, H_b, H_c and H_d own 90% of the ordinary share capital of S between them, and none owns less than 5%.

H_a, H_b, H_c and H_d are called members of the consortium. S is not a member of the consortium but is known as the consortium owned company.

A company which is a 75% subsidiary cannot also be a consortium owned company: in this situation normal group relief provisions apply.

(b)   Consortium relief is a form of group relief which is available when either the surrendering company or the claimant company is a member of the consortium, and the other is:

- a trading company which is a consortium owned company; or
- a trading company which is a 90% subsidiary of a consortium owned company; or
- a holding company which is a consortium owned company.

These three situations can be illustrated as follows:

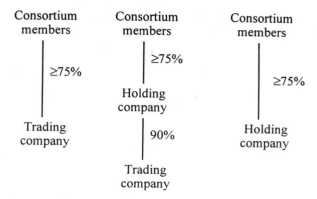

(c)   The losses may be surrendered in either direction. There are, however, restrictions on the amount of consortium relief that may be surrendered.

When a consortium member incurs a loss, the maximum amount that can be surrendered is the amount which covers its share of the consortium owned company's profits.

When a consortium owned company (or its 90% trading subsidiary) incurs a loss, the maximum amount that it may surrender to a consortium member is the proportion of the loss that corresponds with that member's shareholdings.

2.2   Example: consortium relief

Blue Ltd is owned by a consortium of UK resident companies as follows::

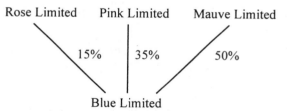

In year ended 31 March 2000 their results were:

	Schedule DI Profit/(Loss) £
Rose Ltd	(30,000)
Pink Ltd	(42,000)
Mauve Ltd	15,000
Blue Ltd	100,000

Calculate the corporation tax liabilities of all three companies, on the assumption that the maximum amount of consortium relief is claimed.

2.3   Solution

Blue Ltd	£	£
Schedule D Case I		100,000
Losses surrendered:		
Rose Ltd		
Loss available	(30,000)	
Maximum surrender £100,000 × 15%	15,000	(15,000)
Not available for surrender	15,000	

Pink Ltd

Loss available	(42,000)	
Maximum surrender £100,000 × 35%	35,000	(35,000)
	──────	
Not available for surrender	7,000	
	──────	

PCTCT		50,000
		──────

Corporation tax liability	
£50,000 × 20%	£10,000

Rose Ltd

Corporation tax liability	£nil
	─────
Loss carried forward under S393(1)	£15,000
	──────

Pink Ltd

Corporation tax liability	£nil
	─────
Loss carried forward under S393(1)	£7,000
	─────

Mauve Ltd

PCTCT	£15,000
	──────
Corporation tax liability	
£15,000 × 20%	£3,000
	─────

2.4   Example: consortium relief

If Blue Ltd, the consortium owned company in the above example makes a loss of £100,000 and the members each have profits of £60,000. What is the maximum amount of the loss that can be surrendered to each company?

2.5   Solution

	£
Rose Ltd may claim £100,000 × 15%	15,000
Pink Ltd may claim £100,000 × 35%	35,000
Mauve Ltd may claim £100,000 × 50%	50,000

Note that each member company must have sufficient profits to absorb the loss.

When a consortium owned company incurs a loss, the amount available for surrender is reduced by any possible S393A claims against current period's profits.

Conclusion   Consortium relief is very similar to group relief. However, note the restrictions on the amount of loss surrendered, and the fact that the surrendering company must reduce the loss available for surrender by any potential current period S393A claim when the surrendering company is a consortium owned company.

3   CHARGEABLE GAINS

3.1   Introduction

There are two provision concerning capital assets that members of a group can take advantage of. These concern:

- the transfer of assets within a group; and
- rollover relief.

3.2   Definition of a group

- These provisions apply to 75% groups. The 75% requirement applies only to the ordinary share capital. Non-UK members are excluded from the group.

- A group can consist of a parent company and its 75% subsidiaries, and also the 75% subsidiaries of the first subsidiaries. However, the parent company must have an effective interest of over 50% in all group companies. The 50% test applies to both distributable profits and any assets available to ordinary shareholders on a winding up. This can be illustrated as follows:

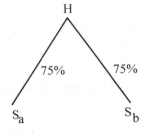

H, S_a and S_b are members of a group, as S_a and S_b are 75% subsidiaries of H.

H
|
| 75%
|
S_a
|
| 75%
|
S_b

H, S_a and S_b are members of a group. S_a is a direct 75% subsidiary of H, S_b is a 75% subsidiary of S_a and H has a 56.25% (75% x 75%) effective interest in S_b.

Note: H, S_a and S_b do not form a group for group relief purposes.

- A company which is a 75% subsidiary of another company cannot itself be a principal company

H
|
| 75%
|
S_a
|
| 75%
|
S_b
|
| 75%
|
S_c

S_c is not a member of the group (H has an effective 42.19% interest in S_c)

S_b and S_c do not by themselves form a separate group as S_b cannot be a principal company

3.3   Transfer of assets within a group

(a)   Where one group company transfers an asset to another group company they do so without a chargeable gain or allowable loss arising. The transfer takes place at a price that gives no gain and no loss to the transferor company, ie, at cost plus indexation allowance. This is irrespective of any price actually paid for the asset. This relief is automatic; no claim is needed. When the asset finally leaves the group, a chargeable gain may arise.

The asset leaves the group when either:

- the asset is disposed of outside the group; or
- the company owning the asset leaves the group within six years of the transfer.

(b)   When the asset leaves the group, the chargeable gain is calculated by reference to the original cost to the group (or 31 March 1982 value if appropriate) plus indexation allowance and the proceeds of sale when the asset finally leaves the group.

(c)   When the asset is disposed of outside the group the gain is assessed on the company which disposes of the asset.

This can be illustrated as follows:

Green Ltd acquired an asset on 1 April 1983 for £100,000. The asset is transferred to Jade Ltd, a wholly owned subsidiary on 1 October 1993 for £120,000, when the asset was worth £180,000.

On 1 December 1999 Jade Ltd sells the asset outside the group for £350,000. Calculate any chargeable gain arising on the disposal of the asset.

The transfer from Green Ltd to Jade Ltd takes place at such a price as gives Green Ltd no gain and no loss, ie

	£
Cost	100,000
Indexation allowance April 1983 to October 1993 $100,000 \times \dfrac{141.8 - 84.28}{84.28} (0.682)$	68,200
	168,200

When Jade Ltd sells the asset outside the group its cost is deemed to be £168,200.

	£
Proceeds	350,000
Less: Cost	(168,200)
	181,800
Less: Indexation allowance October 1993 to December 1999 $168,200 \times \dfrac{165.6 - 141.8}{141.8} (0.168)$	(28,258)
Gain	153,542

(d)   When a company leaves the group it will be assessed in respect of any chargeable gains arising on assets acquired from other group members within the six years preceding the date that the company leaves the group.

The company leaving the group is deemed to have sold and re-purchased any assets acquired from other group members at the market value on the day it actually acquired them.

The gain is treated as accruing in the accounting period in which the company leaves the group.

3.4 Example: Intra-group transfers: company leaving the group

Yellow Ltd sold its wholly owned subsidiary, Orange Ltd on 15 April 1999. Yellow Ltd had purchased a building on 1 August 1989 for £180,000. On 1 December 1995 the building was transferred to Orange Ltd for £230,000. Its market value on the date of the transfer was £375,000. Orange Ltd still owned the building on 15 April 1999.

Both companies prepare accounts to 31 March each year.

What is the effect of the sale of Orange Ltd?

3.5 Solution

When Orange Ltd leaves the group, the company still owns an asset which it had acquired from Yellow Ltd in the six years preceding Orange Ltd's departure.

Orange Ltd is treated as if it had sold the building on 1 December 1995 at its market value, and then immediately reacquired it.

	£	£
Proceeds		375,000
Less: Cost: Cost to Yellow Ltd	180,000	
Indexation allowance		
August 1989 - December 1995		
$180,000 \times \dfrac{150.7 - 115.8}{115.8} (0.301)$	54,180	
		(234,180)
Chargeable gain		140,820

Note that Orange Ltd's cost is the original cost to Yellow Ltd plus the indexation allowance from the date of purchase by Yellow Ltd to the date of transfer to Orange Ltd.

The chargeable gain is assessed on Orange Ltd in the year ended 31 March 2000 ie, in the accounting period in which Orange Ltd left the group.

3.6 Rollover relief (replacement of business assets)

When a person sells a qualifying asset and reinvests the proceeds in another qualifying asset, rollover relief is available and the cost of the new asset is reduced by the chargeable gain on the disposal of the first asset.

Members of a 75% group are treated as one for the purposes of rollover relief and all the trades carried on by the members of the group are treated as a single trade. Thus a disposal by one group company can be rolled over against a qualifying reinvestment made by another group company.

It is common practice for groups to route all acquisitions and disposals through one company to ensure that losses and gains can be set off. Careful thought about this is needed when replacement of business assets relief is relevant. Unless the 'group disposal company' uses the asset for its own trade (which is unlikely in practice) there will be no rollover because the asset was not used for trade purposes **by the disposer.**

Conclusion   These provisions relating to capital assets are very important for group members.

The ability to transfer capital assets around a group has significant implications for tax planning. Capital losses cannot be group relieved. However, if all chargeable assets to be disposed of are transferred to one group member, on a no gain/no loss basis, when the assets are disposed of outside the group any losses made on disposals can be netted off against any gains.

3.7   Pre-entry losses

A company (H) could acquire a subsidiary company (S) which has capital losses brought forward or assets that it could dispose of at a loss. The intention would be for H to transfer to S (at no gain no loss) assets it wishes to dispose of that are showing a capital gain so that S could then dispose of these assets and use its own capital losses to set against the gain on disposal.

Legislation has been introduced to block this loophole.

When S joins the group we have to identify:

(a)   S's losses on disposals before it joined the group; and

(b)   for disposals of assets after S joined the group the proportion of losses on those disposals that relate to the pre-entry period of ownership of the assets.

The calculation of (b) above needs a little care and is covered below.

3.8   Calculation of the pre-entry portion of a loss

When S disposes of an asset that it acquired prior to joining the group, we have to calculate the amount of the loss that is pre-entry.

There are two ways of calculating the loss:

(a)   Time apportion the actual loss; and

(b)   Elect within two years of the end of the accounting period of the disposal for the loss to be the **smaller** of :

    (i)   the loss which would have arisen if S had sold the asset on the date it joined the group; and

    (ii)   the loss on the actual sale.

3.9   Example

S bought a plot of land in August 1991 for £500,000. S joined H's group in August 1996 when the land was worth £350,000 and sold the land in August 1999 for £300,000. What is the pre-entry proportion of the loss?

3.10   Solution

Step 1   Calculate the total loss.

	£
Proceeds	300,000
Cost	500,000
Total loss	200,000

Step 2 Calculate the time apportioned pre-entry loss.

$$£200,000 \times \frac{\text{Aug 91} - \text{Aug 96}}{\text{Aug 91} - \text{Aug 99}}$$

$$= £200,000 \times \frac{5}{8} = \qquad \text{£} \quad 125,000$$

Step 3 Calculate the loss with the election.

(a)   Loss if sold on date of joining group

	£
Notional proceeds	350,000
Cost	500,000
Notional loss	150,000

(b)   Loss on the actual sale   £200,000

∴ Lower loss which would be elected =   £150,000

Step 4 S wants the pre-entry portion to be as small as possible because that part of the loss is restricted. It will therefore **not** make the election and the pre-entry loss will therefore be £125,000 per Step 2.

3.11   Using the loss

The pre-entry loss can only be used against gains on assets which S disposed of before joining the group or it owned before joining. (Note there is no restriction/time apportionment of gains). The usual restriction on carrying losses back applies.

It can also use the loss against gains on assets acquired since joining the group provided the asset was purchased from outside the group and has been used solely for a trade that S was carrying on before joining the group.

Note that the basic rationale here is that S's pre-entry loss can only be used against losses directly connected with S's own business.

The balance of S's loss £(200,000 – 125,000 = 75,000) can be used without restriction. H could transfer an asset to S at no loss/no gain which is immediately sold by S at a gain and set against the loss of £75,000.

3.12   Pre-entry gains

Similar rules to those for pre-entry losses apply where a company (H) that has unrealised capital losses, acquires a subsidiary company (S) that has a realised capital gain.

Without the rules, company (H) could transfer the assets showing a capital loss to company (S) that then disposes of them. Provided everything happens within the same accounting period, the losses could then be offset against the capital gain.

The rules identify any capital gains that have been realised before a company joins a group, and restricts the capital losses that can be set against them.

3.13 Using the gains

The only capital losses that can be set against pre-entry gains are:

- Losses that arose before the company joined the group, and
- Losses arising from assets held before the company joined the group.

4 GROUP CHARGES

4.1 Introduction

Companies in a group can pay charges and interest to other group members without accounting for income tax to the Inland Revenue.

4.2 Definition of a group

These provisions apply to a 51% group.

A 51% group exists where one company
- owns more than 50% of the ordinary share capital of another company; and
- has the right to receive more than 50% of any profits available for distribution; and
- has the right to receive more than 50% of any assets available for distribution on a winding up.

Group members must be UK resident.

4.3 The relief

(a) An election can be made to pay charges on income and debenture interest between members of a 51% group gross. The company paying the charge or the interest pays the gross amount to the recipient company, and no entry is made on the CT61 return.

The company receiving the payment makes no entry on the CT61 return, and as no income tax has been suffered, there is none available to offset against the corporation tax liability. The advantage of making this election is its beneficial effect on the cash flow of the group; it will not have any effect on the overall corporation tax liability of the group. Note that the election cannot be excepted for individual payments of charges on income or interest.

(b) Group charges and interest can be paid under this election by the parent company to its 51% subsidiaries, by the 51% subsidiaries to the parent and between subsidiaries.

(c) In a consortium, group charges and interest can be paid under this election by the consortium owned company to the consortium members only. It is not possible for the consortium members to pay charges or debenture interest to the consortium owned company without accounting for income tax.

> **Conclusion** Certain members of a 51% group may elect to pay charges or interest to other group members without accounting for income tax. These provisions are also available to members of a consortium and consortium owned companies.

The main advantages of the group charges or interest election are:

- a reduction in administration; and
- a cash flow benefit to the group as a whole.

5 SELF TEST QUESTIONS

5.1 What is the definition of a group for group relief purposes? (1.2)

5.2 What types of loss may be surrendered under the group relief provisions? (1.5)

5.3 A surrendered loss is relieved against the available profits of the claimant company. How are the available profits calculated? (1.6)

5.4   What is the definition of a consortium-owned company? (2.1)

5.5   When is consortium relief available? (2.1)

5.6   What is the definition of a group for the purposes of chargeable gains? (3.2)

5.7   When capital assets are transferred within a 75% group, what is the base cost for the company receiving the asset? (3.3)

5.8   When capital assets are transferred within a 75% group, which events may trigger a chargeable gain? (3.3)

5.9   Why does a group often route all acquisitions and disposals through one company? (3.6)

5.10   Which members of a 51% group can pay charges on income gross to other members, without accounting for income tax? (4.3)

6   EXAMINATION TYPE QUESTION

6.1   Longbow Ltd

Longbow Ltd wishes to acquire Minnow Ltd, and has made an offer to the shareholders of that company which it would like to finalise on 1 October 1999. The share capital of Minnow Ltd is owned equally by A Ltd, B Ltd and C Ltd.

The forecast results of Longbow Ltd and Minnow Ltd for the year ended 31 March 2000 are as follows:

	Longbow Ltd £	Minnow Ltd £
Adjusted Schedule DI profit/(loss)	220,000	(140,000)
Trading losses brought forward	-	(9,000)
Capital gain	-	50,000
Capital losses brought forward	(10,000)	-
Interest received on Debenture Stocks (gross)	5,250	-

Longbow Ltd purchased £150,000 of 7% Debenture Stock issued by an unrelated company on 1 August 1999. On 30 April 2000 the company is to purchase a new freehold factory for £120,000.

Minnow Ltd's capital gain is in respect of the proposed sale of a freehold office building for £150,000 on 10 February 2000. One-quarter of the building has never been used for the purposes of the company's trade.

You are required to calculate the corporation tax liability for both Longbow Ltd and Minnow Ltd for the year ended 31 March 2000 if:

(a)   Longbow Ltd acquires one-third of Minnow Ltd's share capital from A Ltd on 1 October 1999.

(b)   Longbow Ltd acquires two-thirds of Minnow Ltd's share capital from A Ltd and B Ltd on 1 October 1999.

(c)   Longbow Ltd acquires all of Minnow Ltd's share capital from A Ltd, B Ltd and C Ltd on 1 October 1999.

7   ANSWER TO EXAMINATION TYPE QUESTION

7.1   Longbow Ltd

(a)   One-third of Minnow Ltd's share capital acquired

Minnow Ltd

	£
Capital gain	50,000
Loss relief	50,000
PCTCT	-

Longbow Ltd

	£
Schedule DI profit	220,000
Schedule DIII (150,000 at 7% × 8/12)	7,000
	227,000
Consortium relief (140,000 - 50,000 = 90,000 × 1/3 × 6/12)	15,000
PCTCT	212,000
Corporation tax at 20%	42,400
Income tax 5,250 at 20%	1,050
Corporation tax liability	41,350

Note:

Minnow Ltd is a consortium company, and one-third of its trading loss can therefore be surrendered to Longbow Ltd. Minnow Ltd must take into account its own current year profits when calculating the loss to surrender, and this is restricted to the corresponding period of 1 October 1999 to 31 March 2000.

(b)   Two-thirds of Minnow Ltd's share capital acquired

Minnow Ltd

The company's PCTCT will be the same as above.

Longbow Ltd

	£
Schedule DI profit	220,000
Schedule DIII	7,000
	227,000
Consortium relief (140,000 - 50,000 = 90,000 × 2/3 × 6/12)	30,000
PCTCT	197,000
Corporation tax at 30%	59,100

Tapering relief 1/40 × (750,000 - 197,000)	13,825
	45,275
Income tax 5,250 at 20%	1,050
Corporation tax liability	44,225

Notes:

Minnow Ltd is an associated company, and so the lower and upper limits for corporation purposes are reduced to £150,000 (300,000/2) and £750,000 (1,500,000/2).

(c)   All of Minnow Ltd's share capital acquired

Minnow Ltd

	£
PCTCT	Nil

Longbow Ltd

	£
Schedule DI profit	220,000
Schedule DIII	7,000
Capital gain	2,500
	229,500
Group relief (140,000 × 6/12)	70,000
PCTCT	159,500
Corporation tax at 30%	47,850
Tapering relief 1/40 × (750,000 - 159,500)	14,763
	33,087
Income tax 5,250 at 20%	1,050
Corporation tax liability	32,037

Notes:

(1)   Minnow Ltd is a 75% subsidiary.

(2)   Minnow Ltd should transfer the freehold office building to Longbow Ltd prior to its disposal. This will be an intra-group transfer of an asset, and will not result in a chargeable gain.

(3)   Longbow Ltd's brought forward capital losses can then be used against the gain.

(4)   Rollover relief can be claimed based on the freehold factory to be purchased by Longbow Ltd.

(5)   Longbow Ltd's chargeable gain on the disposal of the freehold office building will be as follows:

	£
Capital gain	50,000
Less rolled over - 75% business use	37,500
	12,500
Capital losses b/f	10,000
	2,500

The cost of the new freehold factory (£120,000) exceeds the business proportion of the proceeds from the disposal of the freehold office building (150,000 × 75% = £112,500). There is therefore no further restriction on the gain to be rolled over.

27 CLOSE COMPANIES AND INVESTMENT COMPANIES

INTRODUCTION

Close companies are controlled by a few shareholders, and because of the shareholders' position, the company could be used as a vehicle to avoid tax. In order to prevent this, special provisions apply to certain payments made by close companies.

Investment companies need special provisions as they do not generally have any trading income from which to deduct their management expenses.

1 CLOSE COMPANIES

1.1 Definition of a close company

(a) A close company is any UK resident company which is under the control of:

- five or fewer participators together with their associates; or

- participators who are directors (regardless of number) together with their associates.

A participator is primarily a shareholder.

Associates include spouses, ancestors, lineal descendants, siblings and business partners.

Note that:

- participators and their associates are treated as one participator when determining the number of participators; and

- when there are several participators associated with each other, they must be grouped together so as to produce the smallest number of participators.

(b) If a company is controlled by a non-close company, it cannot itself be a close company. Quoted companies with at least 35% of the voting power of the company held by the public are usually not close companies.

(c) The definition of a close company given above is intentionally fairly brief, as the rules for determining a close company are not examinable. It is the implications of being a close company, given below, that are important for examination purposes.

2 CONSEQUENCES OF CLOSE COMPANY STATUS: BENEFITS IN KIND FOR PARTICIPATORS

2.1 Introduction

(a) When a close company incurs expenditure on the provision of any benefits in kind, (eg, a motor car or services) for participators or their associates, the company is treated as making a distribution (ie, dividend) to the participator amounting to the expense incurred, less any contribution from the participator.

(b) The expense incurred by the company in providing the benefit is disallowed for *Schedule D Case I* purposes.

- The amount treated as a distribution is the cash equivalent which would have been assessed on the participator, if he had been a director or employee earning at least £8,500 per annum.

- The distribution is treated like a dividend in the hands of the participator ie it must be grossed up at the rate of 100/90, and higher rate tax must be paid (if applicable).

(c)   This provision does not apply if

- the participator (or his associates) is also a director of the company or employee of the company earning at the rate of £8,500 or more per annum and is assessable under Schedule E on the benefit provided; or

- the benefit is living accommodation provided by reason of the employment.

2.2   Activity

Gerald is a participator but not an employee or director in Tiger Limited, a close company. On 1 January 2000 the company paid £900 for private medical insurance for Gerald and his family. Gerald earns a salary of £40,000 per annum from another, unrelated, company.

What are the consequences of the payment?

2.3   Activity solution

Gerald is treated as receiving a distribution of £900.

Individuals receiving a distribution are given a tax credit of: distribution received × 10/90.

Gerald will therefore receive a tax credit of £900 × 10/90 ie, £100.

He must pay income tax on the gross amount at 32.5%.

Gerald will therefore pay income tax of:

(£900 + £100) × 32.5% = £325 less the tax credit of £100.

Amount payable = £225 (£325 − £100).

2.4   Consequences of close company status: loans to participators

(a)   When a close company makes a loan to a participator (or an associate of a participator) it must pay the Inland Revenue an amount of tax equal to 25% of the loan. If the loan is repaid, the Inland Revenue will repay the amount of tax already paid.

(b)   The tax is due 9 months after the end of the accounting period. The tax will not have to be paid on any part of the loan that is repaid to the company before the tax falls due.

(c)   If the loan (or any part of it) is repaid after the tax falls due, the Revenue repay the tax nine months after the end of the accounting period in which the loan (or part of it) is repaid.

(d)   These provisions do not apply if the loan is made to a director or employee of the company if;
- he works full time for the company;
- he owns 5% or less of the share capital; and
- the loan does not exceed £15,000.

Nor do these provisions apply if the loan is made in the normal course of business by a lending institution.

(e)   If the loan, or any part of it, is waived, the following consequences apply:

- the amount waived, grossed up, is treated as income in the hands of the participator, in the year in which the waiver takes place.

  This income is taxed as a dividend in the hands of the participator ie it must be grossed up at the rate of 100/90, and higher rate tax must be paid (if applicable).

- The company can recover the tax originally paid on the amount waived.

2.5   Activity

Lion Limited, a close company lends £100,000 to a participator on 1 December 1996. He repays £28,000 on 1 July 1998. The company waives the remainder of the loan on 1 January 2000.

The participator is a higher rate tax payer.

What are the consequences of the above transactions?

2.6   Activity solution

(1)   Loan made by Lion Limited on 1 December 1996

   Lion Limited pays tax equal to 25% of the loan

   (£100,000 × 25%)   £25,000
                                                                 ———————

(2)   £28,000 repaid 1 July 1998

   Lion Limited recovers tax at the rate of 25%

   (£28,000 × 25%)   £7,000
                                                                 ———————

(3)   £72,000 waived 1 January 2000

   Lion Limited recovers tax at the rate of 25%

   (£72,000 × 25%)   £18,000
                                                                 ———————

The participator's income for 1999/00 includes £72,000 × 100/90 = £80,000. He will have to pay higher rate tax on this amount, but is treated as having a tax credit of 10%.

Tax due by participator:

	£
£80,000 × 32.5%	26,000
Less: £80,000 × 10%	(8,000)
	———————
	18,000
	———————

Conclusion   When a close company provides a benefit to a participator which is not assessed under the Schedule E rules, the benefit is treated as a distribution.

When a close company makes a loan to a participator, the company must pay tax equal to 25% of the loan. The tax can be recovered by the company when the loan is repaid or waived.

3   CLOSE INVESTMENT-HOLDING COMPANIES

3.1   Introduction

A close company holding investments could be used as a tax avoidance vehicle by higher rate tax payers, as the company holding the investments would be charged tax at the small companies rate of 20%, whereas if investments were held personally, the investments would suffer tax at the higher rate of 40% (or 32.5% in respect of dividend income).

In order to prevent this tax avoidance, close investment-holding companies are always taxed at the full rate of corporation tax, whatever the level of their profits.

> **Definition**   A close investment-holding company is any close company which:
>
> - is not a trading company; and
> - is not a member of a trading group.

> **Definition**   A trading company is one which exists wholly or mainly for the purposes of trading and carries on its trade on a commercial basis.

3.2   Consequences of being a close investment-holding company

The small companies rate and marginal relief are not available to close investment-holding companies. All profits are taxed at the full rate of corporation tax.

> **Conclusion**   The profits of a close investment holding company are taxed at the full rate of corporation tax.

4   INVESTMENT COMPANIES

4.1   Introduction

Companies whose business is mainly concerned with making investments, and whose income is derived from those investments areas taxed in a similar manner to trading companies. However, special rules apply to management expenses; as an investment company may not have sufficient trading income to relieve these expenses, they can be deducted from the company's total profits chargeable to corporation tax.

> **Definition**   An investment company is statutorily defined as 'any company whose business consists wholly or mainly in the making of investments and the principal part of whose income is derived therefrom.'

Note that this definition includes both close and non-close companies.

4.2   Profits of an investment company

The profits of an investment company are calculated in the same way as for a trading company; the same rules for the various sources of income and capital gains apply.

4.3   Management expenses

(a)   Management expenses of investment companies can be deducted from their total profits chargeable to corporation tax.

(b)   Expenses which the courts have allowed as management expenses include the following:

- directors' fees and commissions, provided they are not considered excessive;
- salaries of management;
- audit fees;
- office rent and rates; and

- bank interest.

(c) The following may be carried forward and treated as management expenses of the next accounting period:

- unrelieved management expenses;

- unrelieved charges on income incurred wholly and exclusively for business purposes; and

- unused capital allowances.

Note that excess management charges may only be carried forward, or, group relieved in the accounting period in which they are incurred (see chapter on groups and consortia), there is no question of excess management charges being carried back to the previous period.

Capital allowances available on plant and buildings commercially let will be given in taxing the Schedule A 'business'.

(d) A Schedule A loss can be treated in the same way as management expenses. The reliefs for Schedule A losses (see Chapters 25 and 27) are available to companies generally but are likely to be of most practical relevance to investment companies.

4.4 Rate of corporation tax

Investment companies are taxed in the same way as other companies, and can take advantage of the small companies rate and marginal relief. However, if the company is a close investment-holding company all profits, whatever their level, will be taxed at the full rate of corporation tax (see earlier in this chapter).

4.5 Example: investment company

Cheetah Limited has the following results for the year ended 31 March 2000:

	£
Rental income	70,000
Deposit account interest receivable	20,000
Chargeable gains	3,000
Management expenses:	
Property management	35,000
Other	60,000
Capital allowances:	
On property	2,300
Other	1,600
Debenture interest payable (gross)	2,000
Directors' remuneration	3,000

Calculate the corporation tax liability.

4.6 Solution

Step 1 Calculate the chargeable profit before management expenses.

	£	£
Income		
Rents		70,000
Less: Capital allowances	2,300	
Property management expenses	35,000	
		37,300
Schedule A		32,700

Schedule D Case III net (20,000 – 2,000)	18,000
Chargeable gains	3,000
Chargeable profits before management expenses	53,700

Step 2   Set management expenses against the profit figure:

	£
Management expenses:	
General management expenses	60,000
Directors' remuneration	3,000
Capital allowances	1,600
	64,600
Less: Chargeable profits as above	(53,700)
Excess carried forward and treated as management expenses of y/e 31.3.2001	10,900
Profits chargeable to corporation tax	Nil

Conclusion   An investment company may deduct management expenses from total profits chargeable to corporation tax.   Unrelieved management expenses, capital allowances and trade charges may be carried forward to the next accounting period.

5   SELF TEST QUESTIONS

5.1   What is the definition of a close company? (1.1)

5.2   What are the consequences of a close company providing a benefit in kind to a participator if the benefit is not taxed under the normal Schedule E rules? (2.1)

5.3   What are the consequences of a close company making a loan to a participator? (2.4)

5.4   What are the consequences of a close company waiving a loan that it had made to a participator? (2.4)

5.5   What is the definition of a close investment-holding company? (3.1)

6   EXAMINATION TYPE QUESTIONS

6.1   Investment Company Ltd

Investment Company Ltd has the following income and expenses for the year ended 31 March 2000.

	£
Rental income from unfurnished lettings	270,200
Bank deposit interest receivable	2,600
Expenses:	
Repairs and insurance of let property	5,600
Audit fee	2,000
Directors' fees, salaries, rent of office, capital allowances on office equipment, stationery, telephone ($\frac{1}{3}$ relating to management of the property, $\frac{2}{3}$ to management of the company)	150,600

In addition, the company realised a chargeable gain, which after indexation allowance amounted to £60,000 and paid debenture interest of £2,000 (gross amount) during the year.   The amount of debenture interest payable (gross) during the year was £2,400.

Calculate the profits chargeable to corporation tax.

6.2   Bream

Bream is a participator in Test Valley Ltd, a close trading company which prepares accounts to 31 December each year. In June 1997 the company loaned Bream £72,000 for the purchase of a yacht. In January 1999 Bream repaid £20,000 and in March 2000 the company waived the outstanding amount of the loan.

Requirement

Show the effect of these transactions on Test Valley Ltd and on Bream.

7   ANSWERS TO EXAMINATION TYPE QUESTIONS

7.1   Investment Company Ltd

PCTCT for Investment Company Ltd

	£	£	£
Sch A rent		270,200	
Less: Repairs etc	5,600		
Management ⅓ × 150,600	50,200	55,800	214,400
Sch D III Bank deposit interest (2,600 − 2,400)			200
Chargeable gain			60,000
			274,600
Less: Management expenses £(2,000 + 100,400)			102,400
Profits chargeable to corporation tax			172,200

Notes:

(1)   If the management expenses, together with any other charges paid wholly and exclusively for the purpose of the business, exceed the amount of profits from which they are deductible, the excess can be carried forward (without time limit) to the succeeding accounting periods.

(2)   Unrelieved management expenses are NOT losses; the amount carried forward is treated as having been disbursed in the future accounting period in which it is relieved, and thus no claim is required.

7.2   Bream

The effect of the transactions on Test Valley Ltd and on Bream is as follows

Test Valley Ltd

June 1997	Company liable to pay tax equal to 25% of the loan within 9 months of the end of the AP (ie, on 30 September 1998) £72,000 × 25%	£18,000
January 1999	Company becomes entitled to repayment of tax to extent loan repaid ie £20,000 × 25% Repayment is due on 30 September 2000	£5,000
March 2000	Company becomes entitled to repayment of the balance of the tax ie £52,000 × 25% Repayment is due 30 September 2001	£13,000

Bream

£

March 2000   Loan waived grossed-up and assessable
as dividend income in 1999/00
Amount waived   52,000
Tax credit available of: 10/90   5,778
                                                 ———————
Gross amount on which higher rate assessable   57,778
                                                 ———————

28 COMPANY RE-ORGANISATIONS

INTRODUCTION

This chapter deals firstly with the taxation on the purchase by a company of its own shares, and then the taxation effects of a company reorganising its capital are explained, and finally the effects of a company going into liquidation or a receiver being appointed are covered.

1 PURCHASE BY A COMPANY OF ITS OWN SHARES

1.1 Introduction

A company is allowed to purchase its own shares, subject to various conditions and authority being given in the company's articles of association.

If a shareholder disposes of his shares to a third party, then he is liable to capital gains tax on any chargeable gain arising on the disposal. There are no taxation effects on the company when its shares are disposed of to a third party.

If, alternatively, a shareholder sells his shares back to the company, any payment he receives in excess of the amount originally subscribed for the shares is treated as a distribution.

The effect of this is:

- The distribution carries a tax credit equivalent to 10% of the gross distribution (10/90 of the net distribution).

- The gross distribution is treated as income for the shareholder, who may be subject to a higher rate tax liability. The tax credit will mean that basic rate taxpayers have no further liability. However, the tax credit is never repaid, and so non-taxpayers cannot claim a refund. They will only receive the net distribution.

1.2 Exemptions

There are two situations where the purchase by a company of its own shares is not treated as a distribution by the company.

The exemptions apply when shares are purchased

- for the benefit of the company's trade; or
- for the purpose of paying inheritance tax.

In these situations, any gain made by the shareholder will be subject to capital gains tax.

1.3 Exemption for the purchase of shares for the benefit of the company's trade

This exemption applies where the purchase by the company of its own shares is made wholly or mainly for the purpose of benefiting a trade carried on by the company concerned. Situations where a benefit will be considered to have accrued to the company's trade include:

- when the proprietor of a company is retiring to make way for new management;

- when an outside shareholder who provided equity wishes to withdraw his investment;

- where a shareholder dies and his personal representatives or beneficiary do not wish to keep the shares; or

- when there is disagreement over the management of the company and the dissident shareholder is bought out because he is having an adverse effect on the running of the company.

1.4   Conditions for relief

Various conditions must be satisfied before the exemptions apply:

- the company is unquoted;

- the company is a trading company, or the holding company of a trading group. Companies whose trade consists of dealing in shares, securities, land or futures are excluded.

- the vendor is resident and ordinarily resident in the UK;

- the shares must have been owned by the vendor or his spouse throughout the five years ending with the date of purchase by the company.

- as a result of the purchase, the vendor and his associates must have reduced their shareholding in the company to 75% or less of their percentage share before the disposal.

- as a result of the purchase the vendor must not be connected with the company.

  A person is connected with the company if he owns, directly or indirectly more than 30% of

  - the issued ordinary share capital;
  - the total of its issued share capital and loan capital; or
  - the voting rights in the company.

- the transaction is not part of a scheme to avoid tax.

1.5   Example - reduction in a shareholder's interest

Michael owns 200 of the 500 issues shares in Leather Limited. The company buys back 60 of his shares.

Will relief be available to Michael?

1.6   Solution

Michael has sold 30% of his shareholding.

In order for the disposal to attract CGT treatment, he must reduce his holding to 75% or less of his percentage share before the disposal.

	Total	Michael
Before disposal	500	200
Purchase by company	(60)	(60)
After purchase	440	140
Percentage before $\frac{200}{500}$		40%
Percentage after $\frac{140}{440}$		31.81%
75% of percentage before		30%

As 31.81% is greater than 30% the 75% reduction test is not met and the purchase of the shares is treated as a distribution.

Note that although Michael has disposed of 30% of his holding, and now owns 28% ($\frac{140}{500}$) of the original number of shares issued, it is his percentage holding of the reduced number of shares (440) that is relevant.

The purchase of Michael's shares also fails to qualify for the special treatment because his shareholding of 31.81% is greater than 30%, and so he will still be connected with Leather Limited.

1.7   Exemption for the purchase of shares for the purpose of paying inheritance tax

This exemption applies where the sale proceeds received by the shareholder from the company are used to meet an inheritance tax liability arising on a death.

The vendor must show that the IHT could not have been paid without causing undue hardship, if he did not sell the shares.

1.8   Revenue clearance

Before the company makes the purchase, it is useful to seek clearance from the Revenue that the proposed transaction will, or will not, meet the above conditions. A shareholder may find that it is more beneficial if the purchase is treated as a distribution, in which case clearance can be asked for to confirm that the proposed transaction will not fall within one of the exemptions detailed above.

> **Conclusion**   The purchase by a company of its own shares is usually treated as a distribution. When the shares are disposed of either to pay an IHT liability on death, or for the benefit of the company's trade, the disposal will attract CGT treatment, providing certain conditions are met.

2   REORGANISATIONS

2.1   Introduction

Companies and groups may find that they want to reorganise their structure for commercial reasons. It is important that you are aware of the more common types of reorganisations and the taxation consequences of them.

2.2   Types of reorganisations

There are two main types of reorganisation that you should be aware of:

- Company X might transfer its shareholding in a subsidiary to company Y in return for the issue of shares in company Y to the members of company X

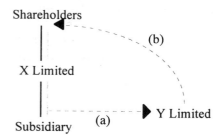

(a)   X Limited transfers shares in subsidiary to Y Limited in return for
(b)   an issue of shares in Y Limited to members of X Limited.

- Company X may transfer a trade or business to a newly formed company, company Y. Shares in the new company Y will then be issued to the shareholders in company X.

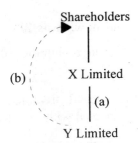

(a)   X Limited transfers a trade or business to Y Limited in return for

(b)   an issue of shares in Y Limited to X Limited's members.

Alternatively, a company could transfer a trade or business to a wholly owned subsidiary in exchange for shares in the subsidiary - this is known as a 'hive down'.

2.3   Taxation implications of reorganisations

(a)   When a trade is discontinued, any trading losses that have not been relieved are usually lost. However, relief is given where a company ceases to carry on a trade and another company begins to carry it on, providing that the same persons own at least three quarters of the trade at two times, one within a year before and the other within two years after the transfer.

Unrelieved trading losses of the transferor company can then be taken over by the new company for relief against future profits of the transferred trade. Capital allowances also continue as if there had been no discontinuation of the trade.

(b)   Capital losses cannot be transferred to the new company:

(c)   The chapter on groups of companies explained that companies in a 75% group transfer assets between each other on a no gain/no loss basis. There is a similar provision available when companies resident in the UK, but not in a 75% group, transfer a business, or part of one from one company to another. In this situation, chargeable assets are transferred on a no gain/no loss basis, providing that:

- the transfer is for bona fide commercial reasons;
- no consideration is paid to the transferor company; and
- the transfer is not to avoid tax.

(d)   When a reorganisation takes place, shareholders holding shares in one company often receive shares in another company in their place. This is not a disposal for capital gains tax purposes, and the new holding is deemed to have been acquired on the same date as the original holding. Note, however, if the shareholder receives any cash in the reorganisation, this will be a chargeable event (see the capital gains tax section of the study text for further details).

(e)   In order for the tax reliefs to apply, the reorganisations must be for bona fide commercial reasons and not in order to avoid tax. It is therefore sensible to obtain Revenue clearance for the scheme before embarking on a reorganisation.

3   LIQUIDATIONS AND RECEIVERSHIPS

3.1   Receiverships

A receiver is a person appointed by a secured creditor to run the company and/or sell assets until sufficient funds have been realised to discharge the secured loan. The appointment of a receiver is not necessarily followed by liquidation.

As the appointment is effectively a management change, it has no corporation tax consequences. Corporation tax will be paid on profits and gains, and loss relief given in the normal way.

3.2   Liquidations - Accounting periods

A new accounting period always begins at the commencement of a winding up (ie, when the resolution to wind up is passed by the company, or, if no resolution is passed, the date of the filing of the successful petition). Accounting periods end annually thereafter. The date of cessation of trading is irrelevant once the winding up has commenced.

3.3   Corporation tax position

During a liquidation the corporation tax position is as follows:

(a)   Any gain on the realisation of chargeable assets during the liquidation will be assessed on the company in the relevant accounting period.

(b)   The Schedule D Case I assessment which includes (or ends with) the cessation of trade will be adjusted to include the closing stock at market value.

(c)   Debtors and creditors at the cessation of trade will normally be adjusted by the liquidator to their realised value. This will affect the Schedule D Case I assessment for the accounting period including the cessation.

(d)   Plant and machinery will be treated as if it had been sold at market value on the cessation of trading, and balancing charges and allowances brought into the Schedule D Case I assessment computation for the accounting period including the cessation.

(e)   Relief is available for trading losses of the liquidator in the normal way, ie:

•   against other income of the same or preceding twelve month period;
•   against future profits of the same trade.

4   SELF TEST QUESTIONS

4.1   If the purchase by a company of its own shares is treated as a distribution, what are the taxation effects? (1.1)

4.2   What are the two situations where the purchase by a company of its own shares are not treated as a distribution? (1.2)

4.3   How is the purchase by a company of its own shares treated for tax purposes if the transaction is not treated as a distribution? (1.2)

4.4   When does the exemption for the purchase of shares for the benefit of the company's trade apply? (1.3)

4.5   What are the conditions for the relief for the purchase by a company of its own shares? (1.4)

4.6   When does the exemption for the purchase of shares for the purpose of paying inheritance tax apply? (1.7)

4.7   What are the two main types of reorganisation that a company might effect? (2.2)

4.8   What are the taxation implications of a reorganisation? (2.3)

4.9   As part of a reorganisation, can capital losses be transferred to the new company? (2.3)

4.10   What are the taxation implications on the shareholder when a reorganisation takes place? (2.3)

4.11   What is the corporation tax position when a liquidation takes place? (3.3)

5   EXAMINATION TYPE QUESTION

5.1   Grange Limited

Joe subscribes for 100,000 £1 shares in his family company, Grange Limited, at par in November 1985. This represents a 25% holding in the company. In August 1999 Joe sells the shares back to the company at £7.30 per share, as he is ready to retire, and the family do not want the shares to go to outsiders.

Joe has earned income of £50,000 in 1999/00 and made no other capital disposals during the year. Advise Joe of how the sale of shares will affect his tax liability for 1999/00 if:

(1)   the transaction is treated as a distribution; and

(2)   the transaction is not treated as a distribution.

6   ANSWER TO EXAMINATION TYPE QUESTION

6.1   Grange Limited

(a)   **Transaction treated as a distribution.**

Income tax payable

	£
Dividend plus tax credit: £630,000 × 100/90	700,000

	£
Income tax @ 32.5%	227,500
Less: Tax credit (700,000 @ 10%)	70,000
Income tax payable	157,500

The amount to be treated as a distribution is the difference between the sale proceeds and the amount originally subscribed for. The distribution is therefore 100,000 × £7.30 = £730,000 - £100,000 = £630,000.

(b)   **Transaction not treated as a distribution.**

	£
Proceeds	730,000
Less: Cost	(100,000)
Less: Indexation allowance to April 1998 $100,000 \times \dfrac{162.6 - 95.92}{95.92}$	(69,516)
Capital gain	560,484
Taper relief (two years) × 85%	476,411
Less: Annual exemption	(7,100)
	469,311
Capital gains tax at 40%	187,724

The shares are treated as a business asset for the purposes of taper relief because Joe has a holding of at least 25% (the question does not state whether or not he is a full-time working director or employee).

Note: the exemption for the purchase by a company of its own shares effectively converts income into capital. As can be seen by the question, this is not always advantageous.

In an exam question, consider the effects of both situations.

Although this question did not state that retirement relief was available this would have had a major effect on the outcome:

Capital gain (assume no non business assets)		560,484
Less: 100% × £200,000	200,000	
50% (560,484 – 200,000)	180,242	
		(380,242)
		180,242
Taper relief (two years) × 85%		153,206
Annual exemption		(7,100)
		146,106
Capital gains tax at 40%		58,442

29 OUTLINE OF INHERITANCE TAX

INTRODUCTION

This chapter introduces inheritance tax (IHT), which is essentially a tax that is levied upon the value of a deceased person's estate.

1 BASIC PRINCIPLES

1.1 Introduction

(a) Since IHT is primarily a tax that is levied upon the value of a person's estate at the date of their death, it is quite different to most of the other taxes covered at Paper 11. Years of assessment or financial years have little relevance to IHT.

(b) Because it would be easy to avoid IHT by making a gift of property just before the date of death, IHT also taxes certain gifts made during a person's lifetime. The first two chapters on IHT will, however, concentrate on the charge at death.

1.2 The rates of tax

(a) For deaths occurring on or after 6 April 1999, the tax rates are:

    (i)   Nil% on the first £231,000 of a person's estate
    (ii)   40% thereafter.

(b) Although different rates and thresholds apply to earlier years, only the above rates of IHT will be applicable to questions set for Paper 11. For examples in this study text it will be assumed that the £231,000 nil band also applied before 6 April 1999.

1.3 Activity

Sara died on 15 June 1999 leaving an estate valued at £376,000 which was bequeathed to her brother.

Calculate the IHT liability.

1.4 Activity solution

		£
Chargeable estate		376,000
Inheritance tax payable	231,000 at Nil	
	145,000 at 40%	58,000

1.5 Chargeable persons

Definition   Individuals are chargeable persons.

(a) For IHT purposes the concept of residence (see chapter 37 on overseas activities) has little relevance. What is important is a person's domicile. A person is domiciled in the country where they have their permanent home. The question of domicile will be looked at in more detail in chapter 33.

(b)   A person domiciled in the UK is chargeable to IHT in respect of their worldwide assets. For persons not domiciled in the UK only their UK assets are chargeable to IHT. This aspect of IHT will be looked at in more detail in chapter 33.

(c)   The following may also be chargeable persons:

(i)   Companies are not chargeable persons, but in certain circumstances participators of a close company may be chargeable in respect of gifts made by the company.

(ii)   Trustees of settled property (trusts).

1.6   Husband and wives

Husband and wives are separate persons as regards IHT just as they are for other taxes. They therefore each have a band of £231,000 which is charged to IHT at nil%.

1.7   Chargeable property

Definition   Chargeable property consists of all property to which a person is beneficially entitled, other than excluded property.

(a)   The value of a person's estate at death therefore consists of the aggregate value of all property to which the deceased was beneficially entitled immediately prior to death.

(b)   The estate also includes any property acquired as a result of death. The most important example of this is the proceeds of a life assurance policy which matures upon death.

However, this is only the case where the life assurance policy is in the name of the deceased. The value of a life assurance policy will be ignored if:

(i)   It has been taken out and paid for by somebody other than the deceased. For example, a wife may take out and pay for a policy which matures on the death of her husband. The proceeds would not be included as part of the husband's estate.

(ii)   The policy has been written in trust for another person. For example, a husband may take out and pay for a policy which has been written in trust for his wife. Upon the husband's death, the proceeds of the policy will be paid direct to the wife, and will not form part of the husband's estate.

1.8   Excluded property

(a)   As already stated, the overseas property of a person not domiciled in the UK is excluded property.

(b)   Unlike CGT where, for example, motor cars and principal private residences are not chargeable, there are few other exclusions from IHT. The most important example, as regards Paper 11 is that of a reversionary interest (refer to the following section on trusts).

(c)   There are some other categories of excluded property, but none are particularly important as regards Paper 11. They are as follows:

(i)   Property owned by servicemen who die as a result of injuries etc sustained on active service.

(ii)   Property of overseas servicemen posted to the UK.

(iii)   Certain overseas pensions, gratuities, and lump sums paid on death.

(iv)   Certain UK government securities owned by individuals living abroad.

(v)   Savings of persons who are domiciled in the Channel Islands or the Isle of Man (which are tax havens off the UK coast).

2   TRUSTS

2.1   Introduction

Although the concepts involved in trusts can be quite difficult to grasp, it is necessary to have an understanding of them in order to study IHT. Note that the terms "trust" and "settlement" are virtually interchangeable.

2.2   What is a trust?

Definition   A trust is an arrangement whereby someone (known as the settlor) transfers assets to trustees to hold for the benefit of one or more persons (the beneficiaries).

(a)   The beneficiaries will receive income and/or capital from the trust either now or at some future date.

(b)   A trust can be created on death as part of the settlor's will, or during the settlor's lifetime by means of a trust deed. The trust deed sets out the trustee's powers and duties.

2.3   The purpose of trusts

(a)   The use of a trust allows a settlor to give away the benefit of property, whilst retaining some control over that property. In respect of trusts created during lifetime, it is not uncommon for the settlor to become one of the trustees in order to retain control.

(b)   A typical example is where a settlor sets up a trust whereby the income from the trust property goes to his wife during her lifetime. Upon the wife's death the trust property will pass to their children absolutely (ie, the trust terminates and the assets of the trust are distributed to the children).

This arrangement means that the settlor's wife has income to live on during her lifetime (perhaps following the settlor's death), but that the assets ultimately pass to their children.

This is an important consideration if, for example, the wife remarries following the settlor's death.

2.4   Interest in possession trusts

Definition   An interest in possession exists where a beneficiary has the immediate entitlement to any income generated by the assets of the trust.

(a)   In an interest in possession trust the trustees have to distribute all of the trust's income. They cannot accumulate the income, and do not have any choice as to which beneficiary is to receive the income as shares are specified in the trust deed.

This is subject to the trustees being able to claim for expenses and other outgoings payable out of the trust income.

(b)   In the previous example, the wife was entitled to all of the trust income. This would therefore be an interest in possession trust.

(c)   It may be the case that the trust does not generate any income, but that a beneficiary has the use of trust assets.

For example, trust property may consist of a house which a beneficiary is entitled to live in under the terms of the trust. The trust will not have any income, but it is still an interest in possession trust.

(d)   The beneficiary who receives the trust income (or has the use of the trust property) under an interest in possession has a life interest, and is known as the life tenant.

(e)   The beneficiary who receives the capital of the trust at some future date (becomes absolutely entitled) has a reversionary interest, and is known as the remainderman.

(f)   The settlor may specify an age or an event as to when the remainderman will become absolutely entitled.

For example, the life tenant may be entitled to receive the trust income only until he or she marries or reaches the age of 21 after which the trust property passes to the remainderman.

(g)   There is no reason why the life tenant and the remainderman cannot be the same person. Property may be held in trust for a minor until he or she reaches 18 or 21.

2.5   Discretionary trusts

[Definition]   A discretionary trust is one where no interest in possession exists.

(a)   In a typical discretionary trust the trustees may have power to decide:

(i)   Whether or not trust income is to be accumulated.
(ii)   How the trust income is to be shared between different beneficiaries.
(iii)   How the capital of the trust is to be shared between different beneficiaries.

(b)   The trustees will have complete discretion as to how to deal with the income and capital of the trust, subject only to the duties imposed by the trust deed.

2.6   Accumulation and maintenance trusts

[Definition]   An accumulation and maintenance trust is a special type of discretionary trust where income is accumulated for a beneficiary or used for his or her maintenance at the discretion of the trustees.

A trust can only be an accumulation and maintenance trust if:

(a)   There is no interest in possession on property held within the trust.

(b)   All the beneficiaries of the trust have a grandparent in common.

If this is not the case, then the trust can only be an accumulation and maintenance trust for 25 years.

(c)   The beneficiaries will become entitled to the trust assets on or before reaching the age of 25. The property leaving the trust can either pass absolutely to a beneficiary or into a life interest trust for a beneficiary.

3   THE ESTATE AT DEATH

3.1   Introduction

Sufficient information has now been covered in order to calculate the IHT liability arising on a person's death.

3.2 Proforma for an estate

2001/02   0% = 242k
              40% = 242 >

Below is the proforma layout for a deceased's estate:

	£	£
FREE ESTATE		
Personalty		
Leasehold property		x
Stocks and shares		x
Business assets		x
Personal chattels		x
Debtors		x
Life assurance policy proceeds		x
Cash and bank balances		x
Less: Funeral expenses	x	
Other allowable debts	x	
		(x)
		x
Realty		
Freehold property	x	
Less: Mortgage secured thereon	(x)	
		x
Net free estate		x
SETTLED PROPERTY		
Interest in possession trust		x
Chargeable estate		x

The term "free estate" denotes property to which the deceased possessed an absolute power of disposal.

3.3 Settled property

(a)   The value of settled property subject to a life interest is included in the value of a deceased's estate.

This is despite the fact that the life tenant does not possess an absolute title to the assets of the trust.

(b)   At first this may seem strange, but compare the position of a person who owns investments worth £100,000 to that of a life tenant of a trust that has investments worth £100,000.

Both will enjoy the income from the investments, and in each case investments can be sold and replaced by new investments (the trust deed permitting).

The only difference is that the beneficiary does not actually have access to the assets of the trust, and cannot use them, for example, to pay for a holiday.

Thus by deeming that the life tenant is the beneficial owner of life interest property (even though, under trust law, he clearly is not the owner) the legislation is able to bring life interest property within the scope of IHT.

(c)   Since discretionary trusts and accumulation and maintenance trusts do not have an interest in possession, it is not possible to identify a person who should be treated as owning the trust property.

         The value of such trusts is therefore excluded from a beneficiary's estate. Instead such trusts are subject to complicated regimes which make them directly liable to IHT.

3.4   Funeral expenses and other deductible debts

(a)   Debts are deductible if they were outstanding at the date of death and if they had been incurred for valuable consideration or imposed by law.

         This will include all outstanding taxes such as income tax and CGT, although not the IHT due on death itself.

         Gambling debts and outstanding commitments under deeds of covenant will not usually be deductible since no valuable consideration will have been received in return.

(b)   The cost of administering the estate or establishing the value of the estate at death is not allowable as it is for professional services carried out after the death. By contrast, unpaid accountants fees for work prior to death (eg, for preparing the annual tax return) would be allowed. Where work spans the date of death the expense must be apportioned.

(c)   If a debt is secured against specific property it is deducted from that property. This will be the case with a mortgage secured against freehold property.

         It is necessary to differentiate repayment mortgages from endowment mortgages. A repayment mortgage is a straightforward loan, and will be a liability in the deceased's estate.

         An endowment mortgage is different in that it includes an element of life assurance. The life assurance will repay the mortgage upon death, and therefore an endowment mortgage is not deducted as a liability.

(d)   If a debt is not payable until after the date of death, then it is deductible but is discounted (reduced) because of the future date of payment.

(e)   Debts contracted abroad are deducted from non-UK property. This is the case even if the non-UK property is not chargeable to IHT.

(f)   The costs of a reasonable funeral (including the tombstone) are allowable, even though the cost is incurred after the date of death.

         What is reasonable depends upon the deceased's station in life.

3.5   Activity

Simon died on 31 December 1999. At the date of his death Simon owned the following assets:

(a)   Freehold property worth £125,000.
(b)   Leasehold property worth £58,000.
(c)   10,000 shares in a quoted company valued at £42,000.
(d)   Four paintings worth £25,000.
(e)   A loan of £16,500 due to Simon by his uncle.
(f)   A motor car worth £13,000.
(g)   Bank deposits of £12,200.
(h)   UK government stocks valued at £9,500.
(i)   Simon was the life tenant of an interest in possession trust. The assets of the trust were worth £80,000 on 31 December 1999.

At the date of his death Simon owed £800 for gambling debts. His funeral expenses amounted to £1,200.

All of Simon's estate was left to his daughter.

Calculate the IHT arising upon Simon's death.

3.6   Activity solution

Simon - Inheritance tax computation.

		£
FREE ESTATE		
Personalty		
Leasehold property		58,000
Quoted shares		42,000
Paintings		25,000
Debtor		16,500
Motor car		13,000
Bank account		12,200
UK government stock		9,500
		176,200
Funeral expenses		1,200
		175,000
Realty		
Freehold property		125,000
Net free estate		300,000
SETTLED PROPERTY		
Interest in possession		80,000
Chargeable estate		380,000
Inheritance tax payable	231,000 at Nil	
	149,000 at 40%	59,600

Gambling debts are not deductible.

3.7   Responsibility for payment of the IHT liability

(a)   It is necessary to keep the free estate and the settled property separate, since different people will be responsible for the respective IHT liabilities:

     (i)   The personal representatives (executors or administrators) pay the IHT due on the free estate.

     (ii)   The trustees pay the IHT due on the settled property.

(b)   Apart from this division, the order of the assets in the proforma is not particularly important.

3.8   Rate of IHT on the estate

(a)   In order to apportion an IHT liability between the different people who are responsible for paying it, a rate of IHT on the estate is calculated.

(b)   The rate of IHT on the estate is calculated as follows:

$$\frac{\text{IHT payable}}{\text{Chargeable estate}} \times 100$$

3.9   Activity

Calculate the rate of IHT on Simon's estate (as per the previous activity), and show who is to pay the IHT liability.

3.10   Activity solution

Rate of IHT on Simon's estate

$$\frac{59,600}{380,000} \times 100 = 15.684\%$$

The IHT payable by the personal representative is:

300,000 × 15.684% = £47,053

The IHT payable by the trustees of the interest in possession trust is:

80,000 × 15.684% = £12,547

4   EXEMPT TRANSFERS

4.1   Introduction

Whether an estate is fully chargeable to IHT (as in the examples looked at so far) or is partially chargeable or even completely exempt, will depend upon who the deceased has left his or her estate to.

Certain gifts are exempt.

4.2   Husband and wives

(a)   Transfers between spouses are normally wholly exempt from IHT.

For example, if upon her death a wife leaves her estate entirely to her husband, then regardless of the value of her estate there will be no IHT liability.

(b)   The exemption also applies if an interest in possession trust is set up under the will (or an intestacy) with the spouse as life tenant.

(c)   Where the recipient spouse is not domiciled in the UK, however, the exemption is limited to £55,000. There is no restriction if both spouses are not domiciled in the UK.

(d)   The inter-spouse exemption is the one most often met in practice, and is therefore the most likely exemption to be examined.

4.3   Activity

Ace died on 31 December 1999 leaving a widow and two children. He left an estate valued at £440,000. Under the terms of his will he left £175,000 to his widow, and the balance to his children in equal shares.

(a)   Calculate the IHT arising upon Ace's death.

(b)   How would your answer change if Ace's widow was not domiciled in the UK?

4.4   Activity solution

(a)

		£
Value of estate		440,000
Less: Exempt legacy		175,000
		265,000
Inheritance tax payable	231,000 at Nil	
	34,000 at 40%	13,600

(b)

		£
Value of estate		440,000
Less: Exempt legacy		55,000
		385,000
Inheritance tax payable	231,000 at Nil	
	154,000 at 40%	61,600

4.5   Gifts to charities

Gifts to registered charities are totally exempt.

4.6   Gifts to political parties

(a)   Gifts to qualifying parties are totally exempt.

(b)   To qualify a party must either have:

(i)   Two elected members of the House of Commons at the last General Election, or

(ii)   One elected member and at least 150,000 votes cast for that party.

4.7   Gifts for the public benefit or for national purposes

(a)   Gifts to non-profit making institutions are, with Treasury approval, exempt.

(b)   Examples could include land and buildings of outstanding beauty, or of historic interest.

(c)   Undertakings are required concerning the use, preservation and public access of the property.

(d)   Gifts to a number of national institutions are also exempt. These include:

(i)   The British Museum.

(ii)   The National Gallery.

(iii)   Approved museums, libraries and art galleries.

(iv)   The National Trust.

4.8   Gifts to housing associations

Gifts of land to housing associations are exempt.

5   THE ALLOCATION OF THE ESTATE

5.1   Introduction

Although not strictly to do with IHT, a question may require a statement showing the allocation of a deceased person's estate between the beneficiaries.

5.2   IHT is borne by the residue of the estate

(a)   Specific gifts of UK property do not bear their own tax (IHT).

(b)   The IHT is instead borne by the residue of the estate.

5.3   Example: Specific gifts of UK property

Jane died on 31 July 1999 leaving an estate valued at £365,000. Under the terms of her will Jane left £100,000 to her brother, and the balance to her two children in equal shares.

(a)   Calculate the IHT arising upon Jane's death.
(b)   Show how Jane's estate will be allocated between the beneficiaries.

5.4   Solution

(a)

	£
Chargeable estate	365,000
Inheritance tax payable 231,000 at Nil	
134,000 at 40%	53,600

(b)   Jane's brother will receive the full £100,000 as this is a specific gift of UK property.

Jane's children will receive £105,700 each as follows:

	£
Value of estate	365,000
Less: Specific legacy	(100,000)
Less: IHT	(53,600)
	211,400

211,400/2 = 105,700

5.5   Grossing up gifts on death

(a)   Where there are specific gifts which are exempt, and the residue of the estate is chargeable, then this does not cause a problem.

The exempt legacy is simply deducted from the value of the estate, and the IHT is deducted from the residue of the estate as per the previous example.

(b)   Where there are specific gifts of UK property which are chargeable, and the residue of the estate is exempt, then it is necessary to gross up the specific gifts.

The logic behind this is that a specific gift of UK property is effectively "net" of tax.

5.6   Example: Grossing up gifts on death

Alex died on 30 September 1999 leaving an estate valued at £546,000. Under the terms of his will Alex left £273,000 to his son Raymond, and the residue of the estate to his widow.

(a)   Calculate the IHT arising upon Alex's death.
(b)   Show how Alex's estate will be allocated between the beneficiaries.

(c)   Show how the situation would change if Alex's widow was left £273,000, and Raymond was left the residue of the estate.

5.7 Solution

(a)   Only the £273,000 specific gift to Raymond is chargeable.

£231,000 of this is chargeable at nil%.

The balance of £42,000 (which is the net figure) is chargeable at the rate of 40/60 rather than 40%.

	£
Inheritance tax payable 231,000 at Nil	
42,000 at 40/60	28,000

(b)   Raymond will receive the full £273,000.

Alex's widow will receive £245,000 as follows:

	£
Value of estate	546,000
Less: Specific legacy	(273,000)
Less: IHT	(28,000)
	245,000

(c)

	£
Value of estate	546,000
Less: Exempt legacy	273,000
	273,000

	£
Inheritance tax payable 231,000 at Nil	
42,000 at 40%	16,800

Alex's widow will receive the full £273,000.

Raymond will receive £256,200 as follows:

	£
Value of estate	546,000
Less: Specific legacy	(273,000)
Less: IHT	(16,800)
	256,200

6   VALUATION RULES

6.1   Introduction

The basic rule for valuing property for IHT purposes is that of open market value.

Definition   Open market value is the price which property might reasonably be expected to fetch if sold in the open market at that time.

The following points must be considered when establishing a sale in the open market:

(i)   The valuation assumes that there has been adequate publicity prior to the sale.

(ii)   The price is not reduced to take account of the fact that the whole property is placed on the market at once.

(iii)   The opinion of a suitably qualified expert will normally suffice in order to establish what constitutes open market value.

For example, an estate agent's opinion will be accepted on the value of land and buildings.

(iv)   The Inland Revenue can set aside any valuation that they consider to be unreasonable.

6.2   Valuation of quoted shares and securities

(a)   At the close of business each day the Stock Exchange publishes two prices for each quoted share or security. These are:

(i)   The bid price (the price that a share or security can be sold for).
(ii)   The offer price (the price that a share or security can be bought for).

It will also list the prices at which certain transactions took place during that day. These are the day's bargains.

(b)   The value of quoted shares and securities is the lower of:

(i)   The quarter up price, and
(ii)   The average of the day's highest and lowest recorded bargains.

The quarter up price is the lower closing price (the bid price) plus one quarter of the difference between the offer and bid prices.

(c)   If a person dies on a Saturday or a Sunday when the Stock Exchange is closed, then the valuation is done for both the preceding Friday and the following Monday.

The lowest of the two valuations is then taken.

6.3   Example: Share valuation

Alex died on 16 December 1999.

Included in his estate were 12,000 shares in Oak plc which were quoted at 488 - 492 on that day.

Recorded bargains were 484, 486, 490 and 492.

You are to calculate the value of the shares for IHT purposes.

6.4   Solution

The IHT valuation is the lower of:

(i)   488 + 1/4 (492 - 488) = 489p
(ii)   1/2 (492 + 484)   = 488p

The shares will be valued at 488p, which gives a total value of 12,000 x 488p = £58,560.

Note the following points:

(i)   The prices given are in pence.

Chapter 29   Outline of inheritance tax

(ii)   Apart from the highest and lowest prices, the other day's bargains are irrelevant.

6.5   Securities quoted ex dividend or ex interest

(a)   The valuation of quoted shares and securities on death must be made cum dividend or cum interest. That is, including the proportion of dividend or interest accrued up to the date of death.

(b)   Unless a question states otherwise, it can be assumed that prices or values given are cum dividend or cum interest.

(c)   Where prices or values are given ex dividend or ex interest, then an adjustment must be made as follows:

      (i)   If shares are quoted ex dividend then the whole of the next dividend should be added to the valuation.

      (ii)   If securities are quoted ex interest then the whole of the next interest payment, net of 20% tax, should be added to the valuation.

6.6   Example: Securities quoted ex interest

Joe died on 2 December 1999. Included in his estate were £10,000 10% Debenture stock quoted at 90 - 94 ex interest. Interest is paid half yearly.

Calculate the value of the debenture stock for IHT purposes.

6.7   Solution

The normal quarter up rule gives a price of:

90 + 1/4 (94 - 90) = 91

The valuation is £9,500 as follows:

			£
10,000 at 91 =			9,100
Add: Interest due 10,000 x 10% x 6/12	500		
Less: 20% Income tax	100		
		400	
			9,500

6.8   Valuation of unquoted shares and securities

(a)   Unquoted shares and securities are more difficult to value for IHT purposes, as there is no ready market like the Stock Exchange.

(b)   An examination question will usually state the value of unquoted shares and securities.

(c)   Shareholdings are generally valued as follows:

      (i)   A shareholding of 50% or less will be valued on a dividend yield basis.
      (ii)   A shareholding of over 50% will be valued on an earnings basis.
      (iii)   A shareholding of over 90% will be valued on an assets basis.

(d)   The value will have to be agreed with the Inland Revenue's Share Valuation Division.

Official ACCA *Textbook, published by AT Foulks Lynch*

6.9 Valuation of unit trusts

Units in unit trusts are valued at the manager's bid price, which is the lower of the two published prices.

6.10 Activity

Li died on 19 August 1999. Included in her estate were 100,000 units in the ABC unit trust.

The trust was quoted at 90 - 96 on 19 August 1999.

Calculate the value of the unit trust for IHT purposes.

6.11 Activity solution

The bid price is 90p, so the valuation of the units in the ABC unit trust is £90,000 as follows:

100,000 at 90 =   £90,000
                                            ————

6.12 Valuation of land and buildings

(a) A valuation for land and buildings will be given in an examination question.

(b) The personal representative will usually take a professional valuer's opinion, whilst the Inland Revenue will take the District Valuer's opinion.

(c) Appeal can be made to the Land Tribunal.

6.13 Valuation of life assurance policies

(a) Where a person's estate includes a life assurance policy that matures on his or her death, the value of the policy is the amount of the proceeds paid out by the life assurance company.

(b) Where a person's estate includes a life assurance policy that matures on the death of somebody else, the value of the policy is its open market value (not the surrender value).

6.14 The valuation of overseas property

(a) Overseas property is valued on the same basis as property situated in the UK.

(b) The value is converted into sterling at the appropriate exchange rate for the date of death.

(c) The value can be reduced by the additional expense (resulting from its overseas location) incurred by the personal representatives in realising the asset.

This relief is restricted to a maximum of 5% of the initial value of the asset.

6.15 The valuation of trust property

Property in a trust is valued in exactly the same way as any other property.

There are, however, two aspects of valuing an interest in possession trust that require further consideration.

6.16 The valuation of a life interest

(a) As already seen, where the life tenant of an interest in possession trust is entitled to all of the trust income, then that person is effectively treated for IHT purposes as owning the trust property.

(b)   If there is more than one life tenant, then each is treated as owning a respective share of the trust property.

For example, a trust might have two life tenants who share the income of the trust equally. Each of them would be treated as owning 50% of the trust property.

(c)   It might be the case that a person is entitled to a specified amount of the trust income. This amount is known as an annuity, and the person an annuitant.

The annuitant is treated as owning that proportion of the trust property that would yield the annuity.

If there is a life tenant the value 'owned' by the life tenant is the value of the trust property after deducting the annuitant's portion.

(d)   There are maximum and minimum values that can be given to an annuitant's share of trust property. The examiner has stated that this aspect will not be examined.

6.17   Example: Valuation of an annuitant's interest

Under a trust set up by his mother, Chi is entitled to all the income of the trust after the payment of an annuity of £4,000 p.a. to his sister. The annual income of the trust is £13,000, and the assets of the trust are valued at £130,000.

6.18   Solution

The sister's share is calculated as follows:

$$130,000 \times \frac{4,000}{13,000} = £40,000$$

Chi's share is £90,000 (130,000 - 40,000).

6.19   Accrued income due to a deceased life tenant

(a)   A life tenant is entitled to the income from an interest in possession trust up to the date of his or her death.

(b)   An adjustment may therefore be necessary if the value of trust property includes accrued income, as follows:

(i)   The gross amount of accrued income is deducted from the value of the trust.

(ii)   The accrued income (net of 10%, 20% or 23% income tax) is added to the value of the deceased's free estate.

6.20   Activity

Dawn died on 31 May 1999 leaving a free estate valued at £235,000.

Dawn was the life tenant of an interest in possession trust that had property consisting of £60,000 10% debenture stocks quoted at 99 - 103. Interest payment dates are 30 June and 31 December.

Calculate the value of Dawn's free estate and the value of the trust for IHT purposes.

6.21   Activity solution

The value of the debenture stock includes five months accrued interest from 1 January 1999 to 31 May 1999, which is £2,500 (60,000 x 10% x 5/12).

The value of Dawn's free estate will be £237,000 as follows:

	£	£
Free estate		235,000
Add: Accrued interest	2,500	
Less: Income tax at 20%	500	
		2,000
		237,000

The value of the trust will be £57,500 as follows:

	£
10% debenture stock	
£60,000 100p (99 + 1/4 (103 - 99)	60,000
Less: Accrued interest	2,500
	57,500

7 RELATED PROPERTY

7.1 Introduction

Related property valuation rules are a special set of rules to cover situations where it is appropriate to value a person's assets as a proportion of an enhanced combined value.

7.2 What is related property?

(a) Property is related to the property in a person's estate if:

    (i) It belongs to that person's spouse (this is the most likely situation in the examination).

    (ii) It is settled property of which that person's spouse has a life interest (an interest in possession).

    (iii) It is owned by a charity, qualifying political party, national body (as listed under exempt transfers) or housing association, and is so owned as a result of an exempt transfer by that person or that person's spouse.

    In this situation, the property continues to be related for five years after the exempt body has disposed of it.

(b) In simple terms, related property is therefore property that is owned by somebody that could have been the recipient of an exempt transfer.

(c) Property owned by a person's children or other family members, even if under the age of 18, is never related property.

(d) In the examination, the related property rules normally apply to unquoted shares.

However, the rules apply wherever a person owns a proportion of an asset and the spouse or certain exempt bodies (see above) own another proportion.

The rules might therefore also apply to collections of antiques and parcels of land.

7.3   The need for the related property valuation rules

(a)   Consider the following scenario:

(i)   On 1 July 1999 Joe owned 60% of the share capital of XYZ Ltd, an unquoted company. This shareholding was valued at £600,000.

(ii)   On 2 July 1999 Joe gave 30% of the XYZ Ltd shareholding to his wife. This transfer, being to a spouse, was exempt from IHT.

A 30% shareholding in XYZ Ltd is valued at £200,000,

Two 30% shareholdings are worth less than a 60% shareholding because 60% holding gives control, whilst a 30% holding is only a minority interest.

(iii)   On 3 July 1999 both Joe and his wife died in a car crash.

Without the related property rules, the estates of Joe and his wife would each include shares valued at £200,000 based on 30% shareholdings.

Under the related property rules, each estate would include a proportion of the combined valuation based on a 60% shareholding. This is £300,000 (600,000 x 30/60).

(b)   Although the related property rules are designed to prevent such tax savings schemes, they will apply even if there has not been an exempt transfer of assets to a person's spouse.

For example, the related property valuation of £300,000 would still apply to the shareholdings of Joe and his wife on 3 July 1999, even if the wife had originally purchased her 30% shareholding from another shareholder, rather than receiving it as a gift from Joe.

(c)   The same principle applies to transfers to exempt bodies. The value of a 51% shareholding (giving control) could be reduced by transferring a 2% shareholding to an exempt body. This would leave a 49% shareholding (a minority interest).

The loss of control would not matter if the person inheriting the 49% shareholding already had, say, a 10% shareholding.

(d)   The related property rules only apply if their use results in a higher valuation than the unrelated valuation.

(e)   As will be seen in the next chapter, the transfer of unquoted shares will usually attract 100% relief (business property relief).

This means that tax saving schemes involving unquoted shares are often not necessary.

7.4   Related property rules: Unquoted shares

The related property valuation is calculated as follows:

$$\frac{\text{Number of shares (transferor)}}{\text{Number of shares (transferor)} \times \text{Number of shares (related)}} \times \text{Combined value} = \text{RP value}$$

7.5   Example: Related property - Unquoted shares

FAD Ltd, an unquoted company, has an authorised share capital of 50,000 £1 shares held as follows:

	Shares	%
George	17,500	35
George's wife	15,000	30
Others	17,500	35
	50,000	100

The values of shareholdings have been agreed for IHT purposes as:

Holding	*Value per share*
Up to 25%	£2
26% to 50%	£4
51% to 74%	£6
75% or more	£8

On 31 December 1999 George died.

Calculate the value of George's shareholding.

7.6   Activity solution

George and his wife own 65% of the shares in FAD Ltd, so the combined value of their shareholding is £195,000 (£6 x (17,500 + 15,000)).

The value of George's shareholding is:

$$\frac{17,500}{17,500 + 15,000} \times 195,000 = £105,000$$

An easier approach would have been to say that a 65% shareholding is valued at £6 per share, and so George's shareholding is valued at 17,500 x £6 = £105,000.

The related valuation is greater than the unrelated valuation of £70,000 (17,500 x £4).

7.7   Related property rules: Other types of asset

The related property valuation is calculated as follows:

$$\frac{\text{Value of transferor's property}}{\text{Value of transferor's} + \text{Value of related}} \times \text{Combined value} = \text{RP value}$$
$$\text{property} \quad \text{property}$$

7.8   Example: Related property - Other types of asset

Sara owns two antique chairs which are part of a set of six. Her husband owns another three, and her daughter owns one.

The value of the chairs is as follows:

1 chair	£5,000
2 chairs	£15,000
3 chairs	£25,000
4 chairs	£40,000
5 chairs	£60,000
6 chairs	£90,000

Calculate the value of Sara's two chairs for IHT purposes.

7.9   Solution

Sara and her husband own five chairs between them, and five chairs have a combined value of £60,000.

The value of Sara's two chairs is:

$$\frac{15,000}{15,000 + 25,000} \times 60,000 = £22,500$$

The related valuation is greater than the unrelated valuation of £15,000.

Note that basing the calculation on two out of five chairs would not give the same answer and is not the correct technique (60,000 x 2/5 = £24,000).

8   SELF TEST QUESTIONS

8.1   What are the rates of IHT? (1.2)

8.2   Which people will be liable to IHT on their worldwide assets? (1.5)

8.3   What property is chargeable to IHT? (1.7)

8.4   What is an interest in possession trust? (2.4)

8.5   How does a discretionary trust differ from an interest in possession trust? (2.5)

8.6   What settled property is included in a deceased person's estate? (3.3)

8.7   Who is responsible for paying the IHT liability? (3.7)

8.8   When is it necessary to gross up on death? (5.5)

8.9   How are quoted shares valued? (6.2)

8.10   What is related property? (7.2)

9   EXAMINATION TYPE QUESTION

9.1   Fred

Fred died in a car crash on 4 October 1999.

Under the terms of his will, Fred's estate was left as follows:

(1)   £120,000 to his wife.
(2)   £50,000 to charity.
(3)   The residue of the estate to his son Joe.

At the date of his death Fred owned the following assets:

(1)   His main residence valued at £200,000.

(2)   A flat in London valued at £150,000. An endowment mortgage of £70,000 was secured on this property.

(3)   Four shops valued at £50,000 each. Fred's wife owns two adjacent shops valued at £60,000 each. The combined value of all six shops is £370,000.

(4)   A villa situated overseas worth 200,000 dollars. The exchange rate on 4 October 1999 was 10$ to £1.

(5)   A half share of partnership assets which are valued at £400,000 in total.

(6)   20,000 shares in ZAM plc. The shares were quoted at 198 - 206 on 4 October 1999, with bargains on that day of 196, 199 and 208.

(7)   8,000 units in the CBA unit trust, valued at 130 - 136.

(8)   Bank balances of £57,850.

Fred's outstanding income tax liability was £7,500, and his funeral expenses amounted to £2,000.

Fred was also a beneficiary of two trusts:

(1)   Under a trust set up by his father, he was entitled to all the income of the trust after the payment of an annuity of £1,250 p.a. to his brother. The annual income of the trust is £3,000, and on 4 October 1999 the assets of the trust were valued at £60,000.

(2)   Under a trust set up by his mother he was one of the beneficiaries who could receive the income at the trustees discretion. On 1 July 1999 he received a payment from the trust of £5,000. The assets of the trust were valued at £85,000 on 4 October 1999.

You are required to:

(a)   Calculate the IHT that will be payable as a result of Fred's death.

        You should assume that no reliefs other than the spouse and charity exemptions are available.

(b)   Show who is liable for the tax.

(c)   Show how the estate will be allocated between the beneficiaries.

10   ANSWER TO EXAMINATION TYPE QUESTION

10.1   Fred

(a)   Inheritance Tax computation

	£	£
FREE ESTATE		
Personalty		
Partnership share (400,000/2)		200,000
Shares in ZAM plc 20,000 @ 200p (note 1)		40,000
Units in CBA trust 8,000 @ 130p		10,400
Bank balances		57,850
		308,250
Less: Income tax due	7,500	
Funeral expenses	2,000	
		9,500
		298,750
Realty		
Freehold property - Main residence		200,000
Flat (note 2)		150,000
Shops (note 3)		231,250
Villa (200,000/10)		20,000
Net free estate		900,000

Less: Exempt legacies -	Wife	120,000	
	Charity	50,000	
		170,000	
		730,000	

SETTLED PROPERTY

Interest in possession (note 4)	35,000
Chargeable estate	765,000

| Inheritance tax payable | 231,000 at Nil | |
| | 534,000 at 40% = | 213,600 |

Rate of IHT on estate = 27.922% (213,600/765,000 × 100)

Note 1

The shares in ZAM plc are valued at the lower of:

198 + 1/4 (206 - 198) = 200p

1/2 (196 + 208) = 202p

Note 2

Since the endowment mortgage would have been repaid upon Fred's death, it is not deducted from the value of the flat.

Note 3

The shops are valued using the related property rules as follows:

$$\frac{200,000(50,000 \times 4)}{200,000 + 120,000(60,000 \times 2)} \times 370,000 = £231,250$$

This figure is higher than the unrelated valuation of £200,000.

Note 4

The value of the trust is £60,000. Fred's share is:

$$60,000 - \left(\frac{1,250 \times 60,000}{3,000}\right) \qquad = \qquad £35,000$$

Note 5

The trust set up by Fred's mother is a discretionary trust as Fred does not have the right to receive the income of the trust.

Its value does not therefore form part of Fred's estate.

(b)   IHT of £203,827 (730,000 at 27.922%) will be due from the estate and paid by the personal representatives.

IHT of £9,773 (35,000 at 27.922%) will be due by the trustees of the trust.

(c)   Fred's wife and the charity will receive £120,000 and £50,000 respectively.

Joe will receive £526,173 as follows:

	£
Value of free estate	900,000
Less: Legacies	(170,000)
Less: IHT	(203,827)
	526,173

Official ACCA *Textbook, published by AT Foulks Lynch*

30 RELIEFS AVAILABLE ON DEATH

INTRODUCTION

This chapter is concerned with the various reliefs that may be claimed against the value of an estate at death, and also the post mortem reliefs that may be claimed after the date of death.

1 BUSINESS PROPERTY RELIEF

1.1 Introduction

Business property relief is the most important of the reliefs that will be covered in this chapter, and features in the majority of examination questions on IHT.

1.2 The rate of relief

(a) Business property relief is given at the rate of 50% or 100% depending on the type of property involved.

(b) As the name implies, business property relief applies to relevant business property.

(c) The relief works by reducing the value of the business property included in a person's estate by the relevant percentage.

(d) There is no upper limit to the amount of relief that can be claimed.

(e) Business property relief also applies to business property situated overseas.

(f) The relief is mandatory if the qualifying conditions are met, so no claim is necessary.

1.3 100% Business property relief

Business property relief at the rate of 100% is available in respect of the following assets:

(a) Property consisting of a business or an interest in a business (such as a share in a partnership).

(b) Shares in an unquoted trading company. This includes shares quoted on the Alternative Investment Market.

1.4 50% Business property relief

Business property relief at the rate of 50% is available in respect of the following assets:

(a) A majority shareholding (over 50%) in a quoted company. The shareholding must give control of the company.

(b) Land, buildings, plant and machinery owned by an individual but used for business purposes by:

- A company of which the individual has control.
- A partnership of which the individual is a partner.

Relief is also available where assets are owned by a trust and are used in business by the life tenant, but this aspect of business property relief is not likely to be examined.

1.5 Related property rules

(a) The related property rules can be used in order to establish a controlling shareholding in a quoted company.

For example, if both a husband and his wife own 26% of the shares in a quoted company, then business property relief at the rate of 50% will be available in respect of each of their shareholdings.

(b) Business property relief at the rate of 100% applies to all shareholdings in unquoted trading companies.

As stated in the previous chapter, this limits the impact of the related property rules as regards unquoted shareholdings.

1.6 Activity

You are required to state whether the following assets, which are owned by David, will qualify for business property relief, and if so the percentage relief that will be given:

(1) 45% of the ordinary share capital of ABC plc, a quoted trading company.

(2) 15% of the ordinary share capital of DEF Ltd, an unquoted trading company.

(3) A factory owned personally by David, but used by a partnership of which David is not a partner.

(4) 35% of the ordinary share capital of GHI plc, a quoted trading company. David's wife also owns 12% of the share capital, and David's daughter owns a further 6%.

1.7 Activity solution

(1) There is no entitlement to business property relief as ABC plc is a quoted company, and David does not have control.

(2) Business property relief is available at the rate of 100% as DEF Ltd is an unquoted trading company.

(3) There is no entitlement to business property relief since David is not a partner.

(4) There is no business property relief since GHI plc is a quoted company, and David does not have control. Including his wife's related holding only results in a total shareholding of 47% (35 + 12).

1.8 Minimum period of ownership

(a) A very important condition that has to be satisfied before business property relief is available is that the property concerned must have been owned by the person claiming the relief throughout the preceding two years.

(b) The reason for a two year qualifying period is that it prevents a person purchasing business property just before the date of their death, in order to claim 100% relief and thus avoid IHT.

(c) In the case of property consisting of a business or an interest in a business, it is the business that must be owned for two years, and not the underlying assets of the business.

For example, the balance sheet of a sole trader may include assets which have only been owned for a few months. Provided the sole tradership has been run for two years, business property relief at the rate of 100% will be available.

(d) There are three exceptions to the two year qualifying period rule. These are not examined that often, but are as follows:

(i) Where business property is inherited from a spouse, then the period of ownership is deemed to include the period that the spouse owned the property.

For example, Peter inherited business property from his wife on 1 January 1998, but he himself died on 30 June 1999. Peter's wife had owned the property for one year.

Although Peter has only owned the property for 18 months, business property relief will be available since his wife's one year period of ownership can be included to make a total period exceeding two years.

(ii) Where business property has replaced other relevant business property.

In this case the combined period of ownership must be at least two years out of the preceding five years.

Business property relief is given on the lower of the two property values.

For example, Marsha had owned ordinary shares in JKL Ltd, an unquoted trading company, for four years until, on 31 December 1998, that company was taken over by MNO Ltd, another unquoted trading company. The consideration on the takeover consisted of ordinary shares in MNO Ltd.

Marsha died on 30 June 1999, at which date her shares in MNO Ltd were worth £160,000. Her shares in JKL Ltd had been worth £110,000 on 31 December 1998.

The shares in MNO Ltd are replacement property, and so business property relief at the rate of 100% will be available. However, the relief will be restricted to £110,000, and so £50,000 (160,000 - 110,000) will be chargeable to IHT.

(iii) Where business property was eligible for business property relief at the time that it was acquired, and was either acquired as a result of death, or is now chargeable as a result of death.

For example, on 30 June 1999 James was given business property by his uncle that was eligible for business property relief. James died on 30 September 1999.

Although James has only owned the property for three months, business property relief will be available as the property was eligible for business property relief at the time it was acquired, and is now chargeable as a result of James' death.

1.9   Non-qualifying businesses

(a) If a business or a company is wholly or mainly engaged in investment activities, then it does not qualify as relevant business property, and business property relief will therefore not be available.

(b) Investment activities consist of the following:

(i) Dealing in securities, stocks and shares.
(ii) Dealing in land and buildings.
(iii) Making or holding investments, which includes the holding of land that is let.

1.10   Excepted assets

(a)   Even if a business or a company is a qualifying business, not all of its assets will necessarily be eligible for business property relief.

(b)   Business property relief is not available in respect of assets that are classed as excepted assets. An excepted asset is one that:

(i)   Has not been used wholly or mainly for business purposes during the preceding two years, and

(ii)   Will not be required for future use in the business.

(c)   Examples of excepted assets are:

(i)   Land and buildings which are let out.
(ii)   Investments.
(iii)   Large cash balances in excess of reasonable business requirements.

(d)   Where a company is concerned, the proportion of the value of the shares qualifying for business property relief is found by multiplying the value of the shares by the fraction:

$$\frac{\text{The company's eligible business property}}{\text{The company's total assets (before deducting liabilities)}}$$

(e)   The aim of this anti-avoidance provision is to prevent someone obtaining business property relief on non-business assets by transferring them into their business just prior to death.

1.11   Example: Excepted assets owned by a company

Wendy died on 31 May 1999.

Included in her estate were 40,000 shares in STU Ltd, an unquoted trading company, which Wendy had owned since 1989. On 31 May 1999 the shares were worth £80,000.

At 31 May 1999 STU Ltd had assets worth £500,000. Included in this figure is property valued at £50,000 which is let out.

Wendy's other assets amounted to £290,000.

Calculate the IHT arising upon Wendy's death.

1.12   Solution

Wendy - Inheritance tax computation

	£
Shares in STU Ltd	80,000
Business property relief	
$80,000 \times \frac{450,000 \,(500,000-50,000)}{500,000} \times 100\%$	72,000
	8,000
Other assets	290,000
	298,000
Inheritance tax payable 231,000 at nil	
67,000 at 40%	26,800

1.13   Binding contracts for sale

(a)   Business property relief is not available if the asset concerned is subject to a binding contract for sale.

(b)   The most common example is where a partnership agreement provides for the interest of a partner to be sold to the other partners in the event of death.

Although the partnership share of a deceased partner is subject to IHT, no business property relief will be available.

2   AGRICULTURAL PROPERTY RELIEF

2.1   Introduction

Agricultural property relief is very similar to business property relief, but since it only applies to agricultural property is not quite so important for examination purposes.

2.2   The rate of relief

(a)   Agricultural property relief is given at the rate of 100%.

It is available in respect of the following assets:

(i)   Property where there is vacant possession (that is owner occupation).
(ii)   Property which is let on a lease commencing on or after 1 September 1995.

The examiner has stated that a question will not be set involving property let on a lease commencing before 1 September 1995.

(b)   As for business property relief, there is no upper limit to the amount of relief that can be claimed. However, relief is restricted to the agricultural value of the property, which may be less than the full commercial value.

For example, where planning consent has been given to develop farm land, its commercial value will probably be far in excess of its agricultural value.

(c)   Where agricultural property forms part of a business, then agricultural property relief is given before business property relief. Double relief is not available on the same value.

Subject to the relevant conditions being met, business property relief will be available on the value of business assets not qualifying for agricultural property relief.

Therefore in the previous example, if a business is being carried on then business property relief might be available in respect of the excess of the commercial value of the farm land over the agricultural value.

(d)   Unlike business property relief, agricultural property relief only applies to agricultural property situated in the UK (and also the Channel Islands and the Isle of Man).

(e)   The relief is mandatory if the qualifying conditions are met, so no claim is necessary.

2.3   Property qualifying for relief

The types of asset which qualify for agricultural property relief are:

(a)   Farm land.
(b)   Farm buildings, including the farmhouse.
(c)   Cottages.

Items such as farm animals and farm equipment do not qualify for agricultural property relief, but may qualify for business property relief.

2.4   Minimum period of ownership

(a)   If a person is farming in their own right, to qualify for the relief the property concerned must have been owned by that person throughout the preceding two years.

(b)   If the property is let, then the property concerned must have been owned by the landlord throughout the preceding seven years to qualify for the relief.

(c)   As for business property relief, there are exceptions to the minimum qualifying periods. Again, these are not examined very often, but are as follows:

   (i)   Where agricultural property is inherited from a spouse, then the period of ownership is deemed to include the period that the spouse owned the property.

   (ii)   Where agricultural property has replaced other relevant agricultural property.

   In order to meet the two year test, the combined period of ownership must be at least two years out of the preceding five years.

   In order to meet the seven year test, the combined period of ownership must be at least seven years out of the preceding ten years.

   Agricultural property relief is given on the lower of the two property values.

   (iii)   Where agricultural property was eligible for agricultural property relief at the time that it was acquired, and was either acquired as a result of death, or is now chargeable as a result of death.

   The land must be occupied for agricultural purposes by the person entitled to the relief.

2.5   Shares in farming companies

(a)   Agricultural property relief will be available in respect of shares in a farming company provided that:

   (i)   The shareholding gives control of the company.
   (ii)   The shareholding meets the two year (or seven year) test.

(b)   Agricultural property relief is only given against the agricultural value that can be attributed to the shares.

   The proportion of the value of the shares qualifying for agricultural property relief is found by multiplying the value of the shares by the fraction:

$$\frac{\text{The company's eligible agricultural property}}{\text{The company's total assets}}$$

2.6   Example: Shares in a farming company

John died on 31 October 1999.

Included in his estate was a 75% shareholding in Arable Ltd, an unquoted trading company which owns farm land. The farm land has been let to tenants for the previous nine years. The most recent tenancy commenced on 1 January 1998.

John had owned the shares in Arable Ltd since 1993. On 31 October 1999 the shares were worth £300,000. The balance sheet of Arable Ltd at that date was as follows:

	£
Farm land	350,000
Other assets	150,000
	500,000

The agricultural value of the farm land was £300,000. The other assets of £150,000 were all used in Arable Ltd's trade of providing services to local farmers.

John's other assets were valued at £280,000.

Calculate the IHT arising upon John's death.

2.7   Solution

Since Arable Ltd's farm land has been let out for the previous nine years, agricultural property relief is available.

Agricultural property relief is available as John's shareholding is a controlling one.

John - Inheritance tax computation

	£
Shares in Arable Ltd	300,000
Agricultural property relief	
$300,000 \times \dfrac{300,000}{500,000} \times 100\%$	(180,000)
Business property relief	
$300,000 \times \dfrac{150,000}{500,000} \times 100\%$	(90,000)
	30,000
Other assets	280,000
	310,000

Inheritance tax payable	231,000 at nil	
	79,000 at 40%	31,600

Note that business property relief is only available in respect of the non-agricultural value of the shares. Even then, the £50,000 value of the land not qualifying for APR does not qualify for BPR as it is an excepted asset.

2.8   Binding contracts for sale

Agricultural property relief is not available if the asset concerned is subject to a binding contract for sale.

3   QUICK SUCCESSION RELIEF

3.1   Introduction

As the name suggests, quick succession relief applies where property is charged to IHT twice in a short space of time.

The obvious situation is where two members of a family die within a few years of each other, the first person to die having made a bequest to the second person.

3.2   The relief available

(a)   Quick succession relief reduces the tax arising on the second transfer by an appropriate percentage of the tax charged on the earlier transfer.

Note that quick succession relief is different to the two reliefs looked at so far in this chapter, since it gives a tax credit against the IHT liability of an estate, rather than a reduction in the value of an estate.

(b)   The relevant percentages are as follows:

Period between the two transfers	*Percentage reduction*
Less than one year	100%
1 - 2 years	80%
2 - 3 years	60%
3 - 4 years	40%
4 - 5 years	20%

No relief is therefore available if the second transfer is more than five years after the date of the first transfer.

(c)   It is not actually necessary for the property received on the first transfer to still be owned at the date of the second transfer.

This makes sense, because the second person's estate will still be higher following the first transfer whether the original property is retained, or is exchanged for other property or is converted into cash.

3.3   Computation of the relief

Quick succession relief is computed using the formula:

$$\text{Tax paid on first transfer} \times \frac{\text{Net transfer}}{\text{Gross transfer}} \times \text{QSR\%}$$

The formula can also be shown as:

$$\text{Net transfer} \times \frac{\text{Tax paid on first transfer}}{\text{Gross transfer}} \times \text{QSR\%}$$

3.4   Example: Calculation of quick succession relief

Jane died on 30 September 1999.

Included in her estate were quoted shares valued at £100,000. Jane inherited these shares as a specific gift on the death of her father on 10 November 1995 when they were worth £50,000. Her father's executors paid IHT of £80,000 on an estate valued at £400,000.

Jane's other assets amounted to £280,000.

Calculate the IHT arising upon Jane's death.

3.5   Solution

Quick succession relief is available in respect of the quoted shares based on a percentage of 40% as Jane died between three and four years after inheriting them.

The quick succession relief is calculated as:

$$80,000 \times \frac{50,000}{400,000} \times 40\% = £4,000$$

The inheritance of £50,000 is a net figure since it is a specific gift of UK property.

The current value of the quoted shares is irrelevant to the calculation of quick succession relief.

Jane - Inheritance tax computation

		£
Quoted shares		100,000
Other assets		280,000
		380,000
Inheritance tax payable	231,000 at nil	
	149,000 at 40%	59,600
Quick succession relief		4,000
		55,600

3.6   Trust property

Quick succession relief is also available on trust property where there is an interest in possession, but it is unlikely that this aspect of the relief will be examined.

4   POST MORTEM RELIEFS

4.1   Introduction

It is possible to make adjustments to the value of an estate in respect of the sale of assets following the date of death.

Three different reliefs are available.

4.2   Quoted investments sold within 12 months of death

(a)   If an estate includes quoted shares or securities, then relief may be claimed if the personal representatives sell any of those investments at a loss within 12 months of the date of death.

(b)   The claim applies to any shares or securities quoted on a recognised stock exchange, and to units in an authorised unit trust.

Unquoted shares and shares dealt with on the Alternative Investment Market do not qualify.

(c)   The disposal must be by the personal representatives.

Disposals by a beneficiary of the estate do not qualify.

(d)   All quoted investments sold during the 12 month period following the date of death must be taken into account. It is not possible to only consider those investments sold at a loss.

It may therefore be sensible tax planning for the personal representatives to postpone the sale of investments standing at a profit until after 12 months have expired.

(e)   The loss (or profit) is calculated as the difference between the probate value (value per the estate) and the gross sale proceeds.

No relief is therefore given for any selling expenses such as brokerage.

(f)   The net loss is deducted from the value of property in the estate at death, and the IHT on the whole estate is recalculated.

In examinations, it is usually acceptable to simply calculate the tax saving.

4.3   Example: Sale of quoted investments within 12 months of death

An estate valued at £400,000 included the following quoted investments which were all sold by the personal representatives within 12 months of the date of death:

	Probate value £	*Sale proceeds* £
ABC plc	150,000	165,000
DEF plc	80,000	58,000
GHI plc	15,000	12,000

Calculate the IHT saving if relief is claimed for the sales within 12 months of death.

4.4   Solution

Since all sales within the 12 month period have to be included, the net loss is £10,000 as follows:

	£
Probate value (150,000 + 80,000 + 15,000) =	245,000
Sale proceeds (165,000 + 58,000 + 12,000) =	235,000
	10,000

A claim by the personal representatives will result in a £4,000 (10,000 at 40%) reduction in the IHT liability of the estate.

4.5   Reinvestment of sale proceeds

(a)   Relief is restricted if the personal representatives reinvest the sale proceeds by buying further quoted investments.

(b)   The aim of this restriction is partly to prevent the personal representatives from bed and breakfasting investments (selling and then buying back immediately) so as to establish a loss for IHT purposes.

(c)   The net loss is reduced by the following amount:

$$\text{Net loss on disposal} \times \frac{\text{Amount reinvested}}{\text{Sale proceeds}}$$

The figures for the amount reinvested and for the sale proceeds exclude purchase and selling expenses respectively.

(d)   Only amounts reinvested during the period running from the date of death to two months after the date of the last qualifying sale during the 12 month period are included.

Although not strictly reinvestment, purchases made before a sale takes place are also included.

4.6   Example: Reinvestment of sale proceeds

Following on from the previous example, the personal representatives reinvested £47,000 of the sale proceeds in further quoted investments one month after the date of the last sale.

Calculate the relief that will now be available.

4.7   Solution

The net loss of £10,000 will be restricted to £8,000 as follows;

	£
Net loss	10,000
Less: $10,000 \times \dfrac{47,000}{235,000} =$	2,000
	8,000

The IHT saving will be reduced to £3,200 (8,000 at 40%).

4.8   Land and buildings sold within four years of death

(a)   This relief is similar to that applicable to the sale of quoted investments.

(b)   If an estate includes land and buildings, then relief may be claimed if the personal representatives sell any of these at a loss within four years of the date of death.

(c)   The claim applies to both freehold and leasehold property, although the relief for short leasehold property is restricted. This aspect is not likely to be examined.

(d)   The disposal must be by the personal representatives.

(e)   As for quoted investments, all sales of land and buildings during the four year period must be taken into account. However, the following sales are ignored:

    (i)   A sale during the fourth year following the date of death if it results in a profit.

    (ii)   A sale (whether it results in a profit or a loss) if the difference between the probate value and the selling price is less than the lower of:

        -     £1,000, or
        -     5% of the probate value.

(f)   As for quoted shares, no relief is given for any selling expenses such as estate agents fees.

The sale must be an arm's length transaction, and the best consideration that could reasonably have been obtained at the time of sale will replace the actual proceeds if it is greater.

(g)   Reinvestment in further land and buildings will result in the relief being restricted.

The net loss is reduced by the following amount:

$$\text{Net loss on disposal} \times \frac{\text{Amount reinvested}}{\text{Sale proceeds}}$$

The figures for the amount reinvested and for the sale proceeds exclude purchase and selling expenses respectively.

Only amounts reinvested during the period running from the date of death to four months after the date of the last qualifying sale during the three years following death are included.

Note that the reinvestment period is only three years, and not four. This mismatch has arisen due to the way in which the relief was extended from three years to four years, in order to give personal representatives more time to dispose of property in a depressed property market.

4.9   Example: Sale of land and buildings within four years of death

Tony died on 1 May 1999 leaving an estate valued at £500,000. Included in this figure are the following land and buildings which have subsequently been sold by the personal representatives:

	Probate value £	*Sale proceeds* £	*Date of sale*
Property A	91,500	90,000	15.6.99
Property B	9,000	9,400	30.8.99
Property C	115,000	100,000	31.10.99

The personal representatives reinvested £47,500 of the sale proceeds by buying property D on 15 January 2000.

Calculate the IHT saving if relief is claimed for the sales within four years of death.

4.10   Solution

	£
Property A	
Loss (91,500 - 90,000)	1,500
This is included as the loss is greater than £1,000.	
Property B	
Profit (9,000 - 9,400) = £400	
This is ignored as the profit is less than 5% of the probate value (9,000 x 5% = 450)	
Property C	
Loss (115,000 - 100,000)	15,000
	16,500
Less: Restriction	
$16,500 \times \dfrac{47,500}{(90,000 + 100,000)} =$	4,125
	12,375

A claim by the personal representatives will result in a £4,950 (12,375 at 40%) reduction in the IHT liability of the estate.

Note that the proceeds from the sale of property B are ignored when calculating the restriction.

4.11   Related property sold within three years of death

(a)   Where an estate includes property which has been valued using the related property rules, then relief is available if that property is sold within three years of the date of death.

(b)   The relief only applies where the property is sold for less than its probate value (using the related property rules).

(c)   The relief operates by cancelling the related property valuation and substituting it with a normal valuation. The property is therefore valued at the date of death, but the related property rules are ignored.

The actual sale proceeds are irrelevant as regards the revised valuation.

(d)   A claim may affect entitlement to business property relief in respect of shares in a quoted company.

For example, a deceased's estate includes 45% of the share capital of a quoted company. If the deceased's spouse also owned 6% of the share capital, then business property relief at the rate of 50% would be available.

Claiming to have the related property valuation for the 45% shareholding replaced by an unrelated valuation would probably not be beneficial as business property relief would then not be available.

4.12   Activity

Simone died on 15 July 1999 leaving an estate of £400,000.

Included in her estate are two paintings which form part of a set of five. The other three paintings in the set are owned by Simone's husband.

The paintings are valued as follows:

1 painting	£8,000
2 paintings	£18,000
3 paintings	£30,000
4 paintings	£45,000
5 paintings	£70,000

The personal representatives of Simone's estate sold the two paintings to an unrelated third party on 15 October 1999 for £25,000.

Calculate the IHT saving if relief is claimed for the sale of related property.

4.13   Activity solution

The five paintings in the set have a combined value of £70,000.

The related property value of Simone's two paintings is:

$$\frac{18,000}{18,000 + 30,000} \times 70,000 = £26,250$$

The paintings are sold for £25,000, which is less than the related property valuation of £26,250, and so relief can be claimed. The paintings will then be valued at the unrelated valuation of £18,000.

A claim by the personal representatives will result in a £3,300 (26,250 - 18,000 = 8,250 at 40%) reduction in the IHT liability of the estate.

5   TAX PLANNING AND MAKING A WILL

5.1   Introduction

There are a number of straightforward tax planning measures that can reduce the impact of IHT.

It is therefore important for a person to make a will so that their estate is distributed in a tax efficient way.

5.2   IHT planning for husband and wives

(a)   Where possible, each spouse should hold chargeable assets at least equal to £231,000.

This will ensure that each spouse utilises their nil rate band when they die.

(b)   The above planning is negated if the couple's wills are drawn up so that property is left to the other spouse upon death.

The aim should be for each spouse to leave chargeable assets of at least £231,000 to, for example, their children so that the £231,000 nil rate bands are utilised.

(c)   The assets involved in such tax planning should be those not covered by a 100% relief such as business property relief.

Such property will not utilise the nil rate band.

5.3   Example: IHT planning for husbands and wives

Bob is 66 years old and has a chargeable estate valued at £60,000.

His wife Flo is 67 years old, and has a chargeable estate valued at £440,000.

Bob and Flo have both made wills which, upon the death of either of them, leave all their assets to the surviving spouse.

The couple have two children.

You are required to advise Bob and Flo of tax planning measures that they could take in order to reduce their potential IHT liability.

5.4   Solution

The present position is that upon the death of either Bob or Flo, the property of the deceased spouse will pass to the surviving spouse. This would be an exempt transfer.

The IHT payable on the death of the second spouse would be £107,600 as follows:

		£
Chargeable estate of surviving spouse (60,000 + 440,000)		500,000
		———
IHT liability 231,000 at nil 269,000 at 40%		107,600
		———

There are two main tax planning measures that the couple could adopt.

(1)   During her lifetime, Flo should transfer assets worth £171,000 to Bob.

They will then benefit from two nil rate bands of £231,000.

(2)   The couple should redraw their wills, since leaving their estates to each other negates the above advice should one spouse die before the other.

Subject to retaining sufficient assets to provide an income to live on, property should be left to their children under the terms of each will sufficient to utilise the £231,000 nil rate band.

Their revised IHT position were they to die would probably be:

	Bob £	Flo £
Chargeable estate	231,000	269,000
IHT liability		
231,000 at nil		
38,000 at 40%	–	15,200

This is an IHT saving of £92,400 (107,600 - 15,200).

5.5   The choice of assets

When choosing between different investments, their IHT treatment will be an important consideration.

For example, the availability of business property relief at the rate of 100% will mean that an investment in unquoted shares will not usually be subject to IHT.

An investment in quoted shares only attracts relief if the shareholding gives control, and this will not normally be the case.

However, the commercial merits of an investment must also be considered, and it is not worth making a poor investment simply to save tax.

5.6   Missing a generation

(a)   Rather than leaving property to children, it can make sense to miss them out and to leave the property instead to grandchildren.

(b)   There will be no immediate saving of IHT, but a charge to IHT on the death of the children will be avoided.

(c)   Such planning is particularly relevant if the children already have sufficient property in their own right.

(d)   The income tax benefits of this arrangement may also be attractive, due to the restriction that applies to parental gifts.

5.7   Varying the terms of the deceased's will

(a)   There are three ways in which the terms of a will can be varied after the testator's death.

The one most likely to be relevant in the examination is a deed of variation, which is also known as a deed of family arrangement.

(b)   A deed of variation is a voluntary agreement whereby the beneficiaries under the terms of a will agree to change the provisions of that will.

(c)   As far as examination questions are concerned, the reason for making such a change is usually for tax planning purposes. Typical situations would be:

(i) Where an estate has been left to the surviving spouse without utilising (or fully utilising) the deceased's nil rate band of £231,000.

Provided that the surviving spouse is left with sufficient property to provide an income to live on, part of the estate could be diverted to, say, the children.

(ii) Where an estate has been left to children who already have sufficient property of their own.

Part of the estate could be diverted to grandchildren, thus missing out a generation.

The making of a deed of variation therefore provides an opportunity for tax planning which is similar to that looked at in the previous section.

In real life, the reason for making a deed of variation is often to redistribute the deceased's estate on a fairer basis.

(d) A deed of variation must:

(i) Be in writing.
(ii) Be signed by all the beneficiaries that are affected by the deed.
(iii) Be executed within two years of the date of death.
(iv) Not be made for a consideration.

To be effective for IHT purposes, a written election must then be sent to the Inland Revenue within six months of making the deed of variation.

(e) The effect of making the election is that for IHT purposes the deceased's will is treated as being re-written.

Therefore, a beneficiary whose benefit is reduced under the revised terms of the will, is not treated as making a gift of property that might be subject to IHT.

(f) The other two ways of varying the terms of a deceased's will are:

(i) By a deed of disclaimer.

This is similar to a deed of variation, but is more limited in that it simply consists of a beneficiary disclaiming a legacy (gift) to which they are entitled.

The legacy is then distributed according to the terms of the will, and will therefore probably form part of the residue of the estate.

A deed of disclaimer must be in writing, and must be executed within two years of the date of death.

(ii) Application can be made to the courts by the family and dependants of the deceased if they feel that they have not been adequately provided for under the terms of the deceased's will.

5.8   Activity

Joan is 67 years old, and was widowed on the death of her husband six months ago.

The husband had a chargeable estate valued at £160,000, and this was left entirely to Joan.

Joan now has an estate valued at £500,000, which will pass to her two children when she dies. Joan's children are both quite wealthy, and are concerned about the IHT liability that will arise upon Joan's death.

Joan has six grandchildren.

You are to advise Joan and her children of tax planning measures that they could take in order to minimise the impact of IHT.

5.9   Activity solution

The following tax planning measures should be considered:

(a)   The will of Joan's husband can be varied by a deed of variation during the next 18 months followed by an IHT election within 6 months of the deed.

(b)   Assuming that Joan does not require the £160,000 from her husband's estate, this amount will then pass to her children or grandchildren as if under the terms of her husband's will.

(c)   This will not result in an IHT liability since his nil rate band of £231,000 does not appear to have been utilised.

(d)   The potential IHT liability that would arise on Joan's death will be reduced by £64,000 (160,000 at 40%).

(e)   For IHT purposes it is usually beneficial to miss out a generation when making gifts of property.

Property is then only taxed once, rather than twice, before being inherited by the third generation of a family.

(f)   Since Joan's children are already wealthy, it would therefore appear to be beneficial for the grandchildren to inherit the £160,000 from the estate of Joan's husband.

(g)   If required, this property could be held in trust (for example an accumulation and maintenance trust) until the grandchildren reach 18 or 21.

6   SELF TEST QUESTIONS

6.1   What types of business property qualify for relief at the rate of 50%? (1.4)

6.2   As regards business property relief, what are excepted assets? (1.10)

6.3   Which assets qualify for agricultural property relief? (2.3)

6.4   How is quick succession relief calculated? (3.3)

6.5   What relief is available for quoted investments sold within 12 months of the date of death? (4.2)

6.6   In what situation is this relief restricted? (4.5)

6.7   What are the de minimis limits for sales of land and buildings within the four years following death? (4.8)

6.8   What relief is available for the sale of property which at the date of death was valued on a related property basis? (4.11)

6.9   Within what period must such a sale be made to qualify for relief? (4.11)

6.10   How may the provisions of a will be changed? (5.7)

7   EXAMINATION TYPE QUESTION

7.1   Martin

Martin died on 31 July 1999. At the time of his death, Martin owned the following assets:

(1)   15,000 £1 ordinary shares in ABC Ltd, an unquoted trading company with an issued share capital of 100,000 shares.

Martin's wife also owns 15,000 shares in ABC Ltd.

Both these shareholdings were acquired five years ago.

The relevant values of ABC Ltd's shares, as agreed by the Inland Revenue, are as follows:

Shareholding	Value per share
	£
15%	10.00
30%	13.00

ABC Ltd has assets worth £3,000,000 of which £500,000 are investments in quoted shares.

(2)   100,000 £1 ordinary shares in DEF plc, a quoted trading company with an issued share capital of 20,000,000 shares.

DEF plc's shares were quoted on the Stock Exchange at 208 - 216 on 31 July 1999, with recorded bargains of 196, 222 and 228 for that day.

(3)   A holiday cottage valued at £120,000.

Martin had inherited this 18 months ago on the death of his uncle. The gross transfer was £90,000 and IHT of £22,500 was paid.

(4)   Bank and cash balances of £150,000.

(5)   Other assets valued for IHT purposes at £200,000.

Under the terms of his will, Martin left £100,000 in cash to his wife, and the residue of his estate to his daughter.

Martin's wife is not domiciled in the UK.

Following Martin's death, the following occurred:

(1)   On 30 September 1999 the executors of Martin's estate sold the 15,000 shares in ABC Ltd for £180,000.

(2)   On 15 December 1999 the executors of Martin's estate sold the 100,000 shares in DEF plc for £185,000.

(3)   On 18 December 1999 the executors of Martin's estate bought 10,000 shares in GHI plc, a quoted company, for £55,500.

You are required to:

(a)   Calculate the IHT liability arising as a result of Martin's death on 31 July 1999.

(b)   State what IHT reliefs will be available as a result of the disposals by the executors of Martin's estate on 30 September 1999 and 15 December 1999.

8   ANSWER TO EXAMINATION TYPE QUESTION

8.1   Martin

(a)   The IHT liability due on Martin's estate will be as follows:

	£	£
Shares in ABC Ltd (working 1)		195,000
Business property relief (working 2)		162,500
		32,500
Shares in DEF plc (working 3)		210,000
Holiday cottage		120,000
Bank and cash balances	150,000	
Exempt legacy - wife	55,000	
		95,000
Other assets		200,000
Chargeable estate		657,500
IHT liability 231,000 at Nil		
426,500 at 40%		170,600
Quick succession relief (working 4)		13,500
		157,100

Only £55,000 of the legacy to Martin's wife is exempt since she is not domiciled in the UK.

WORKINGS

(W1)   The shares in ABC Ltd are valued using the related property rules, and the value is therefore based on a 30% shareholding.

15,000 × £13.00 = 195,000

(W2)   Business property relief is calculated as follows:

$$195,000 \times \frac{2,500,000 \, (3,000,000 - 500,000)}{3,000,000} \times 100\% = £162,500$$

(W3)   The shares in DEF plc are valued using the lower of:

208 + 1/4 (216 - 208) = 210p, or

1/2 (196 + 228) = 212p

The valuation is therefore £210,000 (100,000 at 210p).

(W4) The quick succession relief is calculated as follows:

$$22,500 \times \frac{67,500}{90,000} \frac{(90,000 - 22,500)}{} \times 80\% = \pounds13,500$$

(b) Sale of shares in ABC Ltd on 30 September 1999

The shares in ABC Ltd were valued as related property in Martin's estate.

They have been sold within three years of 31 July 1999 for £180,000 which is less than their valuation using the related property rules of £195,000.

The executors of Martin's estate can claim for relief based on the unrelated value as follows:

	£	£
Original valuation		195,000
Business property relief		162,500
		32,500
Unrelated valuation (based on a 15% holding)		
15,000 × £10.00 =	150,000	
Business property relief		
$150,000 \times \frac{2,500,000}{3,000,000} \times 100\% =$	125,000	
		25,000
Reduction in value		7,500
Reduction in IHT liability 7,500 at 40% =		3,000

Sale of shares in DEF plc on 15 December 1999

The shares in DEF plc are quoted investments.

They have been sold within 12 months of 31 July 1999 for less than their value at that date.

The executors of Martin's estate can claim for relief as follows:

	£
Net loss (210,000 - 185,000)	25,000
This is restricted as a result of reinvestment	
Less: $25,000 \times \frac{55,500}{185,000} =$	7,500
	17,500
Reduction in IHT liability 17,500 at 40% =	7,000

31 LIFETIME GIFTS

INTRODUCTION

(a)   The previous two chapters have looked at the IHT charge that arises upon a person's death.

   If IHT only applied to a person's estate at death, then it would be quite easy for a person to avoid IHT by giving away their property before they died.

   IHT therefore extends to gifts made during a person's lifetime.

(b)   The predecessor to IHT was capital transfer tax, which applied to all gifts made during a person's lifetime although these rules were eventually relaxed.

   IHT was introduced in 1986, and generally only applies to those gifts made within seven years of death.

1   TRANSFERS OF VALUE

1.1   Introduction

During a person's lifetime, IHT only arises if a transfer of value is made.

> **Definition**   A transfer of value is any gratuitous disposition made by a person which results in a diminution in value of that person's estate.

Put simply, a transfer of value is a gift which reduces the value of a person's estate.

However, the term "disposition" is somewhat wider than a "gift", since it covers any act which reduces the value of a person's estate.

1.2   Activity

Norman owns 99 ordinary shares in a company which has a share capital of 100 shares. Norman's son owns the other one share.

If Norman were to change his 99 shares from voting shares into non-voting shares, would this be a disposition?

1.3   Activity solution

Control of the company has effectively passed from Norman to his son.

Although no actual gift has been made, the value of Norman's estate has fallen.

This is therefore a disposition.

1.4   The lack of gratuitous intent

(a)   A disposition is not a transfer of value unless there is gratuitous intent.

   A good example is where a person mistakenly sells a picture to an unrelated third party for £100, when in fact the picture proves to be worth £100,000.

   This is simply a bad bargain, and is unlikely to be treated as a transfer of value.

(b)   It must be shown that a transaction:

(i)   Was made at arm's length between unconnected persons, or

(ii)   It was on terms that would have been made in such circumstances.

(c)   Where a transaction is with a connected person, it will therefore be much more difficult to prove the lack of gratuitous intent.

It will be necessary to demonstrate that the same terms would have applied to a similar transaction with an unconnected person.

(d)   A connected person has already been defined for the purposes of CGT. Briefly, a person is connected to:

(i)   His spouse.

(ii)   Relatives

(iii)   His wife's relatives.

(iv)   Business partners.

(e)   Commercial transactions which result in a diminution of value are not treated as transfers of value.

This would include Xmas presents that an employer gives to his or her employees.

(f)   Expenditure on family maintenance is also not treated as a transfer of value.

This would cover school fees paid for a minor child by the parent or guardian.

1.5   Activity: Gratuitous intent

John has:

(a)   Sold a house valued at £120,000 to a purchaser who paid £105,000.

(b)   Been burgled, as a result of which he lost goods worth £10,000. These were not insured.

(c)   Lost £5,000 to his daughter in a card game.

Which of the above are likely to be treated as transfers of value?

1.6   Activity solution

(a)   John's estate has diminished in value by £15,000. However, provided this was an arm's length transaction with an unconnected purchaser, it will not be a transfer of value.

It might be the case that John sold the house below market value in order to achieve a quick sale. If the sale is to a connected person, it might therefore be possible to establish that the terms were what would have been expected in an arm's length transaction with an unconnected person.

(b)   John's estate has diminished in value by £10,000, but clearly there is no gratuitous intent. This is therefore not a transfer of value.

(c)   John's estate has diminished in value by £5,000 as a result of a transaction with a connected person.

In order to establish that this is not a transfer of value it would be necessary to show:

(i)   That John was in the habit of playing cards with a number of people, including his daughter.

(ii)   That sometimes he lost, and sometimes he won.

(iii)   That the conditions in the game when he lost £5,000 were quite normal.

(iv)   That it would have been possible for John to have lost a similar amount to an unconnected person.

1.7   Diminution in value

(a)   In calculating a transfer of value, it is the diminution in value of a person's estate that is relevant.

(b)   In many cases, the diminution in value of a person's estate will be straightforward.

For example, a parent gives a son £20,000 in cash. The parent's estate has diminished in value by £20,000, and this is therefore the transfer of value.

(c)   However, in other cases it is necessary to compare:

(i)   The value of the donor's estate before the gift, and
(ii)   The value of the donor's estate after the gift.

(d)   This will be relevant where the value of an asset in its entirety is worth more than the sum of its individual parts. For example, a set of three paintings might be worth £3,000 in total when valued as a set, but individually the paintings may only be worth £750 each.

The diminution in value rule is particularly important where shares in unquoted companies are concerned.

1.8   Example: diminution in value

Adam owns 51,000 shares (a 51% holding) in GHI Ltd.

On 30 April 1999 he gave 2,000 of the shares (a 2% holding) to his son.

The relevant values of GHI Ltd's shares are as follows:

Shareholding	Value per share
	£
51%	15
49%	11
2%	4

Calculate the transfer of value made by Adam on 30 April 1999.

1.9   Solution

	£
Value of shares held before the transfer	
51,000 × £15	765,000
Value of shares held after the transfer	
49,000 × £11	539,000
	————
Value transferred	226,000
	————

Adam has therefore made a transfer of value of £226,000. This is despite the fact that a 2% shareholding in isolation is only valued at £8,000 (2,000 × £4), and that this is the amount by which the son's estate will have increased.

The reason for the large difference between the isolated value and the diminution in value is due to Adam moving from being a controlling shareholder to being a minority shareholder. The diminution in value takes into account the fact that the 49,000 shares retained by Adam have fallen in value.

Note that for CGT purposes the deemed sale proceeds would be taken as the value of the gift in isolation, which in this case would be £8,000. The relationship of CGT with IHT will be looked at in more depth in chapter 33.

1.10 Valuation rules

(a)   In computing the value of the donor's estate both before and after the gift, the valuation rules used are the same as those applicable to a person's estate at death (see chapter 29).

(b)   In particular, the related property valuation rules also apply to lifetime gifts.

Where the rules apply, it is necessary to compare:

(i)   The donor's proportion of the combined value of the related property before the gift, and

(ii)   The donor's proportion of the combined value of the related property after the gift.

1.11 Example: Related property - Unquoted shares

ABC Ltd has an authorised share capital of 100,000 £1 shares held as follows:

	Shares	*%*
Joy	30,000	30
Joy's husband	30,000	30
Others	40,000	40
	100,000	100

The value of shareholdings have been agreed for IHT purposes as:

Holding	*Value per share*
Up to 25%	£4
26% to 50%	£7
51% to 74%	£12
75% or more	£15

On 30 June 1999 Joy made a gift of 20,000 of her shares to her son.

Calculate the transfer of value for IHT purposes.

1.12 Solution

Before the gift, Joy and her husband owned 60% of the shares in ABC Ltd, so the combined value of their shareholding was £720,000 (£12 × (30,000 + 30,000)).

After the gift, Joy and her husband own 40% of the shares in ABC Ltd, so the combined value of their shareholding is £280,000 (£7 × (10,000 + 30,000)).

The transfer of value is £290,000 as follows:

	£
Value of shares held before the transfer	
$\frac{30,000}{30,000+30,000} \times 720,000 =$	360,000
Value of shares held after the transfer	
$\frac{10,000}{10,000+30,000} \times 280,000 =$	70,000
Value transferred	290,000

Alternatively, it is possible to say that a 60% shareholding is worth £12 per share, whilst a 40% shareholding is worth £7 per share. The calculation is then as follows:

	£
Value of shares held before the transfer 30,000 × £12	360,000
Value of shares held after the transfer 10,000 × £7	70,000
Value transferred	290,000

The related property valuation is used because it is higher than the unrelated valuation, which is £170,000 as follows:

	£
Value of shares held before the transfer 30,000 × £7 (30% shareholding)	210,000
Value of shares held after the transfer 10,000 × £4 (10% shareholding)	40,000
Value transferred	170,000

1.13   Activity

Alex owns two antique pictures which are part of a set of five. His wife owns the other three pictures.

The value of the pictures is as follows:

1 picture	£10,000
2 pictures	£22,000
3 pictures	£38,000
4 pictures	£56,000
5 pictures	£84,000

On 15 July 1999 Alex gave one of his pictures to his son.

Calculate the transfer of value for IHT purposes.

1.14   Activity solution

Before the gift, Alex and his wife owned all five pictures, and these had a combined value of £84,000.

After the gift, Alex and his wife own four pictures, and these have a combined value of £56,000.

The transfer of value is £19,133 as follows:

	£
Value of pictures held by Alex before the transfer $\dfrac{22,000}{22,000+38,000} \times 84,000 =$	30,800
Value of pictures held after the transfer $\dfrac{10,000}{10,000+38,000} \times 56,000 =$	11,667
Value transferred	19,133

The related valuation is greater than the unrelated valuation of, which is calculated as follows;

	£
Value of pictures held before the transfer	22,000
Value of picture held after the transfer	10,000
Value transferred	12,000

1.15 Chargeable transfers

Definition A chargeable transfer is any transfer of value not covered by an exemption.

(a) A charge to IHT arises when a person makes a transfer of value which is not covered by an exemption.

(b) There are a number of exemptions available in respect of lifetime transfers, and these will be covered in the next chapter.

(c) However, one very important exemption (see below) depends upon the length of time that the donor lives after making a lifetime transfer.

2 POTENTIALLY EXEMPT TRANSFERS (PETs)

2.1 Introduction

As stated at the beginning of this chapter, IHT generally only applies to lifetime transfers made within seven years of death.

2.2 What is a PET?

(a) The majority of lifetime transfers are PETs.

A PET is a lifetime transfer which is made by an individual to any of the following:

    (i)   Another individual.
    (ii)   An interest in possession trust.
    (iii)   An accumulation and maintenance trust.

There are some other situations where a lifetime transfer is a PET, but these are not likely to be examined.

(b) The only type of lifetime transfer made by an individual which is not a PET is therefore one made to a discretionary trust.

This type of transfer will be looked at later in this chapter.

(c) Transfers made on death are never PETs.

2.3 The implications of the donor dying within seven years of making a PET

(a) If the donor lives for more than seven years after making a PET, then the transfer is completely exempt from IHT.

Therefore, at the time that such a transfer is made, it has the potential to be exempt. Hence the term "potentially exempt transfer".

(b) It would be impractical if IHT was due at the time that a PET was made, with a refund being made once the donor has lived for seven years.

Therefore, IHT in respect of PETs is not due until they become chargeable, which will only be when the donor dies within seven years of making the gift.

(c) A PET made more than seven years before the donor dies thus has no IHT implications whatsoever.

2.4 Activity

Daniel made the following gifts during his lifetime:

(a) £20,000 on 31 October 1991 to an accumulation and maintenance trust.
(b) £40,000 on 31 August 1992 to a discretionary trust.
(c) £25,000 on 30 September 1992 to his daughter.
(d) £60,000 on 31 May 1996 to an interest in possession trust.

Daniel died on 30 June 1999.

Which of Daniel's lifetime gifts would have been PETs, and which of these will be chargeable as a result of his death.

2.5 Activity solution

(a) The gift is a PET. It will not be chargeable as it was made more than seven years before 30 June 1999.

(b) The gift is not a PET as it is made to a discretionary trust.

(c) The gift is a PET, which will become chargeable as a result of Daniel dying within seven years.

(d) The gift is a PET, which will become chargeable as a result of Daniel dying within seven years.

2.6 PETs becoming chargeable

(a) Even though the IHT on a PET is not due until it becomes chargeable, the value of the transfer is fixed at the time that the gift is made.

(b) The nil rate band of £231,000 is available in respect of chargeable lifetime transfers.

Only one nil rate band of £231,000 is available, and it will be utilised according to the order that transfers are made.

(c) The availability of the £231,000 nil rate band will often mean that no IHT is due in respect of chargeable lifetime transfers.

However, the utilisation of the nil rate band will result in a correspondingly higher charge to IHT for the estate at death.

2.7 Example: PETs becoming chargeable

Fred died on 30 June 1999 leaving an estate valued at £350,000.

Fred had made the following lifetime transfers:

(a) £60,000 on 31 July 1991 to his son.
(b) £90,000 on 30 November 1996 to his daughter.
(c) £190,000 on 30 April 1997 to his son.

Calculate the IHT arising as a result of Fred's death on 30 June 1999. You should ignore any reliefs and exemptions that might be available.

2.8   Solution

(a)   The PET made on 31 July 1991 is more than seven years before 30 June 1999, and is therefore completely exempt.

(b)   No IHT arises at the time that the PETs on 30 November 1996 and 30 April 1997 are made.

They will become chargeable as a result of Fred's death within seven years. The IHT liability is as follows:

	£
30 November 1996	90,000
Inheritance tax payable 90,000 at nil	Nil
30 April 1997	190,000
Inheritance tax payable 141,000 at nil	
49,000 at 40%	19,600

Only £141,000 (231,000 - 90,000) of the nil rate band is available.

Estate at death	350,000
Inheritance tax payable 350,000 at 40%	140,000

None of the nil rate band is available in respect of the estate at death.

2.9   Responsibility for the payment of the IHT liability

The IHT liability that arises on PETs becoming chargeable is always the responsibility of the donee.

In the example above, Fred's son would have been responsible for the IHT liability of £19,600 in respect of the PET made on 30 April 1997.

3   CHARGEABLE LIFETIME TRANSFERS

3.1   Introduction

A lifetime transfer made by an individual to a discretionary trust is not a PET.

Such a gift is chargeable at the time that it is made, and is therefore a chargeable lifetime transfer.

3.2   The reason for the lifetime charge

(a)   Discretionary trusts do not have an interest in possession, and therefore they cannot form part of a beneficiary's estate.

(b)   Discretionary trusts are therefore penalised in two ways:

(i)   Various IHT charges are raised on the trust itself. These charges are considered in detail in chapter 34.
(ii)   Lifetime transfers to discretionary trusts are immediately chargeable.

3.3   The rates of tax

(a)   Chargeable lifetime transfers are immediately charged to IHT at half of the full rate of IHT, so the rate of tax will be either 0% or 20% as appropriate.

(b)   An additional charge to IHT arises if the donor dies within seven years of making a chargeable lifetime transfer.

This charge is at the full rate of IHT (0% or 40% as appropriate), although credit is given for any IHT already paid.

(c)   Should the donor live for more than seven years after making a chargeable lifetime transfer, then an additional charge to IHT does not arise.

However, any IHT paid during lifetime at the rate of 20% is never refunded.

3.4   Example: The rates of tax

Zoe died on 30 September 1999 leaving an estate valued at £550,000.

On 15 July 1997 Zoe had made a transfer of £283,000 into a discretionary trust. The IHT due in respect of this gift was paid by the discretionary trust.

Calculate the IHT arising as a result of Zoe's gift on 15 July 1997, and her death on 30 September 1999. You should ignore any reliefs and exemptions that might be available.

3.5   Solution

(a)   The gift to the discretionary trust on 15 July 1997 is a chargeable lifetime transfer, and IHT of £10,400 will be due as follows:

	£
15 July 1997	283,000
Inheritance tax payable 231,000 at nil	
52,000 at 20%	10,400

(b)   Zoe's death on 30 September 1999 is within seven years of making the chargeable lifetime transfer. Additional IHT of £10,400 will therefore be due as follows:

15 July 1997	283,000
Inheritance tax payable 231,000 at nil	
52,000 at 40%	20,800
Less: IHT paid	10,400
Additional liability	10,400
Estate at death	550,000
Inheritance tax payable 550,000 at 40%	220,000

None of the nil rate band is available in respect of the estate at death.

3.6   Grossing up of chargeable lifetime transfers

(a)   In the above example, the IHT was paid by the donee (the discretionary trust). The diminution in value of Zoe's estate was therefore £283,000, being the amount of the gift.

If the IHT was instead paid by Zoe (the donor) then the diminution in value of her estate would be the gift plus the IHT payable.

(b)   Where the IHT is paid by the donor, the gift is considered to be the net figure, and this must be grossed up in order to find the gross amount of the transfer.

Since the rate of IHT on lifetime transfers is 20%, grossing up is done using the fraction 100/80.

(c)   Grossing up is straightforward where the £231,000 nil rate band has already been utilised.

For example, a net gift of £100,000 would be grossed up to £125,000 (100,000 × 100/80). The IHT due is £25,000 (125,000 × 20%).

(d)   The calculation is slightly more complicated where the £231,000 nil rate band has not been fully utilised.

(e)   Note that the concept of grossing up has no relevance to PETs.

3.7   Example: Grossing up

On 31 July 1999 Kevin made a gift of £180,000 into a discretionary trust.

His only previous gift was one of £83,000 into a discretionary trust on 1 January 1998.

In both cases Kevin paid any IHT that was due.

Calculate the IHT liability in respect of Kevin's gifts. You should ignore any reliefs and exemptions that might be available.

3.8   Solution

Both gifts are chargeable lifetime transfers. No IHT is due in respect of the gift on 1 January 1998, although it utilises £83,000 of the nil rate band.

	£
1 January 1998	83,000
Inheritance tax payable 83,000 at nil	Nil

The gift on 31 July 1999 must be grossed up since Kevin paid the IHT liability.

31 July 1999

	£	£
Net chargeable transfer		180,000
IHT liability 148,000 at nil	Nil	
32,000 × 20/80	8,000	
		8,000
Gross chargeable transfer		188,000

Only £148,000 (231,000 - 83,000) of the nil rate band is available.

Kevin's IHT liability is therefore £8,000.

3.9   Responsibility for the payment of the IHT liability

(a)   The donor is primarily responsible for the IHT on chargeable lifetime transfers.

Grossing up will then be necessary.

(b)   The donor can, however, agree with the donee that the donee is to pay any tax due.

(c)   If a question is silent as to whether the donor or the donee is to pay the IHT, then it should be assumed that it will be paid by the donor.

(d)   Where an additional charge to IHT arises as a result of the donor dying within seven years of making the chargeable lifetime transfer, then the additional IHT liability is always the responsibility of the donee.

Whether the donor or the donee paid the IHT during lifetime is irrelevant.

(e)   The additional charge to IHT is calculated using the previously calculated gross transfer.

The net figure is not grossed up again using an IHT rate of 40%.

3.10   Activity

Following on with the example of Kevin, calculate the additional IHT liability if Kevin were to die on 31 December 1999.

3.11   Activity solution

The additional IHT liability will be £8,000 as follows:

	£
Gross chargeable transfer	188,000
IHT liability 148,000 at nil	
40,000 at 40%	16,000
IHT already paid	8,000
Additional liability	8,000

The discretionary trust will be responsible for the additional IHT liability.

3.12   The seven year cumulation period

(a)   Whereas PETs are completely ignored once the donor has lived for seven years, this is not the case with chargeable lifetime transfers.

(b)   Each time a chargeable lifetime transfer is made, it is necessary to take into account all other chargeable lifetime transfers made within the previous seven years in order to calculate the IHT liability.

(c)   There is thus the concept of a seven year cumulation period.

(d)   After seven years, a chargeable lifetime transfer will drop out of the cumulative total.

(e)   The seven year cumulation principle is probably the most difficult aspect of IHT to grasp, but it is quite important.

3.13   Example: Seven year cumulation principle

Alex died on 31 December 1999 leaving an estate valued at £250,000.

During his lifetime Alex had made the following chargeable lifetime transfers into discretionary trusts:

£103,000 on 30 June 1991.

£180,000 on 30 June 1997.

In each case, any IHT liability was paid by the relevant discretionary trust.

Calculate the IHT arising as a result of Alex's lifetime transfers, and his death on 31 December 1999. You should ignore any reliefs and exemptions that might be available.

3.14   Solution

(a)   Both of the gifts to the discretionary trusts are chargeable lifetime transfers, and IHT will be due as follows:

	£
30 June 1991	103,000
Inheritance tax payable 103,000 at nil	Nil

	£
30 June 1997	180,000
Inheritance tax payable 128,000 at nil	
52,000 at 20%	10,400

The chargeable lifetime transfer made on 30 June 1991 is taken into account when calculating the IHT due in respect of the chargeable lifetime transfer made on 30 June 1997, as it is within the seven year cumulation period.

(b)   Alex's death on 31 December 1999 is within seven years of the chargeable lifetime transfer on 30 June 1997. Additional IHT will therefore be due as follows:

30 June 1997	180,000
Inheritance tax payable 128,000 at nil	
52,000 at 40%	20,800
Less: IHT paid	10,400
Additional liability	10,400

(c)   The chargeable lifetime transfer on 30 June 1991 is more than seven years before Alex's death on 31 December 1999, and it therefore falls out of the cumulative total. Only the chargeable lifetime transfer made on 30 June 1997 is taken into account when calculating the IHT due on Alex's estate.

Estate at death	250,000
Inheritance tax payable 51,000 at nil	
199,000 at 40%	79,600

3.15   Interaction of chargeable lifetime transfers and PETs

(a)   When calculating the IHT due on chargeable lifetime transfers, PETs are initially ignored.

(b)   Upon the subsequent death of the donor, PETs that become chargeable will have to be taken into account when calculating the additional IHT liability due on chargeable lifetime transfers at death.

(c)   This may mean that a chargeable lifetime transfer will lose some or all of the nil rate band that it previously utilised.

(d)   However, where a chargeable lifetime transfer has been grossed up, the gross figure is not altered.

3.16   Example: Interaction of chargeable lifetime transfers and PETs

Simone died on 31 October 1999.

During her lifetime Simone made the following gifts:

(a)   £125,000 to her son on 30 November 1996.

(b)   £260,000 to a discretionary trust on 30 April 1997. Simone paid the IHT liability arising on this transfer.

Calculate the IHT arising on Simone's lifetime transfers. You should ignore any reliefs and exemptions that might be available.

3.17   Solution

(a)   Simone's gift to her son on 30 November 1996 is a PET, and is therefore initially ignored.

(b)   Simone's gift to the discretionary trust on 30 April 1997 is a chargeable lifetime transfer, and has to be grossed up since she pays the IHT liability. IHT of £7,250 will be due as follows:

	£	£
Net chargeable transfer		260,000
IHT liability 231,000 at nil	Nil	
29,000 × 20/80	7,250	
		7,250
Gross chargeable transfer		267,250

(c)   Upon Simone's death on 31 October 1999, the PET becomes chargeable as it is within seven years of the date of death.

	£
30 November 1996	125,000
Inheritance tax payable 125,000 at nil	Nil

(d)   The PET becoming chargeable has utilised some of the nil rate band that was previously utilised by the chargeable lifetime transfer. The additional liability on death will therefore be £57,250 as follows:

	£
Gross chargeable transfer	267,250
IHT liability 106,000 at nil	
161,250 at 40%	64,500
IHT already paid	7,250
Additional liability	57,250

4   CLOSE COMPANIES

4.1   Introduction

Companies controlled by one person or a small group of individuals could be operated with a view to tax avoidance.

Such companies are therefore subject to special rules.

4.2 What is a close company?

[Definition] A close company is a company:

    (a)   Controlled by five or fewer participators, or

    (b)   Controlled by any number of participators if they are directors.

(a)   A participator is broadly a shareholder, although the definition is somewhat wider than this.

(b)   The definition of a close company is not examinable.

4.3 Transfers of value made by close companies

(a)   A close company is a chargeable person for IHT purposes.

(b)   A charge to tax can therefore arise if a close company makes a transfer of value.

(c)   However, the charge is calculated by apportioning the transfer of value amongst the participators in the company.

(d)   The apportionment is in proportion to the participators' interests in the company.

(e)   Any participator whose estate has increased in value as a result of the transfer, can deduct the increase from the transfer of value apportioned to him or her.

(f)   The value apportioned to each participator is treated as a net figure, and this must therefore be grossed up.

(g)   The transfer is a chargeable lifetime transfer, rather than a PET.

(h)   The company is primarily liable for the IHT liability. If it does not pay, then the participators will be liable, although liability is in each case limited to the tax on the amount apportioned to that participator.

4.4 Example: Transfer of value by a close company

The share capital of STU Ltd, is owned equally by Albert and Barry.

On 31 December 1999 STU Ltd gave investments that it owned worth £546,000 to a friend of Barry's.

Neither Albert or Barry has ever made any lifetime transfers of value.

Calculate the IHT liability arising in respect of the gift made by STU Ltd. You should ignore any reliefs and exemptions that might be available.

4.5 Solution

Albert and Barry will both be apportioned £273,000 of the transfer of value. Since they have made no previous lifetime transfers, the IHT due will be £10,500 as follows:

		£	£
Net chargeable transfer			273,000
IHT liability	231,000 at nil	Nil	
	$42,000 \times 20/80$	10,500	
			10,500
Gross chargeable transfer			283,500

4.6 Alterations in share capital

Alterations in the share capital of a close company are treated as dispositions by the participators.

4.7   Example: Alterations in share capital

Annie owns 70% and Betty owns 30% of the share capital of AB Ltd, with each share carrying one vote.

The company's articles of association are altered so that Betty's shares carry 3 votes, whilst Annie's continue to carry one.

What are the IHT implications of this change?

4.8   Solution

The value of Annie's estate has fallen as a result of the alteration to the voting structure. She has lost control of AB Ltd since she now has 7/16ths of the votes compared to Betty who has 9/16ths.

Annie will be treated as making a disposition to Betty.

5   SELF TEST QUESTIONS

5.1   What is a transfer of value? (1.1)

5.2   When will a disposition not be a transfer of value? (1.4)

5.3   How is diminution in value calculated? (1.7)

5.4   Which lifetime transfers are PETs? (2.2)

5.5   When will a PET become chargeable? (2.3)

5.6   Who is responsible for the IHT liability when a PET becomes chargeable? (2.9)

5.7   What is a chargeable lifetime transfer? (3.1)

5.8   What rates of IHT apply to a chargeable lifetime transfer? (3.3)

5.9   When is it necessary to gross up a chargeable lifetime transfer? (3.6)

5.10   How is a transfer of value made by a close company charged to tax? (4.3)

6   EXAMINATION TYPE QUESTION

6.1   Kevin

Kevin died on 28 June 1999. At the date of his death Kevin owned the following assets:

(a)   100,000 £1 ordinary shares in RST Ltd, an unquoted company with an issued share capital of 500,000 shares.

Kevin originally bought 200,000 shares in RST Ltd in June 1991.

He gave 100,000 of the shares to his son on 30 September 1998.

Kevin's wife also owns 100,000 shares in RST Ltd, which she acquired in June 1991.

The relevant values of RST Ltd's shares (both at 30 September 1998 and 28 June 1999) are as follows:

Shareholding	Value per share £
20%	2
40%	3
60%	5

(b)   100,000 £1 ordinary shares (a 1% holding) in MNO plc, a quoted company

Kevin originally bought 300,000 shares in June 1982.

He made a gift of 200,000 shares into a discretionary trust on 28 December 1998. Kevin paid the IHT arising on the gift.

MNO plc's shares were quoted on the Stock Exchange at 138 - 146 on 28 December 1998, with recorded bargains of 128, 150 and 156 for that day.

On 28 June 1999 they were quoted at 158 - 168, with recorded bargains of 155 and 165.

(c)   Other assets valued at £400,000.

Kevin left his entire estate to his son.

Calculate the IHT arising as a result of Kevin's lifetime gifts, and his death on 28 June 1999. You should ignore all reliefs and exemptions that might be available (including business property relief).

7   ANSWER TO EXAMINATION TYPE QUESTION

7.1   Kevin

(a)   Kevin's gift to his son on 30 September 1998 is a PET, with no IHT due at that time.

Upon Kevin's death the PET becomes chargeable, and will be valued using the related property rules. Before the transfer Kevin and his wife between them owned 60% of RST Ltd, and after the transfer they owned 40%. IHT of £187,600 will be due as follows:

	£
Value of shares held before the transfer	
200,000 × £5	1,000,000
Value of shares held after the transfer	
100,000 × £3	300,000
	700,000
IHT liability 231,000 at nil	
469,000 at 40%	187,600

Kevin's son is responsible for the IHT liability.

(b)   The gift to the discretionary trust on 28 December 1998 will be a chargeable lifetime transfer.

The gift must be grossed up since Kevin paid the IHT liability. The calculation of the IHT liability ignores the PET.

	£	£
Net chargeable transfer		
200,000 × £1.40 (working)		280,000
IHT liability 231,000 at nil	Nil	
49,000 × 20/80	12,250	
		12,250
Gross chargeable transfer		292,250

The additional IHT liability due on Kevin's death will be:

	£
Gross chargeable transfer	292,250
IHT liability 292,250 at 40%	116,900
IHT already paid	12,250
Additional liability	104,650

The PET made on 30 September 1998 now fully utilises the nil rate band of £231,000. The discretionary trust will be responsible for the additional IHT liability.

(c)   The IHT liability due on Kevin's estate is as follows:

	£
Shares in RST Ltd	
(based on a 40% holding) 100,000 × £3	300,000
Shares in MNO plc 100,000 × £1.60 (working)	160,000
Other assets	400,000
Chargeable estate	860,000
IHT liability 860,000 at 40%	344,000

WORKING

On 28 December 1998 the shares in MNO plc are valued at the lower of:

138 + 1/4 (146 - 138) = 140p

1/2 (128 + 156) = 142p

On 28 June 1999 the shares are valued at the lower of:

158 + 1/4 (168 - 158) = 160.5p

1/2 (155 + 165) = 160p

32 LIFETIME EXEMPTIONS AND RELIEFS

INTRODUCTION

This chapter deals with the various exemptions and reliefs that are available in respect of lifetime transfers.

Some of the exemptions and reliefs also apply to the estate at death, and so have already been covered in chapter 30. Other exemptions and reliefs are specific to lifetime transfers.

The administration of IHT is also covered in this chapter.

1 EXEMPTIONS AND RELIEFS SPECIFIC TO LIFETIME TRANSFERS

1.1 Tapering relief

(a) It would be somewhat unfair if a gift made seven years and one month before the date of the donor's death was exempt, whilst a gift made six years and eleven months before the date of the donor's death was fully chargeable.

(b) Therefore gifts made between three years and seven years of the date of the donor's death qualify for tapering relief.

(c) The relief applies to both PETs and chargeable lifetime transfers.

(d) Tapering relief reduces the IHT otherwise payable by a percentage reduction.

The IHT liability is calculated as normal, and this is then reduced by a percentage according to the length of time between the date of the gift and the date of the donor's death.

(e) The percentages are as follows:

Years between the gift and death	Percentage reduction
3 to 4	20%
4 to 5	40%
5 to 6	60%
6 to 7	80%

(f) For chargeable lifetime transfers, any IHT already paid is then deducted.

No refund is made if the tax already paid is higher than the amount now due.

1.2 Example: Tapering relief

Brian dies on 31 December 1999.

He had made the following lifetime gifts:

£250,000 to his son on 31 October 1995.

£273,000 into a discretionary trust on 30 November 1996. Brian paid the IHT liability arising on this transfer.

Calculate the IHT arising on Brian's lifetime gifts. With the exception of tapering relief, you should ignore any exemptions and reliefs that might be available.

1.3   **Solution**

(a)   Brian's gift to his son on 31 October 1995 is a PET, and is therefore initially ignored.

(b)   Brian's gift to the discretionary trust on 30 November 1996 is a chargeable lifetime transfer, and has to be grossed up since he pays the IHT liability. IHT of £10,500 will be due as follows:

	£	£
Net chargeable transfer		273,000
IHT liability 231,000 at nil	Nil	
42,000 × 20/80	10,500	
		10,500
Gross chargeable transfer		283,500

(c)   Upon Brian's death on 31 December 1999, the PET becomes chargeable. Tapering relief will reduce the IHT payable by 40% as the PET was made between four and five years before the date of Brian's death.

	£
31 October 1995	250,000
Inheritance tax payable 231,000 at nil	
19,000 at 40%	7,600
Tapering relief: 7,600 at 40%	3,040
	4,560

(d)   The PET becoming chargeable has utilised the nil rate band that was previously used by the chargeable lifetime transfer. Tapering relief will reduce the IHT payable by 20% as the chargeable lifetime transfer was made between three and four years before the date of Brian's death. The additional IHT liability on death will therefore be £80,220 as follows:

	£
Gross chargeable transfer	283,500
IHT liability 283,500 at 40%	113,400
Tapering relief: 113,400 at 20%	22,680
	90,720
IHT already paid	10,500
Additional liability	80,220

1.4   **The annual exemption**

(a)   The first £3,000 of value transferred in each tax year is exempt.

        Note that this is one of the few situations where the tax year has any relevance to IHT.

(b)   The annual exemption is used up by PETs as well as by chargeable lifetime transfers.

        This is despite the fact that a PET might become completely exempt.

Therefore, where more than one transfer is to be made during a tax year, it would be good tax planning to make chargeable lifetime transfers prior to PETs. This will ensure that the optimum use is made of the annual exemption.

(c)   The annual exemption is allocated on a strict chronological basis.

For example, a gift of £10,000 is made on 30 April 1999, with a further gift of £7,000 being made on 15 May 1999. The annual exemption for 1999/00 of £3,000 will be allocated to the £10,000 gift made on 30 April 1999.

(d)   If an annual exemption is not fully used in a tax year, it can be carried forward to the next tax year. It is only possible to carry the annual exemption forward for one year.

The annual exemption for the current year is used before the annual exemption brought forward.

(e)   The annual exemption is only used after other relevant exemptions and reliefs have been applied.

For example, business property relief is applied before the annual exemption. This ensures that the annual exemption is not wasted if 100% relief would otherwise be available.

(f)   Where a chargeable lifetime transfer is to be grossed up, then the annual exemption is applied to the net transfer. The net transfer, after the deduction of the annual exemption, is then grossed up.

1.5   Activity

Julie has made the following gifts:

(a)   £600 on 31 August 1997 to her son.
(b)   £800 on 31 October 1997 to a discretionary trust.
(c)   £2,100 on 31 May 1998 to a discretionary trust.
(d)   £1,100 on 30 November 1998 to a discretionary trust.
(e)   £5,000 on 30 April 1999 to her daughter

You are to show how Julie's annual exemptions will be utilised.

1.6   Activity solution

31 August 1997 - PET	600
Annual exemption 1997/98	600
	Nil
31 October 1997 - CLT	800
Annual exemption 1997/98	800
	Nil

£1,600 (3,000 - 600 - 800) of the annual exemption for 1997/98 is carried forward.

31 May 1998 - CLT	2,100
Annual exemption 1998/99	2,100
	Nil

30 November 1998 - CLT			1,100
Annual exemption	1998/99 (£3,000 – 2,100)	900	
	1997/98 b/f	200	
		___	
			1,100
			___
			Nil

The unused part of the 1997/98 annual exemption (1,600 - 200 = £1,400) is lost, and so the amount carried forward to 1999/00 is nil.

30 April 1999 - PET	5,000
Annual exemption 1999/00	3,000
	___
	2,000

1.7   The small gifts exemption

(a)   Outright gifts to individuals are exempt if the total gifted to that individual in any one tax year is £250 or less.

(b)   Unlike the annual exemption, if the limit of £250 is exceeded then no relief is given.

(c)   A donor can give up to £250 each tax year to as many individuals as he or she wishes.

1.8   Activity

Simon made the following gifts during 1999/00:

(a)   £120 to his son Alex.
(b)   £450 to his son Bertie
(c)   £245 to his son Charles
(d)   £70 to his friend Diana
(e)   £650 to his friend Eric
(f)   £60 to his son Alex
(g)   £320 to his friend Diana

Which of the gifts qualify for the small gifts exemption?

1.9   Activity solution

Alex   The total gifts are £180, so the gifts are exempt.

Bertie   The gift is more than £250, and so no part of the £450 is exempt.

Charles   The gift is not more than £250, and so is exempt.

Diana   The total gifts are £390, and so neither of them is exempt.

Eric   The gift is more than £250, and so no part of the £650 is exempt.

1.10   Gifts in consideration of marriage

(a)   Gifts in consideration of marriage are exempt up to the following limits:

(i)   £5,000 if made by a parent of either party to the marriage.
(ii)   £2,500 if made by a grandparent or a remoter ancestor of either party to the marriage.
(iii)   £1,000 if made by anybody else, such as a brother or a sister.

(b)   The marriage must actually take place for the exemption to be available.

(c)   Both the marriage exemption and the annual exemption can be claimed for the same gift if it is large enough.

The marriage exemption should be used first, since its use is more restricted.

1.11   Activity

Larry and Livia are to get married on 15 June 1999.

The couple's parents and grandparents are to each make a wedding gift to Larry and Livia.

What is the maximum possible gift that each relative could make without affecting their nil rate band?

None of the relatives have made any previous transfers of value.

1.12   Activity solution

Each parent will be entitled to a £5,000 exemption for a gift in consideration of marriage, together with two annual exemptions of £3,000. Each parent could therefore make a gift of £11,000 without affecting their nil rate band.

Each grandparent will be entitled to a £2,500 exemption for a gift in consideration of marriage, together with two annual exemptions of £3,000. Each grandparent could therefore make a gift of £8,500 without affecting their nil rate band.

1.13   Normal expenditure out of income

(a)   IHT only taxes transfers of capital, not dispositions of income.

(b)   Therefore, a transfer of value is exempt if:

(i)   It is made as part of a person's normal expenditure out of income, and
(ii)   That person's standard of living is not affected as a result of the gift.

(c)   A typical situation where this exemption can be used is where premiums on a life assurance policy are paid on behalf of someone else.

Each year, the premiums will be regarded as coming out of income, and will therefore have no IHT implications. When the policy matures it will not form part of the donor's estate.

1.14   Relief for the fall in value of lifetime gifts

(a)   The value of a lifetime gift is fixed at the time that it is made.

(b)   However, relief can be claimed where a lifetime gift becomes chargeable as a result of the donor dying within seven years, and the value of the gift has fallen between the date of the gift and the date of the donor's death.

(c)   This relief applies to both PETs and chargeable lifetime transfers.

(d)   For relief to be available:

(i)   The property must still be owned by the donee at the date of the donor's death, or

(ii)   The property must have been sold in an arm's length transaction to an unconnected person prior to the date of the donor's death.

(e)   The relief operates by reducing the value of the transfer to:

(i)   The value at the time of the donor's death, or

(ii)   Where the property has been sold, to the amount of the sale proceeds.

(f)   It is important to appreciate that a claim for relief does not affect the donor's cumulative total.

(g)   No relief is given in respect of property that consists of plant and machinery or tangible moveable property with a predictable useful life of less than 50 years.

1.15   Example: Relief for the fall in value of lifetime gifts

Tim died on 30 June 1999.

On 30 April 1997 Tim had made a gift of 100,000 shares (a 1% holding) in ABC plc, a quoted company, into a discretionary trust. Tim paid the IHT arising on the gift.

ABC plc's shares were worth £3.33 each on 30 April 1997, and on 30 June 1999 were worth £3.03 each.

Calculate the IHT liability arising in respect of Tim's lifetime transfer on 30 April 1997.

1.16   Solution

(a)   The gift to the discretionary trust on 30 April 1997 will be a chargeable lifetime transfer, and this must be grossed up as the IHT liability is paid by Tim. IHT of £24,000 will be due as follows:

	£	£
30 April 1997		
100,000 × £3.33		333,000
Annual exemption 1997/98	3,000	
1996/97	3,000	
		6,000
Net chargeable transfer		327,000
IHT liability 231,000 at nil	Nil	
96,000 × 20/80	24,000	
		24,000
Gross chargeable transfer		351,000

(b)   At the date of Tim's death, the value of the shares in ABC plc has fallen to £3.03. The discretionary trust can therefore claim to have the additional IHT liability arising on 30 June 1999 calculated on this valuation. The additional IHT liability will therefore be:

	£
Gross chargeable transfer	351,000
Less relief for fall in value	
100,000 × £0.30 (3.33 - 3.03)	30,000
	321,000

IHT liability	231,000 at nil	
	90,000 at 40%	36,000
IHT already paid		24,000
Additional liability		12,000

Note that Tim's cumulative total is still £351,000, despite the claim for the fall in value of the lifetime gift.

2   OTHER EXEMPTIONS AND RELIEFS

2.1   Introduction

Many of the exemptions and reliefs that apply to an estate at death also apply to lifetime transfers.

These exemptions and reliefs have already been looked at in detail in chapters 29 and 30.

2.2   Husbands and wives

(a)   Transfers between spouses are normally exempt from IHT.

(b)   Where the recipient spouse is not domiciled in the UK, the exemption is limited to the cumulative total of £55,000.

Any gifts in excess of this figure will be PETs.

2.3   Other exemptions for lifetime transfers

The following are completely exempt:

(a)   Gifts to charities.
(b)   Gifts to political parties.
(c)   Gifts for the public benefit or for national purposes.
(d)   Gifts to housing associations.

The detailed rules covering these exemptions were all dealt with in chapter 29.

2.4   Business property relief

(a)   Business property relief applies in exactly the same way to lifetime transfers of business property, as it does to business property forming part of a person's estate.

(b)   The relief applies to the same types of asset, the relief is 50% or 100% according to the type of asset transferred, and the same qualifying conditions apply.

(c)   However, for business property relief to be available in respect of:

(i)   PETs that become chargeable as a result of the donor dying within seven years, and

(ii)   Any additional IHT arising on a chargeable lifetime transfer as a result of the donor dying within seven years.

there are two further conditions that must be met.

The two further conditions are that:

(i)   The business property transferred must be retained by the donee from the date of the transfer to the date of the donor's death.

There are two exceptions to this condition, which are where:

- The donee dies before the donor, or

- The donee sells the property, but then reinvests the proceeds in further business property.

(ii) The property must still qualify as business property at the date of the donor's death (or the donee's death if earlier).

For this purpose, the two year minimum period of ownership is ignored.

(d) If these conditions are not met:

(i) In the case of a PET, business property relief is simply not given.

(ii) In the case of a chargeable lifetime transfer, any relief originally given is withdrawn. If the original transfer was grossed up, then the business property relief is withdrawn by adding it to the gross chargeable transfer as previously calculated.

2.5 Example: Business property relief

Michael transferred £1,000,000 of shares (a 60% holding) in a quoted company into a discretionary trust on 30 June 1998. Michael paid any IHT arising on the gift.

On 30 April 1999 the trust sold the shares, and have not reinvested the proceeds.

Michael died on 31 December 1999, having made no other lifetime transfers.

Calculate the IHT arising in respect of Michael's lifetime transfer on 30 June 1998.

2.6 Solution

(a) Michael's gift to the discretionary trust on 30 June 1998 is a chargeable lifetime transfer, and has to be grossed up since he pays the IHT liability.

Business property relief at the rate of 50% is available since the shareholding is a controlling one in a quoted company. IHT of £65,750 will be due as follows:

	£	£
30 June 1998		1,000,000
Business property relief 1,000,000 × 50%		500,000
		500,000
Annual exemption 1998/99	3,000	
1997/98	3,000	
		6,000
Net chargeable transfer		494,000
IHT liability 231,000 at nil	Nil	
263,000 × 20/80	65,750	
		65,750
Gross chargeable transfer		559,750

(b) As a result of Michael dying within seven years of making the gift, additional IHT will be due. The discretionary trust has sold the shares, and so business property relief previously given will be withdrawn. The additional IHT liability on death will therefore be £265,750 as follows:

	£
Gross chargeable transfer	559,750
Business property relief withdrawn	500,000
	1,059,750
IHT liability 231,000 at nil	
828,750 at 40%	331,500
IHT already paid	65,750
Additional liability	265,750

2.7 Agricultural property relief

As for business property relief, two further conditions have to be met for agricultural property relief to be available in respect of lifetime transfers.

The conditions are that:

(a)   The agricultural property transferred must be retained by the donee from the date of the transfer to the date of the donor's death.

There are two exceptions to this condition, which are where:

-   The donee dies before the donor, or

-   The donee sells the property, but then reinvests the proceeds in further agricultural property.

(b)   The property must still qualify as agricultural property at the date of the donor's death (or the donee's death if earlier).

2.8 The order in which exemptions and reliefs should be applied

(a)   Exemptions which offer complete exemption should be claimed first.

This will include:

(i)   Gifts to spouses, charities and political parties.
(ii)   Normal expenditure out of income.
(iii)   Business and agricultural property relief

(b)   If relevant, the exemption for a gift in consideration of marriage should be claimed next.

(c)   Finally, the annual exemption should be claimed.

2.9 Activity

Mark died on 31 December 1999, having made the following lifetime transfers:

(a)   £231,000 into a discretionary trust on 30 June 1995.
(b)   £10,000 to his son on 31 July 1995 in respect of his wedding.
(c)   £40,000 to his wife on 31 August 1996. Mark's wife is not domiciled in the UK.
(d)   £10,000 to his nephew on 30 September 1996 in respect of his wedding.
(e)   £90,000 to charity on 31 December 1997.
(f)   £20,000 to a qualifying political party on 31 January 1998.
(g)   £50,000 to his wife on 31 May 1998.

Calculate the IHT arising on Mark's lifetime gifts.

2.10   Activity solution

Note that because the sequence of gifts made by Mark is straightforward (a gift into a discretionary trust followed by PETs) the answer only shows the IHT liabilities arising as a result of Mark's death.

		£	£
(a)	*30 June 1995* Discretionary trust		231,000
	Annual exemptions 1995/96	3,000	
	1994/95	3,000	
			6,000
			225,000
	Inheritance tax payable 225,000 at nil		Nil
(b)	*31 July 1995* PET to son		10,000
	Marriage exemption		5,000
			5,000
	Inheritance tax payable 5,000 at nil		Nil
(c)	*31 August 1996* - Gift to wife		Exempt
(d)	*30 September 1996* - PET to nephew		10,000
	Marriage exemption	1,000	
	Annual exemption 1996/97	3,000	
			4,000
			6,000
	Inheritance tax payable 1,000 at nil		
	5,000 at 40%		2,000
	Tapering relief 2,000 at 20%		400
			1,600

Only £1,000 of the nil rate band is available
(231,000 - 225,000 - 5,000).

(e)	*31 December 1997* - Gift to charity	Exempt
(f)	*31 January 1998* - Gift to political party	Exempt

(g)	*31 May 1998* - Gift to wife			50,000
	Exempt 55,000 - 40,000		15,000	
	Annual exemptions 1998/99		3,000	
	1997/98		3,000	
			21,000	
				29,000

Inheritance tax payable   29,000 at 40%   11,600

Only £15,000 of the gift is covered by the spouse exemption since Mark's wife is not domiciled in the UK. The exemption is therefore limited to a cumulative total of £55,000.

3   TAX PLANNING DURING LIFETIME

3.1   Introduction

IHT planning during a person's lifetime generally involves making gifts of property as early as possible on the basis that PETs will be completely exempt after seven years, and that tapering relief will in any case be available after three years.

3.2   Other points to consider

(a)   It may not be worth making a gift of property if it will result in a substantial capital gains tax liability. CGT gift relief only applies to business assets unless the gift is a chargeable (IHT) lifetime transfer.

No capital gains tax liability arises in respect of assets transferred upon death.

(b)   There is little point for IHT purposes in making gifts of property that would otherwise qualify for 100% relief.

This will often be the case where business and agricultural property is concerned.

(c)   In deciding as to which assets to transfer, it is better to make a gift of those assets which are expected to increase in value.

This is because the value of a gift is fixed at the time that it is made.

(d)   Where the recipients of a gift are too young to be entrusted with an outright gift, the transfer can be made into an interest in possession trust or an accumulation and maintenance trust.

(e)   Maximum use should be made of exemptions available such as the annual exemption and the marriage exemption.

4   ADMINISTRATION OF IHT

4.1   Introduction

This section deals with who pays the IHT, its due date of payment and the rules regarding interest on tax paid late.

The instalment option which applies to certain categories of property is also dealt with.

4.2   Persons responsible for the payment of IHT

(a)   The rules on the persons responsible for the payment of IHT have already been covered in the relevant sections of the text, but it is useful to summarise the position.

(b)   For chargeable lifetime transfers, IHT is paid by either the donor or the donee.

Remember that if a question is silent on this point, then it should be assumed that the IHT is paid by the donor, and that grossing up will therefore be necessary.

(c)   For IHT arising on the death of the donor, the rules are as follows:

(i)   Additional IHT arising on chargeable lifetime transfers made within seven years of death is paid by the donee.

(ii)   IHT arising on PETs becoming chargeable is paid by the donee.

(iii)   IHT on the deceased's free estate is paid by the personal representatives out of the estate assets, with the burden normally borne by the residue of the estate.

(iv)   IHT on settled property is paid by the trustees out of the capital of the trust.

(d)   Where IHT remains unpaid, the Inland Revenue can look beyond those primarily responsible for the liability.

For example:

(i)   Personal representatives can become liable in respect of any of the IHT liabilities arising as a result of death.

Their liability will, however, be limited to the estate assets in their possession.

(ii)   Beneficiaries under the deceased's will can become liable if the personal representatives do not pay the IHT on the estate.

Their liability is limited to the IHT on the assets that they have inherited.

4.3   Accounts

(a)   IHT is dealt with by the Capital Taxes Office, which is a part of the Inland Revenue.

(b)   For IHT there is not a system of regular returns as for income tax and corporation tax.

(c)   Instead, the onus is generally on the person making a chargeable transfer to declare it by delivering an account to the Inland Revenue.

(d)   The account must specify details of the property transferred and its value.

(e)   The time limit for the delivery of an account is as follows:

(i)   In respect of chargeable lifetime transfers, it is 12 months from the end of the month in which the transfer is made.

(ii)   In respect of PETs becoming chargeable upon the death of the donor, it is 12 months from the end of the month in which death occurred.

In this case, the onus for the delivery of the account is on the donee.

(iii)   For personal representatives dealing with a deceased's estate, it is 12 months from the end of the month in which death occurred or, if later, three months from the date of their appointment.

The account must specify all property forming part of the deceased's estate, including any interest in possession trusts of which the deceased was a beneficiary. In addition, the personal representatives have to include details of any chargeable lifetime transfers made by the deceased within seven years of his or her death.

(f)   Where the value of an estate does not exceed £200,000 and the deceased has made gifts of not more than £75,000 of cash or quoted securities in the seven years prior to death, then the personal representatives do not normally need to deliver an account.

4.4   Determinations and appeals

(a)   Where the Inland Revenue believe that IHT is payable, they will issue a notice of determination (similar to an assessment).

This may be based on an account submitted or may be an estimated figure.

(b)   The notice of determination will be served on the transferor or the person who appears to be liable to pay the IHT.

(c)   An appeal can be made against a notice of determination within 30 days of it being served. Otherwise the notice becomes final.

(d)   Appeals are normally made to the Special Commissioners, from where an appeal (on a point of law only) can be made to the High Court, then the Court of Appeal, and finally the House of Lords.

4.5   Due dates for the payment of IHT

(a)   For chargeable lifetime transfers, the due date is the later of:

(i)   Six months from the end of the month in which the transfer is made, and
(ii)   30 April following the end of the tax year in which the transfer is made.

(b)   For IHT arising on:

(i)   PETs becoming chargeable as a result of the donor's death, and,

(ii)   Additional IHT arising on chargeable lifetime transfers as a result of the donor's death.

The due date is six months from the end of the month in which death occurred.

(c)   For IHT arising on an estate at death the due date is the earlier of:

(i)   Six months from the end of the month in which death occurred, and
(ii)   When the personal representatives deliver their account.

(d)   Note that the due date is generally earlier than the date that an account has to be delivered.

4.6   Activity

You are required to state the due dates in respect of chargeable lifetime transfers made on the following dates:

(a)   25 March 2000
(b)   20 July 1999
(c)   30 October 1999

4.7   Activity solution

(a)   The due date is 30 September 2000.
(b)   The due date is 30 April 2000, as this is later than 31 January 2000.
(c)   The due date is 30 April 2000.

4.8   Interest on overdue IHT

Interest on overdue IHT runs from the due date to the date that the tax is paid.

4.9   Example: Interest on overdue IHT

Robert died on 15 July 1998.

His personal representatives delivered their account to the Inland Revenue on 31 July 1999, and paid the IHT due of £50,000.

Assuming that the rate of interest on unpaid IHT is 10%, calculate the interest on overdue IHT.

4.10   Solution

Although the personal representatives have delivered their account on time (12 months from the end of the month of death), the due date for the payment of IHT was 31 January 1999 (6 months from the end of the month of death).

Interest on overdue IHT will run from 31 January 1999 to 31 July 1999 as follows:

$50,000 \times 10\% \times 181/365 = £2,479.45$.

4.11   Repayment supplement

The rules for overpaid IHT are the same as the rules for underpaid IHT.

The repayment supplement runs from the date that IHT was overpaid to the date that it is repaid by the Inland Revenue.

4.12   The instalment option

(a)   IHT on certain property can be paid in ten equal annual instalments.

(b)   The instalment option applies in respect of:

    (i)   The transfer of a person's estate on death.

    (ii)   Chargeable lifetime transfers where the IHT is paid by the donee.

    (iii)   PETs becoming chargeable upon the death of the donor, provided that the donee has kept the property until the date of the donor's death (or the donee's death if earlier).

    Certain replacement property is permitted.

(c)   The instalment option applies to:

    (i)   Land and buildings.

    (ii)   A business or an interest in a business.

    (iii)   Shares and securities in a company controlled by the transferor.

    This applies to both quoted and unquoted companies, and it is irrelevant whether or not the shares qualified for business property relief.

    (iv)   Unquoted shares worth at least £20,000 and being at least 10% of the company's issued share capital.

    (v)   Unquoted shares if the IHT on those shares together with the IHT on any other instalment property represents at least 20% of the total IHT payable, or where the IHT cannot be paid at once without undue hardship.

(d)   Note that business property relief at the rate of 100% is available for most unquoted shareholdings. Since no IHT is then due, the instalment option is irrelevant.

(e)   The first of the ten instalments is due for payment:

    (i)   For transfers on death, and liabilities arising as a result of death, six months after the end of the month of death.

    (ii)   For chargeable lifetime transfers, on the normal due date.

(f)   Despite making an election for the instalment option, the whole amount of the IHT liability remaining unpaid becomes due immediately if the property in question is sold.

(g)   For land and buildings and shares in an investment company, interest on overdue IHT is charged on the full outstanding balance.

For other types of property, interest on overdue IHT is only charged if the instalment is paid late.

4.13   Example: Instalment option

John died on 30 June 1999 leaving the following property:

(a)   Freehold property worth £250,000.
(b)   A 40% shareholding in a quoted company worth £150,000.
(c)   Bank balances of £100,000.

John had made no lifetime transfers.

Calculate the IHT due on John's estate, and show how much of this can be paid under the instalment option.

4.14   Solution

(a)   *Estate at death*

	£
Freehold property	250,000
Shares in quoted company	150,000
Bank balances	100,000
	500,000

Inheritance tax payable   231,000 at nil
    269,000 at 40%   107,600

(b)   The rate of IHT on the estate is:

$$\frac{107,600}{500,000} \times 100 = 21.52\%$$

(c)   The IHT of £53,800 (250,000 × 21.52%) on the freehold property can be paid under the instalment option, with the first of the ten annual instalments being due on 31 December 1999.

The balance of the IHT of £53,800 is due on 31 December 1999. The shares in the quoted company do not qualify for the instalment option since this is a minority shareholding.

5   SELF TEST QUESTIONS

5.1   When is tapering relief available? (1.1)

5.2   When can the annual exemption be carried forward? (1.4)

5.3   When is the small gifts exemption available? (1.7)

5.4   What is the exemption for a grandparent making a gift in consideration of marriage? (1.10)

5.5   When is relief for the fall in the value of a lifetime gift available? (1.14)

5.6   What further conditions must be met for business property relief to be available in respect of a lifetime transfer? (2.4)

5.7   Who are the persons responsible for the payment of IHT? (4.2)

5.8   What is the due date for IHT arising on a chargeable lifetime transfer? (4.5)

5.9   Over what period does interest on overdue IHT run? (4.8)

5.10   What types of property qualify for the instalment option? (4.12)

6   EXAMINATION TYPE QUESTION

6.1   Paul

Paul, due to ill health, is expected to die in the near future. You should assume that today's date is 31 December 1999.

The current value of his estate, and a forecast value for 12 months time, is as follows:

	Present value £	Forecast value £
20,000 shares (a 1% holding) in BCD plc a quoted company.	50,000	45,000
8,000 shares (a 2% holding) in GHI plc, a quoted company.	70,000	85,000
30,000 shares (a 10% holding) in NOP Ltd, an unquoted company.	65,000	60,000
Main residence	230,000	250,000
Holiday cottage	130,000	110,000
	545,000	550,000

All of these assets have been owned for at least two years.

Under the terms of his will, Paul has left all of his assets to his son.

His son has two children.

Paul's wife is also ill, and is not expected to live for more than three months. She does not have any assets of her own, but Paul is confident that his son will look after her upon his death.

Paul has made the following transfers of value during his lifetime:

(a)   On 1 November 1991, he made a gift of £171,000 into a discretionary trust. The trust paid any IHT arising on the gift.

(b)   On 1 October 1996, he gave his son £100,000 as a wedding gift.

(b)   On 1 November 1996, he gave his son a business valued at £250,000. Paul had run the business for 10 years, and his son has continued to run it since.

You are required to:

(a)   Calculate the IHT liabilities that would arise if Paul were to die on 31 December 1999. Your answer should show the relevant due dates.

(b)   Advise Paul of why it might be beneficial to change the terms of his will.

If the changes were not made by Paul, would it be possible for his son to subsequently make the changes after the date of Paul's death?

(c)   Paul's son is considering selling the business that was given to him by Paul for its current value of £175,000.

What are the IHT implications if the sale took place before Paul were to die.

(d)   How might the IHT liabilities arising on Paul's estate be reduced if his executors were to sell certain assets following the date of his death?

7   ANSWER TO EXAMINATION TYPE QUESTION

7.1   Paul

(a)   The gift to the discretionary trust on 1 November 1991 is more than seven years before the date of Paul's death, and therefore no further IHT is due.

It is, however, within seven years of the other lifetime transfers, and will reduce the nil rate band available by £165,000 (171,000 - 3,000 - 3,000).

The wedding gift of £100,000 on 1 October 1996 was originally a PET, and no IHT would have been due at that time.

As a result of Paul's death within seven years it now becomes a chargeable transfer, and IHT of £7,360 will be due on 30 June 2000 as follows:

		£	£
1 October 1996			100,000
Marriage exemption		5,000	
Annual exemptions	1996/97	3,000	
	1995/96	3,000	
		11,000	
			89,000

		£
Inheritance tax payable	66,000 at nil	
	23,000 at 40%	9,200
Tapering relief	9,200 × 20%	1,840
		7,360

The gift of the business on 1 November 1996 will qualify for business property relief at the rate of 100%, and no IHT liability therefore arises.

Estate at death

	£
Value of estate	545,000
Business property relief 65,000 × 100%	65,000
	480,000

		£
Inheritance tax payable	142,000 at nil	
	338,000 at 40%	135,200

Only the gift on 1 October 1996 is relevant when calculating the nil rate band available to Paul's estate. The IHT of £135,200 will be due on 30 June 2000.

(b)   At present, Paul has left all of his estate to his son.

The following tax planning points should be considered:

(1)   Paul should leave £231,000 of his estate to his wife. In due course this will utilise her nil rate band which would otherwise be wasted, and will save IHT of £92,400 (231,000 × 40%).

(2)   If Paul left an additional amount to his wife, then she could use her annual exemptions of £3,000 by making gifts to the son or grandchildren.

(3)   Paul could leave some property to his grandchildren, and thus miss out a generation.

It would also be possible to put this tax planning into effect after Paul's death by making a deed of variation.

This must be made within two years of the date of death. An election must be submitted to the Inland Revenue within six months of the deed's execution, and must be signed by all the beneficiaries affected (probably just Paul's son).

(c)   If the business was sold before the date of Paul's death, it would no longer qualify for business property relief.

At the date of Paul's death the gift would become chargeable, with the charge being based on the sale proceeds of £175,000. This is because relief can be claimed for the fall in the value of a lifetime gift.

The IHT liability will be £70,000 (175,000 × 40%.)

Additional IHT of £56,800 (142,000 × 40%) will also be due on Paul's estate, since none of the nil rate band would then be available.

(d)   If the executors sell quoted investments within 12 months of the date of Paul's death they can claim to have the selling price substituted for the value at the date of death.

The IHT liability can therefore be reduced by £2,000 (50,000 - 45,000 = 5,000 × 40%) if the 20,000 shares in BCD plc are sold within 12 months of the date of Paul's death.

The shares in GHI plc are forecast to increase in value, and should therefore not be sold by the executors within the relevant period.

If the executors sell land and buildings within four years of the date of Paul's death they can also claim to have the selling price substituted for the value at the date of death.

The IHT liability can therefore be reduced by £8,000 (130,000 - 110,000 = 20,000 × 40%) if the holiday cottage is sold within four years of the date of Paul's death.

The main residence is forecast to increase in value, and should therefore not be sold by the executors within the relevant period.

33 ADDITIONAL ASPECTS OF INHERITANCE TAX

INTRODUCTION

This chapter deals with the 'foreign element' of IHT and certain anti-avoidance provisions that apply where gifts are made subject to reserving a benefit for the donor or where gifts are made by a series of associated operations. This IHT part of your studies then concludes with a review of the rules whereby IHT and CGT interact.

1 INTRODUCTION

The final chapter on IHT is concerned with aspects of IHT that are of slightly less importance than those covered in the preceding four chapters.

2 OVERSEAS ASPECTS OF IHT

2.1 Introduction

In chapter 29 it was seen that a person's domicile is important when establishing their liability to IHT.

A person domiciled in the UK is chargeable to IHT in respect of their world-wide assets.

A person not domiciled in the UK is only chargeable to IHT in respect of their UK assets.

2.2 Domicile

(a) The concept of domicile is one of general law.

Essentially, a person is domiciled in the country in which they have their permanent home.

(b) A person can only be domiciled in one country at a time.

(c) At birth, a person acquires a *domicile of origin*.

Irrespective of where they are born, a person will acquire their father's domicile at birth.

However, a mother's domicile is acquired where a person's parents are not married.

A domicile of origin is retained until it is changed to either one of dependency or one of choice.

(d) A *domicile of dependency* can be acquired by a child under the age of 16.

If the domicile of the child's father changes (or mother if the child is illegitimate), then the domicile of the child will also change.

(e) A *domicile of choice* can be acquired by anybody aged 16 or over.

To acquire a domicile of choice it is necessary for a person to:

(i) Sever all ties with the country in which they are currently domiciled, and

(ii) To demonstrate the intention of residing permanently in the country in which they wish to acquire domicile.

Long residence in a country by itself is not sufficient to establish a domicile of choice. There must be the intention to reside in that country permanently.

A person who is currently domiciled in the UK, and who wishes to acquire domicile in, say, France, would have to :

(i)   Sever all ties with the UK by, for example, selling his or her property in the UK.

(ii)   Demonstrate the intention of residing permanently in France by, for example, buying property in France, booking a grave plot in France, drafting a will under French law.

2.3   Deemed domicile

For IHT purposes only, a person can also be deemed to be domiciled in the UK for one of two reasons:

(a)   If a person ceases to be domiciled in the UK under general law, they will still be treated as UK domiciled for a further three years.

        This is to prevent a person changing their domicile just before they die in order to avoid IHT.

(b)   If a person has been resident in the UK for at least 17 out of the previous 20 tax years.

2.4   Activity

Graham has been domiciled in the UK since birth. On 1 June 1996 he emigrated to France with the intention of remaining there permanently. He died on 31 August 1999

Jack is domiciled in Germany. He became UK resident on 1 May 1981. He died on 1 March 2000.

To what extent, if any, will these two individuals be liable to UK IHT?

2.5   Activity solution

Graham ceased to be domiciled in the UK on 1 June 1996. For IHT purposes he was deemed domicile for a further three years until 31 May 1999. As his death occurred after this, he will only be liable to UK IHT on his UK assets.

Jack was resident in the UK for 19 tax years (1981/82 to 1999/00). He is therefore deemed to be domiciled in the UK, and will be liable to UK IHT on his world-wide assets.

2.6   The location of assets

Since a person who is not domiciled in the UK is only liable to UK IHT on their UK assets, it is important to establish where assets are situated. There are no specific IHT rules as regards the location of assets so the common law rules apply. The rules are as follows:

(a)   Land and buildings, freehold or leasehold, are situated where they are physically located.

(b)   Chattels are situated where they are physically located at the relevant time.

(c)   Debtors are situated where the debtor resides, unless it is a debt evidenced by a document under seal when it is situated where the deed is kept.

(d)   Bank accounts are situated at the branch which maintains the account.

(e)   An interest in a partnership is situated where the partnership business is carried on.

(f)   Goodwill is situated where the business to which it is attached to is carried on.

(g)   Registered shares and securities are situated where they are registered, or where they would normally be dealt with in the ordinary course of business.

(h)   Government securities are situated at the place of registration.

(i)   Bearer shares and securities are situated where the document of title is physically kept.

(j)   Life policies are situated in the country where the proceeds are payable.

(k)   Property held in trust follows the above rules, regardless of the residence of the trust or the residence of the trustees.

2.7   Activity

Sam died on 30 June 1999.

Although Sam had lived in the UK for six years, he was domiciled in the USA at the time of his death.

Sam's estate, which was left entirely to his daughter, consisted of the following assets, all of which are shown in sterling:

(a)   Freehold property situated in the UK worth £140,000.

(b)   Leasehold property situated in the USA worth £60,000.

(c)   20,000 shares in USA Inc., a company quoted on the US stock exchange at 300 - 320 with recorded bargains of 300, 307 and 316.

(d)   Antiques worth £40,000 which are situated in Sam's US residence.

(e)   A loan of £15,000 due to Sam by his sister who is resident in the USA. The sister used the loan to buy property situated in the UK.

(f)   A motor car worth £15,000 that was bought in the USA, but is now situated in the UK.

(g)   Bank deposits in sterling of £100,000 with the UK Branch of a US Bank.

(h)   UK government stocks with a nominal value of £15,000, quoted at 96 - 98.

(i)   US government stocks valued at £16,000.

Calculate the IHT that will be payable as a result of Sam's death.

2.8   Activity solution

Sam - Inheritance tax computation.

		£
FREE ESTATE		
Personalty		
Motor car		15,000
Bank account		100,000
UK government stocks (15,000 at 96.5)		14,475
		129,475
Realty		
Freehold property		140,000
Chargeable estate		269,475
Inheritance tax payable	231,000 at nil	
	38,475 at 40% =	15,390

2.9   Double taxation relief

(a)   Double taxation relief applies where an asset situated overseas is subject to both UK IHT and tax overseas.

(b)   The relief may be given under a double taxation agreement entered into by the UK with another country.

If there is no double taxation treaty, then relief is given unilaterally in the UK.

The contents of specific double taxation treaties are not examinable.

(c)   Double taxation relief for the overseas tax suffered is given as a tax credit against the IHT payable on the overseas asset.

Relief is restricted to the lower of:

(i)   The overseas tax paid, and

(ii)   The UK IHT payable on the overseas asset.

This is based on the average rate of IHT, and so it is necessary to work out the rate of tax on the estate.

2.10   Example: Double taxation relief

Peter died on 15 August 1999 leaving an estate valued at £300,000.

Included in this figure is property situated overseas valued at £60,000. Overseas IHT of £18,000 was paid on this property.

Peter's estate was left entirely to his son.

Calculate the IHT that will be payable as a result of Peter's death.

2.11   Solution

		£
Chargeable estate		300,000
Inheritance tax payable	231,000 at nil	
	69,000 at 40% =	27,600
Double taxation relief (working)		5,520
		22,080

WORKING

The rate of IHT on the estate is 9.2% (27,600/300,000 × 100).

The double taxation relief is therefore the lower of:

The overseas tax paid =	18,000
The UK IHT paid 60,000 × 9.2% =	5,520

3 GIFTS WITH RESERVATION

3.1 Introduction

Definition The gift with reservation rules are an anti-avoidance provision designed to prevent the making of lifetime gifts where some benefit is reserved.

3.2 The need for the gift with reservation rules

(a) Because most gifts made more than seven years prior to death escape any charge to IHT, it is good tax planning for a person to dispose of assets at a reasonably early age.

(b) However, a person may not want, or be able, to completely give up the use of property.

A typical situation might be where a parent makes a gift of their main residence to a son or daughter, but then continues to live in the property rent free.

(c) If it were not for the gift with reservation rules, such a gift:

(i) Would be a PET, and would thus escape a charge to IHT if the parent were to live for more than seven years.

This is despite the fact that the parent continues to have the use of the property rent free.

(ii) Would not be part of the parent's estate upon their death.

(d) The gift with reservation rules prevent this abuse of the PET concept.

3.3 The treatment of a gift with reservation

(a) At the time that a gift with reservation is made, it is treated as a normal lifetime transfer.

It may therefore be a PET or a chargeable lifetime transfer, as appropriate.

(b) However, property subject to a reservation is still treated as belonging to the person who made the gift (the donor).

It will therefore be part of the donor's estate upon his or her death, and will be included at its value at that time.

(c) Because property subject to a reservation can be treated as both a PET and also form part of the donor's estate, it is possible for a double charge to IHT to arise.

This will be the case where the donor dies within seven years of making the PET.

In this situation there is relief for the double charge. The IHT liability for the donor should be calculated twice:

(i) Firstly, ignoring the PET, and
(ii) Secondly, ignoring the property subject to a reservation in the estate at death.

The basis that gives the highest charge to tax is then used.

(d) If the donor were to die more than seven years after making the gift with reservation, then the PET will not become chargeable.

In this case, the property subject to a reservation is simply included as part of the donor's estate.

3.4   Example: The double charge to tax

Mary made a gift of a cottage to her son Andrew on 31 March 1995.

The cottage was worth £280,000 at that time.

It was a condition of the gift that Mary would have the free use of the cottage for six months each year.

Mary died on 30 June 1999 leaving an estate, excluding the cottage, valued at £400,000. The cottage was valued at £350,000 at that date.

Calculate the IHT due on Mary's death.

3.5   Solution

Mary has the free use of the cottage for six months of the year, and this is a gift with reservation.

The PET on 31 March 1995 is within seven years of death, and will therefore be chargeable. It is therefore necessary to prepare two computations:

(1)   *Treating the gift as a PET.*

	£	£
31 March 1995		
Value transferred		280,000
Annual exemptions 1994/95	3,000	
1993/94	3,000	
		6,000
		274,000
Inheritance tax payable 231,000 at nil		
43,000 at 40%		17,200
Tapering relief (4 to 5 years) at 40%		6,880
		10,320
IHT due on estate at death (excluding the cottage)		
400,000 at 40%		160,000
Total IHT liability		170,320

(2)   *Treating the gift as part of the estate*

In this case, the PET is ignored.

	£
IHT due on estate at death	
Estate	400,000
Cottage (valued at 30 June 1999)	350,000
	750,000
Inheritance tax payable 231,000 at nil	
519,000 at 40%	207,600
Total IHT liability	207,600

Treating the cottage as part of Mary's estate produces the highest charge to IHT, so the total IHT liability will be £207,600.

3.6   Removal of the reservation

(a)   Where the reservation ceases before the donor dies, then the removal of the reservation is treated as a PET at that time.

In the previous example, Mary might have given up her right to the free use of the cottage. The cottage would then no longer be subject to a reservation.

The PET will be based on the value of the property at the date that the reservation is removed.

(b)   The property will no longer be treated as part of the donor's estate.

(c)   Again, there is the possibility of a double charge to IHT, since two PETs will have been made in respect of the same property.

However, a numerical question is unlikely to be set involving this situation.

3.7   Avoiding a gift with reservation

(a)   A gift with reservation will arise where property is given away, and possession and enjoyment of that property is not assumed by the donee to the entire or virtually the entire exclusion of the donor.

Spending a few days each year rent free in a property that has been given away would not therefore be treated as a reservation.

(b)   The following situations will also not create a reservation:

(i)   Where full consideration is paid for any use of the property.

For example, where a house has been given away, but is still lived in by the donor. The payment of a commercial rent will avoid the gift with reservation rules.

(ii)   Where the circumstances of the donor have changed in a way that was not foreseen at the time of the gift.

This situation would be applicable where a house has been given away, and at a later date the donor becomes ill. If the donor goes to stay with his or her family in the house, then this will not fall under the gift with reservation rules.

4   ASSOCIATED OPERATIONS

4.1   Introduction

Definition   The associated operations rules are an anti-avoidance provision designed to catch schemes to avoid IHT by reducing the value of a gift by using a series of transactions.

4.2   What is an associated operation?

The associated operations provisions may be applied where:

(a)   There are two or more operations which affect the same property.

An asset may be transferred piecemeal, so that the total value of the individual transactions is less than the value of the whole asset.

(b)   There are two operations, one of which is undertaken with reference to the other.

A person may transfer part of an asset which, although of little value, significantly reduces the value of the remainder. The remainder is then transferred at a reduced value.

Again, this would allow an asset to be given away at less than its full value.

4.3   Example: Associated operations

Joan owns three paintings worth £20,000 each, but £100,000 as a set.

In June 1999 Joan sells a painting to her friend Jane for £20,000. In July 1999 she sells Jane another painting for £20,000, and then in August 1999 she sells her the third painting for £20,000.

What transfers of value has Joan made?

4.4   Solution

Each painting when looked at in isolation appears to have been sold for its commercial value, and therefore no charge to IHT arises.

However, the combined value of the three paintings is £100,000, and only £60,000 has been received as consideration. Under the associated operations rule the transactions may be looked at as a whole, and Joan will be treated as making a transfer of value of £40,000.

4.5   The application of the rules

(a)   Associated operations are treated as one transaction, and any resulting transfer of value is treated as being made at the time of the last associated operation.

In the previous example, Joan would be treated as making a PET of £40,000 in August 1999.

(b)   It is much more likely that the associated operations rule will be applied where transactions are with a connected person.

(c)   The longer the length of time between the various transactions, the easier it will be to defend against an allegation of associated transactions.

It will be possible to argue that there was no intention of making further transactions at the time of the first transaction.

4.6   Example: The length of time between associated operations

Jed owns two antique vases which are worth £25,000 each, but £100,000 as a set.

On 1 July 1999 Jed gave one of the vases to his wife.

On 2 July 1999 Jed gave the other vase to his son.

On 3 July 1999 Jed's wife gave her vase to the son.

What transfers of value have been made?

4.7   Solution

Ignoring the associated operations rule, the following transfers of value will have been made by Jed:

The gift on 1 July 1999 is exempt as a transfer between spouses.

The gift on 2 July 1999 will be valued using the related property rules:

Value of vase before the transfer

$$\text{Transfer of value } 100,000 \times \frac{25,000}{50,000} = 50,000$$

This will be a PET

The gift on 3 July 1999 will be a PET valued at £25,000.

The two vases worth £100,000 as a pair have therefore been transferred by Jed to his son, although there is a potential IHT liability on only £75,000 (50,000 + 25,000).

Under the associated operations rule the transactions may be looked at as a whole, and Jed's wife will treated as making an additional transfer of value of £25,000.

The associated operations rule will almost certainly be applied due to the short period between the three transactions.

Even if the transactions were spread over a longer period, the associated operations rule would be invoked if the transfer from Jed to his wife was made on condition that she then make the gift to their son.

4.8 Situations where the associated operations rules will not apply

The associated operations rules will specifically not apply:

(a)   In respect of leases, where there is more than three years between the grant of a commerical lease and the subsequent transfer of the freehold.

(b)   In respect of transfers between spouses, where property is transferred in order to utilise the annual exemption or the marriage exemption provided the donee spouse acts from his or her own choice in making a gift.

For example, where a son or daughter is to get married, both spouses may want to make use of the £5,000 marriage exemption. If the husband has no capital, and the wife makes a gift to him of £5,000 in order to make the gift to the son or daughter, then this will not normally be treated as an associated operation.

4.9 Example: Leases

Maud owns freehold property worth £250,000.

On 31 July 1997 she granted a lease to her son for a full market rent.

On 31 December 1999 Maud gave her son the freehold of the property. This was only valued at £150,000 because she no longer had vacant possession.

What are the IHT implications of the two transactions?

4.10 Solution

The grant of the lease at a full market rent on 31 July 1997 is a commercial transaction and has no IHT implications.

The gift of the freehold on 31 December 1999 will probably be caught by the associated operations rule. The transfer of value will therefore be £250,000 rather than £150,000.

If Maud had waited until 1 August 2000 (three years from 31 July 1997) to make a gift of the freehold of the property, then the associated operations rule would not have applied.

5   RELATIONSHIP OF CGT WITH IHT

5.1   Introduction

There are two aspects of CGT that will be briefly looked at.

5.2   Valuation rules

(a)   For IHT purposes, lifetime transfers are valued according to the diminution in a person's estate.

The related property rules may increase this valuation.

(b)   For CGT purposes, however, the value of a lifetime transfer (a gift) is the value of the property actually transferred.

It is very important that this difference is understood.

5.3   Example: Valuation rules

Eddy owns 100,000 shares (a 10% holding) in WXY Ltd.

On 31 July 1999 he made a gift of 50,000 of the shares in WXY Ltd to his daughter.

Eddy's wife also owns 50,000 shares in WXY Ltd.

The relevant values of WXY Ltd's shares are as follows:

Shareholding	*Value per share* £
5%	8.00
10%	10.00
15%	13.00

(a)   Calculate the value of the PET for IHT purposes.

(b)   Calculate the deemed sale proceeds for CGT purposes.

5.4   Solution

(a)   The value of the PET will be calculated using the related property valuation rules as follows:

	£
Value of shares held before the transfer (based on a 15% holding) 100,000 × £13.00	1,300,000
Value of shares held after the transfer (based on a 10% holding) 50,000 × £10.00	500,000
Value transferred	800,000

(b)   For CGT purposes, a gift of a 5% shareholding has been made.

The deemed consideration is therefore £400,000 (50,000 × £8).

The diminution in Eddy's estate, and the related property rules are irrelevant.

5.5   Interaction of IHT and CGT

(a)   A gift to another individual which has been subject to a claim for gift relief could result in that person being subject to a charge to both IHT and CGT.

(b)   Therefore, where IHT is paid on such a gift, it is allowed as a deduction when calculating the CGT liability upon the donee's disposal of the asset.

5.6   Example: Interaction of IHT and CGT

On 31 December 1997 Yaz made a gift of business property worth £295,000 to her daughter Jo.

Yaz and Jo made a joint election to hold over the chargeable gain of £65,000 arising on the gift.

Yaz died on 30 April 1999 having made no other lifetime transfers except to use her annual exemptions. Assume that the business property did not qualify for business property relief and that the annual exemptions were already used.

Jo sold the business property for £360,000 on 31 August 1999. Assume that the indexation factor from December 1997 to April 1998 is 0.020.

Jo is a 40% income taxpayer and makes no other disposals in 1999/00.

Calculate the CGT liability that will arise upon Jo's disposal of the business property on 31 August 1999.

5.7   Solution

When calculating her CGT liability, Jo will be able to deduct the IHT payable as a result of the PET becoming chargeable.

The IHT liability on the PET is £25,600 as follows:

	£
Value transferred	295,000
Inheritance tax payable 231,000 at nil	
64,000 at 40%	25,600

Jo's CGT liability is £31,092 as follows:

	£	£
Sale proceeds		360,000
Deemed cost	295,000	
Gain held over	65,000	
		230,000
		130,000
Indexation 230,000 × 0.020		4,600
		125,400
IHT liability		25,600
Chargeable gain		99,800
Taper relief (acquired by Jo before 17 March 1998 so deemed to be held for two years) × 85%		84,830
Annual exemption		7,100
		77,730
Capital gains tax at 40%		31,092

6 SELF TEST QUESTIONS

6.1 In what circumstances will a person be deemed to be domiciled in the UK? (2.3)

6.2 For IHT purposes, what are the rules governing the location of chattels, debtors, bank accounts and registered shares and securities? (2.6)

6.3 How is relief for double taxation restricted? (2.9)

6.4 What is a gift with reservation? (3.2)

6.5 Where a gift with reservation has been made, how is a double charge to IHT avoided? (3.3)

6.6 How can a gift with reservation be avoided? (3.7)

6.7 What is an associated operation? (4.2)

6.8 In what situations will the associated operations rules not be applied? (4.8)

6.9 In what respect are the valuation rules for CGT purposes different from those for IHT purposes? (5.2)

6.10 How does IHT interact with CGT? (5.5)

7 EXAMINATION TYPE QUESTION

7.1 Mary

Mary Day is a wealthy widow who has asked for your advice in respect of a number of gifts that she is planning to make in the near future.

Her only previous gift was one of £250,000 into a discretionary trust two years ago.

The proposed gifts are as follows:

(a) A gift of a holiday cottage worth £100,000 to her nephew Paul.

As a condition of the gift, Mary would have the free use of the cottage for six months each year.

(b) A gift of an antique clock worth £10,000 to her granddaughter Jane in respect of her forthcoming wedding.

(c) A gift of 20,000 £1 ordinary shares in DEF Ltd into a discretionary trust for the benefit of her nieces and nephews.

DEF Ltd is an unquoted trading company with a share capital of 200,000 £1 ordinary shares.

Mary currently holds 30,000 shares in the company.

A 5% holding is worth £10 per share, whilst 10% and 15% holdings are worth £13 and £16 per share respectively.

Mary acquired the shares one year ago.

(d) A gift of agricultural land and buildings with an agricultural value of £160,000 to her son David.

The land was bought ten years ago, and has always been let out to tenants.

The most recent tenancy agreement commenced in 1998, and comes to an end in six months time. Mary has obtained planning permission to build ten houses on the land.

The value of the land with planning permission is £280,000.

David owns the neighbouring land, and the value of this will increase from £200,000 to £250,000 as a result of the gift.

Mary will pay the inheritance tax arising from the gift into the discretionary trust (gift c).

Any inheritance tax arising on the other gifts will be paid for by the respective donee.

You are required to advise Mary of the inheritance tax implications arising from the above gifts.

Ignore annual exemptions.

8   ANSWER TO EXAMINATION TYPE QUESTION

8.1   Mary

Mary's previous chargeable lifetime transfer for £250,000 will have fully utilised her nil rate band of £231,000.

(a)   Where an individual makes a gift of property but reserves a benefit, it will be a gift with reservation.

Short holiday visits to the cottage would not be caught by the rules, but six months free use would.

Mary could avoid the gift with reservation rules by paying a commercial rent for the use of the cottage.

The gift of the cottage will be a PET of £100,000, but Mary will still be treated as beneficially entitled to the cottage.

It will therefore be included as part of her estate when she dies, and will be included at its value at that date.

This might give rise to a double charge, since the cottage is a PET and also part of Mary's estate.

Relief for the double charge will be given if this is the case.

(b)   The gift of the clock is in consideration of marriage, and will therefore qualify for an exemption of £2,500.

The balance of the gift will be a PET of £7,500.

(c)   The gift of 20,000 shares in DEF Ltd will be a chargeable lifetime transfer of £380,000 as follows:

	£
Value of estate before the gift:	
30,000 shares valued at £16 each	480,000
Value of estate after the gift:	
10,000 shares valued at £10 each	100,000
Diminution in value	380,000

The gift must be grossed up since Mary is to pay the IHT liability.

The gross value of the transfer is therefore £475,000 (380,000 × 100/80), and the IHT due will be £95,000 (475,000 – 380,000).

Business property relief is not available because Mary has owned the shares for less than two years.

(d)   The gift of agricultural land will be a PET for £280,000.

The increase in the value of David's land is irrelevant.

If the PET becomes chargeable as a result of Mary dying within seven years, agricultural property relief should be available at the rate of 100%. This is because she has owned the land for seven years.

Agricultural property relief will amount to £160,000, being based on the agricultural value.

Relief will only be available if David still owns the land, and it is still agricultural property, at the date of Mary's death.

34 TRUSTS

INTRODUCTION

Students tend to find this area of the syllabus difficult to understand, mainly, it seems, because the areas covered are so unfamiliar.

Concentrate on the different types of trust and then work through the ways in which trusts are assessed to

- income tax;
- capital gains tax; and
- inheritance tax.

1 INTRODUCTION

1.1 Introduction

 A trust is an obligation binding a person (**the trustee**) to hold or deal with property settled by one person (**the settlor**) for the benefit of another person or persons (**beneficiaries**).

Trusts are sometimes referred to as settlements: the terms can for all practical purposes be considered interchangeable.

1.2 Trustees

Trustees stand in the shoes both of the creator of the trust (the settlor), who may be living or dead, and of the beneficiaries. They are regarded as a **continuing body of persons** distinct from any individuals who may occupy the position of trustee at any given time and irrespective of the number of persons occupying the position of trustee. Among other things they are **assessable** in their capacity as trustees to UK taxes arising on both the income and capital of the trust.

1.3 Classification of trusts for tax purposes

Two main types of trust may be identified

(a)   **A trust with an interest in possession**

The settled property is held on trust, or for sale, for the benefit of persons entitled to a determined share of the trust property.

This can be illustrated as follows:

Property is held on trust to pay the income to Bella until she marries or dies, then to Seth for life, and then to Zorba absolutely.

Bella has an interest in possession which will terminate on her marriage or death. She is the life tenant.

Until Bella dies or marries, Seth does not have an interest in possession. He has what is known as an interest in remainder.

Zorba, the remainderman, never has an interest in possession; until he takes the property absolutely as against the trustees following the death of Seth, he only has a reversionary interest.

An **interest in possession** is a present beneficial entitlement of a life tenant to the income from, or enjoyment of, the settled property.

A **reversionary interest** is the interest of the remainderman in settled property subject to an interest in possession.

(b)   **Discretionary trusts**

This is a trust where a beneficiary only has a hope, rather than a right, of receiving some benefit which is usually at the complete discretion of the trustees. **No** interests in possession in the settled property can exist until the trust is ended at the discretion of the trustees. An important example of a discretionary trust is an **accumulation and maintenance** trust.

A **tax effective** accumulation and maintenance trust is one where a beneficiary's ability to obtain either an absolute title to the settled property or an interest in possession in the settled property is **contingent** upon him or her reaching a specified age (not exceeding 25 years) or marrying. Until a beneficiary acquires an absolute interest or interest in possession, all income of the trust must be **accumulated** unless applied for the maintenance or education of the beneficiary.

2   INCOME TAX IN RELATION TO TRUSTS

2.1   Introduction

The income of a trust with an interest in possession is subject to income tax at the basic rate of 23%. The starting rate of 10% does not apply to trusts. However, a trust's savings income is taxed at the rate of 20% and dividends are taxed at the rate of 10%. The income of a discretionary trust is generally taxed at the rate of 34%, but there are complicated rules where such a trust receives savings income or dividends. Trustees are **not** entitled to claim personal allowances to set against trust income.

Trusts are subject to self-assessment under the same system applying to individuals and, where appropriate, will make payments on account on 31 January in the tax year and 31 July following the tax year.

Taxed trust income passing to a beneficiary is subject to all rates of tax as part of his statutory total income. Further liability (eg, at higher rate) or repayments of tax deducted at source can arise.

2.2   Duties of trustees with regard to income tax

Each fiscal year the trustees must

- complete an annual return in the required form

- calculate and account to the Inland Revenue for income tax on the trust income under the self-assessment system.

- produce for each beneficiary a certificate showing the gross share of trust income and the tax deducted at source thereon.

2.3   Position of beneficiaries

Each beneficiary must include in his income tax return his gross share of the trust income.

As all trust income will have already suffered tax, the beneficiary is entitled to take credit for that tax, as notified by the trustees, in respect of his gross share of the trust income when computing any further personal liability or repayment for the year.

For interest in possession trusts (not discretionary trusts), all trust income of the tax year is **distributable** to beneficiaries. When computing a beneficiary's personal liability, it is his grossed up distributable share of the trust income for the tax year which must be brought into his computation. Grossing up will be at the 20% lower rate or special 10% rate of tax to the extent that the trust income is made up respectively of savings income or dividends, otherwise at the basic rate of income tax.

In the case of discretionary trusts, the beneficiary's gross share of the trust income will be the amount **actually paid** to him or for his benefit (eg, maintenance advances in the case of accumulation and maintenance trusts) grossed up at the rate applicable to trusts (ie, 34%).

2.4   Statements of trust income - trusts with interests in possession

This can be prepared along the lines of a personal tax computation, with an additional column showing tax deducted or retained at source on income and payments.

- **List** the statutory total income of the trust (as calculated for an individual) classifying, where appropriate, under a Schedule or Case. Where tax has been deducted at source this amount should be noted.

  UK bank deposit interest and building society interest on accounts held by the trustees of interest in possession trusts is credited to accounts, as for individuals, with lower rate income tax deducted at source.

- Dividends from UK companies have a 10% tax credit.

- **Deduct** gross charges on income (eg, annuities and covenants) authorised by the trust instrument.

  Where a charge is paid subject to basic rate relief at source this should be noted.

- **Deduct** income tax from the statutory total income.

- **Deduct** the expenses of the trustees for the management of the trust. These expenses exclude any management expenses that may be deductible in calculating the Schedule A assessable amount of property income.

- The balance represents the net trust income available for distribution to the beneficiaries.

2.5   Example: Interest in possession trust

The Ironstone Trust provides that after payment of an annuity of £500 (gross) to Potter, the sole beneficiary (life tenant) of the remaining income is Clay. The following assets are held in the trust:

Sandpit House, a freehold residence let unfurnished for an annual rental of £4,200
A building society deposit account
Several holdings of Local Authority Loan Stock.

Relevant matters involving the trustees for 1999/00 were

(1)   Receipts:

Rental of Sandpit House on 29 September 1999
Building society interest on 1 June £850 and 1 December 1999 £950
Local authority loan stock interest received (net)

30 June 1999	£360
31 December 1999	£440

(2)   Payments: £

Relating to Sandpit House:

Water rates (April and October 1999)	370
Fire insurance – 6 April 1999	30
Roof repairs	152
Annuity to Potter on 1 January 2000 (net amount paid)	385
Trust administration expenses incurred by trustees	150

Show for 1999/00

(a)   the statement of trust income, indicating the net amount available for distribution to Clay

(b)   the amount of income tax which the trustees must pay to the Inland Revenue.

(c)   the amount of trust income that will be brought into Clay's income tax computation.

2.6   Solution

(a)   **Ironstone Trust: Statement of trust income 1999/00**

Income	£	£	*Income tax paid, payable or retained at source* £
Schedule A:			
Rents receivable	4,200		
Less: Allowable expenses (370 + 30 + 152)	552		
		3,648	839
Building society interest £1,800 $\times \dfrac{100}{80}$		2,250	450
Local authority loan interest (gross)			
£(360 + 440) $\times \dfrac{100}{80}$		1,000	200
		6,898	1,489
Less: Charges on income:			
Annuity to Potter £385 $\times \dfrac{100}{77}$		(500)	(115)
Total (taxable) income		6,398	1,374
Less: Income tax			
Non savings income			
£3,148 (3,648 − 500) × 23%	724		
Savings income £3,250 × 20%	650		
		(1,374)	
		5,024	
Less: Trustees' expenses (of administration)		(150)	
Net trust income for beneficiary		4,874	

(b)   The income tax payable by the trustees is:

	£
Total liability	1,374
Add: Basic rate relief on annuity obtained at source on payment	115
Total tax payable	1,489
Less: Tax credit on interest	650
Tax to be paid	839

(c)   In order to establish the gross amount of trust income received by Clay, it is necessary to split the trust income into its various components as follows:

	£
Savings income less tax (3,250 – 650)	2,600
Other net income less tax (3,148 – 724)	2,424
	5,024
Less: Trustees' expenses	150
	4,874

The trust expenses are treated as set off against savings income in priority to other income.

The trust income that Clay received is therefore made up of:

	£
Savings income less expenses (2,600 – 150)	2,450
Other income	2,424
	4,874

The gross amount to be brought into Clay's income tax computation is

	£
Savings income ($2,450 \times \dfrac{100}{80}$)	3,062
Other income ($2,424 \times \dfrac{100}{77}$)	3,148
	6,210

2.7   Statements of trust income - discretionary trusts

There are two additional rules to remember when completing the computation for a discretionary trust.

(1)   Trustees are charged at the rate of 34%.

(2)   Dividends from UK companies are taxed at a special rate of 25%.

(3)   Income that discretionary trustees use to meet trust management expenses is not liable to tax at the rates of 34% or 25%. Instead, it is liable at the normal dividend rate of 10% (if the income is dividend income), the lower rate of 20% (if the income is savings income) or 23% (for other income). For this purpose expenses are treated as set off firstly against dividend income, then savings income and finally other income. This complicated rule can be clarified by means of an example.

2.8   Example: Discretionary trust

The facts are as in the above example except that the Ironstone Trust is a **discretionary trust**.

Calculate

(a)   the income available for distribution to discretionary beneficiaries

(b)   the income tax which the trustees must pay to the Inland Revenue.

2.9   Solution

(a)   In this example, £150 expenses will be treated as coming out of savings income, so £150 × $\frac{100}{80}$ of income was needed to pay the expenses. The remainder of the trust income is taxed at 34%. The net trust income is

		£	£
Total income as in above example			6,398
Less: Income tax			
at 34% (£6,398 – 150 × $\frac{100}{80}$)		2,111	
at 20% £188		38	
			2,149
			4,249
Less: Trustees' expenses (actual amount paid)			150
Income available for distribution to beneficiaries			4,099

(b)   Income tax payable by trustees:

	£
Total liability	2,149
Add: Basic rate relief taken at source on annuity	115
Total tax payable	2,264
Less: Tax credit on savings income	650
Tax to be paid	1,614

2.10   Certificates of deduction of tax at source

For trusts with an interest in possession, the trustees must issue to every beneficiary for each tax year a certificate of tax deduction setting out the details to be included in the beneficiary's income tax computation.

Since the trustees of a discretionary trust need not distribute the whole net income of a trust, a beneficiary's share of trust income will be the grossed up by the amount of any income actually **paid** to him by the trustees during the fiscal year.

The grossing up will be at the rate of 34% (ie, 100/66) regardless of the source of income in the trust.

Conclusion   The correct identification of a trust is important for income tax purposes, as different trusts are taxed at different rates. The various categories of income are assessable in the same way as for individuals (eg,, Schedule A income - the assessable amount is the net amount due in the tax year computed on business principles). Trusts, like individuals are subject to self-assessment. Remember that trusts do not have personal allowances.

Special care needs to be taken over the treatment of trustees' expenses.

3   CHARGEABLE GAINS IN RELATION TO TRUSTS

3.1   General considerations

Trustees are **chargeable persons** for the purposes of chargeable gains and a liability may arise where there is a disposal of a chargeable asset.

Normal principles apply for the computation of gains and losses.

As for individuals, indexation is only given up to April 1998. Taper relief may be available for disposals made after 5 April 1998.

The distinction between interest in possession and discretionary trusts is largely unimportant for chargeable gains purposes. It is more important to consider the circumstances in which disposals of settled property are made.

Trustees make **disposals** of settled property for chargeable gains purposes where

- they actually **dispose** of settled property, usually by sale to persons other than beneficiaries or other trustees (eg, when investments are sold).

- they are **deemed** to transfer settled property (eg, when property ceases to be settled property and vests absolutely with the beneficiaries).

The transfer of property into a trust is **not** a disposal of settled property chargeable upon the trustees. It is an **actual** disposal of unsettled property by the settlor to the trustees. However, it is convenient to consider such disposals within this section.

The **death** of an individual is **not** a disposal for chargeable gains purposes.

A deemed disposal of settled property arises on the **death** of the **life tenant** of an interest in possession trust, but this is not a chargeable disposal for chargeable gains purposes.

Gifts hold-over relief is available to defer gains arising from the following.

(a)   Transfers by settlor to a trust if the transfer is chargeable to IHT **when made**, ie, transfers into a **discretionary** trust.

(b)   Transfers of qualifying business assets.

The claim for hold-over relief made by the transferor does not need the consent of the transferee trustees.

(c)   Transfers of property, under (b) above, by trustees to a beneficiary.

In this case the normal joint claim is required for the relief.

Where tax does arise on chargeable gains made by the trustees of settled property, the first £3,550 of net gains are exempt (ie, half the normal (1999/00) annual exemption for individuals).

The balance is chargeable at the CGT rate for trusts, which is 34% for 1999/00.

3.2   Commencement of any trust

(a)   In the settlor's lifetime

This will be a chargeable disposal unless a specific chargeable gains exemption or relief can be utilised (eg, where a house which was previously the settlor's only or main residence is put into trust).

Since the settlor and trustees are **connected persons** the disposal by the settlor and acquisition by the trustees, will be at the **market value** on the date of the transfer.

If relevant, gifts hold-over relief may be claimed by the settlor. The trustees will acquire the assets at their current market value (less the hold-over gain where appropriate.)

(b)   Following the death of a settlor

Since the death of the settlor will not be a disposal for chargeable gains purposes no tax will arise.

As the assets are valued at death at their current market (probate) value, the trustees will acquire the assets at probate value from the personal representatives.

3.3   Example: Creation of a trust

Chicken, a wealthy farmer and landowner who died on 1 July 1999 set up two trusts.

(a)   On 6 May 1999, he created the Chicken Trust comprising 50,000 25p ordinary shares in Paxo Ltd which he had originally bought for £20,000 on 1 April 1984. On 6 May 1999, their market value was £45,000. The Chicken Trust is an accumulation and maintenance trust for the equal benefit of his twin grandchildren, Egbert and Clara. Paxo Ltd is Chicken's family trading company.

(b)   By his will, the Roost House Trust, an interest in possession trust with his wife Isobel as life tenant and his son George as remainderman. The trust comprised 15,000 £1 ordinary shares in Coop plc which Chicken had acquired in May 1985 for £21,000 and which on death were valued at £28,000.

Show the chargeable gains position, resulting from the creation of both trusts assuming hold-over relief is claimed where appropriate.

Take the indexation factor from April 1984 to April 1998 as 0.818.

3.4   Solution

(a)   Chicken Trust (discretionary trust created in settlor's lifetime)

1999/00

	£
6.5.99 Market value of Paxo shares	45,000
Cost (April 1984)	20,000
Unindexed gain	25,000
Less: IA (April 1998–April 1984) 0.818 × £20,000	16,360
	8,640
Less: Hold-over relief	
(claim by Chicken only)	8,640
Chargeable gain	NIL
Chargeable gains acquisition cost to trustees: £45,000–8,640 =	£36,360

(b)   **Roost House Trust** (interest in possession trust created on settlor's death).

1.7.99:

Since Chicken's death is **not** a disposal for chargeable gains purposes, neither gain nor loss arises and the trustees acquire the Coop plc shares at their probate value of £28,000.

3.5   Disposals of settled property other than to beneficiaries or other trustees

Where trustees dispose of settled property, usually by way of sale other than to beneficiaries or other trustees, chargeable gains or allowable losses can arise.

3.6   Example: Disposals of settled property

Facts as in the above example and the trustees of the Chicken Trust sold 10,000 ordinary shares in Paxo Ltd for net proceeds of £12,500 on 10 September 1999. The proceeds were not re-invested.

You should assume that the 50,000 shares in Paxo Ltd do not qualify as a business asset for the purposes of taper relief.

Show the chargeable gains position of the Chicken Trust after the disposal of the above mentioned shares.

3.7   Solution

Chicken Trust 1999/00

	£
Sale proceeds (10.9.99)	12,500
Cost of shares sold (6.5.99) $36,360 \times \dfrac{10,000}{50,000}$	7,272
	5,228
Annual exemption	3,550
	1,678
Capital gains tax at 34%	571

Taper relief is not available since they have not been held by the trust for three complete years post 5 April 1998. Holdover relief has been claimed, so only the holding period of the trust is relevant.

3.8   Deemed disposals of settled property

Deemed disposals of settled property arise where property passes **absolutely to the beneficiaries as against the trustees**. This will occur where

- a life tenant of an interest in possession trust either dies or otherwise gives up his interest in possession and the property passes to the remainderman

- the trustees give absolute title to the beneficiaries of an accumulation and maintenance trust (eg, when a beneficiary reaches his 25th birthday)

- the trustees of any other discretionary trust at their discretion distribute all or part of the settled property to a beneficiary.

For chargeable gains purposes, the settled property is **revalued** to the current market value on the date of the deemed disposal.

If the deemed disposal is occasioned by the **death** of a life tenant, then the disposal is not a disposal for chargeable gains purposes and no gain or loss will arise in respect of the gain arising **since acquisition** by the trustees. However, any gain held-over on the entry of the property to the trust will crystallise and become assessable.

If the deemed disposal is occasioned by **any other event**, the disposal is a chargeable disposal. (Any gain arising may be held-over if the property qualifies and the beneficiary and trustees jointly lodge a claim.)

3.9   Example: Deemed disposals of settled property

Facts as in the above examples, and assume the following events take place

30 November 2002	Chicken's twin grandchildren attain the age of 25 and the trustees distribute the settled property of the Chicken Trust to them absolutely.
31 March 2003	Chicken's wife dies and the settled property of the Roost House Trust passes absolutely to George.

Market values of the investments held in trust are

On 30 November 2002	Paxo Ltd	140p a share
On 31 March 2003	Coop plc	220p a share

Show the chargeable gains position arising from these events for both the trustees and beneficiaries assuming all appropriate claims are made, and that rates and reliefs remain the same as for 1999/00.

3.10   Solution

(a)   **Chicken Trust**

	Paxo Shares £
Deemed proceeds (30.11.02) 40,000 at 140p	56,000
Cost of shares sold (6.5.99) $36,360 \times \dfrac{40,000}{50,000}$	29,088
	26,912
Less: Hold-over relief – joint claim by beneficiaries and trustees	(26,912)
Chargeable gain	Nil

No tax payable by trustees

As a result of the deemed disposal the chargeable gains positions of the beneficiaries regarding the property are

	Egbert £	*Clara* £
Allowable cost of shares (50% each) Paxo Ltd: Market value (£56,000)	28,000	28,000
Less: Held-over gain (£26,912)	13,456	13,456
	14,544	14,544

(b)   **The Roost House Trust**

The disposal of the Coop plc shares on 31 March 2003 will not be a disposal for chargeable gains purposes since the disposal arose because of Mrs Chicken's (the life tenant's) death.

No gain or loss will arise, and the remainderman George will take over the shares at their market value on 31 March 2003 ie, $15,000 \times 220p = £33,000$.

Conclusion   Trustees are chargeable persons for the purposes of chargeable gains and normal principles apply for the computation of gains and losses. Note carefully the treatment of the following:

- creation of the trust;
- disposals of settled property; and
- deemed disposals of settled property.

Note which disposals are not treated as disposals for chargeable gains purposes.

4   INHERITANCE TAX IN RELATION TO TRUSTS

4.1   Introduction

IHT can arise, subject to available specific exemptions and reliefs, on both transfers of unsettled property into a trust and subsequent transfers of trust property.

Trustees are accountable for any liabilities arising on transfers of trust property, but unless they agree otherwise, the settlor (or, if he is dead, his personal representative) is responsible for paying tax on transfers into trust, since immediately before transfer the property was not settled property.

Lifetime transfers of property into a discretionary trust (except for transfers into an accumulation and maintenance trust) can never be PETs. Tax on such transfers is therefore chargeable when they are made at the lifetime rate of IHT of 20%.

It is necessary to consider the IHT treatment of trusts with interest in possession separately from that applying to discretionary trusts.

4.2   Trusts with interests in possession

Two situations need to be considered:

(a)   the transfer into settlement, and
(b)   a transfer of settled property caused by a termination of the life-tenant's interest in possession.

Under (a) above, IHT **will** be charged at normal rates if the settlor dies within seven years of the transfer.

IHT can be avoided in whole or in part on this occasion if a specific exemption or relief is available. In particular where the life tenant of the trust is the spouse of the settlor, the inter-spouse exemption applies. This exemption is available because the spouse as the life tenant acquires an **immediate beneficial interest** (in possession) in the settled property. In contrast, it would not apply if the spouse was made the remainderman since his or her interest is only reversionary until the interest in possession terminates.

Under (b) above IHT **will** be charged at normal rates if

- the termination of the interest in possession is caused by the death of the life-tenant. The capital value of the trust immediately before the death is included in the life-tenant's estate and charged at the estate rate on death. The tax is borne by the remainderman and is payable by the trustees

- the interest in possession is terminated by a lifetime transfer (a PET) and the life-tenant then dies within the subsequent 7 years. The PET becomes chargeable, as a result of the death, in the normal way and subject to any available exemptions IHT is borne and payable by the transferee.

4.3 Example: Interest in possession trusts on death

John Largebut died on 1 November 1999. There are the following circumstances arising on his death.

(a) He was the life tenant of his uncle's estate. The total value of this trust at 1 November 1999 was £94,625.

(b) John Largebut was the remainderman of his sister's estate, the life tenant being his brother Timothy. At 1 November 1999 Timothy is still alive and the value of his sister's estate is £15,915.

What is the IHT position arising under each of the above mentioned circumstances?

4.4 Solution

(a) John Largebut had a beneficial interest at death in his uncle's estate, and the capital value of the trust will be brought into the computation of IHT on his death as settled property, and the tax computed at normal IHT rates by reference to the accumulated value of Largebut's gross lifetime transfers in the seven years before his death plus the value of his free estate passing on his death. The tax will be payable by the trustees of the uncle's trust and borne by the remainderman.

(b) Although John Largebut would have become absolutely entitled to the capital of £15,915 had he lived, the transfer of the reversionary interest is excluded property for IHT purposes and no tax will arise.

4.5 Introduction to discretionary trusts

The IHT provisions for discretionary trusts contains two basic occasions of charge. As the property may remain within the trust for many years, a charge is levied every tenth anniversary of the settlement, basically at 30% of lifetime rates. This is intended to approximate to the charge that would have arisen had the property been owned outright and passed from generation to generation.

In addition there is a charge to IHT if property ceases to be subject to the discretionary trust regime (the exit charge). As that property will have been subject to the ten year anniversary charge, it would be inequitable to charge IHT at full lifetime rates; also, the ten year anniversary charge may have been very recent. The charge on property ceasing to be subject to the discretionary trust regime is therefore based on the rate charged at the previous anniversary, but scaled down to reflect the time that must pass before the next ten year anniversary.

Thus, if a trust was created in January 1986 and terminated in February 2000, there would be a ten year anniversary charge in 1996, and on the termination in 2000 the rate would be 4/10 of the previous ten year anniversary rate, as only four years had passed.

A discretionary trust is a separate entity for IHT purposes, and has its own cumulative IHT record. It was considered that it would be too advantageous if its clock started from zero, whatever the settlor's IHT history. Therefore, each trust is treated as an offshoot from the settlor, effectively starting with the settlor's cumulative total of transfers immediately before the trust was made.

4.6 Charges on property in discretionary trusts

A ten yearly charge is levied on the amount of property in the trust at each tenth anniversary of the trust. An exit charge is levied when property is distributed from the trust.

There are three main occasions which require an IHT computation, and these will now be dealt with in order, as follows:

- Exit charge before the first ten year anniversary.
- Periodic charge at ten year anniversary.
- Exit charge between ten year anniversaries.

The examiner has stated that a question will not be set involving the computation of the tenth anniversary charge or an exit charge. However, a written question could be set.

4.7   Exit charge before the first ten year anniversary

(a)   A charge to IHT arises if property leaves the trust. The amount liable to tax is the value of property in the trust before the disposition, less the value of property in the trust after the disposition. If the tax is to be paid from the property ceasing to be trust property (i.e. by the recipient), then the value of trust property before less trust property after is the **gross** transfer. If the tax is to be paid out of property remaining trust property (i.e. by the trustees), then the value of trust property before less trust property after must be grossed up by the effective rate of tax.

(b)   This can be illustrated as follows:

The trustees of Molescroft discretionary trust advanced £10,000 to Ben, the IHT to be paid by the trustees from the property remaining within the trust. One year later an interest in possession in the remaining funds, valued at £75,000, was appointed to Carol.

The advance of £10,000 is the net advance, and must be grossed up.

The appointment in favour of Carol is a gross transfer of £75,000; the IHT is to be found out of the £75,000.

(c)   If an exit charge to IHT arises before the first ten year anniversary an effective rate of tax must be calculated. A hypothetical transfer is used to compute the effective rate as follows:

- The hypothetical transfer of value is the value immediately after the settlement of the property then comprised in it.

- The hypothetical cumulative total of transfers is the cumulative total of transfers made by the settlor in the seven years ending on the settlement date.

- The effective rate of tax is the rate of tax at the lifetime rate that would be charged on the hypothetical transfer assuming the hypothetical cumulative total of transfers.

- Having calculated the effective rate of tax the rate of charge on the gross transfer is:

$$30\% \times \frac{x}{40} \times \text{effective rate}$$

where x = the number of complete successive quarters that have expired between the settlement date and the date of the charge.

(d)   This can be illustrated as follows:

On 1 April 1997 Daniel set up a discretionary trust. He transferred £120,000 into the trust paying the IHT himself.

He had a gross cumulative total of transfers in the previous seven years of £131,000. On 23 July 1999 the trustees advanced £20,000 to Mary; Mary is to pay the IHT arising.

The effective rate is calculated on a hypothetical transfer of £120,000 (the value of the property in the trust at the date of settlement) with a hypothetical cumulative total of transfers of £131,000, using current scales.

	Gross £	Tax £
Cumulative total	131,000	–
Transfer	120,000	4,000
(20% [£251,000 – 231,000])	251,000	4,000

Effective rate of tax $\dfrac{4,000}{120,000} \times 100\% = 3.333\%$

Tax charged on the advance to Mary:

Advance – gross   £20,000

Number of complete quarters between settlement (1 April 1997) and advance (23 July 1999) = 9

Rate of tax $= 30\% \times \dfrac{9}{40} \times 3.3333\% = 0.225\%$

Tax charged $= £20,000 \times 0.225\% = £45$

4.8   Charge at ten year anniversary

(a)   The ten yearly periodic charge is levied on the value of the property in the trust at each tenth anniversary. The rate of tax is 30% of the effective lifetime rate that would be charged on a hypothetical transfer of value made by a taxpayer with a hypothetical cumulative total of transfers.

The hypothetical transfer is basically the value of property in the trust immediately preceding the anniversary.

The hypothetical cumulative total of transfers is the aggregate of:

- the cumulative total of transfers made by the settlor in the seven years prior to the date of the trust; and

- capital paid out of the trust in the previous ten years.

(b)   This can be illustrated as follows:

On 1 April 1990 Charles settled £100,000 on discretionary trusts for his grandchildren. His cumulative total of transfers immediately prior to the settlement was £106,000. On 1 April 1997 the trustees made a payment of £70,000 to his grandson Ian. On 31 March 2000 the value of property remaining within the settlement was £130,000. (All transfers are stated gross.) The ten year periodic charge is calculated as follows:

	£
The hypothetical transfer is the value of property in the trust immediately preceding the transfer	130,000

The hypothetical cumulative total is the aggregate of:

(i)	the settlor's cumulative total in the seven years immediately before the settlement	106,000
(ii)	capital distributed – payment to Ian	70,000
		176,000

Rate of tax on a hypothetical transfer of £130,000 with hypothetical cumulative total of £176,000 at half-scale rates:

	Gross £	Tax £
Cumulative total	176,000	Nil
Transfer	130,000	15,000
(20% [£306,000 – 231,000])	306,000	15,000

Effective rate of tax $\dfrac{15,000}{130,000} \times 100\% = 11.538\%$

The ten-year charge is levied on the value of trust property at the anniversary date at 30% of the effective rate.

The charge is 30% × 11.538% × £130,000 =   £4,500

4.9   Exit charge between ten year anniversaries

The rate of exit charge between ten year anniversaries is the appropriate fraction of the rate at which tax was charged on the previous ten year anniversary.

The appropriate fraction is x/40, where x is the number of complete quarters that have elapsed since the ten year charge.

Note that the appropriate fraction is x/40, whereas for a new discretionary settlement, in the case of an exit charge before the first anniversary, the appropriate fraction was x/40 × 30%. Although use of the same terminology for different figures may cause confusion there is no discrepancy in the charge, since between anniversaries the 30% multiplier has already been taken into account in calculating the rate of tax on the ten year charge.

4.10   Accumulation and maintenance trusts

The accumulation and maintenance trust is a privileged trust for IHT purposes. This means that

- the 10 year anniversary charge will not apply

- exit charges will not be raised where either a beneficiary takes property (from the trust) absolutely or becomes entitled to an interest in possession, or dies before reaching the specified age.

An accumulation and maintenance trust will only acquire privileged trust status if the following conditions are **all satisfied:** namely the trust is one where

- one or more persons (beneficiaries) will, on or before attaining a specified age **not exceeding 25**, become absolutely entitled to the settled property, or to an interest in possession in the settled property, and

- (prior to that time) **no** interest in possession subsists in the settled property and the income from it is **accumulated** so far as not applied for the maintenance, education or benefit of any beneficiary, and

- **either:** not more than 25 years have elapsed since the settlement commenced, *or*

   all the persons who are, or have been, beneficiaries are, or were

   (1) either grandchildren of a common grandparent, or

   (2) children, widows or widowers of such grandchildren who were beneficiaries but died before becoming entitled to their interest.

Conclusion | The inheritance tax provisions for discretionary trusts appear quite tricky; the best approach is to consider the three occasions of charge:

- transfer of property into a trust;
- ten year anniversary charge; and
- the exit charge.

Work through the provisions for each of these events in turn until you feel you understand the straightforward computational aspects.

5   TAX PLANNING

5.1   Income tax

The normal rate of tax for discretionary trusts at 34% is lower than the top of rate of tax (40%) for an individual.

The tax saving only arises where income is accumulated, and for this reason there are no savings as regards an interest in possession trust where all income is appropriated to beneficiaries.

5.2   Capital gains tax

The rate of tax is 34%, which is less than the top rate of tax for individuals.

The availability of holdover relief will often avoid any CGT charge on setting up a trust.

However, this depends either on the trust being a discretionary trust or the property settled being 'business' property.

5.3   Inheritance tax

The main scope for tax planning with an interest in possession trust is that assets may be given away without giving up control. There is therefore more incentive to make gifts of assets earlier in life, when there is less chance of them becoming chargeable as a result of being made within seven years of death.

The IHT position as regards discretionary trust is generally unattractive. There is some scope for tax planning where transfers into a discretionary trust are kept to below £231,000 (including the settlor's chargeable lifetime transfers), since no IHT charge should then arise unless the value of the trust property rises above the nil rate band.

6   SELF TEST QUESTIONS

6.1   What are the two main types of trust? (1.3)

6.2   What rate of income tax do discretionary trusts pay? (2.1)

6.3   What rate of capital gains tax do trusts pay? (3.1)

6.4   What are the capital gains tax consequences of the death of the settlor? (3.2)

6.5   IHT can arise on transfers of property into what type of trust? (4.1)

6.6   How is an exit charge before the first ten year anniversary calculated? (4.7)

6.7   How is the periodic charge at the ten year anniversary calculated? (4.8)

6.8   How is the exit charge between ten year anniversaries calculated? (4.9)

7   EXAMINATION TYPE QUESTION

7.1   George Doyle

(1)   Under the terms of a trust created by George Doyle the trustees have a discretionary power to pay income to Mr Doyle's niece Mary. The following is a summary of the trustees' cash book.

	Year ended 5 April 2000
Receipts	£
Sale of shares in Crown plc	5,500
Building Society interest	3,360
Payments	£
Income paid to Mary	858
Trustees' expenses	69

George Doyle transferred 1,400 shares in Crown plc into the trust on 4 July 1986, when they were quoted at 60p each. The trustees sold these shares on 7 April 1999 for £5,500.

You are required in respect of the year 1999/00 to calculate

(a)   the income available for distribution to beneficiaries and the CGT payable by the trustees.

(b)   the amounts to be included in the certificate of tax deduction given to Mary.

(2)   The above George Doyle decided to transfer in February 2000 some unquoted securities to the trustees of the settlement. These comprise 1,000 of the 2,500 ordinary shares in Diadem Ltd acquired in 1980 for a net cost of £750 and having a current market value of 566p per share and a market value at 31 March 1982 of 100p per share. He has made the election for gains and losses on all assets held on 31 March 1982 to be computed by reference to the market value on 31 March 1982.

George has asked you to explain the capital gains consequences of making this transfer and also to explain the capital gains situation when the trust terminates and Mary becomes absolutely entitled as against the trustees to the shares.

Take the indexation factor from March 1982 to April 1998 as 1.047.

You are required to give a brief explanation.

8   ANSWER TO EXAMINATION TYPE QUESTION

8.1   George Doyle

(1)   **Trustees of George Doyle Trust**

(a)   Income available for distribution to beneficiaries 1999/00

(1)   Income tax

	£	£
Building Society interest £3,360 × $^{100}/_{80}$		4,200
Less: Income tax		
At 34% (£4,200 − 69 × 100/80)	1,399	
At 20% £86	17	
		1,416
		2,784
Less: Trustees expenses		69
Income available for distribution to beneficiaries		2,715

(2)   Capital gains tax

	No of shares	Indexed cost £	Proceeds £	Gain/ loss £
1985 Pool				
4.7.86 Transferred at MV	1,400	840		
Indexed rise to April 1998				
$\frac{162.6-97.52}{97.52} \times £840$		561		
		1,401		
7.4.99 Sale			5,500	
Cost	(1,400)	(1,401)	(1,401)	
Chargeable gain c/d	–	–	4,099	4,099
Less: Annual exemption				(3,550)
				549
CGT @ 34% payable by trustees				187

No taper relief is available, since the shares (which are a non-business asset) have not been owned for a sufficient period after 5 April 1998.

(b)   Amounts to be included in Mary's certificate of tax deduction

	£
Gross income	1,300
Tax (£858 × $^{34}/_{66}$)	442
Actual income received	858

(2)   **George Doyle**

		£
(i)	Transfer of shares to trustees in 1999/00	
	MV at time of transfer 1,000 × 566p	5,660
	Less: 31.12.82 MV – 1,000 × 100p	1,000
	Unindexed gain	4,660
	Less: IA	
	(Apr'98 – March'82)	
	1.047 × £1,000	(1,047)
		3,613
	Less: Holdover relief	(3,613)
	Chargeable gain	Nil

The trustees have a capital gains acquisition cost of

	£
MV of shares on acquisition	5,660
Less: Held-over gain	(3,613)
Deemed cost	2,047

(ii)   Transfer of shares to Mary when trust terminates

	£
MV at time of transfer, say	8,500
Less: Deemed cost of acquisition	(2,047)
	6,453
Less: Holdover relief	(6,453)
Chargeable gain	Nil

The beneficiary (Mary) will acquire the shares as follows

	£
MV on acquisition	8,500
Less: Held-over gain	6,453
Deemed CG cost	2,047

35 VAT

INTRODUCTION & LEARNING OBJECTIVES

Value added tax (VAT) is a tax on goods and services consumed in the UK. It is levied on goods and services produced in the UK and on imports into the UK. The basic principle of VAT is that it is a tax borne by the final consumer.

It is a tax that is easily overlooked in the exam.

When you have studied this chapter you should have learned the following:

- The scope of VAT: taxable transactions and taxable persons;
- Definition of supply, and the various sorts of supply;
- Registration;
- Output and input tax;
- The tax point;
- The detail required in a tax invoice;
- Bad debt relief; and
- Partial exemption.

1   BACKGROUND OF VALUE ADDED TAX

1.1   Introduction

Value added tax (VAT) is a tax on consumer expenditure, and is thus classified as an indirect tax.

VAT is the common consumer tax adopted by European Union (EU) member states. Its main features are set out in a series of Directives made by the EU Council of Ministers, which have been translated into statutes and statutory instruments made by Parliament.

VAT is administered by the Commissioners of Customs and Excise partly through a centralised unit and partly through a network of local VAT Offices situated in most major towns. The division of responsibilities broadly results in VAT Central Unit dealing with tax returns and payments and repayments of tax while the outfield deals with the registration and deregistration of traders and the carrying out of tax audits known as 'control visits'. This latter function arises from the fact that VAT is a self-assessed tax.

The Commissioners of Customs & Excise are referred to in this chapter as 'the Commissioners'. In practice, their functions are largely carried out by customs officers based at VAT Central Unit and the local VAT Offices.

The main structure of VAT is set out in VATA 1994. Many of the detailed provisions concerning the operation of VAT are contained in orders, rules and regulations made by statutory instrument under enabling provisions contained in VATA 1994.

VAT is charged on the supply of goods and services in the UK where the supply is a **taxable supply** by a **taxable person** in the course or furtherance of a business **carried on by him.** VAT is also charged on **imported goods** and **acquisitions** of goods from another EU member state.

The meaning of these terms is discussed below.

1.2   Taxable transactions

It has already been said that VAT is a tax on consumer expenditure. To be more specific, it is a tax on three different classes of transaction, each of which has its own collection procedures:

(a)   **Supplies of goods and services.** VAT is charged on supplies of goods and services made in the UK by traders known as 'taxable persons'. Tax is charged by the taxable person who makes the supply and he periodically pays the amounts so charged to the Commissioners. This tax is known as 'output tax'.

(b)   **Imported goods.** VAT is charged when goods are imported into the UK from a country other than another EU member state. In broad terms, the importer pays any tax due direct to the Commissioners.

(c)   **Acquisitions**. If a UK registered trader imports goods from another EU member state - an 'acquisition' - he has to account for VAT as if he had sold the goods (to himself). The actual sale was zero rated in the seller's member state, being to another member state. The deemed sale in the purchaser's member state enables the VAT rules of the purchaser's state to apply.

The transactions which comprise a supply of goods and services and the manner in which output tax is calculated is described later.

1.3   Taxable persons

It will be noted that taxable persons play an important role in the administration of VAT in that it is they who collect output tax on behalf of the Commissioners.

The economic purpose of VAT is to tax personal (not business) consumption of goods and services and it is therefore necessary to ensure that VAT does not enter into the business costs. This is done by providing taxable persons with a credit mechanism whereby (subject to certain exceptions) they are able to recover the VAT which they have paid. This is known as 'input tax', and represents:

(a)   tax chargeable on goods and services supplied to them by taxable persons;

(b)   tax paid to the Commissioners on the goods which they import; and

(c)   tax chargeable on acquisitions from other EU member states.

Since taxable persons collect output tax from their customers and recover their input tax from the Commissioners, VAT has (in theory) a neutral effect on business costs.

Not all traders are taxable persons. The manner in which traders are identified as taxable persons and the manner in which input tax is recovered from the Commissioners is described later.

2   SUPPLIES

2.1   Introduction

VAT is charged on supplies of goods and services made in the UK. This part of the chapter defines what is meant by a 'supply', sets out the conditions to be met before a supply is within the scope of the tax, describes the manner in which supplies of goods are distinguished from supplies of services, and shows how supplies which are charged to tax are segregated from those which are not.

2.2   Definition of supply

'Supply' is the all embracing term given to the infinite variety of transactions met in the commercial world. In broad terms it may be said to comprise 'the passing of possession of goods pursuant to an agreement' and anything else done for consideration.

2.3   Chargeable supplies

A supply within the foregoing definition must meet four conditions before it is within the scope of VAT:

- it must be made by a taxable person;
- it must be made for a consideration;
- it must be made in the UK; and
- it must be made in the course or furtherance of business.

(a)   **Supplies made by a taxable person**

VAT is charged on supplies made by taxable persons, and it follows that supplies made by traders who are not taxable persons are outside the scope of VAT. The manner in which a trader is identified as a taxable person is described later.

(b)   **Supplies made for a consideration**

The consideration made for a supply may comprise money, something other than money (eg, a barter transaction) or a combination of both (eg, a part exchange deal).

The general rule is that all transactions must be made for a consideration before they are treated as a supply. There are two exceptions. Goods are supplied whether or not there is a consideration if:

- they form part of the assets of a business and are transferred or disposed of in accordance with the trader's directions so as to no longer form part of those assets. This would include, for example, a gift to anyone or an appropriation for the proprietor's personal use; or

- they are held or used for the purposes of a business and are used for a private or non-business purpose in accordance with the trader's directions. This would include, for example, private use of a business motor car by the proprietor or one of the employees.

The following gifts of goods are outside the scope of VAT:

- goods which cost the trader £15 or less and do not form part of a series of gifts;

- industrial or commercial samples unless the recipient is given more than one sample of the same item.

(c)   **Supplies made in the UK**

VAT is charged on supplies made in the UK and it follows that supplies made outside the UK are outside the scope of VAT. Different rules apply to goods and services in determining whether they are supplies in the UK.

Goods are supplied in the UK if they are located here and either removed to another place in the UK or exported. Thus, a motor car manufactured in Birmingham is supplied in the UK whether the manufacturer delivers it to a customer in London or a customer in Zurich.

Services are supplied in the country where the trader belongs and the place where they are actually performed is irrelevant.

(d)   **Supplies made in the course or furtherance of business**

VAT is charged on supplies made in the course or furtherance of any business carried on by the trader who supplies them.

The term 'business' has been widely construed by the courts to include any occupation or function actively pursued with reasonable continuity, regardless of profit motive, unless it is carried on solely for pleasure and social enjoyment.

Once an activity has been identified as a business, any supply made while carrying it on is likely to be made in the course or furtherance of business. No distinction is made between revenue and capital, so the sale of surplus plant is just as much a supply as the sale of trading stock.

2.4   Supplies of goods and services

Supplies which meet the foregoing conditions are divided into supplies of goods, supplies of services, and supplies of neither goods nor services. VAT is charged on supplies of goods and supplies of services. Supplies of neither goods nor services are outside the scope of VAT.

(a)   Supply of goods

The following supplies amount to a 'supply of goods':

- Transferring the ownership and possession of goods, either immediately (eg, on a sale of goods) or at a specified future time (eg, under a hire purchase agreement where ownership passes when the goods are fully paid for).

- Applying a treatment or process to another person's goods.

- Supplying any form of power, heat, refrigeration or ventilation.

- Granting a freehold interest in land or a lease for a term exceeding twenty-one years.

(b)   Supply of services

Anything done for a consideration which is not a supply of goods is a supply of services. This includes the grant, assignment or surrender of any right. The hire, lease and rental of goods amounts to a supply of services.

(c)   Supply of neither goods nor services.

The following supplies are specifically excluded from the scope of VAT by treating them as neither a supply of goods nor a supply of services.

- The assets of a business, or part of a business, transferred as a going concern.

- Goods and services supplied by one group company to another if both companies are included in the same group registration.

2.5   Exempt and taxable supplies

VAT is charged on taxable supplies.

Definition   A taxable supply is a supply of goods or a supply of services as defined above which is not an exempt supply.

From this definition it will be seen that it is necessary to divide supplies of goods and services between exempt supplies on one hand and taxable supplies on the other in order to determine whether tax should be charged.

(a)   Exempt supplies

The position of an exempt supply in the scheme of VAT is as follows.:

- **No** tax is charged on it.
- It is **not** taken into account in determining whether a trader is a taxable person.
- Input tax attributable to it is not normally available for credit.

As regards the last item, therefore, the position of an exempt supply is significantly different from a supply of neither goods nor services, which is merely ignored for all VAT purposes.

Those goods and services which are classed as exempt supplies are listed later.

(b)   **Taxable supplies**

> **Definition**   Any supply of goods or services which is not an exempt supply is a taxable supply, and it is with this category that VAT is primarily concerned.

2.6   The rate of tax

Taxable supplies are charged to tax at one or other of two rates: the zero-rate and the standard rate.

(a)   **The zero-rate**

The zero-rate is a tax rate of nil. Thus, although no tax is charged on a supply taxed at the zero rate, it is in all other respects treated as a taxable supply. It is therefore taken into account in determining whether a trader is a taxable person, and input tax attributable to it is available for credit. In these two respects it has the opposite effect to an exempt supply. The zero-rate applies to goods and services generally regarded as necessities. It also applies to goods supplied for export.

Those goods and services which are classed as zero-rated supplies are listed later.

(b)   **The standard rate**

The standard rate is a tax rate of 17.5% based on the tax **exclusive** value of the goods or services supplies. This is equivalent to 7/47 of the tax **inclusive** value (ie, consideration) of the goods or services supplied. This fraction is known as the 'VAT fraction'.

Any taxable supply which is not charged to tax at the zero-rate is charged to tax at the standard rate.

There is an exception. A supply of fuel and power (eg, electricity) for domestic or charity use bears a VAT rate of 5%.

> **Conclusion**   A taxable supply is a supply of goods or services (other than an exempt supply) made in the UK.

A taxable supply is either

- standard rated (taxed at 17½%); or
- zero rated (taxed at 0%); or
- in the case of domestic fuel and power, taxed at 5%.

An exempt supply is not chargeable to tax.

3   TAXABLE PERSONS

3.1   Introduction

A taxable person is someone who is, or is required to be registered for the purposes of VAT. A trader is liable to be registered if the value of his **taxable** supplies exceeds the statutory limits, but he may be voluntarily registered in other circumstances if he so requests.

A person is entitled to be registered only once, and his registration includes **all** the businesses he carries on, however diverse they may be. Separate businesses carried on by the same partners, even though they may have separate partnership agreements, will have a single registration. A 'person' for this purpose is either:

(a)   a natural person ie, an individual;

(b)   a body corporate eg, a company registered under the Companies Act 1985; or

(c)   an unincorporated association eg, a partnership.

This section sets out the circumstances when a trader may be registered or deregistered for the purposes of VAT, the tax consequences of deregistration, the notifications which taxable persons are required to make, and the special registration provisions applicable to groups of companies and partnerships.

3.2   Registration by reference to historical turnover

Unregistered traders are required to keep a continual eye on their taxable turnover. At the end of every month they must calculate their taxable turnover for the year then ended. A trader is required to register if his taxable turnover (standard and zero rated) for the year then ended exceeds £51,000.

A trader can claim exemption from registration if the Commissioners are satisfied that his taxable turnover in the following year will not exceed £49,000.

Taxable turnover for a period comprises:

(a)   Amounts received or receivable in respect of taxable supplies made in the period, other than supplies of capital assets (eg, surplus plant sold).

(b)   Value of supplies of services received from abroad deemed to have been supplies by the trader in the period.

A trader liable to registration may claim exemption from registration if his taxable turnover largely comprises zero-rated supplies. Exemption is given if this does not prejudice VAT revenue ie, if the trader would regularly receive repayments of tax if he were to be registered.

A trader liable to registration must notify the Commissioners not later than thirty days after the end of the month in which taxable turnover in the previous year exceeds the statutory limit. He is registered from the end of the month following the month in which turnover exceeded the limit, or an earlier agreed date.

3.3   Example

Harry commenced trading on 1 January 1999. His monthly taxable supplies were as follows:

	1999 £	2000 £
January	2,700	3,590
February	2,800	3,660
March	2,900	4,030
April	3,000	4,100
May	3,040	4,770
June	3,110	4,840
July	3,180	4,810
August	3,250	4,780
September	3,320	4,840
October	3,390	4,910
November	3,450	4,980
December	3,530	5,150

In addition, in October 1999 he sold surplus plant for £1,100.

From what date is Harry liable to register for VAT?

3.4 Solution

At the end of October 2000 his taxable turnover for the past year is:

	£
Value of supplies for registration purposes:	
Supplies to customers	51,310
Supply of plant (disregarded)	-
	51,310

Harry is thus liable to register, and must notify the Commissioners by 30 November 2000. He will be registered from 1 December 2000, or such earlier date as may jointly be agreed.

3.5 Registration by reference to future turnover

The historical turnover limits described above are subject to an overriding provision. If at any time, a trader who makes taxable supplies has reason to believe that his taxable turnover for a future thirty day period is likely to exceed £51,000, he must notify the Commissioners no later than the end of that period and is normally registered with effect from the start of that period. Thus, if a trader starts a new business with reasonable expectations, or an established trader expands his business, this provision could well require him to register immediately.

3.6 Activity

Charles leaves his job on 31 December 1999, signs a lease for new business premises on 1 January 2000 and opens for business on 20 March 2000. He estimates, from the outset, that taxable supplies will be in the region of £55,000 per month.

When, if at all, is Charles liable to register?

3.7 Activity solution

Charles is liable to registration because supplies for the thirty days to 18 April 2000 will exceed £51,000. He must notify the Commissioners of his liability to registration by 18 April 2000 and is registered with effect from 20 March 2000.

Note: Charles does not make taxable supplies during the period 1 January 2000 to 19 March 2000. The future limit does not apply to such traders so that a liability to registration cannot arise during this period. However, Charles could apply for intending trader registration (see later in this chapter) at any time during this period if he so wished eg, to accelerate claims for input tax credit.

3.8 Disaggregation

There is a provision to prevent a business from being artificially split into small units thereby avoiding VAT registration because one or more units fell below the turnover limits.

Where the Commissioners are satisfied that persons are carrying on separate activities which could properly be regarded as part of a single business, then they will issue a direction.

There is no requirement for the Commissioners to establish that the main reason for the separation of the activities was to avoid registration for VAT.

The direction will state that the persons named therein are carrying on activities listed together, ie, a partnership is deemed to exist. However, a direction cannot have retrospective effect.

For example, if a husband and wife run a pub together, but the wife operates the pub catering separately, both activities will be considered as one business if a direction is made. The turnover from both activities will be taken into account for the registration limits.

3.9 Deregistration

A registered trader ceases to be liable to registration when he ceases to make taxable supplies. He must notify the Commissioners of this event within thirty days and is then deregistered from the date of cessation or a mutually agreed later date. For example, if James closes down his business on 10 January 2000, he must notify the Commissioners on or before 9 February 2000 and is then deregistered from 10 January 2000 or an agreed later date.

A trader is eligible for **voluntary** deregistration if the value of his anticipated taxable turnover for the ensuing year does not exceed £49,000. The twelve month period is measured at any time and the onus is on the trader to satisfy the Commissioners that he qualifies under this provision. The trader is deregistered from the date of his request or a mutually agreed later date. Thus, if Edward reckons that taxable turnover for the year to 31 December 2000 will be £40,000, and applies for deregistration on 1 January 2000, he is deregistered with effect from 1 January 2000 or an agreed later date.

Where a trader disposes of his business as a going concern, and thereby ceases to make taxable supplies, he is liable to be deregistered under the foregoing provisions. However, instead of doing so, both the transferor and the transferee may make a joint election for the transferor's registration to be transferred to the transferee. Where this done, the transferee assumes all rights and obligations in respect of the registration including the liability to pay any outstanding tax.

3.10 Tax consequences of deregistration

Traders are deemed to supply their business assets (eg, plant and trading stock) when they cease to be a taxable person. The deemed supply is based on the replacement cost of the goods concerned. Individual items are not deemed to be supplied if they did not qualify for input tax credit when acquired.

For example, Frank ceases business on 1 December 1999. Trading stock was valued at £5,250 and the only unsold assets was a car which cost £2,750. Input tax credit is disallowed on motor cars, so this asset is ignored for the purposes of the deemed supply. Output tax on trading stock would be £5,250 @ 17.5% = £918.75.

3.11 Voluntary registration

(a) **Actual traders**

A trader who **makes** taxable supplies, but is not currently liable to registration under the historical or future registration provision, is eligible for voluntary registration. The Commissioners will register him, if he so requests, from the date of his request or a mutually agreed earlier date.

(b) **Intending traders**

A trader who carries on a business and **intends** to make taxable supplies in the course or furtherance of that business is not liable to registration under the future registration provisions while his intention is unfulfilled. He is, however, eligible for voluntary registration. The Commissioners will register him, if he so requests from the date of his request or a mutually agreed earlier date.

3.12 Benefits of voluntary registration

Input VAT can be recovered if a person is registered. It will therefore be beneficial to voluntarily register where:

- the person makes mainly zero-rated supplies.

  Input VAT will be recovered, and no VAT will be charged on zero-rated outputs.

- the person makes supplies mainly to registered customers.

  Input VAT will be recovered, and although output VAT will be due, this will be recoverable by the customers. It should therefore be possible to charge output VAT on top of the pre-registration selling price.

In addition, registration may give the impression of a more substantial business, than is otherwise the case.

3.13   Partnerships

A partnership registration continues when a partner retires or a new partner is admitted provided that the firm continues to exist. However, the dissolution of a partnership will result in a deregistration, even if a former partner carries on the business as a sole trader. The former partner is required to register in his own name, although a joint election could be made for the partnership registration to be transferred to him. Admissions and retirements must be notified to the Commissioners.

3.14   Transfer of a business as a going concern

Where a business carried on by a taxable person is transferred as a going concern this is not treated as a supply of goods or services, but rather as a change in the taxable person carrying on the business. The transferee can even apply to retain the VAT registration number if the transferor ceases business entirely. However in this case the transferee would also inherit any liability for VAT unpaid by the transferor.

The business must be sold as a going concern to another taxable person, or to someone who becomes a taxable person immediately after the sale. Otherwise, output tax will be payable on the supply (see the tax consequences of deregistration).

3.15   Special provisions

(a)   **Groups of companies**

Two or more companies can elect to be treated as a group of companies if one company controls the others or one person controls them all. The effects of a group registration are as follows:

- goods and services supplied by one group company to another are outside the scope of VAT;

- supplies made to or by group companies are treated as made to or by a nominated group company known as the representative member;

Consequently, only the representative member is registered and it is responsible for submitting VAT returns and paying VAT on behalf of the group.

Group VAT registration is restricted to companies that are established or have a fixed establishment in the UK.

An application for group VAT registration has immediate effect, although the Commissioners have 90 days during which they can refuse the application. The application will be refused if the companies concerned are ineligible for VAT grouping, or where the membership of the group would pose a threat to VAT revenue. The Commissioners can remove a company from a VAT group on similar grounds.

It is not necessary to include all members in the group treatment. For example, a company in the group in a net repayment position for VAT could stay outside the VAT group and submit monthly (instead of quarterly) returns to accelerate its cash flow and thereby the cash flow of the group.

Care will have to be taken when deciding whether or not to include a company in a group VAT election where that company makes exempt supplies.

If the company is included, then the group will become partially exempt. It will be necessary for the group to compare its existing recovery of input VAT with the recovery if the company is included. It might be the case that the total exempt input VAT is below the *de minimis* limits (see later in this chapter), in which case inclusion would probably be beneficial.

A further factor to consider would be that supplies of goods and services to the exempt company would be disregarded if the company was part of the group VAT registration. This would be beneficial, since the input VAT on these would otherwise be irrecoverable.

(b)   Companies organised in divisions

In some cases a large enterprise operates not as a group of companies but as a single company with a number of divisions. If the divisions are largely autonomous units dealing in different products and having separate accounting systems, it may be difficult to produce one VAT return for the whole company. In these circumstances the company can apply to be registered in the name of its separate divisions.

Conclusion A trader may be required to register by reference to his historical turnover or his future turnover. Traders may also register voluntarily. A registered trader ceases to be liable to registration when he ceases to make taxable supplies. A registered trader may deregister voluntarily if the value of his anticipated taxable turnover for the next year does not exceed £49,000.

4   OUTPUT TAX

4.1   Introduction

Output tax is the tax charged on supplies made by a taxable person. This section deals with two matters:

(a)   The manner in which the tax due on an individual supply is calculated; and

(b)   The manner in which the tax due to the Commissioners for a prescribed accounting period is calculated.

4.2   Value

Tax is charged on the value of the goods or services supplied. Where the consideration for a supply is paid in money, value represents the trader's tax-exclusive selling price less the amount of any cash discount offered. Thus if Anthony's tax-exclusive selling price is £1,000, and he offers a cash discount of 3.75% for payment within seven days, VAT is charged on £962.50 (ie, £1,000 less 3.75% thereof = £37.50). This is **not** amended if the customer fails to qualify for discount and has to pay the higher net amount of £1,000.

Open market value is the tax-exclusive amount which a customer would pay if the price is not influenced by any commercial, financial or other relationship between himself and the seller. VAT is charged on open market value in the following circumstances:

(a)   The supply is made for a consideration which comprises something other than money eg, a barter transaction whereby chickens are exchanged for petrol.

(b) The supply is made for a consideration which comprises partly money and partly something other than money eg, a new car is sold for £1,000 plus a used car taken in part exchange.

(c) The supply is made to a connected person for a consideration below market value and the Commissioners issue a direction that VAT is to be accounted for on future supplies by reference to open market value.

4.3 The time of supply (the tax point)

Tax is charged in accordance with the legislation in force at the time when goods and services are treated as being supplied. As a general principle, goods are treated as supplied when they are collected, delivered or made available to a customer and services are treated as supplied when they are performed. This is known as the basic tax point.

The basic tax point is amended in two situations:

(a) **A tax invoice is issued or a payment is received before the basic tax point.** In these circumstances the date of issue or date of payment is the time when the supply is treated as taking place.

(b) **A tax invoice is issued within fourteen days after the basic tax point.** In these circumstances the date of issue of the invoice is the time when the supply is treated as taking place. The fourteen day period can be extended in a particular case if the Commissioners so agree.

An invoice is 'issued' when it is sent or given to a customer. Thus, preparing an invoice does not by itself create a tax point until something positive is done with it, such as posting it to the customer.

The legislation sets out special rules for certain supplies of goods which do not fit naturally into the above scheme. In particular:

(a) **Goods on sale or return.** The time of supply is the earlier of the date when the sale is adopted by the customer, twelve months after dispatch of the goods or the date of a tax invoice being issued and a payment received.

(b) **Continuous supplies.** Supplies such as electricity (goods) and tax advice (services) do not have a basic tax point. The time of supply is the earlier of a tax invoice being issued and a payment received.

If the supplier wishes he may issue a tax invoice once a year in advance showing the periodical payments and their due dates. In this case there is a separate tax point for every amount due being the earlier of the due date and the date on which payment is received.

(c) **Periodical payments.** Payments under long term contracts such as leases and royalty agreements do not have a basic tax point. Basically, the time of supply is the earlier of the time when a tax invoice is issued or a payment is received.

(d) **Sales under hire purchase.** The goods are taxed at the standard or zero rate. The interest charges thereon are exempt when disclosed as a separate amount. The time of supply for the full value of the goods will follow the normal rules ie, the time that the goods are collected, delivered or made available.

4.4   Activity

On 30 November 1999, Oak Ltd ordered a new felling machine, and on 16 December 1999, paid a deposit of £25,000. The machine was despatched to Oak Ltd on 31 December 1999. On 12 January 2000 an invoice was issued to Oak Ltd for the balance due of £75,000. This was paid on 20 January 2000.

What is the tax point for

(a)   £25,000 deposit; and
(b)   the balance of £75,000.

4.5   Activity solution

(a)   **£25,000 deposit**

The basic tax point is the date of despatch, 31 December 1999. As the deposit was paid before the date of despatch, this is the actual tax point ie, 16 December 1999.

(b)   **The balance of £75,000**

As an invoice was issued within 14 days of the basic tax point, this is the actual tax point ie, 12 January 2000.

4.6   Tax invoices

Registered taxable persons making supplies to other taxable persons are required to issue a document known as a tax invoice not later than thirty days after the time when a taxable supply of goods or services is treated as being made. The original tax invoice is sent to the customer and forms his evidence of input tax; a copy must be kept by the supplier to support his calculations of output tax. A tax invoice need not be issued if the supplies are zero-rated or if the customer is not a taxable person. A tax invoice is a normal commercial invoice which contains the following particulars:

(a)   an identifying number;
(b)   the date of supply (see above);
(c)   the supplier's name and address and VAT registration number;
(d)   the customer's name and address;
(e)   the type of supply made;
(f)   a description which identifies the goods or services supplied;
(g)   the value and rate of tax for each supply;
(h)   the total tax-exclusive amount;
(i)   the rate of any cash discount offered; and
(j)   the amount of tax payable.

The Commissioners have the power to approve as tax invoices self-billing arrangements under which a taxable person who is a customer may make out tax invoices on behalf of his supplier who is himself a taxable person.

4.7   Accounting for output tax

The output tax due from a customer is shown on the tax invoice issued to him. The supplier must account to the Commissioners for all such tax charged during a prescribed accounting period. The following provisions apply when a customer fails to pay a supplier:

(a)   If there is a good commercial reason (eg, goods damaged in transit), the supplier may issue a credit note reducing the value of the supply and tax due thereon to an amount agreed with the customer. The tax so credited is deducted from the amount due to the Commissioners.

(b)   If the customer is bankrupt or insolvent, and thus unable to pay, the supplier may claim bad debt relief, (see below).

(c)   If non-payment arises for any other reason (eg, the customer disappears), relief is available. This is discussed below.

An alternative form of accounting is available for traders satisfying certain conditions. Such traders continue to issue tax invoices in accordance with the normal rules, but output tax for a prescribed accounting period represents the total amount of VAT included in payments received from customers in the period. Similarly, input tax is the total amount of VAT included in payments made by the trader. This is known as cash accounting and is described in detail later in this chapter.

4.8   Bad debt relief

The relief is claimed by including the amount to recover in the total of input tax on the VAT return.

Relief is given where:

(a)   a supply of goods and services has been made for consideration in money or by barter; and
(b)   output tax has been accounted for and paid by the supplier; and
(c)   the whole or part of the debt has been written off as bad in the supplier's books; and
(d)   at least 6 months has elapsed since the time that payment was due.

If there has been a series of supplies any payments made by the customer must be allocated on a FIFO basis unless the customer allocated a payment to a particular supply **and** paid in full.

On a claim by the supplier, relief will be given for the VAT chargeable by reference to the outstanding amount. The outstanding amount is simply the amount of the debt that has been written off as bad, less any amount subsequently received in respect of that bad debt. Claims for bad debt relief are subject to a three year time limit.

Following a bad debt relief claim, the customer is required to repay any VAT which they have claimed on the supplies for which they have not paid. The supplier must notify the customer that bad debt relief is being claimed, and this notification then serves as an instruction to the customer to repay the input VAT. Notification must be made within seven days of the bad debt claim.

4.9   Retailers

In broad terms, a retailer is someone who supplies goods and services to the general public rather than to other traders. He is not necessarily a shopkeeper. Thus, a hairdresser is just as much a retailer as a newsagent or garage proprietor.

Retailers only have to provide a tax invoice if a customer requests it. Such an invoice can be less detailed than normal if the consideration for the supply is £100 or less. This must show the following information:

(a)   the retailer's name, address and VAT registration number;
(b)   the date of supply;
(c)   a description of the goods or services supplied;
(d)   the consideration for the supply; and
(e)   the rate of tax in force at the time of supply.

4.10   Secondhand goods

Retailers who sell virtually any kind of second-hand goods are entitled to calculate their output tax on what is referred to as the margin (ie, sale price of the goods less cost price of the goods) rather than the sale price.

The following points should be noted:

(a)   Goods may **not** be sold under the scheme if a **tax invoice** is received in respect of the purchase or issued in respect of the sale.

(b)   Expenses incurred in respect of the goods are not taken into account in calculating the margin. Thus, if Anthony buys a used car for £1,250, spends £225 in putting it into a saleable condition, and sells if for £2,100, the margin is £2,100 – £1,250 = £850.

(c)   Output tax is calculated by applying the current VAT fraction to the margin. Thus, Anthony must account to the Commissioners for 7/47 × £850 = £126.60.

(d)   If cost exceeds the sale price, no output tax is due. Thus if Bernard buys a used car for £1,400 and sells it for £1,250, he is not required to account to the Commissioners for output tax.

(e)   A system of 'global' accounting is available for businesses dealing in low value margin scheme goods (eg, postage stamps). Rather than accounting for output tax item by item, traders can account on the basis of total purchases and sales in each tax period.

4.11   Deemed supplies

The following events are treated as a supply for tax purposes:

(a)   Goods supplied without consideration eg, gifts of goods and goods consumed privately by a sole proprietor.

(b)   Business assets used for private or non-business purposes eg, using a business car for non business travelling.

(c)   Fuel provided for private use for an employee, sole trader, or partner, at less than the original cost to, or manufacturing cost to, the taxable person.

The value of the supply is:

- cost for item (a);
- full cost of providing the service for (b); and
- scale rate for (c) as follows:

	Three month period	
	Scale charge	VAT
	£	£
Diesel engine		
2,000 cc or less	196	29.19
More than 2,000 cc	248	36.93
Petrol engine		
1,400 cc or less	212	31.57
1,401 cc to 2,000 cc	268	39.91
More than 2,000 cc	396	58.97

This table will be given to you as part of the tax rates and allowances on the examination paper.

Conclusion   Output tax is charged on the value of goods or services supplied by a taxable person. The critical areas of VAT for examination purposes from this section are:

- the time of supply
- the rules on and importance of tax invoices; and
- accounting for output tax.

5   INPUT TAX

5.1   Introduction

Input tax is the VAT paid by a taxable person on goods and services supplied to him and on goods which he imports. Input tax is recoverable from the Commissioners provided certain conditions are met. This section describes the conditions to be met.

5.2   Conditions for obtaining input tax credit

The strict wording of the legislation, and case law derived from it, indicate that a number of conditions must be met before VAT is available for credit as input tax:

(a)   **The claimant must be a taxable person when the VAT was incurred.** However, credit is available in respect of:

- goods acquired in the three years before registration or before a company is incorporated and held in stock at that date:

- services acquired in the six months before registration or before a company is incorporated; and

- services relating to a registration period supplied after a taxable person has been deregistered.

(b)   **The supply must be to the taxable person making the claim.** There is an exception for business use petrol purchased by the employee of a taxable person where the employee is reimbursed. Businesses are allowed to recover the agreed VAT element in mileage allowance paid to employees even though the VAT-able supply was made to the employee, not the claimant.

(c)   **The supply or importation must be supported by evidence.** This will normally be the VAT invoice.

(d)   **The claimant must use the goods or services for business purposes.** Thus, personal expenses cannot be eligible for input tax credit. An apportionment is made where goods and services are acquired partly for business purposes and partly for private purposes.

Where goods or services supplied to a company are used by that company in connection with the provision of domestic accommodation to a director of that company, the goods or services will not be treated as supplied for business purposes. The input tax will, therefore, not be available for credit.

(e)   **The amount due for credit is the tax properly chargeable on the supply**. Thus, if A charges VAT of £100 on an invoice issued to B, and the amount due is only £50, B can obtain input tax credit for £50. If he has paid £100, he must recover the amount overpaid from A.

(f)   **The tax must not be excluded from credit.** See below.

5.3   Input tax excluded from credit

Input tax on the following goods and services is excluded from credit:

(a)   **Business entertainment.** This means hospitality of any kind eg, food, drink, accommodation or recreational facilities.

Irrecoverable input tax on entertaining cannot be deducted for income or corporation tax purposes.

(b)   **Motor cars.** Input tax credit is generally allowed **only** when new cars are acquired for resale by a motor dealer, for hire in certain circumstances to disabled person, or to be converted into vehicles which are not motor cars.

The general rule, therefore, is that input tax on the purchase of a motor car is not recoverable. However, taxi firms, self-drive hire firms, and driving schools are able to recover input tax on the purchase of cars used for those purposes. On the sale of the car output tax must be accounted for on the full selling price.

The rule is also relaxed for cars bought wholly for business use. In particular this will enable input tax on cars purchased by leasing companies for leasing to be recovered. Where a business leases a car which it uses partly for private motoring, only 50% of the input tax on the leasing charge is recoverable.

Input tax remains irrecoverable on the purchase of all other business cars where there is any private use.

5.4   Partial exemption

Traders who make both taxable and exempt supplies are given credit for only part of the input tax they incur. The amount available for credit is calculated by one or other of the following methods:

(a)   **Standard method**

This works by analysing input tax under the following three headings:

- Input tax on goods and services wholly used for the purpose of making taxable supplies. This tax is wholly available for credit.

- Input tax on goods and services used wholly for making exempt supplies. This tax is wholly disallowed.

- The remainder eg, non-attributable input tax on overheads. The amount available for credit is found by apportionment.

The non-attributable input tax available for credit is found by using the fraction:

$$\frac{\text{Total taxable supplies}}{\text{Total supplies}}$$

Supplies of capital goods are excluded when calculating this proportion.

The ratio is computed as a percentage and, if not a whole number, rounded up to the next whole number.

If input tax wholly or partly attributed to exempt supplies is below the following *de minimis* limit, all such tax is available for credit. This tax is known as exempt input tax. The limit is an amount not exceeding £625 per month on average for any VAT account period.

In order to reclaim all input tax, the exempt input tax must not be more than 50% of the input tax incurred on all purchases.

(b)   **Special method**

Any other method may be adopted with the Commissioners' agreement.

Traders are required to rework their input tax credits on an annual basis. Any under or over-declaration is then accounted to the Commissioners or reclaimed from them.

5.5 **Example: partial exemption**

Arnold carries on activities which give rise to:

(a)   taxable supplies; and

(b)   exempt supplies for which input tax is wholly disallowed subject to the *de minimis* limit.

Relevant figures for the quarter ended 30 June 1999 are:

Activity	Attributable Input tax £
Standard rated supplies (£96,000)	10,500
Zero rated supplies (£32,000)	3,500
Exempt supplies (£37,200)	4,000
	18,000
Overheads	5,000
Total input tax	23,000

Calculate the recoverable input tax for the quarter ended 30.6.99

5.6 **Solution**

Input tax for the period is calculated as follows:

		£	£
(a)	Wholly allowable: Directly attributable to zero and standard rated taxable supplies (10,500 + 3,500)		14,000
(b)	Wholly disallowed Directly attributable to exempt supplies	4,000	
(c)	Non-attributable input tax is £5,000 Percentage apportionment:		

$$\frac{96,000+32,000}{96,000+32,000+37,200} \times 100 = 78\%$$

		£	£
	Recoverable: 78% × £5,000		3,900
	Not recoverable: £5,000 – £3,900	1,100	
	Input tax not recoverable	5,100	
	Recoverable input tax for quarter ended 30.6.99		17,900

Note: the average exempt monthly input tax is £5,100 divided by three ie, £1,700. Since this exceeds £625 the above apportionment applies.

5.7 **Input tax credit and cash accounting**

The normal rule is that input tax on supplies and importations is available for credit in the prescribed accounting period in which the tax became chargeable.

However, an alternative form of accounting, cash accounting, is available for traders approved by the Commissioners. Such traders are entitled to credit for the total amount for VAT included in payments made to suppliers in a prescribed accounting period.

For a trader to be eligible to use the cash accounting scheme his taxable turnover must not exceed £350,000 p.a., all his returns due to date must have been submitted, if any tax remains outstanding he has agreed with the Commissioners to pay it by specified instalments and for the past year he must not have been convicted of a VAT offence nor been subject to a VAT penalty for conduct involving dishonesty.

A trader must leave the scheme if his taxable turnover exceeds £350,000. The cash accounting scheme cannot be used for goods which are invoiced more than six months in advance of the payment date, or where an invoice is issued prior to the supply actually taking place. These measures prevent the creation of an early input tax claim for the customer, long before the supplier (using the cash accounting scheme) has to account for the output tax.

5.8   Interaction with capital allowances

With the exception of motor cars (see above) there are no special rules applicable to a trader's plant and machinery as opposed to his trading stock.

Thus VAT paid on purchases of capital items such as plant and equipment is available for credit as input tax except where used for the purposes of a business making only exempt supplies. When capital goods are sold second hand by a taxable person VAT is chargeable on the sale as on any other supply.

Where capital goods are used by a taxable person the VAT charged on them can be recovered and capital allowances are calculated on the net cost to the business ie, the tax-exclusive price. Where the capital goods are used by the business which is not registered for VAT or whose supplies are exempt no tax can be recovered and capital allowances are calculated on the tax-inclusive price. This is also the position for business cars. Where supplies of a business are partially exempt, then only part of the tax will be recovered and the tax not recovered can be added to the tax-exclusive price to arrive at the cost for capital allowances.

Tax charged on the sale of capital goods is ignored for capital allowances purposes - only the net proceeds are deducted from tax written down value.

5.9   Imports

VAT is charged on imported goods from countries outside the EU as if it were a duty of customs. As a general principle, therefore, it is collected at a port or airport at the same time as customs duties, excise duties and other import levies. It follows, therefore, that the Commissioners collect VAT direct from the importer.

The system of immediate payment of tax can cause serious inconvenience to importers dealing with a large volume of individual consignments. However, approved traders can pay tax arising in a calendar month by direct debit on the fifteenth day of the following month under the Duty Deferment System.

Where imported goods are immediately removed to a bonded warehouse or free zone, payment of VAT is broadly postponed until the goods are removed from bond or the free zone.

Goods may be brought in to the UK without payment of tax provided they are exported within stated time limits. The goods remain under strict customs control while they remain the UK.

5.10   Acquisitions from EU member states

Supplies of goods between member states are not regarded as imports and exports, but as acquisitions and supplies.

The supply of goods is zero-rated.

When goods are acquired in the UK, then output VAT must be accounted for. However, an equivalent amount (subject to the partial exemption rules) can then be recovered as input VAT.

The date of acquisition is the earliest of:

- The date that the invoice is issued.
- The 15th of the month following that in which the goods are removed.

This results in VAT being accounted for at the rate applicable to the member state of the acquirer.

On supplies to buyers who are not registered for VAT, the supplier treats the supply as if it was made in his own member state, and adds VAT at the rate applicable to that state.

However, if sufficient supplies are made to non-registered buyers in any particular member state, then registration may be required in that state. The registration limits for that state will apply. The supply will then be deemed to be made in that member state, and that state's rates of VAT will be used.

The above rules do not apply if the acquisition was one of zero-rated goods.

| **Conclusion** | Input tax, which is the VAT paid by a taxable person on goods and services supplied to him and on goods which he imports is recoverable provided certain conditions are met. |

The most important areas from this section, for examination purposes are:

- the conditions for obtaining input tax credit;
- non-deductible input tax;
- the cash accounting scheme.

6   CHAPTER SUMMARY

This is the first chapter on VAT.

The following areas were covered:

- the scope of VAT   -   taxable transactions and taxable persons;

- supplies
  - chargeable supplies
  - supplies of goods and services
  - exempt and taxable supplies

- taxable persons
  - registration
  - deregistration

- output tax
  - the tax point
  - tax invoices
  - accounting for output tax
  - bad debt relief

- input tax
  - conditions for obtaining input tax credit
  - non-deductible input tax
  - partial exemption
  - cash accounting scheme

7   SELF TEST QUESTIONS

7.1   What is a chargeable supply? (2.3)

7.2   What is the consequence of making an exempt supply? (2.5)

7.3   What are the consequences of deregistration? (3.10)

7.4   In what situations may a trader register for VAT voluntarily? (3.11)

7.5   In what situations is the basic tax point amended? (4.3)

7.6   What particulars must a tax invoice contain? (4.6)

7.7   How can relief be obtained for the VAT element of a bad debt? (4.8)

7.8   What are the conditions for obtaining input tax credit? (5.2)

7.9   What is the standard method for working out the input tax credit when both taxable and exempt supplies are made? (5.4)

7.10   How is VAT accounted for on imports from outside the EU? (5.9)

8   EXAMINATION TYPE QUESTION

8.1   Ken

(a)   Ken has a market stall, and sells mostly fruit and vegetables and a small amount of other food.

He started trading on 1 December 1999, and anticipates his turnover will be as follows:

	£
One month ended 31 December 1999	25,000
Quarter ended 31 March 2000	42,000
Quarter ended 30 June 2000	45,000
Quarter ended 30 September 2000	48,000

Assume that the amounts accrue evenly.

You are required to advise Ken if he should register for VAT, and if so, when the Commissioners should be notified.

(b)   Toby's input tax and supplies made in the quarter to 31 December 1999 are analysed as follows:

		£
(a)	Input tax wholly re-taxable supplies	23,250
(b)	Input tax wholly re-exempt supplies	14,000
(c)	Non-attributable input tax	28,000
(d)	Value (excluding VAT) of taxable supplies	250,000
(e)	Value of exempt supplies	100,000

Calculate the deductible input tax assuming that Toby uses the standard method of attributing input tax.

9   ANSWER TO EXAMINATION TYPE QUESTION

9.1   Ken

(a)   Traders become liable to register for VAT at the end of any month if the value of taxable supplies in the previous 12 months exceed £51,000.

Ken will therefore be liable to register for VAT from 29 February 2000, and he must notify the Commissioners by 30 March 2000. Ken will be registered from 1 April 2000.

(b)   Deductible input tax

	£
Attributable input tax	23,250

Non-attributable input tax $\times \dfrac{\text{Value of taxable supplies}}{\text{Value of total supplies}}$

$£28,000 \times \dfrac{250,000}{250,000 + 100,000}$ (72%)	20,160
Deductible input tax	43,410

The exempt input tax is £21,840 (28,000 – 20,160 + 14,000) and as this amounts to more than £625 per month on average it is all non-deductible.

36 VAT

INTRODUCTION & LEARNING OBJECTIVES

This is the second of two chapters on Value Added Tax. It deals with the administrative aspects of VAT and the important groups of zero rated and exempt supplies.

When you have studied this chapter you should have learned the following:

- VAT returns and records;
- Assessments and appeals;
- Penalties;
- Zero-rated supplies; and
- Exempt supplies.

1 TAX RETURNS AND RECORDS

1.1 Normal accounting system

Taxable persons account for tax by reference to prescribed accounting periods. Traders who pay tax normally have a prescribed accounting period of three months, while traders who normally receive repayment of tax have prescribed accounting periods of one month.

To ensure that the flow of VAT returns is spread evenly over the year, the three-month tax periods are staggered. The Commissioners do this by allocating tax periods according to the class of trade being carried on.

A trader may apply for tax periods which fit in with his own financial year, even where this is not based on calendar months. Applications should be made to the Commissioners when notifying liability to, or applying for, registration.

Substantial traders (those with a VAT liability exceeding £2 million p.a.) must make monthly payments on account.

The payments on account are based on the previous year's VAT liability, and each payment is 1/24th of that annual figure. The payments on account are then taken into account on the quarterly return.

The trader's first prescribed accounting period starts on the effective date of registration and his final period ends on the date this registration is cancelled.

Tax returns are issued by VAT Central Unit. Returns must be completed and returned to VAT Central Unit together with any tax shown to be due within one month of the end of a prescribed accounting period. Any tax shown to be repayable to a trader is repaid to him by VAT Central Unit, normally within fourteen days or so. Delayed repayments of tax attract repayment supplement.

The Commissioners can deny claims for overpaid tax to be refunded if it would 'unjustly enrich' the claimant. For example, this might apply where the refund cannot practically be passed on to the claimant's customers who have been charged tax incorrectly.

On the other hand, a trader has a statutory right to claim interest from the Commissioners, where, as a result of an error on the part of Customs, too much VAT was paid or underclaimed or where he was prevented from recovering VAT at the proper time.

1.2   Annual accounting system

An alternative accounting system is available for traders approved by the Commissioners. In brief, traders have a prescribed accounting period (described as an accounting year) of twelve months which may be expected to coincide with the financial year for accounting purposes. A return for an accounting year must be furnished within two calendar months after it has ended. Nine payments on account are made at the end of the months 4-12 inclusive of the financial year and a balancing payment when the return is furnished. Each payment on account represents 10% of the estimated tax due for the financial year. Annual accounting is only available to traders with an annual turnover not exceeding £300,000.

Traders with an annual turnover not exceeding £100,000 are entitled under the annual accounting scheme instead to make three quarterly payments each of 20% of the previous years net VAT liability. In addition, if the annual liability is below £2,000 the trader can choose not to make interim payments but pay the full actual liability for a year two months after the year end.

1.3   Example: annual accounting

John's financial year ends on 31 December 1999 and his annual turnover is about £140,000. He applies to adopt the annual accounting scheme and approval is given. The Commissioners estimate his tax liability for the year at £3,600. In the event, his liability is £3,821.

What returns and payments must he make for the year?

1.4   Solution

He must furnish a return no later than 29 February 2000. Payments are made as follows:

		£
Monthly payments commencing 30 April 1999	9 @ £360	3,240
Final payment no later than 29 February 2000	£(3,821 – 3,240)	581
		3,821

1.5   Failure to furnish returns or pay tax

Failure to submit a return or pay tax gives rise to a liability to either civil penalties or default surcharge. It may also lead to the issue of an estimated assessment against which there is no right of appeal.

1.6   Records and accounts

Records and accounts must be kept of all goods and services received and supplied in the course of a business. No particular form is specified but they must be sufficient to allow the VAT return to be completed and to allow the Commissioners to check the return. Records must be kept up to date and must be preserved for six years. In practice the main records which must be kept are as follows:

(a)   Copies of all tax invoices issued.
(b)   A record of all outputs eg, a sales day book.
(c)   Evidence supporting claims for input tax credit.
(d)   A record of all inputs eg, a purchases day book.
(e)   VAT account.

Conclusion   Traders generally account for VAT by reference to three month tax periods, though certain traders may have a twelve month tax period instead. VAT is a self-assessed tax and a taxable person must keep sufficient records and accounts to allow the VAT return to be completed and to allow the Commissioners to check the return.

2 ASSESSMENTS AND APPEALS

2.1 Control visits

VAT is a self-assessed tax, and it is not unnatural that the Commissioners should wish to conduct spot checks to ensure that traders are properly carrying out the obligations placed upon them by the legislation. These spot checks are known as control visits. From the Commissioner's point of view their principal purpose is to provide an opportunity for officers to verify the accuracy of tax returns rendered by reference to the prime records available. They also serve as a deterrent to fraud. From a trader's point of view, control visits provide an ideal opportunity to sort out any difficulties which have arisen in practice.

The Commissioners have power to enter business premises, inspect documents, including profit and loss accounts and balance sheets, take samples, and inspect computers.

2.2 Assessments

An officer may find that a tax return is incomplete or incorrect. If so, he can issue an assessment to collect the tax which has been underpaid by the trader or overpaid by him.

An assessment must be made to the officer's best judgement.

An assessment must be made within two years from the end of the prescribed accounting period to which it relates, or if later, within one year after the necessary evidence came into the officer's possession. This is subject to an over-riding three year time limit. The three year time limit is increased to twenty years where tax has been lost due to fraud or dishonest conduct (eg, a criminal conviction or a civil default).

Interest may be charged in certain cases (see below).

2.3 Appeals

Appeals in connection with VAT are made to an independent tribunal - the VAT Tribunal.

An appeal cannot be entertained unless the trader has rendered all the returns he is due to make and has paid the tax thereon.

The normal time limit for appealing is thirty days.

If a taxpayer is unable to resolve the matter with the Customs and Excise, he should complete and sign a notice of appeal and send it to the appropriate tribunal centre within the specified time limits.

A VAT Tribunal consists of a chairman sitting either with two other members (majority decision necessary) or with one other member (chairman has casting vote) or alone.

Costs may be awarded against the unsuccessful party to an appeal unless the winning party's conduct makes this inappropriate.

An unsuccessful party to an appeal may appeal to the High Court on a matter or law, and thereafter the Court of Appeal and House of Lords.

2.4 Refunds

Claims can be made for the refund of VAT overpaid, or for input VAT not claimed. Claims are subject to a three year time limit.

3   PENALTIES AND INTEREST

3.1   Introduction

The examiner has stated that a detailed knowledge is only required in respect of:

- interest;
- the default surcharge; and
- the serious misdeclaration penalty.

The other penalties are therefore only summarised below.

3.2   Criminal penalties

Offence	Maximum penalty
Fraudulent evasion of VAT. Provision of false information with intent to deceive.	Unlimited fine and/or 7 years' imprisonment.
Where a person deals in goods where he has reason to believe that VAT will be avoided on the supply.	3 × Tax evaded or £2,000 if greater

3.3   Civil penalties

Default	Penalty	Notes
Any action or omission involving dishonesty for the purpose of evading VAT	100% of VAT evaded	2
Failure to notify liability to registration	Greater of £50 or 15% of relevant tax	1, 2, 4
Tax invoice issued by unregistered person	Greater of £50 or 15% of relevant tax	1, 2
Failure to keep records, furnish information or produce documents	Daily penalty	1,3
Failure to furnish tax returns or pay tax due thereon	Daily penalty	1
Failure to preserve records	£500	1

Notes:

(1)   No penalty arises if there is a reasonable excuse for the conduct concerned. An insufficiency of funds is not a reasonable excuse.

(2)   This penalty may be mitigated (ie, reduced) up to 100% if appropriate (eg, where the person co-operated in the investigation of his tax affairs).

(3)   The daily penalty depends upon the number of previous failures in the previous two years, thus: no previous failures (£5), one failure (£10) and two or more failures (£15).

Maximum penalty: 100 days at the appropriate daily rate. Minimum penalty: £50.

(4)   The minimum penalty for failure to register on time is £50.

The maximum penalty is a percentage of the tax due (depending on the period of delay between the date when the trader should have been registered and the date the Commissioners were notified).

Delay period	%
Registration up to 9 months late	5
Registration over 9 months up to 18 months late	10
Registration over 18 months late	15

3.4   Interest

A charge to interest will arise if:

- the Commissioners find that VAT has been underdeclared or overclaimed on previous VAT returns; or

- under declarations or overclaims from previous returns are notified as voluntary disclosures by declaring them to the VAT office.

Note that interest is not charged in respect of voluntary disclosures if the under declaration or overclaim does not exceed £2,000.

Interest is charged from the date outstanding VAT should first have been paid to the date shown on the Notice of Assessment or Notice of Voluntary Disclosure.

Any interest charged by the Commissioners will be limited to a maximum of three years prior to the date shown on the Notice of Assessment or Voluntary Disclosure.

3.5   Repayment supplement

If a trader is entitled to a VAT repayment because his input tax for a period exceeds his output tax for a VAT period and the repayment is delayed, a supplement of the greater of 5% of the repayment and £50 will be paid to him.

3.6   Default surcharge

A default occurs if a return is not submitted on time or a payment is made late. On the first default, the Commissioners serve a surcharge liability notice on the taxpayer. The notice specifies a surcharge period, starting on the date of the notice and ending on the anniversary of the default.

If a trader defaults in the surcharge period, there are two consequences:

- the taxpayer is subject to a surcharge penalty if a payment is made late; and
- the surcharge period is extended to the anniversary of the new default.

The surcharge depends on the number of defaults in the surcharge period:

Default in the surcharge period	Surcharge as a percentage of the tax unpaid at the due date
First	2%
Second	5%
Third	10%
Fourth or more	15%

Surcharge assessments at rates below 10% will not be issued for amounts less than £200.

Where the rate of surcharge is 10% or more, an assessment will be issued for either £30 or the actual amount of the calculated surcharge, whichever is the greater.

In order to escape a surcharge liability notice the taxpayer must submit four consecutive quarterly returns on time accompanied by the full amounts of VAT due.

3.7 Example: default surcharge

Mark's return for 30 June 1999 is late, and the tax of £14,500 is not paid until 16 August 1999. His return for the following period is submitted late and the tax of £16,200 not paid until 9 November 1999.

What are the consequences for Mark?

3.8 Solution

Return period ended 30.6.99.

First default: surcharge liability notice issued.

Return period ended 30.9.99.

First default within the surcharge period.

Penalty of £16,200 × 2% = £324 becomes payable.

The surchargeable period is extended to 30.9.2000.

3.9 Misdeclaration penalty

(a) Misdeclaration penalty is imposed whenever there has been a significant or repeated lack of care in preparing VAT returns. The penalty rate is 15% of the tax that would have been lost if the error had not been discovered.

(b) Penalty is considered when large or repeated misdeclarations are discovered **by the Commissioners.** A misdeclaration means

- a trader has claimed a repayment which is too large on a VAT return; or

- a trader has failed to tell the Commissioners within 30 days that a centrally issued assessment is too low.

Note: there is no penalty if an error is disclosed voluntarily.

(c) Errors will normally be measured against the trader's **gross amount of tax,** or 'GAT'.

[Definition] GAT is the sum of output tax and input tax that should have been declared on the return.

(d) A penalty will normally result if an error:

- equals or exceeds 30% of the GAT; or
- equals or exceeds £1 million; or
- is one of a series of errors.

(e) A penalty for repeated errors will never be issued without first issuing a warning notice, known as a penalty liability notice (PLN)

A PLN is issued if a misdeclaration is assessed which:

- equals or exceeds 10% of GAT; or
- equals or exceeds £500,000

A penalty will only be issued if all the following conditions are met.

- The Commissioners have issued a PLN

- Two or more errors have been made on separate VAT returns in the eight VAT periods following the issue of the PLN. This includes the period in which the PLN is issued.

- Each of the qualifying errors must exceed the 10% of GAT or the £500,000 test.

A penalty of 15% of the tax that would have been lost may then be issued.

(f)   There is no penalty if a trader discloses an error before the Commissioners begin enquiries into his VAT affairs.

A trader should deal with errors that he discovers as follows:

- If the net errors discovered in a period are £2,000 or less, he can note them in his VAT account and correct the error on his current VAT return:

- If the net errors exceed £2,000 he must advise his local VAT office.

(g)   No penalty is charged if the trader can convince the Commissioners, or a VAT Tribunal that he has a reasonable excuse.

Conclusion   There are various penalties and surcharges that are imposed on taxpayers; of these, the most important for exam purposes are:

- interest;
- default surcharge; and
- misdeclaration penalty

4   ZERO RATING

4.1   Items that are zero-rated

The most important zero-rated items are briefly described below:

Food

Food of a kind used for human consumption is zero-rated unless it comprises either:

(a)   A supply in the course of catering. This is the provision of food on the supplier's premises (eg, in a restaurant) and hot take-away food.

(b)   Food described in the excepted items, which broadly comprise confectionery, alcohol, soft drinks, crisps and similar products.

Sewerage services and water

The supply of water (eg, by a waterworks) is zero-rated.

Books and other printed matter

This group zero-rates a wide range of reading material (eg, newspapers, books, maps and sheet music).

Construction of dwellings, etc

[Definition] A major interest in a building is a freehold interest or a lease for a term exceeding twenty-one years.

Zero-rating applies to the following categories of supplies:

(a)   The grant of a major interest in a building by the person constructing the building provided the building is:

- designed as a dwelling; or
- intended for the use solely for residential purposes or charitable purposes.

(b)   The supply of services other than of an architect, surveyor, consultant or supervisor in the course of constructing a building as defined in (a) above.

(c)   Goods supplied with services are zero-rated provided the following tests are met:

- the goods are supplied by the same person who supplied the services; and
- the goods comprise either materials, builder's hardware, sanitary ware or articles of a kind ordinarily installed by builders as fixtures.

Zero-rating does not extend to the services of reconstructing, altering or enlarging an existing building.

Zero-rating does not apply where an existing building is being extended or annexed if the extension or annexed area has internal access to the existing building.

International services

There is no general zero-rating for the export of services as there is for the export of goods. Certain broad categories of services are, however, zero-rated: eg, services relating to land outside UK; services to persons belonging outside the UK.

Transport

Transporting passengers by road, rail and sea or air is generally zero-rated provided the vehicle or ship is designed to carry over eleven passengers (eg, not taxis).

Drugs, medicines and appliances

Drugs supplied on prescription by a chemist are zero rated. Certain appliances and equipment supplied to the disabled are zero-rated.

Imports and exports

This group zero-rates certain imports and exports.

Charities

Gifts to, and supplies by, certain charities are zero-rated.

Clothing and footwear

Young children's clothing and footwear are zero-rated provided they are unsuitable for older persons.

4.2   Exported goods

Goods removed from a place in the UK to a destination outside the UK may be zero-rated in certain circumstances. In order to benefit from zero-rating, an exporter must hold specified evidence of export. This may take the form of an export document (eg, a bill of lading), or a Customs form stamped at the place of export from the UK or the place of importation overseas.

| Conclusion | Zero-rated supplies are taxable at 0%. If a taxable person has zero-rated outputs but standard rated inputs, he will be able to reclaim the VAT paid on the purchases. Do not attempt to commit to memory all of the details under the zero-rated category, just try to remember the main ones: ie,

- Food (other than in the course of catering and certain other items of confectionery etc)

- Construction of residential dwellings;

- Transport (most forms of passenger transport);

- Most exported goods; and

- Children's clothing.

5   EXEMPTION

5.1   Items that are exempt from VAT

The most important items are:

Land

This group exempts the grant, assignment or surrender of an interest in land, a right over land or a licence to occupy land. There are a number of exceptions. The following are taxed at the standard rate: freehold sale of a new (or uncompleted) building unless designed solely for residential or charitable use; hotel sleeping and catering accommodation; holiday accommodation in houses, caravans, etc; parking facilities; sports, concert, or theatre tickets; and a number of other similar supplies.

Insurance

This group broadly exempts insurance premiums, insurance brokers' commission and services provided in handling claims.

Postal services

This group exempts all forms of postal deliveries by the Post Office

Finance

This group exempts a wide range of financial services: dealing in money, bonds, bills of exchange, etc, making loans, hire purchase, dealing in securities such as shares, underwriting share issues and banking services such as providing current, deposit and savings accounts.

Education

This group exempts education provided by schools and universities.

Health

This group exempts the services of registered doctors, dentists, opticians, etc, dental technicians, chemists, licensed hospitals and other institutions (not health farms).

Sports

This group exempts entry fees to sports competitions used to provide prizes or charged by non-profit making sporting bodies.

5.2 Landlords option to tax

Exemption will normally apply where rent is charged on commercial letting property. The result would be irrecoverable input tax for the landlord. This situation can be avoided by the landlord electing to waive exemption, effectively opting to be taxed. Of course, if all his tenants are fully taxable persons the overall tax position is improved by opting to be taxed since tax on the landlords inputs and the tenants inputs is thereby fully recovered.

However, the election must be made for an entire building so if some tenants cannot fully recover the tax this places them at a disadvantage.

Once made, an election can take immediate effect and is irrevocable for a minimum of 20 years. The election will apply to a sale of the building although the new owner, if he uses it to make exempt supplies, (ie, rents), will have an independent right to make an election to waive exemption, and thereby receive the input tax on purchase.

Conclusion It is important to differentiate between zero-rated and exempt supplies. A person making only exempt supplies is not able to recover VAT on purchases.

Again, try to remember the main exempt categories ie,

- Land - grant assignment or surrender of an interest in land. But sale of a new freehold building for non-residential/charitable use is standard rated;
- Insurance;
- Postal services supplied by the Post office;
- Financial services eg, loans, banking services, interest etc; and
- Education and health.

6 CHAPTER SUMMARY

This is the concluding chapter on VAT. The following areas were covered:

- accounting for VAT;
- the annual accounting system;
- records and accounts;
- assessments and appeals;
- criminal and civil penalties;
- the default surcharge;
- the misdeclaration penalty;
- zero-rated supplies; and
- exempt supplies.

7 SELF TEST QUESTIONS

7.1 What is the purpose of a control visit? (2.1)

7.2 Within what time limits must assessment to VAT be made? (2.2)

7.3 How are VAT appeals dealt with? (2.3)

7.4 On which defaults do civil penalties arise? (3.3)

7.5 What are the principal occasions when a charge to interest will arise? (3.4)

7.6   How does the default surcharge operate? (3.6)

7.7   When will a misdeclaration penalty be imposed? (3.9)

7.8   What are the main categories of zero-rated supplies? (4.1)

7.9   What are the main categories of exempt supplies? (5.1)

7.10   What option is available to a landlord where rent is charged on a commercial letting property? (5.2)

8   EXAMINATION TYPE QUESTION

8.1   Alan and Roger

Alan and Roger commenced in partnership as chartered architects on 1 February 1999 and the values of their supplies were as follows.

Month	Fees for services invoiced £	Sales of unsuitable office equipment £
1999		
February	2,750	
March	6,000	
April	3,700	
May	3,500	
June	3,100	
July	2,000	
August	1,900	
September	6,200	1,500
October	3,200	
November	3,300	
December	15,400	
2000		
January	-	
February	35,700	
March	29,400	

Alan and Roger informed the Commissioners of their liability to register by telephone on 12 October 2000 and submitted the VAT Registration Form on 28 November 2000.

You are required:

(a)   to discuss when Alan and Roger are liable to be registered for VAT.

(b)   to detail from what date they will be deemed to have registered and explain how any penalties would be computed

9 ANSWER TO EXAMINATION TYPE QUESTION

9.1 Alan and Roger

(a) **Date of liability to register for VAT**

Year	Month	Fees invoiced £	Annual cumulation £
1999	February	2,750	2,750
	March	6,000	8,750
	April	3,700	12,450
	May	3,500	15,950
	June	3,100	19,050
	July	2,000	21,050
	August	1,900	22,950
	September	6,200	29,150
	October	3,200	32,350
	November	3,300	35,650
	December	15,400	51,050
2000	January	-	51,050
	February	35,700	84,000
	March	29,400	107,400

Capital assets of the business are disregarded.

The statutory tests for registration liability are set out as follows:

(i) If, at the end of any month, the value of taxable supplies in the period of one year ending exceeds £51,000, liability to register applies.

(ii) If, at any time, there are reasonable grounds for believing that the value of taxable supplies in the period of 30 days then beginning will exceed £51,000, liability to register applies.

Under (i) above liability can be avoided if the Commissioners are satisfied that for the period of one year just beginning the limit of £49,000 will not be exceeded ie, the turnover has been uncharacteristically high.

If (i) above applies the trader must notify the Commissioners within 30 days of the end of the relevant month and is registered from the end of the month following the relevant month or from an earlier date if agreed. The relevant month is the month at the end of which the trader became liable to be registered.

If (ii) above applies the trader must notify the Commissioners before the end of the 30-day period in which his taxable supplies are likely to exceed £51,000. He will then be registered from the start of the 30 days.

Applying these tests to Alan and Roger it is clear that they should be registered following the period to 31 December 1999. Registration would then be due from 1 February 2000.

(b) **Penalties for late registration**

As explained in part (a) above registration was required by 1 February 2000.

There is a minimum penalty of £50 for failure to register on time. The maximum penalty depends on the period of delay between the date when the trader should have been registered and the date the Commissioners were notified. It is calculated as a percentage of excess of the output tax over the input tax for the period of delay as follows:

Delay period	Percentage
9 months or less	5%
Between 9 and 18 months	10%
Over 18 months	15%

The Commissioners are not notified until they receive the VAT Registration Form (ie, on 28 November 2000). Thus, a 10% penalty can be imposed.

The penalty can be avoided if there is a reasonable excuse for failing to notify. Any penalty can be mitigated up to 100% if the Commissioners or, on appeal, a VAT tribunal think fit.

37 OVERSEAS ACTIVITIES

INTRODUCTION

A person's residence and domicile are relevant factors when considering the implications of various taxes, as is the location of assets in some cases.

This chapter deals with the overseas aspects of income tax, capital gains tax and corporation tax.

1 BASIC RULES FOR CHARGING INCOME TAX

1.1 The UK residents' rule

This rule stipulates that all persons **resident** in the UK are assessed to UK tax on their income arising throughout the world. However, the question of ordinary residence and domicile may affect the **basis** of assessing income.

1.2 The UK income rule

This rule stipulates that all income arising in the UK is assessed to UK tax irrespective of where the recipient is resident. However, interest on Government securities is exempt if the owner is not ordinarily resident in the UK.

2 RESIDENCE, ORDINARY RESIDENCE AND DOMICILE

2.1 Introduction

Before progressing to a detailed examination of the treatment of various classes of income, it is necessary to consider the meaning of three terms – **residence, ordinary residence and domicile** – which are fundamentally important in determining whether or not a liability to UK tax exists and, if so, the basis of assessment.

Statute does not specifically define these terms, but the following are accepted definitions as applied by the Revenue and the Courts.

2.2 Residence

(a) **Individuals – ascertainment of residence**

The residence status of an individual is a question of fact. A person is resident if

- he is **physically present** in the UK for a period (or periods) of **six months or more** in any fiscal year, or

- he has paid **frequent and substantial** visits to the UK. The Revenue regard stays of **three** months a year, on average, for **four** consecutive years as frequent and substantial. This test is essential in order to catch the person who deliberately visits the UK on a regular basis over a number of years but in any one fiscal year does not satisfy the six months rule.

(b) **Individuals – establishing non-residence**

A UK resident can **establish** that he is **no longer resident** in the UK, by being absent from the UK for a period which includes a complete year of assessment.

(c)   **Individuals - coming to the UK**

The residence status of people coming to the UK depends on their length of stay:

- A person coming to the UK to take up permanent residence, or with the intention of staying for at least two years, will be treated as resident from the date of arrival to the date of departure.

- A person coming to the UK for a temporary stay will only be resident in any tax year if he spends more than 183 days in the UK during that year.

2.3   Ordinary residence of individuals

This is a question of **habit and intention**. It depends on where the individual **normally** resides as opposed to his place of occasional residence. Thus, the term ordinary residence implies residence with some degree of continuity, ignoring incidental or temporary absences. An individual who has previously been resident and ordinarily resident in the UK may still be regarded as ordinarily resident (but not resident) for a year which he spends wholly abroad, if it is clear that his intention is to return to the UK (ie, his ordinary place of residence). If he is absent from the UK for at least 3 years he will be regarded as having lost his ordinary residence status.

Persons coming to the UK

(a)   A person who visits the UK in four or more consecutive years will be regarded as **ordinarily resident** for each of those years if the visits average three months or more a year.

(b)   Longer term visitors to the UK will be regarded as ordinarily resident as follows

Circumstances	*Ordinary resident*
Intends to remain for more than 3 years	From date of arrival
Remains for more than 3 years having intended otherwise	From 6 April following third anniversary of arrival

2.4   Domicile

Domicile denotes the country considered to be an individual's *permanent home*. It is a common law concept and not defined in statute. Furthermore, it does not necessarily correspond with the meaning of either ordinary residence or nationality. An individual may have only one domicile at any given time which is primarily a domicile of origin but this may be altered (with difficulty) to a domicile of choice.

(a)   Domicile of origin – an individual will be domiciled at birth in the country in which his or her father is domiciled. However, an illegitimate child, takes the domicile of his or her mother.

(b)   Domicile of choice – an adult may substitute a domicile of choice for a domicile of origin, but to do so is, in fact, extremely difficult and practical steps must be taken to substantiate such a claim.

If a taxpayer currently domiciled in the United Kingdom is proposing to settle in, say, Portugal with the intention of acquiring a domicile of choice in Portugal, the points set out below are among those which will, or may, help to support the case for a change in domicile.

- He should make it generally known that he is leaving the United Kingdom permanently, with the intention of making a new home in Portugal.

- He should, as far as practicable, resign from clubs, associations and societies in the United Kingdom.

- Assets owned in the United Kingdom should, as far as possible, be disposed of.

- He should not make frequent visits to the United Kingdom, and should not return at all in the first year following his departure.

- In Portugal he should join new clubs, associations and societies, and acquire Portuguese assets, including a residence.

- He should make a new will under Portuguese law and acquire a Portuguese burial plot.

- As a final and usually conclusive step, he should consider applying for Portuguese naturalisation.

An infant cannot by his own actions change his domicile until he reaches the age of 18 or, if earlier, marries. Meanwhile he has a domicile of dependency (eg, his domicile of origin will change if his father changes his domicile by choice).

3 NON-RESIDENTS

3.1 Eligibility for personal allowances

UK personal allowances are normally available only to individuals who are **resident** in the UK.

However, British subjects (including Commonwealth subjects) and Citizens of all states in the European Economic Area (EEA), may claim for UK personal allowances despite not being resident in the UK.

Non-residents who can claim allowances may use them in full against any income chargeable to income tax in the UK.

3.2 Exempt UK income

Interest on all British Government stocks (gilt edged securities) is exempt from UK income tax if they are beneficially owned by persons not ordinarily resident in the UK.

4 OVERSEAS INCOME OF UK RESIDENTS

4.1 Introduction

A person who is **resident** in the UK is liable to UK tax on his world-wide income **including income from overseas sources**. The basis of assessment for any overseas income may also be affected by a person's ordinary residence status or domicile.

The various sources of overseas income are now considered in detail.

4.2 Schedule D Case IV and V

(a) Assessable income

Schedule D Case IV taxes income from **foreign securities,** eg, interest from a loan secured by a mortgage on property.

Schedule D Case V charges income from **foreign possessions**. The term possessions will include all sources of foreign income other than those taxed under Schedule D Case IV or Schedule E; it embraces such items as rental income from a foreign property, dividends from foreign companies, foreign pensions and profits derived from a business carried on wholly outside the UK, ie, controlled abroad. For most practical purposes there is no difference in the treatment of Case IV and Case V income.

(b)   **Basis of assessment – arising or remittance basis**

Assessments under Cases IV and V may only be made on individuals who are **resident** in the UK.

All income under Schedule D, Case IV or V is assessed on an actual basis.

The assessment is made upon the **full amount of income arising** (irrespective of remittances) **in the fiscal year**.

However

		Basis
(a)	where income is derived from foreign pensions	Income arising, less 10%.
(b)	income (including that in (a) above) of an individual who, being resident, is either	Income **remitted** to the UK in the year of assessment.
	• not domiciled in the UK, or is	
	• a British subject not ordinarily resident in the UK.	

(c)   **Foreign dividends and savings income**

Foreign dividends and savings income is taxed at the same rates as UK dividends and savings income. Foreign savings income is therefore taxed at 20% where it falls below the higher rate threshold of £28,000 (for 1999/00) and at 40% where it is above the threshold. Foreign dividends are similarly taxed at 10% below the higher rate threshold, and at 32.5% above the threshold.

4.3   Overseas trades

Adjusted trading profits of trades, professions and vocations are assessed under Schedule D Cases I and II where the trade is carried on **wholly or partly in the UK** by an individual who is resident in the UK for tax purposes.

The taxation of profits arising overseas from a business carried on **wholly abroad** is assessed under Schedule D Case V in the hands of a UK resident individual.

4.4   Overseas trades: travelling expenses

Certain travelling and subsistence expenses will be allowable deductions when computing the adjusted trading profits.

The allowable expenses are

(a)   travelling from any place in the UK to the place where the trade is carried on overseas, and return trips, and

(b)   board and lodging at that overseas place, and

(c)   the cost of the spouse and children (under age 18) visiting the overseas place of work up to two return trips in any year of assessment, once the trader has been absent from the UK for 60 or more continuous days.

The relief is only available to individuals who

(a)   carry on a trade, profession or vocation **wholly** overseas, and

(b)   do **not qualify** for the remittance basis of assessment.

4.5 The three Cases of Schedule E

Emoluments are assessed under one of the three cases of Schedule E (or partly under one and partly under another) having regard to an individual's residence and ordinary residence status, and the location of the place where duties are performed, ie,

Case I   Any emoluments for any year of assessment in which the person is resident and ordinarily resident in the UK.

Case II   Any emoluments, in respect of duties performed in the UK, for any year of assessment in which the person is not resident, or if resident not ordinarily resident, in the UK.

Case III   Any emoluments in respect of duties performed outside the UK, for any year of assessment in which the person is resident in the UK (but not ordinarily resident).

Receipts basis: the charging provisions

As regards any year of assessment, income tax is charged

(a)   under Cases I or II, on the **full** amount of emoluments RECEIVED in the year of assessment;

(b)   under Case III, on the **full** amount of emoluments RECEIVED IN THE UK, in the year of assessment

4.6 Schedule E: employee working outside UK

(a)   **The treatment of non-residents**

Revenue practice is to treat an employee who is absent from the UK undertaking **full-time** duties under a contract of employment as not resident (and not ordinarily resident) from the day following the date of departure to the day before his return to the UK provided

- the absence includes a complete tax year, **and**

- interim visits to the UK do not revive a person's residence status under the six months, or three months habitual and substantial visits rules.

By being not resident such an employee will be **exempt** from UK tax under Schedule E in respect of earnings from duties performed outside the UK.

The following should be remembered.

- As a non-resident, the employee will not be entitled to UK personal allowances. However, if the employee is a British subject (or a person in one of the other specified categories) a claim for the benefit of the allowances can be made.

- Where a taxpayer is married, the residence status of himself and his wife are determined independently. Thus, it is possible that a husband who is working full-time overseas may be non-resident whilst his wife is resident.

(b)   **The treatment of UK residents**

If the taxpayer cannot be treated as non-resident his overseas emoluments will be assessable under either

- Schedule E Case I – if he is resident and ordinarily resident in the UK, or
- Schedule E Case III, on a remittance basis.

For example, Jackson, a British subject, is given two alternative job offers in Zambia each for a period of 18 months. One commences 1 January 1999 and the other 1 July 1999.

How will the tax treatment differ?

Contract **1** : 1.1.99 – 30.6.2000 – includes the complete tax year 1999/00 : Jackson will be non-resident from 1.1.99 to 30.6.2000 and will be exempt from assessment under Schedule E Case I.

Contract **2** : 1.7.99 – 31.12.2000 – does not include any complete tax year : Jackson will remain both resident and ordinarily resident in the UK throughout the absence and assessable under Schedule E Case I.

This example demonstrates why careful planning is necessary when working overseas.

4.7   Travelling and subsistence expenses

The rules regarding allowable **travelling and subsistence expenses** in relation to work done overseas are as follows:

Where there is a separate overseas employment (ie, with a non–resident employer), travelling costs to or from the UK at the beginning and end of the employment, and overseas board and lodging expenses borne by the employer are allowable as a deduction from eligible emoluments if included as part of the emoluments. If reimbursed they are not assessed as benefits.

Travel costs, both within the UK and outside the UK, for a spouse and children under 18 visiting a spouse working overseas are allowable provided:

(a)   the employer bears the cost, and
(b)   the employee has worked overseas for at least 60 continuous days.

Up to two return trips are allowable each year of assessment.

Irrespective of the number of days spent outside UK, the employee working outside UK can make an unlimited number of return visits to any place in the UK, without incurring a taxable benefit when the cost is borne by the employer. This is provided the overseas absence was wholly and exclusively for the employment and all the duties thereof can only be performed outside the UK.

There is a £10 per night de minimis exemption where an employer reimburses an employee's personal incidental expenses while on an overseas business trip.

5   CAPITAL GAINS TAX

5.1   Introduction

Individuals are subject to capital gains tax on disposals of assets situated anywhere in the world if they are resident or ordinarily resident for any part of the tax year in which the disposal takes place.

In addition, individuals remain subject to CGT in respect of assets acquired before leaving the UK, if they leave the UK for a period of less than five complete tax years. This makes it difficult for people to avoid CGT by selling assets during a period of temporary residence abroad.

However, the five-year rule only applies if an individual has been UK resident during at least four out of seven tax years immediately prior to the year of departure.

If the anti-avoidance rules apply then:

- Gains made during the year of departure are chargeable in that year whether before or after the date of departure.

- Gains made after that year whilst overseas are chargeable in the year that the person resumes residence in the UK.

The rules do not apply to gains on assets acquired after a person has become resident abroad.

A person that comes to the UK and is treated as resident here from the date of arrival, is only subject to CGT on disposals made after that date.

A further exception to the basic rule is where a person is carrying on a trade, profession or vocation in the UK through a branch or an agency, and an asset which has been used by the branch or agency is:

- disposed of; or
- removed from the UK

or the UK trade, profession or vocation ceases.

5.2   Individuals domiciled abroad

If an individual is resident or ordinarily resident in the UK, but not UK-domiciled, he is assessed:

- on his UK gains on an arising basis
- on his non-UK gains on a remittance basis.

For the purposes of the above rule, assets are deemed to be located on the same basis as for inheritance tax (covered in chapter 33).

6   DOUBLE TAXATION RELIEF FOR INDIVIDUALS

6.1   Introduction

Under UK tax legislation an individual who is **resident** in the United Kingdom is liable to UK **income tax** on his world–wide income.

An individual who is resident **or** ordinarily resident in the UK (or is deemed to be so resident) is liable to **capital gains tax** on chargeable gains arising from disposals of property, wherever located.

In the case of income (or gains) arising in another country, there may well be a liability to tax in that country as well as in the United Kingdom. It is necessary that there should be some relief for such double taxation.

Double taxation relief may be given either bilaterally under a double taxation agreement between the UK and a specific overseas country, or unilaterally by the UK, irrespective of any agreement relief.

On dividends, the overseas tax for which relief is allowed is the **direct withholding tax** on the income. Relief is not available for any other overseas taxes; in particular, individuals cannot obtain relief for any underlying tax on the profits out of which the dividend was paid.

On, say, rents or income of an overseas trade (assessable under Schedule D Case V) the overseas tax will usually be that charged by the foreign country by direct assessment.

6.2   Double taxation agreements

Under these agreements, which must be studied individually in practice, certain classes of income from the overseas country in agreement, received by UK residents are given complete exemption in the overseas country for the local equivalent to the relevant UK tax and reciprocal relief is given by the Inland Revenue for the UK taxes on similar income derived from the UK by residents of the overseas country. The agreement may also extend to tax on capital gains for individuals, or corporation tax on gains for companies.

Classes of income which are not wholly exempted from the foreign tax under a double tax agreement are usually granted relief by allowing the foreign tax suffered by the UK resident as a deduction from UK liability on the same source of income.

Where tax on overseas income is not relieved by a double tax agreement, unilateral relief will normally be available.

6.3   Tax credit relief

Foreign income (inclusive of any withholding tax suffered) is classified as dividends, savings or non-savings as appropriate and included in the personal tax computation under the appropriate Schedule and Case (usually Case IV or V of Schedule D).

Where there is no double taxation agreement or where the agreement does not give relief by exemption double taxation relief is allowed as a credit against the total UK tax liability, such credit being the lower of

(a)   the foreign withholding tax on the foreign income, and

(b)   the UK income tax on the gross foreign income.

6.4   Example: double tax relief

Swot, a 21 year old bachelor, is resident in the UK and a university student. For 1999/00 his only taxable income is an overseas dividend. The dividend arising in 1999/00 was £5,100 net, with foreign tax withheld in the country of origin being £1,275.

Calculate the UK income tax liability.

6.5   Solution

UK income tax computation 1999/00

		£
Schedule D V income:		
Overseas dividend		5,100
Add: Withholding tax (20% of gross amount)		1,275
Total income		6,375
Less: Personal allowance		4,335
Taxable income		2,040

Chargeable:	£	
£2,040 at 10%		204
Less: DTR, being lower of		
(1) foreign tax suffered	1,275	
(2) UK tax on foreign income	204	204
UK tax liability		Nil

The foreign tax unrelieved (£1,071) cannot be repaid or carried forward.

6.6   Tax credit relief continued

Where the individual has foreign income as part of his total income it is treated as the top slice of his income and DTR computed accordingly.

Where foreign income is received from different sources, the taxpayer may choose which source of foreign income is to be regarded as the top slice to gain maximum DTR.

6.7   Example

Andy earns £22,000 p.a. from his employment in the UK, and also has the following overseas income for 1999/00:

- Rental income of £7,000 p.a. (gross) on which overseas tax at the rate of 35% is payable.
- Bank interest of £3,570 p.a. (net) from which overseas tax at the rate of 15% has been deducted.

Calculate the UK tax liability for 1999/00.

6.8   Solution

Income tax computation 1999/00

	£	£
Schedule E		
Salary		22,000
Schedule D Case V		
Rental income		7,000
Bank interest $(3,570 \times {}^{100}/_{85})$		4,200
		33,200
Personal allowance		4,335
Taxable income		28,865
Income tax:		
1,500 at 10%		150
23,165 (28,865 − 4,200 − 1,500) at 23%		5,328
3,335 (28,000 − 1,500 −23,165) at 20%		667
865 (4,200 − 3,335) at 40%		346
28,865		6,491
Double taxation relief		
Rents (see working)	1,757	
Bank interest (4,200 × 15%)	630	
		(2,387)
		4,104

WORKING

The rate of foreign tax on Andy's rental income (35%) is greater than the rate of tax on his bank interest (15%), so the rental income is treated as his top slice of income. The double taxation relief is therefore the lower of:

	£	£
• The overseas tax paid - 7,000 at 35% =		2,450
• The UK tax on the overseas income.		
6,135 at 23% =	1,411	
865 at 40% =	346	
		1,757

You should note that both the bank interest and the rental income are, for different purposes, considered to be the top slice of income.

7   CORPORATION TAX: OVERSEAS OPERATIONS

7.1   Liability to UK corporation tax

Companies resident in the UK are chargeable to corporation tax on all profits and chargeable gains wherever they arise (remittance to UK is irrelevant).

7.2   Residence

The following rules relate to the residence of a company.

(a)   **Companies incorporated in the UK.**

A UK or foreign company incorporated in the UK will be deemed resident in the UK for tax purposes.

(b)   **Foreign incorporated companies.**

An overseas incorporated company will be deemed resident in the UK, if its central management and control are exercised in the UK.

7.3   Examples

(a)   X Ltd is incorporated in the UK. The directors hold monthly board meetings in France where major policy decisions are made.

X Ltd is regarded as resident in the UK. If a company is incorporated in the UK it is immaterial where meetings are held and decisions are made.

(b)   Y Ltd is incorporated in Holland. The directors hold frequent board meetings in London, where the managing directors are based.

Y Ltd would probably be regarded as resident in the UK for corporation tax purposes. Although not incorporated in the UK, it would appear that the company is centrally managed and controlled here.

(c)   Z Ltd is incorporated in Germany. The directors hold weekly meetings in Germany, and quarterly meetings in London where the non-executive directors are based.

Z Ltd would probably be regarded as resident in Germany. The company is not incorporated in the UK, and it appears to be centrally managed and controlled in Germany.

Companies which are resident in the UK, but which would be regarded as resident in another country, for the purposes of a double tax agreement are treated as not resident in the UK.

7.4   The taxation of overseas income

The normal provisions in tax treaties (based on the OECD model treaty) is that an overseas country will normally only tax income arising in its country from the commercial operation of a UK resident company if

(a)   a trade is carried on **within** its boundaries, and
(b)   the profits are derived from a **permanent establishment** set up for that purpose.

The term 'within a country's boundaries' is important, because trading **with**, as opposed to **within**, another country will avoid any liability to overseas profits taxes. Trading with another country usually includes the export of UK produced goods which are sold other than through a permanent establishment owned by the UK company which produced the goods.

The term 'permanent establishment' within an overseas country includes a place of management, a branch, an office, a factory, a workshop or any mine or other place of extraction of natural resources.

A UK resident company that possesses a permanent establishment trading within an overseas country will normally be charged to tax on its overseas profits arising, by both the Inland Revenue under the UK residence rule, and the overseas tax authority under their own tax code.

The operations of an overseas located branch or agency will normally be regarded as part of those of its UK resident head office. On the other hand, scope clearly exists for an overseas located subsidiary company of a UK parent company to be regarded as non-resident as far as the UK is concerned, since the subsidiary would be incorporated outside the UK **and** effective management and control could be clearly shown to be undertaken overseas. Non-resident status would exempt the profits of the overseas subsidiary from UK tax, but the dividends arising on the UK parent's shareholding would be assessable under Sch D Case V (income from an overseas possession).

Any overseas taxes imposed are classified for UK tax purposes as

(a)   **withholding tax**: any direct tax imposed at source by the overseas country (ie, withheld)

(b)   **underlying tax**: this is tax calculated on overseas profits out of which (after underlying tax) a dividend is paid (subject to withholding tax) to the UK investing company.

7.5   The structure of the overseas operation

The basic question to be considered by any UK resident company setting up overseas is whether to operate through a branch, or through an overseas resident subsidiary company.

The two alternative forms can be compared from a UK taxation viewpoint as follows.

Since overseas branch trading profits are assessable under Schedule D Case I, the company can claim UK capital allowances in respect of branch assets.

Since an overseas branch's trading profits form part of the total Schedule D Case I trading profits of the company, any branch trading losses are eligible for UK loss relief and UK losses can relieve overseas branch profits.

Non-resident overseas subsidiaries can usually obtain greater overseas (local) tax advantages than branches because they are set up in the foreign country employing essentially locally based personnel. Such advantages might be lower rates of overseas tax, and easier allowability for overseas tax purposes of UK costs reasonably allocated to the overseas operations in the form of management charges.

Dividends payable by a non-resident subsidiary to its UK parent company will be assessable on the parent under Case V. The profits of an overseas subsidiary, perhaps taxed at a lower rate than applies in the UK, can be accumulated overseas.

7.6   Transfer pricing

Where sales are made to a non-resident group company at an undervalue, then a true market price should be substituted for the transfer price. Under self assessment, this adjustment should be made by the company concerned.

There are detailed rules for determining which companies are caught by the transfer pricing rules, but the basic test is one of control.

The Inland Revenue has introduced advance pricing arrangements. These enable a company to agree in advance with the Inland Revenue that its transfer pricing arrangements are acceptable.

The rules also apply if purchases are made from a non-resident group company at an overvaluation.

The transfer pricing rules prevent companies from transferring profits to a non-resident group company (in a country with a low tax rate), and correspondingly reducing profits chargeable to UK corporation tax.

8   DOUBLE TAXATION RELIEF FOR COMPANIES

8.1   Introduction

Double taxation may be mitigated for UK **resident** companies in one of three ways

(a)   **bilaterally,** under a Double Taxation Treaty between the UK and a specific overseas country

(b)   **unilaterally,** irrespective of any treaty relief

(c)   electing to exclude tax credit relief.

8.2   Treaty relief

(a)   **Introduction**

A double taxation agreement may provide for full recovery of any foreign tax covered by the agreement, by means of a tax credit to a UK resident company, so long as the relief does not exceed the equivalent UK tax charge.

(b)   **Standard pattern of agreement**

It is common practice for agreements to provide:

- for certain income to be taxed only in the country of source, eg, income from land and buildings, or

- for the income to be taxed only in the country in which the company is resident, eg, royalties.

(c)   **The relief**

Relief under treaties will be given either

- by one country **reducing the rate** of tax on the source of income or gain, or

- by one country **exempting** the source of income or gain from tax, or

- by the UK – the country in which the recipient company is resident – giving a **tax credit** for foreign taxes suffered against UK corporation tax payable.

8.3   Unilateral relief in the UK

Where an agreement does not provide relief for a particular category of income or where there is no double taxation agreement, relief is given to UK resident companies by way of a tax credit against the UK corporation tax liability on the doubly taxed profits. This is the same as the tax credit relief given under a double taxation agreement.

8.4   Computation of tax credit relief

For the purpose of relief, overseas tax is converted into sterling at the rate of exchange applying at the time the overseas tax becomes payable.

Although relief for overseas **withholding tax** is always available, relief for any **underlying tax** is given only where the UK resident company receiving the relevant dividend controls, directly or indirectly, at least 10% of the voting power of the overseas company paying the dividend.

Overseas income is included in the corporation tax computation under Case I, III or V of Schedule D as appropriate. Any withholding tax is added back to amounts received so that the gross figure is included. Where relief for underlying tax is available, this will be added back in addition to withholding tax.

The amount of DTR is limited to the **lower** of

- relievable foreign tax on overseas income, and
- UK total corporation tax payable on the overseas income.

8.5 Election to exclude tax credit relief

The company may elect that relief is not given as a tax credit. The overseas income arising abroad (ie, the amount before overseas taxes are deducted) is reduced by the overseas taxes paid, ie, effectively the overseas taxes are regarded as allowable business expenses for UK tax purposes.

Such an election will be made only if the tax credit relief is less beneficial. This is unlikely, as the tax credit relief is a deduction of all or some of the overseas taxes from the UK tax liability, whilst the election basis can confer relief from UK tax only at the highest marginal rate of UK corporation tax. Of course, it would be beneficial where the UK company has no liability to corporation tax, as when a loss is sustained.

8.6 Example: Tax credit relief

Probe plc, a UK resident company, has the following income for the year ended 31 March 2000.

	£	£
Adjusted trading profits from UK business		1,400,000
Income from shares held in an overseas company		
Amount of dividend received		93,500
Withholding tax (15%)	16,500	
Underlying tax (45%)	90,000	106,500
		200,000

Probe plc owns 15% of the voting shares in the overseas company.

Calculate the UK corporation tax payable.

8.7 Solution

Corporation tax computation: year ended 31 March 2000

	£	£
Schedule D Case I		1,400,000
Schedule D Case V		
Dividend received	93,500	
Add: Overseas taxes relievable	106,500	200,000
PCTCT		1,600,000
Corporation tax		
£1.6m × 30%		480,000
Less: Double taxation relief:		
Lower of:		
(1) overseas tax on overseas income	106,500	
(2) UK CT on overseas income 30% × £200,000	60,000	60,000
UK corporation tax payable		420,000

Note: the excess of overseas tax over the UK corporation tax liability on overseas income ie, £46,500, represents the effect of a higher rate of overseas tax, and no further double tax relief is available.

8.8 Source by source basis of DTR

It is important to realise that a major limitation affecting DTR is that it cannot exceed the total corporation tax attributable to the overseas income. It is thus an elementary tax planning point that the total corporation tax attributable on the overseas income must be kept as high as possible in order to maximise DTR.

The manner of computing any credit for DTR is on a 'source by source' basis, not a global basis.

8.9 Example: DTR

Suppose a UK company, chargeable at the full rate of corporation tax, receives overseas income and suffers the following overseas taxes in its year ended 31 March 2000.

£10,000 from Syria at 66%
£10,000 from Jersey at 20%.

What is the UK corporation tax payable on overseas income?

8.10 Solution

Effect on UK tax and DTR is

				£	£
UK tax on overseas income: £20,000 × 30%					6,000
Less:	DTR – lower of UK CT or overseas tax on *each* source **separately**				
	(i)	Syria	30% × £10,000 = £3,000	3,000	
			66% × £10,000 = £6,600		
	(ii)	Jersey	30% × £10,000 = £3,000		
			20% × £10,000 = £2,000	2,000	5,000
UK corporation tax payable on overseas income					1,000

Notes:

(1)   The £1,000 corporation tax payable is, in fact, all in respect of the Jersey income at 10% [the excess of UK tax rate (30%) over Jersey tax rate (20%)].

(2)   There is no UK tax on Syrian income, since it has already suffered tax at least equal to the UK rate.

(3)   Because UK DTR is not on a global basis, the surplus 30% on Syrian income cannot be used to reduce the UK tax on the Jersey income - instead, it is wasted.

(4)   The source rule not only applies to sources arising in different countries, but also to different sources arising in the same country.

8.11 Method of calculating underlying tax

It has been seen above that for DTR purposes any relievable underlying tax is added to the gross amount of the overseas dividend. UK corporation tax is then charged on this total.

The case of *Bowater Paper Corporation Ltd v Murgatroyd* decided that the calculation should be based upon the company's after-tax profits per the financial or commercial accounts, not on the profits as adjusted for tax. It is the profits (after tax) available for distribution to the shareholders, that is the relevant profit.

The actual formula applied to obtain the rate of underlying tax is

$$\frac{\text{Actual tax paid} \times 100}{\text{Actual tax paid} + \text{relevant profit}}$$

8.12 Example: DTR with underlying tax

The following details are given in respect of Stilton Ltd for the accounting year ended 31 March 2000

	£
UK trading income	1,660,000
Dividend received from Edam b.v. a Dutch corporation (net of 4% withholding tax)	105,600
UK capital gains after indexation	30,000
Patent royalty paid (gross)	20,000

The following additional information is also available

(1) Stilton Ltd owns 15% of the voting power of Edam b.v.

(2) The profit and loss account of Edam b.v. for the accounting period giving rise to the £105,600 dividend received by Stilton Ltd shows:

	£	£
Profit before tax		8,325,000
Tax charge – current	1,860,000	
– deferred	2,340,000	4,200,000
Profit after tax		4,125,000

(3) Following agreement of the Dutch company tax return, the tax actually payable for the above period was £1,500,000.

Compute the corporation tax payable for the year ended 31 March 2000, assuming all possible reliefs for double taxation are claimed.

8.13 Solution

Corporation tax computation – year ended 31 March 2000

	Total profits £	UK profits £	Overseas income £
Schedule D Case I profit	1,660,000	1,660,000	
Schedule D Case V (Working)	150,000		150,000
Chargeable gain	30,000	30,000	
	1,840,000	1,690,000	150,000
Less: Charges paid (gross)	20,000	20,000	-
PCTCT	1,820,000	1,670,000	150,000

Corporation tax			
£1,820,000 × 30%	546,000	501,000	45,000
Less: DTR – lower of:			
(1) overseas recoverable taxes (Working)			
£4,400 + £40,000 = £44,400	44,400	-	44,400
(2) UK corporation tax on			
overseas income (£45,000)			
Corporation tax payable	501,600	501,000	600

Charges have been set against UK profits so as to maximise double taxation relief.

WORKING - Computation of underlying tax and Schedule D Case V income

Applying rule in the Bowater case the rate
of underlying tax is

$$\frac{£1.5m \times 100}{£1.5m + £4.125m} = 26.667\%$$

		£
(i)	Gross overseas income	
	Dividend received	105,600
	Add: Withholding tax	4,400
	Gross dividend	110,000
	Add: Attributable underlying tax	
	£110,000 × 26.667/73.333	40,000
	Schedule D Case V income	150,000

(ii)   Alternatively the amount of underlying tax can be computed
without computing the rate as a preliminary.

ie, $\dfrac{\text{Gross dividend} \times \text{Actual tax paid}}{\text{Relevant profits}}$

being: $\dfrac{£110,000 \times £1.5m}{£4.125m} = £40,000$

9   CONTROLLED FOREIGN COMPANIES

9.1   The anti-avoidance provisions

The Revenue had been concerned for a number of years that companies resident abroad but owned by UK resident companies are outside the scope of UK tax on their foreign profits. UK companies have felt encouraged to set up foreign companies (controlled foreign companies (CFCs)) instead of overseas branches if the local rates of tax are significantly below the UK rates. The profits of a branch would fall under UK tax as part of the UK resident company's profits, whereas the foreign company's profits would only be caught (under Schedule DV) when the company remitted dividends to the UK parent.

Anti-avoidance provisions apply to UK resident companies holding an interest (directly or indirectly) in a CFC if all the following conditions apply.

A CFC is a company:

(a)   resident outside the UK,

(b)   controlled by UK residents,

(c)   resident in a territory in which it is subject to a low level of taxation. (i.e. it pays less than three-quarters of the tax that would be payable if it were UK resident); and:

(d)   the UK company is entitled to at least 25% of the profits of the CFC on an apportionment (see below).

If these conditions are satisfied for an accounting period of a CFC, then, subject to a range of exclusions (see below), the CFC's chargeable profits and creditable tax for that period are apportioned between the persons who hold an interest in the company during that period.

9.2   Exceptions

The provisions will not apply for an accounting period if the CFC:

(a)   pursues an acceptable distribution (dividend) policy (generally at least 90% of **taxable** profits less capital gains and foreign tax being distributed);

(b)   engages in exempt activities (mainly arm's length trading with third parties);

(c)   is quoted on a recognised stock exchange in the overseas country of residence with at least 35% of the voting power held by the public;

(d)   has profits not exceeding £50,000 (reduced pro-rata for accounting periods of less than 12 months);

(e)   satisfies the motive test i.e. does not exist wholly or mainly to reduce UK tax by diverting profits from the UK.

9.3   Low tax countries

There is a statutory list of excluded countries (ie, those that are not classed as 'low tax' areas).

9.4   Example: CFC

Hat Co is incorporated and resident in Tanama. It is an unquoted wholesale clothing company. It obtains its goods from associated manufacturing companies, except for 10% obtained from local craft centres. All the company's goods are exported to the UK where the major customer is Titfer-Tat Ltd. The voting share capital of Hat Co is held as follows:

	Shares
Tim Trilby (UK resident and domiciled)	500
Titfer-Tat Ltd (UK incorporated and resident)	300
Doshiba Bank Co (incorporated and resident in Japan)	200
	1,000

The results, converted into sterling, for Hat Co for its accounting year ended 31 March 2000 show

	£'000
Profit before tax	3,000
Less: Tax payable for the year	480
Profit after tax	2,520

No withholding tax in charged in Tanama.

You are required to explain why Hat Co is a controlled foreign company.

9.5   Solution

Hat Co is a controlled foreign company because:

(a)   it is resident outside the UK;

(b)   it is controlled by UK residents ie,

	UK residents	*Non-UK residents*
Tim Trilby	500	
Titfer-Tat Ltd	300	
Doshiba Bank Co		200
	800	200
	80%	20%

(c)   it is subject to a lower level of taxation in Tanama than that which would apply in the UK ie,

	£
Notional UK corporation tax liability	
Profit before tax	3,000,000
£3,000,000 × 30%	900,000
75% thereof	675,000
Overseas tax paid	480,000

Since the overseas tax paid is less than three quarters of the corresponding UK tax the company is subject to a lower level of taxation.

9.6   Apportionment of profits

Subject to the various exclusions, the chargeable profits of a CFC are apportioned between the persons who hold an interest in the company. A UK company that is entitled to at least 25% of the profits must then include details in its self assessment tax return, and will be charged to corporation tax on the apportioned profits. However, credit will be given for an apportioned amount of the CFC's overseas tax.

9.7   Acceptable distribution policy

The easiest way for the apportionment rules to be avoided is by the CFC adopting an acceptable distribution policy. This requires at least 90% of the **taxable** profits to be distributed by way of dividend within the 18 months following the end of the relevant accounting period.

10   FOREIGN COMPANIES TRADING IN THE UK

10.1   Liability to UK corporation tax

An overseas company will be liable to UK corporation tax if it trades in the UK through a branch or agency situated in the UK. It will only be liable in respect of profits arising in the UK.

A liability will not arise where an overseas company is merely trading with the UK, whereby goods are simply sold to persons carrying on a business in the UK.

10.2   Drawing a distinction

The distinction between trading with the UK and trading in the UK can be difficult to draw.

Having a permanent establishment in the UK or concluding contracts in the UK will normally result in the overseas company being liable to UK corporation tax.

To avoid becoming liable to UK corporation tax, an overseas company with a presence in the UK would have to confine its activities to, for example, gathering information, advertising, and maintaining stocks of goods for supply to UK customers.

11 SELF TEST QUESTIONS

11.1 When is a person regarded as UK resident? (2.2)

11.2 Explain the meaning of domicile. (2.4)

11.3 What is the basis of assessment for Schedule D Case IV and V income? (4.2)

11.4 When are the travel costs for a spouse and children allowable? (4.7)

11.5 In what alternative ways can a UK company structure its overseas operations? (7.5)

11.6 How is underlying tax calculated? (8.11)

11.7 What is a controlled foreign company? (9.1)

11.8 When will the provisions introduced for CFCs not apply? (9.2)

11.9 What is an acceptable distribution policy for a CFC? (9.7)

11.10 When will a foreign company be liable to UK corporation tax? (10.1)

12 EXAMINATION TYPE QUESTION

12.1 Factory Overseas

X Ltd is a UK resident company which has, to date, traded only in the UK. The directors have decided to establish a factory overseas and seek advice on the taxation implications of this proposal. In particular, they wish to know whether the overseas trade should be conducted through a foreign-based subsidiary or simply as a branch of the UK company.

You are required to draft an appropriate memorandum to the board of the company highlighting the taxation implications of **each** of the two alternatives.

13 ANSWER TO EXAMINATION TYPE QUESTION

13.1 Factory Overseas

To: Board of Directors of X Ltd

From:

Date:

Taxation implications of establishing a factory overseas

The factory would be a 'permanent establishment' overseas and the profits will suffer foreign tax. Relief will be given for the foreign tax up to the full amount of UK corporation tax on that income.

Overseas branch of UK company

(1) The company would be liable to UK corporation tax on all profits of the branch under normal Schedule D Case I.

(2) Since the branch is considered as part of the UK company, any branch losses would automatically be relieved.

(3) Capital gains arising would be subject to UK corporation tax.

(4) The overseas branch would not effect the upper and lower limits for small companies rate purposes.

Foreign based subsidiary

(1)   The parent company will only be liable to UK corporation tax on amounts received as dividends or interest from the subsidiary.

(2)   Relief for losses would not be available between the parent and a non-resident subsidiary.

(3)   Capital gains arising in a non-resident subsidiary would not be subject to UK corporation tax.

(4)   Management control must be exercised overseas for the subsidiary to be accepted as a non UK resident.

(5)   The overseas company will be an associated company for small company rate purposes, and therefore effect the upper and lower limits.

(6)   If the foreign based subsidiary is a controlled foreign company the profits of the subsidiary may be apportioned to X Ltd.

38 PERSONAL FINANCIAL PLANNING

INTRODUCTION

Tax planning often involves investment considerations. The tax planner must therefore be familiar with the various forms of investment, their risks and suitability, and the statutory regulation governing investment business.

1 INVESTMENTS AND THEIR CHARACTERISTICS

In deciding upon the financial assets in which to invest the investor will need to consider the characteristics of the different forms of investment and how they match with the investor's own requirements.

The principal investments for the private investor include:

- Bank and building society accounts
- National Savings products
- Gilt edged securities
- Other fixed income securities
- Equities
- Unit Trusts
- Investment Trusts
- Open ended investment companies
- Individual savings accounts
- Life Assurance
- Pensions
- Real Property
- Enterprise investment scheme
- Venture capital trusts

In deciding upon the suitability of a particular investment the investor must take account of the following features:

(a)   the risks associated with the investment;
(b)   its liquidity, ie, the ease of encashment;
(c)   its tax efficiency; and
(d)   whether it is income producing or whether it is more suitable for capital growth.

We will review these features in turn.

2 RISK

2.1 Types of risk

The risks associated with investment are various and can be categorised in different ways. The main risks are:

(a)   the risk that the investment will fall in value; examples:

   (i)   a share price falls. This might be as a result of a fall in the stock market generally, known as market risk; or the fall might be as a result of some event or circumstance specific to that company, known as investment specific risk.

(ii)   a gilt-edged investment or other fixed interest security falls in value as a result of a rise in interest rates. This is interest rate risk.

(iii)   the income from a variable rate building society account falls as a result of a fall in interest rates. This is also an example of interest rate risk.

(b)   the investment becomes worthless eg, the company becomes insolvent or the issuer of a bond fails to pay the interest or to repay the capital. This is known as default risk.

(c)   the real value of the investment and of the income from the investment fall because of inflation - inflation risk.

There is probably no investment which is entirely risk free. Even British Government investments, which are the safest form of sterling investment, will be affected by inflation.

2.2   Risk and reward

The two principles governing the return on investment are

1   the greater the risk the greater the return expected by investors; and
2   the longer money is tied up the greater the return expected by investors

One of the objectives in constructing a portfolio is to determine the level of risk which is acceptable to the investor and then to maximise the return for that level of risk.

2.3   The riskiness of different types of investment

Risk can be regarded as a spectrum with British Government securities at one, the very safe end, and speculative unquoted shares and derivatives such as option and futures at the other, the very risky end.

The following list gives an indication of the relative riskiness of different types of investment.

1   No default risk, no risk of fall in value and some protection against inflation:

- Index linked National Savings Certificates
- Index linked Gilts held to redemption

2   No default risk, no risk of fall in value but at risk from inflation

- Other National Savings products
- Conventional gilts held to redemption

3   No default risk but with a risk of fall in value

- Gilts sold before redemption

4   Low risk investments

- Accounts with banks and building societies
- Life assurance policies
- Loan stocks and other bonds issued by secure companies

5   Medium risk investments

- Collective investments eg, unit trusts, investment trusts and open ended investment companies
- Loan stocks of less secure companies

6   High risk investments

- Direct holdings of shares in quoted companies

7   Very high risk investments

- Unquoted shares
- Futures and Options

3   LIQUIDITY

3.1   The meaning of liquidity

Liquidity means cash and the liquidity of an investment means the ease with which the investment can be converted into cash ie, the ease with which the investment can be sold, or cashed in, and the speed with which the proceeds are received.

3.2   Liquid investments

The most liquid investments are bank current accounts and building society instant access accounts on both of which money is at call.

Deposit and notice accounts require a period of notice to be given or, alternatively, a penalty is paid for instant access.

Gilt edged securities are very liquid. They are easy to sell through the Stock Exchange and the proceeds are usually available the following business day.

National Savings products such as National Savings Certificates are also easy to cash in early, although there will be a penalty in the form of a lower return than if the Certificate was held to maturity. The proceeds are available within a few days.

3.3   Shares and unit trusts

The liquidity of shares is variable.

For blue chip equities, where there is an active market, the stockbroker acting on behalf of the investor will be able to sell the shares immediately.

But for smaller, less well known, companies it may take some time to find a buyer.

The shares in private unquoted companies may be almost impossible to sell.

Units in unit trusts can easily be sold back to the unit trust managers with proceeds being available within a few days.

3.4   Life assurance

Life assurance policies must be regarded as being illiquid. Surrendering or selling a policy before the end of its term may not be straightforward and in the early years the amount received may only be a small proportion of the premiums paid.

3.5   The importance of liquidity to the private investor

A private investor should always maintain some liquid funds in order to meet emergencies, or to take advantage of investment opportunities etc. This liquidity should be in the form of bank or building society accounts.

Being forced to sell investments at short notice in order to raise cash is not sensible investment policy. Investments should be sold when the timing is right, for example, in order to take a profit.

Irrespective of how easy it may be to sell a marketable investment such as shares or gilts, the price obtained will only be the current market price and selling in order to raise cash may result in an untimely loss.

4 .   TAX MATTERS

4.1   Tax Exemptions

Some investments offer some form of tax exemption or incentive. These include:

- Gilt edged securities } both are exempt from capital gains tax
- Qualifying corporate bonds
- National Savings Certificates interest is free of income tax
- Individual Savings; Accounts dividends, interest and capital gains are tax free
- Pensions - contributions are deductible from income and the investment fund is tax free
- Enterprise investment scheme and venture capital trusts - 20% income tax relief is available on contributions; capital gains are tax free

However, a word of warning: a common fault among investors is to allow the tax exemption to outweigh the investment considerations.

The guiding rule should be: if a particular course of action is appropriate from a commercial or investment point of view then it should be undertaken in as tax efficient manner as possible. For example, if the investor decides to invest in a particular unit trust then buying the units through an ISA would be tax efficient. But investing in an ISA, which entails exposure to stock market risks, simply because of the tax exemptions is not sensible.

4.2   Income Tax and Capital Gains Tax

The rates of income tax and capital gains tax have been similar since 1988. For 1999/00 the rates of tax on savings income (other than dividends) and capital gains are exactly the same. However, capital gains do offer some advantages, especially to the higher rate tax payer.

(i)   The capital gains tax exemption of £7,100

(ii)   Taper relief

(iii)   Timing: income tends to arise when the payer, such as the government or company or bank, decides. Capital gains arise on disposals the timing of which are usually within the power of the investor.

5   INCOME VERSUS CAPITAL GROWTH

5.1   Investment objectives

Investors tend to invest in order to produce (i) income; (ii) capital growth; or (iii) a mixture of both.

By income we mean a regular cash inflow in order to meet expenses. This cash inflow is usually in the form of interest or dividends. But it could also be achieved through liquidating capital.

Capital growth can be achieved through equity growth, growth in the value of ordinary shares, or through compounding of interest.

5.2   Income

Investments which would be suitable for producing income are:

- building society and bank accounts
- high coupon gilt edged securities
- other high coupon bonds
- guaranteed income bonds
- high yielding equities
- National Savings Income Bonds
- income shares of split level investment trusts

Investment trusts often have a capital structure consisting of different types of share. Some shares, may offer capital growth, and will pay low (or nil) dividends, whilst others will aim at high income at the cost of capital growth.

5.3 Capital growth

Investments suitable for capital growth are

- equities
- unit trusts, investment trusts and open ended investment companies
- capital shares of split level investment trusts
- National Savings Capital Bonds
- Life assurance endowment policies (either with profits policies or unit linked policies)
- National Savings Certificates

6 THE FINANCIAL SERVICES ACT 1986

6.1 The Financial Services Act 1986

Investment business, which includes the provision of investment advice and the management of investments, is regulated primarily by the Financial Services Act 1986 (FSA86).

The main areas covered by the FSA86 are:

- Definition of investment business
- Authorisation of investment businesses
- Conduct of business rules

The main thrust of the FSA86 is one of self regulation but within a statutory framework. Under the FSA86 a formal structure of regulatory bodies has been developed.

6.2 The authorisation of investment businesses

One of the key requirements of the FSA86 is that any person carrying on investment business must either be authorised or be exempt.

Authorisation will be through one of the bodies described below.

6.3 Penalty for conducting unauthorised investment business

There are both criminal and civil penalties for conducting unauthorised investment business:

Criminal: maximum penalties: 2 years imprisonment and/or an unlimited fine

Civil: any agreement entered into by the unauthorised person is unenforceable by him and the other party is entitled to recover any money paid out to him.

7 THE REGULATORY BODIES

7.1 The Financial Services Authority

The overall regulatory body under the FSA86 is the Financial Services Authority (FSA). The FSA is independent of the government but it exercises statutory powers transferred to it by the Treasury.

Under the FSA are other regulatory bodies which have been granted their regulatory status by the FSA. These other bodies fall into one of two groups:

(i)   Self Regulating Organisations (SROs): and
(ii)   Recognised Professional Bodies (RPBs).

An investment business will obtain its authorisation in one of three ways:

(i)   From the FSA directly
(ii)   From an SRO
(iii)   From an RPB.

In practice very few businesses are authorised by the FSA directly.

7.2   Self Regulating Organisations (SROs)

The SROs are the regulatory bodies for companies and other organisations whose investment business is not ancillary to any other professional business. There are THREE SROs:

(i)   **The Securities and Futures Authority (SFA)**

        For businesses involved in dealing and advising on marketable securities and financial and commodity derivatives (ie, options and futures)

(ii)   **The Investment Management Regulatory Organisation (IMRO)**

        For investment managers and advisers including the trustees and managers of collective investment schemes

(iii)   **The Personal Investment Authority (PIA)**

        For firms dealing with private investors.

        A draft Financial Services and Markets Bill has recently been published. This will establish the FSA as the sole 'super' regulatory body. It is expected that the Bill will be enacted during 2000.

7.3   Recognised Professional Bodies (RPBs)

Certain professional firms, for example accountants and solicitors, have traditionally given investment advice to clients as part of their overall professional service. Instead of having to apply for membership of an SRO such firms may apply to their professional body for certification to carry on certain types of investment business under the regulation of the RPB.

The RPBs include:

- The Association of Chartered Certified Accountants
- The Institute of Chartered Accountants in England and Wales
- The Institute of Chartered Accountants in Scotland
- The Institute of Chartered Accountants in Ireland
- The Law Societies of England, Scotland and Northern Ireland

Under the changes to take place during 2000, regulation is to be transferred from the RPBs to the FSA. However, it is possible that the professional bodies concerned may still be involved in the monitoring of member firms carrying on investment business.

7.4   The ACCA investment business rules

Practising firms of Certified Accountants can apply to the Association to carry on investment business.

A firm means either a sole practitioner or a partnership where all the partners are members of RPBs and at least one partner is a member of the Association.

The volume and types of investment business carried on by firms will be subject to restrictions among which are:

- The firm's main business must be accountancy; the Association has agreed with the FSA that this means that the amount of investment business is restricted to 20% of fee income. If a firm has investment activities in excess of this level then it will need to apply to the FSA or an SRO for full authorisation.

- There will be restrictions on the types of investment business carried on. For example, market making in investments is prohibited

- There may be restrictions on the holding of clients money.

8   THE MEANING OF INVESTMENT AND INVESTMENT BUSINESS

8.1   The meaning of investment

The FSA86 defines the meaning of investment. This list includes what might be regarded as traditional investments as well as some more esoteric instruments.

Investments include

- Shares and stock in the share capital of any company wherever incorporated
- Debentures, loan stocks and similar instruments
- Government, local authority or other public authority securities
- Warrants to subscribe for shares or debentures
- Units in collective investment schemes, eg, units in unit trusts
- Long term insurance contracts such as life assurance endowment policies and insurance based insurance products.

It is important to note that the direct holding of the following **are not investments** within the meaning of the FSA86 although they are commonly regarded as investments:

- Building society and bank accounts
- Real property
- Gold and other metals
- Works of art

However collective investments in such assets, for example property unit trusts, are an investment.

8.2   The meaning of investment business

The following activities constitute investment business:

- Dealing in investments either as principal or agent. This will include an accountant purchasing shares or unit trusts on behalf of a client and in the clients name.

- Arranging deals in investments. This might include introducing the client to another authorised person with whom there is some sort of commission sharing arrangement

- Managing investments

- Giving investment advice. This can be interpreted extremely widely

- Establishing or operating a collective investment scheme

The following activities are excluded:

- Dealing as principal where the dealer is not holding himself out as an investment business, eg, individuals dealing on their own account.

- Employees share schemes

- Trustees and personal representatives

8.3   Appointed representatives of authorised persons.

The FSA86 requires that intermediaries advising etc. in the fields of life assurance, pensions and collective investment schemes must act either as an entirely independent intermediary or as a company representative

This is known as the principle of **polarisation.**

An independent intermediary acts as the agent of the client and will recommend the most appropriate policies from the whole market.

A company representative might be employed by an investment provider(such as a life company) or may be a separate entity tied to one company. A company representative may only advise on and sell the products of the company he represents.

Company representatives can range from individuals to large organisations such as high street banks and building societies.

Independent intermediaries must be authorised under the FSA86 by an SRO, by a RPB or by the FSA.

A company representative will not be separately authorised. The company to which they are tied has responsibility to ensure that they are fit and proper persons and that they comply with the FSA86. Such representatives are known as **appointed representatives**.

8.4   Appointed representatives and ACCA firms

The ACCA has decided that neither firms nor any partners in a firm should accept appointments as appointed representatives as such an appointment would be inconsistent with a firm's duty of independence.

8.5   Investment advisers summarised

(i)   Sources of independent advice are:

- Chartered Certified accountants
- Chartered accountants
- Solicitors
- Actuaries
- Stockbrokers
- Independent Financial Advisers

(ii)   Advisers who do not offer independent advice are appointed representatives.

9   REGULATIONS AFFECTING INVESTMENT ADVICE

9.1   Introduction

In conducting investment business firms must comply with regulations laid down by the FSA and the ACCA.

Overlaying all the rules of the various SROs and RPBs are the FSA's 10 Statements of Principle. These 10 Statements apply to all authorised persons and act as a distillation of the fundamental aspects of the standards of conduct of business and financial standing expected of financial service firms and their employees.

The detailed rules which ACCA firms must observe are contained in the Association's Investment Business Rules.

9.2   **The 10 Statements of Principle**

The 10 Statements of Principle are:

1   **Integrity**

A firm should observe high standards of integrity and fair dealing.

2   **Skill, care and diligence**

A firm should act with due skill, care and diligence.

3   **Market practice**

A firm should observe high standards of market conduct.

4   **Information about customers**

A firm should seek from customers it advises any information about their circumstances and investment objectives which might reasonably be expected to be relevant in enabling it to fulfil its responsibilities to them.

5   **Information to customers**

A firm should take reasonable steps to give a customer it advises, in a comprehensible and timely way, any information needed to enable him to make a balanced and informed decision. A firm should similarly be ready to provide a customer with a full and fair account of the fulfilment of its responsibilities to him.

6   **Conflicts of interest**

A firm should either avoid any conflict of interest arising or, where conflicts arise, should ensure fair treatment to all its customers by disclosure, internal rules of confidentiality, declining to act, or otherwise. A firm should not unfairly place its interests above those of its customers and, where a properly informed customer would reasonably expect that the firm would place his interests above its own, the firm should live up to that expectation.

7   **Customer assets**

Where a firm has control of or is otherwise responsible for assets belonging to a customer which it is required to safeguard, it should arrange proper protection for them, by way of segregation and identification of those assets or otherwise, in accordance with the responsibility it has accepted.

8   **Financial resources**

A firm should ensure that it maintains adequate financial resources to meet its investment business commitments and to withstand the risks to which its business is subject.

9   **Internal organisation**

A firm should organise and control its internal affairs in a responsible manner, keeping proper records, and where the firm employs staff or is responsible for the conduct of investment business by others, should have adequate arrangements to ensure that they are suitable, adequately trained and properly supervised and that it has well defined compliance procedures.

10   **Relations with regulators**

A firm should deal with its regulator in an open and co-operative manner and keep the regulator promptly informed of anything concerning the firm which might reasonably be expected to be disclosed to it.

9.3   Know your client

Before performing any service or making any recommendation firms must take reasonable steps to ascertain sufficient information regarding their clients to be able to form a full picture of their financial state of affairs and their investment objectives. This will be carried out through a detailed fact find.

9.4   Best advice

The adviser must give the best advice and recommendations to the client taking into account all relevant circumstances.

Transactions recommended or effected for a client must be suitable for the client in the light of the facts disclosed by the client and other relevant facts about which the firm is or should be aware.

9.5   Best execution

Best execution means that a firm must

(i)   take reasonable steps to ascertain the best price available for the customer in the relevant market for transactions of that kind and size at that time; and

(ii)   deal at a price which is no less advantageous, unless there are circumstances which require it to do otherwise in the customers interests.

9.6   Churning and switching

These rules are designed to prevent a firm from making or recommending unnecessary transactions in order to generate business.

A firm must not make a personal recommendation for a private customer to deal or to deal on behalf of a discretionary customer if the dealing would be regarded as unreasonably frequent in the circumstances.

A firm must not make or recommend a switch for a private customer within or between packaged products unless it believes on reasonable grounds that the switch is justified from the customers viewpoint.

10   SELF TEST QUESTIONS

10.1   Give two examples of investment risk. (2.1)

10.2   What is meant by 'liquidity'? (3.1)

10.3   Give two investment suitable for income. (5.2)

10.4   Give two investments suitable for capital growth. (5.3)

10.5   What is the penalty for conducting unauthorised investment business? (6.3)

10.6   Name the 3 SROs (7.2)

10.7   What type of body is the ACCA? (7.3)

10.8   What is meant by polarisation? (8.3)

10.9   Can ACCA firms be appointed representatives? (8.4)

10.10   What is churning? (9.6)

39 INVESTMENT ADVICE

INTRODUCTION

An investment adviser must approach his, client in a structured and professional manner. He will carry out a fact find to determine his client's current state of affairs and investment objectives.

In the light of the information obtained he will advise on financial planning, an investment portfolio and, if necessary, any borrowings required.

This chapter covers the investment advice process.

1   THE APPROACH TO INVESTMENT ADVICE

1.1   Introduction

An investment advisor will approach the investment advice along the following lines.

(a)   A fact find would be carried in order to establish a client profile, or financial picture of the client.

(b)   In the light of the facts established any necessary financial planning would be advised, eg, pension and life cover

(c)   A portfolio would be constructed taking into account

(i)   The sum available for investment
(ii)   The client's requirements for income and/or capital growth
(iii)   The time over which the client wishes to invest
(iv)   The client's age
(v)   The client's attitude to risk
(vi)   The client's tax position.

1.2   Know the client

No advisor, in whatever field of activity, can advise their client unless they know their client. The Financial Services Act 1986 places a statutory duty on investment advisers to take reasonable steps to find out such facts about the client that will be needed to offer advice.

The following checklist covers the sort of points about which an adviser would ask:

Personal details	- age - family circumstances - profession, employment or trade
Income	- source and size - pension provision
Assets	- capital assets - investments
Liabilities	- indebtedness - family responsibilities, eg, education
Expectations	- career, both calls on capital and future rewards - trusts and legacies

Investment requirements   - investment objectives
                               - investment fields to be avoided

1.3   Essential financial planning

Before considering investment in gilts, shares etc the investor must ensure that the following basic financial planning matters have been dealt with.

(a)   **Emergency funds**

The need for liquidity was explained in an earlier chapter.

(b)   **Protection in case of death, illness and injury**

Does the investor have dependants? If so, adequate life assurance is essential to clear the mortgage and other debts and to provide future income. Such protection may be provided by a pension scheme.

Some form of Permanent Health Insurance should be considered to provide income should the investor be prevented from working through illness or injury. This is particularly important for the self employed who do not have an employer to protect them.

(c)   **Provision for retirement**

Are adequate pension provisions in place? If not then this must be a priority.

(d)   **Home ownership**

Renting one's home is sometimes appropriate but generally owning one's home is more sensible. Residential property usually proves to be a good long term investment.

(e)   **Pay off debts**

If an investor has a capital sum to invest then a higher return might be obtained by paying off debts, especially those debts with high non tax deductible interest, such as overdrafts.

A particular consideration will be a mortgage. Should this be paid off or at least reduced to £30,000. Certainly, the interest on the loan over £30,000 is non deductible, but it is probably the cheapest money an individual can obtain. On the other hand, the tax relief is only at 10% and this is to be withdrawn from 6 April 2000.

If the mortgage is high then there is merit is paying part of it off in order to reduce the interest burden on income. Otherwise it is probably a matter of personal preference.

(f)   **Make a will**

If an individual dies intestate then his estate will be distributed according to the rigid laws of intestacy.

A will ensures that the estate will devolve according to the deceased's wishes and it can also be used for tax planning.

1.4   Investment objectives

The investment objectives of income or capital growth were explained in the chapter on Personal Financial Planning.

2   CONSTRUCTING A PORTFOLIO

2.1   The building blocks

An investment portfolio is simply a collection of financial assets which has been put together for a reason.

The principle reason for holding a portfolio, rather than putting all the available funds into just one investment, is to reduce risk.

A portfolio is constructed from investments having different degrees of risk, income and growth in order to provide the level of return and degree of risk which is acceptable to the investor.

The main building blocks of a portfolio are:

(a)   variable interest deposits, eg, bank and building society accounts. These provide exposure to interest rates, they provide liquidity and for the most part are reasonably secure.

(b)   fixed income investments to provide a secure income and security of capital. Examples are gilt edged securities and, at a greater risk but higher return, corporate securities.

(c)   equities to provide growth of income and capital.

Where appropriate tax efficient investments would be used such as ISAs, National Savings Certificates and Enterprise Investment Scheme shares.

2.2   Tax considerations

(a)   **Higher rate taxpayers**

Higher rate, and to a lesser extent basic rate, tax payers should ensure that where they have decided on a particular type of investment they make use of any tax exemptions.

Examples:

- Part of the building society investment should be in an ISA
- National Savings Certificates
- Equities, unit trusts and corporate bonds should be held through an ISA

(b)   **Non taxpayers**

Non taxpayers should ensure that income is either received gross or that any tax suffered at source is recoverable. Because of the cash flow advantage, gross income is preferable.

Examples:

- Election should be made to receive bank and building society interest gross
- The National Savings Income Bond pays interest gross
- Gilt edged securities pay interest gross.

Tax credits on dividends cannot be reclaimed by non-taxpayers, and so shares and securities will normally not be an appropriate investment for such people.

2.3   Example of a growth portfolio

A portfolio for a higher rate taxpayer looking for long term growth might be:

10% in building society accounts and other cash investments. Full use is made of an ISA.

20%-30% in fixed income securities. These might include National Savings Certificates, low/ medium coupon gilts with a 5-15 year maturity, Index linked gilts. For a higher return, but greater risk there might also be corporate bonds issued by well rated companies.

60%-70% in equities. Core holdings will be blue chips, unit trusts, open ended investment companies and investment trusts, held where possible in an ISA. There will also be some smaller companies to provide the opportunity for higher growth. In addition there would be some overseas exposure probably through unit trusts, open ended investment companies or investment trusts.

It should be stressed however that this is simply an illustration. An investment adviser would construct a portfolio precisely tailored to the clients requirements.

2.4   Portfolio for a basic rate pensioner requiring income.

70%-80% in interest earning assets, for example:

- bank and building society accounts. Monthly income options are often available. Use would be made of an ISA.

- High coupon gilts

- National Savings Income Bond

- Guaranteed income bonds.

20%-30% in equities probably through unit trusts, open ended investment companies or investment trusts. ISAs will be used if the income tax relief exceeds the manager's charges.

3   SOURCES OF PERSONAL FINANCE

Rather than having funds to invest, an individual may have to borrow money. Sources of finance and their main features include:

- Mortgages
  - cheapest (lowest interest)
  - tax relief currently at 10% on first £30,000
  - longest term (usually up to 25 years)
  - choice of repayment methods
  - secured on main residence

- Other secured loans
  - cheap
  - can be long term (10-15 years)

- Unsecured loans
  - more expensive
  - probably no longer than 5 years

- Hire purchase and store finance
  - usually more expensive
  - 1-5 years

- Overdrafts
  - rates vary
  - repayable on demand
  - should be regarded as purely short term finance

- Credit cards
  - very expensive
  - should be avoided as a source of finance

4   SOURCES OF BUSINESS FINANCE

4.1   Introduction

Business finance sources fall into one of two categories:

- Equity finance (share issues); and
- Debt finance (short term and long term).

Money raised through equity is permanent, ie, it does not have to be repaid. Dividends can vary from year to year and can only be paid if the company has distributable profits. However, the dividends are not deductible from profits for tax purposes. Also raising equity from external sources means having outside shareholders.

Borrowings have to be repaid and the company needs to plan for that event. Interest payments are usually fixed and must be paid, even if they push the company into loss. The interest is deductible from profits for tax purposes usually on an accruals basis.

4.2   Sources of equity finance

Sources of equity finance are:

(a)   Share issue to the public in general through the Stock Exchange. Only large companies will be able to do this.

(b)   Share issue to the founders of the company and their associates (friends and relatives). Many private companies start this way with the founders providing the initial finance.

Tax relief under the enterprise investment scheme may be available if the qualifying conditions are met.

(c)   Venture capital from

(i)   independent public companies, eg, 3i or several other investment trusts;

(ii)   independent managers who raise capital from other providers and are rewarded by commission and profit sharing

(iii)   Government sources

(iv)   Venture capital trusts.

4.3   Long term debt finance

Long term debt finance will be used for purchases of long term assets and the provision of long term working capital.

Sources include:

(a)   term loans
(b)   mortgage loans
(c)   debentures and loan stock
(d)   convertible loan stock which gives the holder the right to convert it into shares in the company.

4.4   Short term debt finance

Sources of short term debt finance include:

(a)   bank overdrafts
(b)   short term loans
(c)   trade credit

    (d)   invoice discounting

    (e)   debt factoring

    (f)   HP and leasing.

Invoice discounting is where a company raises finance by selling its sales debts, but guarantees their collection. Effectively, finance is raised by using the sales debts as security.

Debt factoring is where a company raises finance by selling its sales debts, usually outright.

5   SELF TEST QUESTIONS

    5.1   List the main headings of a financial fact find. (1.2)

    5.2   What are four of the essential matters in financial planning? (1.3)

    5.3   What are the three components of a balanced portfolio? (2.1)

    5.4   List three investments suitable for a non taxpayer. (2.2)

    5.5   What are the main features of a mortgage? (3)

    5.6   When are overdrafts repayable? (3)

    5.7   For how long are unsecured loans normally taken out? (3)

    5.8   List two sources of venture capital (4.2)

    5.9   What are the differences between equity and loan finance? (4.1)

    5.10   State two sources of short term debt finance. (4.4)

40 TAX PLANNING - SUMMARY

INTRODUCTION

Tax planning points are generally dealt with in the appropriate part of the text. Some of the more important planning areas are summarised below.

Employment versus self employment

Where a taxpayer has a choice, the following points should be considered:

Employed	*Self-employed*
• Income tax and NIC payable on current year basis, as salary is received.	Class 2 NIC payable during year. Income tax and Class 4 payable on 31 January following the tax year. Payments on account are made on 31 January in the tax year, and 31 July following the tax year. Profits are assessed on a current year basis.
• Higher NIC burden	Lower NIC burden
• Some benefits in kind are favourably taxed, and do not generally attract NIC.	
• Expenses are deductible if incurred wholly or exclusively and necessarily in the performance of duties.	Expenses are deductible if incurred wholly and exclusively for the purposes of the trade.

Remuneration packages

The following points should be considered in relation to remuneration packages:

• Pension scheme:	Contributions by employer are tax deductible.
	Pension offers employee security.
• Benefits in kind:	No NIC for employees (generally).
	NIC for employer on cars and fuel (to be extended to all taxable benefits from 6 April 2000).
	Income tax charge on employee.
	Generally deductible for employer (though restrictions on cars costing over £12,000).
• Bonuses:	Treated like salary.
	Deductibility is delayed if accrued in accounts and paid more than 9 months after period of account.
• Incentive schemes	Tax advantages for employees.

Director in a family company versus sole trader

Their tax positions are compared below:

Director

Sole trader

Profits may be:

All profits taxed at 40% on taxable income exceeding £28,000.

- paid out as remuneration;
- paid out as dividends;
- retained in the company.

Class 2 and Class 4 NIC payable.

Corporation tax is 20% on profits up to £300,000, and 30% on profits over £1,500,000 (marginal rate between two figures is 32.5%).

If profits paid out as remuneration, Class I NIC payable. Employer's NIC is deductible.

- Benefits in kind may be tax efficient

No equivalent.

- No equivalent.

A choice of accounting date early in the tax year (ie, 30 April) maximises the length of time between earning profits and paying the related tax liability.

- Tax due 9 months after the end of chargeable accounting period.

Tax due as per above.

Ways to extract profit from a company

Remuneration

- Deductible against profits
- NIC payable
- Earned income in hands of shareholder

Dividends

- No tax implications for company
- Investment income in hands of shareholder

Liquidation

Profits are retained in company and then it is liquidated.

Potential double capital gains charge:

- company on the sale of its assets;
- shareholders on liquidation (shares are treated as disposed of for the amount paid to the shareholders).

Timing of dividend payments

- The date of payment of a dividend dictates into which tax year the shareholder receives income, and the date that any higher rate tax is payable.

Disposal of shares

When shares in a private company are disposed of, the following should be considered.

- Retirement relief may be available.

- Capital gain on the sale may be reduced by paying out dividends before the sale.

- If shares are sold at undervalue or gifted, disposal proceeds are deemed to be market value (gift relief may be available). Such a disposal may have inheritance tax implications.

Tax planning for groups

- One company should deal with capital disposals so capital gains and losses can be netted off.

- Losses within a group should be relieved primarily in companies paying tax at the marginal rate of 32.5%.

- Group members are regarded as one person for replacement of business asset purposes.

- If a VAT group is formed, VAT will not arise on intra group transfers.

- Holding company should aim to have a 75% effective interest in every company so that losses may be relieved in all members of the group.

Student Questionnaire

Invoice number: . . . .

Because we believe in listening to our customers, this questionnaire has been designed to discover exactly what you think about us and our materials. We want to know how we can continue improving our customer support and how to make our top class books even better - how do you use our books, what do you like about them and what else would you like to see us do to make them better?

1 Where did you hear about AT Foulks Lynch ACCA Textbooks?

☐ Colleague or friend ☐ Employer recommendation ☐ Lecturer recommendation

☐ AT Foulks Lynch mailshot ☐ Conference ☐ ACCA literature

☐ Student Newsletter ☐ Pass Magazine ☐ Internet

☐ Other ....

2 Overall, do you think the AT Foulks Lynch ACCA Textbooks are:

☐ Excellent ☐ Good ☐ Average ☐ Poor ☐ No opinion

3 Please evaluate AT Foulks Lynch service using the following criteria:

	Excellent	Good	Average	Poor	No opinion
Professional	☐	☐	☐	☐	☐
Polite	☐	☐	☐	☐	☐
Informed	☐	☐	☐	☐	☐
Helpful	☐	☐	☐	☐	☐

4 How did you obtain this book?

☐ From a bookshop (name) ☐ From your college (name) ☐ From us by mail order

....

☐ From us by telephone ☐ Internet ☐ Other ....

5 How long did it take to receive your materials? .... days.

☐ Very fast ☐ Fast ☐ Satisfactory ☐ Slow ☐ No opinion

6 How do you rate the value of these features of this Textbook?

Paper No .... Title ....

		Excellent	Good	Average	Poor	No opinion
1	Syllabus referenced to chapters	☐	☐	☐	☐	☐
2	Teaching Guide referenced to chapters	☐	☐	☐	☐	☐
3	Step by step approach and solutions	☐	☐	☐	☐	☐
4	Activities throughout the chapters	☐	☐	☐	☐	☐
5	Self test questions	☐	☐	☐	☐	☐
6	Examination type questions	☐	☐	☐	☐	☐
7	Index	☐	☐	☐	☐	☐

Continued/...

7 Have you purchased any other AT Foulks Lynch ACCA titles?
If so, please specify title(s) and your rating of each below:

Title	Excellent	Good	Average	Poor	No opinion
....	☐	☐	☐	☐	☐
....	☐	☐	☐	☐	☐
....	☐	☐	☐	☐	☐
....	☐	☐	☐	☐	☐

8 Have you used publications other than AT Foulks Lynch ACCA titles?
If so, please specify title(s) and your rating of each below:

Title and Publisher	Excellent	Good	Average	Poor	No opinion
....	☐	☐	☐	☐	☐
....	☐	☐	☐	☐	☐
....	☐	☐	☐	☐	☐
....	☐	☐	☐	☐	☐

9 Will you buy the AT Foulks Lynch ACCA Textbooks again?

☐ Yes   ☐ No   ☐ Not sure

Why? ....

10 Please write here any additional comments you might have on any of the above areas or tell us what you would like us to do to make the books even better:

....

....

....

....

11 Your details: these are for the internal use of AT Foulks Lynch Ltd only and will not be supplied to any outside organisations.

Name
....

Address
....

....

Telephone
....

Do you have your own e-mail address?   ☐ Yes   ☐ No

Do you have access to the World Wide Web?   ☐ Yes   ☐ No

Do you have access to a CD Rom Drive?   ☐ Yes   ☐ No

Please send to:

Quality Feedback Department
FREEPOST 2254
AT Foulks Lynch Ltd, 4 The Griffin Centre, Staines Road, Feltham, Middlesex, TW14 0BR.

Thank you for your time.